The German Army at Ypres 1914
and
The Battle for Flanders

With love to my daughter Alison and my son-in-law Jim
as a new and exciting chapter of their lives opens.

By the same author:

The German Army on the Somme 1914–1916
The German Army at Passchendaele
The German Army on Vimy Ridge 1914–1917
The German Army at Cambrai
The Germans at Beaumont Hamel
The Germans at Thiepval

With Nigel Cave:

The Battle for Vimy Ridge 1917
Le Cateau

The German Army at Ypres 1914 and The Battle for Flanders

by

Jack Sheldon

Foreword by
Professor Hew Strachan

Pen & Sword
MILITARY

First published in Great Britain in 2010 and reprinted in this format in 2021 and 2024
by
Pen & Sword Military
an imprint of
Pen & Sword Books Ltd
47 Church Street
Barnsley
South Yorkshire
S70 2AS

ISBN 978 1 39901 452 6

A CIP catalogue record for this book is
available from the British Library.

Typeset in Ellington by
Phoenix Typesetting, Auldgirth, Dumfriesshire

Printed in the UK on paper from a sustainable source by CPI Group (UK) Ltd, Croydon,
CR0 4YY

Pen & Sword Books Ltd incorporates the imprints of Pen & Sword Aviation, Pen & Sword
Maritime, Pen & Sword Military, Wharncliffe Local History,
Pen & Sword Select, Pen & Sword Military Classics and Leo Cooper.

For a complete list of Pen & Sword titles please contact
PEN & SWORD BOOKS LIMITED
47 Church Street, Barnsley, South Yorkshire, S70 2AS, England
E-mail: enquiries@pen-and-sword.co.uk
Website: www.pen-and-sword.co.uk

Contents

Foreword

First-hand German accounts of the fighting on the Western Front in the First World War are dramatically (an adverb of particular force in this context) different from those written by British participants. Very often conveyed in the historic present tense, their sentences are short and direct, devoid of the convoluted and passive constructions so beloved of more academic German prose of the same vintage. Using pathos, they cast the dead as heroes, putting direct speech into their mouths and not infrequently closing their observations with an exclamation mark for added and rhetorical effect.

For British readers these German accounts can seem 'over the top': rarely have they been taken seriously by those few Anglophone historians anxious to explore the 'other side of the hill'. They have been given equally short shrift by their German counterparts. The products of the 1920s and '30s, they are seen as tainted by fascism and encrusted with the 'stab in the back legend' so fervently promoted by German militarists. But the consequence of such superciliousness has been to rob us of an enormously rich and extensive primary source. The German army produced a vast body of regimental histories after the First World War, the best of them incorporating first-hand accounts and most of them written by participants in the actions they described. True, some of them took their tone from the more hyperbolic volumes of the series, *Schlachten des Weltkrieges*, or 'battles of the world war', of which *Ypern 1914*, written by Werner Beumelberg, is – as Jack Sheldon points out in this book – one of the more egregious examples. Sponsored by the Reichsarchiv, the body responsible for the German official history, *Schlachten des Weltkrieges* was designed to appeal to a more popular market, but some of the series undoubtedly rose above the expectations of the genre – just as did some of the regimental histories.

These points matter because in 1945 the Royal Air Force destroyed the bulk of the Prussian military archives, leaving subsequent historians much more reliant on the published materials of the inter-war period than would otherwise have been the case. To dismiss the accounts so wonderfully exploited (and fluently translated) by Jack Sheldon in *The German Army at Ypres 1914* is wilfully to deepen our ignorance and lack of understanding of an institution central to modern military history. Moreover, the German Sixth Army – one of two Bavarian armies mobilised in 1914 – took a major part in the fighting at Ypres. Unlike those of Prussia, the Bavarian archives were not destroyed in the Second World War, and so Jack Sheldon has been able to work in some unpublished material of particular force: look at the revealing memorandum printed in chapter 6 and issued on 30 October 1914 by Krafft von Dellmensingen, the Sixth Army's chief of staff and himself no mean historian of the war.

The German Army at Ypres 1914 is a tactical narrative of German operations at the regimental and battalion level. That was the significance of 1st Ypres: it was the moment when the generals of 1914 confronted the end of manoeuvre, when corps-level movements and aspirations to higher strategic control were confounded by the tactical constraints of positional warfare. Flanders had long been one of the richest areas of Europe – agriculturally, commercially and (increasingly) industrially. It had enabled the armies of the French revolution to march on their stomachs, and the Germans followed Napoleonic precepts in the autumn of 1914. They scratched Belgium's fertile soil for winter root crops, turnips, beet and mangel wurzels, in order to compensate for the collapse of supply. The German cavalry played an effective part in the opening stages of the battle (contrary to the reputation accorded them in British accounts) but found their movements hampered by hedged and fenced fields, by railway lines and urbanisation. Such a landscape was particularly well adapted for defence, and all the allied armies – Belgian, French and British – proved themselves in their exploitation of the opportunities it presented. But the consequences were horrific: it can be argued that proportionately the casualty levels at 1st Ypres outstripped those of the Somme and Passchendaele, and with them the 'old' armies of 1914 ceased to exist.

Many of the accounts used by Jack Sheldon refer to the effectiveness of sniper fire: German soldiers removed the tell-tale spikes from their *Pickelhaube* helmets, and officers put their swords to one side and picked up rifles to make themselves less conspicuous. But the big killer was field artillery, particularly the French 75 mm gun firing shrapnel over open sights at ranges of less than 1,000 yards. German reserve artillery could not compete: deficient in training, it too often fired short and it was under-equipped. According to Jack Sheldon, one officer, lacking telephone line to speak to his guns let alone to other formations, had to use a whistle to give fire control orders, and another had to collocate his guns with the infantry so that he could communicate.

The first battle of Ypres became the stuff of legend in post-war Germany. The fighting at Langemark, characterised as a *Kindermord*, a slaughter of the innocents, was portrayed as a heroic and self-sacrificial action by German student volunteers, advancing into battle with patriotic songs on their lips. Plenty of the accounts cited by Jack Sheldon testify to the role of music in sustaining German morale, and General Berthold von Deimling announced that musicians who played during attacks would be awarded the Iron Cross. But the armies of 1914 were old not just because they were the last representatives of a disappearing order but also because they used reservists to bring their units up to strength – not so much adolescents fresh from school as middle-aged fathers whose military service lay several years in the past but who were now recalled to the colours.

The legends grew from rumour, fed even at relatively high levels of command. One corps headquarters reported that the Germans had taken Calais. Many accounts testify to the fixed belief that Belgian *franc tireurs* were actively engaged in the fighting, although recent scholarship has debunked this myth as robustly as it has that of the *Kindermord* at Langemark. From the British perspective the German version of the battle in turn punctures some standard wisdom. It testifies to the effectiveness of the navy's ship-to-shore gunnery in the battle on the Yser canal; it praises the martial qualities of the Indians, so often portrayed as failing to cope with the rigours of a northern European winter; and it pays tribute to the value of the British army's colonial experience. German reservists were more complimentary about the British infantry than were many of their more senior officers, seeing them as long service soldiers, hardened by fighting in South Africa and on the north-west frontier of India, and forgetting that many of them were also 'old', ex-regulars to be sure but also reservists.

Historians concerned to engage with issues of morale in the armies of the First World War have tended to gallop forward to 1917, to the mutinies and the revolutions which then preoccupied all those in command. However, it was in the second half of 1914 that armies really confronted the 'shock of battle' for the first time, and they all reeled under the blow. They had no precedent for what they encountered, no compass to guide them. Some struggled to hold on to religious faith, to faith in the nation and to love of family. But others sought ways out of the battle, from desertion to self-mutilation. Jack Sheldon's references to the loss of junior leaders to 'grip' units and to give them direction makes it even more surprising that the German army endured through the winter – and was to do so for four more years.

Hew Strachan
Chichele Professor of the History of War,
All Souls College, University of Oxford.

Introduction

The intense and costly fighting in late 1914 between the River Lys and the sea at Nieuwpoort, known to the British as the First Battle of Ypres, was the final phase of the war of movement. Ever since the Battle of the Marne, both sides had made strenuous attempts to turn the flank of the other, in the course of a campaign erroneously referred to ever after as the 'Race to the Sea'. Successive German attempts to thrust westwards, astride the Somme, around Arras and to the west of Lille faltered and then foundered in the face of increased Allied resistance, which was facilitated by the advantage of interior lines and the intact rail network within France. On 5 October, following a heated meeting between Falkenhayn and the Chief of Staff of Sixth Army, Generalmajor Konrad Krafft von Delmensingen, when it was obvious that the hopes of a breakthrough around Arras were running into the sand, the decision was taken to concentrate massed cavalry to the north, in order to manoeuvre and to fall on the rear of the French army.

The attempt was made, but it was soon obvious that the cavalry lacked the punch to achieve the desired aim. That, it was assessed, would require nothing less than the deployment of an entire army, something the hard-pressed German army was ill placed to find. The Sixth Army had already been redeployed north from the Metz area and had carried out a succession of right hooks, which had depleted its resources and left it increasingly fixed in position from the Somme north to the Lys. Falkenhayn's staff searched for a solution and, such was the desperation of the situation and the determination of Falkenhayn to leave no stone unturned in his quest for victory, that he hit on the solution of assembling, under the command of Duke Albrecht of Württemberg, four of the six new third-rate reserve corps, which were forming up in Germany. His former Fourth Army was dissolved and, in its place, a new Fourth Army was created.

Although this army was to include III Reserve Corps under General der Infanterie von Beseler, together with all its accompanying heavy artillery, once Antwerp fell, the decision to employ a great mass of half-trained, ill-equipped formations at such a critical time and place was a gamble of breathtaking proportions. In essence, the plan was to force the line of the Ijzer in strength, brushing aside Belgian opposition and then to swing round south in a broad sweep, combining the resources of Fourth and Sixth Armies to catch the Allies near St Omer and crush them once and for all. Unfortunately for Falkenhayn, the Belgian army, though severely pressed and far from a first class fighting force, managed to extract some 80,000 men from Antwerp and redeploy them along the Ijzer where, reinforced by French marines, they held out for a critical seven day period. At that point, faced with the final collapse of Belgian resistance, the French army, abandoning any ambition to thrust along the coast of Flanders towards Oostende, placed the whole of its 42nd Division in position to cover the northern section of the front, which King Albert of the Belgians finally caused to be inundated and so denied to any future offensive German operations.

The importance of operations along the Ijzer is here emphasised, because there is a tendency to regard 'First Ypres' as a wholly British affair. This was far from the case, because it was very much an Allied defensive effort. At the height of the battle, for example, not only was the British army holding only half the length of front line that the French army was responsible for, but every time there was a crisis on the British sector, it was the French army which rushed to the rescue to buttress the places where it sagged. This was particularly the case once the German emphasis switched from the coastal plain to the thrust along the Menen road and later the attack south of Ypres by the so-called Army Group Fabeck.

Inevitably, over the years, this battle, which saw the final, complete transition from manoeuvre to positional warfare all along the Western Front, has generated more than its fair share of myth and legend, so it is worth exploring some of the main topics briefly. Both sides, for example, claimed that the artillery fire of the opposition was extremely heavy and that their own was relatively ineffective. The Germans repeatedly assert that they continually had to launch attacks against 'carefully constructed defensive positions, protected by obstacles'. The British, for their part, dismiss such claims as nonsense given the lack of time and resources available to prepare suitable trenches and obstacle belts. Of course, in turn, these British denials ignore the enormous advantage enjoyed by the defence when it is conducted from even the most rudimentary trenches against troops advancing in the open. Striking examples from the American Civil War, as far back at the Battle of Malvern Hill in July 1862, or Cold Harbor in June 1864, demonstrated the truth of this, even when the defenders were only armed with rifled muskets, firing a mere three rounds per minute, but British historians prefer to skim over that simple fact.

However, of all the myths pertaining to Ypres 1914, perhaps none is more entrenched than the assertion first put forward in the British Official History that the musketry of the British infantry with their rapid fire 'mad minutes' convinced the Germans that they were, 'opposed by lines of machine guns'. This completely false notion, which has been repeated ever since by British authors, appears to have been based, quite improperly, on one single extract from the translated version of the 1918 monograph *Die Schlacht an der Yser und bei Ypern im Herbst 1914* [Ypres 1914]. This account, couched in the somewhat breathless style of the *Boys Own Paper*, was a wartime production intended to boost morale on the home front, rather than be regarded as a serious work of military history but, at the time the British Official History was being compiled, there was little else available from the German perspective. So, in the same way as a similar study concerning Mons and Walter Bloem's book, *The Advance from Mons*, were mined for material which suited the British case in that volume of the history, when referring to the defence of Geluveld by 1st Battalion Queen's Regiment on 31 October 1914, the Official Historian chose to quote this statement from the monograph, 'over every bush, hedge and fragment of wall floated a film of smoke, betraying a machine gun rattling out bullets'.

Even the translation was inaccurate. It actually reads, 'Everywhere amongst bushes, hedges and ruins could be seen steam from machine guns, fired until they were [red] hot'. Choosing this one quotation was seriously misleading. In the German version it appears on p 60, by which time there have already been six references to British small arms fire and, before the end of the monograph, there are five more, only two of which refer to the fire of machine guns alone. A much more typical quotation, one faithful to almost all German descriptions of the British defensive tactics during the battle, could have been taken from p 21 of the monograph, 'The British, most of whom had experience gained through long years of campaigning against cunning opponents in close country, let the attackers get to close range then, from hedges, houses and trees, opened up withering rifle and machine gun fire from point blank range'.

There are echoes of that statement throughout the German literature for one very simple reason: that is the way the infantry battle was fought. One of the hardest things for the modern visitor to visualise is how changes in agricultural practice have altered the landscape in Flanders. Hundreds of kilometres of hedges, which once surrounded small fields, have been grubbed up and trees are no longer coppiced for firewood. In 1914 the defenders – French and Belgian, as well as British, exploited these hedges and scrubby wooded areas for the concealment and the canalisation of offensive movement they offered. In addition, for the Allies in general there were shortages of small arms ammunition and difficulties of resupply, especially to the front line, so there was little scope for blasting off in 'mad minute' fashion at long range. Such tactics would have achieved very little and led to individual riflemen firing off all their ammunition in short order, with very limited scope for replenishment.

No, in contrast to the myth, the watchwords for the defending infantry were fire discipline and conservation of ammunition; both of which were best achieved by allowing attackers to get close to defended localities and then pouring lacerating fire into them at short range for as brief a time as possible. Quite apart from these considerations, it is ludicrous to suggest that an army, even one as inexperienced as the German Fourth Army, could possibly mistake rifle fire for the firing of machine guns of the period, with their distinctive low cyclic rates. Not only did they deploy their own Machine Gun 08 on the same scale as the British army and so were well aware of the firing signature of such weapons, they were so attuned to the characteristics of the French machine guns, for example, that they swiftly learned to wait for the moment when the twenty five round strip of bullets was fired off and to move during the pauses for reloading.

The primary German contribution to the mythology of the battle was probably the description of the outcome of the battles of the new reserve corps as *Kindermord* [Massacre of the Innocents]. Within days of the end of the battle it was being asserted that up to three quarters of all those engaged were students or senior school boys who left their studies, signed up as volunteers *en masse* and advanced to their death singing *Deutschland über alles*. A widely publicised communiqué issued by Supreme Army Headquarters and dated 11 November 1914 set the myth in motion and it rapidly gained momentum. Post war, virtually every regiment which fought in Flanders included references to the singing of patriotic songs and anthems on the battlefield in their histories. Some of these claims, which refer to the use of singing as an aid to mutual recognition at night, have the ring of authenticity to them; others which attempted to associate themselves more closely with the wording of the communiqué, or to claim to have been the first to burst into song, less so, but examples of all three will be encountered in the body of this account.

The question concerning the composition of the regiments which manned the new divisions has been subject to careful examination. During the 1980s, for example, Karl Unruh in his book, *Langemarck: Legende und Wirklichkeit,* analysed the make up of the regiments and verified the number of students known to have been serving in the armed forces during the autumn term of 1914 and the spring term of 1915. In so doing, he completely demolished the assertions that volunteers were in the majority in these new formations and that students accounted for most of the volunteers, pointing out that, of the 40,761 students involved, a proportion would have been reservists and not volunteers and that, even if every single student had fought with the four reserve corps (an unlikely scenario), they would not have contributed more than one third of the numbers.

However, the image of setting aside books to pick up rifles was such a romantic and seductive idea, that it soon became an enduring part of life in interwar Germany. The 'Spirit of Langemark' was continually fostered and ruthlessly exploited by the Nazis in a bid to inspire future generations and this went way beyond its use within the military. There was, for example, a 'Langemarckhalle' at the Olympic stadium in Berlin, built for the 1936 games and compulsorily visited by all German athletes so as to motivate them to greater efforts, whilst German endeavours as widely different as the establishment of the Mercedes and Auto Union Grand Prix racing teams and the early attempts to climb the North Wall of the Eiger were underpinned by references to Langemark. Of course the linkage between German student bodies and Langemark was firmly established before the Nazis came to power and despite the fact that, demonstrably, volunteers of whatever origin only make up a minority of those buried there, one of the main features of the dedication of the German cemetery at Langemark on 10 July 1932 was the ceremonial handing over of the key to the main gate to the president of the association of German students.

The fact that, in accepting this symbol, German students assumed particular responsibility for the care and maintenance of the cemetery at Langemark has helped to perpetuate the myth right up to the present day, even amongst the Anglophone audience. Lyn MacDonald, for example, possibly influenced by the panelling in the entrance to the cemetery, which portrays a largely spurious image of those who lie within, has a paragraph in her book, *1914: The Days of Hope,* in which she states that German soldiers, 'advanc[ed] in massed formations across the fields near Langemark . . . the British firing line saw that they were advancing arm in arm . . . and they heard the sound of . . . voices singing . . . The caps they wore . . . were not the regulation headgear of German soldiers . . . They were the caps of German students, and the Kaiser's young soldiers were wearing them as they had worn them striding the streets of Heidelberg . . . Three out of four of the new men were under military age . . . A huge majority of the rank and file had joined in groups from universities or high schools'.

A few points, in addition to the general remarks above, need to be made about this. First, the carriage of rifles and equipment, not to mention the numerous obstacles to movement on the Langemark battlefield, would have made it extremely difficult to advance 'arm in arm' and singing is easily drowned out by the intense noise of small arms fire and shells exploding; second, two of the regiments of the division concerned (51st Reserve) were raised hundreds of kilometres away from Heidelberg, in Meiningen and Gotha in the case of Reserve Infantry Regiment 233 and Kassel for Reserve Infantry Regiment 234. It is true that there were numerous volunteers in the ranks of Reserve Infantry Regiment 234, including a fair proportion of students, but they were mainly from the University of Göttingen. It is extremely improbable, therefore, that any students who happened to find themselves in their ranks studied in Heidelberg. Furthermore, the objective of this regiment in the early battles was not Langemark but Mangelaar, off to the north.

It is true that Reserve Infantry Regiments 235 and 236, which later formed 102 Reserve Infantry Brigade, came from the Rhineland, but Reserve Infantry Regiment 235, raised in Koblenz, was made up as follows: Headquarters and 1st Battalion from the Ersatz Battalion Infantry Regiment 28; 2nd Battalion from the Ersatz Battalion of Infantry Regiment 68 and 3rd Battalion from the Ersatz Battalion Infantry Regiment 160. Similarly, the three battalions of Reserve Infantry Regiment 236, raised in Cologne, were derived primarily from the ersatz battalions of Infantry Regiments 25, 16 and 65 respectively. This does not rule out the possible presence of students in these two regiments, indeed the history of Reserve Infantry Regiment 235 states that there were students from the University of Bonn in its ranks, but they must have been in the minority and these were the regiments which assaulted Langemark directly.

Further proof that the formations deployed in this area were not full of students comes from the example of Reserve Infantry Regiment 213, raised in the north of Schleswig Holstein and part of the neighbouring 46th Reserve Division. In its history it complains that although official communiqués in late 1914 referred constantly to the presence of large numbers of kriegsfreiwillige [wartime volunteers] in the ranks of the new regiments, as far it was concerned, 'Regiment 213 was assembled almost one hundred percent from time served soldiers, reservists and men from the two main Landwehr categories'. Because none of the German sources mention the wearing of unofficial headgear, it is not possible to comment about that, though it is highly improbable. Suffice it to say that this is a clear example of the way myths gain with the telling.

The battle for Flanders in late 1914 was extremely hard fought, with serious losses on both sides. It was regarded finally as over on 22 November 1914, but the failures a week previously had effectively brought large scale German offensive operations to a halt and there were many in the German army who felt that the game was up as soon as the assault by Army Group Fabeck stuttered and then stalled early in November. By the end of the battle, the French army had sustained further heavy casualties to add to the catastrophic losses of the Battle of the Frontiers and the Belgian army was a shadow of its former self. The British army had lost more than 54,000 valuable long service soldiers and the German army somewhere around 80,000. This great casualty count is clear proof that neither side in this landmark battle had any monopoly on courage or sacrifice and that the men of the Fourth German army were too inexperienced to know they could not prevail and too courageous not to go on trying to advance even when it was hopeless.

Jack Sheldon
Vercors, April 2010

jandl50@hotmail.com

Author's Note

Sources used for this book include items from the archives in Munich. Units and formations from Bavaria played a significant part in the battle between Geluveld and Messines in autumn 1914 and much information is available in the *Kriegsarchiv*, which also houses an almost complete set of histories of the Bavarian army. The loss of Prussian documents following an air raid by the Royal Air Force on Potsdam in April 1944 is a permanent obstacle to the detailed study of events between 1914 and 1918 but, fortunately, much that was stored elsewhere survived and it is possible also to draw on the wealth of regimental histories written between the wars. This means, in turn, that it is possible to reconstruct the battles from the German perspective with a high degree of confidence in the resulting accuracy.

It remains the author's opinion that, in general, the material in the regimental histories can be relied on as an accurate portrayal of the events which occurred on the battlefield. Their quality is, inevitably, uneven, though the majority are very sound. Everything depended upon the ability of the authors concerned and the amount of time and effort put into them. A number of the histories relating to Flanders 1914 appeared late, well after the Nazis came to power in Germany, but the majority were already published before 1933. Many of the histories contain extremely critical remarks about the chain of command and deficiencies in the way the campaign was prepared and conducted; all of which leads to the clear conclusion that they were mainly put together by men of principle and independent mind.

Certain eye witness accounts and other descriptions in the text are linked to a particular locality on the battlefield. Each chapter includes at least one map of the area concerned. The figures on the 'Eyewitness Maps' relate to the numbers in bold associated with that section of the relevant chapter. In some cases different witnesses were located in the same area, so they share a number. The only exception comes in Chapter 8, which contains an additional map showing eyewitness locations on 11 Nov 1914. Place names are something of a problem when describing events in Flanders. The familiar names such as Ypres, Messines and Passchendaele have been retained, but other places have been rendered in their modern Flemish forms.

The Germans never differentiated between English, Scottish, Irish or Welsh soldiers and units, referring to them all as *Engländer*. The word *Engländer* has been translated throughout as 'British' for troops from the United Kingdom.

German time, which was one hour ahead of British time, is used throughout the book.

Acknowledgements

I wish to express my grateful thanks to Professor Hew Strachan, who has kindly written the Foreword to this book, the first full account of German operations in Flanders during the autumn of 1914. By demonstrating conclusively the global nature of the Great War of 1914–18, Professor Strachan's work has been extremely influential in recent years. This viewpoint generally held sway in German writing between the wars, but tended to be lost or obscured in the majority of Anglocentric studies of that conflict, so we all benefit enormously from his expert analysis and insights. In Germany I was helped greatly by the friendly, cooperative staff at the *Kriegsarchiv* in Munich and should like to thank especially its director, Dr Lother Saupe and Frau Brigitte Jakobi, who makes working in the reading room there a particularly pleasant experience. Once again Dr Alex Fasse provided me with expert interpretation of obscure references and abbreviations, for which I am most grateful.

Members of the internet Great War Forum have stepped forward readily and offered me their expertise and assistance. I should like to mention in particular Robert Dunlop for providing me with scans of numerous crucial British war diaries; David Filsell for sharing his unpublished research and maps of the situation south of the Menen road at the end of October 1914; Mick Forsyth for suggested translations of linguistic obscurities; Paul Hederer for providing me with much needed, but rare, published German material; Richard Hargreaves for help with Royal Navy terminology and access to the Official History of the War (Naval Operations); Ralph Whitehead for contemporary news clippings, discovered during his painstaking work on German casualties and Eddie Lambrecht, who placed his magnificent collection of photographs at my disposal.

As ever, I appreciate the careful editorial work and helpful suggestions of my editor, Nigel Cave, and the contributions of all at Pen and Sword Books. Finally, where would I be without the help and support of my wife Laurie? Not only has she spent hours turning my rough sketches into maps and kept the supply of tea to my study going, but she was also happy to amuse herself in Munich, whilst I buried myself in the dusty archives during the days leading up to Christmas 2009. My love for her knows no bounds.

Prologue

O n the face of it, the raising, equipping and training of the reserve corps which made up the bulk of Fourth Army was a feat of organisation of the highest class. The one thing of which there was no shortage in Germany in 1914 was manpower. Just as in other belligerent countries, men flocked to join up – especially to the artillery, because there was a totally erroneous view that service in that arm was intrinsically less dangerous and definitely more interesting than life in the infantry.

Major Franz Rubenbauer Bavarian Reserve Infantry Regiment 16[1]

"In order to make best use of surplus manpower, the government decided in August 1914 to call for the training of volunteer formations in every German contingent and what a reaction this call achieved! Thousands responded. They came from every class and walk of life and every trade and profession competed with one another. Just as one hundred years before, it was a case of, 'the King called and everyone came!' The result was a national experience of such a profound nature that there can hardly ever have occurred its equal. It was a display of a single, united, determination to defend all that was best: the Fatherland and its freedom! Millions of souls had but one intention; millions of hearts beat as one. That was the spirit of those days.

"The recruiting centres could hardly cope with the flood which broke over them. Every barracks, the school buildings and all other available large scale accommodation was filled to overflowing with volunteers. They certainly lacked training, but they burned with the desire to close with the enemy. So the men were there, but an army is not made up of men alone! There were deficiencies of all kinds. The necessary weapons and equipment were only assembled with difficulty; the military training cost an enormous amount of work but, with good will, much was achieved. Systematic peacetime training was out of the question, but this was partly compensated for by the intelligence of those under training, their high quality and their patriotic enthusiasm."

Manning aside, inevitably corners had to be cut in order to have all the new formations ready for deployment within two months of the outbreak of the war, as a glance at the reported difficulties makes abundantly clear. Rubenbauer may have made light of them, but the problems of improvising so many formations when the metaphorical cupboard was bare were enormous. Reserve Infantry Regiment 201, for example, noted that, 'The companies lacked suitable junior leadership, namely, leutnants and senior and junior NCOs. The available command structure, drawn mainly from the Landwehr and Landsturm, had themselves to be trained before they could train others.'[2] Much the same point was made by Reserve Infantry Regiment 236, 'The question of command presented enormous difficulties. The senior retired officers were completely out of date and had no understanding of contemporary armaments or modern command on the battlefield. There were also no trained staffs. To help him to solve the outstanding military and administrative tasks, the only active duty officers the regimental commander [Oberst Wilhelmi] could only call on were Leutnant Rive, of Infantry Regiment 65, as regimental adjutant and Leutnant Heldt, of Infantry Regiment 160, as adjutant of the 2nd Battalion.'[3]

Lack of equipment was bemoaned by numerous other regiments. 'Initially, equipping the battalions with uniforms was extremely unsatisfactory. There were particular deficiencies in footwear . . . Very few rifles were available; those on charge had to be passed around between the platoons during training. The helmets and knapsacks for the 1st Battalion were not delivered until the day before deployment into the field, so the men had no opportunity to get used to the weight of their packs during training marches . . . ' (Reserve Infantry Regiment 204).[4] 'Not until 28 September, that is to say one month after the regiment was raised, did the last of the rifles arrive. Bayonets were issued on 1 October. Until then there had been none at all. There was still no personal equipment or wagons and no digging implements. Only about one third of the clothing was field grey, the remainder comprised blue cloth, cotton drill or civilian outfits. There was a complete lack of helmets, groundsheets and coats.' (Reserve Infantry Regiment 205).[5]

Even where clothing was found, it was often in a very poor state, having been stored unchecked and in unsuitable places for decades. As a stop gap, 'Men were dressed in items which bore the names and regimental numbers of men who had served more than forty years previously – in 1871 to be precise' (Reserve Infantry Regiment 212).[6] These complaints were echoed by Reserve Infantry Regiment 208, raised in Hanover, 'Only with the greatest difficulty were the battalions clothed and equipped. To begin with there were absolutely no weapons to be had.'[7] The situation was much the same for Reserve Infantry Regiment 209 in Stettin, 'There was a lack of clothing and equipment, so we had to exercise with lightweight civilian boots and belts over our civilian jackets. There were no rifles for a long time . . . until the early days of October there were no helmets, knapsacks or digging tools.'[8] Reserve Infantry Regiment 210 encountered identical problems. 'By 10 September, when the regiment was meant to be ready to march out of barracks, there were not enough rifles for each man to have one and it was not until the day before we deployed that 400 spades per battalion were made available.'[9]

The deficiencies were not limited to clothing and equipment. Just as serious was the lack of training pamphlets, ammunition and other aids. 'There was an almost total lack of pamphlets. There was insufficient live ammunition to permit shooting practice . . . even the provision of rifles was only achieved gradually. Elements of the officer corps were overage . . . Altogether only four officers were from the active list' (Reserve Infantry Regiment 206). Down in Mannheim, Reserve Infantry Regiment 239 discovered that, 'Difficulties piled on difficulties. Pamphlets, upon which the trainers could have based their instruction, were simply unavailable and could be sourced nowhere. As late as 25 September, that is to say almost a complete month later, forty eight men of 8th Company were still going around in civilian clothes . . . Boots? There were none! Nor were there any caps, rifles, bayonets, ammunition pouches or belts, nothing was available. On 7 September the regiment was still deficient 1,500 rifles. [During training] if one section was practising with the eight available, another had to work on estimating distances with some old soldier. It is true that, between 20 September and 1 October, a few dozen officers of the Landsturm were posted to the regiment, but these old and bold landsturmers had never even seen a Model 98 rifle, let alone handled one'.[10]

Unsurprising to note, all these problems and a lack of time to overcome them, meant that the standard of training and equipment of these new formations was abysmal. The history of Reserve Infantry Regiment 214 from Rostock later lamented,

'It is hardly surprising, as was later to become only too clear, that the training fell short of that desirable as preparation for war. Useless military rituals, which really made no sense in the context of such rushed training, were introduced into the programme by day and night. Who cannot recall all the hours spent practising standing to attention, or learning to salute and other such trivia; or, on the parade ground, repeatedly taking up positions, 'to repel cavalry attacking from the left flank'. We can only look back with fury at this time when our superiors got worked up when a particular drill movement was not properly executed or when someone, 'a volunteer, *naturally*', found himself in the wrong position. This was training based on peacetime requirements, on the depths of peacetime; something which was interrupted only occasionally for weapon training or route marching. When the troops marched away, despite all the so-called preparation, they were totally unable to operate in the way they should have been able to from the start, quite apart from the fact that events turned out entirely differently from the way we had trained.'

Those officers who were drawn from the active army, or whose service was recent, strained every sinew to overcome deficiencies amongst the leadership, but it was an uphill task, even within the reserve jäger battalions, where it might be imagined the overall high standard of these units would compensate for any difficulties. Reserve Jäger Battalion 16, a unit raised in Freiberg in southeast Saxony, later noted, 'By dint of constant visiting, the commander kept himself up to date on the state of training. This was very necessary because, for the most part, the company commanders had not seen service for more than a decade, were only used to the old drills and retained only a shadowy memory of those. In one company, close order drill was restricted to a constant repetition of the order, 'Right incline. Quick march!' [11]

Some idea of the immense effort required to overcome many of these difficulties was later provided by the paymaster of Reserve Infantry Regiment 236, who undertook the duties of quartermaster during these early difficult days.

Zahlmeister Schramm Reserve Infantry Regiment 236 [12]

"For mobilisation purposes in the event of war, planned reserve formations held their entire requirements of clothing and equipment right down to the smallest item and all in the correct sizes. These stocks were kept carefully in separate company stores; whilst hidden away from unauthorised eyes, in safes, were the mobilisation files, which contained the mobilisation calendar, together with numerous annexes and war stocks of maps. All this meant that the apparatus developed during long serious work in peacetime was guaranteed to work.

"On the other hand nothing at all was ready for the unplanned formations called into life during mobilisation in 1914. To clothe the flood of kriegsfreiwillige who came to the army, there were peacetime uniforms for a proportion, but no wartime field grey clothing. In addition there were no weapons – neither rifles, nor machine guns and no personal equipment, such as knapsacks, bread or ammunition pouches etc. There were also no vehicles, no field kitchens and all the other mobilisation stores necessary to equip the troops. All the necessary instruction pamphlets were also lacking. Reserve Infantry Regiment 236 was hard hit by all these problems.

"When, on 31 August 1914, the three battalions arrived in their new quarters, it was only possible to clothe and equip the former soldiers, who were temporarily concentrated in one company per battalion. The kriegsfreiwillige were given blue peacetime uniforms, but not one item of personal equipment, not even a belt. They had to carry small essential personal items in a ground sheet slung over their shoulders. A large proportion of the men only had personal underclothing and wore unsuitable footwear. In order to get round the most urgent needs, underwear and boots were purchased in the department stores of Cologne.

"The troops did not present a very military impression, underlining how much had to be achieved if they were to meet the terms of the Ministry of War timetable and be ready for action by 10 October. During urgent discussions with the Clothing Stores of VIII Corps, which took place at once, it transpired that their entire stocks had already been issued. The accelerated equipping of unplanned formations to reinforce formations already in the field, together with the demands of reserve formations which were being raised in and around Koblenz – for example, our sister regiment [Reserve Infantry Regiment] 235 – had completely exhausted their holdings . . .

"The VIII Corps transport and supply depot was also unable to equip the regiment with the necessary field equipment: vehicles, harnesses, digging implements etc. Its stocks had been laid down precisely and were only available for planned formations. Beyond those [requirements] there was hardly a single vehicle and there was a complete lack of rifles and bayonets. These were not issued until twenty four hours before the regiment deployed to the training area at Ohrdruf."

Reserve Infantry Regiment 209 put much of the blame on poor organisation and the inability of those remaining in charge of such matters in Germany to exert a firm, centralised, grip in this novel situation. 'It does not seem inappropriate to state that 'St. Bureaucracy' and false economy were the biggest unnecessary blocks on progress during the training period. In addition, order and counter-order in all manner of places, ranging from the improvised Corps Headquarters and Quartermasters' Departments (in peace time locations and in the field), through to the Ministry of War, caused enormous delays and confusion.'[13] If the situation was bad for those struggling to form, equip and train infantry formations and units, in many ways the position was far worse for the artillery.

Kriegsfreiwillige Kettlitz 7th Battery Reserve Field Artillery Regiment 44 [14]

"On 17 September we went to fetch our horses from Großbeeren. At 2.30 am, thirty four of us from 7th Battery climbed on board a small wagon. It was an awful journey in the dark. The wagon was so narrow that some of us could only stand on one leg, whilst others were forced stand on someone else's corns. It was a relief to debus. About 4.00 am the horses had been rounded up and each of us was put in charge of two horses, which we were to lead back home. The intention was that we should ride, but when, after considerable effort, we succeeded in mounting, it was no easy thing to maintain our seats, because more than one of these so-called saddle horses had waited for precisely that moment to regain his autonomy.

"Very swiftly the fields to our left housed a number of horses whose violent movement had given expression to their wish for freedom; whilst, to the left, a game of hide and seek had been arranged in the woods for those who had dismounted involuntarily. These were moments when the 'old hands' unleashed a veritable torrent of abuse against the stupid kriegsfreiwillige but, of necessity, turned their attention to rounding up the strays. A highly amusing hunt ensued, but I cannot remember if we succeeded in rounding up all the 'rebels'."

Hardly had the novice drivers made their way back to the regiment and dealt with the horses, than an order arrived which caused great consternation in all ranks.

Vizewachtmeister Wolter Reserve Field Artillery Regiment 44[15]

"In the middle of a day of normal preparation and duty an order suddenly landed on 18 September, stating that the entire regiment was to move the following morning to Jüterbog [training area] for live firing. Immediately the barracks resembled a disturbed ant heap, because we were a long way short of being ready to move and everyone was running and scurrying about in all directions trying to collect equipment and pack it. Later that evening word arrived and was greeted by general rejoicing, that we did not have to move out until 25 [September] and only to Zossen,"

It is hard to imagine the scenes had the earlier order been carried out. Even a week later there were major problems when the regiment left barracks on their way to firing camp.

Zahlmeister Schrader 1st Battalion Reserve Field Artillery Regiment 44 [16]

> "The then regimental commander, Oberst Wuthmann, was close to despair when he observed his regiment on the march, cursing it roundly and graphically. This was not altogether a surprise, because neither man nor horse was used to the duties with which they had been burdened. As far as the kriegsfrei-willige were concerned, ninety percent had never sat on a horse in their entire life. For an old gunner the sight of the regiment on the move conjured up a mixture of melancholy and mirth. It was impossible to know whether to laugh or cry."

It was extremely fortunate that the regiment received a draft of 300 drivers between 26 and 28 September, so the inadequate horse management of the earlier volunteers was not as badly exposed in the field as it might otherwise have been. That said, there were still major difficulties. Horses often fell sick, or even died, as a result of being in the hands of inexperienced drivers in the dreadful conditions of weather and terrain encountered later, as one old Landwehr artillery officer noted.

Leutnant Hans Osman [17]

> "I soon had to come to the sad conclusion that our kriegsfreiwillige, despite the way they conducted themselves under fire, were only that – kriegsfrei-willige. With very few exceptions, it never occurred to them to take care of their horses when it rained. Those meant to be looking after them had tucked themselves away somewhere where they were protected from the weather. The short technical military term for this was that it was a bloody disgrace and the said bloody disgrace brought a violent thunderstorm pouring down on the heads of the entire column. Within seconds the silent bivouac looked like a disturbed antheap. Initially the lads all thought that we were moving off some-where, but they soon found out what the score was. The unteroffiziers, whose ears were ringing, passed the word on with interest and the ensuing wave of activity raised my spirits a little. Returning to our stacks of straw, having groomed and covered up our horses correctly, I finished by pointing out to our vet that if he had not annexed all of the blankets, I should not have woken from the cold and discovered what was happening – and he, too, might have been able to sleep on undisturbed."

If care of the horses was frequently well below standard, the state of gunnery training, even at the end of the preparatory period, was truly woeful and the regiments departed, to be faced with the task of mastering the necessary skills whilst in contact with the enemy. Not only had time been lacking to work up the gun crews sufficiently, live ammunition had been rationed on average to a mere forty shrapnel and ten high explosive shells per battery. If the situation had not been so serious, it would have been laughable; and a high price was paid in Flanders, as artillery fire arrived in the wrong place, or on friendly troops, or failed altogether.

The situation in Bavaria, however, though still poor, was slightly easier. The Bavarian army, having mobilised a large number of formations at the beginning of the war, declined to find another complete corps. Instead it raised the new 6th Bavarian Reserve Division and, therefore, it did not need to dilute its junior leadership quite as much as was the case within the Prussian formations. There was also more experience in the ranks. Bavarian Reserve Infantry Regiment 17, which was based on Augsburg, but with companies scattered over a fairly wide area, was typical, in that it comprised one third reservists, one third ersatz-reservists, who had completed a minimum of their basic training, and one third kriegsfreiwillige. According to Bavarian Reserve Infantry Regiment 16 (known as the 'List' Regiment, after its first commander), 'The section commanders and other ranks comprised experienced unteroffiziers of the reserve, or the Landwehr, who had received special leadership training'.[18] It is also the case that a significant proportion, but still a minority, of the kriegsfreiwillige were students. Bavarian Reserve Infantry Regiments 20 and 21, which made up 14 Bavarian Reserve Infantry Brigade were raised in Nuremberg and Fürth respectively and included numerous students from the University of Erlangen in their ranks.

However, if the quality of the regiments of 6th Bavarian Reserve Division was good and its leadership as reliable as possible in the circumstances, it shared the same difficulties in obtaining sufficient arms and equipment for the new regiments and in training them properly. As the time for deployment approached, there was one particularly acute shortage. There were no *Pickelhauben* to be obtained anywhere so, as a short term expedient, the division adopted Landsturm forage caps with grey covers. This was a disastrous decision. Not only were they constantly confused with British soldiers throughout the battles at Ypres, with inevitable consequences, there was at least one extremely serious incident attributable to this stop gap measure.

During the early dawn of 1 November the men of Bavarian Reserve Infantry Regiment 17 captured Wijtschate and were reorganising prior to pushing on, when Bavarian Reserve Infantry Regiment 21 launched a flanking attack on them, with numerous German guns firing in support. The resulting clash led to a battle of such intensity and with such serious casualties, that the Bavarians had to evacuate the village. Eventually they did recapture it some days later but, by then, the chance, however fleeting, of possibly forcing a break through south of Ypres was gone. On such seemingly insignificant decisions campaigns can turn. This was a classic and tragic case of, 'For want of a battle the kingdom was lost/And all for the want of a horseshoe nail'.

That was all still in the future when the fateful decision was taken to deploy the new formations. Despite all the many and various difficulties they faced, on paper at least, the new formations were regarded as ready for deployment within two months of the outbreak of the war and, at the end of September, the Kaiser appointed two very senior and experienced officers to inspect the various corps during final manoeuvres. When the subsequent reports were written, General der Infanterie Freiherr von Hoiningen gen von Huene, the former commander of XIV Corps, whilst acknowledging the inevitable weaknesses, felt that the new corps would all be equal to the task; that a general willingness to succeed would enable the formations quickly to overcome these deficiencies and that, therefore, they could be regarded as battle ready. His fellow inspector, the Deputy Commander of the Guard Corps, was more guarded and altogether more realistic in his assessment, which he produced on 12 October 1914.

General der Infanterie von Loewenfeld Headquarters Guard Corps [19]

"Everything in the way of training which could be done was done. The infantry, which is still rather cautious in its movements, may be regarded as trained. Within the field artillery, the lack of officers is painfully evident . . . The tactical ability of the commanders, especially at company and battery level, is not good. These appointments have, for the most part, been filled with non-active officers of advanced age. In general they have found it difficult to meet the demands of modern warfare. Furthermore their physical robustness and horsemanship, mounted as they are on mostly untrained and barely broken horses, is in many cases deficient.

"One particular fault is their lack of awareness of the risk posed by enemy artillery, even at long range. This manifests itself in a willingness to manoeuvre ineffectually in mass formations only a short distance from the enemy. In addition there is a lack of awareness of cooperation between the arms in the context of the all-arms battle. This applies not only to the artillery, but also to the infantry."

Despite these obvious problems, such was the demand for fresh formations to enable Falkenhayn to pursue his highly ambitious plans on the plains of Flanders, that he decided that there was no choice but to deploy the newly raised troops without delay. Initially the plan had been to despatch one of the corps to East Prussia and the remainder to the western theatre of operations. It is not entirely clear if the intention had originally been to deploy the new corps to quiet sectors of the front, there to accustom themselves to the demands of modern warfare and to relieve active corps for the potentially decisive battle to the north. There is also some slight evidence that thought was given to sending only two of the corps to Flanders, with two others proceeding to the Dutch – Belgian border and one to Armee Abteilung Strantz, down near Metz. However, time was of the utmost importance, so it is probable that no more than lip service was paid to the need to prepare the corps better and, by 8 October, orders were being issued directing four of them to proceed directly to Flanders, there to be thrown straight into the battle.

It is hard to find other examples in history when such inadequately prepared and equipped troops have been sent into battle at its critical point, with the expectation that they would prevail. Not only was their state of individual and collective training lamentable in many cases, their administrative support was either totally lacking, or completely inadequate. To take one small example, Reserve Infantry Regiment 213,

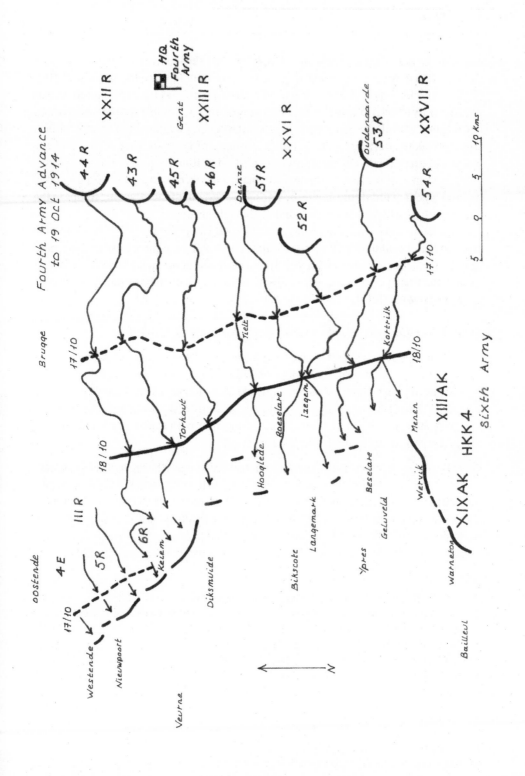

Fourth Army Advance
to 19 Oct 1914

raised in the north of Schleswig Holstein, bemoaned the fact that, 'The field kitchens had not arrived by the time we marched away, so we went to war without them'.[20]They might have added that, at a time when collective cooking was the norm and there was no other truly effective means of preparing rations, this was a most serious problem and it was common to all the new formations. Small wonder, therefore, that despite the best efforts of some quartermasters to obtain a supply of large cooking vessels and the wagons to carry them, administrative support and rationing of the new formations failed as soon as it was put to the test and many men went hungry for days at a time: hardly a way of maintaining morale or getting the best out of the attacking troops in the vile conditions which obtained in Flanders that late autumn.

A charitable view of this enormous gamble is that Falkenhayn and his staff may have assessed that the undoubted high morale and determination of these fresh troops would be more than equal to any defence the Allies could mount on their relatively weak left flank. Others in a position to form a judgement on the wisdom of the policy at the time were much more critical.

Crown Prince Rupprecht of Bavaria Diary Entry 20 October 1914 [21]

"The newly raised corps have been formed by bringing together men from the reserves, Landwehr, and kriegsfreiwillige. In my considered opinion the raising of so many new corps was a mistake. It would have been better to have used the available manpower to reinforce existing corps, whose manpower has been subject to attrition. There, working together with experienced soldiers, better performance could have been expected."

Regardless of such reservations, the decision had been taken; the die had been cast and, for better or worse, tens of thousands of men began to be transported to Flanders to take their chances in one of the most critical battles of the entire war. Only time would tell if the risks about to be run were justified, or if patriotism and youthful enthusiasm were in themselves sufficient to overcome entrenched defences and the power of the magazine-fed rifle, the machine gun and the artillery which lay in wait for them.

Notes

1. Solleder History Bavarian Reserve Infantry Regiment 16 p 4.
2. This and the following extracts from regimental diaries and histories, less those annotated separately, are taken from Unruh *Langemarck* pp 30–35.
3. Mayer History Reserve Infantry Regiment 236 p 82.
4. Schwedt History Reserve Infantry Regiment 205 pp 3- 4.
5. Appel History Reserve Infantry Regiment 205 p 14.
6. Makoben History Reserve Infantry Regiment 212 p 15.
7. Haleck History Reserve Infantry Regiment 208 p 1.
8. Schulz History Reserve Infantry Regiment 209 p 15.
9. Gieraths History Reserve Infantry Regiment 210 p 22.
10. Schatz History Reserve Infantry Regiment 239 p 3.
11. Atzrott History Reserve Jäger Battalion 16 p 14.

12. Mayer *op. cit.* pp 83–85.
13. Schulz *op. cit.* p 15.
14. Boesser History Reserve Field Artillery Regiment 44 p 9.
15. *ibid.* p 11.
16. *ibid.* p 12.
17. Osman *Mit den Kriegsfreiwilligen über die Yser* pp 123–124
18. Solleder *op. cit.* p 7. It is sometimes stated that it was a Bavarian custom to name regiments after their commanders – hence Regiment 'List' – but in fact it was a newly introduced security measure, adopted by the Bavarian army to disguise the fact that a new division was being added to the order of battle. The plan was to use only the new regimental numbers after the formations deployed into the field. However, once the deeds of these regiments became known to the wider public, the names were retained as honorific titles.
19. *Der Weltkrieg 1914–1918 Vol 5* p 274.
20. Tiessen History Reserve Infantry Regiment 213 p 5.
21. Kronprinz Rupprecht *In Treue Fest: Erster Band* p 223.

Preliminary Skirmishing around Ypres October 1914

The early days of October 1914 saw the battles around and to the north of Arras begin to stall, as attempts to push further west failed in the face of increasing French resistance. Already, by 5 October, when Falkenhayn was involved in acrimonious exchanges at Headquarters Sixth Army over the inability of its formations to make better progress, thoughts had turned to how to make better use of the cavalry formations grouped away to the north. It was essential to ensure that they continued to apply pressure and to push out a wide reconnaissance screen, in a final attempt to bring decisive military force to bear on the exposed Allied left flank. Höhere Kavallerie Kommandeure [HKKs = Senior Cavalry Commanders] 1 and 2, comprising Guards, 4th, 7th and 9th Cavalry Divisions, were located on the northern flank of XIV Army Corps, which was currently attempting to get forward through the industrialised area around Lens. During the next few days they would clash with British cavalry northwest of La Bassée in a series of confusing and largely inconclusive engagements.

Despite the presence of all these cavalry formations, such was the demand on their services and, it must be said, inefficiencies in the way they tended to operate, that a further requirement was established for additional cavalry to be deployed on the extreme right flank of the German advance in a screening role. The aim of this deployment was to camouflage the precise movements of the German major formations, in particular the forward deployment of the new reserve formations of Fourth Army, which were scheduled to arrive in the theatre by about mid October. It was also essential to interfere with the freedom of action of the Allies and slow any offensive plans they may have had. In furtherance of this aim, Army Supreme Command ordered HKK 4, commanded by Generalleutnant Freiherr von Hollen, which had begun the campaign by operating forward of Fourth and Fifth Armies in the advance on Sedan and Mezières, to redeploy to the north, where it was to link up with the Bavarian Cavalry Division. 3rd and 6th Cavalry Divisions of HKK 4 detrained in the Mons area; the Bavarian Cavalry Division, which had been operating down near Metz, was transported north to unloading areas near Valenciennes.

Immediately on arrival these forces, augmented by others, such as 'Landwehr Brigade Schulenburg', which was located in Douai and could be spared from other commitments, began to deploy in the rough direction of Lille. The defence status of this major urban conurbation was unknown and there was an urgent need for clarification. Because Bavarian Cavalry Division was located closest, on 4 October a strong patrol, commanded by Rittmeister Fürst Wrede of Bavarian Ulanen-Regiment 1, rode forward in a bold move to obtain the necessary information. Arriving after a somewhat

Eyewitness
Locations
Chapter 1

Map showing locations in the region around Ypres, Armentières, Lille, Roubaix, Tourcoing, Kortrijk and Béthune, with numbered eyewitness location markers (1–10).

Places shown include: Kortrijk, Ledegem, Halluin, Roncq, Tourcoing, Roubaix, Lezennes, Sainghin, Bouvines, Faches, Pont-à-Marcq, Molpas, Seclin, Lille, Menen, Werwik, Comines, Bousbecque, Linselles, Deulémont, Pérenchies, Frelinghien, Prémesques, Armentières, Geluwe, Zandvoorde, Houthem, Geluveld, Hollebeke, Messines, Le Gheer, Warneton, Nieppe, Sailly-sur-la-Lys, Fleurbaix, Fromelles, Aubers, Fournes, Beselare, Dadizele, Zonnebeke, Ypres, Vlamertinge, Dikkebus, St Elooi, Wijtschate, Kemmel, St Jans Cappel, Ploegsteert, Steenwerck, Estaires, Laventie, Neuve Chapelle, Festubert, La Bassée, Paperinge, Cassel, St Sylvestre Cappel, Caëstre, Flêtre, Meteren, Strazeele, Merris, Vieux Berguin, Neuf Berguin, Merville, Forêt de Nieppe, Lestrem, La Bassée Canal, Lillers, Béthune, Hazebrouck.

Scale: 0 5 10 15 km.

adventurous journey during the night, Wrede managed to establish that it did not appear that old fortress of Lille was in a state of defence but that there seemed to be a clear build up of troops in and around the city. Speed was evidently going to be of the first importance.

Even before Wrede's report became available, the formations of the newly constituted HKK 4 were in the saddle and heading north. At 2.00 pm on 4 October, the advance guard of Bavarian Cavalry Division, Bavarian 5 Cavalry Brigade (Chevaulegers = Light Horse) was forced into dismounted action as it veered westwards near Sainghin and came under fire from Lesquin. This slowed its progress, because it had to press its attack north and south of Merchin, which took some considerable time to complete, especially when enemy infantry, believed to have come from Lille, began to pressurise its right flank. This in turn led to the deployment of Bavarian Jäger Battalion 1, with elements of Bavarian 4 Cavalry Brigade (Uhlans) on its right, with orders to fight forward towards Lezennes. During this operation there was an unusual event involving a troop of Bavarian cavalry, namely a mounted charge.

Hauptmann Graf Ingelheim Bavarian Uhlan Regiment 1[1] *1.*

"The approach of a French Hussar squadron was observed from the church steeple in Bersée. The traditional German preference for a charge, rather than dismounted action, prevailed. Exploiting the presence of houses and outbuildings in the area to screen the movement, the squadron, led by the commander, Hauptmann Freiherr von Hirschberg, manoeuvred against the unsuspecting enemy as they advanced along the poplar-lined road from Pont à Marcq to Bersée. Near Molpas the enemy was charged from a distance of two kilometres. Making no attempt to resist, the hussars withdrew and the chase continued over ditches and through fields. Having refused to stand and fight, the hussars bunched up on the road and adjoining fields and spurred their horse in flight back towards Lille.

"The Uhlans pressed the pursuit for several kilometres before the commander called a halt, not wishing to be surprised by superior forces. The bodies of a number of hussars lay dead in the fields and several horses and a large quantity of materiel was the reward for this daring horsemanship. It was a promising start to our operations in Flanders. It was achieved without losing a single man and at the cost of one flesh wound from a lance to the arm of an NCO. The squadron then withdrew from the outskirts of Lille to the Farm La Sauvagerie, where they rested until they were required for further action."

The jägers had heard the sound of battle in Bouvines, where they were enjoying a short rest. Its commander, Hauptmann Franz Spiegel, rode to divisional headquarters in Roncin to be briefed and there followed an efficient minor operation. A timely intervention by batteries of the Horse Artillery Battalion, Bavarian Field Artillery Regiment 5[2], enabled it to bring down a torrent of well directed fire from a flank and, just as night fell, Bavarian Jäger Battalion 1, with 1st, 3rd and 2nd Companies in a first wave and

4th Company, following up echeloned to the left, stormed and took Lezennes. 3rd and 2nd Companies, attacking from west, fixed the defenders (an infantry unit of the French XXI Corps) whilst 1st Company, looping round to the north in an outflanking manoeuvre, completed their defeat and took thirty prisoners. The remainder of the garrison slipped away under cover of darkness.[3] At that, the enemy abandoned Lesquin and Bavarian Schwere Reiter-Regiment [Heavy Cavalry] 2 pursued the withdrawing troops throughout the night. Although the enemy had not resisted hard, the swift elimination of this pocket of resistance underlined the high quality of the Bavarian jägers.

Whilst these clashes had been occurring, 6th Cavalry Division, after a long day in the saddle, had reached an area east of Lille, whilst 3rd Cavalry Division was in bivouac near Orchies. Pressing on in the early morning of 5 October, both 6th Cavalry Division and the Bavarians rode in a huge sweep around the built up areas of Lille, Roubaix and Tourcoing and then paused for the night with the Bavarian Cavalry Division at Linselles and 6th Cavalry Division six kilometres to the northwest at Comines, hard up against the River Lys, which there marked the border with Belgium. Down to the southeast of Lille, 3rd Cavalry Division got as far as Baisieux, but not without becoming involved in minor clashes with French troops probing forward from Lille at Faches, on its southern outskirts. Having been checked, the French troops then bore away northeast to a further skirmish with 1st Battalion Bavarian Reserve Infantry Regiment 1, which had been drafted in to improve the dismounted strength of 3rd Cavalry Division, before pulling back into the security of the city.

It is far from easy at this remove of time to disentangle all the movements and actions of the cavalry during this early phase of operations southeast of Ypres. Though the countryside was much less built up than is the case today, nevertheless the urban areas through which the cavalry on both sides was probing and skirmishing slowed and channelled movement and disrupted command and control, which was in any case always precarious in the German cavalry of the period. Generally speaking, though primitive radio communication was available (when it worked) and there was limited access to the civilian telephone network, the only reliable way for headquarters to remain in touch with their subordinate formations was by despatch rider. Inevitably this produced time delays, less than perfect intelligence and a frequently distorted view of the enemy, their locations and intentions.

Advancing from their harbour areas as dawn broke on 6 October, both 6th Cavalry Division and the Bavarian Cavalry Division advanced to the southwest to complete the sweep of the country to the north of Lille, to establish the status of the Lys crossings at Warneton and Deûlémont and, if possible, to take control of them. One of these patrols was conducted by a troop of 5th Squadron Schwere Reiter-Regiment 2.

Vizewachtmeister Grallinger 5th Squadron Schwere Reiter-Regiment 2[4] **2.**

"On 6 October 1914 I received orders from the regimental commander, Major Freiherr von Eyb, to take eight troopers from 5th Squadron and to patrol forward to the canal crossing at Wambréchies to establish if it was occupied by the enemy. During the carrying out of this mission I was wounded in the right cheek. Due to heavy enemy small arms fire from the fort and cemetery area of Wambréchies, I could not get to the canal bridge so, that evening I returned to the regiment and, on orders of Rittmeister Graf Pocei, went for medical treatment. The doctor promptly sent me back to a casualty clearing station.

When Grallinger arrived, he discovered that there were four officers there, all known to him, as well as almost forty other ranks. These figures may not seem great, but they represented quite a drain on the resources of cavalry regiments and are illustrative of how front line strength was swiftly whittled away during these seemingly innocuous duties. The incident also shows that the Allies were equally clear as to the operational importance of these bridges, so it is no surprise to discover that, from early morning, leading elements of both divisions were engaged in skirmishes with the forward Allied screen, which was acting as an outpost line to the defended Deûlémont crossings. It is impossible to say how this would have been resolved ultimately because, just prior to midday, orders arrived from headquarters HKK 4, located in Kortrijk, ordering their withdrawal with all speed to that area.

Apparently there were unconfirmed reports that strong Allied forces were bearing down on Kortrijk from Gent away to the northeast and the cavalry was needed to counter this new threat. Disengaging with relative ease, the main body headed back for Kortrijk and, by that evening, 6th Cavalry Division was concentrated to the east of the town, with 3rd Cavalry Division out to the southeast and the Bavarian Cavalry Division close to the town on its southern side, with its troops deployed between Aalbeke and the town itself. Prior to this redeployment, the cautious Bavarian Cavalry Division commander, Generalleutnant von Stetten, despatched one of his best formations, 1st Bavarian Schwere Reiter-Regiment, with a section of guns and a cyclist company, off in the general direction of Tielt in order to establish the truth of the reports. It did not take long for this regiment to discover that the report was either totally false or very greatly exaggerated so, the following day, 7 October, the great mass of cavalry moved aggressively westwards once more. Not only had the completely unnecessary movement tired already weary riders and horses even more, a valuable position had to be regained and a day of manoeuvre was lost. Nevertheless, brushing aside minor resistance from enemy dismounted cavalry, cyclist units and members of the Belgian gendarmerie, advanced elements of 3rd Cavalry Division got as far as Ypres that day.

Reserve Hauptmann Ottmar Rutz Bavarian Reserve Infantry Regiment 1 [5] *3.*

"A new day – 7 October – dawned and brought with it a flurry of colourful activity amongst the mounted troops. We were now northeast of Lille, having moved round it in a broad sweep to the east. The place was teeming with cavalry and we kept bumping into the regiments of other cavalry divisions. There were Guards Cavalry, Bavarian Uhlans and Chevaulegers [Light Horse] and the roads were full of horses, riders and wagons. We drew closer to a small town with a great church. It was the well known town of Menen. The whole

[3rd] Cavalry Division was drawn up there, together with its heavy baggage train. It was just as though we were on peacetime manoeuvres.

"After a lengthy halt and then numerous hold ups on the road, including the presence of units crossing the line of march, which caused much cursing and swearing, at long last we marched into the little town and along the length of its main street, under the gaze of its curious inhabitants who crowded the streets. We were to see it later in a very changed situation. Without further delay we carried on along a broad main road to Geluwe and Geluveld. It was a demanding, but fascinating, march. The battalion moved along in the centre of the road, whilst the cavalry stuck to bridle paths to the left and right. Sometimes walking, sometimes trotting, they threw up large quantities of dust, which was a constant trial to us. We were accompanied by wagons which carried those of our men who were exhausted or suffering from foot trouble.

"Away on the horizon the high Gothic towers of a larger town loomed up: Ypres. Apparently cavalry patrols moving near to it had come under fire, so the cavalry halted and orders for an attack by the battalion were issued. However, infantry foot patrols pushing ahead soon reported that there were no enemy in Ypres."

Profiting from that information and far from unhappy that they were not going to have to fight to enter the town, all the regiments of Bavarian Cavalry Division pressed on boldly into the centre of Ypres, making for the great square in front of the famous medi-aeval Cloth Hall. Settling down in the town, thus far totally untouched by the war, the men of 3rd Cavalry Division were about to enjoy an experience unique in the German army on the Western Front. No other German soldiers would ever set foot in the town, except as prisoners of war, so this description of events that day left by a member of 3rd Cavalry Division is probably the only one in existence.

Reserve Hauptmann Ottmar Rutz Bavarian Reserve Infantry Regiment 1[6] 3.

"A marvellous evening mood spread through the ranks. Marching past magnificent properties, beautiful gardens and chateaux, we approached the walls of the town. Crossing ditches, bridges and the moat, we passed through an ancient gateway and entered this famous old town. We first moved through outer streets containing nothing of great significance, then we came to the broad town square in front of the famous Cloth Hall, the giant tower of which reached way up into the darkening sky. Its rich Gothic ornamentation was set off in a refined way by its brilliant, shining windows. The entire square was enclosed by steep, dark, gable ends.

"The companies halted in the middle of the square and piled their rifles together. Shy, but curious, the inhabitants watched all this unfamiliar military activity, with no concept at all of its seriousness. Up until then the war had been conducted a long way away from where they lived. A search had been underway to find accommodation for our men and soon an excellent place had been located. It was an attractive, well appointed, barracks with a pleasant terrace and commodious rooms. Externally it looked like a chateau; nobody would have taken it for a barracks at all. Meanwhile our men looked around the streets and squares with staring eyes. The shops on the main street were as elegant as those of a large city and we could almost feel the proximity of the sea. After attending to the care of my men, I took a stroll through the streets. The side streets were dark and lonely, built in the friendly style of a Dutch suburb. People were out and about on the main street well into the night. It was difficult to communicate with the inhabitants. Only one or two understood French and hardly any of our Bavarians could speak *Plattdeutsch*.[7] I entered some of the well lit shops and benefited by buying things which were very welcome to us, separated as we were from the bulk of our equipment. This included excellent Belgian cigars, which, however, were very expensive and some of the really delicious hard biscuits, which are a speciality of Ypres and similar to others I found later in Kortrijk.

"I found out that on one occasion, about ten to fourteen days previously, a car containing British officers had driven through the town, but we were the first troops to have set foot in Ypres. The people were quite friendly towards me, but they expressed neither sympathy, nor antipathy towards the German advance. Their every third expression was, 'poor Belgium'. I called at one of the most beautiful houses on the main street to make billeting arrangements for myself and several other officers, but the lady of the house explained that a number of other officers had already occupied the house. Never mind! I wandered over to an equally striking building opposite. Having rung the door bell for a long time, the door was finally answered by a friendly cleric, who welcomed us and offered us dinner at 10.00 pm.

"Until then I wandered the streets. I returned to the main square and absorbed the unique sights. All that which lies in ruins and ashes now, then stood tall and straight, in striking splendour, as though it had been built to last for all eternity. The shining lights in the windows had now been extinguished. Several senior officials of the town and the government had been taken hostage. A finance officer had been forced to deliver up the town funds and was only allowed to move about under secure escort. The sound of the footsteps of our Bavarians could be heard coming from the covered walkways of the Cloth Hall, where a guardroom had been established in a chamber on the ground floor and riders clattered over the square delivering messages to the divisional staff, which was located in an hotel next to the Cloth Hall.

"We occupied the whole of Ypres, which was simple because it was surrounded by walls and a moat and was accessible only by a few main roads which passed through the historic gates. I walked a few steps to St Martin's cathedral. Its great dark bulk, with the height of its spire lost in the darkness of the night, bore down heavily on the pointed gable ends of the old houses which surrounded it. I was unable, however, to settle down to appreciate the artistry of it, due to a combination of the hustle and bustle and the excitement of a moment in world history that was to occur only on this one occasion. It was, in fact, a peaceful and moving interlude in the life of what the world has come to know by the name of Ypres – and we were there.

"That evening we did not visualise anything of what was to come; nor anymore did the disturbed and curious inhabitants . . . On my way back to my quarters I talked to a number of them. They had no knowledge of British or French troops and absolutely nothing about the war; they had not received any newspapers for months. 'Where were we marching?' I had no idea myself. In a bookshop I bought a town plan and a map of the surrounding area. I even paid in cash, rather than leaving a credit note. It was just as though we were still at peace. Back in our quarters the friendly priest talked to us about their hopes for a Flemish state and their political humiliation. He could not speak good German, but was better in French.

"He had undergone training at a Jesuit seminary in Austria and had spent a long time in France and Italy, but only a short period in Germany . . . We laid down to rest in good, broad, comfortable French beds. Our departure was sudden and rather like responding to an alarm call. As dawn broke we left the hospitable town and headed down the road towards Vlamertinge. I cast one last glance back at the peaceful scene. As morning fires were lit, the smoke rose comfortingly above the steep gable ends, whilst above them were the towers of the Cloth Hall and the cathedral, the lead roofs and the great gates, which projected a scene right out of the Middle Ages."

Whilst 3rd Cavalry Division had been closing on Ypres, 6th Cavalry Division reached Kemmel and the Bavarian Cavalry Division Dikkebus, four kilometres southwest of Ypres. Pushing forward southwestwards on 8 October into a wide, largely empty space, 6th Cavalry Division got as far as Bailleul. To the north, around Meteren and Flêtre respectively, were the Bavarian Cavalry Division and the 3rd Cavalry Division, with forward elements located at Merris and Strazeele, very close to the important road and railway junction of Hazebrouck. In fact, one platoon sized patrol of 1st Battalion Bavarian Reserve Infantry Regiment 1 actually followed the Bailleul – Hazebrouck railway line right up to Hazebrouck Station, returning unscathed.

According to Rutz,[8] 'The daring platoon commander, Leutnant P., managed to force his way to Hazebrouck Station, overwhelming a French outpost, wounding a senior officer and establishing the fact that there were numerous engines under steam and ready to pull military transport trains. With extreme difficulty the platoon managed to slip out through the French lines under cover of darkness and rejoin the battalion about midnight.' It was, however, obvious that the days of easy movement and coat trailing were rapidly coming to an end. Reports began flowing into Headquarters HKK 4 of strong enemy forces building up at Cassel and around Hazebrouck whilst, off to the east, the complexity of these swirling operations was underlined, when it was discovered that the French 7th Cavalry Division was concentrated around Frélinghien, between

Armentières and Deûlémont. Because this position was virtually in rear of the mass of German cavalry here on the northern flank, this was a matter of considerable concern.

Compounding all the general uncertainty, 9 October dawned to thick fog, which virtually ruled out observation from a distance and led to a series of nerve-wracking close range encounters as mounted patrols from both sides groped about for information. One of these patrols, launched with an offensive mission, was mounted by Bavarian 1 Cavalry Brigade.

Reiter Kaspar Fichtner 1st Squadron Bavarian Schwere Reiter-Regiment 2[9] **4**

"On 9 October I was involved in an eight man patrol. Unteroffizier Brüining also took part and it was led by Oberleutnant Henigst. We started out from near Bailleul with orders to ride thirty kilometres to the north and blow up a railway bridge. We were issued with explosives for the task. The Oberleutnant said that we had been given quite a mission. Whether we should be able to carry it out was, however, questionable, because enemy patrols had already been reported in the vicinity. We rode off at 3.00 pm and, to everyone's delight, the weather was fine. After about half an hour we met up with a Prussian Dragoon patrol, which was approaching from the north. The officer stated that we should not be able to get very far forward, but our Oberleutnant said, 'Well we shall give it a go anyway!' We were pleased he did, because he, a daring patrol leader, was very popular with the troopers.

"We carried on through various villages, then for a time we galloped across country, to an isolated farmhouse, whence we could see enemy cycle troops moving along a main road. We observed for some time then a report was despatched. After that we went on, but by then it was night. We rode on through the pitch darkness and came to a farm, which we surrounded, so that nobody could get away, but there were only two women there. We posted sentries. There were enough oats for the horses and we received an excellent meal. Nothing else happened that night. The following day we left and none too early, because there was thick fog. We headed for Cassel, a really pretty little town set on a hill, but it was occupied by the French, so we carried on to another place and had a short rest before riding on. We then bumped into a civilian riding a bicycle along the road, who told our Oberleutnant that there were two enemy infantry companies and a cavalry squadron in the town and that every village in the surrounding area was occupied. He also stated that 200,000 British troops were said to have arrived in Dunkirk [*sic!*].

"So we did not ride into the town, but went to a nearby estaminet, fed the horses and drank some beer, which was rubbish compared with Bavarian. But we soon had to get going and find out if the villages really were occupied. The Oberleutnant dismounted and, taking two men with him, crept up very close to one through the bushes. The place was occupied and the exits barricaded. The Oberleutnant wrote a report and asked who was willing to ride away with it. Suttner and I volunteered and we were ordered to ride via Godewaersvelde and from there along the line of the railway to Bailleul to deliver the message to divisional headquarters or to a reporting point. Suttner and I rode off at 3.30 pm at a trot, because we had to deliver the message by evening. We were in luck until we reached the railway to Bailleul where we saw an enemy patrol heading our way and rather close. We diverted through Meteren then, fifteen minutes later, we were in Bailleul, but there were no German soldiers to be seen and it was already 7.30 pm.

"We then headed off along the main road towards Dikkebus, thinking that we would certainly meet someone, but we did not get far along it. Coming the other way were two cyclists from the cycle company, who also had a report for division and who insisted that there must be some sort of trace of our troops in Bailleul. We searched the place again, but in vain. We then had to find somewhere to spend the night and all four of us took cover in an empty house outside the town. The next morning the jägers said that divisional headquarters must have advanced, so we took the road to Meteren, but had only gone a short distance when my horse fell. It was pretty well exhausted, so I had to lead it, intending to requisition another horse from a farmer in Meteren. We had not gone more than fifty paces and we were looking at a signpost when a patrol of enemy dragoons rode towards us. They were within 200 metres, so we turned around swiftly and rushed back to the village.

"I was extremely anxious not to be ridden down, so each of us took cover behind one of the trees which was lining the road and opened fire as fast as we could. With his first bullet, Jäger Wagner shot the enemy officer off his horse, but two dragoons rode like the Devil at us across country. Soon both the officer and the dragoons lay dead on the cobbles, two horses had had it and three others were wandering around. We shot them too, because none of them were usable as riding horses and our two horses had run off during all the firing. The second cyclist also rode off during the shooting. We took the officer's revolver, equipment and map case plus all its contents, then the three of us headed back through Bailleul once more and headed for Dikkebus. About midday we met up with a Prussian patrol who informed us that we needed to turn off right and head towards Estaires.

"This we did, arriving at about 3.00 pm in a village where there were about twenty cyclists from Wagner's company. There we were greeted with great joy, because the second cyclist had reported that we must be either dead or captured. The jägers found me a bicycle in a house and later, although they knew nothing of my horse, some Prussian dragoons returned Suttner's horse to him. We then set off for Estaires, because the jägers confirmed that the divisional headquarters was located there. We arrived there at 6.00 pm and delivered our report and the captured map case belonging to the enemy officer. Generalleutnant von Stetten spoke to us and said, 'You have acted with great courage' and directed that names of all three of us be noted – and that is why on 7 November 1914 we received the Iron Cross."

By around 9.00 am the impression had built up that the enemy was withdrawing in a southerly direction, so orders were issued to Bavarian Cavalry Division to close up on Hazebrouck from the northeast and to 6th Cavalry Division to advance on Vieux Berquin to the east of the Forêt de Nieppe. For its part, 3rd Cavalry Division was directed to move south to the east of 6th Cavalry Division and to concentrate at Le Doulieu, five kilometres north of Estaires, where there were crossings over the Lys. It proved to be far from easy to carry out these orders.

Advancing south during the afternoon, 6th Cavalry Division became aware of a threat from the eastern extremity of the Forêt de Nieppe, which was occupied by the enemy, so it was forced to carry out a hasty attack to secure its right (eastern) flank. In the context of this attack, Bavarian Reserve Jäger Battalion 1, which was providing infantry support to the division, pushed boldly on into the wood and captured La Caudescure. However, concern quickly grew about a build up of enemy on this flank so, as evening drew on, the entire division, including its weary infantry, was withdrawn to the area of Bailleul. The Bavarian Cavalry Division also quickly ran into problems with an entrenched pocket of resistance on high ground near La Bréarde, three kilometres north of Hazebrouck on the road towards Steenvoorde. This forced Bavarian 4 Cavalry Brigade to launch a dismounted attack, whilst its infantry element, Bavarian Jäger Battalion 1, together with troopers of Bavarian Schwere Reiter-Regiment 2, attacked forward from Pradelles towards Borre, immediately east of Hazebrouck. Just as the attack of the jägers was developing, the squadrons of Bavarian Uhlan Regiment 1 were galloping forward, led by their commander, Oberst Freiherr von Crailsheim, as far as a prominent farm complex at Le Peuplier, where they dismounted in the shelter of the walls. The regimental history describes what happened next.[10]

"Carbines in hand, we launched ourselves towards l'Egerneest, which the enemy evacuated without a shot being fired. We then brought down fire from the roadside ditch to the south of the place against la Creule and Rittmeister Freiherr von Hirschberg decided to launch an attack on the village, from where the enemy were bringing down rapid fire. Accompanied by Fähnrich Graf Luxburg, Unteroffizier Glück and Gefreiter Kamm, he waded through the stream down in a dip forward of his position, crawled up the slope opposite, then threw himself down in a potato field in order to observe the enemy position through his telescope. Having established its extent, he raised his right arm and waved his section commanders forward but, at that very instant, he felt a blow beneath his right shoulder and a stabbing pain ran along his spine all the way down to his thigh. A bullet had grooved its way the entire length of his upper body.

"At that he shouted to the others who were with him, 'Go back to the squadron!' But make sure that you come back for me; I certainly do not want to be captured.' At that, raising his carbine, the courageous Glück called back,

'I am not leaving my Rittmeister alone! But he suddenly fell back with a soft cry. Blood was pouring out of his nose and mouth; he had been shot through the lungs. Luxburg and Kamm carried him back, whilst Hirschberg, unaided, made his way back down the slope. However, once back at the valley bottom, he attempted to crawl, only to discover to his horror that his lower body was completely paralysed. Troopers from the squadron rushed up and carried him back to the ditch by l'Egerneest where he was bandaged up. Here news reached him that the squadron leader to his right, Rittmeister Freiherr von Lilgenau, had also been seriously wounded as he attempted to advance on La Creule, to the west of the road, with twenty five dismounted troopers – all he had available.

"Initially the streambed and hedges provided some cover, but the last 600 meters were across open ground. Each tactical bound cost him men wounded, then the ammunition started to run short. At about 4.30 pm he was informed that the squadron was to withdraw because the enemy was advancing on the rear of the division. Lilgenau had his men run back to the next cover and onwards to the old positions, whilst he and Fähnrich Bopp stayed out in front. When he began to get to his feet, however, he immediately collapsed, shot through the left lung. Helped by the Fähnrich, who stayed with him, he attempted to return to the squadron in very short bounds. In this he was successful, despite the consequent painful exertion. After a field dressing had been applied, he was even able to make his way to the aid post, to which Rittmeister Freiherr von Hirschberg was carried on a ladder. Meanwhile the 5th Squadron and some horse artillery arrived to assist in breaking clean from the enemy."

This minor and insignificant action, typical of so many during these hectic days, achieved absolutely nothing, but cost the Uhlans two experienced squadron commanders. The Bavarian Cavalry Division as a whole lost ten men killed and five officers and thirty three men wounded during operations on 9 October. Eight men were also missing.

In the meantime, whilst Bavarian 4 Cavalry Brigade was heavily engaged, Bavarian 5 Cavalry Brigade attempted to outflank the enemy to the north via St Sylvestre Cappel. Some progress was being made when, suddenly, at about 4.00 pm, orders arrived there too from HKK4 to break off the attacks. Once again there were reports of strong enemy forces advancing from the northwest towards Steenvoorde on the main road between Cassel and Poperinge. If true, this would constitute a most serious threat to the flank and rear of the Cavalry Corps, so the Bavarian Cavalry Division was pulled back into a holding area north of Caëstre and Flêtre, ready to move to counter it. That same afternoon, in an attempt to secure crossings back across the Lys, 3rd Cavalry Division was directed forward from Le Doulieu to the bridges at Sailly-sur-la-Lys, four kilometres northeast of Estaires, but it never got there. Encountering extremely tough resistance, it was also directed to halt the attempt and to pull back to positions near Steenwerck.

Moving rapidly on 10 October and abandoning the attempt to force a crossing east of Estaires, the entire forces of HKK 4, their northern adventure over temporarily, managed to get back across the Lys and, passing Armentières (with no trace of the elusive French cavalry), swung back southwest. It proved to be yet another long and hard day in the saddle. The Bavarian Cavalry Division, moving via Bailleul and Frélinghien, continued all the way to Laventie where, despite the lateness of the hour and general exhaustion, it had to drive light enemy forces away before it could concentrate for the night. 3rd Cavalry Division advanced along the bank of the Lys until it reached a position to the east of Estaires, which by now was strongly held by the enemy and 6th Cavalry Division moved via Deûlemont and Radinghem-en-Weppes (to the west of Lille) via Perenchies to Prémesques and ultimately into a depth concentration area around Fleurbaix. At Prémesques, the divisional staff had a brush with a squadron of French Chasseurs but, luckily, a troop from 3rd Cavalry Division and a squadron of Jäger Bataillon zu Pferd [Mounted Infantry Battalion] 13, 6th Cavalry Division, arrived at precisely the right moment to avert a minor disaster. The Chasseurs were driven off and a large group of Belgian reservists, estimated at up to 3,000, was captured at the same time.

This lengthy and demanding move had brought the formations of HKK 4 into contact at last with units of HKKs 1 and 2, but there was now such an immense and unwieldy mass of cavalry squeezed into the area between the Lys and the right flank of Sixth Army near La Bassée, that HKK 4 was forced to cross to the northern bank of the Lys once more on 11 October and this time the Bavarian Cavalry Division had to fight its way up to and over the bridges at Estaires, though 3rd Cavalry Division, followed by 6th Cavalry Division, managed to cross at Sailly-sur-la-Lys relatively easily and move back to Bailleul and Steenwerck respectively. The Bavarians had an altogether more difficult day on 11 October. Bavarian 4 Cavalry Brigade and Bavarian Jäger Battalion 1 assaulted Estaires from the south, whilst Bavarian Schwere Reiter-Regiment 2, having crossed the river elsewhere, pushed along the river bank from the east.

Pushed out to the west, Bavarian 5 Cavalry Brigade was meant to attack towards the river from the south via la Gorgue, just west of Estaires, but was soon subject to an attack from Lestrem and it had to turn and beat that off first. After heavy fighting, by about midday Bavarian Jäger Battalion 1 had succeeded in securing the market place in the centre of Estaires and, a little while later, la Gorgue was captured. After that the remainder of the day went smoothly, but all ranks were glad to reach their final objectives between Estaires and Neuf-Berquin and halt for the night. There was, however, little time for rest for the men of HKK 4. If anything the threat first noted on 9 October, of a build up of enemy forces around Cassel and Hazebrouck, had intensified, with a further concentration now reported at Merville, south of the Forêt de Nieppe and west of Estaires so, as a result, on 12 October, HKK 4 ordered its divisions to take up defensive positions against a possible enemy advance, with 3rd Cavalry Division at Meteren, 6th Cavalry Division at Le Doulieu and the Bavarian Cavalry Division in and around Estaires.

Having assessed the situation and appreciated the significance of the Lys bridges at

Estaires for the potential forward movement of the fresh forces arriving in the area of Lille, Generalleutnant von Stetten decided that, instead of following his orders from HKK4, he would deploy his forces mainly to the northwest and not the northeast of Estaires. By around midday Schwere Reiter-Regiment 2 was in position in the southeast part of Neuf-Berquin then, further to the west, Bavarian Chevauleger Regiment 6 was occupying positions around farm buildings along the road to Estaires. The whole of Bavarian 4 Cavalry Brigade was deployed within Estaires itself and Bavarian Jäger Battalion 1 remained back in La Gorgue. 6th Cavalry Division conformed to this deployment and elements of its infantry, Bavarian Reserve Jäger Battalion 1, moved to occupy the vulnerable northwest corner of Neuf-Berquin.

These deployments had been carried out in the nick of time. As the afternoon wore on, pressure built up from what was assessed to be a British and a French Cavalry Division against Neuf-Berquin and increasing amounts of artillery fire began to fall on both Schwere Reiter-Regiment 2 and the Chevaulegers by the main road. In a swiftly mounted counter-action the Divisional Commander ordered elements of Bavarian Uhlan Regiment 2 and Bavarian Jäger Battalion 1 to attack into the left flank of the enemy and, at that, they broke off the action and withdrew to Merville, pursued by men of Bavarian Chevauleger Regiment 6. That morning marked the welcome return of Schwere Reiter-Regiment 1 from Tielt. Under its determined commander, Major von Tannstein, it had been able to establish very swiftly during an extremely challenging independent assignment that there were no enemy forces in the area between Gent and Brugge, which came as a considerable relief to the entire chain of command. There was no time for Schwere Reiter-Regiment 1 to rest on its laurels however. Already by 5.30 am on 13 October it was ordered to cross the Lys and to take up hasty defence between Schwere Reiter-Regiment 2 and the Chevaulegers of Bavarian 5 Cavalry Brigade on the southwest side of Neuf-Berquin.

Advancing with the aid of guides through the dense fog, the dismounted troopers moved into position from about one hundred metres west of the church, in the order 5th, 2nd and 4th Squadrons. In addition, the regiment placed two machine guns which had been subordinated to it where they could bring down defilade fire out to the front. The situation was far from comfortable, however.

Leutnant Freiherr von Dornberg 2nd Squadron Schwere Reiter-Regiment 1 [11] *4.*

"Swiftly we moved into the designated line in front of the edge of the village. There were no trenches at all. We lay down flat on the bare earth. To our rear there was a thorn hedge, which would make a first class aiming point for artillery. For the moment all was still quiet. The jägers, who had spent the night here on outpost duty, were slurping coffee and preparing to depart, but not before they pointed out that yesterday the enemy artillery had concentrated particularly on this spot. Using the spade of one of the jägers, I speedily dug out a shell scrape, because I was located on the extreme left of the squadron firing line, with no cover at all from the hedge. The fog cleared and the visibility improved. At that the firing began. We had obviously been detected when we moved into position. I felt as though I was lying on a presentation platter, but I had to put my head up out of the scrape or I could not observe. Until then I should never have believed myself capable of producing a usable scrape capable of providing cover for my whole person so quickly, but when I noted the quantity of shell fragments lying around I could see that the advice of the jägers had been sound.

There was further fighting around Neuf-Berquin on 13 October. In fact it developed into one of the hardest battles faced by HKK 4 throughout the duration of its operations north of the Lys. Bavarian Schwere Reiter-Regiment 1 was particularly heavily engaged in fending off strong enemy probes. However, despite the fact that the numbers of troopers which they could deploy was very limited and their weaponry less than ideal, the dismounted cavalry more than held their own; the action concluding late in the afternoon, when Bavarian Jäger Battalion 1 launched a flanking attack, which pushed the enemy back to Merville to the southwest.

Gefreiter Kriening 4th Squadron Bavarian Schwere Reiter-Regiment 1[12] **4.**

"There was a farmstead about five hundred metres forward of Neuf-Berquin. This was occupied at about 10.30 am by Leutnant Freiherr von Bonnet and fifteen troopers. These were Unteroffiziers Rogert, Leimböck, Nocker, Strobel, Wugazzer, Graf Holnstein, me and eight others, whose names I forget. From this point we were able to observe the complete enemy approach. Immediately, there were enemy to our front and we opened fire. Initially the enemy advanced in company strength, but there was also cavalry with them. Once our artillery opened fire, the company shook out into a skirmishing line and began to attack our farmstead. We kept our eyes and ears peeled for anything untoward.

"The farmstead was rather large, so we were split up at twenty metre intervals. However, we held the enemy in check. We changed positions frequently, so as to disguise the strength of our garrison. I never saw the enemy gun positions and we did not come under artillery fire at the farm. This only happened when the regiment began to withdraw. We defended the place for a long time until mounting pressure forced us to withdraw. As far as we could tell, the advancing enemy was about six times stronger than the dismounted element of the regiment to our rear. We held out until the enemy were about one hundred metres from the farm than we pulled back. We had gone a bare hundred metres from the farm when we suddenly came under a torrent of fire. Nevertheless we all returned in one piece; how remains a mystery to this day."

As soon as Bonnet's troop evacuated the farmhouse it was occupied by the enemy and, only a short time later, a general attack, complete with artillery support from the flanks, developed against the entire Neuf-Berquin sector. One of the officers of 2nd Squadron later described how events unfolded in a lengthy diary entry.

Leutnant Freiherr von Dornberg 2nd Squadron Bavarian Schwere Reiter-Regiment 1[13] **4.**

"Supported by heavy artillery fire, the enemy advanced in dense firing lines all across our front. Our men fired in an exemplary, calm manner and I could see quite clearly, three hundred metres to the front, men crawling through a beet field. Then the battery opened fire from a place just off to the left, but within our lines. It was quite something to see the shells hammering in at that range, round after round, amongst the prone infantrymen. Already some were running back to the rear. The four guns, firing incessantly, tore great holes in the enemy lines, soon causing them to abandon each attempt to assault. Pursued by rapid fire from us, they disappeared as fast as they could go into the shelter of the farmstead out to the front. I should never have believed that infantry of that strength would be forced to give up their objective having got so close.

"Now, however, began the systematic bombardment of the lines to our rear. One house after another collapsed. It appeared that one of the batteries had been given the task of dealing with our firing line along the hedge and shells were impacting constantly. The effect of the low burst shrapnel was also appalling and each succeeding shell burst about five metres above the ground. Shrapnel balls hammered into the ground in front, behind and to the sides of the position as well as directly on it. One shrapnel pot burst vertically a mere two metres above me; so close that I could feel the blast and heat of it on my face. The enemy squandered great quantities of ammunition on us; it certainly made going for a walk difficult.

"Off to my left 4th Squadron was suddenly withdrawn and I had to cover the gap with my troop. This position, a hedge and field boundary, was about fifty metres in rear of our line. Bent double and one by one, my troop ran back to the hedge. I landed with a thud, having felt a sharp tug at my left foot and had it pulled away from me. A rifle bullet had drilled a groove in the grass immediately beneath my foot. I got to my feet and crossed a wire fence. By spreading out wide, the troop was able to cover across to the Chevaulegers. All the time shrapnel had been bursting above us and now things really began to happen. Together with a few men, I moved to the centre and took cover behind an old rustic hurdle fence, which stood around a ten metre wide dew pond.

"Apparently the enemy artillery thought our guns were located here, but they were a further two hundred metres to the left. It meant that the little space became a real witches' cauldron. All around was the sound ba-bam, ba-bam, as the shrapnel pots exploded and the balls blasted through the branches in the hurdles and sent fragments and splinters showering into the pond. We crouched there for some time, shrouded in really dense powder smoke, then the atmosphere lightened and everyone laughed when two duds splattered into the pond ,sending up a huge geyser of water and soaking us. In fact the only reason they did not explode was probably the soft clay bottom of the pond.

"Mayer II created a most comic image, appearing to dodge fragments as though he was trying to shelter from getting wet. It set the tone for the remainder of the day."

Enemy pressure continued until, at about midday, 1st Squadron was made available to thicken up the defence. When the troopers arrived towards 1.00 pm, the overall commander, Major von Tannstein, directed the squadron leader to place his men in rear of the centre of the line, there to act as a general reserve. For a time the firing seemed to slacken but, by 2.00 pm, it was back to its former intensity. Counter fire by the German artillery, directed at the farmstead to the front, seemed to have the effect of taking some of the pressure off and, about 4.00 pm, the enemy was seen to be pulling back slightly. It was decided to attempt to retake this useful outlier to the defence, so the regimental orderly officer, Leutnant Franz Freiherr von Redwitz, was sent galloping over to 5th Squadron with orders to that effect. There was no room for hesitation, but the assault was launched at an unfortunate moment.

Oberleutnant Freiherr von Perfall 5th Squadron Bavarian Schwere Reiter-Regiment 1[14]
4.

"The squadron had to advance at precisely the moment when the enemy artillery fire was once more coming down very heavily. As a result the squadron suffered relatively heavy casualties. Leutnant Hans Freiherr von Pfetten was seriously wounded, as were eight or nine troopers. Nevertheless not one man hung back when I gave the orders to skirmish forward and two slightly wounded men also stayed in the line. The squadron was soon reorganising and taking up defensive positions in and around the farmstead and its garden."

One difficulty this forward thrust caused was the creation of yet another gap in the thin line of defence in the direction Bavarian Schwere Reiter-Regiment 2. 1st Squadron deployed under Rittmeister Jung to carry out this task and a new reserve was created when 4th Squadron Bavarian Schwere Reiter-Regiment 2 moved forward. Jung's men now formed the extreme right flank of the Bavarian Cavalry Division.

Rittmeister Jung 4th Squadron Bavarian Schwere Reiter-Regiment 1[15] **4.**

"Once in its new position, 4th Squadron received orders to link up with a company of Bavarian Reserve Jäger Battalion 1 on its right and Schwere Reiter-Regiment 2 on its left and to hold the new position at all costs. The enemy, however, did not allow us sufficient time to provide cover from fire for the troopers. The move was directed at about 10.00 am and, only a short time after we reached the new position, enemy infantry detachments began bearing down on us from the direction of Merville, moving in tactical bounds and brilliantly supported by their field artillery, which did not seem to have any need to conserve ammunition. Shortly afterwards, rifle and machine gun fire was opened from the northwest. This had a very damaging enfilade effect on our troopers deployed to counter the threat from Merville. Despite everything, the courageous troopers of 4th Squadron exercised excellent fire discipline and made sure that every round had a worthwhile target.

"Here, for the first time since we were in Lorraine, we learned about the brilliance of the French artillery support for their infantry and, in particular, about their outstanding observation techniques. Shrapnel burst with superb precision just above and forward of our line. Shrapnel balls, fragments and other debris rattled down endlessly on us. One ball hit the squadron commander in the back, fortunately having first been deflected by the branches of a tree, but he was nevertheless hindered in his movements for days to come. About 4.00 pm the enemy attack was halted and the artillery fire died away then, at about 5.00 pm, the squadron was directed to break clean from the enemy and to revert to the command of its own regiment. The squadron was then ordered by the regimental commander to be at readiness (less Bonnet's troop) on the eastern edge of Neuf-Berquin."

This task did not last long, because there was soon yet another enemy attack to be dealt with and 4th Squadron was ordered back into the line.

Oberleutnant Freiherr von Perfall 5th Squadron Bavarian Schwere Reiter-Regiment 1[16]

4.

"Evening had already begun to fall when I observed the enemy infantry, which I estimated to be between one and two companies strong, heading in the direction of our positions. I allowed the columns to approach to within six hundred metres of the squadron then ordered rapid volley fire against them. The enemy deployed and, as the battle developed, they skirmished forward using fire and manoeuvre. When the first waves had closed up to about 250 metres, I ordered a fighting withdrawal by troops. Regaining the regiment was absolute hell. From the rear came heavy fire from the pursuing infantry, together with gun fire. From our rear and half right, came our own rifle and machine gun fire – but we had no casualties!"

This almost miraculous escape was probably due to the fact that Perfall made a timely decision to withdraw in the face of overwhelming odds, assisted by covering fire from other squadrons. Once 5th Squadron was safely back in the line, the fire fight developed all around Neuf-Berquin. The enemy closed up to about 400 metres, but every attempt to close the range foundered in the face of accurate and effective fire by the defenders. As darkness fell finally, enemy small arms and artillery fire died away and the defenders pushed forward patrols and listening posts to prevent surprise. Whilst the Bavarians were tied down in this manner, 6th Cavalry Division to the north of Neuf-Berquin actually managed to push on a further two kilometres, but 16 Cavalry Brigade, 3rd Cavalry Division, faced extremely hard fighting around Meteren, where the enemy pressed in on its regiments from north, west and south simultaneously. However, its dismounted cavalry, stiffened considerably by the men of Bavarian Reserve Infantry Regiment 1, beat off all attacks during the day, the infantry even resorting to launching a series of small forays forward of the village to drive the enemy back and create space for the defence.

Its mounted infantry battalion from Jäger Regiment zu Pferd 7 later described the action from its perspective.[175]

"The defence of the left flank of the position had been allocated to the Mounted Infantry Battalion. Our numerically weaker artillery could not counter the preparatory bombardment with which the enemy prepared the attack and, under its protection, they launched an outflanking assault on the weaker 16 Cavalry Brigade. Advancing along the line of the road from Flêtre, to the west of Meteren, they drove back the men of Bavarian Reserve Infantry Regiment 1 and rushed the village, whilst the road was neutralised by shrapnel and small arms fire. A hasty counter attack launched by the Mounted Infantry Battalion, with fire support from the road, led to the ejection of the enemy and the retaking of the village. There was a steady stream of casualties from the incessant artillery fire and the enemy appeared to be bringing up reinforcements. Everywhere, shells crashed down, shrapnel burst and machine guns poured down fire. In several places, Meteren was ablaze.

"Our left flank was in the air, because there was a wide gap between us and 22 Cavalry Brigade to the south, which was also involved in an intense battle. There were no fewer than three separate assaults by the British on our positions, but each failed in the face of determined resistance by our courageous troops, who kept up their rate of fire and did not yield any ground. The situation became ever more critical at 16 Cavalry Brigade's position to our north, which was increasingly being outflanked by superior forces. Orders then arrived to withdraw from the unequal action and return to Bailleul, but the commanders of the jägers and Bavarian Reserve Infantry Regiment 1 agreed to hold on until it went dark, in order to ensure that the withdrawal could be conducted in good order and not risk it turning into a rout.

"The positions were held until after darkness fell, having been successfully defended throughout the entire day against an enemy six times stronger than we were."

This had been an heroic day of largely defensive battles, but it was a style of warfare for which the cavalry was ill suited so, as evening wore on and the positions of 3rd Cavalry Division were threatened with outflanking from the right (east), orders were given to withdraw closer to the Lys. 6th Cavalry Division and the Bavarian Cavalry Division were also directed to fall back on the general line Estaires – Steenwerck. Having arrived in the new positions, the HKK 4 formations learned that the orders had stemmed in part from a change of direction from Supreme Army Headquarters to Sixth Army.

Henceforth, that army was to go over to defence behind the Lys and, that being the case, the need for HKK 4 to hold open the Lys crossings disappeared.

One of the regimental commanders of the Bavarian Cavalry Division later summed up the day of hard fighting from his perspective in a report.

Major von Tannstein Bavarian Schwere Reiter-Regiment 1[18]

"On 13 October we spent the entire day, eleven hours, under enemy fire. Small arms fire and shells impacted all around us constantly, as we lay there in the open. Together with my staff I was located a mere twenty paces behind the firing line, because a cavalry regimental commander with his few dismounted troopers is only the equivalent of a company commander in the infantry. Naturally we had been ordered to dig in, but that is difficult with bare hands. At that time a cavalry regiment was only issued with eight spades and we had no real idea what to do with them anyway. As a result we only had feeble shell scrapes for protection. Nobody dared to wander about because the firing was ceaseless and unpleasant. The Good Lord protected the regimental staff; that and the presence of a stack of straw, behind which we clustered together and out of whose protection we only emerged to issue orders. As always Hauptmann Jahrreis, the gallant General Staff Officer of the division, came and visited us.

"This was the first time that we learned to cooperate closely with the artillery. Up until then the guns had been under the direct command of higher authority, receiving their orders only from that source. As a result the fire support afforded the troopers was often deficient. The reason for this may have been the fact that, previously, modern means of battlefield communication such as telephone and signalling were not available. Despatch riders could not be employed on the contemporary battlefield, so there was nothing for it but to use runners to maintain mutual links. His Royal Highness Prinz Conrad, a member of my staff, distinguished himself greatly whilst carrying out this duty and making numerous unpleasant traverses of the village streets whilst under fire. It was also new to the horse artillery to have to work closely with their troopers, but everything worked perfectly."

Despite the decision of HKK 4 to withdraw, nevertheless there seemed merit in imposing delay on the enemy bearing down on the river from the north and northwest so, on 14 October, Steenwerck was made into a temporary buttress, with 3rd and 6th Cavalry Divisions going into hasty defence to its northeast and northwest respectively. The enemy advanced against these new positions only cautiously – possibly as a result of the battles of the previous day – and the formations of the Bavarian Cavalry Division began to dig in as best they could to the west between Le Cruseobeau and Estaires. There was, however, action that day to the south of the river, where the wisdom of leaving Bavarian Jäger Battalion 1 at La Gorgue was underlined. After a sharp bombardment, elements of the French 7th Cavalry Division launched a series of attacks but they were held, as were others launched against formations of 9th Cavalry Division of HKK 2 just to the south. In addition a number of patrols were sent out in various directions in the reconnaissance and screening role.

Sergeant Zadow 2nd Squadron Bavarian Schwere Reiter-Regiment 1[19]6.

"When, during the evening of 13 October, the sound of battle died away around Neuf-Berquin, 2nd Squadron was ordered to despatch a patrol comprising one Unteroffizier and four troopers to ride out along the road from Neuf-Berquin to Strazeele until contact was made with the enemy, then to screen and report any possible advance of the enemy the following morning. Unteroffizier Hirsch was appointed patrol commander and they rode away from our positions in Neuf-Berquin. At midnight I, together with four troopers, who by then had been fed, was ordered to go and relieve the other patrol. In total darkness I met up with Hirsch on the road north of the hamlet of La Couronne and assumed the duties of standing patrol. Hirsch informed me that earlier that evening he had come under fire from the area of the level crossing south of Strazeele [i.e. where the railway line from Hazebrouck to Bailleul crosses the road].

"Some of the houses in La Couronne to our rear were ablaze, lighting up the dark night sky. We had to turn back inhabitants, who were attempting to flee with all their belongings, lest they betrayed our presence. Together with one other trooper, I maintained constant surveillance along the road, whilst the other two, who were dog tired, stayed with their horses. Constant rifle and machine gun fire could be heard coming from the southwest. Dawn was just beginning to break on 14th when hoof beats could be heard coming along the road from the north. I immediately stood the patrol to and attempted to establish which troops we were up against. Suddenly, looming up out of the mist not fifty metres away, were the red trousers of the French infantry.

"Whilst we were reacting the first bullet thudded in on the haystack and it was a matter of luck that we came through in one piece, particularly in view of all the confusion; my horse 'Elektra' had its bridle tangled between its forelegs, as opposed to on its head. Hardly had this immediate danger passed, than we were up against an eight man French flank protection team rushing forward across the open ground. Despite the fact that we were outnumbered, we had our lances and therefore felt ourselves superior, because the enemy lacked them. When they rode up to us, they came under fire from our jägers, who had also pushed an outpost forward to this place. Leaving behind some fallen horses and riders, the rest sought safety in flight. I immediately sent a report back about the French approach and it was not long before artillery shells were roaring over head and crashing down on the approach routes of the enemy. Because my task was ended, we rode off to Doulieu and reported back to the regiment having suffered no casualties."

By now it was clear that it was no longer appropriate or viable to maintain light forces north of the Lys, so orders were issued by HKK4 for a complete withdrawal during the night 14/15 October. In view of enemy pressure and the fact that it was far from certain which bridges were still available across the Lys for use by the Bavarian Cavalry Division, as an insurance policy, all the bridging equipment of three regiments was pooled and a member of Schwere Reiter-Regiment 1 was given the task of bridging the river and marking the route to the crossing site. This proved in the end to be unnecessary, nugatory work, but it was a dangerously memorable event for those directly involved.

Leutnant Graf von Marogna-Redwitz Bridging Detachment Commander Bavarian Cavalry Division[20] 7.

"Leutnant Graf von Preysing had found a suitable bridging site at Rue de la Lys. At that I was given the mission of constructing a bridge to enable the division to cross, using the equipment belonging to Schwere Reiter-Regiment 1, Uhlan Regiment 2 and Chevaulegers Regiment 6. So even this aspect of our peacetime training was going to be used and our cavalry bridging equipment was going to be proved for the first time in war. There were only three unter-offiziers and fourteen men of the regiment available to me. I had not trained them personally and I did not even know them well, having completed my engineer training in 1910 and 1911. However the work went well and according to the book. We started at 10.00 am and finished at 2.00 pm when the final part was fixed in position and the whole thing was tested. The divisional engineer detachment then marked the route to the bridge from the nearest road, a bridge guard was mounted and now we waited somewhat keyed up, to see which troops would have the honour first.

"The current was so weak and there was so little tension in the anchor points that both cavalry columns and artillery would have been able to cross without any problem. Having practised on the Isar[21] we were used to hard work . . . Hours passed and nothing stirred. Once, at 6.00 pm, we received a visit from Leutnant von Faber of Chevaulegers Regiment 1, but he had no information for us. As evening drew on, I allowed some of the men to go to a nearby house on the road where we had tethered the horses and cook a meal. I then sent the others in rotation to be fed. At the same time I made my dispositions for the night and had fires and torches prepared ready to light in case there was to be a night crossing.

"At about 9.00 pm, we saw some men moving between the houses and farm to our front. We did not like the look of them, because they seemed to be taking up sentry positions facing us. Preysing and I were both convinced that the regiment could not possibly have departed without informing us, so I thought it wise to send a patrol forward on foot to investigate. Within minutes it reported that there were enemy to our front. What now? With the numbers available to me, there were too few to provide proper bridge security and certainly not to defend it. If our bridge fell into the hands of the enemy it would open the way for them to pass the obstacle of the Lys and fall on the rear of our troops. Should we demolish the bridge without orders? What would happen if one of our columns was to arrive and find that what was meant to be the only remaining crossing was no longer there?

"These were moments of great tension and it was a difficult decision. I ordered all preparations to be made and absolute silence to be maintained. It came as an immense relief to receive an order at 9.30 pm to dismantle the bridge and to rejoin the regiment at Sailly. The second part of the order did not leave us feeling calm, however. The division had pulled back over the Lys, so the assumption had to be that the enemy would be following up. We went to work with all speed, though we were hindered by the darkness. Without light we could not see the lashings, so we had to resort to pocket torches. Bang! Bang! In no time we were being shot at. Haste was essential because the enemy fire was increasing. Our work had been discovered and we had to assume that there would be an enemy attack at any moment from the houses which were only 150 metres away.

"I do not believe that cavalry engineers ever worked faster even in the pitch darkness of night. There was hardly a sound and no cursing and, in barely one hour, the task was complete. Having loaded the wagons all of us, officers and men, were dripping with sweat. Paying no heed to the bullets, we pulled away and the enemy appeared on the far bank, just as the wagons were departing. Luckily they could see as little as us, so they hit nothing and soon we were clear of the danger area. We linked up with German troops in Sailly, but nobody could say where the division was. It would have been pointless to search in the dark, so we decided to halt and eat what was left of our disturbed, but not forgotten, evening meal. My brave orderly had thrust a freshly roasted chicken, hot as it was, in his saddlebag before we left."

This incident is as clear example as could be found for the extreme difficulty of conducting mobile operations in the days before reliable battlefield communications became available. In the event no harm was done but, had the bridge been captured intact, the consequences could have been serious and the incident does not reflect well on any of the superiors of Marogna-Redwitz. As a result of the move back across the Lys, 3rd Cavalry Division moved into concentration areas in and around Armentières. 6th Cavalry Division was located to the west and Bavarian Cavalry Division in and around Sailly-sur-la-Lys for twenty four hours, before pulling back to positions to the south between Armentières and Laventie. This was a short term measure. More of the infantry regiments of Sixth Army were moving into the area and they were far better placed and equipped to hold ground so, their mission apparently complete, HKK 4 was withdrawn to bivouacs around Lille. The withdrawal came none too soon. The entire force, horses as well as men, were totally spent. Bavarian Chevaulegers [Light Horse] Regiment 1 later recalled,

"At 9.00 pm [14 October] orders arrived that we were to act as rearguard to the division and were to move behind the columns of marching infantry to an area to the east of Lille. Already earlier, at around midday, the regiment had been ordered to pull back from Rouge de Bout to Radinghem, so it was possible to get some rest during the afternoon. The march which followed was at least forty two kilometres from Sailly through the foggy night and it drained the very last reserves of strength from the horses. During the previous weeks there had been hardly any rest and, in addition to lengthy marches, they all had considerable patrolling duties behind them as well. As for the troopers, who had been constantly in battle, in the saddle, caring for their horses, or frequently on sentry duty at night, they were visibly exhausted. Hardly any of them had any recollection of the move of the division through the endless streets of Lille in the early grey of dawn. Almost all of them slept the sleep of a cavalryman on the backs of their faithful, patient horses who stumbled along numbly in one long procession.'[22]

Despite the totally unfavourable geography, the cavalrymen of HKK 4 looked back on the events of these two weeks as a highlight of their service. At times completely cut off from their lines of supply, the cavalry divisions had managed to operate effectively in hostile territory and give a good account of themselves whenever they came into contact with enemy forces. The marching performance of their infantry, all of which was Bavarian, was outstanding. In the early days of this short campaign the marches frequently exceeded fifty kilometres in twenty four hours. They were called on to take the main load of the dismounted battles, to act as advance guards, rearguards and generally keep up with the pace of mounted movement. This was no mean feat, especially for the reservists and the Landwehr men in Bavarian Reserve Infantry Regiment 1 in particular, so it was probably fortunate that these men were drawn largely from rural Bavaria where, working the land for the most part, they were used to hard work and difficult living conditions.

With the formations of HKK 4 temporarily out of the line of battle, there now began a phase of operations when both sides made a last, supreme effort to probe for the northern flank of the other and to attempt to complete a major outflanking movement before the proximity of the sea put an end to freedom of manoeuvre. The German XIX Corps having completed the occupation of Lille on 12 October and Sixth Army, believing that it still had the initiative and a preponderance of strength locally, had now secured a firm pivot for subsequent operations and began moving infantry formations of XIII Corps into position to replace the weak cavalry regiments and to check any efforts of the Allies to gain ground eastwards. So, for example, Infantry Regiment 121 of 26th Infantry Division found itself on 14 October, taking a broad sweep around to the east of Lille with orders to occupy Menen. Before it arrived there, however, it discovered that the task had been completed by Uhlan Regiment 20, the divisional reconnaissance regiment.[23]

The German flag was hoisted over the town hall, twenty leading citizens were taken hostage and locked in there as a guarantee of good behaviour and the Württembergers stepped out along the road to Ypres in the footsteps of the men of HKK 4, who had passed that way a week previously. Within a few short hours, patrols had pushed forward as far as Geluveld and Beselare, but the main body was further back around Geluwe and there was no question of the ground being firmly held. The occasional British armoured car patrol and the aggression of the British cavalry made the German hold on this area extremely precarious and soon severely threatened as a more general advance by the British eastwards from Ypres began. Despite the apparent risk, Falkenhayn's plan, just revealed to his Army Commanders, meant that there was a requirement to allow the British to move forward to where they could be trapped. The new largely defensive posture of Sixth Army meant also that there was also a great need for infantry to the south. As a result the barely rested 3rd Cavalry Division was moved forward to the Geluwe area once more on 18 October. Its mission was to screen and hold the position, to be prepared to manoeuvre in support of the move forward of the newly arrived formations of Fourth Army and to hold the advancing British forces in check.

Although the German army had been slow to detect the relief of the British formations on the Aisne, by 11/12 October it was clear that forces were being moved north and that there were also troop movements from Calais. Aerial reconnaissance picked up signs of major unloading and de-training activity in St Omer and generally the density of forces in the entire area between Dunkirk and La Bassée was increasing, with the British detected as established north of the Lys and astride the La Bassée Canal, further reinforced by those elements of the Belgian army which had escaped from the fighting around Antwerp. Naturally, all these shifts in Allied deployments put a completely different complexion on events. Falkenhayn's plans had been predicated on the assumption that it would be possible for XIX and XIII Corps to take and hold the high ground south of the line Lillers – Béthune, while the Fourth Army closed up and took over the main thrust. However, the arrival of additional Allied troops from the direction of Dunkirk not only caused the attack to falter, but its own right flank became increasingly vulnerable to counter action, since it was likely to be at least a week before Fourth Army would be in a position to bring its strength to bear.

In view of the changed situation, Falkenhayn decided to halt the offensive on the right flank of Sixth Army, to swing round to the north and to use the cavalry to cover the moves. In effect these manoeuvres brought a temporary halt to large scale engagements in this area, which was just as well, because serious and worrying shortages of larger calibre shells in particular were already beginning to emerge. However Falkenhayn also hoped to use the new situation to his advantage and to bring about a decisive action. The plan as he explained it to Major von Mertz, chief of the Operations Branch at Sixth Army, was for formations of that army to form a defensive front along the line Menen – Armentières – La Bassée, then to permit the Allies to drive forward as far as Menen, where they would be vulnerable to a thrust from Fourth Army advancing from Gent in their flank and rear. The decision was laid down in a Supreme Army Headquarters directive dated 13 October 1914.

"It is desirable that the two corps, XIX and XIII be not deployed towards the west. Instead their front should face north to counter the enemy attack and then, later, in combination with III Reserve Corps attack the enemy. Supreme Army Headquarters is content with the grouping of these two formations which has been directed by Headquarters Sixth Army." [24]

Instructions were also issued concerning the use of the cavalry formations and future plans for Fourth Army, which was now to advance between Lille and the coast, clearing the enemy in front of it as it moved. As a result, effectively the decision had been taken that the decisive battle was to take place, not on the high ground around Béthune, but to the north and bounded on the right flank by the sea. Not for the first time and certainly not the last, Crown Prince Rupprecht of Bavaria, Commander Sixth Army, was deeply unimpressed with Falkenhayn's planning.

Crown Prince Rupprecht of Bavaria Diary Entry 14 October 1914 [25]

"Major von Mertz, who had been summoned to Supreme Army Headquarters at Mezières, brought us a mission which did not please me much. Whilst III Reserve Corps of Fourth Army is being despatched in an offensive role to Brugge, the remaining corps of Fourth Army are to form the base of a sack into which, it is hoped, the enemy will thrust in an attempt to surround Sixth Army. To this end, Sixth Army is to act purely defensively in a line stretching from Menen via Armentières and La Bassée to the right flank of Second Army. The task we have been given is analogous to that we fulfilled right at the start of the campaign and it is equally as questionable as it was then if the enemy really will enter the open sack. In acting this way, we are yielding the initiative completely to the enemy. They will be able either to attempt to break through somewhere along the over extended length of the Sixth Army frontage, whose sole reserve is 14th [Infantry Division], probably near to its right flank, or – and this is most likely of all – will dig in, in a strong position approximately on the line Poperinge – Bailleul – Béthune, there to await calmly the arrival of reinforcements and to extend their line to the sea. That will mean an end to the war of movement and it will be very difficult to force a decision in the foreseeable future. As before, I am in favour of cutting the Gordian knot; that is to say to launch an attack with the fresh troops of the 14th Division, the XIX and XIII Corps on my right flank. I do not believe that there are overwhelmingly strong forces opposing our current northern flank."

However the directive of Supreme Army Headquarters had not been issued as a basis for discussion. Sixth Army had to conform, adjusting its operational posture as the situation developed and deploying its assets as best it could in support of the major effort off to the north. To that end, XIX Corps was directed to advance to the north and south of Armentières, with 40th Infantry Division north and 24th Infantry Division south of the town. For the Saxon 40th Infantry Division this manoeuvre was ultimately to take the form of a series of bloody encounters across the Lys as it tried to wrest control of Le Gheer and Ploegsteert from troops of the British 4th Division during the three weeks from mid October and so fix strong British forces on its front to prevent them from being used against the Fourth Army thrust to the north. The 24th Division, later into the operation in the case of some of its formations, also saw some hard fighting, but the main effort initially was borne by 40th Infantry Division and Infantry Regiment 104 in particular.

At the same time HKK 4 was deployed to relieve the infantry from Menen to Warneton. 3rd Cavalry Division, still reinforced by Bavarian Reserve Infantry Regiment 1 and with its headquarters established at Halluin, effectively screened off Menen from the Roeselare road round to the Lys via Geluwe. 6th Cavalry Division was clustered around Bousbecque, just south of the river, with its divisional headquarters back in Roncq, whilst the Bavarian Cavalry Division covered along the river from Wervik (Wervicq) west to Comines. There it linked up with 9th Cavalry Division, temporarily resubordinated from HKK 2 to HKK 4, which had responsibility for the river line as far as Warneton.

Naturally, at the time the subsidiary nature of these Sixth Army operations was not transmitted down in those terms to the men on the ground, who were under the firm impression that they were part of a great outflanking movement themselves and who, therefore, strained every sinew to make progress on their own particular front. Furthermore, not being privy to the higher plan, there was some disappointment in the ranks when 40th Division was ordered in the early hours of 15 October to advance to the Lys and to take up defensive positions and hold them securely. Nevertheless, the reaction was fast and decisive and by between 8.00 am and 9.00 am the battalions were shaking out on the far bank in a long line, with Infantry Regiment 181 to the north at Warneton, Infantry Regiment 104 in the centre between La Basse-Ville and Frélinghien and Infantry Regiment 133 to the south, where it became embroiled during the following days in a drawn out battle around the breweries on the outskirts of Frélinghien. The situation was still extremely fluid and a party under Unteroffizier Thümmler of 11th Company Infantry Regiment 181, moving rapidly into position, intercepted and captured a British motorcycle despatch rider during the initial deployment.[26] Patrols from the divisional reconnaissance regiment, Hussar Regiment 20, pushed forward across the river and established the presence of British cavalry from General Allenby's corps, which was making its way forward from the northwest, with orders to reconnoitre the river from Estaires to Menen.

There was some fire across the river from the British troops, but it caused no damage. In the meantime, close inspection of the terrain revealed that for long stretches there were slight rises on the east bank of the Lys, which provided the German troops with the advantage of being able to overlook the flatter approaches on the west bank. They were also able to select places to dig in which stood proud of the surrounding area so, by the time the regiments were visited by the divisional commander twenty four hours later, there were already reasonably prepared defensive positions. The regiments were not permitted to rest on their laurels, however. Orders were soon given to Infantry Regiment 104 to push over the river and develop the hamlets of Pont Rouge and Le Touquet as defensible bridgeheads, so as to provide the basis for a further advance to the west. In response 2nd Battalion Infantry Regiment 104 despatched two companies forward with the mission of securing Pont Rouge, whilst 3rd Battalion moved complete against Le Touquet.

During this operation Vizefeldwebel Staszewky of 9th Company distinguished himself and was awarded the Silver Prinz Heinrich medal, whilst 2nd Battalion succeeded in capturing a five man British cavalry patrol from the Royals. According to Hussar Regiment 18, these troopers made an outstanding impression, were all well equipped and had all seen foreign service.[27] Inevitably there was a swift reaction to this advance. Artillery fire came down against both hamlets, as well as in Deûlemont and Frélinghien on the east bank of the Lys. This caused no casualties, but the lines were beginning to solidify here too. Foot patrols sent forward during the late evening of 17 October established that there were British troops in Ploegsteert Wood and Le Gheer just to the east of it.[28] The establishment of a German presence on the west bank of the Lys had come just in time; almost all British attempts to gain further ground towards the river were thwarted and then, during the night 19/30 October, orders arrived for an attack by XIX Corps to be conducted on 20 October.

The date was no coincidence. It was timed to occur simultaneously with a general assault all along the Fourth Army front from Diksmuide to the Menen road. On the 40th Infantry Division front, familiarity with the ground and the particular demands of the assault led to rapid regrouping. Infantry Regiment 181 on the right was withdrawn and replaced by Jäger Battalion 7 and some dismounted cavalry, whilst 3rd Battalion Infantry Regiment 104 was moved slightly south to form, together with 2nd Battalion Infantry Regiment 134, a 'Regiment Larraß', subordinated to 89 Infantry Brigade and commanded by Generalmajor von Seydewitz. Surprise was the key element in all of this so, in the case of Infantry Regiment 104, whilst its 2nd Battalion moved across fixed bridges and through Pont Rouge onto its start line, 1st Battalion crossed the river upstream in assault boats close to Deûlémont, without being observed.

The German artillery opened up simultaneously at 7.00 am: not only at enemy infantry positions on the edge of Ploegsteert Wood, Le Gheer and Le Bizet, but also at known battery positions near the Armentières – Messines road. H Hour was 9.00 am, but not all regiments were in position to move by then, time having been short. Those who could, however, worked their way forward to the railway line which ran parallel to the river and was about 250 metres to the west of Pont Rouge. Despite the British harassing fire, once there the opportunity was taken to study the ground over which the next phase of the attack was to be launched. In addition, several machine gun positions were established on the embankment where they could provide covering fire for what was a daunting task. Out to the front was a broad, flat, exposed, piece of terrain, more than one kilometre wide and almost devoid of cover. Careful management of the advance and husbandry of manpower were clearly going to be of critical importance.

At about 11.00 pm sufficient forces were in position to continue and then, in sharp contrast to the situation on the Fourth Army front to the north, some progress was made during the day, despite the fact that the terrain was totally favourable to the defence and the British had used the time wisely to create as many obstacles as possible. They had also sited their machine guns so as to create killing zones across the entire area to their front. Heading across the open ground with great aggression, the Saxon soldiers advanced using fire and manoeuvre in sections, half sections and pairs, despite having to cut their way through fences which had been strengthened with barbed wire and using gaps in hedges, whose distance was known to a metre and which were covered by fire.

Inevitably the advance was uneven and patchy so, by the afternoon, with fire from the flanks gaining in intensity, Infantry Regiment 181 to the south was forced into whatever cover was available and Jäger Battalion 7 was forced back to the railway embankment in the north. Nevertheless, despite increased quantities of fire being directed at the forward elements of Infantry Regiment 104, as it went dark the front line had been pushed forward to approximately three hundred metres short of Ploegsteert Wood: no mean achievement in the circumstances. Just as impressive, in contrast to the chaos which was reigning amongst the administrative tail of the newly formed corps to the north, the field kitchens of 40th Infantry Division advanced right up to the railway embankment and, under cover of darkness, fed the forward troops and provided them with coffee and rations for the following day.

Naturally orders for 21 October envisaged the continuation of the attack, with the aim initially of reaching the line Ploegsteert Wood – Le Gheer – Le Touquet. It was then decided that an early surprise attack offered the best chance of success, so orders went out that at 6.30 am the whole line was to advance silently and with no form of fire support. Fortune favours the brave and the plan was completely successful, which speaks volumes for the standard of training and battlefield discipline within the regiment. Benefiting from thick early morning mist and the pre-dawn darkness, the advancing troops closed right up to the British lines before hurling themselves forward to general shouts of *Hurra!* In many cases the defenders had hardly opened fire before they were overrun, but in Le Gheer itself 8th Company was involved in hand to hand fighting with men of the Inniskilling Fusiliers of the British 12 Brigade amongst the houses and the same was true to the south where 1st Battalion had advanced. Three British officers and fifty other ranks were captured by Infantry Regiment 104, together with two machine guns, but lack of similar progress on the flanks left the regiment dangerously exposed.

A swift converging counter attack a short while later, launched by 1st Battalion East Lancashire Regiment and 1st Battalion Somerset Light Infantry of 11 Brigade, north and south respectively of Ploegsteert Wood, recovered the situation. Infantry Regiment 104 later blamed the problems on the flanks for the reverse. Jäger Battalion 7 was unable to get forward and Infantry Regiment 181, having come under came under effective British fire from the King's Own and the Lancashire Fusiliers well short of the British lines, was forced into cover. Infantry Regiment 181, in its defence, pointed out that the ground over which it was moving was barely passable. The going was very muddy through the beet fields and made worse by the rain squalls. When to this was added numerous ditches, fences, hedges and other obstacles, they reported that their movement was severely hindered and greatly canalised; all of which robbed their attack of the necessary momentum.[29] Whatever the situation, both sides fought hard and losses were correspondingly high. Hauptmann Bülau, commanding 5th Company Infantry Regiment 104, was killed[30] fighting at the head of his men and the battle raged for some time, while vain attempts were made to arrange for reinforcements to be rushed forward so as to consolidate at least some of the gains made earlier.

Feeling badly let down that their tactical success and the fighting spirit they had shown had all been for nothing through no fault of their own, eventually the regimental commander felt that he had no alternative but to order the survivors to make their way back to their start point as best they could. On the flanks this was a matter of breaking out through the British and only a minority made it, though Vizefeldwebel Meißner of the Machine Gun Company led back a group of prisoners and two captured machine guns were also recovered to Delbecque Farm. In the aftermath, the British took a total of 134 prisoners and brought about the release of forty five men of the Iniskillings.[31] Even fewer of the attackers would have been able to get back had it not been for the alertness of Major Partzsch, commanding officer 2nd Battalion Field Artillery Regiment 68, who spotted the attempt to break clean and brought down heavy and accurate fire on the British positions at the critical moment, buying some time for the withdrawal to be completed.[32]

The artillery support from the forward batteries also played a significant part in preventing the British pushing forward from the wood edge, though how serious an intent there was of so doing is questionable. Both sides had lost heavily and both needed time to consolidate and take stock. In a somewhat delayed response to the earlier calls for assistance, 1st Battalion Infantry Regiment 134, commanded by Major Liebster, which had been located at Croix au Bois, was rushed forward via Pont Rouge to reinforce Infantry Regiment 104, which by now was considerably reduced in numbers. 89 Infantry Brigade also released 3rd Battalion and Machine Gun Company Infantry Regiment 134 to move in support of Infantry Regiment 181 that same afternoon.[33] For the time being the front was stabilised, even though the hoped-for breakthrough had not occurred. This day was notable for one other reason. It was the last occasion when the 1870/71 colours of Infantry Regiment 104 were carried into battle, Sergeants Löbner and Franke being responsible for those of 1st and 2nd Battalions respectively.[34]

Just to the south, the remainder of 89 Brigade (Infantry Regiment 133 and 2nd Battalion Infantry Regiment 134) moved against the built up area of Frélinghien seriously for the first time. Little progress was made however, nor would it be for several more days. Once again the going was a major problem; a factor which was fully exploited by the British defenders. It was swampy; comprising completely open water meadows, criss-crossed with deep drainage ditches two to four metres wide, up to two metres deep and full to the brim with water. The approaches were also completely dominated from the great brewery which stood on a rise in the ground and was surrounded by a massively constructed high wall, giving it a fort-like appearance. Resolutely garrisoned by well armed troops it held out, impervious to normal shells, until two super heavy howitzers were moved into position a few days later and were able to batter it into near submission.

It was not just XIX and other Army Corps of Sixth Army which launched attacks on 20 October; there was a major reorganisation of the cavalry and a forward deployment to check Allied movement from Ypres and prevent the rear of XIX Corps from being threatened. Three *ad hoc* formations: Groups Stetten (also known as HKK 5) comprised 3rd Cavalry Division, Bavarian Reserve Infantry Regiment 1 and the dismounted element of 16 Cavalry Brigade, together with the Bavarian Cavalry Division; Group Schmettow, made up of 6th Cavalry Division and Reserve Jäger Battalion 1; and Group Richthofen. The organisation of these groups was flexible and other cavalry formations also carried out supporting manoeuvres during this period, making for a complicated picture. On 20 October, for example, in support of the newly formed XXVII Reserve Corps, engaged against Beselare, Group Stetten pushed forward astride the Menen – Ypres road towards Koelenberg, with the detached Bavarian Cavalry Division advancing against the line Amerika – Timbriele.

Because information concerning the situation on the far side of the Lys was somewhat scanty and there was particular concern about the general advance of the Allies in an easterly direction, the Bavarian Cavalry Division was preceded by a number of small scale reconnaissance patrols. One such patrol, mounted from Comines, investigated the situation in the area bounded by the Wervik – Amerika and Comines – Houthem roads. This revealed the news that almost all the farmsteads and other buildings contained small garrisons and, what was of great interest, because it was the first time this regiment had encountered them, from the khaki uniforms of the outposts, it was clear that they would be facing the soldiers of the British army.

Leutnant Graf von Marogna – Redwitz Bavarian Schwere Reiter-Regiment 1[35] *8.*

"Arriving in Comines at 6.00 am, I was given the mission by Major von Tannstein of making my way across the canal and establishing if the enemy was thinning out to our front. I crossed the canal and patrolled forward to the railway line. However, it was already clear from the attitude of the local people that I was not going to obtain good news. Not only were they standing around in defiant groups, they were also casting insolent looks at us and muttering at each other, so it was not difficult to draw the correct conclusions. Sure enough, not 200 metres up the road leading away north, uniformed personnel could be seen. It was not possible to establish what was happening, but it was at least clear that the enemy had not withdrawn.

"It was then that a curiously shaped railway train was seen approaching from the direction of Houthem. Telescope observation was hindered by the morning mist, but having stared at it for a long time, it became clear that it could only be an armoured train. That was enough for this place. I sent a despatch rider back to the regiment and bore off north of the canal towards

Wervik then, just before that place, I turned northwest and followed the road towards Timbriele, but once again I did not get far. About half way towards Timbriele I came under fire from sentries, so there were obviously enemy here. I turned away to the right and headed for Amerika, a place we already knew from our previous special mission.

"We made use of cover as much as possible, which was not too difficult in that close country, even though it was flat. It did not escape my sharp eyed troopers that there were outposts in various locations. It was not possible to say who the enemy were, because they were well concealed and barely visible. I despatched a report back and decided to set up a standing patrol and watch the ground between Timbriele and Amerika. We changed positions several times, but it remained quiet out to the front and there were no troop movements to be seen. Because we were in good cover, we noticed more and more outposts and we also realised why they were so difficult to spot. They were wearing khaki uniforms, so we had the British to our front.

"By now it was afternoon. From time to time shells roared overhead, though where they came from and where they were headed we had no idea. Aircraft also flew low overhead. Because I could add nothing to my observations and our way forward was blocked by pickets, I regarded my mission as complete and returned to the regiment, reporting in person at 5.00 pm."

Armed with that information, the decision was made to abandon an attempt to feint towards Houthem and, instead, Bavarian Cavalry Division moved to occupy positions along a rather more modest line running north–south through Klijtmolen, some 1,500 metres east of Amerika. Group Schmettow, on the same day, advanced either side of the Douve in the direction of Messines, but made little progress as increasing resistance was encountered. Group Richthofen, linking with the right flank of XIX Corps, pressed on with 9th Cavalry Division and Guards Cavalry Division, capturing Ferme de la Croix on the far bank of the Lys, whilst 4th Cavalry Division on the left maintained the junction point with XIX Corps, but barely advanced at all that day. The principal role in the capture of the farm was taken by the Guards Jäger Battalion, under Major Hans von Fabeck, who was later to command Reserve Infantry Regiment 99 at Thiepval during the battle of the Somme in 1916. Working its way forward from Deûlémont to Warneton, which it reached at midday, it detached 1st Company to man the railway embankment to the southwest of the town centre, covering towards Messines, then the remaining companies assembled in the streets of Warneton, where they were under constant artillery fire.

At 3.20 pm, the entire Guards Cavalry Division began to advance against what was said to be dug in British cavalry. 2nd and 3rd Companies, supported by dismounted troopers from Guard Dragoon Regiment 2, attacked towards Chapelle Farm, 1st and 4th Companies, together with elements of the Guards Uhlan Brigade, moved against La Potterie Farm. It took two and a half hours for 2nd and 3rd Companies to reach their objective, after which they swung hard west to face Messines. Meanwhile 1st and 4th

Companies, supported by the Machine Gun Company and Guards Machine Gun Detachment 1, pushed on to a point 500 – 600 metres east of La Potterie Farm, where they were forced into cover. By then fire from La Potterie Farm was too intense to permit further forward movement and the attackers had to take over British outpost trenches and improve the cover they offered – a novel experience for the troopers involved. Still commanded by Fabeck in person, other dismounted troopers, this time from Guard Dragoon Regiment 1, pushed on, reaching Ferme de la Croix as it began to go dark.[36] It was an extremely hard day in unfavourable circumstances and, despite the elite nature of the Guard Jäger Battalion, it proved to be difficult to progress against a hardening British front.

In the meantime, along the 40th Infantry Division sector, the hours of darkness were taken up with the improvement of routes forward and the building of bridges over the water obstacles, so as to facilitate forward movement, but progress was initially elusive and casualties high. During the afternoon of 21 October, for example, Major Larraß, commanding officer 3rd Battalion Infantry Regiment 104, was hit by a bullet fired from the brewery and killed instantly[37] whilst he was conducting a forward reconnaissance of the place, together with Major Freiherr von Halkett 2nd Battalion Infantry Regiment 134 and Oberstleutnant Vollert, commander Field Artillery Regiment 32. Given the weight of fire coming down in the area of the church at the time, it was a miracle that any of the party survived. He was the last of a long line of officers from his family to serve in the army of Saxony and his loss was deeply felt throughout the regiment. The purpose of the reconnaissance had been to determine if it would be possible to move individual field guns forward, so as to be able to fire at the brewery from near point blank range from hidden locations within the village, but this proved to be impossible and other positions just to the east had to be used instead.

Just two days of battle near Le Gheer had cost Infantry Regiment 104 alone twelve officers and 720 other ranks killed, wounded or missing, the great majority irreplaceable men of the active army, who had received their training in peacetime. The front line had been advanced close to Le Gheer and Ploegsteert Wood, but the enemy were still in possession of both places and, with each passing day, their positions grew stronger – as did those of the German formations, who utilised the hours of darkness to develop their trenches and to establish the links to their neighbours to the left and right. Already the lines were beginning to solidify into their final form, as reserve trenches and communications trenches were rapidly dug and revetted as much as possible, whilst the artillery on both sides maintained a rate of fire as high as limited stocks of ammunition would permit. Intensive patrolling began, provoking a sharp reaction each night from the British, who shelled the area heavily from time to time.

One such fire mission brought accurate shrapnel fire down on and around the barn which the regimental staff was using as a command post but, although large numbers of shrapnel balls penetrated the building, by a lucky chance nobody was hit. Just to the south, however, the preparations for the assault on the southern brewery at Frélinghien were gathering pace rapidly. There was now adequate artillery support and a composite regiment, comprising 3rd Battalion Infantry Regiment 104, 2nd

Battalion Infantry Regiment 133 and 2nd Battalion Infantry Regiment 134, under the command of Hauptmann Rühle von Lilienstern of Infantry Regiment 134, was formed to attempt to capture the brewery once and for all. One of the main difficulties was the limited attack frontage, the brewery itself being sandwiched between the River Lys and the Frélinghien – Armentières road.

It was decided, therefore, to begin the attack by launching forward with two platoons of 2nd Battalion Infantry Regiment 134, with Hauptmann Pechwell of Infantry Regiment 133 following up at the head of a second wave, comprising a reinforced platoon of that regiment. At H Hour the attack was launched from the area of the northern brewery and the houses near to the main road, the infantry assault being timed to go in the moment the fire of the super heavy howitzers was lifted. Despite the suppressive bombardment, there was a swift reaction from the British defenders, with artillery defensive fire and small arms fire from all three storeys of the brewery as the men of Infantry Regiment 133 rushed to occupy the houses nearest the brewery and give fire support as the Infantry Regiment 134 team pushed through into the yard of the main building.

According to the regimental historian of Infantry Regiment 133, 'Led by Leutnant Enck, they smashed in the windows and doors and forced their way into the building with its one metre thick walls. The Scots of the 28th [*sic.* 2nd Battalion] Seaforth Highlanders were surprised, although they had also been worn down by the fire of the heavy howitzers. They were fine, upstanding men, who belonged to one of the most highly regarded British regiments.'[38] The church at Frélinghien was set on fire by exploding shells at this time and, although no more progress was made here, the whole of the village of Frélinghien was henceforth firmly in German hands.

North of the Lys, the cavalry continued to inch its way forward as best it could. Group Stetten eventually cleared through Amerika by the evening of 21 October, but the subsequent success in taking Oude Hond (Vieux Chien) was negated when a thrust by the British during the hours of darkness wrested away their precarious hold on that hamlet. The Bavarian Cavalry Division, operating more to the south, achieved the line Timbriele-Houthem and settled down to hold it during the next few days. It enjoyed the occasional success, such as when Pillegrem Farm was captured, but all eight of the engaged cavalry divisions found that they lacked the numbers and the fire power to make any further significant impression on the British lines. General der Infanterie von der Marwitz, who had just been promoted from command of HKK 2 to overall command of all the cavalry, was also forced to accept that reality, though he also placed some of the blame on the terrain in a letter of 22 October.[39]

"I passed a dull day behind the long, over-extended front. I am currently in command of no fewer than eight cavalry divisions, but their deployment could hardly be more different than when on exercise at Döberitz.[40] The entire countryside here is one mass of small enclosed fields and hedges reinforced with wire. How are we meant to attack through that?! The enemy exploits its potential skilfully, firing from inside houses and trenches, which they have dug extremely rapidly. Just recently we were in the same situation when we had a long line to defend. The attackers launched their assaults in vain and had no success.'

This judgement from a senior field commander was also borne out at the lowest levels, as this account of a handful of men holding off greatly superior numbers shows.

Gefreiter Simon Lemmer 1st Squadron Bavarian Schwere Reiter-Regiment 2[41] **8.**

"We first came into contact with the evil British in dismounted action near Houthem and realised how valuable trenches were. The 1st Squadron relieved the Bavarian Jägers around Pillegrem Farm and then held the position. Hardly had the sentries been posted than we were subjected to the first concentration of fire by the enemy, so we crouched down in our trenches, allowing the hail of shells and shrapnel balls to crash down all around us and stuck it out. As soon as the fire slackened the troopers, fourteen of them in all, stuck their heads up and opened fire with the same intensity at the enemy, preventing any thoughts of an attack by them.

"The second time this happened Sergeant Hoffmann was wounded in the arm and I immediately took over his trench, because it was much better and more secure than my own one. For one thing it had overhead cover, proof against shrapnel and, for another, it was located just at the corner of a hedgerow from where there was a good view along the road. It was a clear moonlit night, but the British were not confident enough to launch an attack, so they stuck to bringing down concentrations of fire until, at about 2.00 am, they pulled back along the road into the nearest copse. But it did not do them any good, because I could see them very clearly and every time that a group of fifteen to twenty, accompanied by a machine gun team, rushed across the road, I informed my comrades and directed them to [fire at] where they had taken cover. In this way two British companies near Pillegrem Farm were kept in check by fourteen heavy cavalrymen."

Not everything went the way of the cavalry, however, there were reverses and considerable difficulties in maintaining and supplying them in the frequently exposed positions they had taken up when their advances stalled, as this experience of the mounted infantry of 16 Cavalry Brigade 3rd Cavalry Division records.

Oberstleutnant von Baumbach Jäger Regiment zu Pferd 8 [42] **9.**

"That evening we were in trenches alongside the road to Ypres, proud and happy, but hungry. Although we were quite tired, we had to spend half the night digging in. We had no spades, so side arms, pocket knives and hands were resorted to scrape, dig, tear and cut pieces of turf and throw up a parapet behind which the men might take cover. Opposite and very close to us were the British, digging in with proper spades. How we missed such tools, but we had to manage as best we could. Occasional shots prevented the enemy from acting too boldly and gradually it went dark. There was a need to use ammunition sparingly and the firing gradually died away.

"It was a calm, misty night. Towards 1.00 am we had a surprise. Bean stew was being brought forward to us from Geluwe. It seemed, however, as though the British had either smelled the soup or heard the rattles of the wagon which was carrying it. Perhaps they sensed our hungry anticipation because at precisely the wrong moment – for us – they opened heavy fire on us from their trenches. The guns also began to fire and rockets went up with a great roar. The ration horses made it through the field, but the soup cauldron was tipped out of the wagon and there we found it next morning. We had to go hungry that night but we were very tired so, despite the cold, we were able to sleep a little during the night . . . We were compensated the next morning, however. The British failed to disturb our breakfast."

To the southwest, after the huge losses suffered during the battles around Le Gheer and Ploegsteert Wood on 20 and 21 October, it is perhaps not surprising that there should have been a pause of a few days in that sector. However, 30 October was the day when formations of XXVII Corps made a major push to capture Geluveld. All the other corps of Fourth Army were also heavily engaged, so it was essential that Sixth Army contributed to the extent possible and XIX Corps issued orders to that effect. Infantry Regiment 104 received major reinforcements from Germany on 23 October, no fewer than 32 officers, including Oberstleutnant Gretschel, who assumed command of 2nd Battalion, 131 NCOs and 1,322 other ranks.[43] This filled out the ranks, but of course there was little time to assimilate such large numbers, nor suitable opportunity to do any training while holding the line and improving the positions. In possible recognition of the fact and in the knowledge that Ploegsteert Wood had proved to be an extremely difficult objective, XIX Corps allocated the newly arrived 3rd Battalion Infantry Regiment 106 48 Infantry Brigade 24th Infantry Division, together with the Machine Gun Company of that regiment, to Infantry Regiment 104 for the attack.

In the light of previous experience, commander Infantry Regiment 104 decided to make his main effort against the northeast corner of Ploegsteert Wood and the adjoining St Yvon [St Yves] in an attempt to neutralise the enfilade fire from that direction which had caused so many problems previously. During the preliminaries, the regimental command post was moved to La Basse Ville, to the southwest of Warneton, the better to control the attack of 3rd Battalion Infantry Regiment 106 from the line La Basse Ville – Grande Haye Farm towards the wood.[44] On the morning of 30 October there was artillery preparation all along the front for two hours from 9.00 am, then the battalion moved off, reaching the trenches captured by Jäger Battalion 7 on 20 October without suffering many casualties.

The advance of the entire reinforced regiment was meant to occur as soon as 3rd Battalion Infantry Regiment 106 had drawn level with 1st and 2nd Battalions Infantry Regiment 104 but, frustratingly, there were several postponements and the start line was not crossed until 1.00 pm. The delay was fatal. Fully alerted, the defenders reacted rapidly and decisively as soon as the lines of infantry rose from their trenches and attempted to get forward. It was immediately clear that the artillery preparation had been inadequate, either to destroy or suppress the front line trenches, or to prevent the movement of supports and reserves. To some extent the first wave avoided the worst of the defensive fire, but follow up waves were hit from the right (northern) flank by artillery, rifle and machine gun fire.

The only possible solution was to resort immediately to fire and manoeuvre by pairs or half sections and in this way, at the cost of many casualties and a large expenditure of ammunition, an irregular front line was pushed forward. On the right flank, it was still some three hundred metres short of the enemy position when darkness fell; in the centre it was two hundred metres from the wood. The infantrymen dug in at the furthest point reached, ready to resume the attack on 31 October. In an attempt to deal with the enemy positions around St Yvon, 2nd Battalion Infantry Regiment 106 was introduced to the right of the 3rd Battalion during the night 30/31 October and the commander Infantry Regiment 104, Oberstleutnant Eckhardt, issued orders that no attempt was to be made to get forward before there was a marked reduction in fire from the right flank. Not only did this not occur, the reinforcements from Infantry Regiment 106 made no impression whatsoever and there was no progress at all during the day.

There were several more days of hard-fought and sometimes hand to hand battles before the attempt was finally abandoned to advance the line any further in the Ploegsteert area. Despite the fact that regular troops were involved on both sides, losses had been high, including Oberstleutnant Eckhardt of Infantry Regiment 104 on 2 November. In addition there was a dire shortage of shells for the artillery, so the stalemate on this part of the front had to be accepted and various adjustments were made to facilitate the garrisoning of the trenches and the administration of the forward troops.

Reserve Leutnant Klemm Intelligence Officer Infantry Regiment 133[45] 10.

"Following on from the battles around Frélinghien, 2nd Battalion was moved to positions to the north of Pont Rouge to support Infantry Regiment 104 which was deployed there. Two companies at a time occupied the reserve positions at Ploegsteert Wood on a two day rotation. The front line position hard up against the wood line between Le Gheer and St Yvon [St Yves] was manned by Infantry Regiment 104. When our 5th Company had occupied the reserve trenches, the temporary ones right next to the wood, they suddenly came under fire by heavy British artillery. The losses were so high that we were ordered, this time led by Leutnant Breyer, to make our way through the wet muddy communication trenches to the exposed positions of the 104th.

"Luckily the enemy artillery did not engage the position along the wood edge any more after that. For days it had been under such heavy small arms and artillery fire that for two days it had been impossible to evacuate wounded and fallen comrades and we had had to sit it out surrounded by them. There was also nothing to eat; ration parties, like stretcherbearers, had been unable to get forward and we were reduced to slaking our thirst from puddles of water in shell holes. Some days later we gave up the unfavourable position along the edge of the wood, which offered no fields of fire, and pulled back to the reserve position about eighty metres in rear. Gradually this line was developed more and more. Initially the periods of relief were spent in the sugar refinery at Warneton, but sometimes we were accommodated in Pont Rouge. During the month of December 1914 we were moved further to the left [south] where the famous Christmas truce took place."

With the line fixed in more or less the locations it was to occupy for many months to come, the positions of the garrisons were rationalised. The cavalry began to be pulled out of the line and relieved early in November. The last of the mounted units and formations which had played such a significant role during the early days of the battles around Ypres followed only days later, destined for the most part for more appropriate missions on the Eastern front. Their departure was marked by a special Sixth Army Order of the Day, signed by Crown Prince Rupprecht.

"In battles armed with carbines and faced by fortified enemy positions, the cavalry has never shied away, achieving a series of successes in a style of warfare foreign to it. In so doing it has delivered highly valuable service on that part of the battlefield. For their outstanding bearing and their extraordinary endurance, I proffer my warmest thanks and the expression of my highest recognition to the troops."[46]

Doubtless the thanks were appreciated, but soldiers being what they are several resourceful cavalrymen had already arranged for their own rewards as October drew to a close and some units were already relieved from holding exposed forward positions near Houthem.

Gefreiter Simon Lemmer 1st Squadron Bavarian Schwere Reiter-Regiment 2[47] **11.**

"By the time we were finally relieved at Houthem it was 11.00 pm on 29 October and we still had a good distance to go on foot. That was no easy business for we cavalrymen and, in any case, none of us at that time wanted to have anything to do with that sort of thing, having embarked on the campaign filled with the cavalry spirit. After a march of three and a half hours we arrived in Wervik where we found quarters in an estaminet, because we could not find the area where our squadron was billeted. The following morning we succeeded in tracking the place down and every trooper was delighted to be reunited with his beloved horse. We were then able to attend to our feet, dealing with blisters and powdering them, then turning our attention to cleaning every item of equipment and tack belonging to horse or man.

"When operating in northern France it had always been the policy to provide the dismounted element of the regiment with bicycles and there were a few available to the squadron. During the afternoon, therefore, although almost everyone lay down on the straw to rest their aching limbs, three troopers: Brandl, Weidle and Lemmer, who were not very taken with their surroundings, took a quick decision to take bicycles and go and see what Werwik had to offer. Well, we had not gone far when we came to a large building bearing a sign over its entrance which proclaimed *Brasserie*. I said to the others that that could only mean that it was a brewery[48], so naturally we went straight in to find out what the beer situation was. To my amazement, I bumped into a gunner from the 'Mounted 5th'.[49] He was emerging from the cellar with an easy familiarity as though he had already had dealings with the place.

"We then asked this man how we went about obtaining a barrel of beer and he introduced us to the mysteries of the use of the requisition system. Naturally we immediately obtained a form [from him] and, in exchange [for the promise of future payment], the 'Director' was happy to hand over a one hundred litre barrel. The vouchers were obviously real, no doubt of it, because he jumped for joy when we handed him one. The next task was to get the barrel back to our comrades and we also had the bicycles with us. My pal Brandl then found a two wheeled dogcart and, without more ado, we managed to fasten it to one of the bicycles and to secure the barrel to it with a chain. Weidle and I then balanced the barrel from the left and right and its transport went without a hitch.

"Back at the squadron we were greeted, literally, with roars of approval. Our arrival was noticed by Rittmeister von Poschinger, who was sitting in the sunshine outside his quarters reading a newspaper and he laughed out loud at the sight. We repeated this operation about four times altogether, because there is no such thing as too much beer for a trooper, especially when it could be bought as cheaply as this."

Their task in Flanders more or less complete, the cavalry could afford to settle down and enjoy their beer while they could. On the Sixth Army front, the fighting died down and the lines took on their final shape. Just to the north, however, beer was the last thing in the minds of the men of Fourth Army as they fought for their lives in a series of increasingly desperate battles.

Notes
1. Poseck *The German Cavalry* p 197. N.B. This account and other quotations from this source are paraphrased from the English version of *Die deutsche Kavallerie in Belgien und Frankreich 1914*, which was poorly translated.
2. Kollmann History Bavarian Field Artillery Regiment 5 pp 20–21.
3. Paulus History KB Jäger Battalion 1 pp 15–16.
4. Frauenholz History Bavarian Schwere Reiter-Regiment 2 Band 2 p 66.
5. Rutz *Bayernkämpfe* pp 19–20.
6. *ibid.* pp 20–24.
7. *Plattdeutsch* = Low German, a dialect mostly confined to the coastal areas of Ost Friesland

and up towards Hamburg and the Baltic Sea, which has a close affinity to Dutch and Flemish. The majority of the men of Bavarian Reserve Infantry Regiment 1 were from places more than 1,000 kilometres to the south, where they spoke their own dialect far removed even from Hanoverian High German. It is small wonder, therefore, that there were language difficulties and amazing that any of them at all could speak it.

8. Rutz *op. cit.* p 25.
9. Frauenholz *op. cit.* pp 63–65.
10. Gebsattel History Bavarian Uhlan Regiment 1 pp 64–65.
11. Gonnermann *op. cit.* p 269.
12. *ibid.* p 270.
13. *ibid.* pp 270–271.
14. *ibid.* p 272.
15. *ibid.* pp 272–273.
16. *ibid.* p 273.
17. Poseck *op. cit.* p 204.
18. Gonnermann *op. cit.* pp 275–276.
19. *ibid.* pp 277–278.
20. *ibid.* pp 283–284.
21. The Isar is a major tributary of the Danube, which flows through much of Bavaria and Munich itself.
22. Hutschenreuter History Bavarian Chevaulegers Regiment 1 p 26.
23. Brandenstein History Infantry Regiment 121 p 16.
24. *Der Weltkrieg: Fünfter Band* p 281.
25. Kronprinz Rupprecht *In Treue Fest: Erster Band* p 206.
26. Pflugbeil History Infantry Regiment 181 p 34.
27. Wolff History Infantry Regiment 104 p 94.
28. At this time their identity was not known, but they were from 12 Brigade 4th Division, which had just that day passed through Armentières.
29. Tellingly, their History (Pflugbeil) p 35 also states that they thought that they were up against dismounted cavalry, when in fact they were facing the regular, battle hardened troops of the British 4th Division. It is impossible to say, however, if this misapprehension affected their approach to the attack.
30. Hauptmann Johannes Bülau is buried in the German cemetery at Carvin Block 4 Grave 289.
31. BOH p 150.
32. This was not the only urgent demand for artillery support that day. During the afternoon there were repeated calls for fire support from 4th Cavalry Division operating to the north of 88 Infantry Brigade in the St. Yvon area, so Partzsch had to divide his fire units. 5th Battery Field Artillery Regiment 68 and 7th Battery Foot Artillery Battalion 19 took on most of the shoots to the north, whilst the remainder of his batteries, which he had moved forward to Pont Rouge that morning, fired in direct support of Infantry Regiment 104. See History Field Artillery Regiment 68 p 38.
33. Schatz History Infantry Regiment 134 p 17.
34. Wolff *op. cit.* p 100.
35. Gonnermann *op. cit.* p 311.
36. History Guard Jäger Battalion pp 68–69.
37. Partzsch History Field Artillery Regiment 32 p 80.
38. Niemann History Infantry Regiment 133 p 27. Interesting to note, this version of events entirely contradicts the BOH (p 226). 'The brewery and some houses at Frélinghien, which

had only been occupied with a view to further advance, were abandoned by divisional orders, but otherwise the line remained intact.' For the Germans to have identified and subsequently mentioned the presence of Seaforths, even if they were confused by the numbering system, suggests that their version of events is more likely to be correct. At least it casts doubt on the BOH assertion.

39. Tschischwitz *General von der Marwitz* p 55
40. Döberitz was the name of a large German training area near Berlin.
41. Frauenholz *op. cit.* pp 80–81.
42. Poseck *op. cit.* p 210.
43. Wolff *op. cit.* p 102.
44. Böttger History Infantry Regiment 106 pp 36–38
45. Niemann *op. cit.* pp 28–31.
46. Senftleben History Guards Uhlan Regiment 1 p 143.
47. Frauenholz *op. cit.* p 81.
48. One of almost 3,000 breweries in Belgium at that time.
49. This is a reference to the *reitende Abteilung* [Mounted Battalion] of Bavarian Field Artillery Regiment 5 'King Alfons XIIIth of Spain'. In addition to a normal complement of three field gun battalions, in peacetime this regiment maintained a fourth specially equipped battalion which, on mobilisation, deployed as the horse artillery element of the Bavarian Cavalry Division.

CHAPTER 2

From Antwerp to the Ijzer

Regardless of the wisdom of the policy of introducing large numbers of in-experienced formations into the line of battle at its critical point, the arrival of this great body of troops in theatre meant that there had to be a major re-organisation of the German armies in the west. Fourth Army, commanded by HRH Duke Albrecht of Württemberg, received the following ambitious direction from Supreme Army Headquarters on 9 October:

> "Fourth Army . . . will comprise XXII, XXIII, XXVI and XXVII Reserve Corps. In addition, once Antwerp has fallen, III Reserve Corps and 4th Ersatz Division will also come under command. Leading elements of Reserve Corps XXII, XXIII, XXVI and XXVII will begin arriving west and southwest of Brussels during the morning of 13 October and, with detachments pushed forward at various points within each corps sector, are to assemble along the line Lokeren – Lessines.
> "The Army is tasked, as soon as the corps are ready to move, to by-pass Lille to the north, clear the enemy out of Belgian territory and then to advance with its right flank west of St Omer. Commander in Chief of the new Fourth Army, HRH Duke Albrecht of Württemberg, together with his principal staff officers, is to proceed to the new Headquarters in Brussels, via Mezières, there to report to His Majesty the Kaiser and King and to be briefed by the staff of Supreme Army Headquarters."[1]

In the wake of this directive, enormous numbers of supplementary orders were issued in order to ensure that this massive troop movement to the advancing right flank was properly coordinated. Not only that, as already discussed, it was essential to ensure, subject to the constraints of geography and urbanisation, that Sixth Army operations to the south of the operational area of the new Fourth Army were driven on with vigour. The aim of this was to deny to the enemy the chance of exploiting the defensive poten-tial of the ground and the industrial area to establish a new front and so interfere with the move forward of Fourth Army, whose room for manoeuvre was already constrained by the network of drainage ditches, canals and rivers which criss-crossed the swampy plain of Flanders. After some negotiation between Supreme Army Headquarters and Sixth Army, it was decided that XIX Corps would advance with its left flank passing La Bassée, in the direction of Béthune, whilst XIII Corps would proceed via Lille and advance with its right flank south of the canal Armentières – Estaires – Merville.

Meanwhile, in accordance with his orders, Duke Albrecht of Württemberg arrived at Mezières to be given additional verbal guidance by Falkenhayn. He later recalled that his instructions were that, 'The new Fourth Army is to advance without any

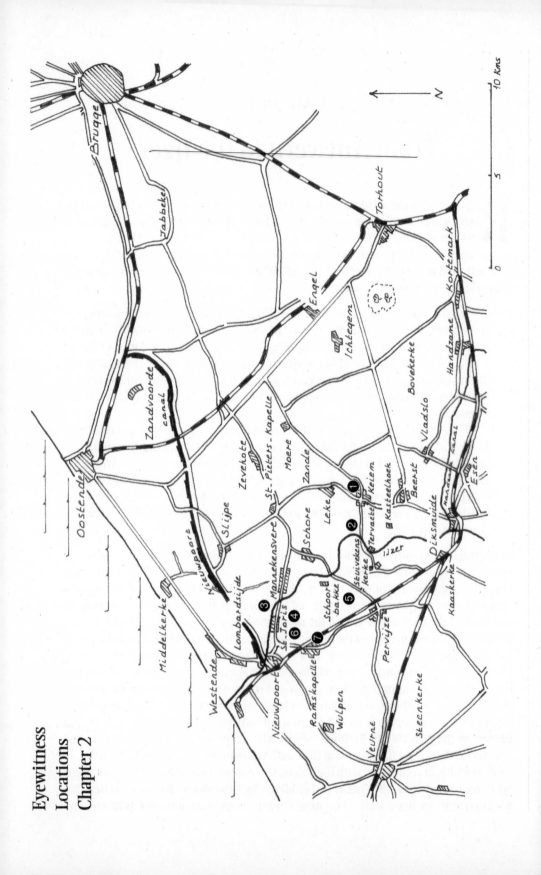

Eyewitness
Locations
Chapter 2

consideration of casualties, with its right wing on the coast. The fortified ports of Dunkirk and Calais are to be isolated – they were to be captured later – and then, leaving St Omer off to the left, to swing down towards the south.'[2] These instructions made it clear that there was to be bold move along the coast and that the intention was to give complete priority to the outflanking manoeuvre between St Omer and the sea. Already, the previous day, the capture of Antwerp had been reported and the formations released as a result had been reallocated. As a result, it appeared by the evening of 10 October that all measures were firmly in place for the continuation of the operations on the extreme right flank of the army but, as was so often the case during this war of manoeuvre, there were substantial changes to the tactical posture of the French, British and Belgian forces during the next few days.

Major von Mertz, of Headquarters Sixth Army, had already raised some concern about the ability of the new formations of Fourth Army to be able to tackle the ambitious mission allocated to them during his visit to Supreme Army Headquarters, but had been informed by Falkenhayn that three factors were in their favour: first, the morale of the troops was excellent (which was probably true, despite deficiencies in their training); second, that the army was to be allocated all the heavy artillery which previously had been involved in siege operations around Antwerp[3]; and third, that if a correct appreciation of enemy intentions had been made and the operations developed as expected, the demands on the new formations would not be particularly great. To any military observer and without the benefit of hindsight, this can be seen at first glance to be a poorly thought out plan. From the outset it demanded good luck to succeed, so it is hardly surprising that it quickly began to unravel.

Doubts even began to appear at Supreme Army Headquarters fairly swiftly. In a directive to Duke Albrecht, issued also on 14 October, it became clear that the Fourth Army might have to become involved in a frontal attack on the Allies.

General Erich von Falkenhayn Chief of the Great General Staff [4]

"Based on all reports to date, it must be assumed that the enemy intended to assemble strong forces south east of Dunkirk, with the intention of enveloping our right wing. Whether this is still the aim is doubtful. In any event, direction has been given that Sixth Army is to withdraw its right flank behind the Lys, roughly along the line Menen – Armentières – La Bassée, and to go into defence. If the enemy threatens it, it will be the task of Fourth Army, once the fresh forces are completely deployed, to thrust against the flank and rear of the enemy. To this end, by the 17th of this month, the new corps are not to be located along the verbally directed line Eekloo – Anzegem. Instead, after III Reserve Corps has moved today to Brugge, the line Ursel – Anzegem is to be occupied. [By the same date] The maximum possible numbers of advance guards are to be in place and ready to move. It is then planned to launch the Army, with Corps Beseler [III Reserve Corps: Commander, General der Infanterie von Beseler] well to the fore and moving offensively along the coast, in an advance towards Merville, with its left flank moving via Menen.

"Corps Beseler, complete with its allocated 4th Ersatz Division and HKK [Senior Cavalry Commander] 4 (which is currently operating in conjunction with Sixth Army southeast of Bailleul and which, therefore, will temporarily remain subject to its instructions) will be subordinated to the Army from this evening.[5] Headquarters Sixth Army has been directed, in the event that Senior Cavalry Commander 4 comes under enemy pressure, to withdraw it in the general direction of Kortrijk. In the most probable situation; *viz.* that the enemy renounce their original intention as soon as they detect the arrival of the fresh troops, it is improbable that there will have to be any change in above mentioned direction of advance. Regardless of whether the enemy choose to stand on the line Dunkirk – Poperinge – Hills east of Bailleul or on the heights southwest of the line Ardres – St Omer – Merville, the Army would be obliged to attack them frontally; whilst it would remain the task of Sixth Army, after a breakthrough from the general direction of Arras, to operate against the flank and rear of the enemy.

"In this event, I should like to draw the attention of Your Royal Highness to the requirement to make the headquarters of the new corps aware of the need to exploit the heavy artillery effectively. There is also a pressing need, because of the necessity to make best use of the strictly limited ammunition, to lay down in advance exactly where the fire is to be placed, so as to ensure that it has a decisive effect. Finally, I wish the marching performance demanded of the fresh troops to match their actual capabilities."

Nevertheless, by 10 October, the day after bells throughout Germany had been rung in celebration of the fall of Antwerp following a two week campaign, the multiplicity of battalions which were destined to man the Fourth Army formations had received their deployment orders and were entraining from the training areas, where they had gathered some two weeks earlier for their final manoeuvres and inspection, and were moving towards Flanders. The new Army Commander lost no time in issuing a special Order of the Day.

Duke Albrecht of Württemberg Commander Fourth Army [6]

"It is with pleasure that I have assumed the command of the Fourth Army with which I have been entrusted. I am completely confident that the corps which have been assembled will bring about the final decision in this Theatre of War; that with good old German courage they will faithfully do their duty to their last breath and that each officer and each soldier is ready to shed the last drop of his blood for the righteous and blessed cause of our Fatherland!"

One week after the process had begun the last of the new formations had detrained and were drawn up in their appointed concentration areas. It had been a close run thing.

Even on arrival in theatre, there were still large gaps in essential equipment, the filling of which demanded the exercise of energetic ingenuity and scrounging skills honed during years of military service.

Hauptmann Baudach Reserve Field Artillery Regiment 44 [7]

"Anyone who was involved in the unloading will have memories of this first wartime episode . . . The order came, 'Harness up! Everyone out! Load up!' Only one ramp, with space to permit two wagons to be unloaded simultaneously, was available for the unloading of horses, wagons and guns. The horses stood, exceedingly stiff after the three day journey, in their wagons, while the kriegs-freiwillige, a large percentage of whom were untrained, struggled to harness them up aided only by the dim light of a hurricane lamp. The experienced drivers were soon ready, having fitted saddles, bridles and collars – even if they did not belong to their horses. The young drivers, on the other hand, struggled with unaccustomed curbs and bridles and found themselves lacking straps, stirrups and headpieces which had been fitted to other horses long before.

"Somehow the corporals and staff sergeants managed to get the animals into a state whereby they could be unloaded, properly harnessed or not, then came piles of baggage: crates of comforts for the troops, reserve clothing, seven days' rations, officers kit and, above all, sacks of oats, bundles of hay and, with each of them, ten pairs of replacement horseshoes tied together. This was the moment I had been dreading. Where were we going to find the vehicles to transport all of this? I rushed over to the officer commanding the station. 'Where I can requisition four large wagons?' 'You will not find any within a ten mile radius!' was the sad reply. We were in Schaerbeek, a small suburb of Brussels. It was pitch black, no houses were to be seen but, away in the distance, was the shadowy outline of a factory chimney.

"Milz, my faithful batman, was waiting on the platform with my horse fully harnessed, not ten minutes after our arrival. 'Right Milz, load your carbine, we have got to requisition some vehicles!' . . . We trotted off along the dark boggy track towards the chimney. Ten minutes later came the challenge, 'Who goes there?' Two resolute Landwehr men, rifles at the ready, barred the way. 'Good friends, comrades! Is this the factory and are our vehicles still there?' I replied, flashing my pocket torch. 'I do not know Herr Hauptmann, we have only been here for an hour ourselves.' 'Take me to the guard commander!' We arrived at a chain link fence and I could see the outline of several assorted Belgian carts. The guard commander, a Landwehr corporal, emerged from a sort of porter's lodge. Naturally he had no knowledge of 'my' vehicles, excusing himself by saying that his company had only detrained that afternoon and he had only been here for the past two hours.

"In the meantime, Milz had gone over to the vehicles and shouted, 'Herr Hauptmann the shaft has been stolen from one and the braking mechanism from the other!' I ordered Milz to ride back at once and to return with four reserve horses and some drivers and set the unteroffizier the task of finding 'my' shaft and brake, which had been 'stolen'. Ten minutes later came the clatter of horses' hooves. Two really large Belgian wagons were harnessed up and we trotted back to the station, where the situation was chaotic. All the equipment which could not be stowed lay around between the tracks in great heaps. A major from the General staff fluttered around, saying that another train was due in, in twenty minutes' time.

"I sorted out the items that we absolutely had to take with us and had them loaded on the requisitioned wagons. It was critical that we took our oats with us but, if they came, there was no question of transporting reserve clothing or six days' rations so, in the end, every gun and every limber had two sacks of oats strapped to them and so we set off on our first march through pitch darkness, twenty eight kilometres to our concentration area.

So, against the odds but as a tribute to the organisational powers of the German army, the general advance began promptly on 17 October, by which date the units and formations of III Reserve Corps, which contained the sole experienced and fully trained troops of Fourth Army, had been on the move for forty eight hours. Unfortunately for the German army, despite the mass of materiel which fell into its hands on the fall of Antwerp, not many prisoners were taken, so there was no prospect of advancing into a tactical vacuum. Approximately 20,000 soldiers were subsequently disarmed and interned in the Netherlands, but the great mass of the Belgian army escaped to the west to continue the battle. In order to understand how this happened, the situation on the left flank of the besieging German forces before Antwerp has to be examined.

Security of the left flank was the responsibility of 37 Landwehr Brigade of 5th Ersatz Division, which was opposed by the 4th Belgian Division and elements of a cavalry division. However the main task of this brigade was to cut the railway line between Antwerp and the west. It was quite beyond the modest capability of this formation to achieve both objectives. After several days of battle of varying fortune, on 28 September it succeeded in capturing the town of Aalst then, once it was relieved by 1 Guards Ersatz Brigade, it attempted to cross the Schelde above Dendermonde. A complete lack of bridging equipment rendered all efforts hopeless and, furthermore, the Belgians strained all their resources to prevent this brigade crossing the river and blocking their movement west. Already, by the night of 1 October, trainloads of equipment, wounded men and medical personnel had left Antwerp for Gent and Oostende and the next eight nights witnessed intense activity, as everything that was transportable was moved west.

The success of the operation depended on the presence of strong defences on the Schelde and, in its fight with 37 Landwehr Brigade, 4th Belgian Division suffered such severe casualties that it had to be relieved by 6th Belgian Division. By 6 October the Allies had decided to withdraw what was left of their forces and the following day 37 Landwehr Brigade succeeded in gaining the left bank of the Schelde at Schoonaarde above Dendermonde, where it was joined by 1 Bavarian Ersatz Brigade, which had been rushed up by rail. As it attempted to advance on Lokeren (being unaware of the overall situation of the Belgian forces), during its move towards that place, it bumped into the marching columns of the Belgian divisions and strong resistance.

When, on 9 October, the German force levels in the area were boosted by the arrival of 4th Ersatz Division, the effort was too late. Only the very final train movements were interdicted. Up to 80,000 men of the Belgian army had got away. Naturally, after a twelve day battle, the victorious German divisions were not going to deny themselves a moment of glory so, despite the drizzling rain, during the afternoon of 10 October, the men of 6th Reserve Division marched through the empty streets and past their Divisional Commander, Generalleutnant von Schickfus und Neudorf. In recognition of their achievement in forcing the crossing of the Nete near Lier on 5 October, Reserve Infantry Regiment 26 was given the honour of leading the parade. However, there was no time to linger and take in the sight of the German flag flying over the cathedral and the blazing oil tanks in the port area. By the same evening orders for an advance early the following morning westwards were already being issued. In a sense this was already too late and events during the coming days and the subsequent battle for the Ijzer were to demonstrate that those who had escaped had retained not insignificant fighting power.

Having spent a few days helping to cover the arrival and initial deployment in Flanders of the newly raised reserve corps, III Reserve Corps concentrated all its forces to the north and prepared to advance along the coast. Orders subordinating it and its allocated 4th Ersatz Division to Fourth Army arrived on 15 October. General von Beseler had intended to bombard Oostende that day and launch an attack with 6th Reserve Division against Touhout, but it was not permitted to cross the line Oostende – Roeselare until further orders had been given by Headquarters Fourth Army. It appears that there was concern that an isolated attack might encourage the Allied forces to manoeuvre and so end up in positions which would be less favourable to the general attack, which was to be launched when the new reserve corps were all ready to proceed. This seems to be a strange, over cautious, decision However, there was nothing for it but for all the III Reserve Corps formations to pause for twenty four hours – during which time the enemy were free to act precisely as they wished. Some reconnaissance was pushed forward as far as the Ijzer, but there was, nevertheless, something of a lack of hard intelligence.

Staging during this enforced halt in Roeselare, some men of 6th Reserve Division heard Belgian civilians calling out that they would not get far. Thinking, wrongly, that the Belgian army had simply dispersed and that the few British army formations arriving in the region would not be able to mount much resistance, the columns stepped out confidently to the northwest early on 17 October, heading towards the coast and so leaving the remainder of the area free for the deployment of the newly arrived formations. Once in position and given the order to move, all the formations began to advance confidently and rapidly parallel to the coast. 4th Ersatz Division was allocated the sector closest to the Channel and, with 5th and 6th Reserve Divisions in that order deployed to the south, III Reserve Corps closed up on the Ijzer. One of the first significant battles for 6th Reserve Division occurred at Keiem, about five kilometres north northwest of Diksmuide.

Oberst von Oertzen Artillery Commander 6th Reserve Division [8] **1.**

"After the fall of Antwerp, 6th Reserve Division went over to pursuit operations as far as the Ijzer, fighting for the first time near Diksmuide, Leke and Keiem. On 19 October Bartsch's company (2nd Company Reserve Infantry Regiment 35) and Dommenget's battery (6th Battery Reserve Field Artillery Regiment 6) combined heroically to beat off a serious Franco/Belgian attack near Keiem. The company suffered sixty one casualties; the battery thirteen men and fifteen horses. During the night the Belgians forced their way into Keiem, then the following morning 12 Reserve Infantry Brigade (Wachsmuth) launched a frontal assault against Keiem. In the meantime, 11 Reserve Infantry Brigade (von Jacobi), which had already thrust past Leke, detached 2nd and 3rd Batteries and deployed them south of Leke to guard the left flank.

"1st Battery (von Chamier) remained in Leke in reserve. That certainly conformed to the demands of the situation, but it was forced to remain there inactive while heavy artillery fire came down. At Charmier's request, General von Jacobi moved this battery to a firing position south of Leke, because at any moment it was expected that the Belgians would begin to withdraw from Keiem. Sure enough, no sooner had von Charmier's guns gone into position, than the Belgians began to stream backwards out of Keiem in dense masses. There they came under the cross fire of all six batteries, some of which were firing shrapnel at ranges of less than 1,000 metres, which caused them a dreadful bloodbath."

These skirmishes were a sign of things to come. Already, by midday 19 October, 1st Battalion Reserve Infantry Regiment 35 was attacked by Belgian infantry advancing from the west and the area of the main road to Diksmuide. Whilst this battle lasted, the Belgians continued to feed forward reinforcements, including some French marines. These attacks enjoyed no success and, once leading elements of Reserve Infantry Regiment 206 of 44th Reserve Division closed up at around 4.00 pm, and went into position to the left (south), 3rd Battalion Reserve Infantry Regiment 35 was released and able to sidestep to the north and go into support behind Reserve Infantry Regiment 26. These initial operations, relatively insignificant though they were, had already cost Reserve Infantry Regiment 35 Reserve Leutnant Kamp and twenty three other ranks killed, together with four officers and 124 other ranks wounded.

The move forward of the troops from XXII, XXIII, XXVI and XXVII Reserve Corps meant that the front was now continuous from the Channel coast to the Swiss border, with the sector of the Ijzer from Keiem north being the responsibility of III Reserve Corps. The orders now given were unambiguous, namely, to advance right up to the Ijzer with all speed and to establish bridgeheads on the far bank with a view to developing operations towards Dunkirk. This early fighting on the near bank of the Ijzer made a deep impression on those involved, even though they were all fully experienced troops. The war diary of Reserve Infantry Regiment 35 contained an annex produced as an after action report by its Machine Gun Company. **2.**

"During the morning of 19 October 1st and 2nd Battalions Reserve Infantry Regiment 35 stormed and captured Keiem. The aggression of the attack forced the Belgians to pull back out of the village in disorder and rush across the open ground towards the Ijzer. But there destruction was lying in wait for them. Whilst the battle was still raging within the village, two guns of Reserve Field Artillery Regiment 6 were advancing left [south] of the village. Oberleutnant von Hanstein, who had ridden forward and was observing events from a barn, had this company double forward and immediately open fire. Together with the artillery the machine guns reaped a dreadful harvest; the enemy running upright cross country presented the best imaginable target. What remained of the Belgians pulled back to the Ijzer where further bitter fighting was to be played out, because the enemy had dug fortress-like positions.

"During 21 October the infantry remained in the captured positions, as did 3rd Platoon Machine Gun Company, which was co-located with 2nd Company. From the morning of 21 October, 1st and 2nd Platoons of the Machine Gun Company remained at the disposal of the Regiment in Keiem. 12 Reserve Infantry Brigade was to force a crossing of the Ijzer. We suffered because of our movement through heavy fire, especially the heavy artillery fire of the enemy. During the night 21/22 October we received the order to advance, with Reserve Infantry Regiment 26 right [north] and Reserve Infantry Regiment 35 left [south] of the road leading west from Keiem to the river.

"The two machine gun platoons in reserve, under their commanders Offizierstellvertreter Hintze and Sergeant Schwandtke, initially went forward to 2nd Battalion and deployed there, about one kilometre from the river amongst 8th Company. Forward of the position was very open country, which, however, was under especially heavy artillery fire. During the night Major von Paczinski called several times for reinforcements. His 1st Battalion had managed to cross the river and man the far bank with two companies. Then, as morning approached, a runner arrived with a report that the west bank could not be held without further reinforcement and, at that, Oberleutnant von Hanstein decided to go forward in order to help hold the crossing come what may.

"Making use of the ditch by the side of the road, we made our way forward, then crossed a narrow bridge over a drainage ditch just before the Ijzer, which was under heavy fire by the enemy. However, doubling forward, both platoons and all their heavy equipment got as far as the river without any losses. Numerous dead and wounded [there] bore witness to the intensity of the fighting. After a short discussion with the commanding officer of 1st Battalion Reserve Infantry Regiment 26 [Major von Paczynski], Oberleutnant von Hanstein gave the order to cross. A provisional bridge, comprising a series of barrels with planks nailed to them, had already been partially destroyed by the enemy and was only kept in use because the engineers had secured it with long ropes. The planks were also slick with wet, sticky, clay, so the machine guns had to be dismantled before they could be taken over.

"Gradually and under constant enemy fire, the platoon crossed the water arriving, despite everything, on the far bank without casualties or having lost anything. There they reassembled their weapons and went into fire positions, one of which was an abandoned enemy machine gun post. Without further delay fire was opened on enemy trenches, columns and buildings to the front. An attempt to prepare the captured enemy machine gun to fire failed. Elements of 2nd Battalion Reserve Infantry Regiment 35 also got across under timely covering fire from the machine guns and, thanks to their great firepower, the position was sustained, despite the overwhelming enemy numerical superiority.

"The place became almost impossible to hold due to artillery fire, probably brought down as a reaction to the effect of our machine guns. We also began to run short of ammunition, though good work from the company overcame that problem and gun teams did their duty under heavy fire, going backwards and forwards over the narrow bridge carrying full ammunition boxes . . . daringly, an ammunition wagon, commanded by Feldwebel Lange, responded to the call for ammunition by driving forward as far as the first bridge and returning unscathed, despite all the firing.

"Meanwhile, a company of Reserve Infantry Regiment 20 [11 Reserve Infantry Brigade] had also succeeded in crossing the open space and closing up on the river and a section of Reserve Field Artillery Regiment 6 trotted up to the bridge and succeeded in opening fire. Unfortunately, their teams of horses got caught in heavy enemy artillery fire as they attempted to withdraw. The commander was seriously wounded and several of the gunners were wounded or killed. As a result, the remainder were forced to take cover and firing ceased. The Machine Gun Company was luckier. That day it suffered only one man killed and two wounded. Two guns were damaged and a box of ammunition was smashed by a direct hit

"After four guns of the Machine Gun Company of Reserve Infantry Regiment 20 had crossed the Ijzer, the Belgians attempted an attack as evening approached. Number 1 Gun was able to bring very effective fire to bear on the enemy from its position. A field of beet in front of 2nd Platoon, where they brought most of their fire down was, as we later discovered, full of dead and wounded men. The attack had been beaten back brilliantly and the firing died away as it went dark."[9]

Whilst all this preliminary skirmishing was occurring, the formations of 4th Ersatz Division had closed up on Westende, right on the Channel coast. Its 13 Ersatz Brigade, which was deployed in amongst the dunes, began to come under fire from ships of the Royal Navy bombarding the coastline and was forced to halt its advance. The large calibre (mostly 6 inch) high explosive shells tore great holes in the flanks of the battalions every time they attempted to move and supply became a real problem. Out to the front were Lombardsijde and Nieuwpoort, both places dominating approaches from the west and both held in strength by the enemy. To the north, 5th Reserve Division was also closing up on the Ijzer. Its leading elements were soon pushing along astride the road between St-Pieters-Kapelle and Schore and could already catch glimpses of the Ijzer. There was some evidence of machine gun fire from the far bank, whilst salvoes of shells were also beginning to land from time to time around Mannekensvere.

Hauptmann Kahler 9th Company Reserve Infantry Regiment 8[10] 3.

"The order to assault the Ijzer was given during the afternoon of 21 October. The company was in the front line and located on the right flank of the regiment. Its objective was the places where the Ijzer dog legs back to the west between Mannekensvere and St Joris. Reserve Infantry Regiment 48 to my right got forward without coming under fire at all. Despite enormous difficulties caused by the fact that the country was crossed by deep drainage ditches, three to four metres wide and full to the brim with water, I succeeded, at the cost of high casualties, to close up with my company on the Ijzer, where we established ourselves. The enemy was separated from us only by the width of the Ijzer – about thirty metres.

"Because of our own artillery fire and this flat terrain, which meant that the entire company was under flanking small arms fire, coupled with the fact that the other elements of the regiment had not reached the Ijzer, I was forced to relinquish this hard won position on the embankment and withdraw to a farmstead about 500metres in rear. At the same time as I sent a message to that effect, I also reported that, as soon as it went dark, I should immediately regain my position along the canal."

Back in the 6th Reserve Division area, where its right flank was now about sixty metres short of the canal and its left was established down towards Schorebakke, Reserve Infantry Regiment 24 was initially held back in reserve while Reserve Infantry Regiment 26 was assaulting the Ijzer. This situation did not last for long, however. As operations developed, its various units were called forward to carry out numerous duties in the forward area. As early as 19 October, 2nd Battalion was deployed along the route between Leke and Keiem to guard against any Belgian attempts to renew its earlier attempts to take Keiem. That same day the commander, Oberst von Schwemler, who had been ill for some time, had to be medically evacuated and was replaced by Oberstleutnant von Kummer. The following day, once Reserve Infantry Regiment 20 closed up on the Ijzer as well, a large gap developed between that regiment and 5th

Reserve Division. In response, three of the rifle companies of its 1st Battalion were sent forward to cover the sector at risk.

During 21 October the whole of 1st Battalion closed up towards the Ijzer and then the following night, 21/22 October, it was also ordered to make an assault crossing, this time near Schoorbakke, as part of an overall thrust by III Reserve Corps. This plan was designed to maintain pressure all along the front and attempt to force the Belgian defenders to give up their defensive lines. This was an extremely tall order, due to the strength of the defences on the far bank in this sector. Nevertheless, the support of 5th Reserve Division was offered and the battalion was allocated a section of two field guns and an engineer company for the operation. In the event, the promised support was not forthcoming, both the battalion flanks were in the air and there was no prospect of success. Instead, the battalion began to dig in where it was. Later that day, seeing that Reserve Infantry Regiment 26 was beginning to make some progress, the commanding officer, Major Fischel, ordered the attack to go ahead. This merely underlined the wisdom of the earlier decision; the attack was shot to pieces by a hail of shrapnel, high explosive shells and small arms fire and the battalion had to be withdrawn temporarily into reserve.

During the early hours of 22 October the 3rd Battalion and the Machine Gun Company moved to relieve Reserve Infantry Regiment 20 in trenches to the west of Leke but, by 9.00 am, reports were arriving that Reserve Infantry Regiment 26 had succeeded in getting one of its battalions onto the far bank of the Ijzer and that reinforcement was urgently necessary. Major Hayner, commanding officer 3rd Battalion Reserve Infantry Regiment 24, took an immediate decision to move in support, an extremely challenging manoeuvre in full daylight over the open ground near the Ijzer, especially in view of the fact that at least twelve wide and deep drainage ditches had to be negotiated with the help of planks. Nevertheless, by midday, the battalion had reached the Ijzer embankment and the engineers succeeded in spanning it with two footbridges made of barrels with planks attached to them.

8th Company crossed first to the far bank, followed by 3rd Battalion and the Machine Gun Company, then the troops deployed left and right along the embankment, despite being under intense fire the entire time. Flanking fire was particularly heavy from Schoorbakke, which of course was strongly held. For the time being a further advance was out of the question and it was soon established that the Belgian army was occupying a group of farm buildings to the front in some strength. Orders arrived in the late afternoon that the strong point was to be captured as it went dark and that 2nd Battalion was also going to be made available for the task. The advance across unknown terrain was far from easy, but the defenders were surprised and did not put up much of a fight. Many of those who tried to escape back to their main position a further 800 metres away were shot down and about fifty prisoners were captured.

The battalions then dug in throughout the night and were further reinforced by three companies of Reserve Infantry Regiment 20 the following day. There was now a substantial and, for the Allies, worrying, presence of German troops on the west bank of the Ijzer and they were in considerable strength, with their bridgeheads being expanded constantly. For the first time serious consideration started to be devoted to a means of countering these incursions, because many of the Belgian units were becoming very worn down and morale in places was dubious. Any lingering thoughts of an Allied advance to the east were set aside. A far more pressing risk was that the Belgians would buckle completely. Their main position now ran along the Nieuwpoort – Diksmuide railway and there was little in the way of defensible ground to the west of this should it fall.

To the south of Schore, Reserve Infantry Regiment 26, commanded by Oberst von Westernhagen, was holding positions hard up against the Ijzer. Top priority was given to bringing forward improvised bridging equipment during the night 21/22 October. Unable to call on the standard collapsible infantry foot bridges, the engineers had to make do with barrels, planks and doors removed from nearby houses and barns. In an attempt to take the defenders by surprise, shortly before 8.00 am the troops swarmed forward over the near embankment and the first crossings were attempted.

Landwehr Leutnant Hoffmann 8th Company Reserve Infantry Regiment 26 [11] 2.

"On 21 October the 8th Company, in which I was a platoon commander, marched away about 1.00 pm from our billets to the east of Leke. We marched with security precautions (I was with the advance guard) as far as Leke, then bore left to Keiem, before heading half right along a field track. A halt was called by farm buildings and the company organised itself behind the farm. Within the farm itself there were engineers, busy preparing temporary bridges. The company was to advance to the banks of the Ijzer and I received orders to advance with my platoon in open order towards the Ijzer bend. The terrain across which we moved was completely open and flat meadowland, criss-crossed by numerous dry ditches, alongside which isolated trees were growing – some of them in rows. Far away to our front we could also see a church tower nestling between houses, only the roofs of which were visible. The village was Pervijze and we marched in the direction of the church tower. There was not a sign of the enemy.

"We kept really well spread out and moved one at a time from ditch to ditch. I moved in the lead, waiting in each ditch until the majority of my men had closed up, then set off once more. Soon the enemy spotted us and we came under fire. A certain amount of shrapnel also impacted in the meadow to our front. I recollect that both the artillery and small arms fire died away and we were able to get well forward before it went dark. We then halted in a ditch. It was bitterly cold. Vizeweldebel Sobbe,[12] who had already demonstrated near Antwerp that he was a cool-headed, keen patrol commander, went forward alone and discovered that in front of the embankment of the Ijzer and parallel with it was a wide water-filled ditch which could not be jumped. Later that night (I cannot remember exactly when) I was relieved by another platoon of the company and pulled back with my platoon to farm buildings to our left rear.

Here I met up with Oberleutnant Schalleyn and the remainder of the company. Some of the bridging equipment had been brought to this point.

"As far as possible accommodation was found for everybody and Schalleyn advised me to lie down and get some rest because we should soon be moving forward once more. I lay down, fully clothed, in one of the available beds, but I had not even warmed up before the order came to move. We pushed forward as far as the previously mentioned ditch, which was bridged with some of the equipment and the First and Second Platoons moved across it and onto the embankment. My orders were to remain together with my platoon at the ditch in reserve. In order to obtain cover, I ordered the men to dig into the steep bank of the ditch on the enemy side. It now began to get light and the Belgians, occupying the far embankment of the Ijzer and having noted our approach, began to bring fire down on our troops whenever they showed themselves above the embankment.

"This developed into a full blown fire fight, although I could see nothing at all of the enemy, who were hidden by the embankment on this side, which was about thirty to forty metres to my front. At one point the fire was particularly intense and, when I looked out, I could see our men standing in the open on the embankment engaging the enemy. The Belgians pulled back and our engineers built a bridge. Leutnant Stade and his platoon were first across. The crossing was in full swing when, suddenly, to our right there was an almighty explosion and huge clouds of dust and smoke rose in the air. A heavy artillery shell, one of ours, had scored a direct hit on a lock keeper's cottage. We all listened intently then a second shell impacted directly in the canal and not far from the first one. A fountain of mud and water shot up into the sky then a third shell landed a little to my left.

"Whilst our men had been steadfast in the face of enemy fire, they proved to be very sensitive to ill-directed artillery fire from our side. The crossing stalled. One by one the men began to pull back, then more and more withdrew from the embankment and some even crossed back across the bridge from the far side. The Belgians took advantage of this moment to re-establish themselves and to bring down heavy small arms fire on us. We attempted to get the artillery fire stopped by waving flags and helmets towards the rear. This seemed to work and I do not recall any more of our own fire coming down after that. Thanks to the combined efforts of all the commanders, most noticeably Oberleutnant Schalleyn and Reserve Leutnant Goedeke, whose 3rd Company had closed up from the left and which had already despatched one platoon under Reserve Leutnant Kautz over our bridge, the troops were once more led forward to the embankment.

"Further forward casualties began to occur. One of these, Offizierstellvertreter Martin, commander of our 2nd Platoon, was severely wounded in the chest. A runner brought orders from the company commander to cross the bridge with my platoon. I mounted the embankment and set off for the bridge, noticing that it was low in the water. One of its supporting barrels had been hit, had filled with water and was dragging the bridge down. Enemy fire continued to be heavy, with bullets buzzing past us like a crowd of swarming bees. I located Oberleutnant Schalleyn further to the right on the embankment. He was surprised to see me, thinking that I was already across. I informed him that the bridge was barely passable, at which he immediately sent engineers forward to carry out repairs.

"Arriving back at the bridge I found that, although the bridge had settled deep into the water, it could be crossed. With my sword tucked under my arm, I crawled over on all fours; my men following me one by one. Once across we lengthened the left hand end of the firing line, which was being dug in on the enemy side of the embankment. Troops of both 3rd and 8th Company were completely intertwined. We remained here under heavy fire, sometimes by artillery, for the remainder of the day. The man next to me in the firing line was wounded quite seriously by a shell splinter. There was, however, not a sign of the enemy. They had clearly pulled back to prepared depth positions. At one point when our embankment was under enemy artillery fire, a Belgian infantryman, a stocky young man, came up over the embankment and surrendered. He had been sheltering in one of the Belgian foxholes on the far side of the embankment, but feared for his life because of the fire. He was extremely anxious, began to sob and shared out the contents of his knapsack with my men. We tried to calm him down, then sent him back alone across the bridge.

"At one point we could see heavy fire coming down on the teams and support elements of a battery, which had gone into fire positions somewhat to our left behind farm buildings, very close to the far bank of the canal. As it went dark, we sorted ourselves out and then, once it was really dark, we heard horns blowing and shouting off to the left, but could not make out what it was about. We found out later that the Belgians had launched an attack on our neighbouring unit. Once everything calmed down and the fire to our front had dwindled as well, our company moved forward a few hundred metres beyond the embankment and dug in. Because our left flank was in the air, my platoon on that side was echeloned back steeply. As far as I can remember, 4th Company, which crossed the bridge after us, was to our right, but I do not know the locations of the remainder of the battalion, nor can I remember where 3rd Company was.

"Throughout the entire night, as we dug in, we were under constant fire from a point half left of us then, as dawn broke, we could see that some Belgians must have taken up position there in a farm house. They attempted to get away one by one during the morning, but were shot at heavily by us every time they tried to escape. One of them, a Belgian engineer lieutenant, was taken prisoner by a patrol, commanded by Unteroffizier Held, which was sent to clear the buildings."

The picture was the same the length of the front that morning. Even where crossings were made, as soon as heads appeared above the far embankment they were met by a torrent of small arms fire, much of it fired at short range, because the first enemy positions were right up on the canal banks. The Belgian second positions were established a few hundred metres in rear, protected by a maze of drainage ditches, obstacles, watercourses and hedgerows. Slowly, fighting hard all the way, the Belgian defence yielded in short bounds. There were heavy casualties on both sides in this fighting, which was occurring a long way short of the next main defensive line. This ran along the Nieuwpoort to Diksmuide railway line, which could just be glimpsed away in the distance. Psychologically this was a difficult moment for the German attackers because, such were the casualties, all ranks could clearly see that if the advance continued at its current speed and cost, none of them would ever get as far as Pervijze.

For the time being, however, there was nothing for it but to hold on, to try to expand the bridgeheads and to attempt to ignore the increasing weight of artillery fire. For the Allies these crossings represented an alarming threat to the integrity of their defences, so every effort was being made to eliminate them. Some idea of the nature of these battles may be obtained from this letter, believed to be that of a feldwebel of 2nd Battalion Reserve Infantry Regiment 35. **3.**

> "So we now held Keiem, but from now on there could be no thought of advancing unstoppably, because Keiem was the point where the appalling terrain, which caused us so much trouble, began. It was as flat as a millpond and was littered every few paces with wide boggy areas and water filled ditches. Two kilometres to the west flowed the canalised Ijzer, behind which were located extraordinarily strong lines of defence. During the next three nights there was an intense artillery duel. We kept down in our trenches with very little to eat and hardly any sleep either. At 9.00 pm on the third day came a report that we were to advance to counter an enemy attack. Off we went forwards. It was a pitch black night and extremely damp and cold. Seemingly endless water meadows stretched out left and right of the muddy track we were following.
>
> "The nearer we approached the river, the more frequently bullets cracked overhead. Only the occasional groan showed that not all of them passed by harmlessly. Finally, we had to divide left and right and move along the ditches through mud a foot deep. There was then a lengthy halt. Bullets sang eerily through the night, clattering into tree trunks, tearing off small branches, splattering against stones and being deflected as ricochets, which made a noise like a toddler wailing its discontent. At long last the silent column began to move once more. We now crossed the 'bridge'. This comprised a barge wedged across the river, to which a few planks had been attached at either end. The planks had become so slippery that it was necessary to crawl across them on all fours. On the far bank we were met by a sentry who whispered, 'Crawl along the river to the left and extend the left flank!'

"It was possible to make out the river, but nothing else. Above our heads came a multiplicity of sounds [from all manner of projectiles]. Gradually we became accustomed to the dark and could see the wall that we were defending. We crawled along it. My hand brushed against something soft and wet. It was a corpse and my hand had grasped its blood soaked face. Every three paces we came across corpses or wounded men groaning. In amongst all that misery came the sharp whip cracks of small arms and the singing and whirring of bullets, mixed in with muffled commands. Eventually we reached the left flank, where things looked bad. The dead lay together in rows, whilst the shooting sounded just like the rattle of hailstones on metal. Someone shouted that the enemy was trying to filter past us. We quickly clambered onto the wall and saw, not twenty paces to our front, dark forms which were getting closer and closer. – Hell that could be a problem. 'Shoot lads! Give them everything you have got!' Crack, crack, crack! Now there were more flashes coming from the other side. We hardly dared expose the tips of our noses.

"Ceaselessly, the enemy tried to make their way to one side to get past us. Gradually we began to run short of ammunition, so we passed a message to the right, 'Bullets and reinforcements to the left as soon as possible!' Passed from hand to hand came cardboard packages full of clips of bullets then, once more, we peppered them until the air stank of powder smoke and we were all deafened. Then came some reinforcements, but they were too few to prevent the outflanking movement. The enemy became ever more numerous and they exploited the darkness to press up more closely. Suddenly dark figures loomed up the other side of the wall. They were four paces away and cast long shadows. They shouted in German, 'Surrender!' That was the furthest they got. There were flashes next to me and the shadowy figures collapsed. 'Fix bayonets!' They threw themselves at our muzzles. Our lads were both in front of and behind the wall. The black shadows scattered as our lads went for them. Within a minute they had all dispersed. 'Back over the wall and keep a good look out!'

"All eyes strained to see over the embankment and every index finger was poised on a trigger. 'Herr Feldwebel! We are being fired at from the flank! They are up on the embankment to the left!' Oh Lord! Where are the reinforcements? I pulled the left flank back to cover down to the river. That was all that could be done. Suddenly there were flashes from the right [east] bank. Don't say they have crossed the river! – Fortunately not. We could tell that they were German rifles from the whip-like crack when they were fired. Now came shouts from the far bank, 'There is a battalion deployed to the left behind the canal. It is firing at the enemy right flank. The enemy is pulling back over the embankment!' The black figures were drifting more to the left; the outflanking had been prevented. Thank God! It came not a moment too soon! We were putting down a solid weight of fire and the shooting from opposite was weakening.

Hurra! That has settled it. 'Stop lads! You cannot see anything now. Dig in and get some sleep. One section per platoon is to stay on guard!'

"Everything was mixed up in the dark. Our lads dug out holes in the embankment. Then everything was calm, or at least as calm as it could be with all our nerves on edge. Day dawned, grey and foggy, gradually lifting the curtain on a scene of tragedy. Row after row of our comrades lay there, most of them shot through the head. My batman lay not far from me. He was a brave, conscientious man who never left my side. The bullet had hit him in the temple. But worse, very much worse, was the scene on the far side of the wall. There were simply heaps of the fallen and the trenches themselves were full of Belgian and French soldiers. Hardly had dawn broke than long rows of wounded and unwounded enemy approached us; piteous-looking creatures in dirty blue jackets with their hands high in the air, all of them victims of the previous night. Many trigger fingers itched, because there was not a great desire to spare the enemy. But, in the end, these pathetic figures, who sought sanctuary through capture, were not worth a bullet. They were led back behind the front. Still early in the morning came the news that to our right 5th [Reserve] Division had forced a crossing of the Ijzer and that the enemy had been pushed back two kilometres all along the line."[13]

In response to an urgent request channelled to General d'Urbal by the Head of the French Military Mission to the Headquarters of the Belgian Forces, that, 'the 42nd Division be moved to the centre, to avoid the risk of the Belgian line being broken',[14] the French army now placed the whole of its 42nd Division on the Allied left flank to bolster the defence and began to give detailed thought to flooding the countryside inland of Dunkirk to prevent further German progress. Meanwhile, on the German side of the battlefield, the priority was to maintain pressure and to advance against the railway embankment to their front. This was the objective of their collective efforts for several days and it was to prove to be a very costly enterprise. Generalleutnant von Schickfus und Neudorf, commanding 6th Reserve Division, made strenuous efforts to exploit the success of Reserve Infantry Regiments 26 and 24 by moving all available forces close up behind the crossing sites, but the weight of enemy artillery fire was against him and rapidly put paid to thoughts of establishing large forces on the west bank of the Ijzer.

Already, during the afternoon of 23 October, the new commander of Reserve Infantry Regiment 24, Oberstleutnant Kummer, was killed just on the bank of the Ijzer; and every time the rifle companies tried to develop the attack towards the northwest, they were thrown back with heavy losses. By the time it went dark, however, there were about two and a half battalions established fairly precariously on the far bank and fighting for their lives to prevent the enemy from eliminating their hard won bridgehead. One of the main difficulties was that of re-supply. Large amounts of small arms ammunition were being expended and it was difficult to move sufficient stocks forward and near to impossible to deliver rations to where they were needed. When, at long last, the field kitchens managed to close up on the east bank of the Ijzer during the evening, large numbers of men of the carrying parties were killed or wounded on the outward or inward journeys and, when the remaining food arrived in the Reserve Infantry Regiment 24 positions some time after midnight, it was stone cold and there was not enough to go round.

In view of the awful conditions of wind, rain and mud to which men under constant fire were being subjected, this was almost beyond endurance and the situation was much the same up and down the line. The regiments debated long and hard whether to pull back to the relative safety of the near bank, but Headquarters 6th Reserve Division insisted, quite correctly, that the positions be held. This was particularly important because 5th Reserve Division, operating a little further north, planned to force three crossings the following night. Had 6th Reserve Division withdrawn, there would have been no hope of success for these follow up actions. So, with some reluctance and despite the appalling wet and windy weather, the forward battalions hung on, while additional troops and guns were manoeuvred so as to support the crossings of additional units.

It was an appalling experience for both sides. The night sky was lit up constantly by flares and the flash of exploding shells, whilst bursts of wild firing disturbed the night repeatedly. After a struggle lasting the entire night and following several failed attempts, the engineers of 6th Reserve Division finally succeeded in building a more substantial bridge in the centre of the divisional sector, but the price was once again high and dawn saw the Ijzer bearing large numbers of corpses sluggishly towards the sea. However, the sacrifice had not been entirely in vain, as two more battalions succeeded in crossing to the west bank to assist in beating off the incessant enemy counter-attacks against the hard pressed perimeter.

Up in the 5th Reserve Division area, by means of an outflanking movement to the north the previous day, Reserve Infantry Regiment 48 managed to get forward, right up to the eastern branch of the Ijzer, whilst Reserve Infantry Regiment 8 did everything possible to consolidate its positions around Mannekensvere by bringing its mortars forward. This was not without danger.

Unteroffizier Noppe Reserve Infantry Regiment 8 [15] *3.*

> "We had just carried forward the last of the mortar bombs when one of our comrades had his right foot torn off by a shell splinter. We lifted a door from a nearby house off its hinges, laid the wounded man on it and carried him several kilometres back along the heavily shot up roads and over bridges across a number of ditches back to the dressing station.

Within a short time all the labour expended and the losses incurred proved to be worthwhile because, on 22 October, a start was made on softening up the enemy positions prior to a forced crossing of the Ijzer on this sector of the front. Despite one mortar bomb from Reserve Infantry Regiment 48 going astray and burying several members of 9th Company Reserve Infantry Regiment 8, the short range bombardment continued and definite progress could be seen on 23 October, once the engineers responsible for operating the weapons had settled down and begun to land the bombs accurately.

Hauptmann Rohrbeck 2nd Company Reserve Infantry Regiment 8[16] 3.

"Once the first bombs came down, the Belgians rushed to get away from the places which seemed to be threatened by the trajectories of the metre long bombs. At that the engineers snatched the rifles of the nearest infantrymen and standing up, as though they were at a hare drive, they began to fire at the Belgians who were running away. Our lads found that most amusing and were quick to follow their example. However, the Belgians began to watch the mortar base plate positions carefully and to open fire at forty metres' range at any of our men who showed themselves after the weapons had been fired. A number of men were shot through the head as a result; 1st Battalion Reserve Infantry Regiment 8 alone suffered six killed and seventeen wounded.

"Despite this it was difficult to hold our men back. In vain Hauptmann Rohrbeck requested the services of a section of artillery or even a single gun to be moved forward and, with the aid of observation from the mortar base plate location, to bring down fire on the Belgians opposite."

Despite this promising start to their assault river crossings during the night of 22/23 October, the regiments did not succeed anywhere in gaining the west bank of the Ijzer. It is not completely clear what went wrong. Possibly the forward regiments under-estimated the difficulty of an opposed crossing at night or perhaps the defences, which were giving Reserve Infantry Regiments 26 and 24 such a hard time further south, were even more effective in this sector. There was the usual pressure from above and renewed attempts were a made in the early morning of 23 October, supported by heavy howitzers and additional artillery assets. With a thunderous roar, heavy shells droned overhead as dawn broke, landing with immense violence on the far bank. Great clouds of smoke and dirt and columns of water were thrown up as huge holes were torn out of the opposing positions.

This short, but devastating, bombardment complete, there was a brief moment of silence, but it really was brief. As strong patrols and groups made for the river bank, they came under lacerating fire at very close range. A fire fight developed between groups of men sheltering behind the embankments on either side and pouring fire at one another from forty metres. At that range it was almost impossible to miss and large numbers of would be assault troops were hit in the head or upper body, rolling back down the bank to be treated by the overworked medical orderlies. Their places were soon taken in the firing line, but there was still no hope of forcing a crossing. Under the cover of all the fire, at about 10.00 am, leading elements of 9 Reserve Brigade of 5th Reserve Division also closed up to the canal. So now the advance had reached the Ijzer throughout its entire lower reaches, but crossings were still elusive.

Everywhere the troops searched around for the means to bridge the canal, but this was far from easy. It did seem that the best chance lay on the left flank of 9 Reserve

Brigade, near to where 6th Reserve Division had forced its crossing, but every attempt to get forward and assemble a bridge was met with devastating fire from houses in Schoorbakke, out on their right flank, and foundered short of the embankment. Additional fire support from the heavy howitzers during the late afternoon took some of the pressure off the attackers, but they were still no closer to a crossing than they had been the previous night. It was a depressing story, one which also applied near the coast, where General von Beseler was beginning to feel that the attempt by 4th Ersatz Division to advance west and seize the lower reaches of the Ijzer stood no chance of success.

The overall perception on the Allied side was, however, quite different. A formal note passed by the Operations Division, Headquarters Belgian Forces, to the French Military Mission during the afternoon of 23 October read, 'Because of the exhausted state of the troops and lack of reserves, it is feared that an attack launched tonight or tomorrow morning can only expand the break in and completely drive in the Belgian centre. If this eventuality occurs, it will be necessary to give consideration to a withdrawal.'[17] This and similar reports finally led to a decision by General d'Urbal to order General Grossetti, commander of 42nd Division, to move the bulk of his division down towards Pervijze and he was allocated additional artillery resources to assist him. Following on from this, substantial additional reinforcements were allocated to the Allied left flank by General Foch, namely a territorial infantry regiment, which was rushed to Veurne, the 31st Infantry Division, cavalry and an additional two groups of 75 mm guns. Following the implementation of these new dispositions and the promise of reinforcement, the Belgians agreed to do all in their power to hold where they were, but the situation remained critical.

Day by day the fire of the Royal Navy was having an increasingly negative effect on the German formations, who found it completely impossible to move or even remain in the area of the dunes whilst being subjected to such a constant weight of accurately delivered fire. In an attempt to respond, heavy 150 mm gun batteries were rushed forward from Brugge, but they did not reach Oostende until late on 23 October and they were not able to begin engaging until the following day. They certainly had some effect, forcing the British flotilla to maintain a respectful distance away from the shore, but this in itself was insufficient to permit an assault on Westende-Bad or Lombardsijde-Bad to be launched with confidence. As an alternative, Beseler planned to withdraw 4th Ersatz Division the following night behind 5th Reserve Division, leaving only weak screening forces on the coast itself. The idea behind this was that 5th Reserve Division would force crossings over the Ijzer and enable 4th Ersatz Division to cross over, attack Nieuwpoort from the landward side and roll up enemy positions along the coast.

Given the continuous presence offshore of the British flotilla, it is not clear why Beseler thought that it would be any easier rolling up the coastline from west to east, rather than the other way round. Not only that, in this still fluid situation, the plan carried with it the risk that, if the Allies detected any weakening of the German position along the coast, they might be tempted into launching a thrust of their own, so as to take advantage of the altered tactical situation. Nevertheless, the corps commander clearly felt that he had to do something in order to regain the initiative, so orders went out for a move of 4th Ersatz Division behind 9 Reserve Brigade to begin the following night. It was not only III Reserve Corps which had plans for this northernmost division, however. That same night instructions arrived from Headquarters Fourth Army, directing that 4th Ersatz Division be withdrawn and sent rapidly to the south as the army reserve near Beselare in rear of XXVII Reserve Corps, which was experiencing considerable difficulties in trying to advance.

This would have been a desperate act. If there really had been a crisis down at Beselare then 4th Ersatz Division would have arrived too late to affect the outcome and, meanwhile, weakening of the northern flank in this way could have had completely disastrous consequences for the entire German front, especially because reliable reports of further Allied reinforcements arriving in Nieuwpoort were at that moment being processed at Headquarters III Reserve Corps. All these arguments were put forward, together with the fact that 4th Ersatz Division was already moving into position behind 9 Reserve Brigade. At that, Fourth Army conceded. Emphasising the need for a speedy victory in the north to ease the pressure on the centre and south of the army front, permission was given to retain 4th Ersatz Division and some other Landwehr formations were sent to Beselare instead. In response, General von Beseler did modify his orders slightly, leaving 13 and 33 Landwehr Ersatz Brigades in positions where they could contribute to the anticipated break through by driving hard against Nieuwpoort when the moment arrived.

As has been noted the prerequisite, namely a crossing in force by 5th Reserve Division of the Ijzer, had not been achieved so, for the time being, the situation in the north was stalled. The Allies were clearly under great pressure, but much of the momentum of the III Reserve Corps advance was leaking away. By the early morning of 24 October, 6th Reserve Division had succeeded in passing all its infantry across the Ijzer, but they were crammed into a tiny bridgehead, vulnerable to shell fire and unable to develop their attack forward. It was case of advance or die and, fortunately, during the early dawn that day, 5th Reserve Division managed at last to get across the Ijzer in three places. It appeared that the enemy had been taken by surprise. It seems also that, following the intense fire fights the previous day, the Belgian defenders had withdrawn to trenches north of Schoorbakke and southeast of St Joris. Apparently the 4th Belgian Regiment of the Line had found German enfilading machine gun fire too much to cope with and had to evacuate, blowing up bridges as they went.[18]

The result of this shift in defensive posture was that 5th Reserve Division suffered far fewer casualties in effecting the crossing than they had expected. Immediately thought was given to the consideration that the attackers might be gaining the upper hand but on the ground the battle continued to be as hard fought as ever. Some ground was being gained along the III Reserve Corps front, but it was happening very slowly and painfully. 6th Reserve Division was still advancing on the distant prospect of the red roofs of Pervijze. 9 Ersatz Brigade crossed over into the bridgehead the following night to expand the 5th Reserve Division area and more progress was made when a position near Schoorbakke was taken after a sharp fight during the afternoon. Progress was still painfully slow, but news from 44th Reserve Division to the south that some of its battalions had crossed the Ijzer as well and were fighting in Stuivekenskerke was very welcome. It meant that the defence had given way along an eight kilometre frontage from Mannekensvere to Kasteelhoek, a fact which gave new heart to the attacking troops.

However, some prisoners who were captured that day, brought with them disturbing news. On being interrogated, they revealed the extent of the move forward of the French 42nd Division from the Reims area for the first time, explaining that its leading elements were already in Nieuwpoort and stating (somewhat inaccurately) that the intention was to press forward eastwards along the coast. As might be imagined, this caused a degree of consternation within III Reserve Corps, because there were now only two Landwehr Brigades to oppose such a move and they were more or less fixed in position, unable to move because of the activities of the Royal Navy. It was a difficult moment for General von Beseler, because his weakening of his right flank had only been approved in the context of the pursuit of a swift local victory. He was further concerned at the thought that the advance just recently achieved by 5th and 6th Reserve Divisions might have been made possible because of an enemy ruse.

Such are the occasions on the battlefield when generals earn their money. Faced with the choice of playing safe by returning forces to his right flank, Beseler took the bolder option and decided that, if the French intended to launch a swift attack, he was too late to react by redeploying his forces, so it was better to strive for a decision in his centre. Meanwhile, he ordered that the entire weight of fire of his heavy artillery was to be directed against Nieuwpoort. Anxious hours followed for Beseler and his staff but, as time passed and there was no enemy sortie out of Nieuwpoort, they ceased to be less concerned and concentrated instead on pushing their own attack forward. There is good evidence that the recent German success and the amount of fire directed at Nieuwpoort led the French to move an infantry regiment and a light infantry battalion round to Pervijze, to block the move forward of 6th Reserve Division, throw it back across the Ijzer and turn to hit 5th Reserve Division in the flank.[19]

Regardless of the exact truth, the main German effort continued to be applied in the centre, with both 5th and 6th Reserve Divisions straining every sinew to get their field artillery across the Ijzer and into locations from where their guns could bring down fire into the depth of the Franco-Belgian positions. The church steeple in Pervijze soon fell, an early victim of this fire. By now the main defensive line of resistance was based on the Nieuwpoort – Diksmuide railway, which ran along a high embankment for most of its length. It also provided useful protection for enemy guns and, as a result, the forward battalions west of the Ijzer suffered very badly from the fire. With each passing day the men were becoming more worn down, tired, hungry and despondent, but there was no relief to be had and no let up in the intensity of operations.

As a result, although 6th Reserve Division pushed towards Pervijze in a further series of limited attacks and 5th Reserve Division attempted to close on Ramskapelle, no genuine progress worth the name was made on 24 or 25 October. Even on 26 October, when there was to have been a general advance against the elusive railway embankment, results were extremely patchy and the casualties continued to mount on both sides. Perhaps this should have been no surprise. 26 October was the seventh day of bitter fighting; seven days during which the infantry had been in action day and night in dreadful conditions, under constant fire. It had been almost impossible to organise any sort of relief anywhere along the front and there was no possibility whatsoever of arranging it for the men west of the Ijzer, who were bearing the main weight of the offensive.

Despite this, 6th Reserve Division, ordered to launch yet another attack as early in the day as possible and benefiting from the combined fire of all the corps heavy artillery, managed to get forward and pressurise the enemy facing 44th Reserve Division to such an extent that they were forced to pull back. 5th Reserve Division, despite being rein-forced by 9 Ersatz Brigade, had almost no success when it attempted to thrust northwards, deeply echeloned, towards Nieuwpoort. Its attack withered away in a storm of small arms fire and shrapnel. However, there was some success when, at about 3.00 pm, Reserve Infantry Regiment 48 managed to close in on Ramskapelle and drive its Belgian defenders back. Its 2nd Battalion pushed on near to where the Koolhof Vaart meets the West Vaart, by the railway embankment south of the town of Nieuwpoort. Here 7th Company soldiers caught a large group of Belgians retreating. After firing at them for several minutes, the Belgians decided that surrender was a better option than trying to escape over open country and one hundred of them were captured.

These and similar incidents were positive proof that the Belgian defence was fast disintegrating, but the German advance had effectively reached its culminating point. Without relief and further reinforcement, its worn out battalions were incapable of further aggressive action. The same could be said of the Belgian forces. However the French reinforcements were starting to have an effect. That evening, despite the fact that their men were totally exhausted and demoralised, there was no more talk of possible retreat. Indeed an order was issued during the night of 26 October, in the name of King Albert, 'Tomorrow the army, reinforced by French troops, will continue the defence of the positions it currently occupies – at all costs.'[20]

On the German side, General von Beseler still wanted next to develop his operations round Nieuwpoort, so as to isolate the garrison and force their withdrawal, but it was to prove impossible. On 27 October yet another attempt was made by 6th Reserve Division to storm forward, but it was hopeless. Every attempt to move was met by a torrent of fire – from artillery near Pervijze, machine guns mounted in armoured cars and heavy shelling from British ships operating off the coast. The attack faltered, the Allied defensive positions seemed to be as far away as ever and Major Hayner, commanding 3rd Battalion Reserve Infantry Regiment 24, had no alternative but to report the depressing news up the chain of command that, 'The attacking spirit of the battalion is completely broken'.[21] The news would have cheered up the Allies, who still regarded the situation along the Ijzer as extremely serious.

Around Nieuwpoort itself on 27 October, whilst the Belgian army reorganised behind the shelter of the Nieuwpoort – Diksmuide railway line, 5th Reserve Division was meant to advance at 9.00 am in order to secure the line of the Nieuwpoort- Pervijze road, which ran along just to the west of the railway. The orders to Reserve Infantry

Regiment 48 of 9 Reserve Infantry Brigade were to push its left flank forward to a point just south of Ramskapelle and to echelon its companies deeply on its right flank, so as to maintain contact at all times with Reserve Infantry Regiment 8 which, for its part, was directed to hold its positions opposite Nieuwpoort. In order to have the best chance of achieving this, the commander Reserve Infantry Regiment 48, Oberstleutnant von Bieberstein, directed that the advance was to begin before daybreak.

2nd Battalion, reinforced by 3rd and 4th Companies, duly set off at 6.15 am. Everyone was wet and thoroughly chilled after a night of driving rain, but the lines of infantry pressed on, ignoring machine gun fire, across the open ground, which was devoid of cover and criss-crossed with deep ditches, and headed for the high embankment that carried the railway line in this area. Initial reasonable progress was not maintained. Reserve Oberleutnant Baltzer, commanding 7th Company, was soon evacuated, shot through the head and Vizefeldwebel Weidner, who took over from him, was forced to respond negatively to an order of 9.45 am, directing him to ensure that 7th Company got forward and gained ground. 'It is now completely impossible to advance in the direction ordered', he informed his battalion commander. 'Our left flank is threatened by machine gun fire, because Reserve Infantry Regiment 52 is too far in rear of us.'[22]

Finally, Reserve Infantry Regiment 48 was forced to take emergency measures and deploy troops to cover its own left flank, because Reserve Infantry Regiment 52 found it almost impossible to move that day. Its 1st Battalion did make about 200 metres of ground in the direction of the Nieuwpoort – Diksmuide railway at high cost, whilst 2nd Battalion gained about 500 metres at a cost of 105 casualties, but it had to be relieved by Reserve Infantry Regiment 20 that same evening. The 3rd Battalion remained in reserve throughout the day, but conditions were so unpleasant and the shelling of the depth positions so heavy that it is hard to say which part of the regiment had suffered the most. On the 6th Reserve Division front there were also difficulties. Prior to its advance stalling, 5th Reserve Division had already reached the line of the railway embankment near Ramskapelle by the end of 26 October and the formations of 4th Ersatz Division were closing up against the vital lock gates at Nieuwpoort. However, to the south, there was absolutely no progress in the 44th Reserve Division sector and the situation for Reserve Infantry Regiment 35 on the left flank was becoming critical.

44th Reserve Division did attempt an attack on part of its frontage, but it was shot to a standstill with bloody casualties and, meanwhile, the gap between it and 6th Reserve Division simply widened. It was all very well for higher headquarters to demand that attacks were to be pressed forward regardless of the situation on the flanks, but this was extremely difficult to sustain over a period of days or nights. A tactic which was acceptable in a fast moving advance was simply foolhardy as the lines began to solidify. Once the 44th Reserve Division attack had been dealt with, a great many guns, French and Belgian, began to bring down heavy fire on Reserve Infantry Regiment 35 and, although the enemy could be seen to be evacuating certain forward positions, a curtain of defensive fire prevented any follow up by the German assaulting troops.

During the evening several units were relieved forward and 3rd Battalion Reserve

Infantry Regiment 20 was returned to its own regiment. The entire battlefield was littered with dead and wounded who cried out for assistance, but there was little possibility of collecting all of them in and many were not evacuated for a further twenty four, or even forty eight, hours. That same evening, at about 10.00 pm, reports came through from 4th Ersatz Division that there had been a particularly large explosion to their front. At the time it was thought that it was the sound of canal bridges being blown, but later it was associated with initial attempts at flooding. In actual fact the first assessment was correct. This explosion was almost certainly the demolition of the swing bridge on the Veurne Lock by Lieutenant François, a Belgian engineer.[23]

The following day there was still no movement possible on this part of the front. Every attempt at patrolling forward was beaten off by enemy small arms fire, whilst the rate of artillery fire seemed to increase with each passing hour and there were no systematic German attempts to counter it. Ammunition stocks were not good, so the shells and shrapnel rounds which were expended were mostly directed toward the railway embankment. Both flanks of III Reserve Corps spent much of the day under fire. To the north, attempts by 4th Ersatz Division to press forward at Nieuwpoort foundered due to the fire support provided to the hard pressed defence by ships of the Royal Navy. Intended originally to facilitate the Allied advance along the coast towards Oostende, by increasing the weight of fire available to the Belgian army, whose own guns were beginning to fail due to overuse and problems with repair and maintenance, the intervention of this flotilla under the Admiral commanding the Dover Patrol began to affect the advancing German troops seriously from about 23 October.[24] When intense German pressure over several days meant that the defence in and around Nieuwpoort was about to give way, only the gunnery of the Royal Navy saved the day. Their shooting was of decisive importance on 27 October in particular.

Rear Admiral Sir Horace Hood flew his flag in HMS *Venerable*, a pre-dreadnought battleship, which had escorted the Portsmouth Battalion Marines Light Infantry to Oostende the previous summer. He could also call on another monitor, two light cruisers and several destroyers, two of which, *L'Intrépide* and *L'Aventurier*, were French.[25] With its twelve inch (305 mm) main armament and secondary six inch (152 mm) guns, *Venerable* could put down a huge, accurate, broadside, especially at the ranges involved. There are differing accounts of how effective the fire was. The British Official History (p 118) suggests that the German accounts claimed later that the 'material effect of [the] naval heavy shells was small', but this is not borne out by other descriptions, such as that of Reserve Infantry Regiment 35.[26]

> "On this day along the coast, 4th Ersatz Division suffered very seriously as a result of a hail of flanking fire from ships' guns of the heaviest calibre. Against these sixteen warships, the German side could only deploy a few 100 mm and 130 mm guns, whose shells did not achieve one single hit against the enemy ships.[27] After the hurricane of fire had lasted for several hours, the battalions which had been advancing across open country towards Nieuwpoort were so battered that they were reduced in strength to one composite battalion. Marine

infantry, stationed at Oostende, with orders to defend against landing attempts along the coast, had to fill in the gaps.[28] For a long time the situation along the coast was critical, but the enemy did not press forward; they also seemed to have been considerably reduced in strength."

There are also reports that naval shelling put the German heavy 150 mm guns located in the dunes at Middelkerke out of action.[29] Regardless of how much direct damage the naval gun fire did, or did not, do, it put paid completely to the attempts by 4th Ersatz Division to control access to the locks at the mouth of the Ijzer, thus enabling the Belgian expert water engineers to carry out the difficult flooding task over the next few days.[30] What is more, the formations and units of 4 Ersatz Brigade were so battered by the hurricane of naval shells that their entire cohesion was broken. In small groups and totally disorganised, the remnants of eight battalions fell back to Middelkerke, leaving only what was left of one battalion still forward. It was fortunate for the German army that neither the Belgians nor the French 42nd Division were in any condition themselves to launch an attack; nor was a convenient embarked force available to attempt a landing on the coast. This was one of those occasions when the value of an intervention by the Royal Navy was not fully appreciated until much later. The bombardment of the coastal area continued until 30 October and, although the action was then broken off, the desired effect had been achieved; time had been bought to enable the inundation to be effective.

Meanwhile, both 5th and 6th Reserve Divisions struggled with both the conditions and the defensive positions to their front. The Nieuwpoort – Diksmuide railway embankment was by now being defended largely by elements of the French 42nd Division, who were putting up stern resistance. In general the German regiments were located between 200 and 500 metres east of the embankment, enduring near intolerable physical conditions and simply trying to consolidate where they were.

Vizefeldwebel Wilde 3rd Battalion Reserve Infantry Regiment 52[31] **4.**

" '3rd Battalion is to remain in the trenches northwest of Grote Henne Farm and is to continue to dig in'. How we dug throughout two nights and how we cursed when our spades hit water only a few spits down. I can still recall a Vizefeldwebel of 10th Company who sat on the edge of his hole, with his feet dangling in the cold water. By the following morning he had such a heavy cold that we would have used an umbrella to shield ourselves from his sneezes if one had been available."

Vizefeldwebel Lehmann 3rd Battalion Reserve Infantry Regiment 52[32] **4.**

"The condition of the water was simply awful. We were forced to drink the salty water out of the canal. At about 6.00 pm news arrived that Unterarzt Schulz had been mortally wounded by a shell. We, Berg and I, had been amused watching the enemy attempting to engage a house near the canal, not realising that there were men inside it. About 10.00 pm we buried our fallen comrade by the bridge. That very morning, true to his helpful, fearless way, he had bandaged up two wounded engineers whilst under shrapnel fire so heavy that the stretcher bearers themselves did not dare to. Now he was dead and laid to rest next to the canal bridge, very near the place which also held the remains of Sergeant Kulisch. It was the old fate of a soldier once more. Which of us knew when it would be our turn?"

This indifference to their fate and feeling of powerlessness spread rapidly through the ranks. Day and night passed in a misery of mud, water-filled holes and saturated clothing. Not even the constant crash of exploding shells, nor the crack of small arms fire, could raise the majority of the men out of a state of listless torpor. However, at Headquarters III Reserve Corps, there was once more great concern. Reports had been coming in that there was an Allied plan to mount a landing in a strength of two infantry brigades along the Belgian coast. Unsurprising to relate – bearing in mind that the report was quite without foundation – nothing actually happened but, while the scare lasted, it caused a swift reaction. The reminder of 4th Ersatz Division was ordered forward once more and the marine infantry directed to return to their stand-by positions at Oostende with all speed. As the marine infantry were force marching back, the British flotilla appeared off shore once more, adding to the anxiety and making life extremely difficult for the German infantry again.

From about 8.00 am to 10.30 am there was a heavy bombardment all along the 4th Ersatz Division front, as well as on the right flank of 5th Reserve Division southeast of Nieuwpoort. This was the day that *Wildfire* was hit, but this success was a poor return for all the effort expended and the damage done to German offensive plans in the area. At 2.00 pm the forward regiments reported that strong columns of infantry were moving from Nieuwpoort in the direction of Pervijze. This was confirmed by air reconnaissance and was interpreted to mean that the main defensive effort was being shifted south to bolster the sector between Ramskapelle and Pervijze, especially as strong forces had also been observed digging in along the road from Nieuwpoort to Veurne. This did not mean that Nieuwpoort was left undefended of course, but General von Beseler felt that there was now an improved chance of capturing it and appropriate orders were issued to what was left of 4th Ersatz Division. However, yet again, naval gunnery prevented any such advance and, eventually, the scheme was shelved and the decision was taken to start to employ 4th Ersatz Division further south. Leaving only 33 Ersatz Brigade in position in a screening role, the following night, once it was safe to move in the open, the remainder of the division was marched south via St-Pieters-Kapelle into a holding position behind the two forward divisions.

On 1 November the news of what had happened west of the Ijzer was officially distributed by Headquarters III Reserve Corps in a message to all subordinate headquarters. 'In order to save his country from certain defeat, the King of the Belgians has caused the lock gates at Nieuwpoort to be blown up and thereby flooded a large piece of territory.' [33] This message was half correct. Contrary to suggestions sometimes made, the decision to flood the polders was indeed Belgian, not French, but the means was not to blow up the lock gates. The correct story is one of skilled, incremental, flooding by Belgian water engineers, who contrived both to inundate selected areas during the course of several successive high tides and also wash away temporary bridges along the Ijzer. King Albert made this difficult decision to flood with brackish seawater some of the most fertile agricultural land in northwest Belgium, because it appeared to be the only way of preventing complete disaster.

The effect of this extraordinary measure, however, was not immediate. It took several days for the flooding to reach the desired level so, until that moment and fortunately reinforced by the French army and marines, there was nothing for it but for the Belgian army to hang on grimly and attempt to beat off all that Fourth Army could muster against it in its continuing attempts to gain ground to the west. On the German side of the battlefield the situation was far from satisfactory. Already, by 27 and 28 October, it was becoming clear on the ground that advancing further west or even remaining west of the Ijzer was gradually becoming less and less practical; The width of the inundated area had increased to 500 – 600 metres and the law of diminishing returns was beginning to apply.[34] Nevertheless, the orders for 29 October stressed yet again, 'At 1.00 pm the entire III Reserve Corps is to storm the Pervijze – Nieuwpoort railway!'[35]

For the first time an objection was raised. Generalleutnant von Schickfus und Neudorf, commanding 6th Reserve Division, formally requested a review of the order. The ground was already saturated, the troops were at the end of their endurance and preparation had been inadequate. Neudorf was known to be an excellent commander and his division extremely reliable. If he had his doubts, there had to be a good reason and Beseler reconsidered the direction he had given. He, however, was himself under great pressure from Commander Fourth Army, so, with reluctance, he had to confirm the order. Nothing was possible in the Nieuwpoort area because of the Royal Navy's gunnery, whilst morning mist hindered the artillery preparation further south but, at the appointed hour, those who could still get to their feet did so and moved forward. However this was an attack in name only. The artillery preparation was insufficient, the defenders fought back strongly, bringing all manner of fire to bear on the few men struggling forward and, although they stuck to their task throughout the afternoon, nothing was achieved. What was worse, the effects of the flooding were by now beginning to be noticed throughout the area.

In common with numerous other commanders located forward, Hauptmann Moeller of Reserve Infantry Regiment 48 reported during the early evening of 29 October, 'The enemy has flooded the ground to our front. The trench encircling the farmstead in which the company is located is filling constantly. It sounds just like a waterfall.'[36] Despite such warnings, either because their seriousness was underestimated, or because it was felt that the following day offered the last opportunity to attempt to get forward across the flooded area, III Reserve Corps issued orders that there was to be a major effort across its entire frontage on 30 October. It is also essential to bear in mind that the III Reserve Corps' battles were not occurring in isolation. 30 October saw a major effort from the reserve corps further to the south, so it was obviously important to maintain pressure all along the Fourth Army front.

"Corps Order 30 October 1914. By order of the Army Commander, all ranks are to be made aware that, if the attack is successful, it will be of decisive importance for the outcome of the campaign. The Corps Commander expects the divisions to press home the attack at all costs and not to permit halts or pauses, even if neighbouring formations are not keeping pace."[37]

This theme was confirmed and expanded further by 5th Reserve Division. 'The attack is to be pressed home at all costs. The railway embankment must be in our possession during the hours of darkness. If a regiment succeeds in carrying out such an attack, all other regiments are to conform immediately. If such an opportunity does not present itself, at 5.20 am precisely, every regiment is to storm the railway embankment.'[38]

The weather was terrible that night. The wind was gusting and rain squalls lashed the flooded area. However, every effort had to be made to conform to the orders, so artillery and mortars both duly opened up on the enemy positions at 4.30 am, then valiant efforts were made to overcome the conditions and close on the embankment. Already by 7.55 am on 30 October, however, Major von Ziehlberg of Reserve Infantry Regiment 26, 6th Reserve Division, was drawing attention to the rapidly deteriorating condition of the battlefield on his front.

Major von Ziehlberg 3rd Battalion Reserve Infantry Regiment 26[39] **5.**

"The water has risen markedly. Since yesterday morning it has increased in depth by about one and a half metres. Because the footbridge erected by the engineers yesterday has been wrecked by the enemy artillery, I have directed the Engineer Company to get bridging material forward during the hours of darkness in case the larger bridge behind the right flank of the battalion is damaged. All companies are standing with their feet in water and ground water is being encountered at the depth of a single spade. It is impossible for the battalion to attack, because the major drainage ditch in front of the embankment is now about ten metres wide. The fighting power of the enemy is undiminished. This morning, during an assault, they opened fire with 35 mm revolver cannons."

Though the situation was also well short of ideal on 5th Reserve Division front, it was still possible for the regiments to advance with difficulty and with varying degrees of success. Despite all the obvious difficulties, the commander of 9 Reserve Brigade, Generalmajor Knoch, who had already thought the previous day that the enemy was pulling back somewhat around Nieuwpoort, ordered 1st Battalion Reserve Infantry Regiment 8 to advance along the road via St Joris and take possession of Nieuwpoort. In so doing the brigade commander was effectively committing the very last of his reserves in support of Reserve Infantry Regiment 48. The 1st Battalion duly advanced, but, when it paused and took cover to the west of St Joris, it met up with some companies of Reserve

Jäger Battalion 3, who stated that Nieuwpoort was still strongly garrisoned by the enemy. Patrols were despatched along the line of the river, the road and the canal to check the situation to the front. They all reported that the bridges were down, that there were strong enemy positions and that they had come under artillery fire from positions to the north and southwest of Nieuwpoort.

In the light of this fresh intelligence the over-ambitious scheme was abandoned and 1st Battalion Reserve Infantry Regiment 8 consolidated in rear of Reserve Infantry Regiment 48. Reports of enemy massing to deliver a counter-attack from the west against Reserve Infantry Regiment 48 later in the day confirmed the wisdom of this decision, but it was not easy in the prevailing conditions to produce any sort of meaningful defensive positions.

Kriegfreiwilliger Knösel 4th Company Reserve Infantry Regiment 8[40] **6.**

> "4th Company was sent forward in reserve. The situation was unclear, so we were told to dig in, in three places. All the trenches and ditches around us were totally full of water but, finally, we came across a slight rise and began to dig. Einjärig-Kriegsfreiwilliger Knösel had everything but a spade, because he had still not learned how to scrounge things. A short time later the wehrmann to his right and the old reservist to his left began to utter curses about 'this lazy, young sprog.' As a result I had a spade pressed into my hands by these old hands and made a pathetic first attempt to dig down. Enemy machine gun fire began to sweep the area and I found this useful weapon of war torn once more out of my hands and later these two, true, faithful comrades laid into me for my hopeless efforts at digging! That is my main memory of the pantomime in the water that was played out at Ramskapelle. We were then driven out that same night by floodwater."

Reserve Infantry Regiment 52 commented later that their movement that morning had been facilitated by thick early morning fog and their 3rd Battalion managed to cover the intervening 400 – 500 metres distance between the positions and overrun a group of Belgian defenders, including a seriously wounded officer. A further advance saw them capturing a further one hundred Belgian soldiers on the embankment itself. One of its companies later reported: **7.**

> "12th Company was occupying trenches parallel to the embankment that was occupied by the Belgians. Between our trenches and the railway there were several wide and occasionally deep drainage ditches. Because observation in the half light of early dawn was probably difficult for the enemy, hardly a round was fired as we crossed the ditches. Immediately before the railway embankment, however, there was heavy fire. Doubling forward, we sought cover behind the embankment, so friend and foe were separated only by the width of the tracks.
>
> "Suddenly German shells started coming down in amongst us and panic

threatened, which would have led to heavy casualties within the company. With great presence of mind, Gefreiter Hermann shouted, 'No, those are Belgian shells!' and the men all calmed down. Meanwhile the Belgians had detected movement amongst the Germans and abandoned caution. Swift action led to some of them being grabbed by the hands and pulled in to be captured, whilst others attempted to escape. Thanks once more to Gefreiter Hermann, few of them made it. There was only one route leading back to the Belgian support positions in the rear. This was kept under constant fire by Gefreiter Herman from behind the embankment. None of the enemy escaped his bullets and, because none could get past alive, the rest finally had to surrender."[41]

Vizefeldwebel Wilde 9th Company Reserve Infantry Regiment 52[42] *7.*

"There was barely controllable impatience in our trenches. Just before 6.00 am the entire line stood up as one man, climbed out of the trenches and ran forwards. Everyone knew what the objective was. Enemy fire was only weak, almost as though they were not expecting our attack. Because there had been no link up with our left hand neighbours in the dark, 9th Company was offering a flank to the enemy and came under a fire from farm buildings this side of the railway. However the fire soon stopped, because the artillery drove the riflemen away. The railway embankment was reached before 7.00 am, but we only spotted one man there. The remainder of the garrison was seen heading through the great gardens towards buildings on the far side of the main road.[43] However, many of those fleeing were knocked out of the battle by our bullets.

"We were on our objective and we waited for orders to be allowed to press on beyond the embankment. We were all in good spirits, because the company had suffered only four casualties, despite the flanking fire. We developed the embankment for defence. By now it was 9.00 am or 10.00 am and then, from the far side of the railway embankment, we were suddenly pelted with bread, sausages, sardines in oil and other useful things. We were somewhat taken aback, being used mostly to having other things fired at us. I went to see what was happening and saw that two soldiers of 9th Company, Buchardt and Vollmann had made their way over small bridge, were inspecting the ground on the far side and found these delicious items in abandoned enemy trenches . . .

"The enemy were also on the look out and there was a fair bit of fire coming from the houses along the road. With a bold dash, the two of them were back in their own positions. However, it was something else that had attracted the enemy fire. The Machine Gun Company had moved up into position and they were soon in the sights of the enemy. Offizierstellvertreter Elger arrived in the 9th Company position, together with his platoon.[44] They took aim swiftly and a few volleys sufficed to drive the enemy riflemen back from the windows.

"Off to our right, heavy fighting had developed in the sectors of Reserve Infantry Regiments 8 and 48. The enemy was well aware that if we could advance beyond the railway embankment and Ramskapelle, their entire position north of Langemark would become untenable. As a result they did everything to reinforce their lines. We could see enemy infantry on the march away to the north, but they were out of range for us. A battery, which clearly was not in the picture as far as the tactical situation was concerned, approached along the road at a full gallop, intending to come to the aid of its hard-pressed comrades. Because it was only 800 metres away, it offered an excellent target to us.

"Elger immediately opened fire with his two machine guns and I issued fire orders to the company, which I was commanding in place of Hauptmann Ziehm, who had taken over command of the battalion following the death of Major Müller. The daring battery had certainly not expected to find itself in such a dense hail of bullets. The heavy losses amongst men and horses forced some of them to turn tail and the remainder to take cover in the roadside ditches . . . We settled down for the night [eventually], hoping to be able to continue the advance the following day."

These minor successes represented the best returns achieved on the III Reserve Corps front that day. Elsewhere, 4th Reserve Division reported that their observers had watched an attempted advance by 6th Reserve Division, that the men were quickly in water thigh deep and that they had been forced to withdraw to firmer ground to avoid the risk of drowning. Generalmajor von Jakobi, commander 11 Reserve Brigade, personally assembled about nine weak assault groups from the entire strength of his brigade and tried to force away along the Schoorbakke – Pervijze road. They fought their way beyond the railway embankment and closed to fifty metres from the village. A final charge saw the survivors disputing Pervijze with rifle butt and bayonet, but casualties had again been high. Major Hayner, commanding officer 3rd Battalion Reserve Infantry Regiment 24 and Hauptmann Neithardt, commanding 10th Company, were amongst the wounded. They were the very last of the original officers who had marched out of barracks with the regiment after it mobilised three months previously.[45] There was no possibility of a further advance without fresh troops, of which there were none and, in any case, the water was rising behind them all the time.

Away to the north, 3rd Battalion Reserve Infantry Regiment 52 ended the day dug in along their sector of the embankment.

Hauptmann Dziobek 3rd Battalion Reserve Infantry Regiment 52[46] *7.*

"From our positions on the embankment we could see Reserve Infantry Regiment 8 advancing to our right, reaching Ramskapelle and entering it. We were in constant contact with each other. Reserve Infantry Regiment 8 was deeply echeloned. To our left all was still and quiet. The neighbouring regiment did not get forward, so our left flank came under a dreadful weight of fire. At my instigation, a machine gun platoon was directed against an especially suspicious building below the railway embankment at a range of 700 metres, then Fischer's platoon moved against it and remained there for the rest of day to provide flank protection. Hauptmann Oehler reported the success to the regimental commander and was promised the Iron Cross First Class.[47] About 11.30 am 9th Company also moved up to the front line, bringing the news that the battalion commanding officer, Major Müller, had been killed. Accompanied by his adjutant, Oberleutnant von Lany, he was on his way forward when he was hit in the heart by a bullet and died on the spot.

"It was our intention to continue on from the railway embankment, when we noticed dense enemy columns about 2,000 metres away and moving between isolated buildings towards the left [south]. At first we thought that we were seeing enemy who had been forced to withdraw, but then we realised that they were negotiating the ditches and closing in towards us. Towards 3.30 pm other columns appeared further to the left. Moving very carefully and paying particular attention to security, they manoeuvred in and out of cover until they reached the road about 600 metres to our front. Although we brought down rapid fire, it did not seem to disturb the enemy at all. It was a very uncomfortable feeling to find ourselves faced with the arrival of potentially unstoppable masses of troops.

"Nevertheless a combination of our fire and that of the machine guns seemed to take the wind out of their sails as far as attacking energetically was concerned. The day passed in state of great tension. A further advance was planned for the next night and engineers were present, ready to bridge a nearby wide water-filled ditch. As it went dark, we pushed patrols forward to the ditch. From time to time our attention was drawn to the positions around Nieuwpoort, as they brought the length of the embankment under fire. We were unlucky when a party of ours, which had been assembled to go and fetch rations, was shelled. Several men, including Gefreiter Hammach, were killed."

During the night 30/31 October, Reserve Infantry Regiment 52 called down various concentrations of fire and prepared to move forward and cross the ditch as dawn broke. It was not to be. After hearing a report from Generalmajor von Jakobi about the state of the inundation and the condition of the troops, the General Staff Officer 6th Reserve Division reported formally to Headquarters III Reserve Corps that the depth of flooding in their sector was so great that there could be no question of continuing to conduct operations forward of the Ijzer. At that, Corps Headquarters made strenuous efforts to ascertain the exact position all along their front. This was difficult, because many localities were already cut off by the rising water. It was clear that there was no time to lose if some of the troops were to be able to withdraw across the Ijzer at all.

The situation on the right flank of 5th Reserve Division was marginally better, but deteriorating all the time The forward battalion commanders were called back to a conference and, whilst they were away, it became obvious that there, too, all the ditches in the area were beginning to fill and overflow, that the water was rising everywhere. There did not seem to be any possible solution so, during the early hours of the morning, General von Beseler took the only possible decision. Orders went out to evacuate the positions and pull back over the Ijzer. This went smoothly and the troops left, leaving behind a great muddy sea, punctuated by the occasional building. A few enemy shells and bursts of fire came down as the columns waded back through the flooded water meadows, but there was no follow up, which was just as well. There was no shortage of obstacles to be negotiated and difficulties to be overcome, as one of the company commanders of Reserve Infantry Regiment 52 noted in his after action report.[48]

"I approached a five metre wide drainage ditch with my company, expecting to find that everyone else had cleared it but, instead, I found that there, some 500 metres from the embankment, 600 men of 10th and 12th Companies and Reserve Jäger Battalion 3 were gathered. The gap was bridged by one wobbly plank. Everyman was weighed down by about a hundredweight of clay on each boot, so there was distinct risk that they would slide off it into the water. This could not continue, otherwise we should find ourselves trapped here by the water when dawn broke. I rushed over, together with a few engineers and hurried to a building where I had noticed some planks the previous day. These were pressed into service to improve the bridge, then everyone was able to cross rapidly."

It was a far more awkward proposition for those involved in moving back heavy or bulky weapons or equipment, even in the case of units in the north of the area where the flooding was not quite so bad.

Leutnant von Schrötter Machine Gun Company Reserve Infantry Regiment 8[49] **6.**

"During the evening of 29 October, we noticed that the water had risen in the trenches so that the men of 3rd Battalion Reserve Infantry Regiment 8 [near Ramskapelle] were forced to spend the night standing in water which was over knee deep. At 5.30 am Friday 30 October, Reserve Infantry Regiment 48 to our left launched an attack. Because we only had one and a half companies facing Ramskapelle, with the remainder manning the front towards Nieuwpoort, we were unable to join in the attack without specific additional orders. Leutnant Scherler, commanding 11th Company Reserve Infantry Regiment 8, and I sent word to 'Daddy' Daum and he arrived, together with Osteroth, at 7.30 am. Out to the front the water had risen considerably. The Belgians had opened the sluices ... In order to assist the 48th, I received orders to advance on Ramskapelle with two companies of 3rd Battalion Reserve Infantry Regiment 8.

"The advance was far from straightforward. To pass the farms northeast of Ramskapelle we had to wade through the water and in front of the railway line the amount of shelling was hellish. Lying on our stomachs parallel to the railway lines we took a short breather. Having crossed further drainage ditches I managed to get Number 1 gun into position through water over knee deep, but without casualties, at the northern end of the village of Ramskapelle. Here I was greeted enthusiastically by the commanders of 9th and 10th Companies Reserve Infantry Regiment 48. My second gun also arrived with its crew intact. I placed Number 1 gun in the final house of the built up area, whilst the two companies of 3rd Battalion Reserve Infantry Regiment 8 extended the line of Reserve Infantry Regiment 48 to the right.

"The enemy heavy artillery was concentrating its shells on the station in particular. The enemy were occupying the farms to the west of Ramskapelle in strength, so a further advance with the weak forces at our disposal was not possible. During the afternoon a field gun drove along the road from Veurne. Using both guns I attempted to prevent it from going into action, but the range was too great. I sent Schütze Sadyn back with a report of the enemy dispositions and a request for ammunition . . . Much later he returned with two machine gunners of 2nd Platoon carrying ammunition. I then went into position with my two guns alongside 3rd Battalion Reserve Infantry Regiment 8, which had dug in in a field to the west of the road to Diksmuide.

"It was an awful job trying to dig with spades in that sticky clay . . . Leutnant Trantow, commander of 12th Company Reserve Infantry Regiment 8, explained to me that one of his platoon commanders, who was a water engineer by profession, was of the opinion that the rising water would overflow the embankment in another six hours. He had reported this. What a pleasant prospect for us! Digging down, we soon struck water. At 1.30 am I was together with the commander of 11th Company Reserve Infantry Regiment 8 when an order arrived ordering 3rd Battalion Reserve Infantry Regiment 8 back across the Ijzer because of the rising water.

"Without infantry assistance, I dismantled everything and pulled back through the village . . . shells were dropping constantly and I was extremely glad to be back at the familiar farm buildings to the east of Blouwhof Farm, where I met up with some members of 3rd Battalion Reserve Infantry Regiment 8, who had to relieve me of some of my ammunition . . . We got back across the Ijzer safely at 5.30 am."

Orders to withdraw reached Reserve Infantry Regiment 8 at 2.30 am 31 October. 'In view of the increased depth of the flooding, withdraw immediately, so that the troops are no longer affected by the water; that is to say, behind the Ijzer. Outposts are to be left west of the Ijzer and an infantry bridgehead is to be maintained . . . '[50] Reserve Infantry Regiment 48 recalled later that it was with chattering teeth that they received the order to withdraw. Unnoticed by the enemy, covered by rearguards which fired in their defence, carrying weapons, ammunition, dead and wounded, each man was heavy laden as they pulled back in single file through knee deep water, through bogs and trenches. They withdrew swiftly over the battlefield for which they had fought so hard during the previous days until they were back over the Ijzer, bitterly disappointed about the turn of events. These operations had cost it 103 all ranks killed, including Major Karl Freiherr von Eynatten,[51] and almost 500 wounded.

This was typical of almost all the formations of III Reserve Corps. They had embarked on this offensive with high hopes in the middle of October. Against all the odds, they had forced crossings of the Ijzer and exerted extreme pressure on the Belgian and French defenders. Throughout the days and nights of incessant battle they had sacrificed every-thing, suffered dreadful casualties, endured unspeakable physical conditions, had to cope with shortages of ammunition and equipment and frequently gone hungry – all in pursuit of a break through which remained always just out of reach. They had often come close to achieving their aim but, finally, they were defeated by flooding to which they had no answer. After giving their all for twelve long days they found themselves forced back to the east bank of the Ijzer by a spreading lake of filthy water. It had all been for nothing.

Notes

1. *Der Weltkrieg 1914–1918 Vol 5* p 276.
2. *ibid.* p 279.
3. The weapons involved were heavy field howitzers, 210 mm howitzers and 100 mm guns. The largest allocations went to III and XXII Reserve Corps, with twelve and eight assorted batteries (mostly heavy field howitzers) respectively. XXIII, XXVI and XXVII Reserve Corps each received three batteries of heavy field howitzers, two of 210 mm howitzers and one of 100 mm guns.
4. *Der Weltkrieg 1914–1918 Vol 5* pp 283–284.
5. The other formations which made up this Corps were 5th and 6th Reserve Divisions.
6. Schakert History Reserve Infantry Regiment 48 p 44.
7. Boesser History Reserve Field Artillery Regiment 44 pp 36–37.
8. History Reserve Infantry Regiment 35 p 50.
9. *ibid.* pp 55–57.
10. Rohrbeck History Reserve Infantry Regiment 8 p 52.
11. Plathe History Reserve Infantry Regiment 26 pp 42 – 45.
12. Vizefeldwebel Hasso Sobbe, in civilian life secretary to a district court in Erxleben, north of Magdeburg, was killed later during the fighting at Poelkapelle on 7 November 1914. He is buried in the *Kamaradengrab* of the German cemetery at Langemark.
13. History Reserve Infantry Regiment 35 pp 54–55.
14. *Les Armées Françaises dans la Grande Guerre, Tome Premier, Quatrième Volume* [FOH] p 322.
15. Rohrbeck *op. cit.* p 52.
16. *ibid.* p 53.
17. FOH p 326.
18. Pul *In Flanders Flooded Fields* p 136
19. Beumelberg *Ypern 1914* pp 166–167 & FOH p 331.
20. FOH p 337.
21. History Reserve Infantry Regiment 24 p 23. In five days of fighting, the 3rd Battalion Reserve Infantry Regiment 24 suffered losses of 391 all ranks, a fairly typical total during the Ijzer battles.

22. Schakert *op. cit.* p 51.

23. Pul *op. cit.* p 182

24. See Repetzky History Reserve Jäger Battalion 3 p 50

25. Later in the action, in recognition of this French cooperation, when Hood withdrew *Venerable* from the bombarding force, he transferred his flag to *L'Intrépide*. This was one of the very few occasions in history when such a thing had been done and, in the case of the French, the first time it had happened without the ship involved having first been taken as a prize. See Pul *op. cit.* p 220

26. History Reserve Infantry Regiment 35 p 62.

27. In fact, this statement is quite wrong. According to the British Official History of the War (Corbett Vol I pp 231–233), on 27 October there were so many German guns in the dunes attempting to engage the flotilla, that it was not safe to come closer than 4,000 yards from the shore. In his determination to provide as much assistance as possible to the force ashore and in the highest traditions of the Royal Navy, Hood commanded his flotilla with considerable skill and daring, despite the treacherous waters and the presence of German submarines, which the destroyers had to chase away from time to time. Despite the constant high speed evasive action of the lighter ships, the British took numerous hits, the worst instance occurring on 28 October when the destroyer, HMS *Syren*, received a direct hit on its forward 6 Pounder, which killed its commander, Lieutenant H O Wauton, and seven ratings and wounded a further seventeen men, ten of them seriously. During the course of this deployment, *Venerable* itself grounded on an ill charted sand bar, though it was floated clear on the next high tide and there were hits which caused casualties in *Brilliant* and *Rinaldo*, whilst *Wildfire*, hit on the waterline by a German 150 mm gun, had to limp out of the action for repairs. Lieutenant Hubert Wauton's body was taken back to Dover and he was buried in Charlton CWGC cemetery (Grave Q H 12), next to which presumably his shipmates lie too.

28. This is probably a reference to a forward deployment from Oostende on 27 and 28 October by elements of Marine Infantry Regiment 2 around Westende. There is a mention of one of their battalions being in position along the coast at this time and coming 'under heavy enemy artillery fire, especially from the sea'. during the days in question. They were relieved fairly quickly, however, and returned to their original priority task. See Goertze History Marine Infantry Regiment

2 p 40. Later the entire Marine Infantry Brigade was involved in a final attempt to advance along the coast on 10 November 1914.

29. Beumelberg *op. cit.* p 172.

30. It also had an effect on morale. A captured German NCO later wrote to his wife that the German solders had had, 'to lead the life of cave dwellers, owing to the terrible artillery fire from the fleet'. Corbett Vol I p 231.

31. Ulrich History Reserve Infantry Regiment 52 p 69.

32. *ibid.* 52 p 69.

33. Plathe History Reserve Infantry Regiment 26 p 55.

34. FOH p 344.

35. History Reserve Infantry Regiment 24 p 23.

36. Schakert *op. cit.* p 53.

37. Ulrich *op. cit.* p 70.

38. Schakert *op. cit.* p 53.

39. Plathe *op. cit.* pp 54–55.

40. Rohrbeck *op. cit.* p 61.

41. Ulrich *op. cit.* p 71.

42. *ibid.* pp 71–72.

43. Presumably this is a reference to the Ramskapelle – Pervijze road.

44. Having transferred later to the German air force as an observer and been commissioned, Reserve Leutnant Erich Elger died on 9 January 1917.

45. History Reserve Infantry Regiment 24 pp 24–25.

46. Ulrich *op. cit.* pp 72–73.

47. He did not live to have it presented. On 10 November, the day before the planned ceremony, he was killed during an assault on Langemark. Hauptmann Fritz Oehler is buried in the German cemetery at Langemark Block A Grave 7594.

48. Ulrich *op. cit.* p 74.

49. Rohrbeck *op. cit.* pp 60–61.

50. *ibid.* p 61.

51. Major Karl Freiherr von Eynatten is buried at the German cemetery at Vladslo Block 1 Grave 2316. Of the other regimental fallen, Leutnant Kurt Solveen is also buried there in Block 1 Grave 66. It is probable that Leutnant Hans Becker, buried at Vladslo Block 3 Grave 204 and Lt Karl Wencker, buried in the *Kamaradengrab* at the German cemetery at Langemark, fell in these battles while serving with Reserve Infantry Regiment 48. In all it is estimated that the Ijzer battles cost the Belgian army 20,000 casualties between 18 and 30 October, whilst those of the German army may easily have exceeded them. FOH p 362.

CHAPTER 3

Bloody Fiasco at Langemark

Commanded by General der Infanterie Freiherr von Hügel, formations of XXVI Reserve Corps launched an attack on a frontage from Moorslede to Staden at 9.00 am on 20 October. Their objective was the area bounded by Zonnebeke in the south and Bikschote in the north. XXVII Reserve Corps was operating to the south in the direction of Beselare whilst to the north, with the intercorps boundary on the edge of Houthulst Wood, was XXIII Reserve Corps. More or less right in the centre of the XXVI Reserve Corps front and located on the railway line from Torhout to Ypres was the village of Langemark. This agricultural community was surrounded by meadows and sandwiched between the Steenbeek and the Broenbeek.

By daybreak on 20 October the formations of 51st Reserve Division were deployed in a wide arc around Oostnieuwkerke, eight kilometres to the east, which was held by weak Allied forces. As soon as it became clear to the defence what was happening, the village was evacuated and the troops fell back to a prepared outpost line either side of Westrozebeke. 51st Reserve Division then reassembled into two great columns and advanced to the west but, by about 10.00 am, they came under accurate artillery fire and were forced to deploy into attack formations once more, the infantry going to ground while the German artillery took up firing positions to the west of Oostnieuwkerke and began to engage the enemy batteries. After a lengthy artillery duel, the infantry regiments launched an attack just after midday, but were soon in some trouble, especially on the right flank, where XXIII Reserve Corps had not made much progress and from where heavy fire from the French troops began to take a toll on the advancing lines. On the right flank the attack faltered; the check soon being transmitted to the units in the centre and on the left of the assault. At this the artillery commander despatched a portion of his batteries right forward, so that they could provide observed direct support from the front.

Having been pinned down for several hours, this intervention meant that the infantry was able once more to get forward and, by around 4.00pm, the German regiments were threatening to envelop Westrozebeke on either side. This was the signal for another hurried evacuation by the defending garrison. Following up close behind and advancing as rapidly as possible to Poelkapelle, men of Reserve Infantry Regiment 235 were able to capture three officers and 103 men of the French Infantry Regiment 41. By the time it went dark, the men of Reserve Jäger Battalion 23 had pushed on as far as the Poelkapelle railway station, which was actually situated about two kilometres north-west of the village itself. From there the Jägers pushed security posts out a few hundred metres more, as far as the southern edge of Houthulst Wood, which still concealed strong enemy forces and thus posed a distinct threat to the Corps right flank. At about the same time XXIII Reserve Corps had pushed up to the eastern edge of Houthulst

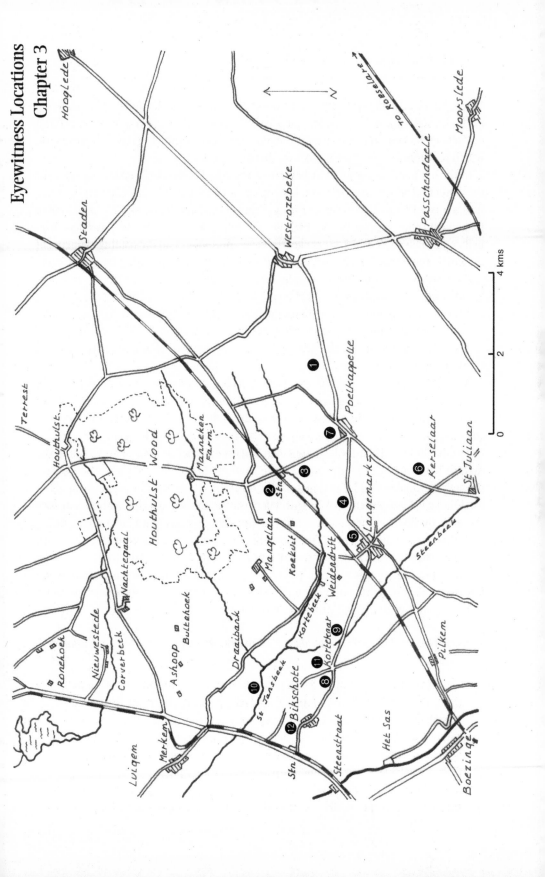

Eyewitness Locations
Chapter 3

Wood, but clearly there could be no question of attempting to advance within it during the hours of darkness. The majority of 51st Reserve Division found some form of billet in Poelkapelle and prepared to continue the assault the following day on Langemark, which was now a mere three kilometres distant.

In the left hand sector of XXVI Reserve Corps it had been an extremely hard day for the men of 52nd Reserve Division. Setting off in two great columns (Reserve Infantry Regiments 238 and 240 to the south and Reserve Infantry Regiments 237 and 239 to their north) they headed for the high ground in the area bounded by Passchendaele, Keiberg, Broodseinde and Zonnebeke. However, no sooner had the leading elements of the northern column passed through Moorslede in the early morning than they came under heavy small arms fire and deployed hastily into firing lines, with the rear regiments continuing to advance to thicken up the position. The remainder of the morning was taken up in an intensely fought battle, during which only slow progress was made. The situation was much the same for Reserve Infantry Regiments 238 and 240, which deployed left and right of the Moorslede – Zonnebeke road and also struggled to continue the advance.

After a fire fight lasting for hours, about 2.00 pm, an infantry assault was launched north and south of Passchendaele by Reserve Infantry Regiments 239 and 237, who succeeded in securing the village after a savage fight at close quarters. Aided by this advance, the southern regiments were also able to get forward in their turn. As a result, by evening Reserve Infantry Regiment 238 had occupied a line of farm buildings on the eastern edge of Broodseinde and Reserve Infantry Regiment 240 was able to pass through the small wood located just southeast of the village itself. Despite the lengthy battle, casualties were reasonably light. There was general satisfaction with the advance achieved that day and morale was high, as the various units contemplated obtaining their first view of the towers of Ypres from the ridges to its east the following day. With patrols pushed forward and other security measures taken all along the front, the troops attempted to snatch as much rest as possible prior to the anticipated exertions of the following day. In a thoroughly confused and fluid situation, however, rumours abounded and spread like wildfire amongst the troops.

Unterzahlmeister Pfitzner Quartermaster's Department 2nd Battalion Reserve Infantry Regiment 240 [1]

"During the afternoon of 20 October the bulky and conspicuous wagons of the quartermaster's department moved up along the road Waregem – Oostrozebeke. The wagons at the rear were located at the village exit. The column waited there for hours, then came a rumour that British cavalry had broken through. All the crews of the wagons in the column were immediately dismounted and a rough firing line was improvised. An enemy aircraft circled high above. 'Attention – aerial darts!' Everyone took cover under trees by the side of the road and, whilst no darts arrived, large quantities of rifle ammunition were fired. The firing line deployed once more. It grew dark and we all felt hungry. There was no meat available; it had all been issued to the field kitchens. I ordered Unteroffizier Malteux, the rations NCO, to go and requisition something from one of the farms located in the direction of march. At that he rode off, together with four other men.

"Night fell; it was absolutely pitch black. Once more 'news' arrived about the threat of an attack by cavalry, so all the lights on the wagons had to be extinguished. All other lights and fires were banned and the entire column was nervous. To top everything else, orders arrived to fix bayonets. In the impenetrable darkness this meant that we were now a danger to one another. Disquiet continued to mount then, all of a sudden, at the tail of the column by the exit to Oostrozebeke, there was a wild burst of firing! Oh, oh, enemy cavalry: here we go! In rear, in the last farmhouse in Oostrozebeke, something could be seen. Was it a light? Was it on fire? Orders flew. Nobody had a clue what was happening; it was impossible to see three paces and all the wagons were wedged together. 'Clear the road! Pick up your weapons!' Hands gripped butts of rifles tightly. We had, after all, learned to shoot! – both at static and moving targets, but at living ones? That was rather different.

"Our eyes stared intently into the darkness and a frosty chill spread up our spines to our necks. The shooting continued. Passed from waggon to wagon from the rear came the message, *'Franctireurs!'* The commander of the baggage column of Reserve Infantry Regiment 240 (Leutnant Wipko?) bawled back, 'Bring the *Schweinhunds* here!' and the cry was repeated all the way back from wagon to wagon. This was followed by a shout of triumph. One had been captured and was being brought over. Then, from the other side, moving as slowly as a hearse, came a strange vehicle. It was a Flanders three wheeled cart, pulled by a horse and led by the farmer. Once more, sharp and penetrating, came the shout of the Leutnant, 'Bring the *Schwein* here!' *'Where is the Schwein?'* Sitting high on his steed and, lacking spurs, forced to use a stick to get it to trot, the Unteroffizier rode up to the Leutnant sweating. Then he reported, 'Here it is, Herr Leutnant!'

"Where?' 'Here!' Everyone crowded round, anxious to catch a glimpse of the criminal and the Leutnant and his posse halted in front of the three wheeled cart. By the beams of pocket torches, a delight to see and still, in death a shimmering pink, lay a dead pig in the cart – it had been requisitioned by the rations Unteroffizier. A huge laugh of relief went up and the tension fell away. In the meantime it transpired that the shooting at the rear of the column was completely harmless and orders arrived to continue the march. The dead pig was loaded onto a baggage wagon and the farmer sent off home. The column set off, not stopping until it reached Izigem. It was already past midnight and time to bivouac. There was no hot water to be had, so the pig was cleaned with cold water and was skinned piece by piece. The meat was then distributed – at

2.00 am there was freshly boiled pork. It tasted excellent, as Comrade Flaskamp can confirm."

During the night orders arrived concerning operations on 21 October. The overall objective was ambitious. The aim was to seize bridgeheads across the Ijzer, north of Ypres, so the three reserve corps were directed to open the way to the river. The omens were not good, however. A battle was still raging around Beselare, where the situation was thought to be critical. XXIII Corps was still held up to the east of Houthulst Wood, though 46th Reserve Division was given the mission of thrusting in a westerly direction, north of the wood, then swinging south to link up once more with 51st Reserve Division. 51st Division itself was given the unenviable task of thrusting west, ignoring the situation on its flanks and securing the approaches to the Ypres Canal. It was generally believed on the German side that Langemark was strongly fortified and stoutly defended, so it was clear to all that this was going to be an extremely tall order.

In addition to the village defences, the landscape in this sector had a number of features which favoured the defence. It was criss-crossed by ditches, dykes and embankments and the numerous farm buildings and slight rises offered superb fire positions, with extensive fields of fire. In short, it was plain to all that the meadows around Langemark would be first class killing zones. The only approach appeared to be to close up on the defenders by means of a violent attack conducted with extreme aggression and at maximum speed. To that end, 51st Reserve Division was directed to advance from Poelkapelle at 9.00 am on 21 October in four large regimental columns in the general direction of Het Sas and Pilkem, with a view to securing the entire sector from Bikschote south. Every available artillery piece was tasked to move forward during the night into firing positions between Westrozebeke and Poelkapelle and from there to bombard Langemark as heavily as possible from first light until the attack went in.

For his part, Commander 51st Infantry Division issued the following order:

"1. The enemy opposing the Corps is located at Langemark and Broodseinde.

2. The offensive will be continued tomorrow. The neighbouring corps to the right will advance completely to the north of Houthulst Wood. 52nd Reserve Division will attack the enemy to the south and, in so doing, will protect the flank of 51st Reserve Division.

3. 51st Reserve Division will attack in four columns as follows:

- Northern Column (Reserve Infantry Regiment 234, Reserve Jäger Battalion 23, half of Cycle Company, 1st and 2nd Batteries Reserve Field Artillery Regiment 51 with a light ammunition column) is to advance from Poelkapelle Station via Koekuit, Bikschote to Steenstraat.

- Second Column (One battalion from Reserve Infantry Regiment 236, Reserve Jäger [Battalion?], 3rd Battery Reserve Field Artillery Regiment 51) from Poelkapelle Station via Goed ter Veste, Weidendrest and Kortekeer to Steenstraat.

- <u>Third Column</u> (Two battalions Reserve Infantry Regiment 236, 4th Battery Reserve Field Artillery Regiment 51) from the northern edge of Poelkapelle village, north of Langemark to Het Sas.

- <u>Southern Column</u> (Reserve Infantry Regiment 235, 3rd Battalion Reserve Field Artillery Regiment 51, Reserve Engineer Company 51 with 51st Reserve Division Bridging detachment on call) from Poelkapelle, south of Langemark to Pilkem then Boezinge.

The columns are to be at their start points, unobserved as far as possible, by 7.00 am. The advance is to begin at 7.00 am.

4. 4th Company Reserve Infantry Regiment 235 is to remain at the disposal of the Corps Commander, together with two field gun batteries (5th and 6th Batteries Reserve Field Artillery Regiment 51) and two thirds of the second light ammunition column.

5. Light ammunition columns are to be deployed as follows:
- 1st Light Ammunition Column, reinforced by the remainder of the 2nd Column, with the Northern Column
- One Third 2nd Light Ammunition Column with the Third Column
- 3rd Light Ammunition Column with the Southern Column

6. The heavy artillery (100mm guns and Field Howitzers) is to reconnoitre positions between Poelkapelle and Westrozebeke, so as to be able to bring fire down on Langemark and are to occupy these positions by 9.00 am.

7. I shall be located to the east of Poelkapelle by the main road. A telephone link is to be established to that point as soon as possible.[2]

Of course it was not intended that this attack would be an unsupported charge. As was made clear in the order, to the south 52nd Reserve Division was directed to outflank Broodseinde and to capture the heights to the west of it, thus putting pressure on the right flank of the troops opposed to 51st Reserve Division; and then to provide flank protection for the overall operation. Nevertheless, this promised to be another hard day of battle against an enemy who was completely clear about what was likely to happen and was now being granted another night to complete all necessary preparations. During the early part of the night such were the immense problems involved in moving the formations of the division forward that serious doubts were raised about whether there would be enough time for them to move into position on their start lines in time. Having buried the first of their fallen in Westrozebeke, Reserve Infantry Regiment 235 later reported,[3] **1.**

"The village was full of hustle and bustle, with every street full to bursting with troops from all arms and services. The 3rd Battalion took the lead when the move began along the main road Westrozebeke – Ypres towards Poelkapelle. In the meantime darkness had fallen. Houses were burning right and left of the road. The first halt occurred just short of the exit to the village. One of the columns had stalled. Curses and swearing! The [exertions] of the day could be felt in the legs; all longed for a place to lie down and sleep. After a further fifty metres there was another halt; nobody knew why. The occasional enemy shell was fired at random. Then came an order, 'About turn! Quick March!' Then it was, 'Forwards!' once more. Artillery drove up from the rear and behind them was a second column, with engineers in the lead. [There were] arguments and incidents – orders – counter-orders – more halts – then, with relief, forward movement again.

"However the movement never lasted long and the road was too narrow. By now three columns were attempting to advance abreast down it. Gradually, the individual riflemen became totally indifferent as a result of the deadening effect of such a night march. At every halt they slumped to the ground. Again and again there was shrapnel fire and more fires broke out. The four kilometres from Westrozebeke to Poelkapelle took a total of five hours! When the students from Bonn finally arrived about midnight to chaotic scenes of activity, they observed wryly, 'Everything seems to be under control here!' It was impossible to move forward at all along the main street, where column upon column was wedged against one another. There was no movement forwards or backwards. The entire division, with all its baggage and equipment, was jammed into this one street in Poelkapelle and all the battalion commanders fumed at the thought that, at any minute, shrapnel fire might be bursting overhead.

"However, there was no artillery fire, but some individuals fired into the houses where French or British stragglers might have hidden in the cellars. Whispers about 'spies' spread rapidly, but otherwise things remained calm and, eventually, order was restored amongst the chaos. Officers from the higher staffs intervened and the leading column was ordered peremptorily to turn off into a side road. A second followed and, gradually, the infantry obtained some space. All the houses were occupied – naturally! A combination of hanging around and confusion left no other course feasible, but any hopes the regiment had of remaining in Poelkapelle disappeared, regrettably, when an order arrived directing it simply to advance on Langemark and find billets there . . . '

Clearing the village and moving off into open country, at long last, towards 4.00 am company commanders were able to order, 'Lie down and sleep. Unteroffiziers are to take it in turns to be awake.' An anonymous member of Reserve Infantry Regiment 234, having described a preliminary operation designed to clear up the start line, continued:[4] **2.**

"Stand by to assault Langemark! . . . By about 6.00 am we were occupying a field to the right of the railway line leading to Langemark. Still enfolded by the night, we sat on our knapsacks and propped our heads in our hands. Our whole beings were consumed by utter weariness. Klaus lay stretched out on the grass snoring. Nobody gave a thought to the day ahead . . . What lay ahead was as dark as the night itself. But there were odd feelings inside . . . what was it? Hunger? Thirst? Neither of those. Desire for sleep? Possibly! No, there was a feeling of anxiety – really sharp anxiety that bit and gnawed away at us . . . "

Vizefeldwebel Frischauf Reserve Infantry Regiment 236 [5] **3.**

"With the grey of dawn there was a constant coming and going. The roads were full of troops. Some were collecting their equipment from the wagons, others were washing at the pumps. The field kitchens drove forward to issue food then, as the companies completed their final preparations, the administrative vehicles left Poelkapelle and galloped back towards Westrozebeke. Despite the fog, the enemy found out what was happening, some shrapnel shells began to explode over the houses and roads and a few men were wounded. Commands could be heard everywhere, but nobody really knew what was happening. One thing, however, was quite clear. The enemy with whom we had not closed up the previous day were close by. Some realised that it was going to be a hard day, but this just raised spirits.

"Doubling forward through gardens with some difficulty, the platoons and companies left the built up area and began to deploy into skirmishing lines. There was an immediate increase in the rifle and machine gun fire of an invisible enemy, who could not be engaged effectively by us. The firing of our batteries, which had closed up at high speed and had gone into position behind our lines, added to the noise of battle. Soon wounded, with pale faces and bright dressings, were returning in ever-increasing numbers. Some of them were being carried on rifles or slung in groundsheets, whilst other propped themselves against houses as their wounds were dressed. At long last my outpost, reinforced by the platoon which had been held back in the trenches they had manned the previous night as regimental reserve, was sent into battle.

"To the left of our regiment, elements of Reserve Infantry Regiment 235 attempted in vain to gain ground along the line of the track to Langemark which branched off the Poekapelle – Kerselaar road. It was necessary here to advance without any sort of cover to where the enemy had prepared a swift, bloody terminus. The *Feldgrauen* lay piled in heaps along the road and in the ditches but, under the watchful eye of their commander, Oberst von Gilsa, they made repeated attempts to force a way forward. However, these courageous men were thrown back repeatedly until they were brought to a halt with heavy losses. At that I was ordered by Oberst von Gilsa to gather my platoon together on the left flank, then to thrust forward along the line of the Haenixbeek in order to relieve the pressure on the 235th.

"We were able to make our way unseen through a line of gardens, to push through hedges and to cross a rising green meadow without coming under particularly heavy fire. Then, when we crossed the crest and tried to jump down into the streambed, we were spotted by the enemy. Salvo after salvo was fired at us and shells almost parted our hair. As though blown apart, we lay there widely scattered. All around there was moaning and groaning; a shell had landed in amongst us as we leapt and now the men became panicky. 'Back!' came a shout, 'Back, behind the hedge!' I could not halt the withdrawal. The overpressure of the exploding shell had hurled me into the stream bed. One of my arms and a leg were stuck in the mud and I had to be pulled out by two of my men. Wounded as I was, I could not move myself. A shell splinter which had hit my stomach had paralysed my right leg. Some of my men carried me back into cover and bandaged me up then I was carried through heavy shell fire through Poelkapelle on a stretcher.

"I saw no more of my platoon. I was delivered, semi-conscious, to the regimental aid post, which was located on the exit towards Spriet; and there the injections of our battalion medical officer, Dr Mirbel, delivered me into a marvellous dreamland."

Brought silently to full alert at 3.00 am, Reserve Infantry Regiment 233, which began the day, together with two batteries of Reserve Field Artillery Regiment 51, in Corps reserve, remarked later that they could have used a little more sleep and something warm inside them. According to their regimental history they had not had a hot meal for three days; they still had not been issued with field kitchens and were reduced to living on scraps of supplies abandoned by the Belgians during their withdrawal.[6] If proof were still needed of the utterly inadequate preparation of these new regiments, it would be necessary to look no further. Dawn broke misty and drizzly, the consequent poor visibility easing the deployment into the forming up places behind the start lines. When the waves of infantry rose ready to move forward from Poelkapelle at about 10.00am, the sun was beginning to break through the early morning fog.

Langemark itself was completely shrouded in the smoke and dirt of a punishing period of preparatory fire by the heavy guns, whilst overhead roared a constant stream of shells on their way to the target. Under their protection the massed infantry bore down on Langemark but, within ten to fifteen minutes of the start of the attack, the German troops came under very heavy, well-directed small arms fire from the houses on the eastern edge of Langemark and elsewhere. The intention of the British 1st Division to launch an attack eastward out of Langemark that same morning seems not to have registered with the German chain of command, nor that many of the early engagements that morning were the work of 1st Battalion South Wales Borderers and 1st Battalion Queen's Regiment advancing on Poelkapelle Station, with 1st Battalion Gloucestershire Regiment in support; not that the precise nature of British deployments made any difference to the outcome. German casualties began to mount rapidly and the advance ground to a halt. Orientation was immensely difficult. Although the terrain was flat, in all directions views were obscured by fences, hedges and stands of trees. Movement was further affected by the constant presence of ditches, swampy meadows and great fields of beet and swede. Farmhouses and other buildings were scattered in such numbers amidst the landscape that it was difficult, especially because mapping was in such short supply, to say where a village began and ended.

After a short pause to assess the situation, junior commanders on the ground ordered that the attack be pressed home, but broken down into section and platoon level actions. All along the attack frontage the infantry could be seen attempting to work their way forward in small groups. All across the full sweep of the meadows appalling sights multiplied as the defenders took an increasing toll of their numbers. Increasingly, small groups of infantrymen began to act independently, digging in as a protection from the weight of fire in some cases but, according to one report, facing entirely the wrong direction.[7] One participant from Reserve Infantry Regiment 235, identified only as 'Unteroffizier B', later wrote in his diary:

> "Who today and during the days that followed had any idea about what was happening and what either we or the enemy intended? Our company commander was as much in the dark as I, or even the dumbest recruit. In fact the last named would have been best placed by far. He knew absolutely nothing and, therefore, could not even get hold of the wrong end of the stick. Quite suddenly bursts of shrapnel spread death and destruction on our positions. There was no holding on any more. There was no order. I have no clue where our platoon commander was, nor did I know if those of us who could still move should launch ourselves further forward, or if it would be better to head to the right and cross the road to see if that offered protection. Men were falling all around me; we were in a witches' cauldron of artillery fire. There was nobody in charge, none who could have stated whether or not we were to hold on at all costs.
>
> "My own thoughts were not to pull back but to go forward and to the right, so that we should leave the artillery fire behind. There were no formed sections or platoons any more, nor was there any sort of unified advance. What I saw and experienced that day and later was amongst the sort of image that the wildest imagination can dream up. What was left of our division, of the four regiments which we had deployed? One thing was sure. In every piece of meadow, behind every hedge, were bands of men, some large, some small; but what were they doing? What could they do? Visibility over the ground was strictly limited by all the hedges. Some claimed to be under fire from the right flank; others from the left. The battle situation was totally unclear. The only leaders left were unteroffiziers; and we knew little more than the men." [8]

Whole sections were seen to fall as accurate shrapnel concentrations burst overhead. Junior officers and NCOs were knocked out of the battle one by one, leaving leaderless groups of infantrymen unsure what to do next. Gradually, farm buildings and other shelters filled up as stragglers gathered and awaited direction and orders. More and more reserves were committed but, as each unit and sub unit closed up towards Langemark, they simply shared the fate of those who had gone before. With great bravery field artillery batteries galloped up close behind the front line positions and engaged machine gun posts and enemy pockets of resistance inside the houses and farm buildings. In places the blue uniformed French territorial soldiers, whose junction point with the British was hard up against Langemark, could be seen pulling back out of the line of advanced battle posts. Some were seen to fall; others simply scattered to avoid the German fire.

More and more reserves pressed forward from Poelkapelle. This display of determination, however, meant that forward units began to become increasingly mixed up, thus compounding an already serious command and control situation. It would be wrong to think that the French were not putting up a good fight. They were well equipped with machine guns and they brought down heavy fire every time that the attacking sections attempted to move. It was not long before the Allied artillery joined in the battle with increased intensity. Although ammunition was already in short supply, this was a clear emergency and soon rounds began to land with unpleasant accuracy amongst the German troops, who were completely exposed in the open and especially vulnerable to that destructive weapon, the shrapnel shell.

Around midday the Corps reserve, Reserve Infantry Regiment 233, was committed, but it was case of throwing even more men forward in a hopeless cause and succeeded only in increasing the already dreadful casualty rate.

Kriegsfreiwillige Kleysteuber 9th Company Reserve Infantry Regiment 233 [9] **4.**

"We advanced on the enemy at about midday. Together with Julius Schleiden from my home town, a few other comrades and Offizier-stellvertreter Grothe, we moved as a covering party about fifty metres in front of the company. We made our way forward by pushing through gardens and hedges. It was flat countryside, [comprising] fields, meadows and numerous gardens, all surrounded by hedges and fences, which made it extremely difficult to advance. Suddenly, we came under fire and bullets whistled all around us. There was, however, absolutely no sign of the enemy. An enemy machine gun joined in and then the fun really began!

"We threw ourselves down and crawled into a ditch and stayed there for a full half hour, whilst the machine gun systematically raked the entire area. Exercising the greatest care, we managed to get to a farmstead, looked for cover behind a ditch and dug in to some extent. We then had a chance to look behind us at our own men and were able to see what havoc the machine gun had wrought. Our dead were lying there in rows and we were not in a secure position either! An aircraft flew over and betrayed our position. Artillery fire began to come down and shrapnel shell after shrapnel shell burst above us – a fuze landed a mere three metres to my left.

"Schleiden and I sought cover behind a willow tree, which was hit repeatedly and splinters of wood splashed into our faces. We felt ourselves all over, but it was nothing. There we stayed for some considerable time under a dense rain of shrapnel balls. In order to get clear of it we moved right, but only succeeded in moving out of the frying pan into the fire. It was even worse there. One man came up to me with a bleeding hand and another was lying behind me. Hit in the leg by a shrapnel ball he was unable to walk and had to pull himself forward with his hands. Sauer arrived, hit in three places. We tried once more to launch an assault, but we were simply beaten back."

This scenario was being played out all over the battlefield and it was not long before the pressure on the attackers began to tell and soon some, leaderless, or simply occupying hopelessly exposed positions, began to fall back. As always, this movement to the rear became infectious. There was a risk of panic as whole companies began to waver but, as was so often the case, the example of junior leaders – platoon and company commanders – managed in most cases to hold the attack together and once again there was certain amount of progress. There was a cost, naturally. Charging forward at the front of his leading troops, Hauptmann Schröter, the courageous commander of 5th Company Reserve Infantry Regiment 235, collapsed, riddled with bullets and died a few moments later.[10] There were attempts made to get out of the main concentrations of artillery fire by dispersing left and right, but with only modest success.

Taking up the main weight of the attack, 2nd and 3rd Battalions Reserve Infantry Regiment 236 pushed on past the northern flank of Reserve Infantry Regiment 235, but they too suffered such heavy casualties that their commander had to deploy the last of reserves forward before 11.00 am – and there was still several hours of daylight to go. It was largely in vain. Within an hour hardly a single officer was still on his feet and, once again, the resolve of the attacking troops seemed to be weakening. In an attempt to bolster the assault, the divisional commander committed 1st Battalion Reserve Infantry Regiment 233 to the advance. It had hardly come within range than it was suffering casualties at the hands of skilled infantrymen in strong defensive positions behind the hedges and in amongst the houses. The fighting continued with undiminished intensity. Survivors amongst the attackers later stated that they had never experienced a hail of fire such as that directed from the buildings on the eastern edge of the village, whilst their gunners admitted that they could not obtain observation over the Allied gun positions to the east of Langemark, making their counter-battery task almost impossible. Allied gunners, on the other hand, only had to direct their shells into one or other of the killing areas to be almost certain of hitting some target.

The day dragged on as the Commander of 51st Infantry Division tried everything possible to inject life into the assault. Orders calling for fresh attacks were despatched forward but, such was the confusion and so serious the fire, some of these never reached the front and, of those which did, the most gallant possible efforts to obey them withered away as the lifeblood drained away from the German regiments before Langemark. In the early afternoon, the thing most feared by the local commanders occurred. One of the regiments – Reserve Infantry Regiment 235 – broke, having suffered immense casualties. All its officers had fallen, killed or wounded; others who tried to step into the breach were also cut down. The bodies of the dead and dying were strewn all over the battlefield as first small groups, then entire lines of infantry, turned and ran. Pursued by enemy artillery fire, the withdrawal was little short of a panic.

'Unteroffizier B' of Reserve Infantry Regiment 235 described later in a scathing manner how the situation developed where he was engaged.

> "On one occasion we had a stroke of luck due to the artillery fire. A shell landed and exploded very close to a group of twelve to fourteen men, forcing them to their feet when otherwise they would have stayed down in cover. I forced them forward and brought them to a place where almost half a platoon was located. Almost simultaneously I could see a detachment advancing some 200 metres to our right. 'On your feet lads! Forwards! We must make contact with them.' Unfortunately I had not taken the most important matter into consideration. There was a Feldwebelleutnant present, whom I had not noticed and who had a totally different opinion to mine. What could I do when he told me roughly that it was senseless to attempt to advance and that we ought to lie quietly where we were. Naturally I fell in with this, especially because the men, having suffered heavy casualties, were much more willing to stay in cover than advance.

> "Some time later it – allegedly – became impossible for us to hold on where we were and on the word of command, 'About turn!' an unstoppable move to the rear began. We moved back until, just before the village, [Poelkapelle] we bumped into the Oberst of Regiment X [Oberst Wilhelmi, Reserve Infantry Regiment 236]. He stopped us in our tracks, turned us about and drove us forwards once more. Had we been gathered together, reorganised, given a clear mission and placed under suitable leadership, things would probably have turned out better. For hours I had not seen a single familiar soul. Soon we set off forwards, then deviated to the right and soon we turned back. There was no sign that men were willing to stand up like German soldiers on campaign, willing to defend what was right and to act as the terror of the enemy. Rather the feeling was that we had been senselessly sacrificed and were being treated like cannon fodder in the most contemptuous meaning of the word."[11]

51st Infantry Division appealed to XXVI Reserve Corps for support and received the very last reserves: one battalion of infantry and one field artillery battery. Staff officers from Divisional Headquarters rushed forward in an attempt to rally the men who were falling back. In this they were moderately successful but, although they succeeded in getting them to advance once more, there was no possibility of reaching as far forward as the previous high water mark of the advance. At this point Oberleutnant Schröder of 7th Company Reserve Infantry Regiment 235 was finally shot down and the 8th Company was reduced to a shattered remnant.[12] As the handful of survivors pulled back, they came across the body of their regimental commander, Oberst von Gilsa, lying dead in a sugar beet field. As Major Bredt moved to take command of the remains of the regiment, the body of von Gilsa was moved to the rear and buried in the monastery garden in Poelkapelle.

All these setbacks were observed with some alarm by the regimental staff of the adjacent Reserve Infantry Regiment 236, whose commander, Oberst Wilhelmi, intervened personally to stem the tide of men flooding to the rear, but this gesture led to him, too, being wounded. Gradually Poelkapelle filled up with stragglers and shirkers who milled around aimlessly until a few officers and NCOs took a firm grip of the situation and led them to occupy positions in the old trenches on the western side of the village. In a day of considerable confusion, 1st Battalion Reserve Infantry Regiment 236 was ordered into divisional reserve and directed to march back to an assembly area near Westrozebeke, but it was not long before it was required to move forward once more, there to be inserted into a gap which had developed between Reserve Infantry Regiments 235 and 236 just in front of Langemark. Moving right up to the edge of the village and suffering many casualties, the men began to dig in, despite the hail of fire to which they were being subjected. Their commander, Hauptmann Schöler, was killed[13] and their ranks drastically thinned by the enemy fire, but some did manage to dig in and hold on in their thoroughly exposed positions.

Kriegsfreiwilliger Willi Kahl 7th Company Reserve Infantry Regiment 236 [14] **4.**

"We had imagined that our baptism of fire would be somewhat different. There can be nothing more depressing that the very public failure of an attack launched as though on exercise against an invisible enemy. Unthinking, section after section ran into the well-directed fire of experienced troops. Every effort had been put into our training, but it was completely inadequate preparation for such a serious assault on battle-hardened, long service colonial solders.[15] Only through consideration of the extraordinary moral tension of the morning of 21 October can there be comprehension of the moment during the afternoon when the enemy hove into view for the first time. Of necessity, due to the increasing loss of our commanders, the individual was thrown back ever more on his own resources and, to some extent, it was possible to proceed beyond the drills which had been learnt and so cope with the hidden terrain and the constant surprises the battle itself threw up.

"We had just reached a meadow on a hillside, which was surrounded by trees and hedges, when the first British caps came into view. That was a relief at long last after the tormenting disappointments of the morning. Forgotten for a moment was that little we had learned about modern battle drills, cover and exploitation of ground. In two ranks and, in some places three, keeling or standing, we poured down fire with an abandon which can only be understood by the excitement of the first great moment of this day of assaults. After hours of demoralising hopelessness, here was a task which was visible and achievable.

"After two rounds fired standing unsupported, as if on the range, the inevitable happened. Just as I was taking the first pressure on the trigger, I was hit in the left buttock and I immediately felt the effects of the last strenuous days of marching – days for which we had not in the slightest been prepared – and the loss of blood from the wound weakened me far more than should have been the case. Everywhere there was confusion. Men were flooding back from the front, it was impossible to miss what was happening. [Was it] withdrawal? [Had there been an] enemy counter-attack? Would we be able to advance once more; would we wounded not have to be cared for? Yet again we were back to the total hopelessness and paucity of thought which had marked our attacks from the very beginning. The gruesome reality was that I was no longer buoyed up by the elation of being close up to the enemy, but was inwardly extremely agitated by my first experience of being wounded, and externally by the total confusion of the events which surrounded me and which seemed to make no sense. How, in the circumstances, could an inexperienced kriegsfreiwilliger make clear decisions?

"As night fell we lay there, dead and wounded alike; left to our fate on this small meadow. Towards morning three unwounded men, who had remained with us, set off to clarify the situation and to fetch medical orderlies, but none returned. At daybreak general uncertainty prevailed. We were unsure where our troops were located and did not even know if the ground behind us belonged to our side or not. One thing was quite clear. Any movement by us could be seen by the enemy and there was constant firing all around us. There was only one solution, namely to lie immobile, covered by a blanket. During the afternoon of 22 October, Gefreiter Bauer of 7th Company, who must have been lying unconscious lower down, got through to us, bringing some food from the knapsacks of the fallen. The danger increased; a shell crashed down in our immediate vicinity. Bauer headed off to fetch medical orderlies, but he too failed to return. That evening we were aware of heavy fighting around us. Unprotected against increasing artillery and small arms fire, huddled in our coats, we heard from somewhere [our side] blowing the signal to attack . . .

"Several of the wounded in this threatened spot did not survive the day. During 23 October some other comrades arrived and gave us water before going to fetch medical assistance but did not return. Now began the worst night of all. The condition of the most seriously wounded was unbearable. More and more we felt ourselves encircled by the opposing firing. Very close by we could hear the distinctive sharp crack of British rifle fire, interrupted by the chatter of machine gun fire. The artillery fire had such a deadening effect on our over-stretched nerves that we fell asleep apathetically, despite the constant threat of danger. Finally, during the morning of 24 October, a German soldier appeared, having discovered us while on patrol. We now found out that our lines were 150 metres to the rear. Gradually we few survivors were evacuated, Kriegsfreiwilliger Gossmann, a friend from my company, amongst them. We were completely stiff from having had to lie motionless day and night on the damp autumn ground. During the successful advance in April 1915 we had a shattering reunion with the fallen, whom the enemy had left unburied throughout the winter months."

This determination not to yield any of the ground which had been so painfully gained saw reasonably strong elements of Reserve Infantry Regiment 236 and isolated sections of Reserve Infantry Regiment 235, including some from the 7th Company, whose leaders had all fallen, clinging on in rough trenches in and around the first houses of Langemark village. Cut off from their reserves and all forms of supply, their situation was precarious in the extreme. There could be no question of a further coordinated assault on the village that day, though the remnants of 7th Company did attempt to capture the land around the gas works. This failed with further losses, though a few British soldiers were captured in nearby houses. An objective assessment of their position by the surviving commanders, after it went dark on the evening of the first day, led to the only feasible decision being taken; namely to take all the wounded and prisoners with them and to fall back on Poelkapelle. Picking their way over fields strewn with dead and dying soldiers, they made their painful way back. Their withdrawal had not been observed by the British defenders, so the only interference with the movement was the occasional artillery concentration fired as part of a general programme of harassing fire.

Vizefeldwebel Sellke 6th Company Reserve Infantry Regiment 236 [16] *5.*

"We succeeded, finally, in reaching the houses on the outskirts of Langemark. The village exuded a magical, irresistible, attraction on us. There is no other way I can explain how our little band managed to fight its way forward, despite everything that had occurred; and that was also true of other groups, which had coalesced out of the different regiments and with whom we linked up later in the village. In this way we met up with Offizierstellvertreter Schwenk, Gefreiters Franz Baumann and Schmelzer, Wehrmann Engels and Reservist Vieren of 11th Company Reserve Infantry Regiment 236, together with a number from the 235th. Perhaps it was all down to the drive to get forward which is drummed into German soldiers. I also presume that Langemark had already been entered from the southeast or northwest, because the fire had reduced markedly in intensity.

"I had only noted something of our own artillery fire during the morning, however several different houses were burning brightly and these could only have been set on fire by our artillery. Once we had crawled through a hedge and crossed a garden, we found ourselves amongst the houses lining the road which joined that running from Poelkapelle to Langemark. Here we had to throw ourselves as rapidly as possible into the ditch by the road, because a loud crash next to us sent dirt and twigs flying into our faces. Here our forward thrust nearly came to an ignominious end because, as we later discovered, there were numerous British soldiers in the first house located not thirty metres from the road. The hedge and the fact that there were no windows or skylights on the side whence we had approached meant that we had not been spotted until we reached the road.

"Because all the houses on that side were on fire and nobody could approach from that direction, there was no danger from the right. For some time we could not move in the ditch without causing dirt to be thrown up round our ears by rounds striking the ground. I had a really unpleasant feeling about this place. When everything quietened down a little, we raced for the shelter of a house. We had still not realised how close the British were because, in a burning village with roofs collapsing, curtains of fire rattling around, breaking beams and cartridges cooking off in the fires, it was difficult to establish where fire was coming from. We had hardly set off than more shots arrived. A very young kriegsfreiwilliger immediately to my right fell backwards onto the road without making a sound and was dead within seconds.

"These were the last shots the British fired at us from that particular house. A few moments later a section of German soldiers came to our aid and together we assaulted the houses from the rear. Some of the British were killed, some were captured and a few succeeded in running away. Because they were soon shielded by the hedges, we only managed to shoot one of them. In this way it was possible for our 'liberators' to get into the relevant house without casualties and without even coming under fire. We were lucky. Capture or death would have been our lot otherwise. Most of the newcomers were from Reserve Infantry Regiment 235. They were being led by Offizierstellvertreter Baehren of our 4th Company. In addition, from our regiment, was Sergeant Sinning, whose courage and unshakeable calmness made a deep impression on me and also Kriegsfreiwilliger Stöcker from 1st Company.

"Forming a group of thirty to forty men, we managed to clear through a few isolated houses, but the approach of darkness precluded any further advance. Instead we began to dig in along a hedge running between the gasworks and the road, because we did not want to relinquish that which we had taken and we hoped to receive reinforcements. We had sufficient light to dig by. To our left the gasometer was on fire and to the right all the houses were ablaze. Because ammunition left behind by the British in the houses kept cooking off, we thought all the time that we were under small arms fire.

"I had an unusual experience whilst we were digging. The man next to me, who was in a trench about knee deep, pushed his rifle experimentally through the hedge to our front when, suddenly, there was a sharp report and it was torn out of his hand. The butt was hurled just past my face and the rifleman leapt up with a yell. A ricochet had smashed through the neck of the butt but, by some miracle, had caused no other damage. The face of the owner of the rifle had a face full of wooden splinters and we had both received the shock of our lives.

"Because we had waited in vain for support, we marched off about midnight. Who ordered the withdrawal I have now no idea. The captured British soldiers had to carry the wounded back. Once we had been marching for some time we met up with our people, who were in the process of digging a position. Naturally, our appearance caused some astonishment because nobody had thought that German soldiers could have held on into the night in Langemark."

Throughout the Corps area all the survivors of this catastrophic day also attempted to withdraw under the cover of darkness, including men of Reserve Infantry Regiment 233, who had been amongst the last to be committed, but who had also suffered badly late in the day.

Leutnant Brendler Reserve Infantry Regiment 233 [17] **6.**

"Darkness fell! – the battle stalled! We could sense that the enemy had beaten off our powerful thrust. The enemy was still harassing the area with shrapnel and firing at the great straw stacks until they caught fire and lit up the battlefield. By the light of these fires we could make out a few figures as they moved around, whilst the enemy, doubtless sheltering in well concealed trenches, immediately brought down fire on them. The [figures] moved towards us; they were men of the 233rd. We went forward and linked up with a further twenty men. Far to our right and left there was no sign of any Germans. In the meantime the night had become inky black.

"Seeking to make contact, we suddenly came under murderously heavy fire which cracked around our ears. There was no need for words of command. Everyone threw himself to the ground and tried to worm his way deep into it. Those who had no spades dug with their helmets or bayonets. None of us had any idea where we were; there were no maps and, even if we had had, we could not have read them in this darkness and the use of light would have been ill advised! (From information I obtained later, I think that we must have bumped into an enemy reverse slope position near Kerselaar.) Behind us field barns and stacks of straw were ablaze and we had been silhouetted against this bright light, so the enemy had been presented with good targets.

"Until this light in our rear faded there could be no thought of changing our situation and we dug out a kidney-shaped defensive position. Out to the right, men scouting around also appeared to have bumped into the enemy. Perhaps it was another little group of ours who thought that they had come under attack? Ever since we moved into the assault we had received orders from neither regiment nor battalion, so it was a matter of acting independently. I then led this detachment, about fifty to sixty men strong and composed of men from all the battalions, back to Poelkapelle. This decision was the correct one, as it transpired the following day.

"We assumed that Poelkapelle was located where the dark night sky was lit up by two burning farmhouses, so on and on we went, feeling our way through the dark night. Now and then came the chatter of small arms fire, which would die abruptly like a light being extinguished, then the night was silent once more. After an hour we reached an outpost. 'Halt! Who goes there?' – accompanied by the sound of rifle bolts being worked. 'Germans, Germans!' we shouted back. In rear of the outpost the outline of a farm building could be made out through the darkness. There was artillery everywhere here. For us, exhausted as we were, there was a great stack of straw to shelter in. Because I wanted to remain here until dawn, my men were quick to crawl in and cover themselves in sheaves.

"First of all I sought out an artillery officer in order to find out where we were – some kilometres west of Passchendaele. This meant that we had drifted to the left during the battle. Now it was time for me to find a place to sleep. On the windward side there was a free hole and there I came across my company commander, Leutnant Stegner. It was joyful reunion after such a hard day! Although dog tired we could not sleep. It was cold and the stars glittered in a clear night sky – and the events of the day would not permit us any rest. Not only that, there were constant crashes out to our front. Then the howling of the French shells filled our ears and drowned out the stillness of the night.

"Before dawn I went and begged some coffee for my men from the gunners. That revived us then we set off in a northerly direction to where Poelkapelle ought to be and where we hoped to find our regiment. Not far from the farmstead we met up with a detachment from Reserve Infantry Regiment 239. Under the command of an officer, they were also looking for their regiment and we continued the march together. Suddenly rounds cracked overhead and, by their rushing sound, we knew that they were meant for us. Quick, take cover! Luckily the beginners over there had shot too high. Packed together as we were, their machine gun could have really done some damage; but, over there, was a village in the midst of green fields. It had to be Poelkapelle!"

Not all groups of survivors were fortunate enough to have an officer or NCO to provide leadership and guidance. The day had been an exhausting, emotionally draining and shattering experience for the majority of those engaged. Not only was there no question of a successful advance to outflank Ypres, the actual German line itself was in an extremely precarious position. Orders had been given by Headquarters 51st Reserve Division to the remnants of the regiments to go into hasty defence and to hold Poelkapelle come what may. However, such was the confusion that the situation on the ground was often quite different from that anticipated by those issuing the orders. The Orderly Officer of Reserve Field Artillery Regiment 51 was walking just north of the village through the pitch black night, when he came across what can only be described as a gaggle of infantryman, standing around swapping tales of disaster, but actually doing nothing in an agony of indecision. According to the historian of Reserve Field Artillery Regiment 51 the conversation then went like this: **7.**

"What are you doing here?'

'Herr Leutnant, we are supposed to dig in, but we do not know what that means.'

'Who is the senior man here?' – no reply.

'Is there no unteroffizier? No gefreiter?' – no reply.

'Which is the senior of you musketiers?' After a long debate this was finally established.

'Right, you take command and the others are to obey you. You are to take up your spades and dig a trench wide enough for you to lie down in. Those of you without spades are to go over to that stack and collect a few armfuls of straw, so that you can lie down dry and comfortable. One of you is to go over to the section on your right and explain the situation. Then, within one hour, with the exception of a sentry, you are all to lie down and sleep. Understood?' The group came at once to life, the mood lightened and one man came up and said, 'Herr Leutnant, if only somebody had told us that in the first place! We just had no idea what we should do. However, now we do know exactly what to do!"[18]

This incident provides a perfect example of the utter inadequacy of the preparation of these formations and units. There had been insufficient time to provide the troops with anything more than the basics of their role and, as a result, the moment that the leaders became casualties (probably as a result of having to expose themselves to risk even more than usual, so as to provide an example of courage in the face of the enemy) minor tactics and battlefield discipline fell apart. Small wonder that there was near-panic that day before Langemark; and this poor morale manifested itself in other ways too. Poelkapelle itself was full of wounded men – but also contained many shirkers, skulking in the various buildings and cellars where there was ready access to large quantities of red wine, which slipped easily down parched throats, but had a swift effect on the empty stomachs of the drinkers, compounding the problem. It was also noted later[19] that many of the medical personnel were more than ready to succumb to temptation.

Meanwhile sporadic firing punctuated the night, leading at one point to yet another totally false rumour that the enemy had broken through to the north, and were threatening to encircle the village. All available personnel gathered in battle order on the streets and the teams of horses were harnessed to the wagons, but order was eventually restored once more. It was all the result of overstretched nerves, exhaustion and inexperience; something which only time in the field and rest could begin to overcome. Inexperience was, however, not confined to regimental level and below. Late on 21 October Headquarters XXVI Reserve Corps issued an order, whose wording suggested either that the higher levels of command were completely detached from reality or, naively, had put an extraordinarily optimistic gloss on reports reaching it via the chain of command.

"Southern Exit, Westrozebeke, 21 October 1914

1. I am delighted that today the Corps, during its first serious battle, has beaten off and driven back the enemy all along the line.

2. Tonight the Corps is digging in in the captured positions, reorganising, and replenishing with food and ammunition. Strong forces, also dug in, are echeloned back on the flanks and are preparing to resume the offensive in the

morning. Throughout the night there is to be constant patrolling against the enemy, timely reporting if they withdraw, including information concerning the direction in which they are pulling back. Should the enemy still be in position along the front in the morning, the attack is not to be launched until a special order has been issued.

During the attack artillery reserves are to be held back until the decisive moment, but individual guns or sections can be used in enfilade against enemy lines of infantry.

3. 51st Reserve Division is to withdraw a large reserve during the night and is to devote itself to deciding when and where its deployment is likely to promise final success.

4. 52nd Reserve Division is largely deployed outside the boundaries of the Corps. The division is to leave only weak forces dug in against the enemy in the Broodseinde sector and the main force is to move in to the area bounded by Mosselmarkt – Kerselaar and Moorslede – Brielen.

5. From day break the heavy artillery is to be ready to fire in its current positions.

6. Headquarters will be located at the southern exit of Westrozebeke from 7.00 am tomorrow.[20]

The men of XXVI Reserve Corps, had they even heard about this order – which given the chaos which reigned is highly improbable – might have been forgiven for wondering how it was, if paragraphs 1 and 2 were even partially correct, that the battlefield was covered with men who were exhausted, disorientated, confused and hungry? Why if the enemy were in retreat, were they still bringing down fire whenever contact was made or suspected? Elsewhere commanders and staffs might also have wondered how on earth substance was to be given to directions to side-step large elements of 52nd Reserve Division in the dark and how, even if this extraordinarily difficult manoeuvre were to be attempted, orders were to be disseminated, moves coordinated and the resulting gap adequately filled. The very existence of such an order simply underlines how far from top to bottom these new formations were from being genuinely able to take their places in the order of battle.

Over on the northern flank of 51st Reserve Division, Reserve Infantry Regiment 234, reinforced by Reserve Jäger Battalion 23, had been heavily involved in the battle around Houthulst Wood. Reserve Infantry Regiment 234 headed in a rapid advance for the village of Mangelaar, south west of the wood, whilst Reserve Jäger Battalion 23 was responsible for providing flank protection along its southern side. Once it was realised that the wood was also being bypassed to the north by regiments of 46th Reserve Division, its defenders withdrew rapidly. It had, in any case, not been prepared for defence, so there was little point in trying to defend it and to risk being cut off. Nevertheless, the morning was punctuated by a series of low level actions, some of which were fought hand to hand, as 1st and 2nd Battalions Reserve Infantry Regiment 234 strained to get forward. Around midday Reserve Infantry Regiment 234 succeeded in taking the village, whilst the jägers continued to press forward a little to the north, in the face of numerous pockets of resistance dotted around their axis of advance. Despite the efforts of the defence, good progress was made during the course of hard fighting and the way was clear as far as the Kortebeek.

Wading through the waist deep water, the jägers gained a further one hundred metres on the far bank and took up positions where they could hear and see both the bitter fighting by Reserve Infantry Regiments 235 and 236 for Langemark off to the south, as well as the formations of the neighbouring corps, as they repeatedly pressed their attacks towards Bikschote. However their somewhat isolated position was vulnerable to artillery fire, which increased throughout the afternoon. Furthermore, the withdrawal of Reserve Infantry Regiment 236 and the partial crumbling away of the forward elements of Reserve Jäger Battalion 23 meant that eventually they, too, withdrew back across the Kortebeek and halted in positions about half way back towards Mangelaar and stretching in the direction of Koekuit. With the exception of some elements of the battalion, which were directed to launch an attack to relieve the hard pressed troops down by Langemark, the remainder passed a relatively quiet night, though losses had been severe. Reserve Infantry Regiment 234 had lost nearly two thirds of its strength, whilst Reserve Jäger Battalion 23 counted two officers and seventeen jägers killed, three officers and eighty eight jägers wounded, with a further twenty four missing. Amongst the fallen was the battalion commander, Major von Winterfeld.

In the early morning of 21 October, the formations of 52nd Reserve Division, organised into two great columns, also began to advance westwards. The northern column, comprising Reserve Infantry Regiments 237 and 239, moved along the line of Roeselare – Ypres railway, deeply echeloned to the right and maintaining contact with 51st Reserve Division. To the south, the aim was for Reserve Infantry Regiments 238 and 240, reinforced by Reserve Jäger Battalion 24, to advance either side of Broodseinde. Having taken that village they were intended to plunge into the wooded area south of Zonnebeke, maintaining contact with XXVII Reserve Corps, which was heavily engaged to the west of Beselare. 'The enemy is to be attacked energetically', stated the divisional operation order for that day.[21] Setting off at 6.30am, and with its 1st Battalion pushed forward as an advance guard, 2nd and 3rd Battalions Reserve Infantry Regiment 237, which were following up at about 750 metres distance, made to outflank Broodseinde to the north. Within half an hour the 1st Battalion was involved in a severe fire fight with mounting casualties. The regimental commander immediately despatched 3rd Battalion to extend the 1st Battalion line to the north, whilst 2nd Battalion moved up to reinforce the centre of the 1st Battalion line.

To its north, Reserve Infantry Regiment 239 was also pushing forward, but everywhere the fields were being swept by heavy fire, meaning that progress was painfully slow and the casualties severe. Whilst the companies were trying everything possible to exploit the geography within their boundaries, the Orders Group of 1st Battalion moved onto a rise south of the road, so as to have an overview of the complete area. There they came under immediate small arms fire. At least this showed that the enemy were occupying the Langemark – Zonnebeke road and the farm buildings in front of it.

The main tactical difficulty was the fact that the ground favoured the defence in many ways, enabling the experienced defenders to lure the raw attacking troops into killing zones where they could be picked off in large numbers. Nevertheless, despite all the problems, with the slight knowledge of the enemy positions so gained, 3rd Company Reserve Infantry Regiment 239 was despatched to work its way forward, making use of hedges, ditches and culverts until it was in a position to launch an attack on Zonnebeke. Inevitably the movement was spotted, effective fire began to be brought down from a flank and enemy artillery fire suppressed all movement. Shrapnel fire was an especially useful weapon against troops in the open and maximum use was made of it that day. The company commander of 2nd Company was hit in the chest by a rifle bullet and numerous other men had to be stretchered away, having suffered wounds from shrapnel balls.

Throughout the morning the situation was the same everywhere. Small groups worked their way forward using fire and manoeuvre and reserves closed up. Men only slightly wounded tried to make their way to the rear, picking their way through huge numbers of dead and dying who were littered all over the sector. During the early afternoon, all this pressure began to pay off and some enemy troops could be seen making their way back in the direction of St Juliaan. Exploiting this potentially brief opportunity, the men of Reserve Infantry Regiment 237 thrust forward. Unfortunately the remaining regiments were in some disarray at that time and the right flank of Reserve Infantry Regiment 239 became involved in the hasty withdrawal of Reserve Infantry Regiment 235. Despite the coolness under fire of Oberstleutnant Bronisch, commanding officer 1st Battalion Reserve Infantry Regiment 239 (who walked calmly around on the Broodseinde crossroads, although he was blown off his feet by a shell and had his coat torn by shell splinters), order could not be restored before the various sub units were back halfway to Poelkapelle, having been pursued all the way by artillery fire. The right flank of Reserve Infantry Regiment 237 was hanging in the air and the troops which had attempted to dig in hastily were subject to such an enormous weight of fire that casualties began to mount alarmingly. Within two hours the position had become untenable and the regiment had to pull back eight hundred metres and dig in once more.

A further attempt was made to advance later that afternoon at about 4.00 pm but, from a start line on the s'Graventafel ridge, only a few hundred metres' progress was made before an increasing weight of small arms and artillery fire brought it to a halt and forced the attackers to dig in where they were. Meanwhile a major battle was still raging around Broodseinde, where Reserve Infantry Regiments 238 and 240 of 52nd Reserve Division were engaged. Reserve Infantry Regiment 238 closed up to the eastern side of the village and waited for the advance to the north of the reinforced Reserve Infantry Regiment 240. Its commander, Oberst von Wartenberg, gave the order for the attack at 11.00 am and, with 1st Battalion Reserve Infantry Regiment 240 left, 2nd Battalion right and the battalions of Reserve Infantry Regiment 238 deeply echeloned on the left flank, to begin with good progress was made. The enemy had apparently been expecting the main effort to come directly against the village and so opened very heavy fire on the hasty trenches being occupied by Reserve Infantry Regiment 238. There were numerous direct hits and losses were severe, but the regiment was forced to hold on and endure the fire until, about 3.30 pm, orders arrived for 1st Battalion Reserve Infantry Regiment 240 to assault the village frontally. Despite the obvious danger, the order came almost as a relief to the hard pressed men. Within minutes the leading sections were clashing with British troops holding out in the first of the buildings.

Unfortunately for the attackers, their artillery support left much to be desired and, as a result, just to the north of the built up area, the enemy held out obstinately against Reserve Infantry Regiment 240. However, repeated attacks by Reserve Infantry Regiment 238 soon led to the waving of white flags and the surrender of numerous surviving infantrymen. Some of the less experienced troops had wanted to rush forward at the sight of the white flags, but those who had been fighting since the beginning of the war insisted on caution in case of trickery. In the event this did not happen; instead, first one at a time, but eventually in more or less complete sections, more than one hundred British troops had surrendered and made their way over to the German lines. This was almost the final act of the day as night fell early on this dark autumn evening. This did not mean the end of the fighting, with minor assaults and counter-attacks being launched by both sides in the darkness.

It had proved to be yet another day of painful losses for Reserve Infantry Regiment 240. The 1st Battalion, which had been particularly exposed, lost its commanding officer, Major von Blücher and Hauptmann Waldschmidt, commanding 1st Company, wounded and Oberleutnant Hieronimus of 4th Company dead.[22] In two days of fighting the commanding officer and all four company commanders had become casualties and command devolved to the adjutant, Leutnant Reunert. [23] There were also particular problems to the south of the village, where British troops appeared to have established themselves along the line of the road from Broodseinde to Keiberg. In pitch darkness Reserve Infantry Regiment 238 fought its way south to take the road. Leaving some troops to guard positions, the remainder continued, but it was almost impossible to distinguish friend from foe. Shells crashed down and small arms fire cracked in all directions. The German troops maintained the pressure against the village and forced the defenders out. Some were captured, others were killed, but large numbers managed to evade both fates, melting away into the darkness of the night.

Following up, 1st Battalion Reserve Infantry Regiment 238, ignoring the effect of a battle which had lasted over twelve hours, pressed forward to the Moorslede – Zonnebeke road and then advanced along the road towards Zonnebeke itself, capturing several farmsteads along the way. During the course of these operations, 1st Company, commanded by Leutnant Mattenklott, captured three officers and 115 other ranks. Despite the fact that the 3rd Battalion Reserve Infantry Regiment 240 had become totally scattered in the confusion, men of its 10th Company, led by Offizerstellvertreter Riedmüller, captured a further three British officers and forty eight other ranks. Shortly after that the advance was halted and security outposts were pushed forward in all directions, in order to ensure that the German troops were not surprised in their turn. In fact such was the general confusion that a heavily laden British stores column blundered into the German lines just before dawn broke. Its personnel were also captured and the stores seized. Sporadic firing continued throughout the night, but there were few casualties, because everyone had managed to find shelter in a building or some sort of trench or shell hole. Those who had food, or could acquire some, ate it. The reminder wrapped themselves in their groundsheets and attempted to get some sleep, though some, haunted by the bloody casualties of the previous day, found it elusive.

As 21 October drew to a close it should have been evident to the entire chain of command that not only had their troops failed to take their designated objectives, they had suffered serious and costly setbacks all along the front. In part this was due to the lack of battlefield experience of many of the units and formations involved, but full credit has to be given to the quality of the defence put up by the Allies and the British army in particular. Contemporary German accounts, striving to put the best possible gloss on events, resorted to statements that the day had seen a mixture of victory and setback, advance and retreat, but that the young recruits had very quickly learned to come to terms with the British defensive tactics. That is one way of putting it. The fact was that the ground had set the attackers a difficult tactical problem; one which they had no means of overcoming with their standard of training and the fire support at their disposal, quite apart from the stout resistance they encountered. The day which began with high hopes had ended in places in near rout and panic.

As night wore on, a greater sense of realism began to emerge at Headquarters XXVI Reserve Corps. It was decided swiftly that, in view of the severe losses and the shaky morale of the survivors, a simple renewal of the frontal assault on Langemark stood no chance of success on 22 October. Careful study of the map suggested that it might be possible to push forward with the left hand formations of the Corps, which had enjoyed success the previous day near Broodseinde, the aim being to drive in the British positions in the direction of St Juliaan, then swing north to roll up the Langemark position from the southeast. Whilst looking good on paper, this ignored the extreme problems being encountered by the right flank of XXVII Reserve Corps, north of Beselare and around Reutel. There was a further problem. 52nd Reserve Division on the southern flank had been dragged so far to the south during the fighting that the junction point between 52nd and 51st Reserve Divisions was extremely vulnerable to British counter-action. As a partial solution, orders were issued that the formations were to regroup and redeploy so that the left flank of the Corps rested on the northern edge of Broodseinde, with the right located near the southern edge of Poelkapelle.

Headquarters Fourth Army concurred broadly with this overall assessment, but differed inasmuch as it decided that there could be no question of Langemark remaining unattacked on 22 October. From its higher perspective, it was essential that pressure be taken off the hard pressed XXVII Reserve Corps. Furthermore, inaction would put at risk the operations of XXIII Reserve Corps, directed further north against Bikschote and the Ypres Canal. Nevertheless, the diminution in fighting strength of XXVI Reserve Corps was recognised and, although there was risk attached, 46th Reserve Division of XXIII Reserve Corps was directed to thrust almost southwards on 22 October, crossing the

Broenbeek and assaulting Langemark from the rear. For its part, XXVI Reserve Corps was ordered to renew the attack on Langemark, once it became clear that 46th Reserve Division had made progress. Fourth Army stressed the need for the utmost urgency and ordered that the 46th Reserve Division attack was to begin at 7.00 am, with a view to completing the capture of Langemark by midday. In response to this new directive, XXVI Reserve Corps released a second order, whose detailed content also left much to be desired in terms of accuracy and its reflection of the actual situation on the ground:

1. The enemy, which advanced against the Corps on 21st, has been outflanked by the corps to our left and right and, in places, has been forced back to the vicinity of the Ijzer. To our north, at 7.00 am, the neighbouring division (46th Reserve Division) will launch an attack on Langemark, with its left flank anchored on Mangelaar.

2. The Corps is to join in with the general attack. 51st Reserve Division is to assemble to the west of the line Poelkapelle Station – Poelkapelle – Stroombeek ready to attack. The evacuation of Langemark by the enemy is to be reported immediately.

3. 52nd Reserve Division is to link up with 51st Reserve Division and is to report direct to Corps Headquarters when the junction point with 51st Reserve Division is established.

4. Both divisions must be in contact with one another and be ready to advance westwards from 8.30 am.

5. The heavy artillery is to remain initially in its present locations and is to reconnoitre positions to the east of Langemark as soon as that place is free [of enemy], from where fire can be brought down by heavy field howitzers and 210mm howitzers against Steenstraat and Boezinge (destruction of the bridges there). The 100mm battery will be given the task during the further advance of taking up a position from where it can bring the road Luzerne – Boezinge under enfilade fire. [24]

Time was very short if this plan was to have any chance of success and, in any case, numerous formations and units were already conforming to earlier orders. The attendant manoeuvrings meant, for example, that 52nd Reserve Division spent the entire day on the move and was in no position to participate in any attack. Nevertheless, the attempt had to be made. In a field of sugar beet alongside the road towards Poelkapelle Station, Oberst von Gilsa, commander of Reserve Infantry Regiment 235, was in the process of giving out final orders when a shell landed in the midst of the group and the German artillery also opened up. 'Forwards!' roared Gilsa, drawing his sword. The trumpeters blew the attack call and the drummers beat out a brisk tempo. At that the companies shook out and attempted to begin the advance, but within a few minutes word was being passed to the rear. 'Oberst von Gilsa has been killed. Where is Major Bredt?'[25] Nobody had actually seen the commander fall. He had collapsed silently, sword in hand, probably the victim of a burst of shrapnel. 'Unteroffizier B', once more: 2.

"Once more we received orders to attack. My heart still beat within me, [my courage] did not fail me and I was able to summon up the strength and resolution that was urgently necessary. 'Father I call unto thee!' There is quite a difference between hearing these words, joining in their singing and to go into battle with them. He who was ready to plunge into this murderous small arms and artillery fire must have made a compact with Him and the world and be ready and prepared to leave this life. The sight out to my front and in the distance looked quite harmless. In large masses, the *Feldgrauen* moved out of their trenches and launched forward. Who could differentiate between those knocked involuntarily to the ground and those who just wanted to take a short breather, prior to continuing? The rows thinned out, becoming less regular.

"Here and there whole sections, or single individuals, could be seen dashing forward and all in the same position – half ducked down, head stretched forward. They threw themselves down into cover, sprang up and rushed forward with a speed which had often been missing during the period of training . . . Then we received our own orders. The next five to ten minutes were absolutely dreadful. There could be no such thing as fire of that density. No longer did I look backwards to the right or the left. Where were my men, my section? Killed, wounded? I simply cannot say. I did not feel the bullet which grazed me and later sent me to the rear. I could see that my hand was bleeding, but it did not incommode me in any way. Anyway there was no good lying there: forward and forward again. We covered a long bound across a bare wide meadow, which had literally been ploughed up by shells and was criss-crossed by heavy small arms fire, then I saw a trench to my front. Assessing quickly where I might find a space, I plunged, half dazed, into cover. I found myself in exactly the same spot I had been on Wednesday [21 October] and where I had lain and waited for evening.

"Before I could think straight or do anything, I had to get my breath back. What marvellous protection the knapsack, that much maligned modern instrument of torture, can offer! As mentioned, we were crammed together under the heaviest artillery fire imaginable, seeking protection in this shallow, narrow trench. Our knapsacks were thereby forced upwards and, naturally, provided protection from above. What a state the mess tins were in afterwards! There were seven holes in them, two from a rifle bullet, the remainder caused by shrapnel. How would it have played out for me, had I considered my equipment a nuisance and left it behind?

"Our digging made progress and because we had survived almost without casualties in the midst of heavy firing for a long period, morale improved visibly and I received hearty laughter in response to the old joke, 'Keep tight hold of your trousers then these cadets will only be able to shoot you through the heart!' and it was passed along the line left and right. It then occurred to me that a German battery of a specially heavy calibre had already landed four shells in the same place and that the mean point of impact was perilously close to our left flank. Angrily, I remarked to the man next to me, 'You would think that they could soon see that they are shooting too short and add 100 metres!' But then, what was that? Droning and groaning another shell arrived and landed not twenty to thirty metres from us, sending a column of dust and earth tumbling into the sky. Then there was another impact, which robbed us of sight and hearing equally dangerously close – a little to our right and just in front. Now came another from behind and we were almost covered in flying earth; this was getting serious! Every one of us lay flat on the floor of the trench, unable to speak, breathless with the shock then, suddenly, came a shout and an order was passed on: 'One man from the left flank go back and report that we are under fire from our own artillery . . . "[26]

By the evening of 22 October Reserve Infantry Regiment 237 was established south of Poelkapelle and west of Passchendaele then, to the south, came Reserve Infantry Regiment 240, Reserve Jäger Battalion 24 and half of Reserve Infantry Regiment 238 in that order. The reminder of Reserve Infantry Regiment 238 occupied Broodseinde and Reserve Infantry Regiment 239 was withdrawn into divisional reserve. Meanwhile, from shortly after 8.00 am, the German heavy artillery brought down fire on Langemark and St Juliaan. Sensing the crisis, the British replied bringing down fire throughout the morning on the Keiberg and around Poelkapelle.

Whilst this artillery battle continued, the attack of 46th Reserve Division was awaited anxiously. Patrols were despatched and ears strained for the sound of battle to the northwest, but there was no sight or sound of any attempt to force crossings over the Kortebeek [Broenbeek on the modern map], a situation which persisted throughout the day. The men of 51st Reserve Division kept their heads down and attempted to improve their positions. Some signs of activity amongst the British positions were observed during the afternoon. Then barely had the formations of 52nd Reserve Division completed their redeployment than the British launched a limited counter-attack. After an hour of intense close quarter battle this was beaten off with severe casualties to the attackers, though there were indications throughout the following night that the British were doing everything possible to wrest the initiative in this area from the German attackers.

The mystery concerning the attack of 46th Reserve Division was not cleared up until later. It had spent most of 21 October engaged in small scale actions along the northern edge of Houthulst Wood, reaching the hamlet of Nachtegaal, near the northwest tip of the wood, by nightfall and halting between there and Ashoop to the southwest, overnight. It then began the preparations for a continuation of the attack towards Bikschote the following morning, but orders arrived during the night that the axis of advance was to be turned through ninety degrees, in order to assist the hard pressed 51st Reserve Division in its battle for Langemark. The situation around Nachtegaal was relatively quiet but, down on the divisional left flank, the noise of the continuing battles around Langemark and Broodseinde could be heard clearly. This underlined the need for speed and the four regiments of the division – Reserve Infantry Regiments 213, 214, 215 and 216 – studied the problem in detail.

Quite apart from the difficulty of making so radical a change in the axis of advance, the ground posed considerable difficulties. The streams and ditches which flowed mostly in a westerly direction presented considerable problems. Crossing the Kortebeek promised to be particularly difficult, as did negotiating the railway embankment, with its obvious potential as a defensive line, to the northwest of Langemark. Despite these reservations, the assault began reasonably early on 22 October, with Reserve Infantry Regiment 213 and Reserve Jäger Battalion 18 in the lead. The aim had been to be on the line of the Kortebeek by 7.00 am, but this had proved to be impossible to achieve. Nevertheless, by that time, leading elements were pressing south towards Mangelaar, to the southwest of Houthulst Wood. This advance guard came under effective enemy fire about 1,000 metres north of Mangelaar and were forced into cover as reinforcements moved up.

By this time Reserve Infantry Regiment 215 began moving forward to the right (west) of Reserve Infantry Regiment 213, but by now the defenders were thoroughly alert to what was happening. Reserve Infantry Regiment 215 had barely left Nachtegaal when its units came under unpleasantly heavy and accurate artillery fire from the direction of Bikschote and were forced to take cover. This was unfortunate. The sub units had still not shaken out at this point and their columns provided the British gunners with dense targets. Casualties mounted rapidly. Caught in the open, there was no alternative but to press forward rapidly and to seek shelter and cover from view in one of the small stands of trees to the south. It was not until 2.00 pm that it was possible to sally out of the wood once more and to attempt to draw level with Reserve Infantry Regiment 213 and Reserve Jäger Battalion 18. The area was dotted with farm buildings, all of which seemed to be sheltering British troops, who quickly brought down heavy fire from their cover.

A rumour spread that the fire was coming from Belgian *Franctireurs*. There was no truth in this, but the anger it provoked acted as a spur to the advancing infantry, who pushed on to the Draaibank area, where they once more came under lacerating British fire from short range of troops concealed behind hedgerows and in buildings. Whilst still engaged in the ensuing heavy fire fight, orders arrived at around 3.00 pm that a passage was to be forced across the Kortebeek and that the final assault was to be launched against Langemark. In response, numerous attempts were made to carry out these orders, but all attempts were in vain. During the next few hours, as a rising tide of casualties thinned the ranks of the leading companies, reinforcements kept moving forward to fill them out once more. Repeatedly the trumpeters sounded the attack call and further attempts were made to close up to the Kortebeek.

After many fruitless efforts, some men succeeded in crossing, making use of improvised flotation aids, but the far bank was now filled with a hopeless mix of minor units and miscellaneous groupings. All command and control was lost and the area was pounded ceaselessly with shrapnel fire. Nevertheless, the attack continued to be pressed home, being countered violently by the British, who were holding out in houses, buildings and trenches throughout the sector under attack. By 4.00 pm, with bullets cracking in all directions, fighting was taking place at very close quarters. Located right amongst his leading troops, Oberst von Oertzen, commander of Reserve Infantry Regiment 215, led his men forward in a wild charge, during which many men fell killed or wounded and succeeded in gaining a foothold in the forward British trenches. There then followed a bitter struggle for every metre gained amongst the hedgerows and farm buildings near Bikschote.

As casualties amounted alarmingly, the advance reached a large field of sugar beet, where Freiwilliger Redecke of 9th Company Reserve Infantry Regiment 215 fell, killed instantly by a burst of five machine gun bullets which tore into him. In a letter home another Kriegsfreiwilliger of 9th Company wrote:[27] **8.**

> "I felt a sense of utter fatigue and exhaustion. I was barely able to pull a few beets out of the ground. I bit into them and I can still remember their earthy taste. We crawled on, the hedges and houses looming up out of the dark background. We could see the flash of the rifles and the machine guns. 'On your feet! Double march!' We made some progress, but the majority were hit. To the rear were burning buildings. I looked around and saw two men still on their feet. We threw ourselves down and pressed our faces against the cold earth. There was an eerie rustling in our ears. It was the sound of bullets cutting through the leafy tops of the beets.
>
> "I scraped a hole for my face with my bare hands then began to return fire. Beside me an old officer groaned and pressed his hand against his body, as though he could reduce the intense pain of a stomach wound by so doing. To my rear, a second assault wave was launched forward. It did not even get level with my position. All I could hear were screams and groans. A third wave threw themselves to the ground to my front. '*Achtung!* – Go!' . . . Dear God, Thy will be done . . . 'On your feet! Go!' Ten metres further on, the entire wave was mown down, a mere fifty metres from the enemy. Close to me someone was screaming out loudly, but I was such a coward that I could not bring myself to go to his aid.
>
> "An Oberjäger kneeled by him and bound him up in the midst of a torrent of fire. That shook me into action. I, too, kneeled up and offered him the contents of my water bottle – the last I had. 'On your feet! Go! Go!' As I hauled myself up something heavy knocked me back down and the leading Oberjäger, who had been so helpful, was also hit. I felt him go stiff in my arms. I do not know how long we were lying there. Off to one side, a wehrmann prayed the Lord's Prayer out loud, adding in several prayers of intercession . . . "

Charge followed charge. Casualties were extremely high amongst the junior leadership until, just as it began to go dark and the overall objective had still not been taken, Major Ryll, of Reserve Infantry Regiment 215, gathered around all the survivors of four or five different regiments and dug in on the outskirts of the village. Taking control of events, Oberst von Oertzen then caused this relative success to be extended. Pushing forward in gathering gloom along the line of the Hanebeek, the advance crossed the line of the railway embankment. Outposts were pushed even further forward during the hours of darkness. Reorganisation was extremely difficult. There was no hot food, because the field kitchens could not get forward and the contents of bread pouches had long since been eaten. The aid posts were overflowing with wounded and it was proving almost impossible to evacuate them.

Musketier Scheidhauer 8th Company Reserve Infantry Regiment 215[28] **9.**

"Never again did I experience so tough an assault as this one. Whistles blew to signal the start. A warrant officer was lying to my front. 'Herr Feldwebel, we must get going!' I pulled at his foot, but he lay there stiffly. He was dead. At the end of the next bound an Unteroffizier was lying down on the ground. I pulled at his clay covered boot. Stiff – dead. I shuddered all over. I raced diagonally across the road into the ditch on the right hand side. It seemed to me as though a woodpecker was pecking at the telegraph pole next to me; fine chippings of wood were falling on me. I then realised that I was lying in the beaten zone of a machine gun and its bullets were gradually felling the pole. Further forward a voice bawled, 'On your feet! Double march!' It was hard to make the decision to move. My rucksack was digging into my neck. Apathetically, I jogged slowly forward. Shot cows were bellowing in the fields. I ran with death at my throat and tore myself free of a wire fence as bullets whistled around me. Beads of nervous sweat stood out on my brow. Near a farm building I met up with an Offizierstellvertreter and about thirty men. Mentally and spiritually we were totally spent . . . "

Although the attack had fallen well short of expectations, it was felt within the chain of command that the German formations in contact still had sufficient offensive strength to permit a renewal of the attack the following day. There was a major effort to resupply the guns overnight then, as dawn broke, Langemark and the surrounding area was once more subject to very heavy bombardment. Before Langemark, 51st Reserve Division was reinforced by Reserve Infantry Regiment 239 which, it will be recalled, had moved back into reserve twenty fours earlier. This welcome addition to its forces enabled the division to despatch it, together with some batteries of Reserve Field Artillery Regiment 52, to its right flank where, together with the rather reduced Reserve Infantry Regiment 239 and Reserve Jäger Battalion 23, it came under the orders of General von Wechmar.

Unfortunately these manoeuvres and the move forward of Reserve Infantry Regiment 239 from the area of Poelkapelle were subject to considerable disruption as the Allies launched one minor night attack after the other. Eventually, after at least three distinct night actions, the so-called Detachment Wechmar moved into position. The axis of advance was to be the Langemark – Boezinge railway and the objective was the Ypres Canal. The orders were to begin the advance astride the embankment as soon as re-deployment was complete. Any hopes of this movement beginning during the hours of darkness were dashed when the clashes earlier in the night caused repeated hold ups and confusion amongst the units moving forward. Dawn had already broken by the time the troops were in position.

It was intended that 46th Reserve Division, forming the left flank of XXIII Reserve Corps, and Detachment Wechmar, on the right flank of XXVI Reserve Corps, were to cooperate closely during the advance and to coordinate their start times. The delay to Wechmar's forces meant that this was not to be. 46th Reserve Division began its attack promptly as planned, but the men of XXVI Reserve Corps were late. This, in turn, meant that the British artillery was able to concentrate its fire initially against 46th Reserve Division and then switch it to meet Detachment Wechmar; whilst the British infantry were also able to offer one another mutual support. This was to prove fatal to the chances of success. With its right flank anchored on Bikschote, 46th Reserve Division soon found itself locked into a desperate engagement which gradually sucked in all its available forces. Here and there there were minor successes. A party, comprising men of Reserve Jäger Battalion 18 and elements of Reserve Infantry Regiment 213, commanded by Major von Loesen, launched a successful attack on Bikschote mill, capturing 150 British soldiers in the process, whilst elements of Reserve Infantry Regiments 209 and 211 became involved in close quarter bayonet fighting on the outskirts of the village.

On the far bank of the Kortebeek, Reserve Infantry Regiments 214, 215 and 216 soon found themselves also involved in a vicious fight at close range with fixed bayonets. Frequently they advanced against volley fire at ranges of less than fifty metres with inevitable consequences for the advancing troops. Perhaps due to their inexperience the attackers pressed home their assaults long after there was any real hope of achieving a breakthrough. Some idea of the cost may be obtained from the fact that the entire three battalions of Reserve Infantry Regiment 215 were soon reduced to only four weak composite companies, commanded by Hauptmann Henkes, Oberleutnant Hofmann, Oberleutnant Heinrich and Hauptmann Kinne. In rear, Major Valentini managed to assemble two hundred stragglers and lead them forward. The other battalions were in scarcely better condition. Almost every single officer had become a casualty and Major Valentini collapsed with a heart attack and had to be evacuated.

Despite all these setbacks the attacks continued into the afternoon. A renewed German artillery bombardment was followed by further efforts, as junior NCOs assumed command of the troops around them and tried to press forward. The St Jans Beek was crossed in one or two places and there were further captures of British soldiers and seizures of equipment, but the attack had shot its bolt. The regiments were visibly melting away in the face of obstinate British defence and, as darkness began to fall, the attackers, silhouetted against the fires of burning buildings, made easy targets for British infantry, who continued to take a heavy toll of their numbers.

Kriegsfreiwilliger Lübkert 4th Company Reserve Jäger Battalion 18 [29] **10.**

"Hardly had we set off than signal for the assault: '*Kartoffelsupp! Kartoffelsupp!*'[30] was sounded and, with bayonets fixed, we pushed on through barbed wire and trenches, through shrapnel fire and a hail of bullets. Many a comrade gave his life here, without even catching a glimpse of the enemy. Despite the heavy fire, General von Rohden [Generalmajor von Rohden, commander 92 Reserve Infantry Brigade] rode into action with the assault columns, inspiring the troops. As we attempted to cross the St Jans Beek, many men lost their balance due to their heavy packs and could only get across with great difficulty."

An attempt by men of Reserve Infantry Regiment 213 and Reserve Jäger Battalion 18 to pull back in the face of this fire almost completely withered away as the blazing Bikschote windmill lit up the battlefield as bright as day. West of St Jans Beek, the regiments had lost more than two thirds of their effectives. The first signs of a British counter-attack led to a rapid decision by the senior German officers on the spot to abandon these untenable gains and they led their surviving men back across the Kortebeek to relative safety. Most of the wounded who were able to move were forced to spend the hours of darkness making their way painfully to the rear, whilst the entire battlefield was covered by the corpses of the fallen. The events of late afternoon and early evening in this area, when Reserve Infantry Regiment 211 was suddenly summoned forward out of reserve near Bultehoek, subordinated to 46th Reserve Division and sent into battle to try to wrest back the initiative, were summarised later by the commander of one of the Jäger battalions involved.

Oberst Riedel Commander Reserve Jäger Battalion 18[31] **10 – 11.**

"About 5.00pm we advanced together with Reserve Infantry Regiment 211 of 45th Reserve Division. [Our] orders were to attack the enemy dug in on the far bank of St Jans Beek. Reserve Infantry Regiment 211 forded the beek, with the Jägers, some of whom crossed by a bridge to their left. The battalion moved forward and then lay down on the ground. Behind a house stood General[major] Herhudt von Rohden. He advised against a further advance and suggested waiting for darkness to fall. However, once the signal, 'Fix bayonets!' was heard by means of a trumpet call from the right, there was no further delay. The battalion advanced, 1st and 3rd Companies shook out and led off, with battalion headquarters next, followed by 2nd and 3rd Companies in a second wave.

"With truly colossal daring, a way was forced through the murderous rate of fire, the front line was reached and a way was forced further forward. Several farmsteads, their buildings on fire, were stormed. After a short pause the battalion pushed on and, as darkness fell, together with men drawn from the entire division and despite heavy enemy fire, the houses of Kortekeer were stormed ... "

1,500 metres to the northwest, the men of Reserve Infantry Regiment 211 were attempting to press on into Bikschote. In the pitch darkness, with disorientated groups of men from both sides stumbling around in the dark, the risk of clashes with friendly troops was ever present. The men of the 211th went around shouting constant challenges in German, causing German trumpet calls to be sounded and resorting to the singing of various patriotic songs as recognition signals. In one of numerous references to the singing of *Deutschland über alles!* during the battle, it was claimed by Unteroffizier Barknecht, of its 4th Company, that Hauptmann Dehrmann, commanding officer 2nd Battalion Reserve Infantry Regiment 211, was the first to direct that it be sung – only a few moments before he fell, mortally wounded from a bullet in the neck.[32] One of the members of 10th Company Reserve Infantry Regiment 211, who was later commissioned, recorded the attack on Bikschote in his diary.

Kriegsfreiwilliger Arndt 10th Company Reserve Infantry Regiment 211[33] **12.**

"The word 'assault' was almost inaudible, but immediately afterwards we heard the calm, strong word of command of our Hauptmann Preis: 'The last section is responsible for maintaining contact. The platoons are to move to the edge of the wood and advance by sections.' We stumbled through the thick undergrowth, rifle bullets striking the trees above our heads. 'On your feet! Double March!' We ran forward, being greeted by the whistle and crack of rifle fire. 'Down!' There was then a short pause for us to catch our breath and control our heartbeats. 'On your feet!' Everyone ran forward as best he could, then, suddenly, we were confronted by a fully unexpected obstacle. It was a stream several metres wide and of unknown depth. Nobody was willing to risk it! There was a confused tangle of bodies lying around.

"Come on lads. Follow me!' It was our Hauptmann shouting. He had spotted the hold up and, rushing forward, plunged up to his belt in the water. His example had the desired effect. Having reached the far bank, I first of all lay on my back and raised my legs. Most of the water ran out of my boots, but unfortunately a great deal ran up my back and only emerged around my neck. Others were doing the same thing; the odd laugh could be heard, then we were all flat on the edge of the ditch pinned down by fire. How long I do not know. Time lost its meaning. We could feel and think about nothing and heard only the angry roar of the enemy shells. It went very dark, then from somewhere came the sound of the signal for the assault: *'Rückt vor, rückt vor, schneller vor, vor, vor, vor!'* [Get forward, get forward, faster forward, on, on, on!].

"Everywhere lines of riflemen got to their feet, from places where nothing had been in sight earlier. [They emerged] from trenches, hedges and furrows in the ground. This [sudden] emergence of rows of unknown individuals and the flash of fixed bayonets in the dying redness of the closing day was extremely eerie. In amongst it all came the screams of the wounded. Our chain of messengers shouted forward some sort of order from the rear. Nobody could make out what was being said, but Hauptmann Preis stood up and shouted something back. We all understood what was required. We sprang up amidst the murderous fire and ran forward, tripping, stumbling, leaping over ditches and hedges and falling over. Sweating freely, we pushed on ever more forward. Left and right comrades were hit and fell spinning to the ground, groaning and whimpering.

"Did we feel fear? Not really, there was no time to be frightened. We felt and thought nothing at all; we just kept running. Perhaps sometimes we moved slower – I really do not know. It is only particular incidents which remain clear. There was one evil house, from which fire had just seemed to be coming. I attacked it with my rifle butt like a mad man. Windows and frames were smashed inwards. On the far side somebody else was also smashing in the door and then stood upright. I saw his spiked helmet, but my neighbour did not and he raised his rifle to his cheek to shoot him. 'Are you mad? He's German!'

"I ran on, how far I do not know. I could see nothing of the enemy, but seemed to have been swept up in a wave of impersonal violence. Here and there I remember flashes and flames coming from the pitch black hedges where machine guns were hammering away then, suddenly, there were twin flashes to my front. Instinctively I threw my body to the left and forwards against a dark wall. There was a hellish crash and cracking sound as a salvo of shells crashed down, wiping out everybody in front or to the side of me. I pressed myself against the potato clamp, probably only for a few seconds, then there was a flash behind me, a rushing howl above me – I believe that I felt the pressure wave – then a crashing, bursting sound to my front. Then all was dark once more. The nervous rattle of the machine guns seemed almost quiet. I ran to the right and found myself on a path full of men running forwards. I ran too and soon was able to see the shadowy outline against the sky of a small town. It was Bikschote, the place we were meant to be capturing.

"The small arms fire diminished somewhat. Sweating profusely we slowed our pace, until we appeared to be moving along the road like a crowd of tourists returning home. It seemed as though we had succeeded; our objective had been reached. The fearful exertions behind us, we continued on our way. Then, suddenly, there were flashes and flames from roofs and windows. Only a few of us seemed to be hit, but we all pushed back rearwards. The idea that we reached our target had been all in vain. I myself dashed into a house and shone a hand torch around. It was a small shop with a room adjacent to it. Perhaps there were enemy on the floor above me, but the thought did not trouble me much. I crept to the window, determined to deal with one of the riflemen on the roof, but there was nothing to be seen. Everywhere was dark, sometimes there was a shot in the distance and, from somewhere, came the faint sound of somebody groaning.

"Feeling tired I sat in the counter and dangled my legs. Next to me was a jar of cheap sweets. I took them out by the handful and ate them. Gradually my thoughts cleared. I could not sit here for ever. With a feeling of resignation I slid off my comfortable counter, put a few more sweets in my mouth and picked up my rifle. It seemed to weigh a ton. Outside in the street, nothing was to be seen, but there was still the sound of heavy small arms fire. I headed out of the place and bumped into numerous comrades, who were taking cover in a road-side ditch. They all had every reason to do so, because shots were coming in from a hedge off to one flank. I forced my way down into the ditch too; nobody volunteered to give me any space. There we lay and there we waited – for what I know not; possibly the arrival of a leader.

"Then, in the distance and from the direction of the firing, came faintly the sound of *Heil Dir im Siegerkranz*,[34] whilst from another direction came *Deutschland Deutschland über alles!* One of us suggested that we sang too, in order that others might recognise us. It was not a bad idea, especially as our shouts of, 'Don't shoot! Own troops!' had had no effect. A song is an unmistakeable sign, so the occupants of our ditch joined in *Heil Dir im Siegerkranz*, with gusto. From the right, we received the response of *Die Wacht am Rhein*. Despite this, enemy shells rained down mercilessly, sometimes at a slow rate, sometimes faster, but always pinning us down. My neighbour was lying suspiciously still and I suddenly realised that I had been lying all this time next to a dead man, which explained why there had been no protest when I jammed myself into the narrow space, making it even more crowded.

"All of a sudden an officer appeared on the road and ordered us to reoccupy the village. A leader at long last! We followed him and pushed on into the village street. Soon shots were cracking off the cobbles; a machine gun was still firing from the church tower. Wisely, the officer said, 'We must work our way around in rear of the houses. Then we shall get the entire gang.' Swiftly we pulled back and circled the village to the east. Once more we found ourselves in the beaten zone of a machine gun and threw ourselves down behind some stacks of straw. However, the fire slackened and we were able to get round the village. In a paddock there were heaps of dead and wounded. We crossed a road and pushed through a hedge, behind which there were dead Scottish soldiers. By now there were only five of us left. We retraced our steps and made our way into the town, which seemed to be firmly in German hands. The officers took up positions in the alleys and attempted to gather in and rally their troops. Coming from one corner were continuous shouts of, '211th, over here!' About two hundred men assembled. I was part of a group of about forty which was allocated to a tall Leutnant who, I believe, was named Müller."

East of Langemark, despite the obvious need for haste, it was not until 10.00 am on 23 October that General von Wechmar could give the order to the formations of his detachment to begin their attack. Moving as swiftly as possible, the lines of infantrymen closed up to the Kortebeek, about 1,500 metres from Langemark, where they came under very heavy fire, which forced them to take cover and dig in once more. Machine gun fire, coupled with repeated concentrations of shrapnel fire from the artillery, took its toll until, by mid afternoon, the severely weakened troops began first to falter and then to pull back. First it was a matter of individuals, then sections headed for the rear. Such movements are infectious and in short order entire lines of infantry were racing to the rear as fast as they could move. It was all the company officers could do to check this retreat along the line of the old positions by Poelkapelle Station. 51st Reserve Division ordered that this line be held come what may.

Not only was the right flank affected. The centre of the divisional line before Langemark also cracked and very soon it too had pulled back precipitately to Poelkapelle. For its part 46th Reserve Division could not hold its forward positions; its units, too, were forced to withdraw. Nobody could say that these formations of units had not done the best they could in the circumstances. Some sub units lost over ninety percent of their strength and the entire battlefield was littered with the dead. Nevertheless, the entire effort had all been for nothing. By the evening of 23 October, not only had the gains of the day been lost, so too had those bought so expensively during the past few days. The Allies, at considerable cost had prevailed. Everyone on the German side could see that there was no prospect of a further successful advance as matter stood, so, whilst the ruins of Langemark continued to smoulder, the German front line was consolidated from the southern edge of Mangelaar – Poelkapelle Station – Poelkapelle – Broodseinde Crossroads.

Luckily some of the guns of the divisional direct support regiment were in a position to provide at least limited cover during the withdrawal, or even fewer of the survivors would have been extricated. Subsequently they were also able to boost the somewhat precarious hasty defence the following night. An 'Oberleutnant K', of 6th Battery Reserve Field Artillery Regiment 46, later described how this was achieved. **12.**

"When, on 23 October, a report arrived that the enemy had established a strong defensive position along the line Drie Grachten – Bikschote – Langemark, the vanguard of our Corps was directed to advance from Houthulst through the wood and in the direction of Mangelaar – Bikschote. That same day my battery went into position near Mangelaar and began to bring fire down on the enemy positions around Bikschote, in preparation for the infantry assault of 46th Reserve Division. Because we were engaging at a range in excess of four kilometres our fire had very little effect – especially on the enemy artillery. As a result, it appeared as though our infantry was about to bleed to death in the course of the assault, so 6th Battery was given the mission of advancing into positions just to the rear of the infantry. I moved into a firing position about 400 metres west of a copse, which was well protected to the front by a hedge.

"We began immediately to dig in, telephone connections back to battalion were laid and the guns were surveyed in. That evening I established that I was exactly 120 paces in rear of the single front line trench manned by Reserve Jäger Battalion 18. Because the jägers informed me that the British were showing definite signs of attacking, I took the opportunity to calculate the precise distance to our trench line. I left my teams of horses two kilometres to the rear, because the entire area was under constant enemy harassing fire, but ensured that contact was maintained by despatch riders. Just as it went dark, heavy machine gun and artillery fire began to come down from our front and left flank though, thank heavens, very little of the latter landed amongst the battery: presumably because the enemy assumed, as I had previously thought, that my position would be behind or up against the wood. However they were successful in cutting both the telephone line and all contact with the light ammunition column.

"This was followed at once by an assault by enemy infantry against our weakly held firing line. Because I received no sort of orders from the rear and because the situation of the hard-pressed jägers to my front had worsened – a fact of which I was only too well aware, due to the way small arms rounds were rattling against my gun shields and observation wagon like dried peas – I began rapid fire with case shot which, as the jägers later told me, had a miraculous effect on the assaulting columns. The British assaults were repeated that night eight to ten times, sometimes with such force that our jägers (who had fallen back into my battery position because all their officers and NCOs had been killed or wounded) could only be prevented from falling back further through the application of much energy by me.

"That night the battery[35] fired 960 rounds, most at ranges of 400 to 800 metres. I was assisted in this task somewhat because I was able to bring down effective fire on the enemy artillery between attacks at 1,400 – 1,800 metres and, in so doing, managed to set fire to two wooden windmills, which cast a flickering light over the battlefield. In doing this I had to give almost all my fire orders by whistle, a system I had practised previously, because the gun line was about one hundred metres distant from my observation wagon, which was off to the side. The noise of battle was colossal, voice commands could not be heard and the telephone system could not be put in working order.

"Ammunition resupply was an interesting feature of this battle. There were no links to the rear. My battalion commander, as well as my wachtmeister, back with the horses, both noted the mad rate of fire of the battery and realised that we could easily run out of ammunition. As a result the first named sent three despatch riders to order the ammunition column to bring up ammunition to me. On the other hand, the wachtmeister, concerned about the battery and not knowing the location of the light ammunition column, decided to send the teams and limbers forward to the position. Although the first of the ammunition wagons got through easily, the horses were not used to the shrapnel fire and the wagons were tipped over, so that we had to carry the ammunition from there by hand. In addition the limbers, which my Wachtmeister brought forward personally, had to be emptied under fire.

"Nevertheless the battery enjoyed unbelievably good fortune. Despite the firing of nearly 1,000 rounds by the morning of 24 October (a performance made possible only because of energetic action by those behind the battery), we were still holding our position and fully supplied with ammunition.

Furthermore, we had suffered no casualties at all amongst men or horses. Through its good shooting and the devotion to duty of its personnel, the battery had so supported the thin line of jägers that they were able that night to regain their trenches and the enemy only launched weak attacks the following day. The following morning the battalion commander was informed that the division had been able to hold on, thanks to my battery and, as a result, I was the first officer of the regiment to receive the Iron Cross."[36]

Interesting though it is, this short vignette, concerning a local tactical success, cannot disguise the fact that the preliminary attempt to take Langemark by storm was a complete and utter failure. Unrealistic demands had been made of men badly commanded, ill-prepared and inadequately supported. It is, perhaps, wrong to speak of a cover up, but it is a constant in military history that the bigger the disaster, the more praise and rewards are heaped on the survivors, if only to deflect frequently justifiable criticism of those responsible. The wanton sacrifice, the callous exploitation of their idealism and courage and, quite frankly, their betrayal, caused by the incompetence of their superiors, was and remains a scandal. The soldiers who attacked Langemark effectively achieved nothing on the battlefield, but they were, nevertheless, awarded an enduring place in the history of the war as myth was laid over legend and the 'Spirit of Langemark' was exploited between the wars for unscrupulous ends.

Notes

1. Lennartz History Reserve Infantry Regiment 240 pp 12–13.
2. Vogt History Reserve Field Artillery Regiment 51 pp 45–46.
3. Hennig History Reserve Infantry Regiment 235 pp 22–23.
4. Knieling History Reserve Infantry Regiment 234 p 51.
5. Mayer History Reserve Infantry Regiment 236 pp 104–105.
6. Brendler History Reserve Infantry Regiment 233 p 18.
7. Hennig op. cit. p 24.
8. Foerster Wir Kämpfer im Weltkrieg pp 98–99.
9. Brendler op. cit. p 24.
10. Hauptmann Ernst Schröter is buried in the German cemetery at Langemark Block B Grave 16564.
11. Foerster op. cit. p 99.
12. Oberleutnant Ernst Schröder is buried in the Kamaradengrab of the German cemetery at Langemark.
13. Hauptmann Friedrich Schöler is buried in the German cemetery at Menen Block H Grave 12.
14. Mayer op. cit. pp 101–103.
15. It is in fact extremely unlikely that the units being attacked had seen colonial duty, but a great many contemporary German accounts assert this and some individuals may well have served abroad in the circumstances described.
16. ibid. pp 110–113.
17. Brendler op. cit. pp 19–20.
18. Schiedt History Reserve Field Artillery Regiment 51 p 57.
19. ibid. p 58.
20. ibid. p 60.

21. Schatz History Reserve Infantry Regiment 239 p 12.
22. Oberleutnant Ludwig Hieronimus is buried in the German cemetery at Langemark Block B Grave 13294.
23. Lennartz *op. cit.* p 22.
24. Schiedt *op. cit.* p 61.
25. Hennig *op. cit.* pp 26–27.
26. Foerster *op. cit.* pp 100–101.
27. Willers History Reserve Infantry Regiment 215 pp 65–66.
28. *ibid.* p 60.
29. Stoffleth History Reserve Jäger Battalion 18 p 35.
30. 'Potato Soup! Potato Soup!' The soldier's method of distinguishing the various trumpet calls was to give them names, much as the British Tommies and the French *Poilus* did for their own calls.
31. Stoffleth *op. cit.* p 37.
32. Hauptmann Arthur Dehrmann died of his wounds on 23 October 1914. He is buried in the German cemetery at Langemark Block A Grave 2923.
33. Fuhrmann History Reserve Infantry Regiment 211 pp 37–39.
34. *Heil Dir im Siegerkranz* [Hail to thee in Victor's Crown] was the unofficial anthem of the German Empire from 1871–1918. Originally written in 1790 by Heinrich Harries in praise of King Christian VII of Denmark, it was adapted, with the word 'Kaiser' substituted for 'Christian' in the German version. It was never recognised by, for example, Bavaria or Württemberg – not that that fact would have troubled these Prussian soldiers. More problematic, bearing in mind that it was being used to distinguish friend from foe, was the fact that it was sung to the same tune as 'God Save the King'!
35. This battery had only four guns. Active and planned reserve batteries had six guns each at this stage of the war, but the second draft of reserve divisions were short of all types of equipment, so they deployed with four gun batteries – a model later adopted by every other field regiment to improve efficiency of ammunition supply as much as any other consideration.
36. Foerster *op. cit.* pp 96–97.

The Battle for Beselare, Geluveld and the Menen Road

Advancing on the extreme left of Fourth Army was XXVII Reserve Corps. This formation, comprising 53rd and 54th Reserve Divisions, was drawn from Saxony and Württemberg. Of its ten regiments (infantry and artillery, six were from Saxony and four from Württemberg. It also had the services of two jäger battalions at this early stage of the war: Reserve Jäger 25 from Dresden and Reserve Jäger 26 from Freiburg in Saxony. As far as its state of training and preparation was concerned, this was as lamentable as that which obtained in the other corps, indeed it appears that Reserve Jäger 26 spent most of its training time on the drill square learning a set of completely useless drill manoeuvres more appropriate to the battlefields of the eighteenth, rather than the twentieth Century. The Corps Commander was the Minister of War for Saxony, General der Infanterie Adolph von Carlowitz. Although Carlowitz was a career officer and a member of the Great General Staff, he had had no experience of command at either divisional or corps level and, during these early battles, it showed.

On 20 October the General, members of his staff and other subordinate commanders were assembled at Moorslede for an orders group, during which Carlowitz made an extraordinary pronouncement.[1]

> "The advance is to continue via Dadizele, Terhand, Beselare and Geluveld. Once that place is captured, it is to be continued on to Ypres. The line Poperinge – Dikkebus is to be secured. Orders group tonight in the town hall at Ypres."

Bearing in mind that the British had laid out forces in delaying and defensive positions along the line Passchendaele – Beselare – Geluveld long before XXVII Reserve Corps even appeared on the Flanders battlefield, the most charitable comment to make about this is that it indicates that both commander and staff must have been detached from reality; not only that, they cannot have been familiar with their own doctrine, nor can they have had any clear idea about speeds of advance in contact, even against the lightest of opposition. It beggars belief that trained military personnel could imagine that such an advance of around twenty five kilometres would be possible at all in the face of enemy interference. Even to march a complete corps that far under peacetime conditions would be no mean feat. To set such an objective for a single day was simply ludicrous, but perhaps not more so than the subsequent stream of orders within the corps which simply demanded the impossible of those whose misfortune it was to have to attempt to carry them out. The Saxon Reserve Infantry Regiment 243 later noted bitterly, 'Hardly a day went by without the issue of yet another fresh attack order to

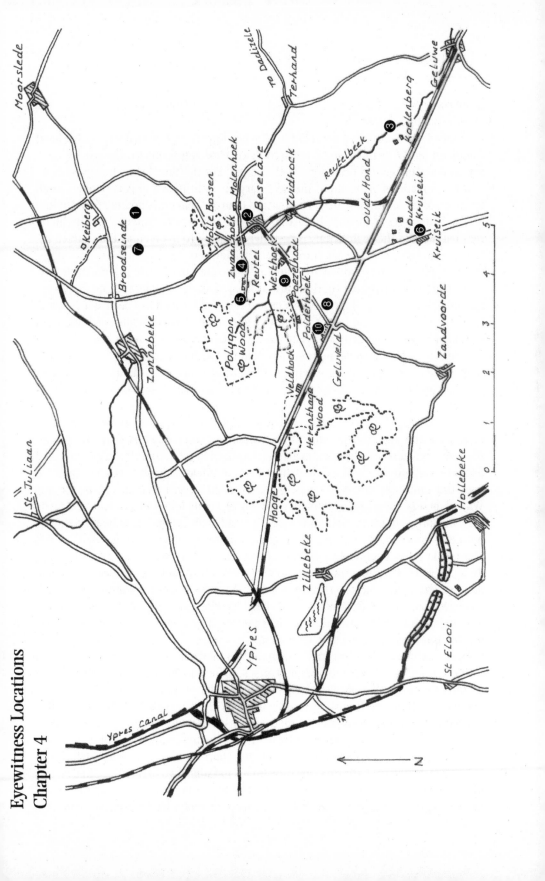

**Eyewitness Locations
Chapter 4**

troops who for weeks had been subject to the greatest imaginable privations and assaults on their morale.'[2]

It must have come as a great relief to all when Carlowitz reported sick with a heart complaint on 27 October, to be replaced by General von Schubert, though, by then, irreparable damage had been done to the corps.[3] For the time being, however, every effort was made to bring about the necessary breakthrough and commanders at all levels did their best to inspire their men and to urge them on. Marching forward into battle, Unteroffizier Siegfried Brase of Reserve Infantry Regiment 241 distinctly recalled hearing the regimental commander shouting to his men as they passed by, 'Throw the lying rabble back into the sea!'[4] They certainly needed the encouragement. Typically, after a difficult fight to gain Rollegem-Kapelle the previous day, there had been an almost total failure of the re-supply system and the men were becoming very hungry. Quartered in a farm, Brase and his men had been able to requisition a large quantity of butter, but only a few bread rolls and some small pieces of cured ham. Brase commented, 'What good was that amongst so many? For the most part we had to feast on generous portions of butter with nothing to spread it on. Later it appealed to me much more when spread on peeled turnips; a discovery of which I was very proud and one which I went round recommending to everyone as something special.'[5]

For the advance on 20 October, 53rd Reserve Division was split into two columns to ease command and control. One of the columns, commanded by Generalleutnant Bierling, divisional artillery commander, comprised Reserve Infantry Regiments 242 and 244 and moved via Dadizele, whilst Reserve Infantry Regiments 241 and 243, operating under the orders of Generalleutnant von Criegern, marched along the axis Waterdam – Zonnebeke. From the first leading elements found themselves held up by delaying forces, but they maintained pressure and made ground, if somewhat slowly, with elements of XXVI Reserve Corps advancing to their north on the planned axis Moorslede – Passchendaele – Brielen. Everywhere there were the signs of battle. Refugees were thronging the roads carrying a few pitiful belongings tied up in great bundles, hasty barricades had been erected in numerous places and the area was full of stragglers, medical units, wounded and sick, together with burnt out farms and other buildings, amongst which dead or riderless horses mingled with cows bellowing in pain because there was nobody left to milk them.

Once leading elements had arrived in the area of Dadizele, reports arrived that British forces were about to launch some type of attack, so Bierling's column deployed, Reserve Infantry Regiment 242 taking up hasty defence on high ground near Strooiboom, some one and a half kilometres northwest of Dadizele. With its 1st and 2nd Battalions in line along the crest where the windmill stood and its 3rd Battalion in reserve, the regiment began to break all records for digging in, in a field of mangel wurzels, because there was an obvious threat of artillery fire. Sure enough, a short time later, shrapnel shells began to burst overhead, the balls shooting forward to land some two to three hundred metres in rear of the positions. The so-called attack failed to develop in any meaningful way and the advance was soon resumed. Away to the west units of 54th Reserve Division were heavily engaged in the Molenhoek area, but gathering darkness prevented any involvement by formations of 53rd Reserve Division. However the advance was disrupted and, in the pouring rain of a pitch black night, Bierling's column found itself crammed miserably into large groups along the Dadizele-Terhand road, unable to move because of heavy artillery fire to its front.

Hours went by. Blazing fires from houses burning in Beselare, which was in the process of falling to formations of 54th Reserve Division, could be seen through the darkness and the column was suddenly jerked back into alert wakefulness as a stray shell crashed down right next to a large contingent from 2nd Battalion Reserve Infantry Regiment 242. Nevertheless, the regiment had hardly been affected by the day's fighting as it was finally ordered to halt where it was and to go into bivouac near Oosthoek and await further orders. As far as the other column was concerned, with all the hold ups and delays, it was already quite late in the day when the men of Reserve Infantry Regiment 243 had moved forward sufficiently to be able to make out in the distance, beyond a wide area of small hedge-lined fields, the road running north from Beselare in the direction of Zonnebeke and Passchendaele. Thoughts were beginning to turn to going into bivouac for the night when, suddenly, the advance guard checked and went to ground. According to Reserve Infantry Regiment 243, at that point the main body was still moving in column and approaching Keiberg when, out of the distance, despatch riders came galloping up to them: **1.**

> "Take cover!' bawled a despatch rider and then there was a whirring, groaning noise . . . something unpleasant passed overhead then, just beyond our columns, a pair of shells crashed down in a field of sugar beet, sending steel splinters and clods of earth flying amongst us. We were not quite sure what was happening. Crawling along the ground, we headed for cover in the ditches by the side of the road and then a third shell roared overhead, exploding behind us. 'On your feet!' We could see our leaders and had only one thought: to follow them forwards – behind the windmill – as far as the hedge which ran along by the village [Keiberg]. There was no time for the pale-faced, uncomprehending men to ask questions. Was it due to shock? Was it fear? After all, we were still in one piece. The next second a second salvo of shells crashed down just where we had been lying."[6]

Having overcome the initial shock of coming under serious fire for the first time, Criegen's column rushed to deploy. Attacking with two battalions of Reserve Infantry Regiment 241 right, with Reserve Infantry Regiment 243, reinforced by one battalion of the 241st left, it closed up on the Keiberg –Waterdam area.

Unteroffizier Siegfried Brase Reserve Infantry Regiment 241 [7] **1.**

> "Perfectly calmly [*sic*.], we bore off to the left. There were about twenty men, including me, under the command of a leutnant. Riding with us was our ober-leutnant, who was now acting company commander, because our Hauptmann

S. had taken over from the battalion commander, who had reported sick.[8] Arriving at the village of Waterdamhoek, we resumed our original direction and arrived on the Keiberg heights, whilst the exchange of artillery fire was already underway. On the hill top we released our worried Belgian guide; some men were detailed to go and clear a group of houses whilst the remainder of us pressed on so as to link up with our neighbours.

"Although we succeeded in doing this, we managed to lose contact with our own battalion; neither our Oberleutnant nor a patrol succeeded in re-establishing the link. On the other hand the close country offered us favourable cover from view. To our front – to our ears, unpleasantly close, though a small wood prevented us from seeing it – an enemy gun was firing and, as it later transpired, a number of us thought that we ought to be dealing with it. In the event we did nothing of the kind and our little detachment was probably too weak for such a task anyway. A few shells from our own artillery had already landed rather close to us, so we had to halt and take cover in a hollow with some men from Baden . . . Ducking down we could hear the uniquely strange sound of branches splintering, as some of our men who had advanced to our right came under fire from enemy infantry as they pushed through a small wooded area."

The bullets fired were directed against the men of Reserve Infantry Regiment 243, who, trying to ignore the shrapnel balls which were flying around, listened for the words of command of their company commanders as they shook out for action. 1.

"On your feet! Double march! and the men doubled across the fields, disappearing in amongst the tall leaves of the beet fields. 'Whizz . . . Crack! . . . Crack!' Strange whirrings, interspersed with sounds like whips cracking could be heard as the enemy rifle bullets cut through the air. Ricochets buzzed overhead, the bullets deflected from their paths as they hit solid objects in the hedges. Involuntarily we ducked and weaved with every unusual sound, though the bullets themselves had long since disappeared beyond us. It became darker then, all of a sudden, came shouts of *Hurra!* What had happened? The first prisoners had been captured. It was men of 7th Company, under Leutnant Sellnick and Feldwebel Möller, who had succeeded in snatching a British seven man patrol and bringing it in triumphantly. Stray bullets still cracked through the air as the night wore on. Brigade ordered that the regiment was to pull back to Keiberg Mill and go firm there, so we assembled as best we could after this first clash with the enemy. We had received our baptism of fire at Keiberg Mill."[9]

In the confusion of the fight, the murky weather and the darkness of the night, numerous isolated groups could only guess exactly what was happening and attempt to contribute in the way judged best by the senior man on the spot.

Unteroffizier Siegfried Brase Reserve Infantry Regiment 241 [10] **1.**

"Having spent a long time sheltering from artillery fire behind a hedge, we eventually met up with other sections of our platoon and then the entire platoon, together with our oberleutnant. Because through the gathering mist a quick glance made it appear as though further lines of infantrymen were following up behind us, our commander decided to launch an attack. This was a risky endeavour because we knew absolutely nothing about the strength or location of the enemy. We opened fire on the enemy at a range of 500 – 600 metres . . . and began to work our way forward in short bounds, just as we had practised on the training area.

"Soon, the faint moans of pain of those who had been hit blended with the noise of battle. The enemy infantry were not alone. To their rear, half right of them, a supporting battery fired four swift salvos. Each time this happened, shrapnel balls whistled past our ears. I myself suddenly received an extraordinarily heavy blow. It felt as though half of me had been blown away. I looked down, but I was still in one piece . . . but a spade, which I had bent over and was using as a rifle rest, was swept away by an ugly fist-sized fragment of the jacket of a shell, as though by an iron broom. It had already crippled the rifle of the man next to me, without injuring him and he stood there, bemused and astounded, holding the two halves of his weapon. The hot fragment now lay harmlessly in front of me where it had scoured the ground.

"My neighbour to my left told me later that he was sure that I had been killed when I appeared to have been thrown backwards half a metre, but then he saw me lying on my left side, as though nothing had happened. Luckily, displaying constant good will, the majority of the bullets cracked away over our heads, thanks in part to the low lying positions we were occupying. Off to our right, however, from our comrades who had pushed up onto a fold in the ground, came the shout: 'The commander of the Württembergers . . . has been killed as well!' Of a group of twenty men, finally there was only the abovementioned oberstleutnant and two of our men still there. One of them, Hans Pfitzner from my section, was shot through both knees but found by the medical orderlies a day and a half later, still alive.

"All the time that we were able to shoot we were detached from this painful scene. Quite correctly, there was criticism on the exercise area whenever one group or the other pushed on too far in front of the remainder, even if the ground seemed to encourage it. With about six to eight men around me, I had others in front and behind me, so could not continue the fire fight and the same applied to those even further in rear. Such unwanted obstacles are always bad. Ones attention turns to parents and Homeland and the effect is like a creeping poison.

"Thoughts of God as my personal saviour drifted into my consciousness, but I suppressed them. For why should the creator of the world favour a poor worm like me before those who were, perhaps, my betters? Were such thoughts not simply naked egotism of a sort which our great thinkers, Spinoza and Kant, had exposed and railed against? At this moment when I found myself most aware of the risk of death, however, even I found myself believing *Ihm ziemt's die Welt im Innern zu bewegen* [Fittingly, He is the innermost motion of the world]. In other words I accepted the unfolding of this massive clash of peoples in its entirety, as something which was being directed by Him in accordance with His great scheme; that all this was an example of His unalterable greatness and righteousness – the result of His love and blessings in support of our special endeavours."[11]

For its part, 54th Reserve Division from Württemberg, commanded by General der Infanterie von Schäfer and comprising Reserve Infantry Regiments 245, 246, 247 and 248, was also present in Flanders from mid October. Following a few preliminary manoeuvres, leading elements had pressed on beyond Terhand by the afternoon of 20 October and were beginning to advance on Beselare. There was a degree of apprehension about what might lie to the front and numerous senior officers took up positions of observation and searched the area to the front through their telescopes. The close nature of the country, dotted as it was with small fields enclosed with dense hedges, made this task extremely difficult but it was at least possible to select routes forward towards Beselare and there were no obvious signs of British opposition.

2nd Battalion Reserve Infantry Regiment 246 was given orders to move directly towards Beselare, advancing until contact was made with the enemy. Around 4.00 pm, by which time they were not much more than 300 metres beyond Terhand, there were suddenly signs of life at Beselare and bullets began to impact on houses at Terhand, despite the fact that the range was at least two kilometres. Meanwhile more and more units of 54th Reserve Division began to arrive in the Terhand area. Three battalions: 1st and 3rd Battalions Reserve Infantry Regiment 245 and 1st Battalion Reserve Infantry Regiment 246, were attempting to find cover in the built up area, together with rear elements of 2nd Battalion Reserve Infantry Regiment 246. The result was a complete jam until, eventually, large groups of infantrymen, rifles in hand, were seen gathered in the protective shelter of the houses, whilst the noise of small arms fire from the west, together with the whirr of ricochets, became ever more prominent.

Platoon and company commanders looked to their battalion commanders for orders; in the meantime the infantrymen waited developments. Eventually, information began to filter back from the advance guard and it became clear that Beselare was being defended in strength and that a German assault was anticipated. The torrent of fire which greeted every attempt to get forward simply confirmed this. Casualties were already being incurred, despite the range, which further increased the respect felt for the British opponents, as did the fact that absolutely nothing could be seen of their positions. Moving in single file, the companies of 1st and 3rd Battalion Reserve Infantry Regiment 245 began to move through the village and shake out into skirmishing lines.

To their right (north) were the leading elements of Reserve Infantry Regiment 246, already engaged in a sharp fire fight with British outposts east of Beselare. Once all were in position, the order to advance was given and, simultaneously, salvoes of British artillery fire began to explode in and around Terhand, causing casualties at once to the units in reserve.

Leaving the care of the wounded and dying to those still in Terhand, the remainder pressed on, exploiting covered approaches as much as possible, until they were closing up on Beselare, with the guns of Reserve Field Artillery Regiment 54 providing close support. Its 1st Battalion later reported, 'Until midday there was all the tension of waiting; but then came orders to bring fire down on enemy trenches and the farm buildings which they had occupied at Zuidhoek . . . That same afternoon we pushed forward, with 2nd and 3rd Batteries going into fire positions just east of Beselare – which was partly in flames – spread out to our front on a one kilometre front. Here the batteries suffered their first casualties but soon we were moving again into positions of readiness, still harnessed up, behind a copse, in front of which the infantry was heavily engaged. Towards evening we linked up with our ammunition column on the Terhand–Beselare road, then went into position with the guns at five metre spacing and shells fuzed for 200 metres, because surprise attacks always had to be assumed at night . . . '[12]

Benefiting from the gun fire, which was coming down heavily on Beselare and its main road junction in particular, the infantry was locked in a close quarter, savage, fight on the eastern perimeter of the village. There appeared to be British small arms fire coming from all directions, not only from within the blazing village, but also from concealed positions in the fields and hedges on either flank. This caused confusion and many casualties amongst the Württembergers who, unsure of their targets, had to resort to pouring fire into any likely places of concealment as they attempted to get into the village itself. Eventually, by dint of moving in short bounds, 1st Battalion Reserve Infantry Regiment 245 began to make limited progress, but not before it had been caught in an extremely heavy concentration of fire on a forward slope on the approaches to Beselare and had suffered a large number of casualties from both British artillery and small arms fire. Its first sight of the towers of the cathedral and Cloth Hall in Ypres viewed from the crest line were no compensation for this brutal baptism of fire.[13]

With his 1st Battalion furthest forward, with 3rd Battalion close up behind, the commander of Reserve Infantry Regiment 245, Oberst Baumgarten-Crusius, personally led the assault of 2nd Company into the northern sector of Beselare, whilst 5th and 6th Companies pressed their attacks home from the east. The remaining companies of 1st Battalion followed up closely and soon the British defenders were forced back into the western part of the village. 7th and 8th Companies joined in, reinforcing the remainder of 2nd Battalion in the eastern section of the village and pressing on into the southeast sector. There were by now almost too many German infantrymen engaged and near total confusion ensued in the shell-torn village with bullets still cracking around. Eventually some sort of order was restored and parties moved house by house, clearing their way towards the areas where the British defence was still holding out.

Whilst its 3rd Battalion was attempting with extreme difficulty to work its way round to the south of Beselare, where the route west towards Poezelhoek and Geluveld opened up, 1st Battalion Reserve Infantry Regiment 246 was heavily involved in this phase of the operations; a kriegsfreiwilliger of 1st Company later provided a description of its ultimate capture, which was complete by 6.00 pm on 20 October. [14] **2.**

"We pushed up close behind the withdrawing British advance guard and moved via Moelenhoek to the northern tip of Beselare, which we reached unscathed. All was deadly quiet in the village. Pressing myself against the wall of a building by the side of the road and with my rifle at the ready, I moved towards the cross roads,[15] coming across the body of a fallen German cavalryman, whose body blocked the clean, cobbled pavement to me. Just as I was going to step over him, I noticed the single shot to his forehead. At that moment shots rang out from all sides, the shock blotting out all sight and sound to me. Cracks, whistling and roaring sounds filled the air, together with the clatter of falling roofing tiles and clouds of dust from the broken ones. There was a main British position a few hundred metres to the west and from there they had suddenly brought down a hellish rate of fire against us.

"What was to be done? Answer: a swift withdrawal to the entrance to the village and take cover in a ditch. Just then a group of soldiers rushed up from Molenhoek, urged on by shouts form the tall figure of Oberst Roschmann in their midst. In quick time we pushed back into Beselare, beyond the cross roads and into a field of tobacco which adjoined the village. There we dug in as quickly as possible. The 3rd Battalion, moving in column with 300 metre intervals, followed this advance party along the line of track which ran southwest about 600 metres east of Molenhoek towards Beselare church. The battalion had tried in vain to make contact with General[Leutnant] von Reinhardt [Commander 107 Reserve Infantry Brigade, killed in action 22 October], so the advance was continued without fresh orders through the southern portion of Beselare, as far as the southwest exit, which was under heavy enemy artillery fire and was still unoccupied by our troops.

"This point was reached a little after 6.00 pm. 10th and 11th Companies in the front line occupied a crest line just north of the Beselare – Geluveld road. The left flank was covered by an 11th Company outpost comprising fifty men, commanded by Offizierstellvertreter Kress von Kressenstein. The remainder of 11th Company linked up with the regiment in the northern part of the village and the farm buildings 650 metres southwest of Beselare church were occupied by elements of Reserve Infantry Regiment 245 shortly before midnight. Once darkness fell extremely heavy enemy fire was brought down on the newly-reached line. This gradually increased in intensity and accuracy. The enemy was in possession of the bend in the road southwest of Beselare, together with the farm buildings to the south of it[16] and Westhoek-Poezelhoek. The positions were was rapidly dug and held throughout the night . . . "

This description reveals what an immense variety of experiences can arise in the course of a single action. As has been noted, the majority of the attackers certainly did not reach the village 'unscathed'. The depth companies of Reserve Infantry Regiment 245, for example, came under such a weight of fire from the direction of Reutel that in some platoons losses were so high that they were virtually wiped out and entire meadows were said to be carpeted in corpses. The situation of the wounded was dreadful. It was impossible to move in the open to attempt to tend or recover them, so they were forced to lie where they had been hit and many succumbed to their wounds during the hours which followed. With the German artillery either involved in changing positions, replenishing ammunition or simply disorientated, it was impossible to respond to the increased British fire which began to crash down on Beselare when it became evident that that place was lost and which inhibited every attempt to exploit the gain further.

Company and platoon commanders urged their men on, but every move forward brought an increase in fire in its wake and the demands were too great for these inexperienced troops, who had already seen their numbers dramatically reduced earlier that day. The impossibility of spotting the British infantry, the accuracy of their fire and that of their gunners, coupled with the feeling of being in an extremely vulnerable salient, all had a negative effect on the nerves of the men of XXVII Reserve Corps and, one by one, then by sections, they began to fall back into the cover of the burning village of Beselare. Both 1st and 3rd Battalions Reserve Infantry Regiment 245 were similarly affected and when Oberleutnants Beverförde and Pfeifer were killed and Oberst Hesse, commanding officer 3rd Battalion, fell, seriously wounded, there was nothing for it but to dig in, in an attempt to reduce the serious losses being generated by shrapnel fire and to hold on to the latest gains. Gradually night fell and the enemy fire was reduced to unaimed harassing fire, which continued to come down heavily, making attempts to sort out the mixed up units very difficult.

Elements of 2nd Battalion Reserve Infantry Regiment 246 were intermingled with 1st and 3rd Battalions Reserve Infantry Regiment 245 to the immediate west of Beselare, whilst 1st Battalion Reserve Infantry Regiment 246 had swung north after passing through the village, its commander, Major Baumann, was wounded and it found itself in the disagreeable position of being completely isolated and under heavy fire. There was only one thing to do – dig in, which is precisely what its hard-pressed survivors did, holding on to the exposed salient their success during the afternoon had brought them. In and around Beselare they were located well ahead of flanking formations and, although it is at least questionable if the British forces opposing them had any serious intent of attacking them, the night was spent in reinforcing the positions taken and preparing for a further advance the following day.

Infantry Regiment 248 had a rather different day on 20 October, having spent most of it in reserve. By mid afternoon, it was concentrated, concealed in a sunken area southwest of Terhand. The battalions were well spread out, waiting to advance, whilst the regimental commander, Oberst Freiherr von Hügel, starved of accurate information concerning the battle out to his front, was reduced to having to make his assessments from the (frequently inaccurate and contradictory) reports of the walking wounded making their way to the rear. No orders arrived from higher headquarters and night began to draw in. Eventually, at around 5.00 pm, after a crescendo of noise was noted, a wounded runner arrived from the formation to the left, requesting assistance in the battle raging around Koelenberg. Hügel immediately requested appropriate orders from 54th Reserve Division but, before a reply could reach him, other orders arrived, directing him to move immediately to Beselare.

Barely had the movement got underway at around 6.00 pm, than counter-orders arrived re-directing him to Koelenberg. The battalions immediately changed direction towards the southwest, but by now it was dark and raining hard, which made matters much more complicated. Out in the distance the blazing church in Beselare glowed a deep red colour and great clouds of smoke enveloped the village. The crash of exploding shells was intermingled with shouts of the infantry fighting at close quarters and the crack of small arms fire and the flashes and reports of shrapnel shells bursting. Almost inevitably mistakes were made. 1st Battalion Reserve Infantry Regiment 248 got disorientated, lost direction and, instead of heading for Koelenberg, found itself mixed up within the boundaries of Reserve Infantry Regiments 245 and 246, which were still engaged in the battle for Beselare. There was nothing else for it, but to report to the brigade commander, Generalleutnant Reinhardt, then to come under his orders, at least temporarily.

The situation was much the same for 2nd Battalion and also 9th and 11th Companies of 3rd Battalion. After wandering around in the dark, they too gravitated to Beselare, linked up with 1st Battalion and spent the night reinforcing Reserve Infantry Regiments 245 and 246. The only troops which reached Koelenberg were regimental headquarters itself, together with 10th and 12th Companies. There they were welcomed by the hard-pressed 1st Battalion Bavarian Reserve Infantry Regiment 1 of 1st Bavarian Reserve Division, but which was operating with 3rd Cavalry Division to boost its rifle strength. It was the following morning before Hügel was able to establish the whereabouts of his missing units, which is hardly surprising given the total lack of communications, uncertainty of the situation and the general confusion of a night following a costly day of battle. The rain had turned into a drenching drizzle which quickly soaked everyone and everything.

The close country was fitfully lit by the blaze of burning buildings, the flash of exploding shells and the occasional flare. Hanging over everything was the noise of the artillery, the British employing harrassing fire and the German artillery bringing down concentrations beyond Beselare, aimed at Poezelhoek and the woods and copses around Reutel. All the roads were clogged with horse drawn traffic of all kinds. There were batteries trying to change position, ammunition columns attempting to locate their units and vying for space with ambulance carts and machine gun sections. Tempers were lost, orders and counter-orders given and the infantry was forced to attempt to move cross country. Terhand was total chaos; horses and their vehicles jammed every road and open space. Eyewitnesses later commented that it was just as well that the village was not singled out for harassing fire. Heavy casualties would have been the inevitable result.

A pre-deployment photograph of Oberst Julius List and a group of officers from Bavarian Reserve Infantry Regiment 16 wearing the ill-fated Landsturm forage caps. At the end of the battle for Geluveld, List and seven others depicted had been killed. Two officers were evacuated wounded and only two survived unscathed, one of whom was the Regimental Medical Officer.

A group of cavalrymen resting by a bivouac tent improvised from groundsheets and lances.

Men of Reserve Jäger Battalion 3 on the march.

Belgian Infantry in hasty defensive positions October 1914. (*Lambrecht Collection*)

A German prisoner being closely escorted to the rear by a mixed group of Belgian soldiers.

Belgian motorised transport including an armoured car of the type used in the delaying battle east of the Ijzer, parked on the main square at Veurne.
(*Lambrecht Collection*)

King Albert visiting forward Belgian positions, November 1914.

A monitor of the Royal Navy Dover Patrol off the Flanders coast, October 1914.

A group of German soldiers posing by a captured London bus of the Metropolitan Electric Tramways company in the main square at Brugge (Bruges). The damaged advertisement is for the play *Diplomacy*, by Victorien Sardou, starring Gerald du Maurier in a revival of the 1879 original. The play ran at Wyndham's Theatre until April 1914, with the Germans substituted for the Russians as the villains of the piece.
(Lambrecht Collection)

A field gun battery of 1st Marine Division moving forward from Oostende, October 1914.
(*Lambrecht Collection*)

A German infantry company taking cover on and around one of the ubiquitous Flanders haystacks prior to an advance.

Officers of Infantry Regiment 172 in a front line trench, believed to be near Shrewsbury Forest, December 1914.
(*Lambrecht Collection*)

A pair of German infantrymen manning a hastily dug trench early in the battle when the spikes on the *Pickelhauben* were still in general use.
(*Lambrecht Collection*)

The temporary resting place of members of 44th Reserve Division, believed to have been killed during the battles around Stuivekenskerke and Pervijse in late October 1914. Of the numerous men buried here at Vicogne Chateau on the west bank of the Ijzer, only one, Wehrmann Albert Kasten, who was killed in action on 24 October with the Machine Gun Company of Reserve Infantry Regiment 208, has a known grave. He is buried in Block 3 Grave 39 of the German cemetery at Vladslo.
(*Lambrecht Collection*)

The initial battlefield grave at Veldhoek of Reserve Oberleutnant Adolf Eckermann, 3rd Battalion Grenadier Guard Regiment 2 'Kaiser Franz', killed in action 11 November 1914. Eckermann now lies buried in the *Kamaradengrab* at Langemark.
(*Lambrecht Collection*)

An early trench of
Grenadier Guard Regiment
4 'Königen Augusta' near
Veldhoek.

A German supply waggon
moving along the Menin
Road near Veldhoek,
Winter 1914/15. Note the
temporary grave at the
side of the road.

Men of Reserve Infantry
Regiment 246 manning a
forward trench near
Polygon Wood,
November 1914.

Men of Infantry Regiment 104 in trenches near Le Gheer, November 1914.

Two views over the area of inundation west of the Ijzer. (*Lambrecht Collection*)

An abandoned German trench in the flooded area west of the Ijzer.

Footbridge spanning the inundations between the Ijzer and Stuivekenskerke, early 1915. (*Lambrecht Collection*)

Fuel tanks damaged by shell fire near Veurne. (*Lambrecht Collection*)

A captured British fire trench connected to the building to its rear by a mouse hole. Zandvoorde, November 1914.
(*Lambrecht Collection*)

The battlefield between Poelkapelle and Langemark, November 1914. The rows of dots in the middle distance are the bodies of some of the German fallen.

A group of British prisoners assembled in Poelkapelle prior to being marched to the rear. On the extreme left is a bearded German jäger wearing a distinctive shako. Second from right is a German cavalryman wearing the *Tschapka* of an Uhlan regiment.
(*Lambrecht Collection*)

British prisoners being marched to the rear by men of Reserve Infantry Regiment 246 after the capture of Reutel.

British Position stormed by Reserve Infantry Regiment 237 near Broodseinde, October 1914.

French Infantry in northwest Flanders, November 1914.
(*Lambrecht Collection*)

French casualties of the battles near Lombardzijde, November 1914. (*Lambrecht Collection*)

French supply convoy on the road between Oostvleteren and Ypres.

The town hall and main
square of Diksmuide, a
scene of intense earlier
fighting, photographed in
December 1914.
(*Lambrecht Collection*)

The wreckage of Messines
village after the battle.

The remains of Messines
abbey after the battle.

The ruins of Zonnebeke, December 1914.

Bikschote church after the battle. (*Lambrecht Collection*)

The destruction of the main square in Bikschote. Late November 1914.
(*Lambrecht Collection*)

Street scene in Beselare, November 1914. (*Lambrecht Collection*)

Survivors of a Reserve Jäger Battalion rally in a ruined hamlet near Langemark. (*Lambrecht Collection*)

Langemark village
in ruins after days
of shelling.

Wrecked gasometer,
Langemark, November
1914. At that time all
the larger villages in
Flanders had their own
gasworks and supplies
piped to the houses.

Views of a section of well revetted Bavarian forward trenches. Wijtschate, winter 1914/15.

Die Eltern [The Parents] by Käthe Kollwitz, located in the German cemetery at Vladslo.

The rationing system failed yet again – by now the troops were suffering greatly from lack of food and drink – but there was nothing for it but to carry on regardless, a situation not improved for the generally inexperienced troops by the constant presence of the stream of wounded making their way back themselves, or being transported by every conceivable conveyance. The rain continued to fall. Soaked overcoats weighed heavily on the wearers and rain dripped down their helmets and ran down their necks. It was hardly conducive to good preparation for yet another day of attacks, yet that was precisely what the latest orders were demanding. As if the conditions were not already bad enough for the chilled men attempting to get a little rest, despite chattering teeth and violent shivers, shortly after midnight torrents of British fire from the eastern edges of Poezelhoek and Reutel announced a limited night attack. Not much progress was made; in fact in places it was hard to know that there had been such an attempt, but for the numerous dead and wounded lying in the fields as a result of all the firing.

Day dawned on a thoroughly dismal scene. The orders were to press on as swiftly as possible with the advance westwards, but on the XXVII Reserve Corps front, and on that of their neighbours to the south, that was barely possible until after midday, apart from isolated ill-prepared attempts which had no chance of success. In fact it took until the early afternoon just to reorganise the units available and to move them into position for a systematic resumption of the offensive then, when the assaults began, they achieved nothing but more appalling casualties. Participating on the left of the Corps southern boundary were the Bavarian troops who, having moved north from the Arras area, had fought the previous day for Koelenberg.

Hauptmann Ottmar Rutz Bavarian Reserve Infantry Regiment 1[17] 3.

"We were now in a new sector. Previously the British had been attacking us and we, using advanced defensive tactics, had caused them heavy casualties. Now it was us who were to storm their defensive positions. Initially it was their positions by the village of Koelenberg on the main road to Ypres that were assaulted. That was on 20 October, when other companies of the battalion were doing the attacking. We closed up that evening, but were not involved in the battle. Dismounted cavalrymen marched on past us; it seemed to be a serious business. We spent the night in the nearby houses.

"21 October, a bloody day indeed, dawned. Heavy British artillery fire started falling and we spent the morning sheltering in the houses. During the afternoon an attack was launched. The companies deployed in the midst of very heavy shrapnel fire. The road to Ypres was reached and crossed. To our right a Saxon regiment advanced. The attack stalled. The commander of 4th Company, Oberleutnant F., my old friend, fell during the assault. Offizierstellvertreter G. of 2nd Company was killed. His men had always regarded him as bullet proof. He had happily survived the worst of days at the Saar Canal, at Lunéville and Einville, standing upright amidst the very heaviest fire. Now he had been mortally hit by a British bullet. In 3rd Company four platoon commanders were wounded, one after the other.

"That was the bloody day of Koelenberg. Night fell and we held the road. Volunteers from Saxony filled out our ranks. The air was suddenly full of firing. Shrapnel balls and shell splinters rattled as they hammered down on the road, whilst rifle bullets, thick as a shower of hail, cracked overhead. It felt as though all Hell had broken loose. We took cover as best we could in the road-side ditches. It seemed as though nobody was meant to quit this place alive but, miraculously, not a single shell found its mark in the ditch. An hour passed then all was quiet. The British had feared that a night attack was in progress. In fact a patrol from 3rd Company, creeping forward to reconnoitre the British positions, had got hung up on the wire. The alarm was immediately raised: hence the terrible burst of firing."

To the south, 3rd Battalion Reserve Infantry Regiment 247 was located in and around the farmstead at Zwaanhoek, located on the road to Passchendaele, about 500 metres north of the centre of Beselare. Many of them were lining the bank on the western side of the road, wondering what the day held in store for them. To its right were the Saxons of 53rd Reserve Division, occupying the so-called Holle Bossen, an area of relatively open woodland to the east of the road. As it became light, they could make out a thin line of trenches a few hundred metres further forward. These were the hard won positions of the remains of Reserve Infantry Regiment 246, together with some men of Reserve Infantry Regiment 245 who had ended up there after the previous evening's battle for Beselare. It was still misty enough to disguise movement when, at around 9.00 am, these men rose out of their slit trenches and began to move forward. They were soon swallowed up in poor visibility, only the sound of small arms fire betraying the fact that they were locked in a fire fight with British troops. This situation persisted for two to three hours, then word arrived that the waiting troops of Reserve Infantry Regiment 247, the only reserves available to XXVII Reserve Corps, were required to reinforce the faltering attack. On the face of it they were sorely needed, because out to the west of Beselare it was evident that something had gone seriously wrong with the command and control of what was already a confused battle. On the ground, such was the splintering, that the alleged attack had degenerated into local efforts by the surviving officers to do whatever was possible with the small groups of the various regiments who had gathered around them. They advanced if they could but absolutely no synergy was being developed and each effort just added to the casualty list.

Fortunately, after much effort, by that afternoon reorganisation and ammunition resupply was largely complete and 2nd and 3rd Battalions Reserve Infantry Regiment 247 were as ready as they would ever be to launch an assault westwards – to complete the capture of Reutel, they hoped. The troops deployed left and right then, following a short pause, the signal for the assault was given. Repeated out left and right, there was an immediate response as dense masses of German infantry rose from cover and immediately came under fire from well-concealed British positions. The troops hesitated but, thanks to vigorous leadership from the company commanders and especially from Major Strelin, commanding officer 3rd Battalion, they were soon pressing forward once more. Dangerously conspicuous in a light coloured coat, he urged his men forward. Despite every effort, however, the attack stalled forward of a copse of pine trees just to the east of Reutel. There was still no sign of the enemy but, employing the old infantry trick of listening for the 'crack' of bullets passing overhead, followed by the 'thump' of the firing signatures, it was soon established that the positions were somewhere in the copse. Leaving elements to continue to engage these targets, the remainder divided into two main groups to continue the advance north and south of the Beselare – Reutel road.

There was no question of systematic fire and manoeuvre, however. The inexperienced troops simply moved in densely packed groups of ten to twenty, where they were easily picked off crossing open ground. Hauptmann Stockmayer, commanding 9th Company Reserve Infantry Regiment 246, was spotted using his telescope to observe when he fell, mortally wounded through the heart.[18] Seizing the initiative, a courageous kriegsfreiwilliger named Steiner bawled, 'Hauptmann Stockmayer has been killed. Listen to my orders 9th Company!' but, before he could attempt to bring order from chaos, he too fell, riddled with bullets.[19] Conscious that the attack was failing, Major Strelin, pistol in hand, urged his men forward. However, the further advance achieved led to total catastrophe. Coming under increased fire from Reutel itself, the attack was forced away to the south, presenting a flank to the British entrenched around the village.

Very quickly the battalion was under fire from three sides and the inevitable result was a slaughter. Major Strelin fell[20] and one by one the remaining junior leaders all became casualties. The survivors clung to whatever local cover they could find then, as night fell and the shattered remnant also had the misfortune to come under fire from their own artillery, there was nothing for it, but to pull back to the start line. The attack, so bravely pressed home, achieved nothing and proved only that ill-prepared, poorly conducted assaults against experienced British infantry were nothing short of suicidal. The men involved in carrying out the attacks could not be faulted for their courage, however. That same afternoon Reserve Infantry Regiment 248 renewed their attack on Poezelhoek on the left of Reserve Infantry Regiment 245, no fewer than five separate times. Unfortunately, on each occasion they exposed a flank to British enfilade fire and they too achieved absolutely nothing. Having pulled back, Feldwebel Buck of 5th Company called the roll at Beselare. Only thirty six men were there to reply, though some did turn up later as stragglers. Major Burgund led the little band off to Dadizele, where it was augmented by some stragglers, but he himself had to report sick. It had been a terribly dispiriting day. The full extent of the casualties for this single day of battle was never established exactly. Indeed, so weakened was the right flank of 54th Reserve Division that the German position itself was in extreme peril until the arrival later of reinforcements from 53rd Reserve Division.

First on to attempt to reach the scene had been Reserve Infantry Regiment 242 which, more or less unscathed, had been directed to assembly areas around Terhand and to remain in Corps reserve for 21 October. Orders arrived about midday for two battalions to move forward in support of 54th Reserve Division, so 1st and 3rd Battalions headed off towards Zuidhoek, some two kilometres west southwest of Terhand. Advancing with difficulty through the hedges and copses of the close country, the units suddenly came under heavy artillery fire from high ground to the south. Immediately Oberstleutnant Hammer, the Second in Command (the commander, Oberstleutnant Pudor, had previously been detached to join Generalleutnant Bierling), altered the direction of the advance, turning to confront the fire which appeared to be coming from a crest line near a burning mill.

After a short battle the hill was taken and the British withdrew. However, no sooner had the battalions crossed the crest line than they came under heavy machine gun fire, which began to tear great holes in the ranks. There was absolutely no sign of the enemy. Hidden away in folds in the ground, behind hedges and in amongst buildings, the British infantry prevented further movement and, without exact knowledge of their positions and suitable fire support, it was obvious that to continue on with the attack would be suicidal. The only alternative was to go firm, so spades were produced and slit trenches began to appear in amongst the beets, but it was evening before any sort of continuous line had been produced. To the south, troops of 3rd Cavalry Division were also still attempting to get forward but, as has been noted, they were dogged by much the same problems. Added to this was the lack of firepower available to the dismounted German cavalry regiments and so for the next few days Oberstleutnant Hammer and his two battalions were subordinated to 16th Cavalry Brigade, assisting it to secure the area between Koelenberg and Kruiseke.

22 October dawned as another dreary day of indifferent weather. The ruins of Beselare were still smouldering and the condition of the forward infantrymen, trying to shelter from the incessant drizzle in wet trenches, was nothing short of desperate. There was talk of hot food but all the troops knew was that they had endured yet another freezing cold and wet night, with nothing but that which was left of their iron rations and food which they had been able to recover from the pouches of the dead to sustain them. There was little action between the infantry of either side; both appeared to have fought each other to a temporary standstill. Needless to say, XXVII Reserve Corps, spurred on by Fourth Army, was still demanding a resumption of the offensive. On the spot, Generalleutnant von Reinhardt, commander 107 Reserve Brigade of 54th Reserve Division, a man with a good overview of conditions at the front, regarded this as impossible. Creating a small reserve, he ordered that the western edge of Terhand be put into a state of defence, convinced that there would be a British attack to exploit the current weakness of the German position. In his opinion the lack of ammunition and food and the strain of the last two days of intense battle in terrible weather had seriously weakened the ability of his men to resist.

Despite these very reasonable reservations, there was nothing for it but to attempt to put the Corps orders into action, so the 54th Reserve Division decided to try to launch an attack round to the south of Beselare in the direction of Oude Hond and Oude Kruiseke. Appropriate orders were taken to the commander of Reserve Infantry Regiment 247, Oberst von Bendler, with the direction that the attack was to be a two battalion front, with his 1st and 2nd Battalions leading and a reserve being made available from the available elements of Reserve Infantry Regiment 248. A superhuman effort succeeded in ensuring that a hot meal was got forward to participating troops. This was wolfed down enthusiastically. It was their first meal for two days and, for many, the last they would ever eat.

At least on this occasion there was some sort of systematic artillery preparation. Beginning at 3.00 pm, the heavy guns began to bombard the road to Geluveld and the village itself, whilst a number of sections of light field guns were ordered to advance in intimate support of the attacking infantry. Advancing behind a light screen, which hardly merited the title of an advance guard and with 1st Battalion Reserve Infantry Regiment 247 right and 2nd Battalion left, for the majority of participants the assault went in by company columns. Leaving Terhand, the ground dropped and the advancing lines could see, away in the distance, the tops of the houses of Oude Hond, with Oude Kruiseke beyond. The British artillery reacted to the movement, bringing defensive fire down to the west of Beselare; however this did not prevent Reserve Infantry Regiment 247 from reaching the area of the Reutelbeek and the wooded areas just to the north of Oude Hond unscathed. Once they pressed on into the open ground beyond, however, it was a different matter and casualties mounted alarmingly.

In leading the way towards the Geluwe – Geluveld road, the commander of 4th Company, Hauptmann Freiherr von Soden, was mortally wounded, dying two days later in a field hospital. His sacrifice and that of other members of the regiment achieved nothing. British defenders manning a series of skilfully sited, mutually supporting strong points around Oude Kruiseke pinned them down with accurate fire and prevented any further forward movement. This stand off continued into the night; the British infantry making use of speculative rifle fire to induce their inexperienced German opponents into thinking that they were under attack and to reply with large quantities of fire which simply depleted their stocks of ammunition and achieved nothing. In the confusion there were several instances of patrols clashing, men falling victim to friendly fire and, in one case at least, to a complete rifle company engaging in an extended fire fight with another sub unit of the regiment, which was located nearby.

This nervousness manifested itself in various other ways. False and inaccurate reports went up the chain of command and a series of confusing orders was received. The artillery persistently fired short into the hastily dug German positions, causing near panic and, later that night, on the flimsiest of grounds – namely that a despatch rider had brought an unsubstantiated report of a British break through near Beselare to Headquarters 54th Reserve Division – a divisional order was issued at one point that the troops deployed forward were to withdraw to Terhand. Contributing to this chaotic picture was the effect on the men of exposure to extreme danger for the first time, the appalling weather, prolonged lack of food and sleep, a breakdown of battlefield administration and the endless nervousness caused by constant friendly fire incidents. Well might Fourth Army lament that, repeatedly, all along the front positions were being given up at night which had, expensively and with extreme difficulty, been captured during the day. It was about this time that higher headquarters had to resort to issuing orders that at night all weapons, with the exception of those of men on sentry duty, were to be unloaded and that fire was only to be opened on the orders of an officer or senior NCO.[21] That matters had deteriorated to this extent was yet another indictment of sending men whose training was criminally deficient, both individually and collectively, into battle against a first class opponent.

That same night, as a final blow at a time when morale was already at a low ebb, Generalleutnant von Reinhardt was killed in action by a single rifle bullet through the forehead. For three days and nights he had tirelessly led his men into action, appearing wherever the fight was hottest. This night was no different and he fell, hit by a stray bullet whilst visiting forward positions along the line of the Beselare – Geluveld road. He was replaced by Oberst von Roschmann but, for the time being, his death brought a pause to operations. Two days later, despite general exhaustion amongst the troops, a further attempt was made to renew the assault on Reutel and Polygon Wood, manned by the British 7th Division. Orders to that effect reached the forward units during the early evening of 23 October. Apart from a general wish to advance towards Ypres, there was mounting concern that the salient, whose tip was in the Beselare area, was extremely vulnerable to determined counter action.

During the hours before dawn on 24 October, increasingly heavy German artillery fire was directed against both places then, at precisely 7.00 am, the leading elements, comprising Reserve Infantry Regiment 244 of the Saxon 53rd Reserve Division and Reserve Infantry Regiment 246 of 54th Reserve Division, rose out of their trenches in to a cold, wet and misty scene and started to move forward. Having learned from recent, bitter experience, Reserve Infantry Regiment 244 chose to advance deeply echeloned against the British 21 Brigade, with its 2nd Battalion in the lead, with 3rd Battalion following up closely in support and 1st Battalion held back under the orders of the regimental commander, in reserve. As was so often the case at this time, the minute that the assault force came into view, extremely heavy British fire was brought to bear in an attempt to break up the attack in its early stages. Initially the movement was checked, but the junior commanders managed to rally their men and, after a short pause, the attack went on.

Hauptmann Dehgen, drawn sword in hand, dashed ahead, leading 5th Company Reserve Infantry Regiment 244 forward in an attempt to cross the danger zone and close up to the British lines as soon as possible, whilst leading sections of the adjoining Reserve Infantry Regiment 246 rushed to conform. At huge cost in men who fell to the well-aimed fire of the defenders, the forward trenches were rushed and the battle degenerated in to a desperate hand to hand struggle. The attack resulted in both regiments suffering extremely heavy casualties. A member of 3rd Battalion Reserve Infantry Regiment 246 later described the action that day.[22] **4.**

> "It was during the evening of 23 October. We were occupying dug in positions behind a wrecked house near Reutel, when our platoon commander arrived with the news: 'Tomorrow morning there will be a general attack all along the line.' We immediately began to prepare our battle equipment, ate the still plentiful rations and tried to get some rest. The following morning,

punctually at 5.30 am, we paraded in section columns on the Reutel – Ypres road and advanced in the half light, taking advantage of all the cover available. Immediately we came under fire from the enemy. This increased ever more as we advanced. Unfortunately some of our men began to shout *Hurra!* even though we were still more than one hundred metres from the British position.

"Everyone joined in the shouting and the result was that we came under lacerating rifle and machine gun fire. Instinctively, each individual took cover behind the houses which lined the road and so, within a few seconds, the attack stalled. The men were then wedged together in densely packed clusters behind every possible piece of cover. Each of them was convinced, despite the fact that the artillery began to fire very energetically, that it would be absolutely impossible to advance further. Casualties had already been heavy, but it was impossible to estimate how many there had been because individuals from other companies had suddenly appeared amongst us. The commander of 10th Company, Hauptmann Schließmann, arrived unexpectedly in our midst, tirelessly firing us up to get forward.

"The masses were gradually untangled as the men, some crawling and some dashing forward in bounds, crossed the lane to close up to the enemy positions. Casualties increased; there were wounded men lying everywhere, but a boundless anger at the enemy rose within us. It came as a sort of relief when, with loud *Hurras!* we hurled ourselves at the enemy trenches – at which point the British, almost without exception, threw down their weapons and put their hands up. They had still been firing at us when we were barely five metres form their trenches. That had a lot to do with the fact that some British soldiers still lost their lives at the point of a bayonet.

"We quickly arranged an escort group which led the prisoners away. We cast a final long look at this dreadful battlefield and saw a sight which we shall never forget. In and around the positions lay hundreds of dead and wounded. It was a sight which would have affected even the toughest and tears could be seen in the eyes of some of our comrades. After we had received some reinforcements, we went on further, reaching the edge of Polygon Wood to our front. The fire had reduced noticeably in intensity and our casualties were a lot lighter. We few, who had been lucky enough to come through unscathed, spread ourselves along the edge of the wood and immediately dug in."

Despite the losses to the German attackers, the fact is that on that day the British defence in the forward positions was assaulted in overwhelming strength and overrun. Having broken through two platoons of 2nd Battalion Wiltshire Regiment by about 8.00am, leading companies of Reserve Infantry Regiment 244 then rolled up the entire front line. In the Reutel area alone, thirteen British officers and well in excess of five hundred other prisoners were captured. However, the impetus of the assault was running out. It is certainly true that the wild charge continued forward to the outskirts of Polygon Wood, driving back a reinforcing company of 2nd Battalion Royal Scots Fusiliers, but courage and inspired leadership alone were insufficient to carry the day. 2nd Battalion Reserve Infantry Regiment 246 was caught in vicious cross fire and lost half its remaining strength; sections, platoons and companies began to get mixed up, rendering effective command and control of the contact battle almost impossible then, to cap it all, the German field artillery yet again managed to fire on their own troops as they crossed the higher ground west of Reutel.

Confusion increased and, noticing their difficulties, the British redoubled their efforts, well placed shrapnel fire taking a deadly toll and the commander of the British 7th Division, Major General Capper, throwing his final reserve – men of the Northumberland Hussars – into Polygon Wood, in what was the first action of any significance for a British territorial unit on the Western Front. Hauptmann Reinmöller and Hauptmann Raiser of Reserve Infantry Regiment 246 both fell wounded and, after all the losses, Reserve Infantry Regiment 246 was reduced in strength to barely one composite battalion. There was little the survivors could do but attempt to dig in where they were, still under fire, with whatever digging tools were to hand and, failing that, with their bayonets.

Oberstleutnant von Holleben[23] and his adjutant, both of Reserve Infantry Regiment 244, were killed and although the fight went on for the edge of Polygon Wood, once a coordinated counter-attack by 2nd Battalion Highland Light Infantry and 2nd Battalion Worcestershire Regiment was in progress, the defenders gradually got the upper hand. There was hardly an officer or senior NCO left on his feet and so there was nothing for it but to pull back. Oberst Straube managed to rally what was left of his regiment in a section of abandoned British trenches on a slight rise about two hundred meters east of the wood and Oberleutnant von Criegern, seizing the initiative, set about securing a position a short distance to the south, making use of every man remaining of 3rd Battalion who approached his location. It was just as well that the battle had also taken a severe toll of the British defenders, because these remnants of the two regiments which had stormed forward that morning were just about at the end of their endurance. Shivering in their shallow trenches as the rain poured down on them they tried to come to terms with what had happened to them and their comrades.

That morning the fighting strength of Reserve Infantry Regiment 244 had been fifty seven officers and 2,629 other ranks. By that evening they were reduced to six officers, seventy seven NCOs and 671 other ranks.[24] It had been an utter catastrophe, with only meagre territorial gains in compensation. Not only was this a tragedy in human terms, the withdrawal of the right wing of the advance had further endangered the position of Reserve Infantry Regiment 246. Moving forward, its regimental adjutant, Leutnant Sautter, annexed every straggler from Reserve Infantry Regiment 244 who came into his area and placed them in line with his own men. It was all in vain. Coming under severe pressure as the day wore on as a result of British small arms fire from the grounds of Polderhoek Chateau, it eventually became too much for the men of Reserve Infantry Regiment 246 and, without orders, they began to withdraw from their exposed positions, pulling back as it went dark all the way to the Reutelbeek; a move made even more difficult in the gathering gloom by general confusion and continuing heavy fire.

In addition to the loss of Major Holtzhausen, commanding officer 3rd Battalion Reserve Infantry Regiment 246, the regiment had lost sixteen other officers, eighteen offizierstellvertreters and 1,800 other ranks: in other words, some seventy percent of its strength; losses in the 2nd Battalion alone amounting to fifty seven killed, 310 wounded and 179 missing. The men were so exhausted and mentally drained that they were almost incapable of carrying out the simplest tasks at that time. One pressing job was the burial of all the fallen, but there were insufficient numbers left in Reserve Infantry Regiment 246 to carry out the task and at the same time hold on to their positions. The following day the services of Pionier Company 54 were requested to carry out this job but, such was the weight of fire, it proved impossible to complete and many of the fallen simply lay and rotted where they had been hit. [25]

Although Reserve Infantry Regiment 241 of 53rd Reserve Division had not been involved directly in the battle that day some of its men witnessed how the events had unrolled:

Unteroffizier Siegfried Brase Reserve Infantry Regiment 241[26] **5.**

"On 24 October, following the intervention at close range of German field artillery, which brought down fire against the enemy trenches despite all the small arms fire, neighbouring troops succeeded in launching an assault which cost the British four hundred prisoners, amongst them many officers. We had sufficient experience – and this was constantly repeated – to know that artillery preparation against the strongly constructed enemy positions was indispensable. Unfortunately, strong enemy reserves [*sic.*] prevented the success from being exploited.

"That day we marched all over the place so as to be able to meet any counter-attacks the enemy might launch. One wooded area, which we traversed and which had come in for special treatment by the enemy, lacked one single undamaged trunk. As though in silent complaint they lay on their sides, their bark damaged right up to head height. Finally, when it went dark, we lay down to rest alongside a forest track. Bullets cracked overhead, disappearing like ghosts in the night. We could hear the occasional German shout of *Hurra!*, then suddenly all was still and clear until, from a German trumpet, could be heard the melody of, *Strömt herbei, ihr Völkerscharen.*[27]

"Not a single soldier dared disturb that rare pleasure. It had, of course, the practical purpose of ensuring that German troops did not clash with one another in the dark. But afterwards the hellish rackets of batteries and rifles rang out once more, without ceasing. Three German guns, which fired the occasional salvo, must have been very close but, despite the spectacle, some of us managed to sleep the sleep of the exhausted, sending up huge snores. Despite the strictest warnings, there was some careless use of pocket torches and it is possible that this led to our downfall, because British patrols were creeping about.

"However it was not us, but amongst our reserve companies, that shells suddenly came down and caused serious casualties. Between 3.00 am and 4.00 am, however a dull thudding sound roused me out of a slight doze and a load of dirt flew into my face. Still everything was quiet, then there was a second strike. This time it was not a dud and there were appalling screams everywhere. Reeling, I got to my feet and made my way with others through the knee deep mud of a trench and out of the immediate impact area. It was not possible to evacuate the poor wounded men before daybreak and, by then, some were beyond help."

All along the XXVII Reserve Corps front a situation of near stalemate had apparently been reached. However, the German chain of command was unwilling to accept that state of affairs and so began a few days of lesser battles, during which little progress was made, but which took their toll on the infantry of the forward regiments in particular. Everywhere it was the same story. Rushed attacks, often lacking systematic reconnaissance or artillery preparation, were launched against the British infantry, which was skilfully husbanding its resources and exploiting superior field craft and defensive tactics to disrupt the German thrusts. On 25 October, there was a further attack towards Kruiseke, which was being held by men of the British 20 Brigade.

Because Kruiseke stands on a small rise and formed a salient in the British line, it was held in some strength. 1st Battalion Grenadier Guards was located to the north of the village, with two companies defending its eastern edge. Beyond these companies, came a reinforced company of 2nd Battalion Scots Guards, with 2nd Battalion Border Regiment and 2nd Battalion Gordon Highlanders spread along the southern edge of the village – later to be joined by 1st Battalion South Staffordshire Regiment. According to British accounts[28] the trenches and ground were in a shocking state because of artillery fire, there were no communication, or even crawl, trenches between the positions and there was no wire. Nevertheless the German army regarded it an extremely tough nut to crack, so this time more thought and effort had been devoted to the preparations. It is, however, true to say that Reserve Infantry Regiment 242, which was to be directly involved in the assault, commented that the necessary frontal infantry attacks launched in order to gain ground, improve positions and so increase the chances of a successful assault on Kruiseke, came at a high cost in casualties.[29] There was, nevertheless, adequate time for the assaulting troops to get into position and, within the limits of ammunition availability, the enemy positions were systematically bombarded for once.

Hauptmann Ottmar Rutz Bavarian Reserve Infantry Regiment 1[30] 6.

"That evening [24 October] I reported to the battalion commander and received orders to reconnoitre the 1st Company front line and its right hand contact point. The 1st Company was occupying positions directly opposite the British position at Kruiseke. After a lengthy search I found my friend, the commander of 1st Company. In amongst his company, he had inserted several squadrons of cavalry in the dismounted role. I then carried out the necessary checks on the company and reported its front line trace to the commander . . .

"We formed up behind farm buildings, ready for the assault! The British positions were to be captured today [25 October] at all costs. The heavy artillery preceded us. At long last! Just what we had been longing for! At daybreak they opened fire. From the roof of a house which was being engaged heavily by the British, together with an artillery observer, I watched the bombardment of the British trenches. The artillery ranged in swiftly. The first heavy shells crashed down on the British positions which were, perhaps, about four hundred metres to our front. First one great fountain of earth was thrown up, followed immediately by another and so it continued.

"The effect was shocking; the British could not withstand it and they leapt up out of their trenches with our machine guns taking them in their sights. Now was the moment of revenge! Shell after shell came down: thump, crash! More and more of the green [*sic.*] clad lads ran for it. Without their weapons! Back into the houses of Kruiseke. At that our guns began to bring their fire down there. Shrapnel and high explosive shells were fired and soon none of the houses was left intact. From the left came the report: the attack is about to be launched. The heavy artillery received orders to cease fire.

"That was it, the assault! The confident decision of our commander was to be carried out. We launched forward: Bavarians, hussars, Prussian and Hessian dragoons.[31] A British machine gun was still firing. Those who were in luck managed to avoid its destructive stream of fire by moving along a drainage ditch or behind a wall. I was hidden by a slight depression in the ground and the curtain of fire passed over me. I then raced for the cover of a wall and continued that way. We rolled up the British trenches from the right, capturing several and numerous prisoners. The battalion rallied in a hollow then moved off by companies to the western edge of Kruiseke, where we came under small arms fire once more. My company was now composed in part of Prussians, whom I had gathered in along the way. The western edge was finally in our hands at 4.00 pm . . .

"The Bavarian battalion was forever linked with the capture of Kruiseke. That evening there was an event of special importance: a British aircraft crashed in flames. The day's work was rounded off to perfection! The roadside ditch was rapidly developed into a trench and lined with straw, so our men were soon able to rest, protected by sentry posts pushed out forward. All the exits to the village were barricaded with everything that was lying by the roadside, with dead horses, cupboards and tables. Whilst we rested, the young troops to our right pressed home their attack, singing *Wacht am Rhein* and *Deutschland über alles*, whilst trumpet calls sounded the charge."

It is interesting to contrast the tone of the Bavarian report, written at the height of the war and employing a considerable amount of poetic licence, with the altogether more measured assessment of the Saxon Reserve Infantry Regiment 242 compiled some ten years later. It is clearly the case that the Bavarians attacked to the south of the men of 53rd Reserve Division and so had a somewhat easier time of it, but it is equally evident that the capture of Kruiseke was a much more complicated, hard fought and drawn out affair than Rutz suggests and was not finally completed until 26 October.[32] Having made the point that, despite all the privations and heavy losses of the past few days, the chain of command was still far too to ready to sacrifice uselessly and carelessly its inexperienced soldiers in attacks against the battle-hardened British, the regimental historian continues: 6.

"That can be the only explanation of the order received towards the evening of 25 October that, despite insufficient artillery preparation, the strongly constructed British position in front of Kruiseke was to be captured. A dark, rainy night began to fall. Trumpets and drums sounded the assault and, bayonets fixed, the companies stormed forward. Bullets from the machine guns located in positions amongst the ruined walls of the village, lashed them. Shells and shrapnel rounds exploded, tearing great holes in the ranks of the brave. However, progress forward was made, through the fences and the hedges, over wire obstacles and trenches. Direction was maintained by [the light of] the burning village.

"A British trench extended along its southern side. It was reached and bitter close-quarter fighting broke out with the trench garrison, degenerating into individual battles. Here there would be a daring charge at a desperately firing machine gun; there a vicious hand to hand fight but, finally, the whole village was captured. All the participating troops were totally mixed up, but the advance continued through the burning village. The British had pulled back, only to return, reinforced and to launch counter-attacks during the night. This was how elements of the battalion which had moved furthest to the west found themselves in a weakly defended set of farm buildings, which were suddenly attacked in strength by the British, cut off and for the most part, captured.

"Very few broke out. Other parts of the battalion, launching a hasty counter-attack against the position the British had captured lost their leaders here, including Oberstleutnant Garten, commanding officer 3rd Battalion. Not until dawn were they withdrawn to their starting positions. Some men of 11th Company, under Hauptmann Matthes, did not receive the order and so stayed where they were in a water filled ditch close up to the enemy and were able to pass useful target information and corrections to the artillery, which increased its rate of fire on the British. Oberstleutnant Hammer, having rallied the remainder of the regiment under cover of the foggy early morning, launched a renewed attack about midday. This time it was successful, though he was one of the first to fall, directly on the British positions.[33]

"This caused deep anger amongst the ranks who, furious, attacked with great aggression. The British were exhausted and surrendered in large numbers, the regimental commander [*sic.*] and more than 400 men were brought in.[34] Many regimental wounded who had had to spend the night in the village, but who had been treated in a knightly manner by the British, who dressed their wounds and placed them in cellars, could now be evacuated. However the hearts bled of all those who wandered about the battlefield which had fallen still by the approaching evening and saw all the brave lads lying there pale and stiff their rifles clenched tightly in their grip, young and old jumbled up: the face of one frozen in a victorious smile; that of another grimacing after a hard fight to the death. It was the fate of a soldier!"[35]

The final stages of the battle for Kruiseke were not restricted to the infantry alone. There was close involvement from 25 Cavalry Brigade, as a member of Leib-Dragoner Regiment 24 later reported: **6.**

"At 11.00 am on 26 October, the British began to leave their front line trenches. When our troopers saw this, without waiting for orders, they rushed forward from their inadequate dug outs under the command of Hauptmann Riedesel Freiherr zu Eisenbach, determined to take revenge on an enemy who had inflicted such heavy losses upon them. Despite being swept at times by machine gun fire, they charged into the British trenches. Before the British knew what was happening and were able to defend themselves [we were amongst them]. A few showed signs of attempting to resist so it was necessary to go in with lead and rifle butts to demonstrate that further resistance was useless. Encouraged, the dragoons pressed on into the narrow trenches and took one hundred prisoners.

"The Royal Scotch Guards [*sic.*] were astonished at the sight of our spurs and one officer, realising that their trenches had fallen to the cavalry, attempted suicide. The assault was continued on beyond these trenches towards Kruiseke, where a great many of the enemy were taken prisoner. Orders were then given to halt any further advance. The edges of the village were all pick-eted and once initial duties were complete, the dragoons helped themselves to captured British preserved rations and cigarettes."[36]

The fall of Kruiseke represented a severe setback to the British army, so no time was lost bringing it into a good state of defence in case of counter-attack. The cavalry units remained for a further three days to assist until they were relieved by infantry of XV Corps, whilst Reserve Infantry Regiment 242, terribly worn down by its high losses, reorganised into three composite companies and was reinforced by Landwehr Regiments 77 and 78 of 1st Landwehr Division, which had been engaged further to the north. The re-supply and rationing was still totally chaotic, forcing the forward troops to subsist on dry bread from their pouches, with swedes and potatoes lifted from the fields and surreptitiously boiled to supplement the last of the iron rations taken from the dead. Despite these handicaps, however, this scratch force managed to advance on

27 October, capturing Oude Kruiseke and continuing to press along the Menen road in the direction of Geluveld.

Meanwhile, north of the Menen road, French reinforcements, recently arrived, pushed forward from the area around Zonnebeke and pressurised units of 53rd Reserve Division which, severely worn down by the events of the previous days, soaked to the skin and also extremely hungry, were forced to stand to in their water filled trenches and shell scrapes and fight off this new assault, which was threatening the flanks of Criegern's brigade. Cramped for space between Keiberg and Mispelaarhoek, units of Reserve Infantry Regiment 243, the 3rd Battalion under Major Friedrich, in particular, found themselves severely pressed, short of ammunition and having to fight extremely hard at close quarters.[37] Fortunately, thanks to timely reinforcement by Reserve Infantry Regiment 244, the attempted thrust was slowed to some extent, but not before some British troops, advancing in parallel, succeeded in crossing the Broodseinde – Beselare road, occupying a group of houses and threatening the rear of 2nd Battalion Reserve Infantry Regiment 243. The situation was becoming increasingly critical and elements of Reserve Infantry Regiment 241 were also rushed forward to plug gaps.

Unteroffizier Siegfried Brase Reserve Infantry Regiment 241[38] 7.

"Some men of our battalion were moved forward during the night to the firing line as reinforcements. Another group, including me, was detailed the following morning to accompany our machine guns to a position further to the left. The gun teams, complete with weapons and accessories and, just like us, moved forward individually with five metre spacing from building to building or other cover to cover. The gun commander was immediately in front of me when, suddenly, just as though we had been pulled by the same cord, we lurched forward, blown by the air pressure of a shell passing just overhead. Further to the rear there were yells and shouts; the shell had come down amongst those following up and they were falling about laughing at us.

"However, we ignored them and hurried on to the place we had been directed to occupy. Having arrived, we infantrymen were superfluous; only the engineers were now needed to help prepare the position . . . our orders were to extend the line to the left, but when I, together with my comrade Körner, attempted to reconnoitre there, we came under such a weight of fire from two sides that it would have been hard to take the decision to place the men there. Much to our relief came a shout that there was a great lack of ammunition in the neighbouring trench and, content with our new task and having attempted to still our hunger with some unripe apples taken from a house in Broodseinde, we left some of our group there and headed off through enemy fire to take several bandoliers of ammunition to our comrades.

"Manning the trench we came across some Schwabian Landwehr men who had been calmly occupying it since the previous evening and were coolly firing at the clay coloured beings opposite whenever they spotted them up trees or attempting to fetch water. In order to help I removed my rifle stock and set about cleaning my rather ancient weapon. British Dum Dum rounds clattered harmlessly on the road to our rear,[39] whilst our machine guns had soon discovered worthwhile targets in the shape of enemy columns. As we later discovered from the war diary of one of our opponents, they were reinforcements which had been called forward from France.

"Suddenly very heavy artillery fire started coming down, initially around one of the buildings we had left back in Broodseinde, but then behind us and falling ever closer to our zig-zag trench, which actually offered almost no protection and we had barely begun to construct small fox holes . . . shouting came from our right. To the left my comrade Körner, who had had a good laugh at my expense a little earlier, was hit by rifle bullets twice in the arm whilst out in the open. Our artillery fell silent, their guns in some cases destroyed, in others they had no ammunition left to fire. We could no longer hear our machine guns either; they had been wrecked by shellfire though, remarkably, their crews, sheltering in their holes, were completely unharmed.

"As a result, the reinforced enemy could continue to work their way forward out on our right flank so, whenever we lifted our heads over the parapet to fire at the enemy, the howl of a shell made us duck our heads rapidly . . . we then noted that the whole of the line to our right was pulling back. The commander of the Jägers, Major B., our former commanding officer when we were in the garrison . . . having decided that to attempt to remain in our indefensible positions was tantamount to suicide, had given the orders for this. We tried also to conform. We had to leave the wounded behind, because to attempt to move them in the open would have put them at risk once more. We found some of them later, gruesomely beaten to death by the enemy . . . "

Orders arrived during the evening of 28 October for a resumption of the offensive. Morale was reportedly still good. XV Corps, under General Deimling, had arrived on the left flank of XXVII Reserve Corps and contact had been established by Reserve Infantry Regiment 247. The overall situation appeared to be promising, a Corps order issued two days previously had announced, 'The enemy has attempted by means of a failed thrust near Broodseinde to free itself of 'encirclement'.' In the East the talk is of a second Sedan and there are rumours that Calais has already fallen.'[40] If that was meant to be truthful then, at best, the statement was over-optimistic; at worst, if it was intended simply to bolster morale, it was deceitful in the extreme. Post war, much was made of the involvement of Bavarian Reserve Infantry Regiment 16 of the newly raised 6th Bavarian Reserve Division in this assault, but naturally the assault on 29 October was not solely the business of the Bavarians, who were actually grouped with Reserve Infantry Regiment 247 to form a 'Group Bendler' under the command of Oberst von Bendler of Reserve Infantry Regiment 247. In fact, the whole of XXVII Reserve Corps, with elements of XV Corps operating on its left, was involved in an assault, designed to

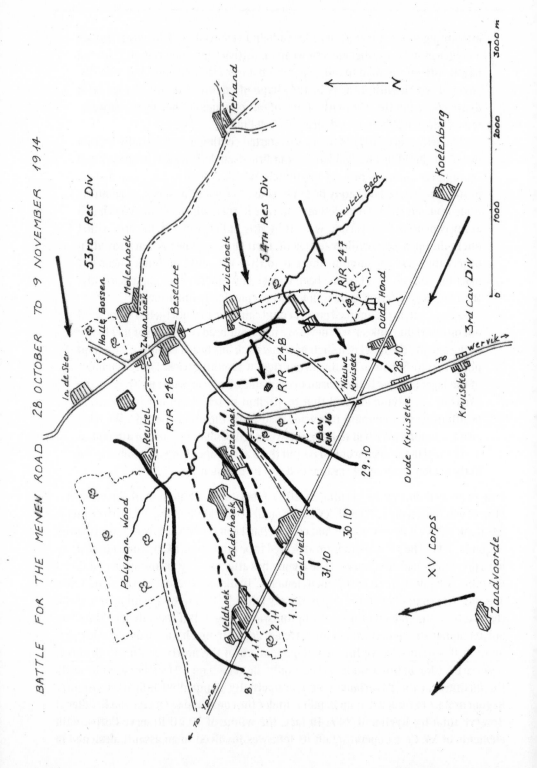

BATTLE FOR THE MENEN ROAD   28 OCTOBER TO 9 NOVEMBER 1914

advance the entire line from Poezelhoek to the crossroads 1 km northwest of Vieux Chien [Oude Hond].[41]

The orders to Group Bendler were to, 'work their way forward during the night 28/29 October, closing right up to the British positions; to direct the engineers to destroy any obstacles and to ensure that their light mortars opened fire immediately before the start of the attack, [which was scheduled for 6.30 am].'[42] The orders continued, 'The attack is to be pressed in the direction of Geluveld. Two battalions of Bavarian Reserve Infantry Regiment 16 will be subordinated to Group Bendler for the attack and are to be ready to move on the Geluwe – Geluveld road, with leading elements located at the crossroads at Koelenberg by 5.00 am, ready to receive further orders brought by runner from Oberst von Bendler . . . You are reminded once more that Bavarian Reserve Infantry Regiment 16 is equipped with Landsturm caps with a green covering.'[43]

These orders reached the forward battalions about midnight. Hauptmann Obermann, commanding 2nd Battalion Reserve Infantry Regiment 247 and who was killed later that day, had previously personally crawled right forward to reconnoitre the enemy positions, so had a clear idea about how he intended to approach the operation.[44] His battalion was on the extreme left in the angle created by the two main roads, with the others ranged out to the north. The waiting troops passed an extremely tense night. Already near exhaustion due to their previous efforts, they also had to ride out yet another disappointment. The planned artillery preparation was abandoned – due, it was said, to the fog. A few of the guns located right forward did manage to get a few shells off, but it was hardly enough to inspire confidence amongst men who had already seen the bloody consequences of insufficiently supported attacks.

There was not much sleep that night for the men of Bavarian Reserve Infantry Regiment 16 either. They received a warning order to be ready to move at immediate notice at about midnight and to 'keep the fact absolutely secret from the local inhabitants' then, at 2.00 am, a further order arrived, 'The Regiment is to assemble forthwith in the Panemolen – Vijfwegen road,[45] front facing south.' Within thirty minutes all units were correctly deployed and ready to march off. The 2nd Battalion was sent off independently to advance via Terhand to Beselare and there to link up with Group Mühry [107 Reserve Infantry Brigade 54th Reserve Division] and to remain under its command for operations the following day. Heading off in the other direction, 1st and 3rd Battalions departed to come under command of Group Bendler, already comprising Reserve Infantry Regiments 242, 247 and 248, together with the Saxon Infantry Regiment 105.

Already, taking advantage of his local knowledge, Hauptmann Obermann of Reserve Infantry Regiment 247 had led his men via a concealed route towards the enemy trenches and so incurred very few casualties initially when these forward British positions were overrun later. Unfortunately his luck then ran out. Moving up to the main road junction to determine the best way of continuing the assault, he was mortally wounded by a burst of machine gun fire from a dug in position some three hundred metres away. He was the second commanding officer of this battalion to fall since the beginning of this brief deployment in Flanders. As Obermann died in the arms of his adjutant, his men did everything possible to consolidate their position and to eliminate the offending machine gun, which was carving great holes in the battalion ranks. After several had fallen in the attempt, a group under Gefreiter Rominger managed to dash across the wide road and, from a position on the north side, silence the machine gun which was being manned by an old soldier who carried on firing to the last. This action had cost 1st Company Reserve Infantry Regiment 247 fifteen killed and seventy four wounded. Amongst the fallen was Oberleutnant Meßbauer, the company commander, and there were many dead Scottish soldiers lying in and around the captured positions.[46]

Reserve Infantry Regiment 247 claimed later that their surviving opponents took to their heels. Be that as it may, the enemy opposite Reserve Infantry Regiment 248 stood their ground, forcing 3rd Company Reserve Infantry Regiment 247 to abandon any thoughts of hot pursuit and to turn their attention to the flanks and rear of the enemy positions to the north of the road. By now the attack was a scene of considerable confusion because Bavarian Reserve Infantry Regiment 16 diverted to the south during its difficult assault and the area became one great confused mass of mixed sub units. There was further confusion caused by the fact that the Bavarians had been issued caps which looked similar to British ones at a distance and, despite the earlier warnings, they came under fire at times from the Württembergers whom they were trying to assist. Some progress was made – the line was advanced in places to a point some 700 metres beyond the junction, but at heavy cost because here a second battalion commander of 108 Reserve Infantry Brigade, Major Jordan, the experienced and courageous commanding officer 3rd Battalion Reserve Infantry Regiment 248, was mortally hit. As he was being carried to the rear in a groundsheet, suspended on a pole and covered in filth and blood, he spotted his regimental commander, Oberst Freiherr von Hügel, and called out to him, 'Herr Oberst, I was certainly not shot whilst withdrawing!'[47] He had nothing to apologise for and, although he was successfully evacuated to a field hospital in Kortrijk, he died of his wounds two days later.[48]

At 6.45 am 1st Battalion Bavarian Reserve Infantry Regiment 16 began to advance west, north of the Menen – Ypres road, skirting Oude Hond. 1st and 3rd Companies led off, with 2nd and 4th in support. Within a few hundred metres of the start line the lines of infantry began to come under artillery attack. Swiftly increasing the spacing within companies, the men of the 1st Battalion began to move forward rapidly in short bounds to get clear of the area which was under fire. In the process, a shell splinter carried away the gilded lion which surmounted the battalion colour and it was lost. One of the platoon commanders provided a detailed account of this first action

Offizierstellvertreter August Haugg 2nd Company Bavarian Reserve Infantry Regiment 16[49] **3.**

"Autumn mists swirled around the woods and copses near Koelenberg. It was 6.00 am 29 October 1914 when 1st Battalion of the List Regiment,[50] following a night march, stacked its weapons behind a wooded slope near

Koelenberg. The company commanders were ordered to the commanding officer. Immediately behind the pyramids of rifle could be seen fresh soldiers' graves, marked by simple wooden crosses, the piles of earth being surmounted by helmets. These, together with the rifle fire we had heard during the night, made us certain that we had arrived in a battle area. It was no easy task for a unit which had been raised as recently as 1 September from untrained manpower to detect and close up with the enemy in the hilly wooded area in front of Ypres and there engage them in open battle. These troops provided flank protection for Haig's army [*sic.*], which was attempting to thrust towards Menen. The previous day the word had been put about that the British located opposite us had shot their bolt, which gave us a feeling of superiority. However, even without this announcement, we should not have felt heavy-hearted when we first stepped onto the uncleared battlefield on 29 October. Jokes were told and we were not at all downhearted.

"Whilst we were still puffing our pipes around the pyramids of rifles, the captains returned. 'Pick up the weapons!' The 1st Battalion was to capture and hold the road junction to our front and the commanding officer, Major Graf Zech, gave out his orders. It was 7.00 am, the sun was still battling the fog. The battalion scattered as it moved through the wooded area and lost cohesion. Hasty defensive positions loomed up in the clearings. Now and then British stragglers were taken prisoner or shot down. It appeared that we were up against 'colonial troops', that is to say British soldiers who had seen service in the colonies.[51] We came under shrapnel fire near a copse, but we passed through the danger area at the double. Just short of the cross roads, an Oberst from Württemberg appeared. Initially he took us for British soldiers because we were wearing forage caps with dull green canvas coverings, rather than *Pickelhauben*,[52] until I called 'Good Morning!' to him in the thickest Schwabian accent possible. We duly linked up and agreed that I, together with my platoon and an assortment of Württemberg and Saxon stragglers, would advance on the road junction. Shrapnel shells burst overhead and suddenly a farmhouse, located by the cross roads at Kruiseke, about two hundred metres to our front, was blown up but, unopposed, we reached the road junction.

"The sun had dispersed the fog and we found ourselves standing before a broad re-entrant. Away on the heights opposite, some three kilometres distant, lay a village with a chateau, approached by a road running along a high embankment. Geluveld! The scrub-covered slopes beneath the chateau were criss-crossed with hedgerows enclosing cattle pastures, complete with small ponds which glistened in the sunlight. Here and there small cottages were to be seen. A road lined with poplar trees linking the small village of Kruiseke and Beselare ran along the heights where we were standing.

"The remainder of our 1st Battalion was deployed behind us, with the 2nd Battalion to its right and 3rd Battalion out to our left. Feeling our way forward, we despatched a patrol to our front and took a sort of possession of the road junction, in that I with my platoon of 2nd Company, together with some Wurttembergers and Saxons – about eighty men in all – dug in behind a hawthorn hedge which ran about two hundred metres to the west of the Geluveld – Beselare road. I then took up a concealed position of observation behind a stack of straw. Suddenly, on the embankment which led towards Geluveld, a six man patrol appeared, carrying their rifles under their arms. It disappeared before we had time to tell if it was friend or foe. About six hundred metres along the valley to our front were a group of small enclosures, surrounded by hawthorn hedges. Just as we were surveying them with a telescope, something whirred past my ear: 'Psst!' Was it a flying beetle? Once more, 'Psst!' By then I realised what it was, but if the shot was coming from in front or behind I could not say.

"Meanwhile it was 8.00 am. The sun was higher in the sky and the 'Pssts' were ever louder. We could see some sort of flashes coming from the hedge to our front. The telescope revealed them as belonging to rifle barrels pointing in our direction. I gave the order, '600 metres; hedge to your front; at the deliberate rate – fire!' The first shots rang out. This relieved the tension and everyone was much calmer. I could see that my men did not wish to be held back behind the hedge any longer; there was a desire to get forward. However, with only eighty men that would have been foolhardy. We remained in the fire fight for thirty minutes without suffering any casualties. Suddenly there came the rattle of machine gun fire and shrapnel rounds burst up in the air, scything down poplars to our rear. I increased the rate of fire. At one point I felt a sharp pain in my left foot. A runner dashed up, trying to pass a message to me but such was the racket that I could not make out what he was saying.

"I tried to get to my feet, but that was impossible; I had been shot through the left foot. I turned around on my stomach and looked to the rear, where a long line of riflemen was emerging out of the undergrowth. What was happening? I looked through the telescope and realised that they were our men. At this I sighed with relief. I saw Leutnant Heß and Feldwebel Feuchter, the other platoon commanders of 2nd Company, together with Leutnant Schmidt, commander of 3rd Company. The trumpets sounded and the drums beat. The 'List' men poured down into the valley and with loud shouts of *Hurra*, the charge went in against the gnarled old hedges. I could not participate; I lay there on my own from 11.00 am until it went dark. The battle raged in the valley below. Men went down, shot like hares; one man threw up his arms then disappeared entirely.

"During the afternoon heavy artillery fire came down. One poplar tree after another was felled. Their branches hid me as the stack of straw caught fire. Down below, I could see the battle develop from bush to bush, from hedge to hedge, climbing up the slopes, ever closer to Geluveld. Ghostly figures, glowing blood red from the dying rays of the sun, flittered about behind the wooded outskirts of Geluveld as the 'List' men took cover on the bushy slopes. The regiment had survived its baptism of fire."

In reality Bavarian Reserve Infantry Regiment 16 had taken very considerable punishment during this action, which was also observed by Ottmar Rutz, identified in print only as a 'Reserve Hauptmann in a Munich Regiment' in his 1917 book *Bayernkämpfe* [Bavarian battles]. In a piece entitled 'The 'Do-or-Die' Assault of the 16th Bavarians' he painted an altogether more sombre account of the events of the day.[53] **8.**

"On 29 October, the reinforcements arrived. They were the Bavarian 16th, Reserve Regiment List, the flower of the youth of Munich, in many cases students, almost all volunteers and full of fresh enthusiasm. All-out attack! The fresh troops advanced as though on the drill square and the British fell back noticeably quickly. We had warned the new troops that the British were cunning, sly, opponents. This demanded the greatest care during the advance to contact. In the meantime we moved further to the left to link up with Prussian troops. The attack seemed to be progressing much better than expected. The British artillery fire caused us no casualties as we stood by, near some mean dwellings, ready to move.

"The 16th stormed forward with youthful impetuousness. I was able to shout greetings to an old acquaintance, who was one of their company commanders, then they pressed on! Suddenly there was an appalling roaring and groaning noise mixed with whistles and cracks. The British, like us during the assault on Kruiseke, were firing heavy artillery. To our front, about two hundred metres away, the first heavy shells crashed down, right in the centre of one of the advancing lines of the 16th. Simultaneously shrapnel balls rained down, shells exploded in grey-green clouds of sulphurous smoke and bullets from British small arms fire whistled through the air. In their careless forward thrust the men of the 16th found themselves trapped in the carefully planned cross fire of British riflemen and machine gunners, firing from the flanks. A Prussian officer came hurrying across from the left and shouted, 'Why aren't the Bavarians getting forward? Why are they lying down out there?'

"Well there certainly was a line of riflemen from the 16th lying down, but they were not resting – they were either dead or wounded. We went into hasty defence and, silently, began to dig in. One heavy shell after another droned towards us. It was extraordinary how they groaned and droned through the air. Some of them came down not thirty metres to our front; the black fountains of earth flew into the air and cascaded down on us. These were moments of great tension. Would the next salvo hit us? Was it all over for us? But no, the next rounds crashed into a house to our rear, sending clouds of red tile dust, looking like a giant flower, into the heights. Off to our right shells and shrapnel bullets rained down on the twigs and branches of a copse. A shell splinter flew across, cutting off the calf of one of our runners. The poor man died as a result.

"The dead and wounded were carried to the rear. My acquaintance, the company commander of the 16th, had been killed. Evening fell. Our doctors came right up to the front line to help. Taking advantage of the twilight we made our way forward to a farmstead, which was already occupied by one of our patrols. A heavy shell had landed right in its dung heap, but the surrounding softness had completely contained it. The perimeter of the farm was immediately put into a state of defence and a trench was dug along the length of the farmhouse and extended to the left and right. It began to pour with rain.

"Numerous patrols went out to bring the poor 16th in – those still alive that is. They had been dreadfully mauled. Some individuals had been wounded five, seven, or even more, times. We filled the barns with the most seriously wounded. The rain grew even heavier. The British, fearing a night attack, brought down idiotic, unaimed fire. This lasted for about an hour and greatly hindered the work of rescuing the 16th . . . "

Much of what Rutz reported was confirmed at the time in a letter written home by a member of 3rd Battalion Bavarian Reserve Infantry Regiment 16, who was recovering in hospital in Heilbronn after being severely wounded during the action.

Einjährigfreiwilliger Gefreiter Ludwig Klein 11th Company Bavarian Reserve Infantry Regiment 16 [54] **8.**

"It was 29 October . . . We set out at 3.00 am . . . After some manoeuvrings, at about 9.00 am, the 3rd Battalion deployed into attack formation with 11th Company of the 16th on the left flank. This was somewhere near Geluwe. The way forward led over German and British trenches. Everyone had gone; there was nothing but corpses lying here and there, items of clothing and British ammunition. By 10.00 am on this day of what was designated a 'general assault', the British had abandoned all of this. Whenever we had a chance we went through everything. Suddenly there was heavy shelling. The thin morning mist had cleared somewhat and the British must have seen us. So we took cover in the old trenches.

"It was soon time to push on forwards. We had already had three men killed. Although it did not look too inviting, I lit up the last of my 'Munich Havanas' [cigars]. More and more shells crashed down near me and the hail of shrapnel grew ever thicker. As I was engrossed reading a British letter, a shell smashed in, not two metres in front of me and the stinking sulphurous fumes right in my face nearly choked me. However, it was nothing really and I was fine. I took it as a sign that I and the others were going to get through the day well, but that was far from the case. We came to a road and because there was no way forward through this heavy fire, we paused. This was where Hauptmann von Lüneschloss (battalion commander) passed on the order to his adjutant . . . Contact to the right lost . . . !

"It was not all that long until the fire slackened off and the ground-shaking thunder eased a bit. I ate some of the previous day's biscuits. At 1.00 pm came the order, '3rd Battalion, form skirmishing line, forwards!' – and off we went – but where to? For most of those involved, it was to their death. It must have been about 1.45 pm (my watch had just stopped), when we came to a gentle rise. A few shots rang out. 'Down!' Were we being shot at by our own side? Surely not! Where from? Nobody could see a thing, but we could certainly hear [the firing] We first waved our firing flags and then took the covers off our caps, in the sure belief that the German infantry had mistaken us for British troops . . .

"Suddenly someone shouted, 'Left, British dug in on top of the hill!' and the order came, 'Up! Double march! Down!' 'Sights at 400. Aim carefully . . . !' Using the first available cover, at first we all fired too short.[55] We were right in their line of fire; were literally swamped by it. My friend Schram was the first to fall; shot straight through the centre of his head. He threw me an unforgettable glance as though he was trying to give me a message of farewell! A moment later came the order, 'Up! Double march!' As I rushed forward I felt a violent blow to the stomach. Realising what had happened, I crawled as best I could in my weakened condition to a nearby ditch along the road towards Wervik. It was a miracle that I reached it still in one piece.

"Just prior to this our company commander, Oberleutnant Peuckert, shouted to the wounded Feldwebel Gies, 'I must have reinforcements'. Hardly had he spoken than he collapsed, hit by a bullet in the head. It was a fine death. He did not suffer at all. I myself lay with my face down in the ditch whilst bullets whistled in all direction over me. Shells crashed down so close that I was sprayed with earth. Eventually, darkness fell and the shelling and machine gun fire died away . . . Let me finish by returning to the assault. According to all the reports, only five men of my 3rd Platoon are still alive; the remainder are all dead. Apparently the situation was somewhat better in the other companies of 3rd Battalion, but they certainly suffered badly. The British had dug themselves in well in a tobacco field on the top of a broad hill and they had fought desperately . . ."

In addition to the work of the German stretcher bearers, who later recovered Klein, along with many others, the British were also involved in clearing the wounded from the battlefield. Numerous wounded German soldiers, including Leutnant Abelein of 4th Company, were captured in this manner. As has been noted, the organic units and formations of 54th Reserve Division endured a day almost as trying, if not quite so deadly, as the Bavarians. In yet another example of the woeful preparation of these troops for battle, their inexperienced divisional artillery repeatedly fired on their own troops, adding to the general confusion and leading a sorely pressed Hauptmann Theinert, commanding officer 1st Battalion Reserve Infantry Regiment 246, to send the following desperate message back to regimental headquarters that afternoon:[56]

"3.00 pm. Report to Regiment. In the past five minutes our own artillery has fired eight rounds into our positions. In the name of all the men subordinated to me, I request your assistance. Enemy artillery fire is coming down heavily on our trenches either side of the lane leading westwards from Reutel. Where are our artillery observers? I am complaining officially about such incompetence. Update at 3.07 pm. Nine or ten shells fired by our own artillery have just landed immediately behind our trench."

The regiment later commented that their gunners candidly admitted to them that they had really only learned to shoot and engage targets efficiently during the winter of 1914–1915. Whilst honest, this is a further lamentable admission that men were committed to battle long before their training was at all adequate. It is impossible to estimate how many lives this cost but there is no doubt that poor artillery support was at least in part responsible for many reverses and failures in these early battles: most noticeably on the battlefields of Langemark, Bikschote and during the long drawn out struggle to capture Diksmuide. Although the price paid on 29 October was extremely high (Bavarian Reserve Infantry Regiment 16 alone lost no fewer than 349 all ranks killed in action that day), progress had been made and there was some satisfaction that well-prepared British trenches, reinforced with timber and provided with some overhead cover had been captured, despite the near-total failure of the artillery support. Losses were severe on the British side, too, and XXVII Reserve Corps took four hundred prisoners.[57] All along the Corps frontage the battered survivors attempted to dig protective cover and consolidate their gains. After the adrenalin rush of the day, reaction set in. No hot food was available for the time being, so the men shivered inside their soaked greatcoats and gathered up everything they could find in an attempt to stay warm. Straw, abandoned British coats and blankets were all pressed into service and a few lucky individuals were able to assuage their hunger with tins of British corned beef or packets of biscuits. Later that night some food did get forward, but it proved to be impossible to distribute it to everyone and many went hungry for yet another night.

It would be reasonable to assume that after such an experience Bavarian Reserve Infantry Regiment 16 would have been withdrawn from the battle, but not a bit of it.[58] Such was the importance of the drive along the Menen road that it was to remain temporarily under command of 54th Reserve Division and was to participate in the renewal of the offensive the following day. Inevitably, after such a long and hard fought battle, there was a delay in issuing orders down to unit level but later that night the divisional orders arrived.[59]

"Today the Division, including attached troops, namely Bavarian Reserve Infantry Regiment 16, Reserve Infantry Regiment 242, 2nd Battalion Reserve Field Artillery Regiment 53 and Landwehr Detachment Waxmann, is to attack the enemy opposite it and is to carry the attack on to Geluveld once the assault has been prepared by the artillery.
– Group Mühry, linking up on the right with 53rd Reserve Division and on the left with Group Bendler, is to advance on the sector southern edge Polygon Wood – Polderhoek – Poezelhoek.

– Group von Bendler, continuing the line is to advance on the chapel just to the south of Geluveld and Group Waxmann is to conform to this from the positions taken up tonight, maintaining close contact with Group von Bendler.

For the purpose of preparing the attack, the artillery is to open fire as soon as observation is possible.

The Divisional staff and reserve will remain initially in Terhand."

Although the intention had been to renew the assault during the morning of 30 October, that proved to be quite impossible and, in the event, fresh orders, which arrived at 3.00 pm, directed 3rd Battalion Bavarian Reserve Infantry Regiment 16 and Infantry Regiment 105 to renew the advance along the Ypres – Menen road towards Geluveld at 4.00 pm. Moving rapidly in short tactical bounds progress was made for a few hundred metres, but there was a swift and violent reaction from the British defenders and shrapnel came down with such great accuracy against the advancing waves that Bavarian Reserve Infantry Regiment 16 later stated that the ranks fell like ripe corn before the scythe and that there were also major problems for the troops who attempted to advance against the windmill on the slopes before Geluveld, who came under intense rifle and machine gun fire.[60] There were also to be major problems in this area the following day.

In an attempt to rebuild momentum, Oberst Feucht, commander Reserve Field Artillery Regiment 54, personally led a section of his guns forward along the main road to provide direct fire support to the attacking infantry by engaging the buildings adjacent to the grounds of the chateau, but little was achieved and the gunners suffered badly as a result. Nevertheless, the attack was reinforced as 1st Battalion Bavarian Reserve Infantry Regiment 16 joined in. Once more some progress was made but the sacrifices were all for nothing when a cyclist arrived from the rear with orders to break off the attack and withdraw to the start line. About 6.00 pm the assault was discontinued; some wondered why it had ever been launched. Amongst the casualties were Leutnant Brenner, 11th Company killed,[61] and Offizierstellvertreters Böhm and Thiemann of 9th and 10th Companies. After the losses of the previous day, these additional casualties could be ill afforded.

At battalion and regimental level there was a growing awareness of the scale of the difficulty involved in attempting to drive directly at Ypres and a realisation that more was being demanded of them and their men than they could reasonably be expected to deliver. Nevertheless, further up the chain of command, where more detached views were being maintained, there was never any doubt that the assault against Geluveld would be renewed yet again on 31 October. During the evening of 30 October, a conference and orders group of all regimental and battalion commanders of 54th Reserve Division was convened in Kruiseke. This occasion made such an impression on officers of the Bavarian Reserve Infantry Regiment 16 that a reconstruction of elements of it appeared later in the regimental history.[62] **6.**

"Oberst von Oldershausen, Deputy Sector Commander, chaired the meeting. 'Gentlemen, are we all present? Then please pay attention! What is our current situation? Who is in the centre?' '1st Battalion [Reserve Infantry] Regiment 16 between the two roads, 600 metres forward of the crossroads.' '3rd Battalion left as far as the Ypres road.' 'To the left of them again is [Reserve Infantry] Regiment 247, with its right flank on the Ypres road.' 'Good! During the night the two battalions are to set out and work their way forward unnoticed towards the British positions – The assault on Geluveld will begin at dawn . . . '

"At that point there was noticeable movement in the back rows when the word 'battalions' was mentioned. The Oberst broke in: 'Do you gentlemen have something to say?' The commanding officer of 1st Battalion Bavarian Reserve Infantry Regiment 16 [Hauptmann Rubenbauer] began, 'Excuse me, Herr Oberst. The word 'battalions' has been mentioned. We in the centre no longer have a battalion; scarcely a recognisable company. The men have been in battle now for forty eight hours and they have had no sleep for three nights. The troops are exhausted. We have no infantry reserves behind the front. I regard it as impossible to conduct a purely infantry assault against the strongly dug in British positions successfully, unless it has been preceded by really heavy artillery preparation.'

"Do you say impossible? – There is no such thing as impossible! We are all soldiers and we must accept the risk of death! . . . Are you saying that the Bavarians are not willing to attack?' 'That has nothing to do with it! But my responsibility to my troops obliges me to draw attention to the fact that without strong artillery support, we shall be unable to sustain the assault!' 'You talk of responsibility? Well just calm down – you do not have any such responsibility! When the order is given the responsibility lies with he who gives it – and who will know how to shoulder it. Your sole responsibility is to ensure that the order is carried out correctly! . . . '

"At that Oberst List got his feet slowly, deepest concern etched in his face. 'If I may add a word – I too am of the opinion that a simple infantry attack conducted against such a cunning, intelligent and strongly dug in enemy will either fail or simply lead to a bloody sacrifice of immense proportions. I would urge that heavy artillery be brought to bear during the course of the night and to continue until the positions are thoroughly softened up for an assault. Only then should we advance with infantry – otherwise what remains of my regiment will be lost as well!' 'A delay in the attack is out of the question. Geluveld must fall tomorrow! – These are the orders. We have our duty to do! What will be, will be! There is no time to be lost!'

"The general impression was that the majority of the commanders present inwardly shared the expressed opinions, but whilst this exchange of views was occurring, the commander of the Battlegroup, Oberst von Bendler, had stepped forward. After a short greeting, he pointed at a sketch of the positions and in a clipped voice began, 'Orders for the attack on 31 October . . . '

The enemy was reckoned officially to be occupying strongly constructed positions straddling the Menen road and to have reserves back in the village itself. Of course, in reality, the British defenders had had no time, opportunity or materials to dig anything but the most rudimentary trenches and to erect barricades with whatever came to hand but, in war, perception is everything and, in any case, the mere occupation of slit trenches or well dug shell scrapes conferred an enormous advantage on steady, well trained troops armed with magazine fed rifles. The primary assault was to be launched by Rubenbauer's 1st Battalion Bavarian Reserve Infantry Regiment 16 and was to aim at the centre of the Chateau grounds, with Reserve Infantry Regiment 248 to the right. Out on the left was the 3rd Battalion, with Reserve Infantry Regiment 247, Infantry Regiment 105 extending the line of attack, south of the main road. As the day wore on, elements of Infantry Regiment 143 also became increasingly drawn in to the battle. Weapons were to be unloaded, bayonets fixed, the battalions were to move forward under the cover of darkness and the artillery 'as far as possible' was to support the attack with fire, which Bendler estimated would last only from 6.30 to 6.40 am! One of the members of 2nd Battalion Bavarian Reserve Infantry Regiment 16, not directly involved in the attack initially, was told off to act as liaison officer to the guns.

Landwehr Oberleutnant Ernst Glunk 5th Company Bavarian Reserve Infantry Regiment 16 [63] **9.**

"Four heavy 210 mm howitzers had the task of softening up the British positions at Poezelhoek and Polderhoek for the assault. This information reached 2nd Battalion during the early morning of 31 October. The battery of heavy artillery had driven forward to well protected positions behind a hill southeast of Beselare. The infantry located forward in trenches were warned to take cover hard up against the forward walls of the trenches because shell fragments could fly backwards and land well in rear of the trench lines. They had established an observation post in a shelled house at Westhoek, just where the road from Beselare bends and I was ordered to proceed there, so as to direct fire onto British positions which I, together with two kriegsfreiwillige, had reconnoitred on a previous patrol. Two artillery officers acted as observer and fire control officer. An infantry major in charge of the attack was also there, as were Oberleutnant Engelbrecht and I.

"A telephone line linked the observation post to the battery and thence to higher headquarters. Two unteroffiziers manned the telephones and runners waited to carry orders. From the upper story we were able to see over the entire countryside as far as the heights by Veldhoek and along the valley of the Reutelbeek down to Geluveld. British trench lines ran along the wall of the park at Polderhoek and snaked in front of the houses and stables south of the park. Hidden away in scrub land along the Scheriabeek British machine guns chattered away, having already done so much damage to our troops yesterday and the day before that. The roar of British batteries came from the park and from the wood adjoining it to the north. That was where the main British position was located, a good thousand metres from our observation post. Muzzle flashes could be seen and clouds of powder smoke rose from the houses in Poezelhoek.

"We opened fire . . . shell fragments and large chunks of metal flew about above the British trenches. The artillery observation officer called the distances off to the Unteroffizier on the telephone. He, in turn, passed them to the battery, together with the number of metres to be added for the next shot. The battery reported back which of the four howitzers would be firing and with what elevation . . . Things got rough for our opponents. Six heavy direct hits smashed into the British trenches and each time parties of British Tommies fled into the safety of the park. It was no wonder; a fragment weighing fifteen kilograms flew all of 1,100 metres back at us. However the British troops were equally tough, digging in once more some few hundred metres behind the old positions.

"Midday arrived. Curse it! The ammunition was running out. There were only ten shells left then, all of a sudden, a strange performance was played out in front of our eyes. Behind the rows of trees and the hedges along the Veldhoek heights, troops came into view. More and more of them descended the hill. They were in regimental strength [i.e. about 2,500] and were spread out over about five hundred metres between the railway line to the north of Geluveld, down towards the the Polderhoek – Veldhoek road and behind the British positions. Were they friend or foe? The distance was too great, still about 1,800 metres. We assumed that they were British reinforcements. Slowly they approached . . . Through the tripod binoculars their helmets and knapsacks came into view. So Germans, Germans! Our joy was great. Now they would either surround the British or throw them back to Polygon Wood.

"However they, unknowing, turned away towards Geluveld. Only then did they realise that they had had the possibility of outflanking the enemy on the left and taking them in rear. Too late! Already the British artillery was bringing down protective fire in front of them. As we later discovered, they were Württembergers from Reserve Infantry Regiments 246 and 247 [sic.]. New troops appeared to our rear in the area of Zuidhoek. The enemy artillery brought down such huge quantities of fire against them that to remain in our observation post became ever more hazardous. Shrapnel balls smashed down through the tiles on the roof, stones were knocked out of the walls, chunks of mortar began raining down and a shell exploded in the cellar. It felt as though all hell had broken loose. The telephone links to the battery and the division were shot up and, because of the lacerating fire, it was impossible to repair them.

"The assault was in full swing. Two hours later we launched our attack on the positions to the north of Poezelhoek. Hit in the left thigh, I hauled myself forward another twenty paces to a stack of straw . . . Meanwhile the daring

16th pushed on, with the British not halting them once more until they were almost at Polygon Wood [*sic.*]. French reinforcements in overwhelming strength had sprung to their assistance."

Hauptmann Rubenbauer, commanding officer of 1st Battalion Bavarian Reserve Infantry Regiment 16, following the death in action of Major Julius Graf von Zech auf Neuhofen[64] on 29 October, later described how the day unfolded around Geluveld itself. By then, it will be recalled, the regiment had been involved in the assault on the approaches to the village for forty eight hours. On the 29 October alone the battalions had been involved in an eight hour battle at close quarters which had seem them clear all resistance up to the edge of the grounds of Geluveld Chateau, capturing hundreds of prisoners in the process but losing heavily themselves, then they had been directly involved in a further vain attempt to win ground to the west on 30 October.

Hauptmann Rubenbauer 1st Battalion Bavarian Reserve Infantry Regiment 16[65] **10.**

"Midnight had come and gone by the time orders for the forthcoming major attack on 31 October reached the forward positions. It was a cold rainy night, lit only by the flames of the burning Beselare and the countless great stacks of straw which dotted the landscape and which had been set alight by the fire of the enemy. Rifle fire cracked overhead constantly, but we did not reply, concentrating instead on silently preparing for the start of the operation under cover of darkness. At 6.30 am precisely, just as ordered, there was the crash of a surprise concentration of fire to the front of 1st Battalion where the British were occupying positions on the southeast edge of the village. As dawn gradually broke there was activity all along our lines. Surging forward from the dense hedgerows and up the slope, the lines of infantrymen, mostly from our 3rd Battalion, worked their way in bounds, wave after wave, up the rising ground.

"British shrapnel fire fell on them like iron rain. A densely held British trench was overrun and about two hundred prisoners were taken. Hardly had they been assembled on the Ypres road ready to be moved back, than enemy shells came down amongst the column of prisoners. Shouting fearfully, they scattered. Dozens of them lay where they had fallen on the road, the remainder rushed wildly down the hill where they were reassembled by our reserves. The attack continued, but more slowly, making forward progress step by step. On the southern slope below the village around the windmill, the British had dug themselves in strongly. The defenders' fire beat off every attempt to close up to it. Salvoes of artillery fire thundered from the direction of the village and machine guns hammered away . . . Each assault was pushed back disdainfully and the battlefield became littered with dead and wounded soldiers as the intense fighting went on hour after hour.

"Finally, at 3.12 pm, our heavy artillery, which had just been brought forward during the previous hour, brought fire down on the windmill. One round, followed by a second, then a third sent it spinning into the air. How it cracked and splintered! That was the turning point. The garrison fled and the way was open. In no time flat our lines rushed it, tumbling forward one after the other. Everyone charged forward against Geluveld. For a moment there was a pause in the enemy fire, rather as if they were taking a deep breath, then down it came again, with renewed strength, like a violent storm. It was clear that the enemy could tell what was at stake! Suddenly the leading troops wavered then fell back into the hurricane of fire which was being directed at them. It was a truly critical moment. The trumpeters from the left to the right flank blew the call for the charge and, their blood up, everyone responded, Emerging from behind hedges and out of cover, the assault was carried forward: line after line pressed on, closing gaps – Bavarians, Saxons and Württembergers. A thousand shouts of *Hurra!* echoed over the battlefield in one great cry of victory, which could be heard above the rattle of machine guns and the thunder of the guns.

"Rolling forward violently in waves like giant breakers crashing ashore the storm formations forced their way into the village. Geluveld was ours! After a short period of fighting from house to house, the enemy pulled back, abandoning their positions. The firing died away, evening fell with early mist gradually clearing to a clear starry night enfolding the bloody Flanders battlefield. Listening posts were sent forward whilst the remainder, nerves trembling and totally worn out dug in.

"Suddenly a runner came rushing up and tumbled breathlessly into the trench, throwing himself exhausted at our feet. 'The regimental commander has been killed!' 'What are you saying – the Oberst?' 'Dead – over there by the hedge in the grounds of the chateau – during tonight's assault – right in the front line!' Good Heavens! We had not even been spared that! We looked at each other and there were tears in every eye. A need for revenge grew silently and bloodily in our hearts. He lay there in the grounds of the chateau, his white face set and determined; in amongst his faithful soldiers. Covered in a blood soaked coat, he was laid to rest there for all eternity at the foot of a severed tree stump, upon which hung his field cap. God grant him peace."[66]

List was not the only senior casualty that day. As dawn broke, the commander of XV Corps, General der Infanterie von Deimling, was joined by General Schäfer, Oberst von Bendler and the artillery commander, Oberst von Feucht, for a meeting at the crossroads at Kruiseke. Either by chance or design, British artillery fire caught this group whilst they were conferring. Bendler and Feucht were both mortally wounded, as were their accompanying adjutants, whilst the remainder of the group were hit, but only lightly wounded. At unit level, during a day of mass casualties, 3rd Battalion Bavarian Reserve Infantry Regiment 16, for example, suffered extremely heavy casualties on top of those of previous days and Reserve Infantry Regiment 247 ended the day with almost all of its officers and, in particular, almost every platoon commander, dead, wounded or missing.

Rubenbauer's account of the capture of Geluveld is of course one man's view of a very hard fought battle of changing fortunes and is, inevitably, both a subjective and a simplified version of events on a day when British resistance was strained almost to breaking point and German losses became almost intolerable. The attack jumped off as ordered at 6.30 am precisely and, where in the centre and on the right the attackers had closed almost up to the British positions near the grounds of the chateau, the men of Bavarian 16th Reserve Infantry Regiment had no difficulty is overrunning the defence and securing that part of the attack frontage. Out to the south, it was a different story. Reserve Infantry Regiment 247 and 3rd Battalion Bavarian Reserve Infantry Regiment 16 found that their attack could make no progress against the area of the windmill and, that being the case, the orders to the men near the chateau were to hold in their current positions: which they did for several hours.

Gradually, more and more German troops were fed into the battle and, during a bitter, attritional struggle which saw elements of three regiments pressing forward, ground was gained painfully slowly, whilst casualties from British artillery and small arms fire thinned out the ranks. The shortage of artillery ammunition referred to by Glunk was typical, affecting the indirect fire support all along the attacking sector. However, despite the lack of really effective gun fire and at the cost of yet more casualties, caused by what was later described as an 'extraordinary hurricane' of fire from rifles, machine guns and artillery, some dogged progress was made. Finally, after hours of attacks which surged forward only to be beaten back, then advance once more, by around 3.00 pm, the area around the windmill to the south of Geluveld was finally secured.

All the 'ebbing and flowing' in the German accounts obviously takes into account the fact that as early as 12.30 pm the surviving men of the King's Royal Rifle Corps (less those captured), the Queen's and the Loyal North Lancashires had been driven out of the village, some 60 pounder guns had been captured and a spirited hasty British counter-attack had been driven off, but it was not until the sudden slackening of the defensive fire and a more general German advance from all the survivors of the regiments in the vicinity during the early afternoon, that the German hold on the village was anything other than precarious. The taking of the prisoners and the guns is clear proof that, at this stage of the battle, the German advance into Geluveld had been significant, if limited, though the British Official History maintains a fairly peevish tone about these events, levelling, for example, the accusation at Infantry Regiment 143 that it was 'To [its] everlasting disgrace' that some of its men 'clubbed and bayoneted' some of the KRRC to death.[67] Even if true, it is hard to see why this incident merited mention in the Official History. It is not hard to find innumerable examples where the butt was on the other skull, so to speak.

Interesting to note, it was about this point that the heroic counter-attack by about 350 men of 2nd Battalion Worcestershire Regiment under Major EB Hankey was launched across open ground from the direction of Polygon Wood. The British Official History, admittedly written before very much was available from German sources, with the exception of the unsatisfactory monograph *Die Schlacht an der Yser und bei Ypern im Herbst 1914* [Translated as, 'Ypres 1914'], provides what appears to be a quite misleading version of events in Geluveld that afternoon. According to the British account, the attack hit 'The Bavarians (16th Reserve Infantry Regiment) and other Germans ... [who] were enjoying the repose of victory, searching for water and looting and [were] in no expectation of such an onslaught. They offered no resistance and were soon fleeing back through the village.'

The British account then describes a further move by Hankey's fourth company which 'extended through the village to the church and churchyard', followed by patrols, 'which established that 'Geluveld was definitely in British hands and concludes, 'The second successful counter-attack had achieved extraordinary results; for the Germans, though in great numerical superiority, ceased their efforts to capture Geluveld. ... It was now about 4.00pm and the German failure near Geluveld was complete.'[68] Now, it is perfectly clear that the Worcesters' action was of decisive importance. A critical situation had been averted and a complete rupture of the British line had been prevented, but to claim that it brought to an end German efforts to capture and hold Geluveld is hard to sustain. Not one single German account – and there are several – supports that interpretation. In fact the only mention of the intervention of the Worcesters at all is contained in the regimental history of the Württemberg Reserve Infantry Regiment 247.[69]

> " ... but we felt that they were weakening. No matter that their artillery was firing as fast as the guns could be loaded, no matter how the rifle fire cracked across the meadows, we got ever closer and, at about 3.00 pm, Geluveld was in our hands. The village itself was in an utterly indescribable, chaotic state. The thunder, of the guns and the chattering of the rifles was continuous then, amidst it all, came the shout, 'The British have forced their way back in!' Only with great difficulty could the commanders bring the situation back under control. Major Gutscher, who by now was commanding the regiment, was wounded in the upper arm by shrapnel but stayed in the village and directed the defence. The streets were filled with rubble and everywhere shells and shrapnel crashed down. For the time being there could be no question of a further advance; the formations were hopelessly intermingled, so the officers did not have a firm grip on their own men and in any case, there was an increase in enemy artillery fire and the exhaustion of the men was too great."

All the rest of the regiments recorded a difficult situation, gradually mastered and night falling on a village firmly controlled by the German attackers – undoubtedly helped by the British decision to withdraw from the village during the early evening and despite a final and inaccurate dig by the British Official History that, 'It was not, indeed, until 5.00 am the next day that even scouts of the enemy showed themselves in Geluveld.'[70] Whether the British were pushed out by force or left before they were, the fact is that, after intense fighting extending over several days, the village, for which so much had been sacrificed by both sides, was finally in German hands, together with almost 1,000 prisoners, three guns and a machine gun. Its possession was, however, not seen by them as an end in itself, merely a springboard to a further advance.

Oberst Klotz Reserve Field Artillery Regiment 54 [71] **10.**

"On 1 November the regimental staff reconnoitred forward in order to be able to direct the advance of the battalions. The regimental command post, together with that of Oberst Freiherr von Hügel [Reserve Infantry Regiment 248] was moved into a small English garden near Geluveld Park. Immediately after the fall of Polderhoek Park, orders were given that 2nd Battalion, together with some of its guns, was to advance to the hill there in support of (and to act as a rearguard to) the infantry. Thrusting forward to fulfil this, 2nd Battalion took up firing positions with all its batteries in the sequence 6th, 5th and 4th; opening fire at more or less point blank range on lines of enemy infantry and their trenches. Due to heavy artillery and machine gun fire, the extremely exposed battalion suffered heavy losses. 3rd Battalion pushed one gun forward to the crossroads, where it could bring fire down along the road in the direction of Ypres then, at 10.30 am, 8th and 9th Batteries Reserve Field Artillery Regiment 54 advanced as well.

"In the meantime the losses amongst the officers, especially in view of their small number, had become so great that replacements were required urgently. Offfizierstellvertreter Lorenz, who arrived wounded at regimental headquarters, was directed to deliver a report to this effect directly to the Ministry of War in Stuttgart . . . It was dark. The trench containing the regimental staff came under intense fire at that moment from several enemy batteries, so the report was written by the light of exploding shells. That evening the regimental staff moved to quarters in Geluveld Chateau. A British aid post had been established on the ground floor and in the cellar. Fighting was still continuing at the far end of the park and orders were given out that evening in the chateau.

"So, Geluveld and Polderhoek were finally captured. The enemy had everywhere been ejected from their positions, but at the cost of huge casualties on our side. There had been no breakthrough of the enemy front and, although there were further attacks during the coming days, including some from other divisions (Guards) and, although certain important points fell into our hands, the line achieved by 54th Reserve Division, which now ran along within Polygon Wood, hardly altered, more or less remaining the same throughout the winter of 1914/15."

Notes
1. Orgeldinger History Reserve Infantry Regiment 246 p 14.
2. Winzer History Reserve Infantry Regiment 243 p 32.
3. To be fair to Carlowitz, it must be stated that he held subsequently a number of command

appointments, both on the Eastern as well as the Western Front. Rising in 1918 to command of Ninth Army in August 1918 during the battles between the Oise and the Aisne, he became one of the very few officers from Saxony ever to command an entire army.

4. Brase *Bei den 241ern.* p 39.

5. *ibid.* p 42.

6. Winzer *op. cit.* p 15.

7. Brase *op. cit.* pp 42–43.

8. That battalion commander and many others. A large number of the older Landwehr officers, appointed to higher commands and deployed with the new reserve formations, were simply not equal to the demands of modern soldiering or the rigours of field service, quickly reported sick and were replaced by more robust officers.

9. Winzer *op. cit.* 243 pp 15 – 16. It is quite probable that the British fire comprised mainly shrapnel fired by a section of 25th Battery XXXV Brigade Royal Field Artillery, whose guns were advanced hard up behind the infantry of 7th Division. See BOH p 156.

10. Brase *op. cit.* pp 43–44.

11. It should, perhaps, be pointed out that Brase was a far from typical junior NCO. In civil life, he held the degree of Doctor of Philosophy. Here he is quoting from Goethe's 1827 poem *Gott, Gemüt und Welt*, in which Goethe makes plain his concept of a personal God, whose place is at the centre of all things and who is the prime mover in the affairs of man. The complete couplet is *Ihm ziemt's die Welt im Innern zu bewegen/Natur in sich, sich in Natur zu hegen* [Fittingly, He is the innermost motion of the world/Nature and He co-existing in mutual devotion]. Goethe's view, as exemplified in this poem, is that man's natural state is one of turmoil and confusion between darkness and light, between choosing God, or choosing evil, but that Christianity, having laid out the choices, leaves it to the individual to make that choice. For Goethe, a convinced Lutheran, it is clear that man's requirement for help has its origins in the need for salvation arising out of a love of God, which in turn demands accept-ance of His will and the primacy of scripture. If Brase was genuinely running these ideas through his head on the battlefield, they must at least have served to divert his attention from the proximity and distinct possibility of death.

12. Reimer History 1st Abteilung Reserve Field Artillery Regiment 54 p 4.

13. Krämer History Reserve Infantry Regiment 245 p 10.

14. Orgeldinger History Reserve Infantry Regiment 246 pp 17–18.

15. Presumably this refers to the cross roads where a minor road crosses the Zonnebeke – Beselare road, about 300 hundred metres north northwest of the church in Beselare.

16. This appears to be a reference to the point where the road turns south at Kortekeer, approxi-mately 1,200 metres northwest of the centre of Geluveld.

17. Rutz *Bayernkämpfe* pp 48–49.

18. Hauptmann Alfred Stockmayer is buried in the German cemetery at Menen Block D Grave 2334.

19. Moser *Die Württemberger im Weltkrieg* p 291.

20. Major Hans Strelin is buried in the German cemetery at Menen Block D Grave 2891.

21. Beumelberg *Ypern 1914* p 66.

22. Orgeldinger *op. cit.* pp 24–26.

23. Oberstleutnant Magnus von Holleben is buried in the German cemetery at Langemark: Block B Grave 13098. The Volksbund has wrongly recorded the date of his death as 20 October 1914.

24. Beumelberg *op. cit.* p 69.

25. Orgeldinger *op. cit.* pp 26 & 32.

26. Brase *op. cit.* pp 52–54.

27. This 1848 song by Otto Inkermann (1823–1862), set to music in 1867 by Peter Johann Peters (1820 – 1870) is in praise of the Rhineland, its wine and women. It has a good, rousing, distinctly patriotic-sounding tune and it was very popular pre-war with German university students. It was also taught to older pupils in Prussian schools. There is no need to doubt that Brase heard it played, just as he records, but a cynic might remark that, when the *Kindermord* myth was gaining momentum rapidly, it was also a 'convenient' melody to have cropped up at that time and place.

28. BOH p 239.

29. Kastner History Reserve Infantry Regiment 242 p 15

30. Rutz *op. cit.* pp 59–61

31. On the basis of this statement, it is possible to reconstruct fairly accurately the make up of this attack. In addition to elements of Bavarian Reserve Infantry Regiment 1 and men of 53rd Reserve Division, the remainder of the attackers appear to have been drawn from 22 and 25 Brigades of 3rd Cavalry Division, the units involved being Dragoner Regiment von Manteuffel (Rheinisches) Nr. 5, Husaren Regiment Landgraf Friedrich II von Hessen-Homburg (2. Kurhessisches) Nr. 14, Garde-Dragoner- Regiment (I. Großherzoglich Hessisches) Nr. 23 and Leib-Dragoner-Regiment (2.Grossherzoglich Hessisches) Nr. 24. It is not possible to say how large the contribution of each formation was, though number and effectiveness would have been fairly low in comparison with the infantry. Quite apart from the smaller size of units, the usual drill, because of the need to care for the horses, was for only every second man to be employed in the dismounted role at any one time.

32. It is the case, however, that at least some of the Bavarians or their attachments were involved in the fighting on 26 October. BOH (p 246) quotes a war diary entry by Dragoner Regiment 23, which confirms this.

33. Oberstleutnant Hermann Johannes Garten, who was aged forty nine at the time of his death, is buried in the German cemetery at Menen Block N Grave 2031. Next to him, in Grave 2032, is Oberstleutnant Max Hammer, who was killed a day later.

34. In the final assault on 26 October, two companies of the Border Regiment were completely overrun and many were captured. The remainder of the prisoners appear, according to Poseck, *The German Cavalry 1914 in Belgium and France* p 212, to have been from 1st Battalion Scots Guards, Poseck putting the figure at 300, an estimate which was accepted by BOH (p246).

35. Kastner *op. cit.* pp 14–15.

36. Poseck *op. cit.* pp 212–213 N.B. The original translation, being of very poor quality, has been paraphrased slightly for clarity.

37. Winzer *op. cit.* p 24.

38. Brase *op. cit.* pp 54–56.

39. Accusations such as this crop up frequently in the literature, totally ignoring the effect such tampering would have on the ballistic quality of the bullets when fired at this sort of range. In general such reports may be dismissed as fantasy.

40. Herkenrath History Reserve Infantry Regiment 247 p 18

41. This is a reference to the major road junction where the Beselare – Wervik road crosses the road between Ypres and Menen.

42. Sollider *Vier Jahre Westfront* p 17.

43. *ibid.* p 17.

44. Hauptmann Ludwig Obermann is buried in the German cemetery at Menen Block N Grave 2593.

45. That is to say, at a point about three kilometres north northwest of Geluwe.
46. Oberleutnant Gebhardt Meßbauer is buried in the German cemetery at Menen Block C Grave 120
47. Reinhardt History Reserve Infantry Regiment 248 p 14.
48. Major Max Jordan is buried in the German cemetery at Menen Block K Grave 3245.
49. Sollider *op. cit.* pp 55–57
50. It was a Bavarian custom, based originally on a need for security, frequently to refer to the new regiments by the name of their commanders; in the case of Bavarian Reserve Infantry Regiment 16 that was Oberst Julius List.
51. There was some justification for this assessment. The British 7th Division comprised mostly veteran troops. Three quarters of the infantry battalion had had recent overseas service and three of the battalions had fought in the South African War.
52. There were several similar instances at this time, providing yet another proof of the hasty improvisation which was typical of the inadequate preparation of these new formations for field service.
53. Rutz *op. cit.* pp 63–66.
54. Kriegsarchiv München HS 1928.
55. This is a common problem. It is notoriously difficult to estimate ranges accurately on rising ground.
56. Orgeldinger *op. cit.* p 33.
57. Herkenrath *op. cit.* p 19.
58. The Commander XXVII Reserve Corps, General von Schubert, did have the grace to half apologise for this in a letter to 6th Bavarian Reserve Division, dated 4 November 1914. 'I hereby express my thanks to the Division for the support afforded XXVII Reserve Corps by Reserve Infantry Regiment 16. It was not possible for me to withdraw the regiment from the line of battle until the fall of Geluveld. I issued an order to this effect on 29 October. The village did not fall completely into German hands until the night 1–2 November, after which the greater part of the regiment marched away'. It is also clear, reading between the lines, that this letter was written following a complaint by the regiment to Headquarters 6th Bavarian Reserve Division about their treatment, because Schubert's letter continues, 'If the regiment was not issued with sufficient ammunition or rations before its departure, the mistake does not lie which the division to which the regiment was subordinated [54th Reserve Division], rather it was their own fault for not sending the necessary wagons to the distribution point'. Schubert then concludes by saying that, although he was in no position to judge deserving cases, he had requested Fourth Army to allocate a number of Iron Crosses for distribution to the regiment. See Kriegsarchiv München 6. Reserve Division. Bd 5.
59. Sollider *op. cit.* pp 29 – 30
60. *ibid.* p 30. Interesting to note BOH p 285 has nothing to say about this attack, which was, naturally, overshadowed by the major push by Army Group Fabeck the same day.
61. Leutnant Joseph Brenner is buried in the *Kamaradengrab* of the German cemetery at Langemark.
62. Sollider *op. cit.* pp 33–34
63. *ibid.* pp 57–59
64. Major Julius Graf von Zech auf Neuhofen, the aristocratic former Governor of the German colony of Togo, was shot through the head whilst crossing the Kruiseke – Beselare road and killed, aged 46. He is buried in the German cemetery at Menen Block N Grave 1947.
65. Dellmensingen *Das Bayernbuch vom Weltkriege II Band* pp 125–127.

66. In fact Oberst List did not remain where he was buried for very long. His remains were transferred after the war to the German cemetery at Langemark and he is buried in the *Kamaradengrab*.
67. BOH p 317.
68. *ibid.* pp 328–331.
69. Herkenrath *op. cit.* p 21.
70. BOH p 332.
71. Moser *op. cit.* pp 297–298.

CHAPTER 5

Diksmuide

XXII Reserve Corps, comprising 43rd and 44th Reserve Divisions, commanded by General der Kavallerie von Falkenhayn and destined to be deployed as the most northerly of the new reserve corps, detrained in the southwest of Brussels on 13 October and began the march north to Flanders on 14 October, the same day that formations of III Reserve Corps started to move west along the Belgian coast. Advancing through the Flanders countryside, there were numerous indications of war – wounded and dead cattle in the fields, abandoned farmsteads and a trail of discarded military equipment. However, the march itself was unmolested and by the night of 18/19 October all the formations and units were well forward and enjoying their final undisturbed night in bivouac for many days to come. Writing home, one member of 3rd Battalion Reserve Infantry Regiment 205 of 44th Reserve Division remarked:[1]

> "We were accommodated in a nunnery. Pigs were requisitioned and slaughtered and the meat was then distributed to the men. In the village everything imaginable was still available for sale. Where we were the nuns even sold us large pieces of ham for one mark each. Very sensibly this was done in the evening, because the ham was so full of maggots it could have moved itself. The nuns had to beat a hasty retreat." Another man complained in his letter:
> "Up until then we had not heard a single bullet fired. This had already become tedious. To march day after day without ever catching sight of the enemy was boring. However, today we had a fine firework display. During the afternoon a British pilot had honoured us with his presence then disappeared once more having arranged two shells as an unfriendly welcome. Now we can see flashes from heavy guns to the west flaring up into the sky like lightning bolts."

These guns were still a good ten kilometres distant, as shown by the first assessment of the enemy which appeared in Corps orders that night. 'Ijzer occupied by the enemy. To the east in the Beerst – Vladslo area; enemy infantry and artillery. In Praet Bos [east of Belhutte], enemy cavalry patrols. Belgian, British and French troops have been identified.'[2]

So, after a relatively trouble free few days, the regiments of XXII Reserve Corps were in position to participate in the general attack of Fourth Army on 20 October, though Reserve Infantry Regiment 201, for example, had already been in action the previous day at Bovekerke, as 43rd Reserve Division advanced west from Torhout in the direction of Beerst, two and a half kilometres north of Diksmuide. By about 10.00 am, leading elements had reached Belhutte when information arrived from Reserve Jäger Battalion 15, scouting ahead north of the road, that enemy cavalry and infantry had

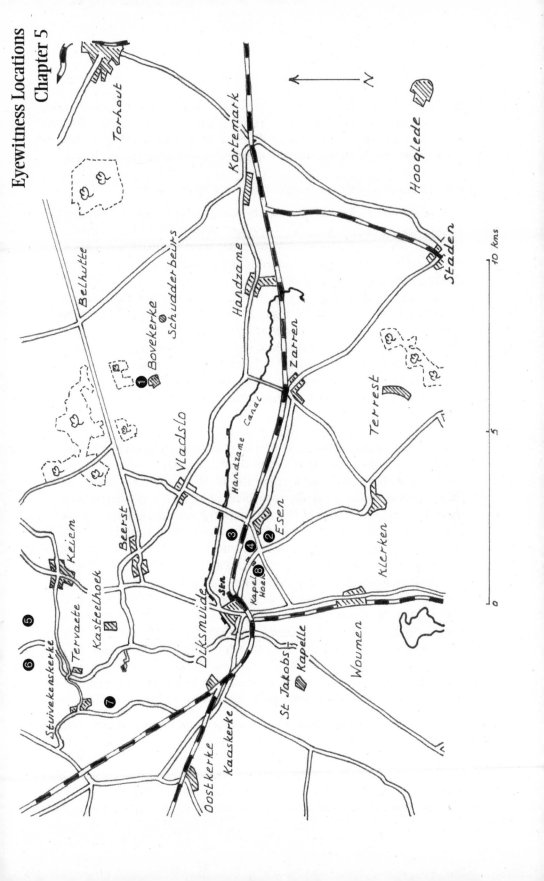

been sighted. At that the battalions of Reserve Infantry Regiment 201 began to deploy, but the enemy, who were clearly there in a screening role, pulled out and orders were given that the regiment was to swing southwest as an advance guard and to head for Bovekerke. A member of the regimental staff later described what happened next.

Leutnant von Frantzius Adjutant Reserve Infantry Regiment 201[3] 1.

"Cavalry and cyclists accompanied the new direction of march, providing flank protection on the right. A fairly straight road led to Bovekerke, which was still about one and a half kilometres away. But, what was that? Was it beginning to rain? Heavy droplets thudded into the ground, but no, those were enemy bullets which impacted all round us. Immediately we rushed right and left into woodland, leaving only the vehicles of the machine gun company which were unable to get off the road. Soon reports were coming in from the point platoon that there was an enemy armoured car at the entrance to the village and that it was firing its machine gun. The battalions deployed swiftly: 2nd Battalion right of the road and 3rd Battalion left. The companies shook out and an attack was launched, just as it had been taught. Occasionally it may have deviated [from the ideal], because 'blue beans' [bullets] were repeatedly cracking by.

"Up and at them! We want to shut them up! So we advanced, ever closer to Bovekerke. We had long left the protection of the wood behind us, nevertheless we continued on our tortured way. The Belgians had not reckoned with this sort of daring. All of a sudden came the sound of the engine starting and the enemy disappeared as rapidly as possible, taking their armoured car with them. With rousing shouts of *Hurra!* we entered the village. Within a few moments we had passed right through it and it was firmly in our hands. The first battle; the first success! Now we knew what war was like; what it felt like to be shot at. We already felt more experienced – just like front line soldiers. Everybody swapped stories, impressions and experiences. It was all so new, it had come on us so swiftly and passed by just as quickly. Nevertheless we had realised that this was a serious business, as I did when a man went down wounded right next to me. *Eine Kugel kam geflogen, gilt sie mir oder gilt sie dir?* [A bullet came flying. Was it meant for me or for you?].[4] This [experience] only drew in the bands of togetherness tighter and more firmly. There was an air of the comradeship of battle: all for one and one for all. Now we really were proper soldiers – and that was the baptism of fire for the volunteers from Berlin."

This was, however, not a totally bloodless encounter for the division. Reserve Infantry Regiment 202 was directed to advance deeply echeloned in the order 1st, 2nd and 3rd Battalions to the left of Reserve Infantry Regiment 201 as it moved towards Bovekerke. As the 202nd closed up on the neighbouring village of Schuddebeurs, 1st Battalion came under fire from its edge. 1st and 2nd Companies shook out and advanced rapidly on the enemy which, once more, comprised cavalry and cycle mounted troops. These withdrew, but others, better hidden and in some strength, maintained a steady and accurate rifle fire, supplemented by some shrapnel. At times the fire was heavy enough to be described as a 'hail' and the men of Reserve Infantry Regiment 202 were forced to dig in for the night, still not having closed right up on Schudderbeurs and, indeed, concerned that they might be subject to an attack. During the ensuing random exchanges of fire, the regiment suffered its first fatal casualties: Grenadiers Schwederski and Hübner of 2nd Company.[5]

3rd Battalion Reserve Infantry Regiment 202 was moved forward to reinforce during the night, then the following morning the attack continued. Moving forward in bounds, progress was made, because the Belgian troops, having imposed delay, had withdrawn under cover of darkness, but it proved to be impossible to prevent the soldiers, as they passed buildings and farms, breaking off to go in search of something to eat, no rations having arrived the previous night. Apparently the farms were all well stocked and the regimental history describes the advance continuing with the grenadiers clutching their rifles in one hand and an apple or other snack in the other. However the picnic atmosphere could not have lasted long, because leading platoons of 1st and 2nd Battalions in particular soon found themselves coming under flanking fire from Kruisstraat.

It was necessary to turn yet again and deal with this situation. Having fought hard from house to house against troops in hasty defence and some snipers, the village was captured and the companies continued to the west, occupying Eindsdijk after minor opposition was dealt with, at more or less the same time that Reserve Infantry Regiment 201 arrived in Vladslo. That afternoon 43rd Reserve Division ordered that Diksmuide was to be captured that same day. To that end Reserve Infantry Regiment 202 was ordered to cross the Handzame Canal[6] and swing ninety degrees to the west, so as to advance westwards, with one flank on the canal and the other on the Esen – Diksmuide railway embankment. It should be mentioned that possession of Diksmuide as soon as possible was of the first importance. Quite apart from the importance of the Ijzer just to its west, it was also a road and rail route centre, the latter being of great importance in 1914. In short it was one of the most important points in Flanders and worth fighting hard for.

Viewed from the area of Esen, the ground rose gently towards Diksmuide. Like so much of Flanders at that time, it was one great mass of hedges, farms, and wide drainage ditches, all of which obstructed, complicated and canalised movement. Rows of poplars lined the roads and the railway embankment, which rose high above the surrounding fields, was extremely prominent. To the north of the embankment was the Handzame Canal, which was a considerable obstacle in itself and was flanked by extremely boggy water meadows. Altogether it presented formidable difficulties to an attacking force yet, without pause, with no time allowed for any sort of meaningful preparation, this was the ground across which the formations of 43rd Reserve Division had to advance – and rapidly if the bridgehead was to be reduced in accordance with the Fourth Army timetable.

As always it was one thing to set an ambitious objective, quite another to secure it, especially when the village of Esen, two and a half kilometres to the east, acted as an outer work to its defences. Hoping that earlier reconnaissance reports that the Belgians were evacuating Esen were correct, the weary and hungry men of 43rd Reserve Division advanced on the village just as it was beginning to get dark. Leading elements of Reserve Infantry Regiments 201 and 203, together with Reserve Jäger Battalion 15, were just about to decide how best to divide the bivouac possibilities of the place as darkness was falling when, suddenly, right in the centre, heavy firing broke out. It was total chaos, nobody could pinpoint the source of the firing and every road and open space was crammed with marching troops and equipment, so it was impossible to move either forwards or backwards. Orders were given, bayonets were fixed but, until some observers from Reserve Jäger Battalion 15 spotted muzzle flashes coming from in and around the church, there was no possibility of counter- action.

Leutnant von Frantzius Adjutant Reserve Infantry Regiment 201[7] 2.

"About 6.30 pm I was standing in front of our regimental headquarters, which had been established in a house near the church, when, all of a sudden, the church clock struck 7.00 pm. I immediately reached for my watch and said, 'That is odd; it is only just 6.30 pm'. At that precise moment, a wild exchange of fire began. Hauptmann von Bonin and I immediately searched our house and found a uniform jacket which had been taken off and dropped on the floor. In the meantime the men, roused by the burst of firing, were in an excitable state and it is entirely possible that some may have loosed off their weapons at random.

"Further searching of the houses led to the discovery of enemy ammunition in various places. There was no doubt that an ambush by *franctireurs* had been attempted. In consequence, the regimental commander ordered the houses to be burnt down as a punishment. The bright light thus produced also prevented renewed ambushes from occurring."

The torching of Esen was controversial, both during and after the war. As can be seen from Frantzius' description, Reserve Infantry Regiment 201, which suffered no casualties at all that night, was convinced that it had come under fire from *franctireurs*, though even he acknowledged that some of the firing and, therefore, retaliation, may have been caused by their own inexperienced, panicky troops. Whatever the truth, the outcome was quite clear. Doors and windows of houses around the church were smashed in and at least one account[8] claims that a civilian was dragged out of one, having been found armed with a rifle. He was summarily shot and then the attention of the troops turned to the church. Finding it locked and barred – its great walls glowing red as it reflected the surrounding flames – and its doors apparently impervious to blows with a pick, it, too, was set alight by men of Reserve Jäger Battalion 15 and, if there were indeed armed civilians or soldiers within, none escaped the flames or the ultimate collapse of the roof.

The Belgian defenders, allegedly profiting from the battlefield illumination caused by the blazing fires in Esen, launched forward a series of weak thrusts from Diksmuide, but all were easily brushed off by the numerous outposts that the regiments of 43rd

Reserve Division had pushed forward for security. Reserve Infantry Regiment 201 considered that this action provided additional proof that the ambush in Esen had been designed to trigger the Belgian counter-action, but it is impossible to comment on the veracity of the statement.[9] However, all the delay that these incidents imposed effectively put paid to any idea of closing up to and crossing the Ijzer in this sector on 20 October and Fourth Army was forced to re-cast the orders, directing that this be done without delay on 21 October.

XXII Corps ordered a concentric attack to be launched, with the formations of 43rd Reserve Division launching assaults from east and south, with 44th Reserve Division directed to advance from the north. There was an underlying assumption that no serious attempt would be made by the Belgians to defend Diksmuide as a bridgehead on the eastern bank of the Ijzer, so this great concentration of force was intended to be precautionary, to ensure that the attack would sweep all before it. Events were to prove swiftly that this assessment was totally at variance with the true facts and the troops committed to it were about to receive an extremely rude shock. Examination of the situation from closer range early on 21 October revealed that in fact the Belgian army was present in and around the town in considerable strength. A Belgian source states:[10]

> "The defence of the bridgehead on the right bank of the Ijzer was entrusted
> to Brigade Meiser (11th and 12th Regiments of the line). 12th Regiment of the
> Line under Colonel Jacques withdrew to the trenches surrounding the town
> and deployed its three machine gun platoons into positions covering the exits
> of the town in the direction of Beerst, Esen and Woumen [i.e. north, east and
> south], in order to be able to sweep with their fire the roads leading from those
> places. Six companies of the 11th Regiment of the Line and two machine gun
> platoons formed the immediate reserve and were located in Diksmuide itself.
> The remaining six companies of the same regiment were in bivouac two kilo-
> metres to the west in Oude Bareel."

The commander of the French Fusilier-Marin Brigade, Contre-Amiral [Rear Admiral] Ronarc'h, had been appointed commander of the entire Diksmuide sector. He had established his headquarters in the station at Kaaskerke and deployed his own brigade so as to man the west bank of the Ijzer. He could call on the fire of over seventy, mostly Belgian, guns and the flour mill near the Ijzer bridge west of Diksmuide, which commanded wide views over the area, proved to be a first class observation post in the days to come. Almost all the available machine guns were then divided into three large groups, sited and dug in to cover the three main approaches to the town from Beerst, Esen and Woumen.

Such a defence, conducted from well constructed trenches and with a considerable quantity of back up available to the commander, was bound to be a serious proposition and so it proved. As a result of divisional orders, Reserve Infantry Regiment 201, reinforced by Reserve Jäger Battalion 15, was directed to assault from the east, astride the Esen – Diksmuide road and Reserve Infantry Regiment 202 was to assault from the south, making direct for the castle. The aim was to have secured the town and the bridge across the Ijzer by nightfall and for both regiments to reorganise along the embankment. As soon as it was light enough to see, the various regiments began to march into their forming up places prior to launching the attack, but the going was extremely difficult and there were endless complications. Reserve Infantry Regiment 201 had difficulty linking up with the jägers and so plans had to be recast to place all four companies of its 1st Battalion in the lead, with 5th and 7th Companies moving into support. Repeatedly, all the units kept coming across water filled ditches, some of which, according to Reserve Infantry Regiment 202, were fifteen metres wide and effectively impassable.[11] In addition the ground was very heavy underfoot and there were innumerable hedges and fences to be negotiated.

Finally, at about mid morning, the attack got underway in the some places, but Reserve Infantry Regiment 201, because of the extra manoeuvres required, was not in a position to move until rather later. At 11.30 am, the attack was finally ordered for 1.30 pm. At first good progress was made, but then problems arose because of fences, hedges, ditches and boggy ground, all of which disrupted movement and took the impetus out of the attack. Then, as if there were not problems enough already, Reserve Infantry Regiment 202 found that it was under fire from its own artillery. The white armbands which were being worn were failing to provide protection and even when a man was sent up a windmill to wave a yellow flag vigorously, this still had no effect on the misdirected fire.[12] However all the movement soon produced a reaction from the Belgian defence and the attackers found themselves coming under machine gun fire and shrapnel fired from batteries located in relative safety on the west bank of the Ijzer. One member of Reserve Infantry Regiment 201 later wrote a vivid account of the events of the day:

Kriegsreiwilliger Karl Classow 1st Company Reserve Infantry Regiment 201 [13] *2.*

"Day dawned on 21 October. We, the members of 1st Company Reserve Infantry Regiment 201, were occupying wet trenches to the left of the Esen – Diksmuide road at the cross roads Esen – Diksmuide – Klerken. It had been a cold and frosty night and our stomachs ached with hunger. If only we could get going out of the misery of these trenches. Down into the earth and waiting was not for we kriegsfreiwillige. Suddenly a runner appeared in the trench with a message that took wings left and right – *Assault!* The word alone brought life to mind and body and I stretched my cramped limbs. The eyes of all the comrades were shining. We made ready – Done! However we had to be patient for some hours more. It seemed a pity to be stuck in this damned trench in the clay and, just to add to our discomfort, the enemy ranged in on us with shrapnel.

"The loads of balls slammed down closer and closer and the nose caps whirred and ploughed in the ground. Then the type of ammunition was changed and shells howled and roared overhead: too far, too near, but certainly closer! Crashes, bangs, lumps of clay and cries of 'medical orderlies!' filled the air. To Hell with this! Just get things moving; let us get in amongst the enemy! At long last came the order, 'Prepare to attack! Unload your rifles! Look in to your section commanders!' [Hauptmann] Graf Saurma-Jeltsch [the company commander] glanced at his watch. '1.30 pm! Forwards!' We leapt up with smiling faces; longing to get going and keen to attack.

"We were about 1,200 metres short of our objective, ground that was flat, but had very restricted fields of view. Moving upright and well spread out, we advanced, with our section commanders out in front. Everything we had learned at Döberitz[14] was put into practice. I looked around. It was a stirring sight! Everywhere to our left and right men of the 201st were advancing, oblivious to enemy shells and shrapnel. We were going to manage it today. Who would be able to withstand our mass? The great moment for which we had been waiting so anxiously was upon us. Up and at the enemy! We were going to win the laurels of victory!

"The enemy greeted us with increasing quantities of artillery fire, but we pressed on. Shrapnel balls and shell splinters came down thicker and closer, whilst bullets started to buzz around our ears. 'Take cover! Fire and manoeuvre by sections! The enemy fire increased. 'On your feet! Double march!' was all that could be heard up and down our firing line. 'Damn it all!' – a thick hedge was blocking our advance. It was too dense to push through and we bunched together to find a weak point before moving through it and shaking out once more. Now there was a water-filled ditch. 'Get through it. Forwards!' Yet another hedge. Where were the other platoons, the neighbours? 'Take cover!'

"An order was shouted through. '1st Company! Work your way forward as far as the meadow to our front!' The number of wounded began to increase. A few quick bounds saw us arrive at the meadow, where we took a breather. This developed into a longer check as we were pinned down by enemy fire. Diving into any furrow or hollow, we pressed our faces to the ground. Graf Sauma kneeled up in a furrow and, pistol in hand, ordered: '1st Company! Fix bayonets!' At that, for the first and also the last time in the 201st, the trumpeter blew the signal to charge and the drummer beat it as well. That raised our morale! We should soon be able to stare the enemy in the face. Where were they hiding?

"Lacerating fire was directed at us. My comrades were twisting, tumbling over and collapsing, but we charged on with bayonets fixed. A quick glance left and right revealed that our ranks had become terribly thin! All cohesion was lost: hedges, ditches, no visibility. Get through! Get over! My breath was coming in gasps; my chest was heaving. There was still absolutely nothing to be seen of the enemy. 'Take cover!' – all the platoon and section commanders were going down dead or wounded. 'Everyone, listen to my orders!' Young white faced men with shining eyes stepped into the breach. Torrents of fire were still coming down. 'On your feet! Double march!'

"Every time we heard these words, we got to our feet, filled with new determination, despite the ever present threat of death. Suddenly a new contin-uous chatter came from the front. Enemy machine guns! They must be hidden behind hedges, walls or trees. Our comrades half left of us were all mowed down as they went forward. Some writhed in agony, others lay silent, not moving, their fingers dug into the soil of Flanders like claws – dead. Dear God! Was it all over here?' 'On your feet . . . !' There was no mercy to be had so, up once more, rush forward another twenty paces and throw yourself down again. Was there no end to it? Then, out in front, I caught the first glimpse of the houses of Diksmuide and, to my right, the road that led to this monstrous place.

"I was in the midst of one great, hellish racket. Where was the fire coming from? I was full of fury. There was still no sign of the enemy, but I was deter-mined to close with them. I hauled myself upright for the umpteenth time and, as I did so, I was thrown sideways by two heavy blows. What was that? Had I been hit? My nerves were strained to breaking point. I felt no pain and there was no blood running down anywhere. 'You have been shot through your knapsack, bawled one of my comrades!' The earth to my front suddenly boiled up as the curtain of fire came down ever closer. Where was there any cover? Quick, dive down behind a small dung heap to my front! When can I, the in-habitant of a great city, have ever imagined that my life would be saved by a miserable little dung heap in Flanders?

"Every time I made the slightest attempt to get up, bullets whistled past. It was impossible to get further forward. I clenched my fists. I was in Hell. Time seemed to stand still but, gradually, the sun sank lower. The battlefield itself seemed to have died . . . then, here and there, a gradual movement to the rear began. Firing flared up occasionally; Death still lay in wait. Some of my comrades must have got further forward. I saw about ten of them pulling back. Had they taken leave of their senses? They were walking upright, with short, dragging footsteps. 'Get down!' I bawled at them, but they just stared back blankly at me. Then they were caught in a burst of fire. Some collapsed imme-diately and remained still. Others hesitated, their weapons under their arms, until the bullets knocked them to the ground also. Appalling!

"All around me men were strewn about, just as motionless as me. Were they dead, wounded, or alive? I looked to my front, consumed by a great feeling of emptiness. Why were we not inside that town that was so close? We had gone forward in the attack, ignoring thoughts of death, full of hope, had pressed on constantly, offering our faces to the enemy repeatedly. Where was our victory? It was a boundless, unspeakable, disappointment. Then despite all the fire, a great calmness came over me. The battlefield began to get increasingly dark. There was movement to my right as ghostly figures, previously immobile and hidden like me behind small dung heaps, began to crawl to the right to the road and there to roll into the cover of the ditches.

"I, too, attempted to crawl along a furrow to get to the safety of the ditch, but came under fire – which was too high. I ran the last few metres and tumbled into the ditch. Full of dead and wounded men, it presented a harrowing sight. Those of us who were still fully fit did our best to patch up the others, until the field dressings ran out. We then evacuated the wounded behind the houses which were located in rear of a line of poplars running diagonally to the road. There, at long last, we met up with two officers and surviving comrades from various companies of Reserve Infantry Regiment 201. Night had cast a mantle over the dreadful battlefield. The officers gave out instructions. 'Man the wall, lie down and relax, but stay awake in case the enemy counter-attacks!'

"We barely exchanged a word. Totally aghast, we kriegsfreiwillige could barely comprehend what had happened as this dreadful day drew to an end. We were utterly drained and exhausted. Strange to relate we almost felt ashamed as we looked around. An old comrade put our thoughts into words, as he spoke in the silence of the night, 'Chins up lads! You have done your duty to the very limit of the possible: fearlessly and sacrificially, but a cruel fate awaited you!' During the night odd individuals arrived and were taken under command by the officers. With the early dawn came the order, 'Assemble at Esen!' Joyfully, we linked up with a number of previously missing comrades there then, silently, we fell in for roll call. The first count revealed a few over seventy men from a company 250 strong, but later we were joined by a few more. Accursed Diksmuide! But the day will come when we shall be the ones gloating and then, hidden enemies of today, then you will get to know us face to face!'

Classow's experience was shared by others in the division. Numerous letters home described the shock of 21 October, when the survivors were eventually withdrawn some days later. Many of the kriegsfreiwillige were well educated men, accustomed to expressing themselves on paper and their thoughts provide a graphic description of events at a time when the spirit of youthful idealism and patriotism was replaced by the shock of the grim reality of war.

Grenadier Eberhard Lattermann 10th Company Reserve Infantry Regiment 202 [15] *3.*

"Today dawned a fine autumn day. With the exception of a few of ours, the guns are silent. At the moment, unlike earlier, we are not on any form of readiness, so I now have enough time to provide you with a rather more detailed report . . . even though the sun is shining and we have our overcoats, it still feels rather frosty, but at least I am still sound of limb, which is by no means the case in general. Just think, as I mentioned in my earlier brief note, right from the very first fight, we and the other companies suffered a lot of casualties. For us it was seven killed and twenty one wounded. In other words, more than ten percent and the other companies suffered even worse. That can happen. On this occasion we launched forward, not having noticed a fortress-like enemy position about 1,200 metres to our front.

"This happened last Wednesday, 21 October. We had advanced by bounds, with our platoon leading, to a point about one thousand metres [from the objective], without seeing the slightest sign of the enemy when, without warning, we came under absolutely murderous rifle fire. We threw ourselves forward a second time and luckily found ourselves in a large drainage ditch. At the cost of wet feet we managed to make progress; in fact the ditch saved us or, rather, prevented us all from being shot to pieces. We opened fire, each of us firing about one hundred rounds: first with sights at 1,300 metres, then at 1,000 metres, but it was all in vain. Awful artillery fire, both high explosive and shrapnel, came down, tearing the great gaps in our ranks I mentioned earlier. It was dreadful.

"During all of this, nothing whatever was heard from our artillery. In fact it took them all of three hours to open fire at all and cause the enemy some casualties. After we had been pinned down, unable to achieve anything for about ten hours – by then our rate of fire was being strictly controlled – we pulled back about two hundred metres under cover of darkness. Here those who remained rallied and buried the dead. We also dug the trenches which we are still occupying; ready to fend off whatever comes our way . . . The first to be wounded was our Hauptmann von Rappart and he was followed by a number of others, despite the fact that they were under cover at the time. It happened during one awful evening when we had taken cover behind a building and shrapnel came down less than one hundred metres behind us. For days now we have been surviving out in the open and as for our personal needs we have been suffering greatly from hunger. There was one thirty hour period when we had absolutely nothing to eat. Every little piece of stale bread was greeted with cheers. The field kitchens just cannot get anywhere near us . . . "

Kriegsfreiwilliger Lothar Eickhoff Reserve Infantry Regiment 203[16] **4.**

"Emerging from the area criss-crossed by hedges, we entered field of beet, which offered absolutely no protection. We then closed up to the railway embankment which ran up to our objective, but which also offered no cover. There were several houses by a level crossing, which were under heavy artillery fire. The infantry, too, brought fire down on them because firing was going on from the windows. I could not pick out a target but fired several rounds anyway . . . We then crossed the railway embankment, coming under heavy fire, because we were particularly conspicuous and I was immediately struck by how many dead and wounded there already were . . . Still under constant small arms fire, we reached a bank which ran at right angles to the railway embankment and were able to take a short break for the first time, because the bank offered us protection.

"From the very start I had been following Offizierstellvertreter Seefeldt because he, who had first learned about war in China, was by far the calmest of all our leaders . . . At the bank he was the only one present. He took the opportunity to reorganise his platoon, together with the men of the other companies. All this was done prone, of course, because anybody who raised his head above the bank was shot at. We must have been close up to the enemy, judging from the accuracy of the fire, but there was not a trace of them to be seen . . . Everywhere men were calling for orders. This was not to be wondered at, after all we had only been soldiers for two and a half months and we simply could not operate independently.

"In the meantime Seefeldt's platoon was joined by a complete company under a Hauptmann, who assumed command. He ordered [us to carry out] two bounds forward. These were carried out brilliantly, but of those who had gone forward, almost all were killed or wounded, because we were met with lacerating fire. The Hauptmann was numbered amongst the fallen. We now found ourselves in a slight dip between two fields of beets. It was, however, very shallow, so nobody dared stir. A few men raised their heads and were shot straight through the head, or bullets hammered in right next to them, bringing a swift end to their efforts. At long last night fell and the fire eased."

Beaten back, bewildered and in a confused state of total defeat, the largely leaderless men began to congregate around Esen and to dig in, though in many cases this was easier said than done. There was a general shortage of digging implements throughout the new formations and XXII Reserve corps was no different. The regimental historian of Reserve Infantry Regiment 203 later noted, 'The lack of digging equipment in the companies was very noticeable. The short infantry spade was the object of all our desires.'[17] A clear exercise of leadership, of command and control would also have gone a long way to restoring the morale and efficiency but so many officers and NCOs were dead or wounded that this was hard to provide and, where some of the junior leadership was still available, at times it appeared to be the blind leading the blind. According to Reserve Infantry Regiment 202: 'During the ensuing dark nights, the platoons stumbled around the beet fields and, with fatal regularity, were caught by accurate fire. This demoralised the kriegsfreiwillige and filled them with feelings of bitterness, because it was never made clear to them what the point of these struggles in the dark was. They simply led to heavy losses and demonstrated a lack of systematic and methodical leadership.'[18]

So the first great attack on Diksmuide had failed. This failure was a direct result of underestimating both the enemy and the inherent strength of defensive positions manned by resolute troops with plenty of weapons and ammunition. Against such a combination the lives of troops, whose courage greatly exceeded their tactical ability, were forfeited in huge and dispiriting numbers, as they threw themselves repeatedly against an unseen, determined and well-equipped enemy. The casualties and the sacrifice of so many of the kriegsfreiwillige had an immediate and detrimental effect on the morale of those who had survived somehow, as this letter home, sent some time later, shows all too clearly.

Kriegsfreiwilliger Freidrich Meese 5th Company Reserve Infantry Regiment 201 [19]

"My dear friend Ernst is missing. That appears to be a clear-cut and concise description and yet it brought a lump to my throat when I read it. Poor, dear lad! Missing: that is a miserable and tough word for those who understand what it means. It immediately conjured up images in my mind of 21 October before Diksmuide. We were beaten back and none of us could understand why. There was a farm to our front, with a road to its right, along which we had advanced cheerfully in full expectation of victory, just as though events were playing out on the drill square. Off we went forward, far too proud to duck at the constant crack of oncoming bullets. Then we found ourselves in the front line. An unteroffizier was shot right next to me. Out to the right J. was shot through the arm and I myself received a bullet through my mess tins.

"We were lined up behind a hedge and were meant to be firing at the enemy, but we could see nothing of them. Then it was 'On your feet! Double march to the farm!' [Bullets] whistled and sang through the twigs, the shack itself was on fire and behind the walls which were still standing were groups of jägers and men of Reserve Infantry Regiment 201 [taking cover] while the machine guns knocked the walls down stone by stone. I bandaged up poor old N, then R, who was shot in the side of the head. It was only by taking great care that this wound could be compressed and he certainly does not know that my bandaging saved his life.

"We then went on, but things began to unravel. There were no leaders and our comrades were going down in rows. Still we continued, because at that point nobody thought that we were not going to win. Suddenly Tac! Tac! Tac! We were hit from the rear by our own machine guns and the entire attack collapsed. Back we went. What a feeling of bitterness there was! Then, taking cover by the last of the stacks of straw, we could hear the cries and groans of one of our badly wounded comrades, lying exposed to the fire. Ignoring the fire I, together with two others, crawled forward but we could not help him. We then pulled back slightly and dug in where we were, fully expecting an enemy counter-attack.

"Our wounded lay out to our front, between us and the enemy and under fire from both sides. Weeks later, when on patrol – in the meantime we had never actually got back to this point – I saw them there and had to crawl over them: row after row of dead. They were the ones who up until then had been numbered among the missing. There were others who were never even seen again, i.e. those few who were fortunate enough to be captured, wounded by the enemy. Of course that is a better interpretation of the word, which is such a miserable and tough one for everyone who knows what it means!"

Everywhere, the idealism of late summer was swiftly being replaced by a sense of loss. However, nothing was to be gained from dwelling at length on the failures of the previous day so, as soon as it became light on 22 October, the difficult process of disentangling the different formations and units began. Gradually the full scale of the casualties and the major incidents became clearer. As far as the Belgian defenders were concerned, the previous day had caused them some concern. They had been under great pressure both here and to the north. Although they did not have it all their own way, the regiments of 44th Reserve Division made much better progress and were able to close right up to the banks of the Ijzer within a few days.

There had been numerous incidents along the way: days of confused fighting, a failed attempt, due to lack of bridging equipment and artillery support, to secure crossings initially over the Handzame Canal and more than one instance of firing on their own men. The overall condition of the forward troops was no better than that in 43rd Reserve Division. The necessity to wade through chest deep drainage ditches meant that they were forced to lie out soaking wet through the long cold nights with almost nothing to eat and certainly nothing in the way of hot meals. The men had no means of warming food in the front line and neither Reserve Infantry Regiment 205, nor Reserve Infantry Regiment 208 had field kitchens or the means to transport rations forward. One kriegs-freiwilliger of Reserve Infantry Regiment 205 later described, in a letter home, the confusion of the night 20/21 October:[20] **5.**

"Suddenly, we came under fire from two sides. We thought that we had either been attacked or that an attempt was being made to break through. There was a storm of small arms fire, more intense than anything we had ever heard. The night was pitch black and it was raining; the whole situation was strange. In order not to be surprised, 1st Platoon 9th Company, i.e. us, had to shake out and deploy to cover the right flank. For a young soldier this was a terrifying experience and we would have done anything not to have to carry it out. We moved, somewhat uncertainly, about one hundred metres. Then we took up a position. At that we came under fire from a range of about two hundred metres. We dug in and fired back from time to time throughout the night, without ever catching a glimpse of the enemy. It then transpired that we had been firing at our own men and *vice versa.* I have never been in such flat country. We lay behind a hedge tired, hungry and soaked to the skin. Whenever there was a pause in the firing we fell asleep. After dawn we were withdrawn and came under rapid small arms fire. The enemy artillery then spotted us then, finally, we came under fire from our own artillery which was firing too short and landed shells amongst us. It was a chaotic withdrawal."

Despite all these problems, more forward progress was made by this division than was possible for their neighbours to the south and it was able to stick to its objective of gaining the west bank of the Ijzer between Stuivekenskerke and Kloosterhoek. After some hard fighting, with considerable casualties on both sides, the defenders evacuated the east bank of the Ijzer on 23 October. This had as much to do with the advance of formations of 6th Reserve Division to the north as with the actual pressure exerted by 44th Reserve Division.

As a result of these operations all along the XXII Reserve Corps front, there had been a series of limited Belgian counter-attacks during the hours of darkness, designed to increase the area under their control. Generally these had achieved little, but in a few cases, such as in the Reserve Infantry Regiment 201 and Reserve Jäger Battalion 15 sectors, some individuals demonstrated their jumpiness by pulling back to the gun lines. This, in turn, affected the steadfastness of some gunners. Without at least an infantry screen out to their front, some batteries elected to undertake a change of position to new gun lines in rear. Better liaison between infantry and artillery could have minimised this, but the losses amongst those who might have conferred had been too high. However the Belgian counter-actions were limited in both scope and time, so by the time dawn broke it was fairly clear that the relative success further north and the pressure to which the Belgian defence had been subjected, meant that there was little chance that the temporary disorganisation within 43rd Reserve Division was going to be exploited in any significant way.

Stragglers linked up once more with their units and, gradually, order was restored. In contrast to the situation further south, there was no immediate pressure to resume the assault directed at Diksmuide which had proved to be so deadly. The experience, dearly bought on 21 October, ought to have shown quite clearly that a further attempt to reduce the Belgian bridgehead would have to be preceded by systematic artillery preparation. It was now apparent that not only was the position properly dug in, exploiting fully all the potential of the close country, with its numerous fences, hedges and watercourses, but also that obstacles had been used to create killing zones, where weapons carefully sited in embankments, the upper stories of buildings and well constructed strong points, could bring deadly crossfire to bear. Not only that, positions and trench lines west of the Ijzer, which could fire into the flanks of German forces advancing north or south along the line of the Ijzer canal, could be seen to be occupied.

Field interrogation of prisoners yielded the information that the defence involved upwards of 4,000 men, who were being reinforced gradually by elements of two French marine regiments. A captured order also indicated the determination of the Belgians to fight hard for the last of their territory:[21]

> "The outcome of the entire campaign may depend upon the resistance we offer. I implore officers and soldiers, regardless of the strains which must be borne, to do much more than their simple duty. The well-being of our Fatherland and each individual depends on it. So resist to the absolute limit of what is possible."

Whilst planning for a future attack went ahead, the regiments continued to improve their fieldworks as best they could with the few tools to hand. At least this kept them occupied and eventually reduced their vulnerability to the continuous harassing fire. The flat trajectory guns of the artillery of 43rd Reserve Division were moved forward and emplaced where they could provide direct fire support as the infantry went forward once more. Machine guns were carefully maintained or repaired and a major effort was made to bring up ammunition, because many sub units had fired off their entire allocations previously. XXII Reserve Corps also moved up more heavy batteries and, given a suitable pause in operations, all might have been well. However, at Fourth Army, there was still no real understanding of the true situation at Diksmuide. There was an appreciation that there had been a major setback, but it was obviously assessed that one more effort would bring about the desired success and, over local protests, a resumption of the assault was ordered for 23 October. It was intended to gain the far bank of the Ijzer. The orders by 43rd Reserve Division stated:[22]

"44th Reserve Division will cross the Ijzer to the north of Diksmuide in rear of 6th Reserve Division, which has already gained a foothold there. It will then thrust south to hit Diksmuide from the rear. 43rd Reserve Division will attack at 9.00 am, following a heavy artillery bombardment. Reserve Infantry Regiment 201 and Reserve Jäger Battalion 15 will attack Diksmuide from the east, Reserve Infantry Regiment 203 from the south and Reserve Infantry Regiment 202, in support of the attack from the south, will take the chateau and, having set it alight, will close up to the line of the canal."

Needless to report, the Belgians and the French forces were ready and waiting when the attack went in. The operations launched to the north came nowhere near to closing up on Diksmuide, nor was there much in the way of support from the south. However, the attack was begun in accordance with orders, the thin ranks of the attacking regiments once more made some progress towards the bridgehead, but the advance was an illusion. Once the attackers had closed up towards the defensive lines, they were swiftly shot to a standstill once more. At about midday there was an unfounded suggestion that the defenders were evacuating the area which, for a short while, gave new heart to the assaulting troops, but they were rapidly disabused of the idea. The attack stalled once more in complete failure. More lives had been lost for nothing and, as it went dark, the survivors pulled back to their starting positions having achieved absolutely nothing but lengthening casualty lists: so much for the second attempt to capture Diksmuide.

The problems faced by 44th Reserve Division were rather different. The Ijzer, for example, posed a very considerable obstacle to movement. In this area it ran canalised on a bed about twenty five metres wide, which was contained by embankments about two metres high. The banks were steep on the eastern side, but on the far bank a roadway ran along parallel to the watercourse. With considerable difficulty the divisional engineers succeeded during the night 23/24 October in throwing footbridges across the obstacle and, from 5.00 am, a steady stream of infantrymen was able to cross and take up position on the far side. Amongst other units, 3rd Battalion Reserve Infantry Regiment 205 got across safely, but there was a delay in passing the crossing orders and, as a result, it was after 7.00 am and daylight before most of the nine battalions which were to cross the Ijzer that morning began to move. Naturally the movement was spotted and, although a considerable force was established on the west bank, every time an attempt was made to advance on the Diksmuide – Nieuwpoort railway, some two to three kilometres distant, each was fired on and stopped at the cost of a considerable number of casualties. That which might have been possible with surprise and under the cover of darkness proved to be impossible by day. The would-be attackers took cover behind every available structure. Some tried to dig in, but the trenches filled with water at a depth of two spades and casualties mounted. By mid-morning Hauptmann Weber, commanding 9th Company Reserve Infantry Regiment 205, was already dead, shot through the head by an unseen rifleman.

A machine gun platoon of Reserve Infantry Regiment 205, which was in position on the embankment, lost two guns to artillery fire, which came down with constantly increasing ferocity against the crossing site. In fact, as the day wore on, the pontoon bridges were under such intense fire that all contact with the east bank was lost. Those elements of Generalleutnant von Dieringshofen's 87 Reserve Infantry Brigade located on the west bank were eventually ordered not to attempt a further advance, because Headquarters 44th Reserve Division was becoming increasingly concerned that a threat was developing against this precarious bridgehead from the south. At around 3.00pm all the main pontoons had been struck by gun fire and were in a sinking condition. This left only two footbridges still in action when, at 6.00 pm, an enemy counter-attack was launched with heavy fire support. During this operation a French infantry battalion succeeded in breaking right through to the Ijzer and driving a wedge between 44th Reserve Division and 6th Reserve Division to the north. The situation was extremely serious, almost desperate, for the hard pressed troops on the west bank and Dieringhausen resorted to ordering his regiments to win or die where they were.

Despite this further check to the plans of XXII Reserve Corps, there was a decision to renew the assault on Diksmuide for a third time on 24 October, but the derailing in the rear area of a goods train bringing forward ammunition for the artillery put paid to that idea and the infantry, enduring dreadful conditions in their forward positions, were thereby granted a stay of execution of twenty four hours. It was clear that no such attack could now be launched until 25 October at the earliest. So, although there was no major attack that day, the German positions forward of Diksmuide were subject to constant harassing fire and numerous patrols were despatched forward, resulting frequently in clashes with the Belgian forces. Despite this involuntary pause, there was no improvement in battlefield administration so the survivors of the previous assaults on Diksmuide were now falling prey to all manner of illnesses, which were exacerbated by their utter exhaustion after six days of continuous operations and appalling weather, all compounded by a lack of hot food and drinks. Men manning trenches have little else to look forward to than their next meal and if it is not forthcoming the fall in morale and efficiency is almost tangible.

During the course of the day news filtered through that both to the north and south some reasonable progress had been made. Although the troops in the front line could probably have not cared less to hear that III Reserve Corps, reinforced by some elements of 44th Reserve Division, was pushing forward west of the Ijzer (a somewhat over-optimistic assessment of the actual situation) and that XXIII Reserve corps was closing in on Bikschote, higher up the chain of command the information had a heartening effect and convinced key decision makers that one more hard push at Diksmuide could shake the cohesion of the entire Allied line. Inevitably, the result was a further demand on the 43rd Reserve Division to launch an all-out 'final effort' against the town. Dawn broke cold and wet on the bedraggled men of Reserve Infantry Regiments 201, 202 and 203 on 25 October. Although the night had passed more or less quietly, there had been little sleep. There was nowhere dry to lie down, overcoats were stiff with accumulated mud and the cold and real pangs of hunger gnawed at their empty stomachs.

It had proved almost impossible to evacuate any of the wounded, some of whom had been lying immobile for three days and were now in a pitiful state. The trenches were full of water and the drenching sheets of rain were making conditions worse by the minute. Unburied corpses contributed to the general air of utter misery and they shuddered from time to time as further bullets slammed into them. All the surviving officers shared the view that it was useless to expect any more from their worn down troops until they had had a period of rest and recuperation. This opinion was passed upwards with all the determination that the regimental commanders could muster, but it made no difference. The formations to the north and south were pressing for the elimination of the bridgehead, XXII Reserve Corps and Fourth Army agreed and so, taking no account of the wretched state of the remnants of the once proud 43rd Reserve Division, orders, which brooked no dissent, were passed down at around midday.

Yet again Reserve Infantry Regiment 201 and Reserve Jäger Battalion 15 were to attack over the same old ground from the east and Reserve Infantry Regiment 203 was to advance from the south. All the divisional artillery was allocated in direct support of one or other of the two axes and, in addition, a large allocation of heavy artillery right up to and including the heavy 420 mm heavy howitzers, was also made. Despite this, the danger area of some of these weapons meant that it was not possible to attempt to engage the forward enemy trenches without the risk of rounds dropping short or the normal fragmentation endangering the advancing troops. Location of the exact points to be neutralised was in any case quite impossible in the prevailing circumstances so, once more, the infantrymen would be very much on their own resources once the attack began.

The bombardment began at 1.00 pm, shells falling on the town with shattering effect and there was practically no response from the Allied artillery. Then, as the rate of fire increased, the companies told off for the attack moved forward to close up to the enemy positions. Having learned their lesson from earlier failures, much of the movement was done by crawling across the sodden fields, exploiting every piece of cover but, despite some of this being carried out lying flat, it was soon obvious that the defenders had not been properly neutralised by the artillery and that they were preparing to resist strongly. To observers further back all seemed to be going well. The town of Diksmuide was one seething mass of explosions, clouds of dust rose in the sky from the shattered tiles as one building after another collapsed into the streets or caught fire. However, what was being hit was what could be, not what mattered, which were the stoutly defended forward trench lines and securely dug in machine guns.

The gun fire was moved forward from the town and, profiting from a lull in enemy small arms fire as the defenders took cover in the depths of their positions, the German infantrymen rose to their feet and attempted to organise themselves for a final charge. At that, the men of Reserve Infantry Regiment 201 and Reserve Jäger Battalion 15 found that there came under intense flanking fire from a machine gun or dug in in a defilade position and, in what was an early example of that *leit motiv* of the Great War, one unsuppressed machine gun effectively took much of the impetus out of the attack as dozens fell before its fire. By the time the remaining attackers had closed to within 150 metres of the outskirts of the town, three or four Belgian trenches crammed with the dead and the dying had been overrun but, crucially, even the direct support batteries had had to lift their fire further forward and the positions on the edge of the built up area came to life, as the defenders manned their fire positions once again.

Knowing what was at stake, the Belgians rushed every available rifleman forward and, as successive attempts were made to charge across the open ground, each was shot to pieces in a torrent of small arms fire. The few German survivors found themselves pinned down unable to move and forced to wait the onset of darkness. Every attempt to move was doomed, the enemy artillery continued to take a toll and it was obvious that nothing could be achieved without a complete reorganisation and, equally, that nothing was to be gained from remaining where they were. They would be vulnerable either to Belgian attacks overnight or to be dealt with from improved Belgian positions the following day. In small groups or by sections they began to make their way back as the night became properly dark. The great majority of the wounded were also evacuated; the dead had to remain where they were. It was no great distance back to their starting positions, so by some time between 6.00 pm and 7.00 pm, those that were left stood around, their senses totally dulled, waiting to see what the coming hours would bring, but emotionally completely drained and physically almost beyond exhaustion.

Needless to say, there were still no rations to be had and the rain began coming down again heavily. However, they did not have long to contemplate the miserable situation. Within the hour orders arrived from divisional headquarters. The failure earlier that day was unacceptable. It was to be renewed forthwith and this time was to be driven home. Hauling themselves wearily into some sort of attack formation, 3rd and 4th Companies Reserve Infantry Regiment 201 set out again for Diksmuide. There was no reconnaissance, no preparation, nothing at all; just the few men left on their feet stumbling forward in to the dark to an uncertain fate. They were never seen again. 1st and 2nd Companies, manning the front line, saw and heard little of what happened to them. The distance was too great for voices to be heard and although the odd flash was seen coming from Diksmuide, it was impossible to ascertain exactly what was occurring.

Initially there was not too much concern but, after some time when not even a runner carrying a report had arrived, there was real concern that something catastrophic had happened. It later transpired that, under the cover of the darkness, the two companies had managed to break right into the centre of Diksmuide and that a wild battle had developed in and around the market place – man against man at close range. The Belgians, with the advantage of local knowledge, manned windows overlooking the square and poured fire down at the attackers below. One of the senior men present, Oberleutnant Dugend, fell seriously wounded and was dragged away by the Belgians. Oberleutnant von Weiher collapsed in a burst of fire and lay in a pool of blood overnight until some of his men found him and carried him away in the early hours of the morning.

During the night 3rd Battalion Reserve Infantry Regiment 202 also penetrated the town, led personally by their regimental commander, Major von Oidtmann. In heavy fighting they got as far as the bridge over the Ijzer, but they too were hunted down in hand to hand fighting and a mere handful fought their way out back to Esen as dawn broke. That the men of this unit went to their deaths was an unlucky twist of fate. As the evening wore on and there was no definite news from Diksmuide, a decision was taken to launch this, the final divisional reserve, forward in order to add weight to the Reserve Infantry Regiment 201 assault force, which was believed by then to be fighting its way through the town. Orders to that effect were sent by runner and the regimental commander, knowing how difficult a mission it was going to be, decided to command it personally. The companies shook out and were swallowed up in the darkness. Not long afterwards a message arrived countermanding the previous one, but it arrived too late. By then the battalion was advancing to its fate.

No attempt appears to have been made to keep this attack silent. Drums and trumpets sounded, shouts of *Hurra!* went up and, with commendable aggression, the momentum so developed carried the attackers across the open grounds, enabled them to overrun all the trenches and obstacles in their way and break into the town, despite being entirely isolated, with both flanks hanging in the air. A vigorous push through the built up area meant that they thrust as far forward as the canal bridge but, once there, the men found themselves right in the centre of a killing zone, surrounded on three sides by enemy fire positions. Right up until the moment he was killed, Major von Oidtmann did everything possible to rally his men and to hold onto what they had gained, in the hope that support would be forthcoming, but it was no use. Casualties continually mounted and as dawn broke, trapped in a tiny perimeter, their ammunition exhausted, the remnants of the battalion, some twelve officers and 300 other ranks, many of them wounded, were captured.

A mere five or six men evaded capture and returned to their former positions, together with a couple of platoons who had carried out detached duties on 25 October and so avoided the fate of the remainder of their comrades. It was not until later in the war, when a copy of a Belgian publication *La Campagne 1914/15* fell into German hands, when it was found on the person of a Belgian prisoner from the 2nd Regiment of the line 1st Belgian Division, that the alleged course of events during the night 25/26 October in Diksmuide became known in any sort of detail. Despite being couched in somewhat flowery prose, it provided an outline, which was later expanded upon after the war when men returned from captivity and were able to provide personal accounts.

"One hundred times over the order 'Hold on unto Death!' was given to those magnificent troops, who stood firm through the storm of fire and iron. Huge quantities of ammunition were got forward, together with oil to lubricate the overworked machine guns. This meant that the Belgians and the French Fusilier-Marins had enough bullets to kill thousands of the *Boche*. Every man felt that the terrible hour of decision was fast approaching and this certainty gave them all the courage of desperation. Hardly had darkness fallen than a new attack began in the northern sector, but it was beaten off. Almost simultaneously a strong thrust in the south foundered as well. Each time that we opened up with small arms fire, our artillery brought down defensive fire in the area just in front of our trenches. The bursting of shells and shrapnel rounds lit up the night sky with an effect like fairy lights. Our mens' morale was excellent. The troops of the courageous Iron Division fought with indescribable bravery; they seemed to be invincible.

"It appeared, however that the enemy were willing to sacrifice whatever it took to ensure victory. It seemed as though large masses of fresh troops had been assembled before Diksmuide and given orders to capture the place at all costs, because there was no wavering in their tenacity. Hardly had one assault been beaten off before another was launched with increased ferocity. What sort of booty could have been dangled in front of them for them to be so willing to go to their deaths? What drink could they have drunk to fill them with such animal aggression and fury? Bloodthirsty, demonic, they stormed forward with the savage fury of animals, hungry for the slaughter, stumbling over corpses, treading on the wounded and, despite being mown down in their hundreds, kept coming forward again and again.

"Occasionally individuals pressed forward to the parapet and then the battle degenerated to a hand to hand fight with bayonets and rifle butts. Stomachs were slashed open, men were throttled and skulls smashed, but with every man in reserve thrown forward to fight in the trenches, the defence never weakened; not one bit of ground was yielded anywhere. Intermingled with scraps of uniforms and weapons lay hundreds of German corpses. Wounded men crawled towards our trenches covered in blood and filth, presenting a picture of total misery which cried out for mercy. The rain turned into a real storm, with the howling wind blending with the thunderous roar of the shells.

"Towards 1.00 am, despite the rifle fire of the 4th Company 11th Regiment, several hundred Germans, commanded by a major (3rd Battalion Reserve Infantry Regiment 202 under Major von Oidtmann, who was killed there) came storming along, adjacent to the Esen road. At a run, carrying all before them, they rushed Diksmuide and then burst into the market square like a howling gale, believing that by yelling, shouting and firing their rifles they would cause complete confusion. This horde then arrived at the bridge over the Ijzer and the first of them were across it before it became clear if they were men pulling back or enemy. Once the chance of error was eliminated, a machine gun opened up on the mob at point blank range. Thirty of them were killed. The remainder of them, with the major at their head, rushed on to the [railway] halt at Kaaskerke [one thousand metres west of the bridge], their yells of *Hurra!* split the night as their trumpeter blew the charge.

"At the Kaaskerke level crossing the yelling band was brought to a halt when the gates were closed just in time and they came under fire from Fusilier –Marins manning nearby trenches. They hurled themselves at them and into the meadows beyond. Threatening them with death, they demanded of the prisoners the whereabouts of the gun lines, but nobody would betray anything, despite the fact that the guns were located not one hundred metres away, but invisible to the enemy in the darkness. After that the group broke up. In the darkness some men became lost and scattered . . . At daybreak they were rounded up in small groups and captured. Only one small group, which was led by the major, offered defiance even after they had killed the last of their prisoners. He paid for this crime by being bayoneted, half his men were mown down and the remainder captured. Four of the prisoners, suspected of murder, were shot then and there on orders of the admiral."[23]

After the war, one member of 10th Company Reserve Infantry Regiment 202 wrote a version of the events of that night:[24]

"During the evening of 25 October, 3rd Battalion Reserve Infantry Regiment 202 was withdrawn from the regimental sector at Woumen to Esen to act as divisional reserve. Following a two hour march in the pouring rain we reached that place. The riflemen were placed to the side of the road leading to Diksmuide and we had to remain at readiness to intervene in the battle for Diksmuide which was raging. Shortly after midnight, orders arrived stating that the battalion was to attack the enemy in Diksmuide and occupy the western exit of that place. Weapons were unloaded, bayonets were fixed and we made our way past burning houses along the road which had been churned up by shells towards Diksmuide. Hardly had we passed our own front line than we were greeted by the first of the enemy fire then, just before we reached Diksmuide itself, we came under lacerating small arms fire from the left flank.

"Instinctively we took cover in the ditch on the right hand side of the road and carried on, one behind the other, in the direction of the town. I was right at the front, with our brave commander, Major von Oidtmann in the lead. 'Forwards men!' he shouted and was the first to leap over the barricade the enemy had erected at the entrance to the town. A number of Belgians rushed out of the nearest houses and charged us, but they were defeated after a short struggle with bayonets. With drums beating and to shouts of *Hurra!* we drove on without stopping, our 10th Company in front. Huge salvoes of fire came at us from the houses and off the roofs. Taking terrible casualties, we pushed on through the town to the canal bridge, where we were met by a hellish rate of rifle and machine guns fire from both sides.

"The attack threatened to stall, but Major von Oidtmann, swinging his sword took the lead and urged us on. With thunderous shouts of *Hurra!* we followed him, charging across the bridge of death. About one third of the daring men who had stuck by their leader made it across the bridge in one piece: perhaps about forty men . . . "

Another member of Reserve Infantry Regiment 202 who emerged from the battle for Diksmuide with nothing worse than painful, but superficial, wounds to the face took advantage of a pause later in the battle to write home at some length, providing his family and posterity with a further version of events on this day of dreadful casualties, courage and failed hopes at Diksmuide.

Kriegsfreiwilliger Lattermann 10th Company Reserve Infantry Regiment 202 [25]

"Let me begin with 25 October. It was just about midday when we suddenly got the word, 'Prepare to move. At 5.00 pm we are moving forward out of these trenches further forward to the front line and from there probably to assault Diksmuide!' 'Thank goodness' I said to myself, 'at long last we are going to get away from this dismal dump where we have already spent a week doing nothing except be on the receiving end of huge quantities of shells, shrapnel rounds and bullets.' Then it was afternoon and the sun went down. Then began an evening and night, which were to play a shocking role in the history of this war. At 5.00pm all the men along a one kilometre stretch of trench were ready to move. They were from Reserve Infantry Regiments 201 and 204 and were hopelessly mixed up.

"To our right the attack had begun; sections moving forward independently. The coordination problems caused by the intermingling were soon obvious. It was extremely hard to differentiate one group from another and runners were kept busy trying to make sure that their battalion and regimental commanders were kept up to date. On one occasion I volunteered to carry a message a distance of 500 metres to our major and ran through such a storm of fire that everyone who saw me bawled, 'Take cover! That man is mad! No, he is just running past!' I had to keep shouting that I was a runner and that I had no time to take cover. I succeeded in remaining in one piece and ending up back by our Leutnant Hentschel, though both my boots were full of water. He was delighted with the success of his volunteer.

"Having passed on my message I set to and emptied my boots and put on dry socks – three pairs of them simultaneously. I wish I had known that they too would soon be soaking wet! Soon it was our turn, that is to say with the trenches to our front empty, we moved forward without being specially ordered to do so until we were hard up behind the front line. Naturally this did not occur without casualties, but soon it went dark and we did not offer such definite targets. Unfortunately, the darkness caused the utmost confusion and we completely lost our cohesion. To begin with we were not sure if we were to remain in the front line trenches but then we received the order, 'Move to the right in single file at five metre intervals and form up.' Unsurprisingly, an order to move like this in the dark was bound to lead to regrettable mis-understandings. Not everybody made it to the rallying point and for that our third platoon and parts of other companies have to thank for their survival.

"We later discovered that an order was sent, detailing us to pull back, but this reached only a few of the platoons. The remainder of us went to the fate which this night attack on Diksmuide held in store for us. Meanwhile, it began to pour with rain. Our officers tried in vain to maintain contact with each other. We waded through waterlogged trenches which our pioneers had attempted to keep passable by placing baulks of timber in them. We were in a very sorry state as we made our way to Diksmuide and I was extremely angry that my feet were wet and cold again. After an hour we reached Esen, which had fallen into our hands a few days earlier . . . and there we stood for two hours dripping wet. We were thirsty, but there was nothing to be done. There was nowhere to sit and although we could have lain down, we should soon have been drenched to the skin.

"If you bear in mind that, in addition, we had been fed extremely poorly for the past week and had had the pleasure to be able to spend the time in trenches, which we ourselves had had to construct, and stay there, sitting or crouching, attempting to sleep and being unable to move without risking being hit by a bullet – not to mention the mass of shells and shrapnel which were sent over, or the attention of *franctireurs* shooting from every bush, tree or ruined building, you will be able to paint an approximate picture of our mood. Finally we got started on an attack against Diksmuide which was about two kilometres away. Because numerous houses were already ablaze, it could be seen for some distance, as could be heard the sound of the enemy firing.

"There was nothing for it but to pluck up courage and press on, with the thought that perhaps the enemy had pulled back from Diksmuide and were occupying their positions in rear . . . Soon we heard. 'Unload all weapons. Fix bayonets!' We formed into so-called assault columns and set off. Soon shrapnel was cracking down among the ranks. Some men were hit and fell screaming terribly to the ground . . . To the left and right machine guns firing from trenches had fired to such effect [during previous attacks] that bodies lay heaped up and numerous young men from Berlin lay there unknown and only roughly covered up with soil. We pushed on and on, always in the greatest danger of being skewered by the bayonet of one of our own man because we could only see a mere one to two paces in front of us. The only illumination came from the fires of Diksmuide, which we had by now reached.

"Here there was an unexpected hold up. The men hesitated. They were unsure about clearing through the town; memories of the shoot out in Esen were still fresh in the memory. Here the leadership played a big role. From our battalion these were the commander, Major von Oidtmann, Adjutant von Renesse, our company commander, Leutnant Hentschel, platoon commander Leutnant Kiefbusch and Unteroffizier Neuendorf. Shouting at the men, they fired them up with new courage and off we went. Nobody hung back, not even those who had fallen over and sprained their ankles etc. This last matter was very easy to achieve because the ground was littered with rubble from collapsed houses, dead animals and human corpses and there was a constant risk of tripping over them, or over other comrades who had themselves lost their footing. This also caused some of them to suffer bayonet wounds, as you can well imagine.

"Anyway, with shouts of *Hurra!* or *Long live Germany!* We raced along the street, without encountering any resistance. We could not see anything of the enemy and there was no fire from the buildings, not that there was much left of them anyway . . . still shouting *Hurra!* we reached the railway embankment of Diksmuide, the much disputed embankment of which so much has been mentioned. I shall have to keep this short, otherwise we shall have quitted our idyllic quarters before I have described everything. It was here at the embankment that we suddenly came under the most murderous machine gun fire from houses which were still in reasonable condition . . . about twenty to thirty machine guns fired as if under single command at us – approximately 500 men drawn from every conceivable battalion of 43rd [Reserve] Division.

"In my considered opinion, the mistake was to drive in a tightly packed group through the streets without scouts, flank protection or patrols, or having first cleared the houses. There we were, powerless, weapons unloaded, having to stand there and be mown down like corn in a field."

Some time after midnight the Belgians launched a counter-attack from Diksmuide, more or less at the same time as leading elements of 2nd Battalion Reserve Infantry Regiment 201 heard about the fate of their 1st Battalion and the commanding officer, fearing the consequences, cancelled the move forward in support of that unit and instead ordered that their front line trenches be occupied in readiness to fend off the Belgian attack. In the event the Belgian threat did not materialise. Probably after all the chaos back in Diksmuide, it proved to be impossible to organise a counter-attack systematically. Meanwhile 3rd Battalion Reserve Infantry Regiment 201 was ordered to go into hasty defence around a small wayside chapel by the road between Esen and Diksmuide and to hold it at all costs. Earlier, certainly before midnight when news of the failed attack by Reserve Infantry Regiment 201 had reached the headquarters of 43rd Reserve Division, orders went out to Reserve Infantry Regiment 203 to launch a further assault from the south to take some of the pressure off the thrust from the east. Nobody had any great faith that this attempt, launched in pouring rain in a pitch black night through the known obstacle course of fences, hedges and ditches, would enjoy success. Nevertheless the orders had to be obeyed and every effort was made to brief and prepare the participants. All this took some time and it was not until around 1.00 am, long after the first attack had ended in bloody failure, that it was launched.

The rain was drenching down in sheets. The attackers were all soaked to the skin; their morale as low as it could be. Nevertheless, weapons were unloaded and bayonets were fixed, shining in the flash of exploding shells. In silence, with the exception of the occasional whispered word of command, this assault force stumbled forward in section columns to attack Diksmuide form the south. In reality not one man in this force had the slightest idea of what confronted them, but orders were orders and nobody dwelt upon the fact. Stumbling, cursing under their breath through the driving rain, the columns began to approach Diksmuide after about ten minutes. They were just about to deploy into assault formation when somebody on the Belgian side must have spotted what was happening. Instantly all Hell broke loose as the defenders opened up on this side of the town with every weapon that could be brought to bear and only a few moments later the first of the artillery defensive fire began to come down amongst the attackers.

The officers and NCOs in the lead were the first to be hit, but they were followed by many others as the approach route was swept by fire. Men were falling constantly, the sections lost their cohesion as the night was filled with the rattle of small arms fire, cries of pain or anger and shells came down with increased frequency. The attack was over before it had begun. It had never seemed to stand much chance of success and so it proved. The remnants fell back on their start line and counted the cost of this latest example of folly. The 1st Battalion alone suffered casualties of twenty four killed, 102 wounded and thirty four missing. For the time being there was nothing more to be done. 43rd Reserve Division had done everything humanly possible to carry out the orders of their superior headquarters. Now it made no difference what orders were given; there was nobody left to obey them. The Belgian army, of which they had formed such a low opinion, had dealt them a severe blow, one from which it was going to be extremely difficult to recover.

Possibly in recognition of this fact, certainly in conformity with developments in the remainder of the Fourth Army area and in tacit recognition of the fact that the offensive against Diksmuide had hitherto been conducted with scandalous incompetence, there was a reorganisation in that sector. It had become clear that attempting to command the forward regiments from locations which, necessarily, were well to the rear, was not working. Brigade headquarters were improvised forthwith. Henceforth 85 Reserve Infantry Brigade, commanded by Oberst von Reuter, would be responsible for Reserve Infantry Regiments 201 and 202, together with Reserve Jäger Battalion 15, whilst Oberst Teetzmann would command 86 Reserve Infantry Brigade, comprising Reserve Infantry Regiment 203 and 204. To complete these important changes, Generalmajor von Runckel was posted in as divisional commander. Although late in the day and long after the damage had been done, it remained to be seen if the new arrangements would bring to an end the appalling series of inadequately prepared attacks.

Early signs were encouraging. All three senior commanders were from active formations, had a well developed sense of what was militarily possible and brought a strong degree of practical, sensible realism to bear on the problem of Diksmuide. In future there would be no question of attacks being launched without the necessary reconnaissance and artillery preparation and care would be taken to advance the German front line so as to shorten the distance over which any assault would have to be launched. To their credit and as a considerable boost to the morale of the forward troops, the commanders moved right up to the most forward positions to assess the situation. Within a very short time they had convinced themselves that almost every aspect of what they had inspected was deficient and that without radical steps being taken there was no prospect whatever of the town falling.

Virtually the entire front line was condemned. For the most part, due to the deficiency of suitable equipment and lack of tactical understanding, the trenches had been inadequately dug in low-lying beet fields. Not only was the protection they offered largely illusory, there was no worthwhile field of fire from most of them and they were also overlooked by Belgian positions, which could bring down accurate fire against them every time there was the slightest movement. This was the first thing to be rectified. That same night moves were made to occupy every farm building and its surrounding area within range, because these places tended to be on firmer ground or to be slightly above the adjacent fields. Engineer advice was then provided to show the infantry how to construct secure trenches with overhead cover and how to develop the positions so that they became linked together and advanced towards the enemy positions. With each passing night there were improvements and an active policy of patrolling was pursued though, for the time being, there was no repetition of the large scale assaults which had proved to be so disastrous.

In addition a special effort was made to quarter the old battlefields to try to reduce the enormous numbers of casualties recorded as missing. Many of the fallen were identified and seriously wounded men were also recovered, despite having spent three or more days lying helplessly in the open. There were some amazing survivals, but not all the stories had a happy ending. During the evening of 27 October, for example, a patrol from 12th Company Reserve Infantry Regiment 201, led by Kriegsfreiwilliger Hennig, came across the commander of 9th Company Reserve Infantry Regiment 201, who had been badly wounded during the attack of 21 October and had been virtually untended ever since. A rescue party was immediately assembled, he was recovered to the dressing station in Esen but, gravely weakened by his experiences, he died on the operating table. One of his soldiers later described what happened.

Kriegsfreiwilliger Hans Otto 9th Company Reserve Infantry Regiment 201 [26] **4.**

"Hans Graf von Wintzingerode was from a family whose seat for 600 years had been a castle in Eichsfeld.[27] In accordance with the old tradition of his family, he became an officer and, from the age of eighteen, was a member of the Fusilier Guards for some years before returning home to run the family estate. At the outbreak of war, he rejoined the army immediately, being posted to us as company commander on 17 October during the march from Alost to Gent . . . When, on 20 October we advanced towards Esen, he rode on his charger, despite the enemy fire and that evening, after orders for the attack the following day reached us, he rode out again by himself. Silent and serious, he returned and spent the night in amongst his men.

"During the assault on 21 October, he was always to the fore. As the enemy fire increased, he never flinched in his determination to press home the attack. Holding his sword aloft, he urged his men forward repeatedly, but death had reaped a dreadful harvest in our ranks. The numbers able to respond to his leadership grew ever smaller then, as we were approaching the enemy positions on the far side of the embankment, an enemy bullet knocked him to the ground and those following him closely were also hit. When the foggy October night drew a veil over the plain of Flanders and the signal to rally was blown, the remainder of the company gathered by the embankment. As far as the enemy fire permitted the wounded were taken to the platelayer's hut, which was about 300 metres from Esen Kapelle but, in accordance with the statements of everyone who had witnessed him fall, it was assumed that the company commander was dead.

"It was not until much later that we discovered that five of our comrades had remained behind at the platelayer's hut to care for the wounded and to evacuate them when the enemy fire eased. They soon heard the groans and cries of wounded comrades and, after crawling around the fields, they brought one after the other into the hut until eventually the cellar, the ground floor and the upper story were full of wounded men. The courageous five then realised that they could not just abandon the wounded and it was their duty to stay and look after them. They bandaged them and cared for them, scavenging around to find food for them. Eventually they thought that they had recovered all the wounded men within range of the platelayer's hut then, during the evening of the third day, by which time we had worked our way forward along the row of poplars, once more we reached the hut, summoned medical orderlies and the wounded could be evacuated.

"Later again, during the evening of 27 October, a patrol found our Hauptmann, seriously wounded by several bullets, but still alive. For six days he had laid out there in the rain and the cold, tended by two or three slightly wounded men who had stuck it out with him and managed to dig down rather deeper into the ground to provide more shelter form the enemy fire. During the daytime all movement had to be avoided, because it just attracted more fire. The very limited rations were shared out, but thirst was the worst thing of all. Enemy patrols came along and took the other wounded men prisoner, but the Hauptman refused their aid, not wanting to draw attention to himself. Once he was discovered he was carefully carried back to the aid post in Esen, but cruel fate, which had torn away so many of our comrades on 21 October, claimed him too.

"Faithful to Germany, his heroism, his endurance alone on the battlefield and his tragic death after successful evacuation will always remain unforgettable for us. Even though he only led us for a few days, in our hearts he will always remain 'our' Hauptmann."

Possibly as a result of the major diversion of enemy effort caused by the ill-fated assault on Diksmuide on 25 October, troops of 44th Reserve Division had managed, despite intense Allied pressure, to maintain and even improve their positions on the west bank of the Ijzer. The outcome of the disaster which had befallen 43rd Reserve Division meant that the southern flank of 44th Reserve Division was in the air. Nevertheless, its commander, Generalleutnant von Dorrer, decided to concentrate as much force as he could muster and push west on 26 October. Hastily a 'Regiment Czettritz'[28] was formed from one battalion of Reserve Infantry Regiment 207, which had been acting as divisional reserve, the corps reserve, 1st Battalion Reserve Infantry Regiment 205 and a company of miscellaneous stragglers. These forces crossed the Ijzer, pushed west and gained approximately one kilometre of ground, as did the remnants of the forces already in place in the bridgehead.

Naturally there was a Belgian counter-action. Fighting was brisk throughout the day and some of the newly-gained territory had to be given up. Nevertheless, there was considerable engineer bridging activity. The numerous footbridges were supplemented by two others, one of which was sufficiently strong to permit two batteries of Reserve Field Artillery Regiment 44 to cross over and take up fire positions on the west bank. Earlier in the day its commander, Oberst Wuthmann, realising that this was a possibility, had gone forward to carry out a personal reconnaissance so, when the orders arrived, it was possible to pass 4th and 5th Batteries across the bridge and for them to take up fire positions rapidly. The state of the ground forced the artillery to place their guns in thoroughly unsuitable locations right on the embankment where they were in full view of the enemy, but the move, conducted one gun at a time and with considerable spacing, succeeded in passing them all over without casualties.

Vizefeldwebel Kirchner 5th Battery Reserve Field Artillery Regiment 44 [29] **6.**

"The embankment that the battery had to pass was under fire by the enemy. Therefore the guns were pulled forward individually and crossed the canal on a pontoon bridge constructed by our engineers. This was the first time that our young drivers had to carry out such a crossing under fire and there was an air of considerable tension and excitement, which only varied according to the temperament of the man concerned. Everything went smoothly and according to the book. During the few days since our baptism of fire we had already experienced being on the receiving end of heavy bombardment and had taught ourselves how to overcome the unpleasant feeling of having to sit there, unable to react, whilst an unseen enemy aimed a hail of iron of all descriptions at us.

"We had also seen enemy wounded and killed, though admittedly only a few of those, at close range and had been fortunate enough only to see at first hand a handful of our own bloody casualties. Now, however, as we turned onto the narrow strip between the dike and the canal bank, we were confronted with a gruesome sight. Lying mostly with their heads towards the embankment lay our comrades and fellow countrymen. The poor, faithful lads must have been hit by a concentration of fire which landed behind them because in most cases the backs of their skulls had been literally torn off. At least forty to fifty men, perhaps more, all appallingly killed in this manner, lay piled up in one small area."

At this stage it was still the firm intention to press on with the attack west of the Ijzer, so although conditions in the bridgehead were dreadful, the units within it just had to hang on in the face of endless artillery fire and Allied counter attacks. Life was particularly difficult for the gunners on the west bank, but their fire was considered to be essential for a major attack planned for 30 October, so they had to make the best of it. The fact that they were fully occupied during the previous days was probably helpful to their morale, which definitely needed to be boosted, judging by this eye witness account:

Kriegsfreiwilliger Nebel 2nd Battalion Reserve Field Artillery Regiment 44 [30] **6.**

"The connection to the rear was via a wooden bridge built by our engineers and which they had to repair constantly because it kept being shot up. The short distance between our teams of horses and the gun line was a path of utter misery. It took about fifteen minutes to cover it and it was littered on either side by dead cattle which were in a shocking state and stank terribly. There was then a group of houses which provided a place for countless wounded, who could not be evacuated to the main aid post, to be held. All the way there was a musical accompaniment, provided by shells whose filling had parted company with their jackets before the end of their trajectories. There were masses of these things which whirred overhead like lidless and empty tin cans.[31] There was a filthy smell from the canal which was full of dead cattle and the occasional corpse of a soldier which bobbed along gently downstream. There were as good as no digging tools and no drinking water. Everything was ruined and the water in the muddy holes was so contaminated that we hardly dared use it for washing – and all the time there was nothing but rain, rain and more rain."

It was apparent to Headquarters XXII Reserve Corps that, for the time being, nothing more could be achieved on the Diksmuide front but there was still a chance of developing operations west of the Ijzer, so 43rd Reserve Division was directed to reorganise its sector, so as to release what was left of Reserve Infantry Regiment 202 to move under command of 87 Reserve Infantry Brigade and reinforce it for a renewed attack in the direction of the Diksmuide – Nieuwpoort railway, which was to be launched by 44th Reserve Division in conjunction with another operation further north by 6th Reserve Division. In order to achieve this, 2nd Battalion Reserve Infantry Regiment 202 was absorbed within Reserve Infantry Regiments 205 and 207, whilst a combined force of 1st and 3rd Battalions operated a little to the south. Crossing the Ijzer to the west of Kasteelhoek, the companies moved into position and attempted as far as possible to dig for cover in the sodden stinking morass, having traversed the boggy area and its innumerable drainage ditches with the utmost difficulty.

The artillery preparation for the attack began on 29 October, with the assaulting troops distributed along a start line which ran from Kloosterhoek to Stuivekenskerke via Gaepaert. At 4.00 pm the attack began on a complete brigade frontage and immediately ran into heavy fire as the attempt was made to cross the open ground and negotiate the various ditches and over water courses. Some progress was made, but enemy small arms fire built up to such an extent that hardly any of the engaged sub units closed to within 500 metres of the railway line. One of the members of Reserve Infantry Regiment 202 later described the attack from his perspective.

Grenadier Petersen 3rd Company Reserve Infantry Regiment 202 [32] *7.*

"The regiments of 43rd Reserve Division [*sic.*] were detailed to support the attack of 44th Reserve Division on the embankment of the Diksmuide – Nieuwpoort railway. One part of 3rd Company was already in position on the far bank of the canal. The remaining one and a half platoons moved together with the other companies of 2nd and 1st Battalions across the Ijzer bridges to the west of Kasteelhoek, then marched some distance along the canal before deploying in a firing line in the direction of the railway line, which was away in the distance beyond the sodden Flanders fields and meadows which were criss-crossed with ditches. We were greeted by black pillars of earth from the exploding shells, white shrapnel bursts and the crack of rifle and machine gun fire, but to begin with we did not suffer many casualties as the advancing lines of infantrymen gathered in a shallow ditch.

"The company commander, Oberleutnant Költz, who was killed the following day, ordered me to find out if the trench opposite was free of enemy. Bent over and following a ditch which ran at ninety degrees to ours, I arrived at the trench. I had been lucky.[33] The only things hit by a bullet were my mess tins. I leapt over the edge and thought that I had landed in a Belgian trench because the soldiers were dressed in black coats, but in fact they were the remnants of Landwehr Regiment 35 [*sic*: in fact, almost certainly Landwehr Brigade Ersatz Battalion 35 of 4th Ersatz Division], who had been involved the previous day in a failed attempt to capture the railway embankment.

"Just after 4.00 pm the companies got to their feet and stormed forward to the railway embankment. We were not fired at. By the light of the afternoon sun, at a range of about 200 meters, we could clearly see the telegraph poles on the embankment. Apparently the Belgians had withdrawn from it. All of a sudden all Hell broke loose. Belgian machine guns were mounted on the embankment then only a few paces later we were pinned down on the hard ground by curtains of fire from these guns. To my right and left I could hear the groans of men who had been hit. Slowly twilight fell. Pressed hard against the earth, with only our knapsacks for cover, we tried to dig into the hard ground, because every movement spotted by the light of a burning farmhouse and the rising moon was met with another burst of machine gun fire.

"Night fell slowly. To my front, a few metres from the wire obstacle, I could see the outline of the pale bearded face of a kriegsfreiwilliger against the night sky. Working in fours we tried to produce a shell scrape which in the daylight would at least provide us with cover from view from the embankment. The following morning some Belgian sections advanced down from the railway embankment, but they were swiftly beaten off with rifle fire. The Belgians began to stir again about midday, so we engaged them from the edge of our scrape. Silently Grenadier Dettmann, who was next to me, fell back, shot through the head. The narrow edge of our scrape had not been thick enough to stop the bullet.

"The three of us left pressed ourselves down on the ground. Flachs had a chest wound, Jakobitz had a graze wound on his back and next to us was the dead Dettmann. The sun burnt down. All the food we had was a dry crust of bread and some pea soup powder from the iron rations. One of our comrades from 1st Company put his head up from an adjacent hole and shouted a witty comment at us then fell back, shot through the head. Eventually the full moon rose once more lighting up our holes. From somewhere came the order, 'Crawl back individually.' In a trench filled with wounded men a few steps behind our scrape I came across comrade Mayer with a serious stomach wound. Together with comrade Barlitza I carried him back in a ground sheet. Again and again we had to throw ourselves down because the Belgians reacted to every movement with machine gun fire.

"On the far side of a broad water-filled ditch we discovered a wehrmann with a leg wound, who begged us in the dark to take him with us, but because we had Mayer to carry, we could not help him. We also did not realise that the increase in width of the ditch represented the start of the flooding caused by opening the lock gates of the Ijzer canal.

These men of Reserve Infantry Regiment 202 were in no position to participate in the resumption of the attack the following day, but that was due to their relative success on 29 October. For the majority of 87 Reserve Infantry Brigade it was a different matter. Luckily it soon began to get dark, but their position was also thoroughly unenviable. Where they were located, the water meadows were soaking wet and there could be no question of digging in. As soon as a spadeful of earth was lifted the hole filled with water. For some of the troops this was their tenth successive night in the open and although some rations were got right forward, large numbers were too ill with diarrhoea and other gastro-intestinal diseases to be able to benefit from it. Despite all these difficulties, however, almost all the survivors were able to hold on through the night with a view to resuming the advance the following day.

At 5.30 am on 30 October, shivering with cold, wet through and in many case far from well, the men of Reserve Infantry Regiments 205 and 207 unloaded their rifles, fixed bayonets and, still in darkness, made a fresh attempt to get forward. Thwarted almost immediately by deep ditches, they splashed their way through with extreme difficulty, only to be detected by the enemy and to come under very heavy fire once more. 3rd Battalion Reserve Infantry Regiment 205 pressed on and thought at once point that it had reached the embankment. There was great disappointment when it was found to be a long earth bank; the real embankment was another 150 metres further on. In reaching this point the battalion has lost almost all its officers. In the end only a small fragment was still charging forward, led by Leutnant Rudolf Schulz with drawn sword. Then he fell and the attack was checked by a hedge which had been strengthened with barbed wire. It was yet another failure.

Leutnant Trebbin 3rd Battalion Reserve Infantry Regiment 205 [34] *7.*

"Only about twenty five to thirty of us reached the objective. Then, directly opposite us on the other side were the Belgians and the French. We soon realised what a desperate situation we were in. Should we let ourselves be captured? No! We put our heads together and decided to stick it out and fight to the last man. Cut off from any possible assistance, we began a fire fight. As soon as an enemy soldier put his head above cover he was hit. We were almost surrounded, so we could not protect our flanks. As a result our ranks were thinned repeatedly when the other side scored a hit and yet another brave lad sunk into the mud of the trench. Unteroffizier Take of 9th Company was hit in the lower jaw and a short time later, Kriegsfreiwilliger Alfred Beck was seriously wounded by a gun shot to the thigh.

"I hauled him clear of the filth and helped him through the hedge so that he would be able to crawl back under cover of darkness. Those still unwounded hung on grimly, but around midday our ammunition ran out. Then, of all bad luck, our own artillery began to bring down fire on our position, causing more casualties. At that, as the commander on the spot, I gave the order to abandon the position and we tried to crawl back to the rear. Salvoes of fire accompanied the movement of each man. Through ditches which were over-flowing with dead and wounded men we made but slow progress. I found Leutnant Badelt suffering from a serious head wound. It was not until it went dark that I could rush back in bounds and after going round in circles for a time, I got back to our lines at 1.00 am."

It is impossible to say how much longer the German army would have gone on trying to make progress west of the Ijzer, because matters moved swiftly out of its control. This last attack, which had cost so many casualties, had moved the line forward a mere two hundred metres on average. Within Reserve Infantry Regiment 205, Major von Treskow was seriously wounded and died that evening, Major von Mülmann was wounded in four places and almost all the company and platoon commanders were killed, wounded or missing.[35] From Reserve Infantry Regiment 208, the commander, Oberstleutnant Czettritz, was seriously wounded and the commanding officer of 2nd Battalion, Oberleutnant Wachsmuth, was dead.[36] All the sacrifice was for nothing, because gradually everyone became aware that the water was rising. The orders were still to hold on, which was done, despite yet more casualties from heavy artillery fire. Night fell once more and was grimly endured but, as day dawned the following day, it was quite clear that the flooding had now spread over an even larger area. 6th Reserve Division pulled back its left flank and, so as to correspond, 44th Reserve Division also withdrew its right flank. An attempt was made to keep hold of the positions closest to the railway embankment and Reserve Jäger Battalion 16 moved forward to carry out this duty, arriving during the late evening of 31 October.

By the morning of 1 November, it was clear that the task was hopeless. The jägers later recalled:[37]

"The water rose higher and higher in the trenches. Gradually the entire No Man's Land disappeared under water, right out to the Pervijse – Kaaskerke railway. Only the track to Lettenberg, which was being occupied by the enemy, remained above the water. The attack of 44th Reserve Division, on whose left flank the battalion was deployed, had to be suspended. However, orders arrived directing us to attach ourselves to a possible advance to be carried out by 43rd Reserve Division on our left. That also did not occur, because in this area, too, the water rose more and more until it was out of the question to be able to move forward.

"With heavy hearts the commanders were forced to withdraw the lines here as well. It had become impossible to remain. At 10.00 pm the battalion disengaged from the enemy. The entire rear area was under heavy fire and water was thrown up violently every time a shell crashed down. It was a clear moonlit night as the jägers crawled back one by one out of their positions, so as to carry out the withdrawal unnoticed. The battle area of the previous days was traversed then the canal was crossed. Never again did the jägers set foot on the far bank . . . enemy small arms fire cracked over the battalion as it marched away. It was the final goodbye of the enemy on this battle front. The column marched away in profound silence. After the exhaustion of the past few days, everyone longed for a rest. The battalion strength had dropped to 514 men."

Whilst the battle had been raging west of the Ijzer, to the south and east of Diksmuide it had been a period of consolidation and reorganisation. There had been a great deal of activity between the positions at night and one positive result of all this patrolling, coupled with careful observation, was that 43rd Reserve Division was able on 29 October to issue an assessment of the enemy situation which was fully accurate for the first time.[38]

"The enemy positions run from the group of houses at In de Dry Cabaret, via the depot by the railway then along the railway embankment just east of Diksmuide [i.e. southwest at this point]. They then follow the Wade-beek [south] in the direction of the bend in the Ijzer to the east of Sint-Jakobs-Kapelle. Pushed forward towards our positions are the garrison of the platelayer's hut, about 300 metres east of the depot, as well as the cemetery, about 300 metres south of Diksmuide by the Woumen road. In rear the Ijzer Line from Kapelhoek to Sint-Jakobs-Kapelle has been fortified. There are other enemy trenches to the north, either side of the Diksmuide – Beerst road. Our own front line runs opposite to that through the most westerly farm buildings at Esen Kapelle, northwest of the buildings at Diksmuidehoek and as far as the northern edge of the chateau about 800 metres south of Diksmuide. This line is to be dug forward constantly towards the enemy under the protection of our artillery."

This information, which was typical of that available in the headquarters, meant that from that moment there would be no more attacks launched vaguely in the direction of the enemy but with no real understanding of what would oppose them. This did not mean, of course, that the prospect of another attack was not viewed with concern. The regiments were so terribly reduced in strength that just to advance would be a most serious proposition. To provide an idea of how difficult the manpower situation was, on 27 October Reserve Infantry Regiment 203 had to report that it had established a shortfall of thirty six officers and 1,316 other ranks. This was virtually half of its starting strength and, worse, the regiment was completely unable to say of the casualties how many were killed, wounded, missing or evacuated sick.[39]

There were obvious deficiencies in divisional administration, but at least a firm grip had been taken of the rationing arrangements. From 27 October, hot food was brought forward to the front line at least once per day and generally twice. This was probably as big a boost to morale as the arrival of additional heavy artillery to improve the quality and quantity of fire support available, though that, too, was a welcome addition to the attacking strength of 43rd Reserve Division which, after another week of general consolidation and preparation, interspersed with deployments of some of its formations to other parts of the corps area from time to time, was about to be called on to complete the unfinished task to its front.

Major Freiherr von Wedekind Commanding Officer 3rd Battalion Reserve Infantry Regiment 201 [40] 8.

"At ten minutes to midnight during the night 9/10 November, the brigade commander, Oberst von Reuter, entered my tiny dugout at the fork in the road next to the ruined chapel and briefed me verbally: 'From midnight tonight you are to begin working your way forward into assault positions. Tomorrow at 1.00 pm the brigade will storm Diksmuide!' A quick look at the watch showed that the whole process was to begin in ten minutes! 'The only chance of that being achieved is to remain calm', I thought to myself. Runners took oral orders to all the companies and also Company Henden. 'Prepare to move with the aim of advancing to a line 200 metres from the enemy position!'

"I went forward along the communication trenches, thick with clay, to 11th and 12th Companies. There, at 12.45 am, I received the detailed written orders, of all headquarters from Fourth Army downwards, for the attack. By

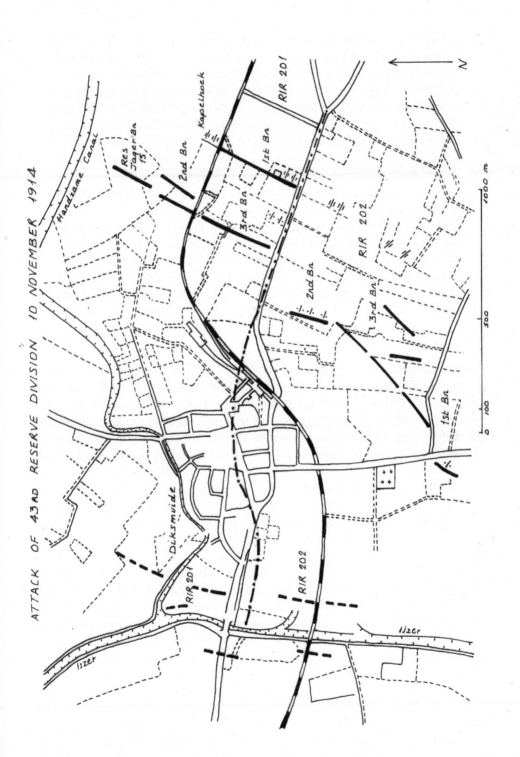

ATTACK OF 43RD RESERVE DIVISION 10 NOVEMBER 1914

the light of a poor tallow candle, I dictated extracts from the orders to the runners and half an hour later I received confirmation that everyone had received them. At about 1.15 am the regimental staff joined me in the support trenches of 11th Company. I reported that the orders had barely reached me and that, therefore, the forward movement had not yet begun. 9th and 10th Companies were able to begin their move and to dig in without coming under fire but, because the situation forward of 12th Company was unknown, 11th and 12th Companies stood by waiting for my order until matters were cleared up.

"Once patrols had established that the trenches, which the enemy had been occupying the previous evening, had apparently been evacuated, these companies, too, received the order to move forward at about 3.30 am. A dark night and fog facilitated the conduct [of the move] and, by 8.00 am, it was possible to report to the regiment that the battalion had moved forward to within two hundred metres of the enemy and dug in. As it became light it was possible clearly to make out two lines of enemy trenches, one behind the other and equipped with loopholes. Valiantly supported by the engineers, our men went to work with a will; the construction of communication trenches to the rear went on despite harassing fire."

The garrison opposing the forthcoming attack was somewhat reduced and worn down compared with that which countered the original attacks. On 10 November, it comprised two battalions of Fusilier-Marins, one battalion from Senegal, whose solders had suffered particularly badly from the cold, wet conditions, and one Belgian battalion. All of these units were well below strength and the defending artillery was down to about thirty percent of its original strength. The odds had shifted significantly in favour of the attackers for the first time and, as dawn broke, the assaulting troops were able to lift their heads above the parapets of their trenches and consider the prospect of Diksmuide to their front with rather more equanimity than had been possible two weeks earlier. The fog was still too dense to enable them to see the outlines of the houses and other buildings to their front, but it provided useful cover as final preparations went ahead.

All concerned had worked hard to get ready but, as has been noted, for some the time was rather short, so maximum use was made of the limited visibility and although there was some desultory small arms fire, it was effectively unaimed and caused the attacking force no problems at all for the time being. At 10.45 am, Generalmajor von Seydewitz issued the confirmatory attack orders. The operation was to be conducted on a fairly narrow front to improve concentration of force. To the north of the town, 4th Ersatz Division was to launch an attack in strength to divert the attention and resources of the defenders, Reserve Jäger Battalion 15 was directed to bring pressure to bear from the northeast but, once again, the main effort was to be made by Reserve Infantry Regiment 201 right and Reserve Infantry Regiment 202 left. The right hand limit of this attack sector was from a point 400 metres north of the railway embankment south to the inter-regimental boundary, which ran along the Diksmuide – Kapelhoek road. To the south, the Reserve Infantry Regiment 202 frontage ran southwest, following the line of the railway to the cemetery about three hundred metres south of the town on the Woumen road and, due to the width involved, all three of its battalions were in line in the order north to south of 2nd, 3rd,and 1st. This dilution carried risks with it, but such had been the earlier losses that the consequent reduction in initial impact in this area had to be accepted.

Reserve Infantry Regiment 201 chose to attack with the whole of 3rd Battalion, reinforced by 5th and 7th Companies in a first wave until leading elements had secured the line of the embankment which shielded the town from the east. At that point and following up closely in support, 1st Battalion, 6th and 8th Companies Reserve Infantry Regiment 201, reinforced by the machine guns and 8th Company Reserve Infantry Regiment 203 would pass through and fight through the town, supported by large quantities of rifle and machine gun fire from the top of the embankment. This was essentially a simple plan, with all the advantages that that confers and it emphasised overwhelming force, properly controlled (which was a welcome innovation) at the critical point.

Armed with the knowledge of previous failure, but buoyed up by the more professional and systematic approach to this operation, the attacking troops waited on their start lines in a mood of grim determination. This time, they felt there would be no rebuff, no stopping until the town had been cleared all the way to the Ijzer and then secured against enemy counter-action. As time passed, the weight of fire being directed against the objective increased dramatically. All the work in concentrating heavy artillery and plentiful ammunition was paying off and, furthermore, much of the gunnery was the responsibility of active units and formations and so was very much more effective than the random fire support provided for the earlier attempts. Heavy and super-heavy guns and howitzers poured fire into the already shattered town of Diksmuide. It was one of the heaviest bombardments of the war to date and soon the town was enveloped in one continuous series of great crashing explosions until it was completely enveloped in dust and smoke, whilst the field and medium artillery joined in by hammering the area of the railway embankment and all the enemy positions which had been so painstakingly recorded during the past week.

Numerous direct hits were scored on enemy trenches, whilst the railway embankment was pounded so hard that sections of track and sleepers were flung into the air like matchwood. Between midday and 1.00 pm the rate of fire rose to a crescendo. It was already too much for some of the defenders in exposed positions forward of the town and observers began to note a move backwards into the illusory protection of the built up area by individuals, small groups and even whole sections. At this sight the morale of the attacking forces visibly improved. There was hardly any enemy artillery fire and virtually none that was effective, the ground to the front presented tempting targets and soon the men of the first attack wave were up on their feet, stretching cramped limbs to get the blood moving again and taking pot shots with some success at the retreating enemy. There was real anticipation building up, then came the moment to launch the assault.

Major Freiherr von Wedekind Commanding Officer 3rd Battalion Reserve Infantry Regiment 201 [41] **8.**

"Standing on a stack of straw, about thirty metres in rear of 11th Company, at exactly 1.00 pm I bawled, 'Go!' and, as one man, the entire company launched forward at a run with loud shouts of *Hurra!* and stormed the enemy forward positions. I shall never forget the tension which had gripped us up to that point and the uplifting scene which then unfolded. Before the defenders – Belgians, Fusilier-Marins and Senegalese infantry – had had a chance to recover from our suppressive preparatory bombardment, they were simply overwhelmed. A few black troops, who attempted to continue to fire their machine guns, were just mown down. Prisoners came streaming back, machine guns were brought in and the names of the beaming attackers who had captured them were established.

"The attack on the Reserve Infantry Regiment 201 front made good progress. It was soon clear that the embankment had been secured and up there, from the standing position, the victorious volunteers were bringing down pursuing fire. The same was true out to the right, but it was a different story on the left! Here it seemed that Reserve Infantry Regiment 202 had come up against stronger resistance. Whilst two runners, ignoring all the fire coming from the left, made their way forward to the railway embankment with orders to consolidate there for the time being, I directed Loeber's machine gun platoon, which could be spared, to get his guns into a position where they could bring down enfilade fire to the left; some keen members of my staff lending a hand to carry the guns in to position.

"I then sent a message back to General von Seydewitz, informing him that 3rd Battalion Reserve Infantry Regiment 201 had stormed the positions and was reorganising along the line of the railway but before the runner was able to return, the staff of 1st Battalion Reserve Infantry Regiment 201, led by Hauptmann Graf Sauna, arrived at my position, together with one of the company commanders, Oberleutnant von Born-Fallois. I briefed them about the situation, took the two companies of 1st Battalion under command and ordered Oberleutnant Born-Fallois to take his company to the left and intervene in the battle there. I indicated to him a general direction of advance of the church tower with my arm then, with shouts of 'Forwards lads. We must take our revenge for the fallen of the 21st!' Fallois and his company charged off in the direction I had ordered.

"This flanking attack soon had an effect. Machine guns started to be captured from other black troops and prisoners began to move to the rear. Reserve Infantry Regiment 202 had been given a breathing space and here, too, the attack began to move forwards."

As Wedekind noted, at long last an attack had been launched after thorough preparation by the guns and success was so swift that the defenders were allowed no time to react before the assaulting forces were in amongst them. Those not directly stormed were also clearly affected by the neutralisation because their shooting was said to have been poor and, in many cases, as soon as the assault closed up on their positions, the great majority surrendered rather than remain to fight it out hand to hand as had happened on previous occasions. Those who chose flight, rather than surrender, especially those who chose to move parallel to, or near the railway embankment, were soon shot down in significant numbers. Some defending machine gun crews did put up a doughty defence in places, but they were isolated, few in number and dealt with one by one using low level fire and manoeuvre. One proof that the German attackers were swiftly gaining experience was demonstrated by the fact that several machine guns were taken out through exploitation of the loading pause. The French machine guns of the period fired a twenty five round strip. Once this was used up there was a gap in firing unless skilful crews operated the weapons in pairs. Individual weapons and their crews were vulnerable to decisive counter-action and none survived very long.

Within thirty minutes of the start of the attack, the railway embankment east of Diksmuide was in German hands and lightly wounded men were conducting prisoners to the rear. The sheer speed of the advance caused some minor difficulty at Diksmuide Station (located on the eastern tip of the town). There the resistance was particularly determined and, in any case, the German guns continued to fire on this section of the town for some time after fire elsewhere had been lifted, so it was not possible immediately to force an entry into the built up area. However, eventually word was passed back to the guns, and the second wave of Reserve Infantry Regiment 201 was able to manoeuvre. This part of the assault, like all fighting in built up areas, was altogether more difficult and costly. Defenders, who had survived the bombardment in cellars and other underground spaces, emerged to man roof tops, heaps of ruins, windows and doorways and took steady toll of the attackers until their firing positions were cleared one by one at the point of the bayonet.

Gradually, however, progress was made and soon the defenders were forced into a small perimeter around the Minoterie [flour mill], located just to the south of the Ijzer bridge on the east bank. The battle here was hard fought, because the upper story and roof of the mill housed the artillery observers and were key to the defence. When the building was eventually captured, its new owners made equal use of the observation it offered and considerable quantities of telephone equipment, documents and maps were captured. Whilst this mopping up continued, the northern part of the town also fell to Reserve Jäger Battalion 15 and 2nd Battalion Reserve Infantry Regiment 201. Once it became obvious that the Germans were closing in on the east bank of the Ijzer, resistance slacked and many of the defenders attempted to rush back across the bridge to safety. By then the advancing troops had taken up dominating fire positions, so not many who attempted to pull back made it to the relative safety of the west bank. Eventually the majority of those who remained ceased to try and surrendered. It had been a long hard fight and certainly anything but easy as this letter by a member of 2nd Battalion Reserve Infantry Regiment 201 indicates.

Kriegsfreiwilliger Meese 5th Company Reserve Infantry Regiment 201 [42]

"One of the Berlin papers wrote, 'Diksmuide stormed and captured!' However it was in fact not as short and sharp as that, because we have been through a failed assault, hard weeks in the trenches and a battle lasting several hours between ourselves and the brave French marines. The Frenchman showed himself to be a thoroughly courageous chap: all respect to the marines! However our artillery, the heavy like the light, produced a brilliant preparatory bombardment. Direct hits in the enemy trenches together with shrapnel and our well directed small arms fire coming down behind on the pressured masses meant that it was soon all over! Later the Blacks held out in the station and would not surrender. We showed them no mercy. We broke down the door and our bayonets had plenty of bloody work to do! Then night fell. The enemy guns hammered away at the town, so we were not able to feel joyful at having taken it. Numerous Belgian or French wounded lay in the houses and, whenever we approached, they all had the words 'Bon Camarade' [*sic.*] on their lips. Yesterday deadly enemies, today comrades – that is war for you!"

Later investigation revealed that at least 500 unwounded prisoners had been captured during the final attack, together with numerous machine guns, always highly sought after items because of the prize money paid for their recovery. There was considerable local satisfaction at the successful storming of the town. Major Freiherr von Wedekind of Reserve Infantry Regiment 201 later summed up the events of 10 November from a narrow regimental perspective. 'It was a marvellous success and one achieved with relatively few casualties. There were beaming faces wherever you looked; hundreds of prisoners and several machine guns were the booty. The important bridgehead of Diksmuide was in our hands and it remained German until autumn 1918.'[43] However, in the general euphoria, justifiable perhaps in the case of the men of 43rd Reserve Division, who had fought so hard and lost so heavily in pursuit of this objective, it was quietly forgotten that the aim in this sector was not simply to secure Diksmuide, but to exploit its rapid possession as a springboard to a significant and wide ranging flanking movement. The skill and courage of its Belgian and French defenders had put paid to that idea.

In truth Diksmuide was a bloody catastrophe for the German army in general and more particularly for the courageous young volunteers, whose lives were thrown away so casually and thoughtlessly in and around it. Langemark became the shorthand for remembered sacrifice in Germany after the war, but the experience of Diksmuide lay equally heavily on those who had suffered there. Kurt Peterson, who had been studying philosophy in Berlin right up until the moment that he and his friends volunteered for service, wrote to his parents in the wake of the failed attack of 25 October. 'After experiencing something like that, it is impossible to see how any of us can learn to smile again: dejection, complete and utter depression . . . '[44]

Notes

1. Appel History Reserve Infantry Regiment 205 p 22
2. *ibid.* p 22
3. Hayner History Reserve Infantry Regiment 201 p 38
4. This a quotation from verse two of *Ich hatt' einen Kamaraden* by Ludwig Uhland, which is the traditional farewell of a German soldier to a fallen comrade.
5. Bergeder History Reserve Infantry Regiment 202 p 17. Of the two men, only Karl Hübner, described as a Kriegsfreiwilliger, rather than a Grenadier, has a known grave. He is buried in the German cemetery at Vladslo Block 1 Grave 1838.
6. This canal, which runs more or less directly east – west, meets the Ijzer immediately north-west of the town of Diksmuide.
7. Hayner *op. cit.* p 40
8. Beumelberg *Ypern 1914* p 73
9. Hayner *op. cit.* p 40
10. Tasnier and R van Overstreten *La Belgique et la Guerre* Vol 3 Brussels 1923. Quoted in Hayner *op. cit.* pp 51 – 53
11. Bergeder *op. cit.* p 18
12. *ibid.* p 18
13. Hayner *op. cit.* pp 47–49
14. Döberitz was the home of a Prussian School of Musketry and a large training area to the east of Berlin.
15. *ibid.* pp 19–20
16. Unruh *Langemark* pp 112–113
17. *ibid.* p 114
18. Bergeder *op. cit.* p 19
19. Hayner *op. cit.* p 50 Meese, having survived all the battles of autumn 1914, was killed in action in May 1915 near Notre Dame de Lorette. He has no known grave.
20. Appel *op. cit.* p 26
21. Beumelberg *op. cit.* p 82
22. Beumelberg *ibid.* p 82
23. Bergeder *op. cit.* pp 22–23. It is of course impossible to comment one way or the other on the suggestion that the German soldiers committed an atrocity or that the Belgians responded in the way described. The fact that this thrust got as far west as Kaaskerke is, however, entirely feasible. Unfortunately, though heroic, it achieved no more than any other of the other attacks that night.
24. Bergeder *op. cit.* pp 23–24
25. *ibid.* pp 25–26
26. Hayner *op. cit.* pp 57–58
27. This refers to Burg Bodenstein above the village of Wintzingerode in Thuringia, which today is the best preserved of all such castles in the Eichsfeld area.
28. Czettritz was the commander of Reserve Infantry Regiment 208 44th Reserve Division.
29. Boesser History Reserve Field Artillery Regiment 44 p 61
30. *ibid.* p 62
31. This man was in the artillery and should have known what he was describing but from his account it would seem rather that he was witnessing the landing of empty shrapnel pots after the contents had been discharged.
32. Bergeder *op. cit.* pp 30–31
33. Oberleutnant Bruno Költz is buried in the German cemetery at Vladslo Block 1 Grave 981.

34. Appel *op. cit.* p 32
35. *ibid.* p 32 Major von Treskow is buried in the German cemetery at Vladslo Block 3 Grave 179.
36. Haleck History Reserve Infantry Regiment 208 p 14
37. Atzrott History Reserve Jäger Battalion 16 p 31
38. Unruh *op. cit.* p 125
39. Unruh *op. cit.* p 126
40. Hayner *op. cit.* pp 67–68
41. *ibid.* p 70
42. *ibid.* p 72
43. *ibid.* p 73
44. *Langemark:ein Vermächtnis* p 51 Peterson, having survived the 1914 battles, was killed on the Eastern Front in August 1915. He has no known grave.

CHAPTER 6

The Attempted Breakthrough by Army Group Fabeck.

Following the early bitter fighting which had not led to the desired breakthrough, the situation around Ypres was reviewed. It was still considered that success on this northern flank would be decisive if it unleashed German formations to fall on the Allied flank thus exposed. Within days it was evident that the offensive operations of Fourth Army under Duke Albrecht of Württemberg were beginning to stall, so a decision was made to concentrate a new 'Army Group Fabeck' from the forces of XV Corps and II Bavarian Corps, together with 26th Infantry Division and the newly raised 6th Bavarian Reserve Division. The command element was based on Headquarters XIII Corps from Württemberg, with General der Infanterie von Fabeck in command and Oberstleutnant von Loßberg as chief of staff. Orders for the reorganisation arrived on 28 October, direct from Army Supreme Command. The so-called, and somewhat confusingly titled, 'Army Group', was to come under the command of the Sixth Army of Crown Prince Rupprecht of Bavaria. This large mass of troops was to be moved rapidly into position and was to launch a fresh assault in a northwesterly direction from a line of departure drawn between Deûlémont and Wervik. The clear objective was to thrust along the general axis Ypres-Poperinge, breaking the British line once and for all. Up until this point, as described earlier, the sector between the Sixth Army, preoccupied with the battles for Arras, La Bassée and Armentières and Fourth Army was held more or less loosely by cavalry formations. The new arrangement was designed to transform German strength in this key area and it was popular with the cavalry, who were not relishing having to fight in the dismounted role and increasingly against the odds. On the eve of the battle, the general in command of all the cavalry south of Ypres wrote to his wife, describing what was about to happen.

General der Kavallerie Georg von der Marwitz Senior Cavalry Commander 2 [1]

"I believe that I can write to you about the forthcoming operations, because they begin early tomorrow morning [30 October 1914]. From the Menen – Ypres road, the enemy position bends away sharply southwest and west. From there to Messines my divisions are dug in facing the enemy. The total length of the frontage is about sixteen kilometres. The regiments have held on to these positions for about eight days now, whilst their horses have been held south of the Lys. Now today comes relief. Two and a half corps under Fabeck are to launch an assault on Ypres via Wervik and Comines. Our men are going to be relieved in the line at about midnight then march back six to eight kilometres to the horses. Instead of them the infantry will be manning the trenches and then tomorrow and, after an absolutely crazy bombardment on the enemy positions, everyone is going to attack with as much surprise as possible.

"If the attack is successful, the enemy line will be pierced and their situation as far as the sea will be untenable. By the time my letter reaches you, you may already have read about a successful battle. It could well be decisive for the northern theatre of operations. I pray to God that he may grant our troops success! The assault may overrun the forward enemy positions with ease then the follow up thrust may develop extraordinary power and send them all packing. On the other hand it could easily stall in front of the front line and then again there may be other positions in rear of the first ones, so that the attack will have to be phased. Based on these thoughts, you should be able to determine from reports of Supreme Army Headquarters how things turned out at Ypres on 30 October."

For the formations involved in the new offensive, there was no time to lose. Whilst the new headquarters was being set up in Linselles, Fabeck and Loßberg rushed around on 28 October, making contact with the various headquarters involved and acquainting themselves with the situation on the Fourth Army front and forward of the cavalry. One particular concern was the quantity of heavy artillery available to the Army Group, as was the extreme shortage of ammunition. By this stage of the war, artillery units further south around Arras and on the Somme were being restricted to two or three shells per gun per day, but even these extreme measures did not free up significant quantities of ammunition for use elsewhere and the lack was to be felt keenly later. In the short term, the only additional units which could be made available were: elements of 1st Battalion Guards Foot Artillery and 1st Battalion Foot Artillery Regiment 4 with heavy field howitzers. There were also some heavy howitzers from II Bavarian Corps and 1st Battalion Foot Artillery Regiment 14, heavy howitzers from half of 1st Battalion Foot Artillery Regiment 19, together with one 300 mm howitzer battery from 26th Infantry Division. The four heavy howitzer batteries of 2nd Battalion Bavarian Reserve Foot Artillery Regiment 3 were held back in reserve initially.[2]

Most of the cavalry and associated jäger battalions operating on the new front were subordinated to one or other of the formations of Army Group Fabeck and incorporated into the altered plans which, because of the urgency of the situation, were issued as early as the evening of 28 October. In broad outline, XV Corps was to attack on the right flank, with its most northerly units advancing just to the south of the Menen – Ypres road and its left flank units along the Comines -Ypres canal where its heavy artillery was also to be placed. On the southern flank, with its left hand formation anchored on Garde Dieu, II Bavarian Corps was to form the *Schwerpunkt* [point of main effort] of the attack. On the extreme left, 26th Infantry Division was to assault with its southern flank on the Douvebeek to the west of Warneton. Cooperating with the planned assault, elements of HKK [Senior Cavalry Commander] 1, supported by three battalions of XIX Corps, was to

Eyewitness Locations Chapter 6

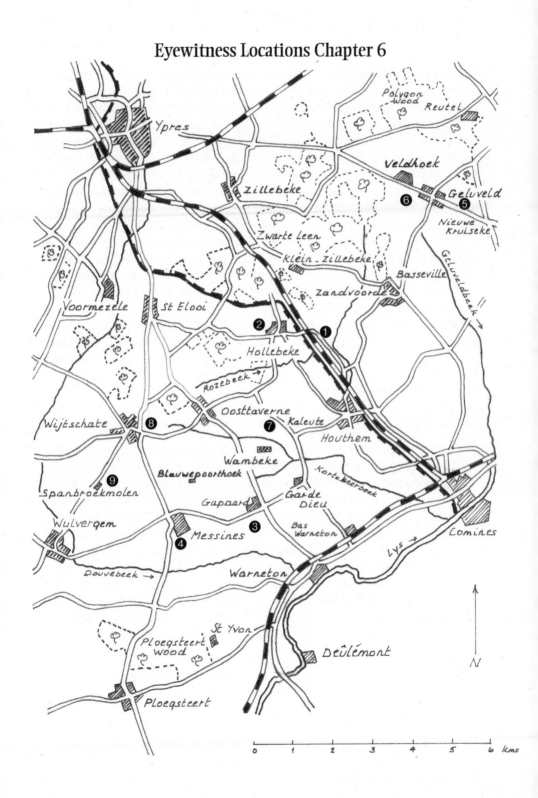

attack St Yvon and Ploegsteert Wood. From this, it can be seen that the primary aim was to force a decisive breakthrough to the south of Ypres. Whether this attempt would achieve more than the thrusts to the north of that place had done remained to be seen.

Clearly all concerned were determined to give of their best to secure the new objective, but the preparation time was severely truncated and the troops who were to carry out the attack had to overcome a number of severe difficulties. The principal negative factor was that all the troops concerned had to spend more or less the whole of 29 October moving into position and, which was worse, the leading elements followed this by lengthy, exhausting, approach marches in pitch darkness during the night 29/30 October, in order to be on their start lines at the appointed hour. As the time for the attack approached, Fabeck was faced with the unpalatable fact that his infantry was already very tired and had had absolutely no opportunity to reconnoitre the ground over which it was meant to advance. Not only that, it was quite clear, even without detailed staff checks, that the artillery resources were inadequate to meet the demands of the forthcoming task.

Fabeck despatched a request for a delay of twenty four hours in order to meet some of these concerns, but Supreme Army Command dismissed the request, insisting instead that the attack went in on 30 October as planned and with the support of Fourth and Sixth Armies on either flank. The chief of staff of Army Group Fabeck later noted some of these difficulties and concerns.

Oberstleutnant Fritz von Loßberg, Headquarters Army Group Fabeck [3]

"We were convinced that the assault of Army Group Fabeck was going to bump up against stiff resistance because the time delay on this previously planned attack to the south of Ypres (the orders for which had only just been given), had provided the enemy time to move up reinforcements. Having strengthened their front along the lower Ijzer by flooding, they were then able to move the formations thus released south to counter Army Group Fabeck and the left flank of Fourth Army. [In addition] with the exception of 6th Bavarian Reserve Division, almost all the units of Army Group Fabeck had been severely reduced in strength as a result of previous battles and, above all, from the very first days of the battle, there was a serious lack of artillery ammunition, which became worse and worse with the onset of offensive operations, thus making reduction of stubbornly defended woods and strongly-built villages increasingly difficult."

No matter what the reservations within the chain of command were, every effort had to be made to fulfil the overall aim of this new offensive. XV Corps, advancing with 30th Infantry Division right and 39th Infantry Division left, had the overall mission of taking over its frontage from the cavalry and launching an attack between the Menen – Ypres road and the Ijzer – Lys canal and breaking through to Ypres and beyond. On the eve of the attack, the corps commander issued a special order of the day, which included this exhortation to the troops:

'Tomorrow, in conjunction with Bavarian II Corps and 26th Infantry Division, we are to attack the British around Zandvoorde and to the east of that place and then push on to Ypres. This breakthrough is of decisive importance for the outcome of the war. Therefore we shall and must be victorious! His Majesty the Kaiser trusts that each will try his utmost to do his duty. We shall make sure that we justify this trust. Brave and undaunted we are going to attack the British, Indians, Canadians,[4] Moroccans and all such rabble. The enemy is becoming worn out and recently, whenever we have gone for them energetically, they have surrendered in large numbers. So let us go forward with God for our Kaiser and our beloved German Fatherland!'[5]

For its part, II Bavarian Army Corps extracted its mission and tasks from the Army Group Fabeck directive and issued its orders during the afternoon of 29 October. Whilst not downplaying the significance of the thrust just south of the Menen – Ypres road, it underlines that the main effort had been shifted to the south for the time being.[6]

"1. General von Fabeck intends to deploy the Bavarian II Army Corps to break through the enemy positions along the line of the canal. To our right XV Corps will also go on the offensive and 26th Infantry Division will attack to our left. Strong forces echeloned in depth behind the inner flanks of these neighbouring formations are in place to prevent Bavarian II Army Corps from being vulnerable to outflanking manoeuvres after it has broken through. A general reserve will be formed from 6th Bavarian Reserve Division and one heavy howitzer battalion.

"2. The *Schwerpunkt* [point of main effort] of the attack is placed on the inner flank of the two divisions and is directed at the village and chateau of Hollebeke. So, once the canal has been crossed, permanent contact is to be maintained between the two divisions. Having gained the heights northwest of Basseville and the Rozebeek sector, the next strong points to the rear are to be assaulted immediately and preferably with fresh troops.

"3. The attack will begin at daybreak 30 October when, without further order, the artillery is to range in. As soon as this is complete and the artillery is ready to start its bombardment, the infantry is to begin immediately to advance so as to force the enemy to man its positions. The artillery is to bring down effective fire against the occupied positions. Harassing fire simply squanders ammunition and is forbidden. Every effort is to be made to profit from the flanking effect of interdivisional cross fire. Artillery operating from the 4th Division sector is to superimpose its fire on the Zandvoorde area.

"4. A field gun battery is to be allocated in direct support of each of the infantry regiments in the front line. When this happens they are removed from the command of their parent artillery formations.

"5. By 6.00 pm 29 October at the latest, Commander 4 Field Artillery Brigade (less his staff) is to report to the Corps command post in Comines and act as artillery adviser until further notice. Placed at his disposal are

Oberstleutnant Gramich and Hauptmann Lehmann from Corps Headquarters, one orderly officer from each of 3 Field Artillery Brigade and Foot Artillery Regiment Gartmeyer and six despatch riders from the cavalry of each division."

Apart from the picture this paints of the main threads of the plan, the order is interesting in other ways. It includes, for example, an order to the corps signals detachment to connect the divisional headquarters by telephone line to corps headquarters, suggesting that that was not standard practice.[7] Furthermore, the fact that an artillery adviser and staff had to be improvised at the beginning of a major offensive shows how the German army was wrestling to come to terms with the need to centralise control of artillery fire on the modern battlefield and to move away from the wasteful dispersal of assets. The attempt to correct these problems and the reservations expressed by Loßberg chime with a widespread feeling that all was not well with the way the German army was organised and deployed to meet the needs and demands of the offensive battle. The desperate straits in which the Fourth Army found itself repeatedly can be laid firmly at the door of inexperience and inadequate training and equipment. The problems experienced by the formations of the other German armies were in some ways more worrying, because they seemed to suggest that pre-war doctrine and development had been wanting and that there had been gaps and deficiencies in the area of all-arms cooperation and training.

In an attempt to correct the more glaring manifestations of these difficulties, the Chief of Staff Sixth Army, Generalmajor Konrad Krafft von Dellmensingen, issued a strongly worded directive, based on instructions from Supreme Army Headquarters, on the eve of the offensive by Army Group Fabeck. Because it deals with matters of fundamental importance to the entire German army, it is worth considering at length.[8]

"During recent days, several promising opportunities have been wasted because entire corps have allowed themselves to be held up by vastly inferior forces. This situation can be traced back to the fact that attacks are not being pressed home with the utter disregard for danger that each attack which aims at a decisive result demands. Naturally it must be recognised that the high officer losses have seriously damaged the offensive power of the army. However, if as a consequence we frequently conduct half-hearted attacks, the enemy will soon lose respect for us. We shall spare the blood of our infantry if we confine ourselves to attacks which are essential and make sure that they are strongly supported by all available artillery and other technical resources. If, however, a decisive attack is ordered, then every commander, including those at high levels, is <u>personally</u>[9] to ensure, including by example, that he is so engaged that the attack will be conducted with the utmost power. Superior officers are also to appear at the front sufficiently frequently to bring their personalities to bear on the troops.

"Valuable advantages are often not being exploited properly because, in the case of formations advancing alongside one another, instead of driving forward ruthlessly within their boundaries, troops are pausing to allow their neighbours to catch up, or halting as soon as they come under enfilade fire from neighbouring sectors. From receipt of this [directive] there is an explicit ban on delaying or halting if the planned advance is delayed or disrupted on neighbouring fronts, or to see what effect the outflanking manoeuvre might have. Even if neighbouring attacks are held up, that is no excuse for failing to act.

"It is a fundamental principle of the French artillery to bring down flanking fire and it cannot be avoided when adjacent formations are advancing simultaneously. The troops must arrange for their own protective measures. It must also be the unvarying case that neighbours may never be left in trouble. Individual units and formations have often suffered heavy casualties because their neighbours delayed far too long before coming to their assistance, or believed wrongly, after reports from the other troops, that they were occupying places which were actually in enemy hands. It is essential, therefore, that reports and information concerning lines reached or points captured are absolutely reliable. If a formation is unable to reach a particular piece of terrain, or cannot do so in time; if it believes that the situation has changed, or that it cannot reach the designated place for reasons unknown to its superior level of command, it is to make the fact known to all relevant places, without fail.

"An extremely threatening squandering of artillery ammunition, far beyond even the most pessimistic estimates, has occurred. This has been caused because many units and formations have constantly engaged inadequately reconnoitred enemy positions with wide-ranging, harassing fire; either that or attempts have been made by bombarding enemy positions for days or hours at a time to eliminate them in that manner, instead of the infantry through daring direct action, forcing a weaker enemy to occupy [and attempt to defend] their positions. For the future it is essential that the troops draw the lesson that careful husbandry of artillery ammunition is of decisive importance; that simply bringing fire down will never have an effect and, furthermore, that fire may only be directed against clearly identified targets and only for strictly limited tactical purposes. As a result, the artillery may not meet every request by the infantry for fire support and may only respond to the senior commander. The infantry must always cooperate with the artillery in the attack; the artillery must never try to attack alone.

"It is very regrettable to note that up to now there has been a constant lack of liaison between neighbouring formations. This is another reason for the undesirable situations described [earlier]. The despatch of liaison officers is only useful when they are furnished with ample means to pass on information. In future, commanders will be held personally responsible for failures of this type.

"Every effort is to be made by all commanders to designate reserves or make them available once again [after redeployment]. Every individual man is to be pressed into service to this end.

"Troops not involved in attacks must spend their time thoroughly reinforcing their positions and developing them with all means available, so that
they are strong enough to enable a minimal garrison to beat off all enemy
attacks. Reserves are to be used constantly to reinforce. Even when battles are
drawn out, it is essential to arrange for troops in the front line to be relieved,
so that they can rest and regain their ability to strike. The men are never to be
left with nothing to do. Every opportunity is to be taken to re-impose discipline
through the use of drill.

"Commanders at all levels who fail to meet the requirements outlined
above will be summarily dismissed. No special consideration will be given to
any individual, not even if previously he has been thoroughly worthy. The
names of all individuals who are not completely fit for their posts are to be
passed immediately to Supreme Army Headquarters through official chan-
nels. Belief in a favourable outcome must always be maintained at a high level.
Every individual must be made to realise what is at stake. Patience will
certainly be required. It will be a long time before a final decision is achieved
but, if every single individual is absolutely determined to see it through to the
end, then all enemy efforts will be for nothing and final victory will be
assured."

On the right of XV Corps, 39th Infantry Division divided its frontage into three main
sectors. Attacking on a narrow front, Infantry Regiment 132 on the right aimed to
capture the rather elaborate farm complex 700 metres east of Zandvoorde. To the left,
82 Infantry Brigade, less one battalion, was allocated the centre and western parts of
Zandvoorde, whilst the centre of the divisional sector was the responsibility of a
composite force of jäger battalions from HKK [Senior Cavalry Commander] 2 under the
command of Major Petersen, commanding officer Jäger Battalion 10. Shortly after first
gunner light on 30 October (i.e. the time when targets could be made out at battle ranges
by ground observers), a group of designated batteries fired three rolling salvoes as a
signal that the preliminary bombardment of the enemy trenches was to begin.[10] For
once this was a substantial, if short, bombardment, with a significant contribution from
concentrated heavy artillery. Precisely one hour later the general advance began, with
2nd Battalion Infantry Regiment 132 maintaining contact with 30th Infantry Division
on its right. As an example of how concentrated the assault was, Oberst Kreyenberg
attacked with his 1st and 2nd Battalions in line, each of them on a frontage of only 350
metres.

Despite being in position on the start line in good time, visibility was so poor that it
was 8.00 am before the guns opened fire and 9.00 am before the two battalions, each
reinforced by an engineer platoon to deal with obstacles and a machine gun platoon,
launched their attacks with two companies forward.[11] The advance was far from easy.
The battlefield was fundamentally flat, offering good fields of fire, though it was punctuated by folds in the ground, hedgerows and copses and criss-crossed by numerous
drainage ditches. It was also dotted with farm houses and agricultural buildings of all

kinds. The advance was subject to heavy flanking fire almost from the start and artillery defensive fire increased in strength constantly. Nevertheless good progress was made and 3rd Battalion, in reserve, closed up behind 2nd Battalion with the regimental band in attendance. By 11.00 am the attackers had penetrated the British positions on part of the 1st Battalion front but, on the extreme right, were stalled by the moat surrounding Zandvoorde Chateau and the bitter defence offered by the 1st Battalion Royal Welch Fusiliers. Nevertheless, at the cost of heavy casualties during virtually hand to hand fighting, the chateau, too, was swiftly taken and, with it, the primary divisional objective for the day.

2nd Battalion endured a far harder morning of fighting, dense thickets and woodland making it difficult to maintain direction and cohesion during the assault. However, once the chateau fell, much better progress was made, partly because units of the British 7th Cavalry Brigade lacked the dismounted strength fully to counter a determined and concentrated infantry attack. In order to encourage the troops to greater efforts, Oberst Kreyenberg ordered the regimental drummers to blow the appropriate calls and beat the drums for the assault. He then followed this by directing the regimental band to play stirring music in support of the attack.[12] Despite the intervention of 3rd Battalion and all the other encouragement, bitter and inconclusive fighting continued for several hours, leaving the men of Infantry Regiment 132 in a dangerously exposed position between Zandvoorde Chateau and Chapelle d'Epines. Finally, an immense effort was made to get a section of 2nd Battery Field Artillery Regiment 66 forward into positions where the enemy positions could be engaged at short range over open sights. Re-launched, the attack was driven home, but at heavy cost, especially amongst the company offices, several of whom fell at the head of their men as they strove to encourage them. Eventually the objectives were all carried and numerous prisoners from the Royal Welch Fusiliers and South Staffordshire Regiment were captured.

Whilst all this was occurring, at 2.30 pm, 39th Infantry Division ordered a continuation of the attack towards Zillebeke. This was to have involved Infantry Regiment 132 in a further advance to a point 800 metres beyond Zandvoorde, but the attack never got going. The day had been too costly in casualties, too hard fought in view of all the British counter-attacks and the men were completely exhausted by the effort. Despite vigorous action by Generalleutnant von Kathen and the remainder of the chain of command, it proved to be impossible to disentangle jumbled sub units so as to attack with any chance of success so, finally, the divisional reserves were stood down and the remaining troops were ordered to dig in where they were.

Also participating in the attack on 30 October was Infantry Regiment 136 of 30th Infantry Division. It had moved into position the previous night, taking up station between Infantry Regiment 99 on its right and one of the formations of 39th Infantry Division on its left. Three companies from each regiment were located forward in the front line as the artillery preparation began at 8.15 am. More or less exactly one hour later, the order to launch the attack arrived at the forward brigade headquarters and slowly, but surely, profiting from good artillery support, the attack began to make progress; Infantry Regiment 136 capturing several small positions and a series of farm buildings as it advanced approximately 600 metres. Already casualties were mounting due to the obstinate defence being put up by the British defenders and Major Borck, commanding officer 2nd Battalion Infantry Regiment 136, was killed at the head of his troops, as were Leutnants Schumann and Brinkmann.[13] By about midday Infantry Regiment 136 has pushed forward as far as Chapelle d'Epines, located about one and a half kilometres south southwest of Nieuwe Kruiseke, but Infantry Regiment 99, which had suffered heavy casualties due to flanking fire from Geluveld, had made little progress and the whole attack in this sector threatened to stall. Ordered to push on at all costs, Infantry Regiment 99 continued to press in the direction of Geluveld then, towards 4.00 pm, Headquarters 30th Division ordered that the line Zandvoorde – Geluveld was to be secured that day

This was easier said than done, with the British infantry continuing to resist fiercely, in some cases from well constructed strong points, based around farm buildings and field fortifications. After hard fighting, Infantry Regiment 136 seized this line but, because flanking units had been less successful, two of its companies had to withdraw from the furthest point reached, in order to re-establish the link with the units to its north and south. A member of the machine gun company, who was involved in the thick of the action that day, later described the manner in which it had unfolded.

Schütze Meister Machine Gun Company Infantry Regiment 136 [14] **1.**

"On the morning of 30 October 1914 there was to be an attack right across the front. That morning the storm broke punctually. The first trench was taken with few casualties and we captured between 600 and 700 prisoners. We then pressed on. As we advanced in bounds, we saw a white flag being waved above the enemy trench, so we stood up and advanced on the enemy. However, it was a trick. Just as we approached to within one hundred metres, we were engaged from there with rifle and machine gun fire. As though an order had been given, we all hit the ground and then we continued forward in rushes, but there were heavy casualties. The second trench was captured and we laid about us with rifle butts. Because the infantry was so tied up, Vizefeldwebel Mehlbräuer pushed on ahead with his platoon. We arrived at a farm which offered cover and he directed that the guns were to be placed in firing positions. He then went on ahead alone out of the farm, probably with the intention of placing a machine gun up on the hill, but the hill was occupied by the enemy. Vizefeldwebel Mehlbräuer did not get very far before we saw him hit and collapse. At that Unteroffizier Berning, who had assumed command of the platoon, gave orders that the guns were to go into action."

After what was a day of hard fighting and painfully high casualties throughout 30th Infantry Division, the following night and morning was described by one member of the same regiment.

Unteroffizier Knauth 6th Company Infantry Regiment 136 [15] **1.**

"That night there was strange, eerie silence. Hardly a single shot was heard and not a word was spoken aloud. A farmhouse to our front was burning and lighting up the trees behind in a marvellous manner. It was not possible to distinguish flames, smoke and sparks, just the glow of the fire, sometimes brighter, sometimes fainter, which showed that a blaze was still burning there behind the walls. There was no crackling to be heard or falling beams to be seen, it was all rather like a theatrical backcloth, with one pointed gable end standing up like a church spire above the remaining blackened walls with their empty window sockets. As dawn broke the flames died out and only a few sad remains of walls stuck up into the sky.

"Emerging like a shadowy figure out of the darkness our company feldwebel appeared and whispered to me, 'One volunteer per section is to go forward on listening duty!' Slowly and silently the thin file of men wrapped in their great-coats disappeared. Within seconds, they had been swallowed by the darkness of the night. Gradually the clouds cleared and the stars emerged. For a great many of us this was the very last time that they would ever be able to look up at the endless starry heaven in all its beauty. At 6.00 am, still under the protection of darkness, a figure came up to our company feldwebel. They spoke together for a short time, then the figure disappeared once more. This was followed by a lively discussion amongst the platoon commanders down in the dugout. Soon all was quiet once more. A short while later my platoon commander arrived.

"Has the attack been ordered?' I asked. 'Yes. The artillery opens up at 7.00 am to prepare the enemy positions for the assault'. That meant a stay of execution of another hour. Gradually it became light and I looked at my watch. Five minutes to go; then, passed on from mouth to mouth came the order, 'Fix bayonets! Make ready!' With a metallic clattering noise the bayonets were fixed. Would I be thrusting with my bayonet once more or not? If I did it would certainly be streaked with blood. A strange feeling came over me. It was not fear; that emerges only when we feel ourselves to be defenceless. But today we would be setting off calmly and sure of victory. If anyone was to fall, he would be falling in battle as a brave soldier, happily carrying out his duty to his Fatherland; as a victor, for not a man doubted that our operation would bring victorious success.

"At exactly 7.00 am there was a dreadful rushing, roaring and groaning sound in the air, just as though all hell had broken loose Our artillery had opened fire. To our front the ground dropped away to the road, then rose gently once more. Our artillery engaged the area on the far side of the road, Wherever the eye could see, smoke and pillars of earth were being thrown up by exploding shells with, between them, the small yellow clouds showing where shrapnel had burst. A road in the distance lined with poplars was brought under heavy fire and very soon a dozen snapped off tree trunks were lying in the road. Only a few hundred metres to our front rounds from a complete heavy battery were landing. It was a gruesomely fine sight. Our 210 mm howitzers were firing rapidly and all the smaller calibre guns, down to the lightest field guns, were contributing to the concert.

"There was almost no sound from the British artillery. On one occasion something whistled over our heads and impacted about two metres away in the soft ground, but the shell did not explode. Rapid small arms fire was then aimed at the British. Now and then the odd individual could be seen, but the enemy also fired back vigorously. One man leapt up out of the trench to take an order to the supporting platoon, but hardly had he broken cover than he gave a shout and fell, groaning terribly. A bullet had hit him in the abdomen. At the risk of their own lives, two men of the supporting platoon dragged him to safety. Shells whistled past, unpleasantly close to our heads then we saw German infantry emerge from the wood to our left and begin to advance. It could not be long before it was our turn. Our comrades down below us did not seem to be under fire, then one suddenly fell, followed by another. They began to run forward and another one went down. The remainder disappeared behind the house that had been burning the previous night. A battalion runner appeared. '6th Company: attack!' he shouted, then disappeared once more. All of a sudden another runner appeared and bawled, '2nd Battalion: attack!' At that our company commander shouted. 'Right, with God's help, let's go!' Reserve Leutnant Knapmann was the first to plunge into the hail of bullets. Followed by my section, I climbed out of the trench as fast as possible and we ran as fast as we could after our Leutnant.

"At first it appeared as though the British had been taken completely by surprise by our attack but no sooner had the other companies appeared than their bullets were whistling most unpleasantly around our ears. We ran as far as the road, but our way on the other side was blocked by a hedge. I ran up to it but, unfortunately, a few strands of wire ran through its twigs. Our company had now taken up a firing line with its front at ninety degrees to the road. To our right neighbouring troops had closed up to the thick hedge, which surrounded the farm to the right of the road. The British there seemed to be firing especially accurately, judging by the fall of shot, which was right in amongst the line.

"Offizierstellvertreter Räbisch ordered, '6th Company! On your feet! Double march!' We took cover again just in front of the house. During the dash forward Räbisch had been grazed on the thigh by a bullet, but he took no notice. Drawing his sword and taking his pistol in his right hand, he entered the house to see if any of the enemy had hidden themselves there. Hardly had Räbisch entered the second room than he gave a groan and collapsed, with blood oozing out from beneath his helmet. Because I could see that simultaneously spurts of chalk were being thrown out of the wall on our side, I assumed that Räbisch had been hit by a German bullet but, by chance I looked out of the window and saw where the shot had come from. Barely one hundred metres behind the house there was an enemy trench, in which the British were running up and down in some excitement.

"In order to be able to maintain the link to 7th Company more easily, Leutnant Knapmann, I and a few other men rushed over the road into the ruins of the second house. The situation here was more or less the same as the other side, but this time there were no window openings in the direction of the enemy. At this point our howitzers opened fire on the trench to our front in order to help us get forward. We watched with uncontrolled joy as we saw how accurately our artillery was landing shells, this time directly on the trench. Not even the toughest British skulls could withstand that for long. Four times in succession there was a roaring sound just over us, so low that we feared the shells would collapse our gable end, but then there were four dreadful explosions one hundred metres to our front, so strong that they made the earth shake and caused the weakened wall above us to rock. Yellow earth and grey smoke rose up from four points along the enemy trench. Then, finally, it got too much for the British. They took to their heels and ran backwards as fast as their legs could carry them.

"Nobody gave an order on our side, but almost everyone rushed out of our houses, shouting *Hurra!* It would in fact have been better had we stayed where we were and simply fired from there, because our shells were still landing in the enemy trench. But who could show such control at a time like that? Then, suddenly, I received an awful blow to the left shoulder, causing me to cry out as I was thrown forwards. I was gasping for breath, my heart was beating fit to burst, my fingers clawed at the grass, my teeth ground together and my right foot came up against a metal object, which I saw later was my bayonet which was lying behind me. I realised that I had been shot in the back by a bullet which had exited through my chest and I thought that my last hour had come. Soon things improved a little. I could breathe once more and my heart rate steadied. I shouted to the man next to me to take my knapsack off. The rear of it was already soaked in blood. Extraordinary to relate, my next thought was, 'Well, you will be spending Christmas at home'.

To the south, II Bavarian Corps had been making rather better, if slow, progress on 30 October. 4th Bavarian Division, commanded by Generalleutnant Graf von Montgelas, successfully stormed and captured Hollebeke at about 4.30 pm after a renewed assault had been arranged at 3.00 pm. Further to the south, 3rd Bavarian Division, under Generalleutnant Ritter von Breitkopf, assisted by 26th Infantry Division from Württemberg (which established itself a mere 1,200 metres from Wijtschate), pushed on west of Wambeke to within two kilometres of the crest of the Messines Ridge. According to German sources, however, there was also very hard fighting by elements of both 3rd and 4th Bavarian Infantry Divisions for Hollebeke Chateau and its adjoining parkland. Whilst Bavarian Infantry Regiment 9, with Infantry Regiment 172 on its right, was thrusting forward to the heights west of Zandvoorde, Bavarian Infantry Regiment 5 was heavily involved in the fight for the area around the chateau.[16]

Even with the direct fire support of two gun batteries, Bavarian Infantry Regiment 5, having first assaulted with two of its battalions in line, found that by midday it had to deploy all its own reserves and call on the support of battalion of Bavarian Reserve Infantry Regiment 5 and a company of Bavarian Jäger Battalion 2 that afternoon, before it was able to enter the grounds of the chateau and take prisoner a captain and two other members of the King's Dragoon Guards.[17] For its part, Bavarian Infantry Regiment 17 noted that it had to deal with several machine gun nests in succession by means of minor platoon and company tactics and the sending forward of reserves repeatedly until, by the time Hollebeke Chateau was finally taken and secured by 6 Bavarian Infantry Brigade, it was past 10.00 pm and long after darkness had fallen.[18]

Reserve Leutnant Hermann Kohl Bavarian Infantry Regiment 17[19] 2.

"The German assault flooded northwest towards Hollebeke. Blow after blow was struck, but enemy machine guns fired mercilessly and tore holes in the ranks. Were we up against the same sort of fanatical opponents we had met at Maricourt?[20]Here they clung on like glue to their ground and refused to yield one single square metre voluntarily. Charge followed charge as the companies crashed in. Bronzed Indian troops lay there, cut down in rows. They were Herculean men, with complete contempt for death, who took not a single step backwards! They preferred to die where they were! Only over their shattered skulls could the sacred charger of Mars advance to victory! Their fearful wrath as they faced death was matched only by the anger burning in the hearts of the German ranks.

"Towards 4.00 pm Wibel's Battalion [Major Moritz Wibel, commanding officer 2nd Battalion] had pushed the attack to within three hundred metres of Hollebeke, Haasy's Battalion [Major Wilhelm von Haasy, commanding officer 3rd Battalion] had crossed the canal and was advancing on the final objective of the day. It was tough, bitter, fighting. The potential of every building, right up to its rafters, was cunningly exploited for its defensive possibilities, the dense woods served as one long endless barrier to progress. Fire blazed down from the treetops, serving its deadly veto on the Bavarians storming forward . . . It was fighting at its hardest and only the good Lord knew to whom the evening would belong.

"The German guns roared, hurling their smashing steel with religious fervour, like a raging storm . . . but one battery fired using incorrect sight settings and hit the rear of Haasy's Battalion badly. With dull thuds German shells came down amongst our own ranks. The commander gave the sign and the trumpeters blew 'Halt!' The battle was paused as runners raced back to the battery position but then, fifteen minutes later, a new performance took centre stage. There was an overture of the loudest *fortissimo* and the battle entered its final phase. The enemy line crumbled and, at 4.30 pm Hollebeke, that blood-soaked bulwark, was in German hands.

"This success was a spur to further action. That evening, despite being worn out by the battles of the day, the Bavarian 17th, in conjunction with the neighbouring troops, stormed the grounds of Hollebeke Chateau. The German *Hurra!* came like a shot out of the distance, echoed off the walls of the chateau and shook the occupants out of their carefree existence. In a tearing hurry, the enemy staff vacated the chateau, abandoning a freshly laid table, complete with silver cutlery and every delicacy. It must have been painful for that Great Nation to leave such sumptuous food to the barbarians, but the Germans were to have no problem dealing with it."[21]

In summary, the first day of the offensive produced mixed and largely disappointing results for Army Group Fabeck. On the XV Corps front, Zandvoorde fell during the morning, followed a little later by its heavily fortified chateau, but the inability of XXVII Reserve Corps to the north to capture Geluveld meant that progress on its right flank was minimal. In an attempt to reinvigorate his attack, its commander, General der Infanterie von Deimling, requested the subordination of the heavy weapons of 2nd Battalion Mörser [i.e. heavy howitzer] Regiment 3, which was located at Comines. However, Fabeck's intention remained to force a breakthrough on the narrow frontage of II Bavarian Corps, so he allocated only one battery to XV Corps, whilst the Bavarians received the support of three of the available batteries. In a further attempt to unlock the right flank, XV Corps then redirected several battalions towards Geluveld, but it made no difference; that village continued to resist stubbornly in the face of a series of attacks which went in repeatedly throughout the remainder of the day.

On the extreme left flank of Army Group Fabeck, the 26th Infantry Division from Württemberg, commanded by Generalleutnant Wilhelm Herzog [Duke] von Urach, had a hard, and not especially successful, day. In this area the terrain was extremely unfavourable for an assault, posing particular problems for the guns of Field Artillery Regiments 29 and 65 which supported it. The difficulties were particularly acute for the direct support guns, which 26th Infantry Division was already routinely allocating to its leading regiments during offensive operations. An unnamed diarist from Field Artillery Regiment 29 underlined the challenges in his entry for 31 October.[22] **3.**

"One section [of guns] had to be advanced even further so as to provide intimate support to the infantry. If the reconnaissance itself was very problematic, the move of the guns into position demanded an even more amazing performance by the gunners. They had to wade knee deep in the mud, whilst the guns themselves sank in up to their axles – and all this was achieved under constant artillery and small arms fire. The daring troop was hindered especially by the fire of some machine guns but, finally, Reserve Vizewachtmeister Engländer succeeded in locating these troublemakers and a few well directed shells silenced them. However, in order to be able to engage the main enemy trenches, it was necessary to change positions again.

"[Everyone] set to work with a will. Making use of long tow ropes, the guns were hauled through deep boggy ground, over churned up tracks and deep, sharp sided, trenches. The section was now a mere three hundred metres from the enemy. Right and left the infantry were poised to launch the assault. Two men worked the guns. Everyone else slithered backwards and forwards under heavy rifle and machine gun fire fetching ammunition and the guns were fired at the fastest rate possible. The enemy did not hold out for long. To shouts of *Hurra!* the infantry advanced and captured the enemy position."

This clearly refers to a forward British position and not Messines itself, which did not fall until later. The regiments of 26th Infantry Division, after their brief foray to Menen and Geluwe, had been involved in a three day battle near Fromelles and had then had to march all the way forward via Quesnoy and Warneton into positions some two kilometres short of Messines. They arrived there during the early evening of 29 October and relieved the weak forces of 6th Cavalry Division. Worn down by the fighting and extremely tired from their previous exertions, the entire formation was in urgent need of rest, but there was no time for that and not even enough for appropriate reconnaissance and preparation. The whole affair was extremely rushed and, to make matters worse, the objective was very challenging. The main enemy line of defence in this sector was established some 1,000 metres east of Messines, where a low, flat topped ridge ran away northeast towards Wambeke. From the crest there were excellent fields of fire and the flat open terrain offered the attackers nothing much in the way of cover or concealment, except for a few ditches and the hedges and fences which surrounded the houses and gardens of the many isolated farmsteads. To the rear the small town of Messines stood out, dominant and threatening.

During the early morning of 30 October, the divisional artillery began to bombard the British positions and Messines itself, provoking an immediate response from the British guns near the town and west of Wambeke. Nevertheless, making use of the cover provided by the fire, the regiments attempted to get forward. Infantry Regiment 122 made straight for Wambeke, whilst Infantry Regiment 125 thrust towards Messines. It was over-ambitious. Its 1st Battalion advancing on Blauwepoorthoek came under withering fire, both from the front and the right flank, halting it and forcing its right flank company to pull back. 2nd Battalion Infantry Regiment 125 was equally thwarted trying to close in on Messines, when it came under effective fire from the direction of Wijtschate. Every effort was made to suppress the defences in Messines, but the light field guns were not effective against the thick walls of the buildings so, until the heavy artillery could be brought to bear and range in correctly (which did not happen immediately), there was little more that the infantry could achieve.

At 2.50 pm, Major Sproesser, commanding officer 2nd Battalion, reported, 'My impression is that the attack is still not sufficiently prepared. Enemy rifle and machine gun fire from the area northwest of Les Quatre Rois is still coming down with undiminished force.'[23] Luckily that was about the time that Infantry Regiment 122 managed to get forward and an opportunity presented itself to renew the main assault. However, as an illustration of how slow the passage of information and orders could be, the regimental commander Infantry Regiment 125 ordered a resumption of the assault on Messines on his own initiative, but a 51 Infantry Brigade order to the same effect did not even arrive at the Infantry Regiment 125 command post until 5.55 pm. By then the second attempt had also run into the sand; Major Sproesser, reporting again at 5.00 pm, 'Under fire from infantry and artillery to the front and machine guns in the right flank, 2nd Battalion Infantry Regiment 125 cannot get forward'.[24]

As Loßberg had feared, Allied resistance had been stronger on 30 October than expected and, in any case, in country which offered numerous advantages to the defence it was a relatively easy matter for small groups of men to impose delay on the advancing formations. The possession of Hollebeke Chateau was of the first importance. It enabled General Ritter von Martini to give orders to II Bavarian Corps to continue to drive northwest, but to switch its focus to the crucial Messines – Wijschate ridge and to plan on introducing the uncommitted regiments of 6th Bavarian Reserve Division (Bavarian Reserve Infantry Regiments 17 and 21) into the line between 26th Infantry Division and 3rd Bavarian Infantry Division and drive on hard and exclusively to Wijtschate.[25]

In the meantime, in order to provide the best possible support, top priority was given to the move forward of heavy artillery, in order to support an all-out assault on Messines the following day. Perhaps as a reflection of the limited progress made, however, a mere three hundred British prisoners of war had been captured. They were drawn mainly from the British 4th and 7th Divisions, though some cavalrymen were also captured and there were reports that the bodies of Indian troops had been discovered north of Messines. As a result, it was felt that the attack had gone in primarily against weakly held British outpost positions; only Messines, Wijtschate and Geluveld seemed to be held in significant strength.

There were also German air reconnaissance reports that day, indicating that strong reinforcements were being readied between Ypres and Poperinge and that there was a great deal of rail traffic forward from Dunkirk in the direction of Hazebrouck. This was a source of concern to the German chain of command, especially in view of the fact that progress on 30 October had not conformed to expectations. There was an urgent need to maintain the pressure on the defence and so, as darkness fell on a confused situation on the 26th Infantry Division front, attempts were made to use reinforcements to carry out patrols, to establish contact with neighbouring units and to decide, on the basis of a closer inspection of the ground, what might be possible the following day. All the work was overturned, however, when, at midnight, 51 Infantry Brigade issued orders for a night attack on Messines to start at 2.45 am.

After a scramble to be ready on time, this attack was launched against the British garrison, comprising the dismounted elements of the 1st Cavalry Brigade, reinforced by the 9th Lancers of 2nd Cavalry Brigade and two companies of the Indian 57th Rifles.

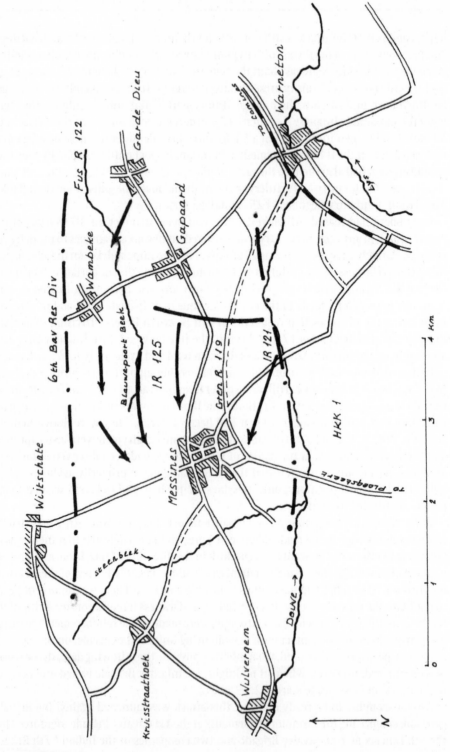

THE ATTACK OF 26th INFANTRY DIVISION 31 OCTOBER 1914

Enjoying for once the fire support of heavy howitzers, the attack gained a certain amount of ground, after some initial ebbing and flowing, though it was only after several hours of hard fighting that news filtered back that 1st and 3rd Battalions Infantry Regiment 125 had succeeded in entering Messines and were consolidating there. At around midday there was a further concentrated effort to clear right through the whole town, but that was still not complete when the regimental commander arrived late that afternoon to take personal charge; this, despite the fact that barricade after barricade had already been stormed with support from point blank range by individual guns of Field Artillery Regiment 29. The British Official History[26] stated that prior to the first assault, some Germans had been, 'disguised by wearing turbans' as they approached forward trenches manned by men of the Inniskillings, the implication being that surprise was gained unfairly. Given the presence of Indian troops awaiting relief, a case of mistaken identity in the dark seems to have been a much more likely explanation.[27]

Despite the relative weakness of the British garrison, the fighting both north and south of Messines and within the village itself took its toll on the attackers. By the afternoon, Grenadier Regiment 119 and Infantry Regiment 125 had already been heavily engaged for almost ten hours and needed reinforcement. This was far from easy to arrange. Infantry Regiment 121 had lost very heavily during the battles near Fromelles a few days earlier. Its 11th Company, for example, was reduced to three junior NCOs and thirty men.[28] Nominally in divisional reserve, it despatched its 9th Company to Grenadier Regiment 119, followed shortly by 5th and 8th Companies, then amalgamated 10th and 11th Companies and placed them under command of Infantry Regiment 125. The commander of the combined company later described their experiences in this hard fought battle.

Leutnant Schröder 10th Company Infantry Regiment 121[29] 4.

"The little town of Messines stood out on the hill to our front like an old fortress on a mountain top. Of course it had no battlements or towers set into its walls but, nevertheless, torrents of fire from concealed trenches and loopholes poured down on the daring attackers who were attempting to storm the heights. Despite this, our neighbouring regiment had succeeded in closing right up to the edge of town from where, out of hastily dug holes, they were conducting a costly fire fight. It was essential to capture the broad sweep of terrain in front of the dominant town, but a frontal attack would have been difficult to carry out and a flanking attack promised greater success.

"10th Company, which was dug in on the flank in the second line was ordered by 51 Infantry Brigade at about midday on 31 October to move over to the right and to take the town in the flank by means of a swift charge. This was a serious mission, because the British had prepared every house for defence. Moving individually or in small groups, the riflemen sprang up out of their trenches and made their way in bounds forward and to the right. This was carried out amidst rapid rifle and machine gun fire and the whole area was also under shrapnel fire. Rushing forward, creeping and crawling in cover behind hedges and garden fences, the riflemen reached the cover of a small hollow.

"Many, including the company commander (who was wounded), had already been hit, but it was essential to press on. To the front of the left flank platoon a small ditch ran directly towards a tile works, which was strongly defended. Everybody piled into the ditch, the platoon commander leading and soon they were about sixty metres from the tile works. A quick order was given and the platoon dashed forward as one at the double, shouting *Hurra!* and entered the yard. The British left in great haste and the building was swiftly prepared for defence.

"The other platoons, advancing in a similar manner, had pushed up against the northern exit to the town and stormed the first of the houses in the face of lacerating fire, which tore holes in their ranks. Messages were sent back requesting reinforcements and ammunition but, instead, the British counter-attacked. The aim was to drive out these people who had forced their way in, threatening their flank and rear, but they did not make much progress and they were sent back home, with bloody heads. Darkness fell, supports came up and, with them, two guns. Assisted by some of our men these were quickly brought into action out on the street. They fired at occupied houses and street barricades with great effect, but the British artillery, unconcerned about their men in the town, brought down heavy fire. This cost us casualties during the night, including the battery commander, who was killed.[30] However, the British dared not attack. Messines had been taken, admittedly with heavy losses, thanks to the energetic flanking attack of the 10th Company."

Whilst the battles of the Messines – Wijtschate ridge had been raging on 31 October, there was equally heavy fighting further to the north in the XV Corps sector, which was later summarised by the commander of the troops deployed closest to the Ypres – Menen road.

Generalleutnant von Altrock Commander 60 Infantry Brigade [31]

"On the orders of 30th Infantry Division, Oberstleutnant von Oldershausen and Infantry Regiment 105, supported by their right hand neighbouring formation, were to capture Geluveld. General von Altrock was to support this attack by means of one of his own launched by Infantry Regiment 99 and one battalion of Infantry Regiment 136 to the west of the Wervik – Geluveld road. On the morning of 31 October, preliminary artillery fire came down on Geluveld. The staff of 60 Infantry Brigade moved to occupy a small house to the west of Oude Kruiseke, whilst the four battalions (three from Infantry Regiment 99 and one from Infantry Regiment 136) were deployed against Geluveld.

"The assault was launched against Geluveld and, a short time later, came a report that the commander of Infantry Regiment 99 [Oberstleutnant Nollau], who was in overall command, had been seriously wounded. At that, General von Altrock and his staff went forward through heavy harassing fire as far as the southern edge of Geluveld where the regimental commander lay severely wounded and where Major Rock [Commanding Officer 3rd Battalion] of Infantry Regiment 99 had been killed. There were severe casualties on both sides, but Geluveld had been captured. That same night General von Altrock went in search of a command post for the following day, but everywhere had been shot to pieces. They were surrounded by all the grimness of the battle-field; everywhere lay wounded soldiers, British as well as German, together with dying cattle who let out bellows of pain. The howl of shells passing over-head, coupled with the crack of small arms fire, provided the aural backdrop. Large numbers of stragglers and shirkers were rounded up.

"It was difficult on 1 November to determine the positions of the battalions because of all the small arms fire that was flying about. General von Altrock selected a small building, *Granat-Haüschen* [Shell Cottage], situated just west of Geluveld as a brigade command post. It was located close behind the infantry firing line and protected by a fold in the ground. Here throughout this and the following days, we were under constant heavy artillery fire. The roof was pierced constantly by shrapnel balls and it kept raining tiles."

This was the second consecutive day of heavy fighting for Infantry Regiment 99. Having attempted the previous evening to press forward by means of a night attack at 10.00 pm, already by 5.00 am on 31 October the regiment was thrusting forward once more in the direction of *Windmühlehöhe* [Windmill Hill], southeast of Geluveld, but the leading elements suffered such heavy losses that they were forced into cover and to attempt to dig themselves in. As it became light, however, the hill began to be bombarded systematically and 2nd Company was ordered to capture it, whilst the remainder of 1st Battalion moved to cover the gap with Infantry Regiment 136. Moving from cover to cover in bounds and despite further painful casualties, by 1.00 pm the men of 2nd Company were ready to begin the final attack, which was timed to coincide with the assault of the Saxon Infantry Regiment 105 against Geluveld village itself.

The intensity of the battle may be judged from the fact that it was almost impossible to pass verbal orders from man to man for the attack. Nevertheless the assault was pressed home promptly and valiantly. Three officers were killed and a further ten wounded in quick succession and casualties amongst the other ranks rose alarmingly but, by 2.30 pm, and following a determined charge led by Reserve Oberleutnant Walter which led to the capture of 200 prisoners and a machine gun, the hill was taken and held.[32] The regiment later felt that but for the intervention of the French and the fact that casualties amongst the junior leadership had been so high, rapid progress could have been made. Given the weight of flanking fire coming from the direction of Polygon

Wood this was probably overoptimistic, especially because resistance from this same direction continued to hinder German operations for some days to come. However, after the frustrations of the previous day, 31 October was day marked by slight, but measurable, progress towards the elusive goal of Ypres.

One gun commander from 2nd Platoon, Machine Company Infantry Regiment 105, later left a very atmospheric account of the events of the day.[33] **5.**

"We were called forward during the night 30/31 October 1914, with the mission of pushing as far forward towards the strong British positions to the right (north) of the Menen – Geluveld road as possible, there to dig in. Our machine gun platoon was commanded by Offizierstellvertreter Tuchscherer, who failed to return from a forward reconnaissance right at the start of our operation. Unteroffizier Gläser, an extraordinarily energetic NCO and one of the first members of our regiment to be awarded the Iron Cross Second Class met the same fate, having been fatally wounded by an enemy bullet.[34] At that, command of the platoon was assumed by the Einjährig-Unteroffizier and Gun Commander Schaarschmidt, who went on to work his way forward with his two guns to within about sixty metres of the British trenches located forward of Geluveld, which was in flames. There he dug in for the remainder of the night, together with a few infantry sections.

"As dawn broke there was a brief artillery bombardment to the south of the road, where the majority of the regiment was located, then the assault of Infantry Regiment 105 was launched. However it was repulsed repeatedly with heavy losses, due to the tough resistance put up by the elite troops to our front. During all of this, increasingly heavy British artillery fire began to come down, but rather than causing damage to our trenches on the right of the road, it seemed to be directed more towards our rear positions. Our rifle and machine gun fire against the trenches opposite us appeared to be more effective because, all of a sudden and quite unexpectedly, we spotted movement there. Initially believing that there was going to be an attack, we opened fire, but the British began waving handkerchiefs and reversed rifles then climbed out of the trench and came towards us with their hands up. There were about fifty of them and they were quickly led to the rear. Given the unclear situation there could be no thought of occupying the trench for the time being and we contented ourselves by searching it quickly.

"A further patrol under Gun Commander Blechschmidt which clambered up the high road embankment, established that our assault trenches were exactly opposite the densely occupied enemy trenches on the far side of the road. Coming to a swift decision we lugged our one remaining machine gun – the other one had been shot up during the battle – up onto the embankment and brought it into action! The field of fire we had from up there was amazing, as was the surprise suffered by the British when we brought our well-aimed fire down along the line of the enemy trench. However we did not remain undisturbed. We were spotted from Geluveld and came under accurate small arms fire from there and from another position almost in our rear. One after the other we fell victim to the fire, until only Blechschmidt and Unteroffizier Schaarschmidt were left operating a half-damaged gun . . .

"Nevertheless when our regiment renewed its attack our fire held the British trench in check and it was soon overrun by the 105th, followed closely by the much disputed village of Geluveld. The following day Blechschmidt and Schaarschmidt were promoted by Oberst Freiherr von Oldershausen and were awarded the Iron Cross Second Class, followed a short time later by the Military St Heinrich's medal in silver."

Unsurprising to relate, by the afternoon of 31 October, the scene to the south of Geluveld was one of great confusion. Despite the fact that some progress had been made, on this critical day it was essential that the German line was pushed forward to the maximum extent possible and so maintain the pressure on the British defence. There was a feeling within the German chain of command, not without some justification, that it was close to cracking, so it was time for every possible expedient to be attempted.

Oberleutnant Krazer and Kanonier Lobeck 3rd Battery Field Artillery Regiment 51 [35] **6.**

"The infantry could not get forward. Deimling decided to push a battery forward and create some space. The Veldhoek heights had to be captured. The General spoke direct to the commander of the 1st Battalion and his battery commanders while standing on the observation wagon of 3rd Battery Field Artillery Regiment 51. He explained the situation and demanded the services of a battery which he wished to deploy in front of the infantry; the intention being to prevent the enemy counter-attack which was being prepared. Lots were drawn and it fell to 3rd Battery. The commander of 3rd Battery, Hauptmann Kirchner, thanked the general for the mission. A small hollow provided cover for the move forward, then it was a matter of galloping onto the hill, with the observation wagon in the lead.

"Following up, Number 1 gun came to a halt in the midst of a hail of fire, perhaps only two hundred metres in front of the astonished British troops. The courageous gunners dragged out two shell baskets and brought the unharnessed gun into action. The gunlayer, Braun, aimed independently at the trench to his front and, without waiting for orders, sent the first shell flying towards the enemy. He was on target from the very first shell, which made bringing up the other five guns easier. Unfortunately the great weight of fire brought down by the British at such short range meant that there were considerable casualties amongst both men and horses. Losses mounted rapidly. The brave Braun received a bullet through the throat but, gradually, the British fire reduced in intensity as they were pinned down in their trenches.

"The ammunition was exhausted about 3.00 pm. Scattered and isolated, the battery was caught close up to the enemy and could only have defended itself with revolvers. Not until evening could Vizefeldwebel Doubs lead the teams forward at least as far as the protective dip slope and there unload. The infantry also got forward at this time – Infantry Regiment 105 – and dug in between and about twenty five metres in front of the guns. When the Saxons saw our ammunition crisis they rushed down to the ammunition stacks and, together with the gunners, had soon transferred all the ammunition forward. On the left flank of the battery was a small hut and there, in amongst wounded British soldiers, we set up an observation post. That night we also buried our dead near this hut.

"The following day brought the fruits of the efforts of the battery. A short fire programme came down on the trenches which were very close, there were shouts of *Hurra!* from the courageous 105th, the bayonets flashed then we gunners were able to watch what was a only a brief infantry battle from very close range. Soon two or three companies of British soldiers surrendered. It was an unforgettable sight when we both joined in shouts of *Hurra*. The infantry were standing on the parapets of the captured trenches and we by our guns. Then the Tommies marched back past us and were able to see at first hand the battery which had closed right up on them . . . For us it was a sad move back to Geluwe then near to Menen. When the battery dismounted we could see all the gaps in the ranks. Instead of five men, there were only three and sometimes as few as two per gun. Hauptmann Kirchner was also wounded. During our march back through Menen we saw the Corps Commander. When the battery was reported to him, he was amazed that we were still there. Visibly relieved he said, "I thought that the British had got you. I thank you all."

During the early months of the war in particular, it was frequent practice for families who had received detailed letters from their relatives or friends serving at the front to pass them on to local newspapers for publication. In the wake of the battles at the end of October, the family of member of Infantry Regiment 105 allowed the use of one such by the *Leipziger Volkszeitung*. It was deemed to be of such general interest that it was later republished by the *Freiburger Zeitung* some weeks later. An extract, though somewhat highly coloured, nevertheless conveys the close quarter, confused and intense nature of the low level infantry battle along the Menen road vividly. It reads: **6.**

" . . . After a march of several days duration, we heard the thunder of the guns on 31 October . . . What we experienced that day was a more appalling scene of war than it is possible for the normal mortal to comprehend . . . There was an eerie silence then suddenly a Hauptmann from the 99th on our left shouted across, 'Prepare to attack! The assault begins at 1.00 pm!' We shook our heads in disbelief, because thus far, anybody raising his head above the edge of the sunken road would have had it shot off. However, we made ready and waited patiently.

"At 12.45 pm the same Hauptmann suddenly shouted, 'Rapid fire!' We looked up and there, one hundred to one hundred and fifty metres away, the clay-yellow forms of the British, wearing caps of the same colour, were pulling back to the village behind them. We gave them all we had. The Hauptmann himself fired and I could hardly load fast enough . . . Suddenly came the call 'Stop!' Our comrades off to the right had followed up towards the enemy trenches and there was chance that we might have hit them. At this point the drums beat for the attack, the trumpets blew and, from thousands of throats, came shouts of *Hurra! Hurra!* We rushed forward like a wild storm, despite the weight of our knapsacks, with bayonets fixed and hunted the British out of their trenches, where they had made themselves extremely comfortable.

"Their trenches were well constructed and equipped. To eat and drink there was corned beef, ham, chocolate, brandy and wine and there were ample quantities of cigars and cigarettes. Most of them were located behind hedgerows and hawthorn bushes. They had excellent overhead cover and featured tables, chairs, woollen blankets and mattresses. They fired at us from these trenches until we were a mere thirty metres away, then they emerged with their hands up and ran towards us to surrender. Despite their raised hands a great many were nevertheless shot down, some of us could not stop ourselves. We took several hundred prisoners . . . the British were better infantrymen than the French. Some had sixteen years' service and most of them eight . . .

"My nerves were on edge and my heart was beating so loud I could hear it, but I stormed on, one amongst a wild horde rushing forward. The enemy was firing from every building. By now the sections included men from all the different regiments and they were attacking every trench and every building. Together with five other men, I overran three British supply wagons. Two men were attempting to guard them. Despite our charge, they would not yield, so we shot them down. We had a quick look in the wagons and found that they contained ammunition, rations and mail – most of which had been posted in London on 22 October . . . '[36]

Away to the south, where the battle for Messines was proving to be a tough examination for the battle-hardened Württembergers of 26th Infantry Division, the attempts by the men of 6th Bavarian Reserve Division (who were as raw as the ill fated troops of Fourth Army operating up to the north), to establish a foothold in Wijtschate, proved initially to be a failure. During the afternoon of 31 October, orders reached Bavarian Reserve Infantry Regiment 21 to move forward to the Wambeke area east of the Warneton–Oosttaverne road, to come under command of 12 Bavarian Reserve Brigade and to prepare to launch a night attack against Wijtschate. This would have been a challenge for any active army formation; to give such an order to men, who had only begun even platoon level training a mere five weeks previously, was distinctly ambitious, especially because they were being required to advance across totally unreconnoitred ground to attack an enemy of unknown size.

The situation was equally difficult for the inexperienced gunners of Bavarian Reserve

Field Artillery Regiment 6, who had been supporting the advance into the west of Hollebeke, but now had to switch their attention to Wijtschate. One of the gunners later described one abortive action in his diary.

Kriegsfreiwilliger Schuster Bavarian Reserve Field Artillery Regiment 6[37] *7.*

"About 5.00 pm on the evening of 31 October, we arrived in Houthem, which was ablaze. Only with difficulty could we get the horses to move forward in amongst all the smoke and flames of the burning houses. The battle had also left its mark outside the village, where medical orderlies were busy tending to the wounded and gathering together the fallen. The fields and ditches were littered with abandoned equipment and shell baskets. Darkness was already falling when the battery went into position in a field surrounded by hedges not far from Kaleute. The gunners then set to, to dig in the guns and ammunition wagons. As far as the falling light permitted, the ground out to the front was observed. In the west this was crowned by a low hill feature. Upon it were situated Wijtschate, with Messines on fire to the south.

"By now it was dark, so the flash of guns firing, the explosions of enemy shells and the sight of burning farms in all directions made a striking, if sad, impression. We did manage to grab a quick meal from the insulated containers; it was the first warm food of the day. It was about 9.00 pm when we opened fire on Wijtschate. The moment when the order 'Fire!' was given was an unforgettable occasion. It was not until midnight that the loud sound of battle began to die away. Wijtschate was a sea of flames and the church tower first tilted and then collapsed. It was now All Saints' Day. For many this religious holiday was also to be their last day! We were manning our guns at 2.00 am when we were ordered to change positions forward.

"In near silence the teams arrived and we moved along a field track at a walk. Because it was narrow and the infantry were also marching forward along it, we had to halt frequently. Finally we arrived at Oosttaverne and three guns of the battery went into position at its western exit. [Our] fourth gun, commanded by Offizierstellvertreter Jaenisch, was sent forward, together with an ammunition wagon, along the road to Wijtschate, so as to accompany the forward troops of Bavarian Reserve Infantry Regiment 17. The gun soon bore off to the left along a track that petered out and we were reduced to carrying on cross country until we unharnessed behind a hedge. The gun was run forward to a point about one hundred metres from a lone house and ammunition was moved forward. The team remained in cover behind the hedge.

"All around it was relatively quiet, though now and again we heard rifle or machine gun fire. We were in an odd sort of position, because we had no contact with the infantry. We aimed at Wijtschate and opened fire. We had barely fired one shell than a hail of small arms fire came from the right. Some flew overhead, the rest rattled against the gun shield. We threw ourselves to the ground and took up our carbines, ready to shoot. The shots came from Rondel Wood about one hundred and fifty metres away. There was enemy in the wood and we had passed through our own lines in the darkness. The first thing, therefore, was to withdraw our gun so that we should not be caught out. Under a torrent of fire which fortunately passed overhead, we hauled the gun and as much ammunition as possible back behind the hedge, but we had to leave the ammunition wagon where it was. We remained behind the hedge, ready to fire to cover the withdrawal of the gun then, when we thought that it was back in safety, we pulled back ourselves, moving in bounds until we were safely back with the battery. The wagon was recovered the following day."

At 10.00 pm the order to attack Wijtschate was also given to Bavarian Reserve Infantry Regiment 17. On receipt it disengaged from the wooded area to the west of Hollebeke and sidestepped to the left to be in position on the start line at 1.00 am about three hundred metres short of the first enemy positions. To have achieved this was no mean feat for inexperienced troops. Linking with Infantry Regiment 122 on the left, the attack jumped off at 2.00 am but, hardly surprisingly, there were problems immediately. The ground was littered with obstacles, most of them natural: ditches, thick hedges and wire. Direction and cohesion was lost repeatedly, so it was probably only due to the fact that the British defence was weak, that the advance reached the ridge and carried on into Wijtschate. Here, in addition to the difficulty of fighting in a built up area, once again the wearing of forage caps by the regiments of 6th Bavarian Reserve Division caused another near disaster.

In the gloom of the early morning, troops of Bavarian Reserve Infantry Regiment 21 advancing from the east, mistook the leading elements for British troops and, according to that regiment, 'a battle with many casualties broke out until it was ended with considerable difficulty by the intervention of individual officers'.[38] This entirely avoidable setback provides yet another proof that on the battlefield a high price was being paid for rushing these troops into action. The furthest point of the advance was probably achieved by men of Bavarian Reserve Infantry Regiment 17, who pressed on to the eastern edge of the village by about 3.30 am. They were in the process of reorganising, an extremely difficult operation in view of the general inexperience of the troops, when Bavarian Reserve Infantry Regiment 21, which had encountered great difficulty in closing up on the town in the dark, launched its attack in error.

Bavarian Reserve Infantry Regiment 17 noted later, 'Towards 5.00 am, elements of Bavarian Reserve Infantry Regiment 21 launched an attack on Wijtschate from the east near Torreken Farm. Despite the waving of flags and unfurling the regimental colour; notwithstanding the giving of German signals and the singing of *Die Wacht am Rhein*, it was impossible to correct the error. Our sister regiment charged in amongst us and wrecked the carefully created order. Only gradually did the officers restore order.'[39] Unfortunately vigorous local British counter action, coupled with an increase in flanking fire and shelling, both from British as well as German batteries, then convinced the commander of Bavarian Reserve Infantry Regiment 17, Oberst Großmann, that the place could not be held without additional reinforcements. These were not forthcoming so, at 9.00 am, he gave the order for withdrawal. Arriving back at their rallying point near Wambeke, the roll was called and it was discovered that Bavarian Reserve Infantry Regiment 17 had suffered thirty percent casualties and there were subsequent accusations that some of the men were suffering wounds caused by Dum Dum bullets.[40]

A member of one of the leading companies later described his experience in a letter home, written on 2 November from a field hospital. The timings he described are somewhat awry and he does not mention the unfortunate clash with Bavarian Reserve Infantry Regiment 21, but he does convey the impression of the confusion experienced by men going into battle for the first time.

Kriegsfreiwilliger Ludwig Engstler 4th Company Bavarian Reserve Infantry Regiment 17[41] 8.

"Do not be shocked, in two days' time I shall be back in action. I have a bayonet wound in my right thigh. I have headed this letter 'All Souls' Day' [2 November]. My God, the words 'All Souls' conceal a tremendous amount. Let me explain it to you. During the evening of 31 October the Oberst said to us, 'Comrades. It all begins today! His Majesty the Kaiser himself has ordered that the town of Wijtschate is to be stormed and held. Both the Kaiser and the Crown Prince [Rupprecht] will be observing the battle. Act like brave Bavarians!'[42] We moved forward joyfully; it was still night when were arrived at our place of battle. The guns were already making a tremendous racket. Everywhere the shells groaned their way to the horizon. The German artillery was the stronger and did not grant the enemy any sort of breathing space. We shook out and launched into battle.

"At that everything opened up on us: guns, machine guns and rifle fire. Our ranks began to thin, as here and there our comrades fell. However the unholy howling and rushing sounds of the shells did not throw us off balance. Forwards! Not a step backwards! It was 12 o'clock midnight. 'Fix bayonets!' We closed our ranks in tightly and went forward like a wall of flashes. Every gap which appeared in the wall was rapidly filled. With shouts of *Hurra!* we pushed on into the town. From all sides a raging rate of fire was poured at us from within the houses. We set fire to them and the flames blazed upwards, illuminating a grim scene. The streets were full of dead and wounded men: dark skinned Indians, together with British, French and Belgians, all lying alongside rows of our courageous Bavarians. We drove the British out of the town, which now belonged to us. The British, however, summoned reinforcements and pushed forward. We came under fire from the entrances to cellars and every other nook and cranny.

"There were too few of us. There were no officers in sight and we just had to pull back. Once more we advanced and once more we retreated. It was a saddened platoon which turned its back on this place of death. 'Are you still alive?' asked one of the few who remained. It seemed to me that I had been granted new life; something which was permitted to very few. I cried with anger when I saw all the misery around me. A man ran past me. I glanced at him and saw that it was Jordan Mattias. Deeply moved, we shook hands in silence. On All Saints Day [1 November] there was a regimental roll call. More than half the regiment was missing. The other regiments who had also fought on this day suffered equally dreadful losses. Today is All Souls Day, when the living remember the dead. However, we are proud that we were present during a great battle, which worked out in our favour [*sic.*] and which the Kaiser and the Crown Prince witnessed. Within two to three days nothing more will be heard about the British troops but this [for us] was less a baptism of fire and more a baptism in blood.

"How did I come to be wounded? We were in the town and pursuing the enemy when, suddenly, I felt something sharp and metallic pierce my thigh. I threw my leg forward quickly, so that it did not penetrate far, then I went back to my opponent. It was a wounded British soldier, who was aiming his rifle at me. His instrument of death flew into the mire and I despatched him to Hell with one thrust. Then we pushed on. It was not until after the roll call that I had my wound dressed and I have now been in hospital for nearly two days. I shall then be out just in time to take part in the decisive battle. May God protect me as he has thus far.

"What did I experience during the battle? I was relieved that it had finally got going. The never ending marching was not at all to my liking. The first time shrapnel burst over us, we all ducked down low, but we soon got used to it. I was very lucky during the assault. Men were falling to my front, my right and my left, but I remained on my feet. I gave up all hope of surviving and, in this fatalistic mood, did not seek cover, but moved around upright. I shall have to stitch up two holes in my clothes caused by these damned British soldiers. In the town we came up against a mixed group of twenty British and Indian troops. There were about twelve of us and we opened fire at once.

"The Hauptmann was stationed at the entrance to the village and called for volunteers to go and collect the wounded and bring them into the shelter of the undamaged buildings. I volunteered for this rather risky task. We carried about two dozen into two houses and made them comfortable. All of a sudden there was firing on all sides. Some of our comrades raced by and shouted to us, 'The British are coming!' We had to pull back. We took the slightly wounded men with us, but we had to leave the others behind. We could not stay there; we realised that it was pointless to stay and be killed, so off we went! I took the arm of my Leutnant and supported him, but suddenly he was shot through the temples and fell dead, so I went and joined the others. A word about the battle in general. It was one of the largest to date. The British were attacked all along the front and suffered similar casualties to us. They were hemmed in a horseshoe – like position and could not get away. You will be able to read more about it in the papers. Most of our officers have fallen."

In fact, as has been noted, this assault failed because it was conducted by troops who were barely trained, over unknown ground and in the dark. There was a major clash between friendly forces and numerous instances of ill directed German artillery fire. It is possible that regular troops with time for preparation would have done better but they, too, would have had problems because the formations to the north were unable to get forward out of the Oosttaverne woods, leaving Bavarian Reserve Infantry Regiment 17 to attempt to cover its open right flank in addition to getting forward. As it was, this failure cost that regiment over thirty per cent casualties, including the following officers, who were all killed in action: Major Hermann Helmes, commanding officer 2nd Battalion, Hauptmann Georg Danner and Landwehr Oberleutnant Theodor Harster, commanders of 3rd and 6th Companies respectively, together with Leutnants Georg Fillweber, Anton Halder, Michael Sacherl and Rudolf Schuster. Within the next two weeks, especially on 4 November, the regiment lost a further twelve officers killed in action, so Engstler's assertion was certainly true by the time the regiment was withdrawn from this disastrous first battle.[43]

This engagement had one other amazing feature. On 12 November the Corps Commander, General der Infanterie Karl Ritter von Martini, signed off a letter to Headquarters Sixth Army about the conduct of one of the soldiers under his command.[44]

"I wish to draw your attention to the following extraordinary action:

During the night 31 October/1 November 3rd Company Bavarian Reserve Infantry Regiment 17 became split up during bitter house to house fighting in Wijtschate. Only a few men reached the edge of the village with the company commander and all but one were killed in the [subsequent] fire fight. The only survivor was Infanterist Johann Zott, whose knapsack was holed by shell splinters. Zott disguised himself in the coat and cap of a dead British soldier, who was lying next to him. He then ran to a position behind the line of British riflemen and went up to where the ammunition wagons and field kitchens were located. He remained there for several hours, drank some coffee with the British soldiers, busied himself around an ammunition wagon and fed the horses.

"As dawn approached, Zott feared that he would be unmasked, so he mounted the saddle horse, drove the wagon forward to the British firing line and emptied the ammunition. It came in useful that Zott, a former seaman, knew a number of English expressions and swear words. Whilst the British soldiers were occupied with the ammunition, Zott mounted suddenly and galloped off past the trenches in the direction of the German lines, under heavy fire from both sides. Luckily he found cover in a small hollow. Here he was able to swap his British clothing for German, because there were dead and wounded

German soldiers in the hollow. Once he had loaded a wounded officer and three wounded soldiers on his wagon, he drove on towards the German position. Towards evening he arrived at Headquarters II Bavarian Army Corps with his wagon and three wounded men – the officer had died on the journey. I have awarded the man, who is a kriegsfreiwilliger from Augsburg, the Iron Cross Second Class." [45]

Naturally the inability to take and hold Wijtschate was not regarded as the final word on the subject. From the war diary of 6th Bavarian Reserve Division, it can be seen that the importance of the place was such that, a full two hours before the withdrawal of Bavarian Reserve Infantry Regiment 17, a decision had been made to move fresh troops forward for a renewal of the attack. [46]

"7.00 am. Enemy in Wijtschate once more. From 12 [Bavarian] Reserve Brigade [Bavarian] Reserve Infantry Regiment 17 is 500 metres east of the built up area; [Bavarian] Reserve Infantry Regiment 21 is on the adjoining hill to the south. In order to speed up the capture of the enemy strong point Wijtschate, another two battalions of [Bavarian] Reserve Infantry Regiment 8 have been released from Corps reserve and have been placed at our disposal. Admittedly this is because it was thought a breakthrough in this area might have been possible. The allocation was, however, urgently needed because [Bavarian] Reserve Infantry Regiment 17 needed a break, so Commander 12 [Bavarian] Reserve Brigade has received fresh troops."

The adjutant of Bavarian Reserve Infantry Regiment 8, who was later to achieve fame as the man who led the recapture of the Schwaben Redoubt near Thiepval on 1 July 1916, takes up the story:

Oberleutnant Herbert Wurmb Adjutant Bavarian Reserve Infantry Regiment 8 [47] **8.**

"It was on All Saints' Day 1914, a beautiful Sunday in autumn, that troops of 6th Bavarian Reserve Division captured Wijtschate but, due'to several unfortunate circumstances, the village had to be completely evacuated once more. However, the divisional commander, [General der Kavallerie] Freiherr von Speidel, did not regard the battle as lost. [Bavarian] Reserve Infantry Regiment 20 and our regiment, less 2nd Battalion . . . was given the mission of renewing the attack at 2.00 pm. The regimental commander, Oberst Hartmann, and I, as regimental adjutant, were despatched in advance to Groenelinde, where we were met by the commander of 12 Reserve Brigade, General[major] Kiefhaber. He issued orders for the assault on Wijtschate. The 1st Battalion (Hauptmann Oskar Prager) and 3rd Battalion (Major Bezzel) advanced as far as Oosttaverne, where they halted, because it was not known whether we or the enemy were occupying Wijtschate. From here 3rd Battalion pushed forward patrols towards Wijtschate.

"The artillery preparation of the attack was provided by the heavy artillery of 6th Bavarian Reserve Division (Reserve Foot Artillery Battalion 6) and 3rd Division. The light field howitzers of Bavarian Reserve Field Artillery Regiment 6 were also involved, but the field guns were distributed as infantry support batteries amongst the two brigades of 6th Bavarian Reserve Division and located in the front line. In accordance with the mission, the 3rd Battalion, together with Reserve Infantry Regiment 17 was to assault and capture Wijtschate. To the northeast of Wijtschate, it was to link up with Bavarian Infantry Regiment 23 at the *Rondellwald*, whilst its left flank was to move along the line of the Oostaverne – Wijtschate road, maintaining contact with Bavarian Reserve Infantry Regiment 21. 1st Battalion was to follow up eche-loned to the right.

"The attack began at 1.45 pm. Zeitler's battery kept up a constant fire on Wijtschate, lifting only when 3rd Battalion began to advance, in the face of very heavy small arms fire from *Rondellwald*. There was a gap of about two kilo-metres with the 3rd Division until that evening, when a battalion from that division had closed it. As a result Major Bezzel requested the Regiment to deploy 1st Battalion in his support. At that a platoon of 2nd Company was sent forward and established that the southern edge of this wood was free of enemy forces and pushed on further to the western edge. Initially this did make much of a difference to 3rd Battalion but, at 2.30 pm, a further attempt was made by the entire company to clear the wood. Meanwhile Reserve Infantry Regiment 17 was withdrawn completely from the firing line, having suffered insupport-able casualties.

"About 2.00 pm the 3rd Battalion was occupying reasonable cover in a hollow some 800 metres west of Wijtschate. Enemy shelling was having no effect. Grehn's patrol from 10th Company, reported, 'Southern sector of Wijtschate is free of enemy, but there are strong groups of enemy in the northern part.' Towards 3.00 pm Major Bezzel ordered an attack on Wijtschate. In order to reduce the risk of casualties, the men were ordered to spread out and to advance individually as far as a fold in the ground a few hundred metres from the eastern edge of Wijtschate and to form up there. Reserve Leutnant Graser, commanding 10th Company, received a head wound and was replaced by Reserve Leutnant Schaurer. Major Bezzel hurried forward with his adjutant, Oberleutnant Bärmann (Infantry Regiment 4) and 10th Company to the track running from Oosttaverne – Wijtschate, passing racks of drying tobacco and under extremely heavy flanking fire.

"There was a short breather in the hollow from where it was possible to observe troops, apparently from Bavarian Reserve Infantry Regiment 21, advancing and then digging in at the southern end of Wijtschate. Once more Major Bezzel repeated his orders for the assault on the village and directed that there be no halt until the western edge was reached. Rushing out in front himself and not far from the houses began he came under fire from a rough brushwood shelter and suddenly felt a heavy blow on the thigh – wounded! He made his way back into the first house he came across, which happened to be on fire, made it his command post and his wound was tended by Infanterist Pfirsching of 10th Company . . . Leutnants Böck (11th) and Mantel (officer commanding 12th) were also wounded and Offizierstellvertreter Hacker, a platoon commander in 9th Company, was killed.[48]

"The adjutant 3rd Battalion [Oberleutnant Heinrich Bärmann] observed the progress of the battle from the roof of the command post. 9th Company had formed a front facing the enemy in the *Rondellwald* whilst, to the left 10th Company appeared to have deployed. Then, once 2nd and 4th Companies had opened fire just before 4.00 pm on the groups of houses and pockets of resistance from the western edge of the *Rondellwald*, 3rd Battalion (primarily 9th and 10th Companies) supported by 3rd Company, which advanced to the south of *Rondellwald* in contact with 3rd Battalion, pressed the attack against the eastern edge of the village and succeeded in capturing a line of enemy trenches by about 5.30 pm. Two light enemy machine guns, which the 3rd Battalion captured and which were placed that evening in a house east of the village, were unfortunately moved to the rear the following day by Bavarian Infantry Regiment 22.

"There was an unfortunate occurrence at 5.20 pm when our own artillery brought fire down once more in the village. Our 10th Company, which had already pressed on into the village, received heavy casualties as a result. Despite every effort by the commanding officer of 3rd Battalion: waving with artillery flags, towels and coats, the artillery continued to fire and to damage 10th Company, such that it had to withdraw. Once the small arms fire from the flank had slackened, Major Bezzel, supported by Infanterist Pfirsching and leaning on his sword, hobbled back to Oosttaverne, whence he was transported back to the homeland. Oberleutnant Bärmann assumed command of 3rd Battalion that evening. He and Leutnant Fritsching, officer commanding 9th Company were the only officers of the battalion still on their feet. Bärmann amalgamated the 9th and 11th Companies into one, Feldwebel Eberling commanded the 10th and Feldwebel Mayer the 12th . . .

"During the night the troops dug in, together with the grenade launcher teams. In accordance with divisional orders the village perimeter was to be held at all costs. Many of the wounded were evacuated, but it was a difficult operation. The shadows darkened and night fell, heavy and serious, on the bloody Sunday that was All Saints' Day 1914, the weapons fell silent and the fallen took their rest."

The War Diary of 6th Bavarian Reserve Division noted, 'At 5.30 pm, as a result of enemy numerical superiority and flanking artillery fire from the north, the village had to be evacuated yet again. Weak elements hung on there, but the remainder had to pull back some 150 metres to the east. The falling of night precluded a further attempt at an assault. Order: The positions achieved are to be held in readiness for a continuation of the attack tomorrow.'[49] All day on 2 November further attempts were taken to storm and hold Wijtschate. The British cavalry, which had been defending it up until then, was finally relieved by French troops, who seem to have wasted little time in withdrawing from the village and leaving it to be occupied by Bavarian Reserve Infantry Regiment 8. Because the entire sector had proved so tough a nut for the 6th Bavarian Reserve Division to tackle unaided, as an emergency measure, 3rd Infantry Division was rushed to the area and the Pomeranian Grenadier Regiments 2 and 9 force marched forward to take over the main responsibility from the largely fought-out Bavarians. Surprising to note, their arrival was not greeted universally with enthusiasm. By now it had become a point of principle to the Bavarians to capture and hold the place themselves and Grenadier Regiment 9 makes the point firmly that, 'On two separate occasions the order to 5 Infantry Brigade to attack was withdrawn, because the Bavarians wanted to storm Wijtschate alone.'[50]

In view of the need to force a decision to the east of Ypres Army Group Fabeck ordered a full scale attack all along its front. In the northern sector, so as to wring every last vestige of effort from his exhausted troops, the commander XV Corps issued a special Order of the Day that showed that every expedient was to be exploited to this end:

"Headquarters XV Corps　　　　　*Wervik, 3 November 1914*

Corps Order!

During the past three days the Corps has captured approximately forty officers and 2,000 British other ranks.

It is clear that the British surrender if they are subject to energetic attack.

I direct, therefore, that the attacks are to be pressed home with bugle calls and with the regimental bands playing.

Regimental musicians who play during assaults will be awarded Iron Crosses.[51]

Signed: von Deimling"[52]

Meanwhile, down at Wijtschate, 3 November began badly. A French local counter-attack was launched against the north of the town and Bavarian Reserve Infantry Regiment 8 was pushed back in the northwest quarter. This time, the support of Grenadier Regiment 9 was urgently sought at about 2.00 pm to help restore the situation, whilst Grenadier Regiment 2 was launched forward as part of a more general attack in the direction of Spanbroekmolen on the far side of the ridge between Messines and Wijtschate.

Unteroffizier Schadow 2nd Company Grenadier Regiment 2 [53] 9.

"Assault! What that word means to a soldier! To our front was a wide expanse of terrain. Wherever the eye could see shells and shrapnel rounds were exploding. First there would be a small cloud in the sky then it would expand. Suddenly there would be a roar and a rush of air, as though an autumn wind was blowing through the twigs. Over there a shell was landing in an isolated house. There was a dull but heavy crash and hundreds of tiles flew through the air. Where the house had once stood there was just a thick black cloud, enveloping red flames which shot skywards. So it was that something which a man had built by the sweat of his brow was flattened in an instant. The rafters still stuck up steeply, but they were being burnt higher and higher by the flames and it was not long until the whole place was one great inferno. Then there was a thunderous crash and only the blackened walls remained to bear witness that people had once lived here.

"In the meantime we stayed in cover and thought once more about our own homes. Of course we knew that our thoughts could not dwell on that for long. Soon we should have to act and an iron sense of duty meant that we had to suppress all our humanity. The minutes ticked by with desperate slowness; time seemed to stretch out. We lay there completely still, looking so peaceful that it was hard to believe that all these men with their serious eyes would soon appear to be utterly transformed. Soon they would stretch their limbs and stand up, the light of battle in their eyes and their trusty weapons gripped tightly, ready to launch themselves wildly into battle. Above and around us raged the artillery battle. The earth seemed ready to burst as each side tried to out do the other's firepower.

"Everywhere where the shells landed they spread death and destruction, producing one glowing crater after another. The grim reaper moved amongst both friend and foe, young and old and claimed a rich harvest. The fire grew ever heavier, the sky was lit up as though by a sea of flames. It was as though the air was being split by hundreds of bolts of lightning – just a few moments now! – 'Fix bayonets!' That wrenched us out of our reverie. Already to our front the trumpets were sounding and the drums beating. Shouts of 'On your feet! Forwards!' rang in our ears. Off in front raced our first platoon, with Hauptmann v Waldow in the lead. With shells bursting in amongst them, they advanced in short bounds. It looked as though they had all disappeared off the face of the earth, as if they were all dead, but repeatedly the grey wave pushed on, pausing frequently to go to ground.

"They finally set foot in the first abandoned line of trenches and were followed up by the Second Platoon and then the Third, though not all our comrades made it as far as the trench. But this was, in any case, no place to linger: press on was the watchword. We launched forward and all hell broke loose once more. Throwing ourselves down, we pressed our faces into the ground and gasped for breath. Then it was time for another bound. Shells crashed down on our ranks; here and there a comrade fell with *Hurra!* still on his lips. Forward, ever forward, we stormed at a breathless pace. Swift commands passed from mouth to mouth, but sometimes they could not be heard; the crash of the shells drowned everything else out. Rifle bullets whistled past us, punctuating the monotonous clatter of the machine guns. Out front our standard bearer (Hornack) went down passing, with the last of his strength, the unfurled colour to a comrade rushing forward to take it up.

"Finally we could go no further and we leapt down into the enemy trenches. Tired out we lay around or sat in an old position – played out men with restless eyes, staring around us, taking no note at all of shells or shrapnel – tired, just so tired! Evening fell. It went darker and darker then the moon rose and the artillery fire died away. Then stooped figures began moving over the bloody ground; the Samaritans of the battlefield. Here they would close the eyes of the dying, there they would offer a water bottle to a wounded man, who would take long draughts from it. 'Thank you, comrade!' We hunched down deeper into our coats and huddled together, but our tired bodies were shrieking for rest. We might have wanted to turn our thoughts to our homes once more but we were too tired, simply too tired. Now and again someone stirred, sighed deeply then slept on towards the morning which would bring further difficult tasks."

The situation in Wijtschate restored, Bavarian Reserve Infantry Regiment 8 resumed responsibility for the forward positions and Grenadier Regiment 9 took advantage of the fact, allowing its forward troops to gather in the cellars of the town and rest overnight. Elsewhere the line barely moved that day but although it was becoming clear that Army Group Fabeck was going to enjoy no further success and that the arrival of the French in force on its front simply reduced the chances further, nevertheless, the battles continued over the next few days. On 4 November, for example, there was an early resumption of the attack by formations of 3rd Infantry Division south of Wijtschate. Because of heavy fire from a flank, it made little progress and finally stalled some two hundred metres short of Hill 75. At 11.30 am 3rd Battalion Grenadier Regiment 2 received orders to move forward and it arrived in the forward positions by 2.00 pm. The attack, supported by the divisional artillery reinforced by the Howitzer Battery of Field Artillery Regiment 38, was due to be renewed at 4.00 pm, but this start time had to be postponed for a further one and a half hours. When the attack was finally launched, several members of the regiment left detailed descriptions of the way the attack unfolded.

Leutnant von Kleist 8th Company Grenadier Regiment 2 [54] *9.*

"We officers wished each other luck, drank a last schnaps and smoked a final cigarette then, punctually at 5.00 pm, the trumpeters blew, 'Fix bayonets!' and a crazy rate of fire was opened. However, because visibility was so poor, nobody could really tell what they were firing at. Five minutes later the order to attack was given and the wild hunt was on. The first objective was a farmstead. What did we care about the artillery? What did it matter who was firing at the farmstead: ours, or the enemy's? The [enemy] had certainly spotted our advance, countering it with a hail of lead and iron. It was complete hell, but we pressed forward and had soon taken the first farmstead. However, shells were coming down accurately and men fell as though they had been mown down. I indicated the second target with my sword, but my arm fell as though it had been paralysed. I put away my sword and pistol and carried on. There was a hedge twenty metres to my front – but what was that? I stumbled on and threw myself down by the hedge. My foot had also been hit and I stayed lying where I was."

Kriegsfreiwilliger von Geibler 8th Company Grenadier Regiment 2 [55] **9.**

"It was midday. We were still under cover in the trench. Finally – about 4.00 pm – a runner arrived from Leutnant von Kleist. 'The platoon is to prepare to move. Move forward to the trench which is currently under fire, then go half right towards a farm – a watermill – and assemble there! The other platoons will be following up!' At long last the relief of an end to all the waiting, to having to lie still. Now it was up and at the enemy! I can still see them in my mind's eye, all my mates, moving on past the 3rd Battalion and shouting wise-cracks and jokes at them, like acquaintances from an exercise as they lay at readiness lining the edge of a sunken road. The move continued. At one point contact was lost between two sections, but this was restored and first the platoon, then the whole company, arrived at the farm. Leutnant von Kleist lay together with Hauptmann von Mutius in a large hole in the ground which had once been a clamp for sugar beet.

"I ran over to him and reported all present. He gave out his orders then I heard Hauptmann von Mutius shout over to the trumpeter: 'Blow, Fix bayo-nets! and put the wind up that lot over there!' At that the trumpeters took up the call which ran along from the right, echoing back quietly amongst the noise of the firing. There was great enthusiasm, almost jubilation, amongst us as bayonets flew out of their scabbards, then it was, 'On your feet, forwards!' and we advanced on the enemy. Initially my platoon advanced half right through a hollow, then straight on and through a hedge – but where was the enemy? They had pulled back. Nevertheless we [received] fire from the front and from the flanks and salvoes of shells fell around and amongst us. We lay there for a short while and then dashed further on.

"To our right was a platoon from another company. I was just about to order another bound forward when shrapnel burst overhead, throwing me to one side. I felt dizzy and faint, but pulled myself together and shouted at the man next to me that I was wounded and that the next most senior Unteroffizier was to assume command. It was not until late in to the night that the wounded were all brought in to the dressing station at Bas-Warneton and there I met up with some comrades from the company. All the platoon commanders of 8th Company had been hit, as had the company commander, Leutnant von Kleist, who took his sword in his left hand after he had been hit and continued to charge forwards until he was wounded again."

Hauptmann von Keßler 1st Battalion Grenadier Regiment 2 [56] **9.**

"Despite an heroic advance, ground was only gained slowly. Murderous rifle and machine gun fire mowed down complete rows of our courageous [men]. In the end all elements of the regiment were merged together. When, at long last, the order to dig in arrived the regiment was located to the west of Wijtschate. Its right flank rested on a narrow gauge railway opposite a park, its left on Spanbroekmolen and its centre pushed forward. The losses within the battalions were very severe, with almost all the officers killed or wounded. The last men of 1st Company were commanded by Vizefeldwebel Langner and the 3rd by Sergeant Gebhardt. Elements of 2nd and 4th Companies assembled by the field kitchens under the command of Vizefeldwebel Preuß of 2nd Company. Other parts were mixed in with the other battalions. The standard bearer, Gefreiter Gutzmer, was seriously wounded and Grenadier Köhler of 2nd Company took over the colour."

It is clear from Keßler's statement that the law of diminishing returns was applying in this area – which did not prevent a continuation of the attacks for several more days, with Grenadier Regiment 9 being pressed into service and Infantry Regiment 42 from 6 November. However, there were no more substantive gains and the lines finally solidified into the shape they would retain during the coming months. It was a similar story further north, where painful progress continued to be made along the line of the Ypres – Menen road. More or less the final distinctive act by the forces of Army Group Fabeck occurred on 8 November. Infantry Regiment 136, commanded by Major von Trott was very near the end of its tether after several days of fighting and very heavy casualties, amounting by this stage to eleven officers, thirteen offizierstellvertreters and 829 other ranks. As a result it was forced to reorganise into two battalions.[57] About this time the regiment received a draft, comprising mainly kriegsfreiwillige, drawn from the ranks of the students of Göttingen University. One of those involved later wrote a detailed account of his experience.

Offizierstellvertreter Böttcher Infantry Regiment 136 [58] **6.**

"We set out during the evening of Monday 2 November 1914. Six companies of kriegsfreiwillige and Ersatz Reservists, some of whom had travelled with me from Infantry Regiment 82 in Göttingen, had been brought together at Strasbourg. Commanded by Hauptmann Nelle, who had already been awarded the Iron Cross First and Second Class, they had carried out tactical exercises and some shooting. Now, after about twelve weeks of training, they were to be sent to reinforce XV Corps, which had suffered severe losses. Having detrained in Lille and spent the night in a school near the memorial to Joan of Arc, they marched via Wervik, where there was another overnight halt, as far as Amerika [two and a half kilometres north of Wervik]. Here the reinforcements were finally allocated to companies. During the evening of 5 November orders arrived to move forward to the positions of Infantry Regiment 136; that is to say to the trenches.

"Under the cover of darkness we set off guided by an Unteroffizier, who knew the area and who had been sent back by the regiment. All we knew was that it was in the direction of Ypres. The main road to Ypres was teeming with arms and services of every kind, as well as field kitchens, ammunition columns etc. Every now and then a shell impacted somewhere nearby. Had the enemy fired more, the situation on that broad road would have been terrible, packed as it was in the darkness. We marched almost as far as Geluveld and then turned off to the left along a track where the mud was almost up to our calves and we had to be careful that we did not stumble into a shell hole and drown. Picking our way carefully through the darkness we passed fields, ditches, meadows and other obstacles, until we reached a small copse where we paused.

"An Offizierstellvertreter of the troops already in position was ordered to spread the newly arrived reinforcements around some of the trenches of the second line. In the darkness of the wood that was no easy task and each of us was happy if we managed to avoid deep holes. I was put in charge of one detachment and was told to deploy them in a particular trench that was already partly full of water. However, bullets whistling past now and then ensured that the men had soon disappeared into the depths. My young soldier-students wanted to know, naturally, where and how far away the enemy were, what the situation was and what role was intended for us. All I knew was that we were in the second line. Our guns were located a short distance behind us. Every time they fired the ground trembled and in response a 'blessing' was sent howling towards us from over there. It was certainly a thorough grounding in warlike operations for us.

"About midday on 6 November we were assembled on a narrow path in the wood then, together with experienced men, were sent to the various rifle companies. Our company, the 4th, was directed to a position on a wooded forward slope. To our front a clearing opened up. The British were supposed to be located on the far side of it. The troops to our left were more or less level with us but, to our right, the battalion was rather more to the rear. A British attack was expected that evening and soon the first shots rang out. Platoon Commander Kulawik was first to spot the danger and shouted, 'Half right, 300 – 400 metres, British troops in the scrub by the clearing! Rapid fire!' Someone shouted back to Leutnant Schott, 'We are under heavy enfilade fire!' We barely had time to take cover in the positions we had prepared and to bring our rifles into our shoulders. After we had been pinned down in this murderous flanking fire for several minutes, a call came, 'About turn, take cover in the thicker wood to the rear!'

"At that everyone flooded to the rear, bent over and pushing through the scrub for about two hundred metres, in order to be able to man a front facing the enemy, who were attacking from the right. We thought it terrible that our first experience of battle was to turn our backs on the enemy. However, the weight of British fire increased. An absolute hail of fire whistled over our heads, striking left and right of us. To add to our enjoyment we came under heavy shrapnel fire as well. Suddenly, however, both the shrapnel and small arms fire died away. Some way off I heard Hauptmann Nelle order an assault. Immediately there were repeated shouts of *Hurra!* and heavy small arms fire broke out, the sound gradually dying away as it became more distant. Night fighting in woods is always a grisly business, especially when it begins with an enemy ambush. The British had to evacuate the high wood, but our casualties were also heavy. Hauptmann Nelle, leading from the front, was wounded in the shoulder right at the start and a great many of the volunteers were killed.

"We occupied the holes and trenches that the British had evacuated but, unfortunately, we could do nothing for the wounded, because a renewed attack was expected at any moment. Here we passed four days and four nights, at times experiencing Hell on earth. The shell and shrapnel fire which lashed us and felled the trees around us was dreadful. It was particularly bad that there were no medical orderlies with us and first aid had to be administered by platoon and section commanders, whilst the evacuation of the severely wounded had to be carried out by the infantrymen themselves. This could only be done at night, because anybody showing himself by day was immediately fired on. This was the time when Unteroffizier Heß, who carried out the duties of company feldwebel here forward, was killed whilst observing. He was the only regular Unteroffizier in the entire company. Offizierstellvertreter Kulawik was so severely wounded in the head that he died whilst he was being evacuated. My faithful batman, Schweineberg, was also slightly wounded.

"Our artillery managed to land several direct hits in the British trenches, forcing them to pull back into the reserve trenches in rear. Naturally we exploited this opportunity to fire on those retreating. Schweineberg, joining in, was just about to fire when, a British soldier swung round in a standing position suddenly and shot at him. He immediately felt a burning sensation in his head, but luckily the bullet had only creased him. This accuracy shown by the long service British soldiers with colonial experience who were deployed opposite the company, verged on the miraculous. On the morning of the fourth day we heard that we were to be relieved that evening at 8.00 pm. However, the closer we drew to that hour, the more critical the situation became. Intense artillery fire began to come down on and around us and crash followed crash, as shells impacted very close by, causing the earth to tremble and walls to crumble. Splinters and bullets flew in all directions and the machine gun, which was laid along the line of the communication trench, began to play its music with fresh intensity. Minute after minute dragged by, each seeming like an eternity. But we were in luck. The thunder of the enemy artillery did not last long. Betrayed by their muzzle flashes, our guns began to fire back accurately and so increasingly gagged the enemy. Finally our relief took place at about midnight."

On 6 November, while the battles were still in full swing around Wijtschate and Veldhoek, the Kaiser decided to inspire his troops with news of the defeat inflicted on Rear Admiral Cradock's squadron at the Battle of Coronel by Vizeadmiral Graf von Spee. This was the first British naval defeat since the war of 1812 and, in a personal message he wrote:

"Our armoured squadron commanded by Spee has defeated a squadron of British cruisers in battle.
– Armoured cruiser *Monmouth* sunk
– Armoured cruiser *Good Hope* seriously damaged [*sic.*]
– Light cruiser Glasgoy [*sic. Glasgow*] escaped, but damaged.
A cheer for our lads in blue. Inform all the troops and have them give three cheers for the navy.

   Wilhelm. [59]

It is impossible to say if the men struggling for control of the Messines Ridge or fighting their way through the thick woods south of the Ypres-Menen road were particularly heartened by the message or even if they ever heard about it. Having entered Valparaiso on 3 November to a rapturous reception, Admiral Spee, in accepting a bouquet of flowers, said, 'These will do nicely for my grave'. He knew that despite the tactical victory, with half his ammunition gone, his fate was sealed. Having raced south with the battlecruisers *Invincible* and *Inflexible*, Vice Admiral Sturdee destroyed all but one of his ships at the Battle of the Falkland Islands on 8 December 1914. Spee lost his life and so did his sons, together with over 2,000 German sailors. Needless to say, that event was not followed by a call for cheers.

Long before that event, any thought of cheers had completely died away amongst all the formations engaged in the north. At Supreme Army Headquarters, efforts were still being made as late as 10 November to introduce fresh troops in the hope of forcing a decision around Ypres but, at Headquarters Army Group Fabeck, both the commander and chief of staff were convinced by the end of 3 November that all hope had gone, that the chance of operational success had slipped away, never to be retrieved. That day XV Corps did take Veldhoek, but II Bavarian Army Corps, in the *Schwerpunkt*, it will be remembered, made hardly any progress and was under extreme pressure from British counter-attacks against 6th Bavarian Reserve Division. Effectively the entire day passed, marked only by disputes for particular geographical features. The artillery ammunition had almost run out, forcing the infantry to carry the main load of the battle and suffering accordingly.

Oberstleutnant Fritz von Loßberg, Headquarters Army Group Fabeck [60]

"The events of 3 November demonstrated to all levels of command, up as far as Supreme Army Headquarters, that there was no way of forcing an operational success in Flanders. The necessary battle reserves and, above all, sufficient stocks of ammunition to press on with offensive operations, were simply not available. In Flanders Supreme Army Headquarters had let slip the final opportunity to gain a victory through the timely deployment of reserves released from elsewhere and the use of all the ammunition which could have been made available. This would probably have been possible had every releasable corps been made available simultaneously with Fourth Army. [These should have been] assembled on the right flank of the army, deeply echeloned and provided with sufficient ammunition, in order to smash with overwhelming force into what were then in Flanders only weak enemy forces between Diksmuide and Armentières.

"As ever, however, after the Battle of the Marne, Supreme Army Headquarters, through its slow decision making and division of the resources of the armies in the west which wore them down, always trailed behind the enemy command processes in Flanders. This made it possible for the enemy to match force with force in battle. The consequence was that the entire German Western Front was more or less condemned to positional warfare. Up to 3 November, tardy decision making by Supreme Army Headquarters led to the succession of frontal attacks by Fourth Army which cost it 49,000 men killed in action or wounded and 13,000 missing. The Sixth Army suffered about 27,000 casualties, of whom 17,250 were caused to Army Group Fabeck alone between 30 October and 3 November.

"The final reserves of ammunition were expended. The battleworthiness of the German Army of the West was considerably weakened. For the time being the German army had no capability to conduct major operations. It was absolutely essential, therefore, to break off offensive operations in the west, to adopt a defensive posture and to go at once to the aid of the Eastern Front, threatened by the weakening of the Austrians. This decision was completely obvious, but still Supreme Army Headquarters could not bring itself to take it, preferring instead to cling on to the idea of attacks in the west; this despite the weakened state of most of the German formations and the lack of ammunition, which all recent experience had shown might perhaps produce the odd tactical success, but had no hope of achieving anything at the operational level."

Stalemate it might have been, but at least from the attackers' point of view it was stalemate with the German army in possession of dominating positions all along the Messines Ridge. There it was to remain until it was blown off it on 7 June 1917, in a position to observe every move the British army made forward of Ypres and, as a result, able to cause it monumental casualties over a two and half year period. Post war in Germany it became overshadowed and forgotten in the wake of all the popular attention devoted to the tragedy of Langemark, but in Bavaria there was continuing pride in what had been achieved at such sacrificial cost, as these words from the pen of one of the divisional padres at the time makes clear.

Feldgeistlicher Oskar Daumiller 6th Bavarian Reserve Division[61]

"From the Bavarian perspective, the 'Spirit of Langemark' is the 'Spirit of Wijtschate' – its hallmarks were an unparalleled disregard of the risk of death; love of and faithfulness to People, King and Fatherland; to Kaiser and Empire, in the most noble and pure sense of the words of the oath sworn on the Colours. We stood together as one for our parents, wives and children; for hearth and home. Our innermost conviction was, 'Germany must live, even if we have to die'.[62] We were the physical embodiment of that rousing call to battle!"

Notes

1. Tschischwitz *General von der Marwitz* p 58.
2. Lossberg *Meine Tätigkeit im Weltkriege* p 94.
3. *ibid.* p 95.
4. This is a strange remark. The first Canadian troops did not arrive at Ypres until January 1915.
5. Glück History Infantry Regiment 126 p 67.
6. Kriegsarchiv München 3. Inf. Div. Bd 6 *Generalkommando II. Bayer. A.K. Korpsbefehl 29.10.1914.*
7. This order is all the more strange, bearing in mind, for example, that General US Grant in his 1864 campaign during the American Civil War would be automatically linked by telegraph to his subordinate headquarters each evening within a very short time of the end of each day's march. It is hard to avoid the conclusion that insufficient attention had been paid before the war to the requirement to exploit every modern means of communication to facilitate command and control of the field army.
8. Kriegsarchiv München Gen-Kdo (wk) II AK Bd 6 A.O.K. 6.Armee *Weisung an die Armee* von 30.10.1914.
9. All underlined words are points of original emphasis.
10. Steur History Infantry Regiment 132 p 84.
11. The fog may have been thicker elsewhere along the attack frontage. Bavarian Infantry Regiment 18 reported that their artillery did not finish firing until 9.30 am and then for some reason there was a thirty minute gap before the 3rd Bavarian Infantry Division began to advance. See Ritter History Bavarian Infantry Regiment 18 p 63.
12. Steur *op. cit.* p 86.
13. Of the three, only Leutnant Wolfgang Schumann has a known grave. He is buried in the German cemetery at Menen Block F Grave 1605.
14. Joermann-Düsseldorf History Infantry Regiment 136 pp 116–117.
15. *ibid.* pp 117–119.
16. Etzel History Bavarian Infantry Regiment 9 p 44.
17. Weniger History Bavarian Infantry Regiment 5 p 32.
18. Riegel History Bavarian Infantry Regiment 17 pp 23–24.
19. Kohl *Mit Hurra in den Tod!* pp 53–54.

20. This is a reference to one of the places on the Somme where the German attacks stalled at the end of September 1914.

21. This account contains a certain amount of poetic licence. The BOH (p 291) describes a 'wheel back of 3rd Cavalry Brigade 2nd Cavalry Division near Hollebeke' that afternoon and states that a squadron of the Royals departed the area of the chateau, 'forced to retire' but in good order at the time the German mid afternoon attack was launched. Even if there was no British staff there to be driven out of Hollebeke Chateau – and the BOH maintains that it was empty at the time the Bavarians arrived – it is entirely feasible, indeed extremely likely, that the British cavalry had being making full use of the facilities it offered.

22. Gerok History Field Artillery Regiment 29 pp 14–15.

23. Stühmke History Infantry Regiment 125 p 42.

24. *ibid* p 43.

25. The actual situation within 6th Bavarian Reserve Division was quite complicated. Bavarian Reserve Infantry Regiment 16 was still engaged to the north against Geluveld, Bavarian Reserve Infantry Regiment 17, which, together with Bavarian Reserve Infantry Regiment 8, of 5th Bavarian Reserve Brigade, 4th Bavarian Infantry Division, had been in Corps reserve, initially received orders at 10.00 am 31 October to move under command of 3rd Bavarian Infantry Division in the Wambeke area, where it fought for several hours that day under the command of Generalmajor Danner's 5th Bavarian Infantry Brigade. (See Großmann History Bavarian Reserve Infantry Regiment 17 pp 12- 13) It was not until 10.00 pm that orders to link up with Bavarian Reserve Infantry Regiment 21 for the attack on Wijtschate were issued.

26. BOH p 305

27. Peculiar assertions like this are dotted throughout the early volumes of the BOH. There is no mention of any such unlikely event in any of the German accounts, which are quick to describe the successful use of subterfuge on the occasions when it was employed, or indeed to mention British examples. Großmann (History Bavarian Reserve Infantry Regiment 17 p 13), for example, relates an instance of a British officer galloping towards them in the early hours of 1 November near Wijtschate, shouting in German, 'Don't shoot. I am a German!' Not that this did him any good; both he and his horse were shot dead.

28. Brandenstein History Infantry Regiment 121 p 18

29. *ibid.* pp 19–20

30. This refers to the death of Hauptmann Heuß of Field Artillery Regiment 65, the last man on his feet that night capable of serving a gun, who fell while firing a howitzer that had been brought into action on the main street through Messines. See Gemmingen History Infantry Regiment 119 p 61.

31. Bossert History Infantry Regiment 143 pp 159 – 160.

32. Petri History Infantry Regiment 99 p 27.

33. Glowgowski History Infantry Regiment 105 pp 30–32.

34. Unteroffizier Alfred Gläser is buried in the German cemetery at Menen Block 1 Grave 1019.

35. Wagner History Field Artillery Regiment 51 pp 82–83.

36. *Freiburger Zeitung* 15 January 1915.

37. Beckh History Bavarian Reserve Field Artillery Regiment 6 pp 26–27.

38. Braun History Bavarian Reserve Infantry Regiment 21 p 13.

39. Großmann History Bavarian Reserve Infantry Regiment 17 p 14.

40. *ibid.* p 15. There were constant accusations on both sides that illegal ammunition was being used. In fact such use is likely to have been rare. Fighting in amongst buildings would have caused many ricochets and wounds inflicted in that way could easily give the impression that ammunition had been tampered with.

41. Dellmensingen *Das Bayernbuch vom Weltkriege II Band* pp 127–128.
42. This is an interesting proof that sometimes exhortations and messages from the highest levels could permeate to the lowest rapidly. The previous evening General von Fabeck had signed off a message to the troops, which read: 'His Majesty the Kaiser has arrived at Headquarters Group Fabeck. [He] is highly delighted with the progress so far and expects further victorious advances all along the line.' Kriegsarchiv München Gen-Kdo II AK Bd 6 *An II. A.K. u. 6. b.R.D.* In fact the Kaiser is unlikely to have been 'highly delighted' with progress. Nobody else in the chain of command was, but this was not the occasion to say so.
43. Großmann *op. cit.* pp 12–15 & 111. Because this sector of the battlefield remained in German hands, the bodies of all these officers were recovered. Danner, Hanster, Halder, Schuster and Sacherl all lie in the *Kamaradengrab* at the German cemetery at Langemark, whilst Major Hermann Helmes and Leutnant Georg Fillweber are buried in the German cemetery at Menen in Block A Grave 379 and Block G Grave 2155 respectively.
44. Kriegsarchiv München HS 1972 General Kommando II. B. Armeekorps Nr 1560 3.11.1914 *Betreff: Besondere Taten.*
45. This was clearly an immediate operational award. News of it appeared as the first item in the Bavarian II Army Corps Routine Order on 2 November 1914. See Kriegsarchiv München 6. Reserve. Division. Bd 87
46. Wurmb History Bavarian Reserve Infantry Regiment 8 p 44.
47. Dellmensingen *op. cit.* pp 128–130.
48. Offizierstellvertreter Max Hacker is buried in the German cemetery at Langemark Block B Grave 13118.
49. Wurmb *op. cit.* p 46.
50. Hansch History Grenadier Regiment 9 p 100.
51. It would be nice to think that the offer was still open three days later, because the temporary commander of Infantry Regiment 171 of 39th Infantry Division (following the necessity for Oberst Freiherr von Imhoff to report sick and be evacuated on 3 November) ordered the 3rd Battalion to dig a trench 'with all speed' during the night of 5 November hard up behind the regimental start line, so that the regimental band could take cover and play during the renewed attack through the swampy woods towards the distant (and unattainable) objective of Zillebeke on 6 November. This was done and the men advanced to the stirring strains of *Preußens Gloria*. Bravery medals were won that day, but it is not recorded if the regimental band or its bandmaster were honoured. See Kaiser History Infantry Regiment 171 pp 87–88.
52. Bossert History Infantry Regiment 143 p 170.
53. Gottberg History Grenadier Regiment 2 pp 80–82.
54. *ibid.* pp 82–83.
55. *ibid.* pp 83–84.
56. *ibid.* p 84.
57. It is interesting to note that of the original complement of officers who marched out to war three months earlier, only five still remained with the regiment and three of those had already been wounded once. Joermann-Düsseldorf History Infantry Regiment 136 p 125.
58. Joermann-Düsseldorf *op. cit.* pp 125–126.
59. Kriegsarchiv München Gen-Kdo II AK Bd 6 *An II A.K. u. 6.b.R.D.* In fact *Good Hope*, like *Monmouth*, sank with all hands, making a combined loss of 1,600 men. To be fair, the ultimate sinking of *Good Hope* was not witnessed by anybody. The message as taken down contains a real howler. It must have been passed over a bad telephone line, or been received by a slow witted operator. It begins *'Unser Panzergeschwader Unterspree . . . '*, which translates as, 'Our armoured squadron 'Lower Spree' . . . (i.e. the squadron was apparently named

after the river which flows through Berlin). What it should have stated was, '*Unser Panzergeschwader unter Spee...*', i.e. 'Our armoured squadron, commanded by Spee...' This just goes to show that no army has a monopoly on mistakes.

60. Lossberg *op. cit.* pp 99–100.
61. Kriegsarchiv München HS 1360 *Geschichte des RIR 20 Seiten 105–106: Beilage III*
62. The quotation is taken from the poem *Soldatenabschied* [The Soldier's Farewell] by Heinrich Lersch (1889 – 1936), whose war poetry had an enormous popular following in Germany – fully comparable with that of Rudyard Kipling in the United Kingdom. Unfortunately for Lersch, his work, which was founded on simple patriotism and the experience of the front line soldier, was pressed into service between the wars by the Nazis and tainted for all time as a result.

CHAPTER 7

Endgame at Langemark

The situation around Langemark on 24 October was one of totally confused chaos and the entire battlefield was littered with dead and dying soldiers. Officer casualties had been especially high so that even where groups of survivors were still in action, they frequently lacked leadership, direction or even any kind of orders to follow. All around Poelkapelle and towards Mangelaar, shattered subunits of Reserve Infantry Regiments 233, 234, 235 and 239 were hopelessly intermingled and occupying shallow trenches more or less randomly scratched out in amongst the beet fields. For obvious reasons the situation could not be allowed to persist so, although there were no immediate plans for further offensive operations on this part of the front, the highest priority was placed on reorganising the tangled bands of men who were still able to fight and re-establishing command and control as soon as possible. Oberst Wilhelmi of Reserve Infantry Regiment 236 had been severely wounded and Oberst von Gilsa of Reserve Infantry Regiment 235 was killed trying to establish some sort of order, so drastic action was required.

That afternoon one of the senior surviving battalion commanders of Reserve Infantry Regiment 233 was directed to assume command of Reserve Infantry Regiment 236.

Major Grimm Commander Reserve Infantry Regiment 236[1] **1.**

"During the afternoon of 24 October, a divisional order arrived at Reserve Infantry Regiment 233, directing me to be at the church in Poelkapelle at 8.00 pm that evening for the purpose of taking over command of Reserve Infantry Regiment 236. I was very reluctant to take leave of my battalion, with which I had shared the bloody baptism of fire. I took with me Kriegsfreiwillige Samwer and Seidler, my two battle orderlies. Both had proved themselves in action. Samwer was the most intelligent of all the orderlies and constantly volunteered for the most dangerous tasks. In January 1915 he was one of the first kriegsfreiwillige to be made an officer. At the appointed place I was met by a guide from Reserve Infantry Regiment 236. The start was ominous. The village was under heavy artillery fire and the main road was dominated by enemy machine gun fire, so we had to take cover.

"The night was well advanced before we were able to set off for the 236th. Our guide became disorientated so, instead of arriving where the regimental staff was located, we found ourselves out front in amongst the battle trenches. Profiting from the error, I immediately familiarised myself with the layout of the position and met up with a number of the men. The first impressions were not promising. There was an air of great nervousness in the trenches. Despite

Eyewitness Locations Chapter 7

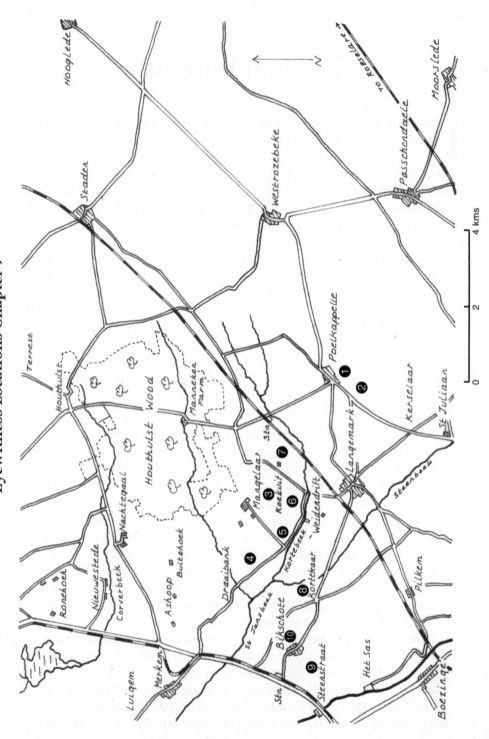

a lack of evidence, there was a general assumption that the enemy was going to attack and, throughout the night, a huge amount of ammunition was wasted shooting at shadows. No sooner would this be stopped in one place than it began again elsewhere.

"When I toured the entire position in the early dawn, I found that it was occupied by members of five regiments. As well as the 236th, there were men from the 233rd, 234th, 235th and 239th. A lack of junior leadership had made it impossible to sort out the situation. With the aid of the battalion commanders it gradually became possible to organise and develop the position. However, it was, for example, necessary for me personally to accompany them around the forward trenches in order to ensure that bread and other rations had been correctly distributed and to check that the sections were gradually being reorganised. At that time there was a generally careless air. The regimental command post, or what passed for one, was made up of planks leaned against a wall, propped up by a couple of posts, roughly covered with turfs and located about one hundred metres from a farm. It was in that farm, incidentally, that I was able to wash and shave for the first time in eight days. I had not looked so smart for ages! The men who occupied the farm had lit the fire, the chimney smoked away merrily and the field kitchen was located behind it. Of course the inevitable happened, there was a concentration of fire one morning, men were killed and wounded and the house caught fire . . . "

This sort of cross posting was occurring in every regiment, Reserve Infantry Regiment 233, the regiment which Major Grimm had just left, could only muster two hauptmanns to command its battalions, so Hauptmann von Germer was sent from Reserve Infantry Regiment 31, 18th Reserve Division, to take over 1st Battalion. He, too, found it to be a difficult assignment, made all the worse by the rapidly deteriorating autumn weather. Wilhelm Brendler of Reserve Infantry Regiment 233 later recalled: 2.

"It was the same grey daily scene . . . Here we were occupying Flanders trenches into which rain had been pouring ever since the previous day, turning all the bottoms of the trenches into small lakes, puddled by the impermeable clay. The walls began collapsing and we were completely plastered with mud. It clung to our boots, our hands and our faces like glue. The Flanders rainy autumn days, accompanied by gusty winds, had now begun. It was not so bad if it was possible to hide away in a hole cut into the forward trench wall out of the wind, or if there was some small dry place in which to squat. But if it was necessary to move from one place to another, great courage had to be mustered to wade through these muddy ponds and lakes where the water was often knee deep . . .

"We had not had a wash for eight days. Corpses, which we had so far not been able to bury, lay all along the Haenixbeek, so there was no question of being able to drink the water, nor was there enough to eat. The field kitchens got as far forward as Poelkapelle at night, though they were shelled every time.

It soon appeared as though the enemy were being informed about their time of arrival! The ration parties had a very difficult job. Slow, harassing fire went on throughout the night, concentrating on the period just after nightfall and covering the entire area. It was very risky to be caught outside a trench and many paid with their lives. That is precisely what happened to my young friend Günther Gräf from Meiningen. Tonight [26 October] all six of our ration party were shot down . . ."[2]

In some places this lack of food was beginning to have a serious effect on morale. Reserve Infantry Regiment 233 had clearly made an effort to organise carrying parties, but within Reserve Infantry Regiment 235, which had suffered especially severely and where the command structure was extremely precarious at this time, a couple of days spent eating raw turnips had led to a deterioration in battlefield discipline. The regimental history notes:

"Despite heavy enemy shellfire on Poelkapelle, the field kitchens moved there during the occasional pauses in firing. Naturally, there was no possibility of organising the orderly collection of rations. Because of the fact that during the previous few days the men had been existing on raw beets, two to three men from the forward sections, and sometimes more, raced to the rear to grab some food from the nearest field kitchen. This endangered the positions very much . . . "[3]

That was something of an understatement but, fortunately, no enemy attacks developed and order and a firmer grip began to be exerted as more commanders arrived. Oberst von Wunsch took over Reserve Infantry Regiment 235 on 25 October (though he himself fell ill and had to be replaced two days later) and the following day what was left of Reserve Infantry Regiments 234, 235 and 236 was concentrated into a 'Group Poelkapelle' under command of Oberst von Busse.

For the time being there was still no question of further offensive operations for these battered formations, but their casualties continued to mount as they clung on in unsuitable, inadequate, badly located trenches, which had simply been dug as a reflection of where the ebb and flow of the battle had come to a halt.

Kriegsfreiwilliger Emil Pouplier 4th Company Reserve Infantry Regiment 234[4] **3.**

"During the day we sent the first platoon back to the village into the support position and sentries were relieved in the trenches at two hour intervals. During the afternoon Klaus went back to the village to find us something to eat and he finally returned about 6.00 pm. He had had to go much further to the rear, almost to Houthulst Wood, but he had brought us a boiled chicken in a cooking pot. Our entire section was huddled together in a trench beneath all sorts of junk which we had dragged over. At lengthy intervals the enemy continued to bring down fire on our area, sometimes with small calibre shells

– most of which fell to our front or on the village to our rear. Restlessly, they combed the entire area.

"We were sitting in a tightly knit group and Klaus was just about to divide the chicken into equal shares, when there was a roar through the air and something landed with an infernal crash on the low parados of our trench. Flash – crash – earth – smoke – everything was chaos. There was a dull ringing in our ears and water began to pour in. As I came round, I could hear 'Father – Our Father . . .' then more shouts and groans. I reached down into the loosened soil and found the tip of a helmet spike which was moving jerkily. I took a firm grip, though I myself could hardly move, and shook and shook until I freed Ernst Austermühle's head. We were effectively trapped. We had pulled a feather quilt up over our knees, but it was now piled high with earth, so that we were buried up to our shoulders.

"Some comrades rushed round from the next traverse and scrabbled and pulled until they could haul the earth covered quilt off us. One by one we crawled sideways through a small hole and into the trench. Only Klaus, who had been sitting in a small hole with his back to the wall of the trench, moved no more. When we got to him we could see that his right thigh had been torn right off and turned almost inside out. His rifle, which had been propped next to him, had been cut clean through just below the breech. His chest was also peppered with shell fragments. Assisted by the medical orderlies, who were swiftly on the scene, we pulled him out and laid him down behind the trench.

"This shell, which had arrived like a bolt out of the blue, had claimed one man killed and four wounded. I stood together with Max Greb in one of the traverses. Neither of us spoke a word. This sudden, cruel, event which had come in the middle of a peaceful evening hit us badly. Again and again the company commander shook his head. All that night, without relief, I stood leaning against the parapet together with Max Greb. About midnight Ernst Austermühle returned from the aid post. He had only needed treatment with a small piece of sticking plaster near his eye. Just before dawn food was brought round the trenches in large milk churns and there was a delivery of mail. Just to our left in the next traverse, one of our comrades was shot through the head and killed as he read a letter.

"Together with Max Greb and Otto Wulf I dug a grave just behind the trench for Klaus, but we had to spend much of the time lying prone, because rifle fire came cracking closely overhead from time to time. We placed the smashed rifle with Klaus in his grave then slowly we threw the earth back in. Once we were finished, all three of us kneeled together next to the grave. Otto Wulf said the Lord's Prayer. Throughout this time the company commander knelt next to us in the trench. With his head hung low, he prayed with us and wept."

The situation was much the same along the sector of 46th Reserve Division, which was located just to the west of Reserve Infantry Regiment 234. Its regiments, too, had been fully occupied during the days following the Langemark disaster with the need to reorganise and bring some sort of order to the battlefield. It was a traumatic time and an immense strain for all concerned, as is demonstrated by this somewhat disjointed letter, written despite constant interruptions and sent by a member of 3rd Battalion Reserve Infantry Regiment 213.

Offizierstellvertreter Franke 12th Company Reserve Infantry Regiment 213[5] **4.**

"Within the past five minutes, 10th Company has suffered one man killed and two wounded. There are two or three trench lines to our front, but bullets still keep cracking over our heads. Naturally, there are shells and shrapnel rounds as well, which at any moment could come crashing down into our little room, which resembles a kitchen. Last night we had to turn out five times because the enemy was either attacking, or at least bringing down heavy fire. Once again, only those in the very front line were permitted to fire. The remainder spent the night with their weapons unloaded and their bayonets fixed, so that they would not be able to fire on the comrades out to the front by mistake. It makes everybody extremely nervous, but the main thing is that it helps to keep things calm.

"The enemy airmen must obviously be reporting accurately because, as soon as they have returned home, artillery fire comes down. Our men have learned to take cover and keep still until the aeroplanes have departed. The fact that I am still alive is a special mercy and one of God's miracles, for which I cannot give sufficient thanks. What have I done to deserve it? May God continue to help me! . . . I have not seen my batman for four days; it is said that he has been wounded. What's that? – a shell has just landed a mere twenty paces to our front without damaging us and now another has come down a bit more to the right and further forward. What is the next one going to do? May God be with us!

"A small goat, which has been accompanying us for days, is still running around; over there some of the fallen are being buried; the Major and his adjutant are moving above ground over to regimental headquarters; over there is a dead horse, grossly distended and with one hind leg sticking straight up towards the sky; over there a dead cow is blocking one of the trenches; knapsacks and bits of uniform are scattered all around – but the worst aspect of it all is the whimpering of the wounded in the night. 'German, over here!' 'Help me!' 'Medical orderlies!' 'Help!' 'Come and fetch me!' It is really hard to find our dead and wounded in the beet fields; our stretcher bearers and other men do their best. In between it all the cattle continue to graze peacefully.

"There is no sign of the local inhabitants and we take everything of possible use from the houses, leaving nothing behind. Doors are removed, beds stripped down and mattresses taken. Barn doors, beams and planks are knocked down and used to provide overhead cover for the trenches. Sometimes we have to burn down buildings to improve our fields of fire: the poor owners! But it is just as I said when I was still at home, I am off on campaign to protect our women and children, friends and colleagues from the destructive terror of war in the Homeland. That to me is sufficient justification. War and all its terror is dreadful. May God protect our Homeland from it! In a small way I am, perhaps, playing my part to prevent it. May God also help us in our justifiable quest for victory and to bring about permanent, blessed, peace!

"Now I need to go and bury the dead! God grant their souls mercy! We are not able to fire volleys for them. There was an extraordinary concentration of fire during the burial. – When will someone be taking my identity discs off me? – There are plenty of potatoes here, but no means of cooking them and the pigs are gorging on them. We are not allowed to light fires, because of the smoke . . . "

Gradually, as the situation was brought under control, some of the worst hit regiments were temporarily withdrawn into reserve and the remainder were warned to be ready to participate in the third major effort to capture Langemark on 30 October. It is difficult to assess what the estimate of the chances of success were at corps level and above but, with Army Group Fabeck poised to make its effort at breakthrough south of Ypres that same day, it was clearly essential to ensure that pressure was maintained all along the front, in case the Allies should be tempted to begin to transfer forces south to counter the new threat. Although 51st Reserve Division was to have participated alongside 46th Reserve Division, it will be recalled that its remaining forces had been concentrated into 'Group Poelkapelle', which had very little fighting power left, so its role was largely limited to active patrolling and holding in place in order to provide a firm shoulder for a thrust southwards by 46th Reserve.[6] 45th Reserve Division, meanwhile, was to attack towards Bikschote.

In view of the relatively low level of training of the participants, their inexperience and the difficulty of rehearsing the patrols quietly and calmly behind the lines, not all these patrols were particularly successful or useful. Reporting on one such effort, the temporary company commander of 4th Company Reserve Infantry Regiment 236 stated:

Vizefeldwebel Remy 4th Company Reserve Infantry Regiment 236[7] **4.**

"A patrol left at 3.30 am under the command of Einjährig-Freiwilliger Menges. Its task was to reconnoitre the ground to our front. The patrol route was out via the brickworks, which lay in front of the position of Reserve Infantry Regiment 234, then left to the tall trees directly in front of the company position. So far only Einjährig-Freiwilliger Menges has returned and reports that there was nothing to be seen of the enemy anywhere along the patrol route. He came under fire near the tall trees and withdrew to our own trenches. Kriegsfreiwilliger Reif was grazed on the head and back by two bullets. Kriegsfreiwilligen Haamann, Flöther and Hölscher have not yet returned."

Reading between the lines this patrol, which was large and, therefore, awkward to control on a reconnaissance mission, did its best to move around in No Man's Land but then, as soon as it was fired upon, the whole operation fell apart. Another such minor task was, however, completed more successfully the following day.

Gefreiter Bischoff 2nd Company Reserve Infantry Regiment 236[8] **4.**

"We set off at 3.00 pm, heading along tracks from where we could observe the lie of the enemy positions. We were under fire from the shot up buildings all the way. However, they were all individual shots and not, as we had originally thought, volleys. We were able to establish that the enemy lines ran more or less parallel to our trenches, which led off to the right of those of 2nd Company. In some places the lines seemed to be camouflaged with twigs. They followed the edge of the damaged village. As far as we could tell, in some places, if not all, there were actually three lines of trenches arranged one behind the other; and in or around the damaged houses there were large numbers of infantrymen. From the shells which landed around us, we were able to say that they had been fired by the French. Furthermore, we were able to discover that an enemy trench ran at almost right angles to those of 2nd Company. We were unable to cross the beet fields because they offered no cover, but we moved to the right until we were in dead ground about twenty metres from our own lines. We then raced to them, pursued by bullets."

The Corps order for 30 October was issued early the previous day, though in some cases it was late reaching the forward regiments. The attack was to begin at 7.30 am. 45th Reserve Division was to assault Bikschote, 46th Reserve Division the line Bikschote (exclusive) – Kortekeer Cabaret – Weidendrift and 51st Reserve Division Langemark itself. Similar efforts were being made up and down the Fourth Army front, probably more in hope than expectation of positive results. The histories of Reserve Infantry Regiments 234, 235 and 236 – 'Group Poelkapelle', the only fighting troops of 51st Reserve Division – may be searched in vain for any mention of this attack, which suggests that, if launched, it never really got clear of the start line.[9] The personal diary of a member of Reserve Infantry Regiment 234 does, however, record a further ill-prepared, forlorn hope arranged the following day, in what must have been the very final effort of any consequence of this division before it was relieved.

Kriegsfreiwilliger Emil Pouplier 4th Company Reserve Infantry Regiment 234[10] **3.**

"Today was supposed to lead to a decision. An attack on a broad front was intended to advance our lines at long last. A few men from each section went back into the village to knock together some assault ladders, so that we could climb out of the trenches quicker. We were linked up with 46th Reserve

Division on our right... The order ran through the trenches and we made final adjustments to our equipment then, a moment later, the company commander bawled 'Go!' We sprang like cats up the ladders and out of the trenches. Left and right our comrades had also climbed over the parapets and we set off slowly, rifles under our arms, in widely extended lines. There was an eerie silence. Not a shot was fired and our artillery did not fire one single shell. That was something quite extraordinary: an assault without artillery preparation? We looked questioningly at one another.

"Off to the left in a field of hops as we advanced we saw a great many dead men lying around – blackened, bloated corpses... We were amazed that there was still no enemy fire. Quietly, in orderly lines, we continued to move forward slowly. We had covered about five hundred metres when the dance finally began. From Langemark itself; from positions left and right of it; from the fields all around came the sound of gunfire then, in front of us, behind us, in front of us once more and behind us yet again, shells crashed down, exploding with great roars and sending pillars of earth and dust flying as high as houses into the sky. We raced to take cover, but we were so close to the exploding shells that showers of earth kept being thrown over us, so we were pinned down for some time.

"Hissing and roaring, this 'blessing' poured down over us. We could do absolutely nothing. We could not fire; we could not see a thing; we just lay there in a field on a forward slope as though we were on a presentation tray. The shells crept ever closer and everywhere they were striking home. Our men were running backwards and forwards, trying to avoid the places where the fire was hottest. It was a crazy form of chaos. It was impossible to hold out. In ragged groups we ran in all directions seeking cover, any cover, anywhere. The company commander, Leutnant Zitzewitz, was with us. He stood behind a tree, searching with his telescope, but the enemy were nowhere to be seen. Completely ignoring the torrent of shells and the appalling whip cracks of the splinters, Leutnant Zitzewitz remained upright by his tree.

"We shouted, 'Herr Leutnant, You must take cover! – but he just looked at us, wild eyed and said, 'Yes, yes' and continued to raise his telescope. All of a sudden there was a dreadful, bursting, crash just to our front. Great clods of earth flew up and smashed down on us. We pressed our noses hard into the ground then, when we eventually raised our heads once more, we saw our Leutnant lying there on his back, in the grass, next to the tree. We crawled up to him and saw that there was small hole in the breast of his uniform jacket. As though it had been aimed at his chest, a shell splinter had pierced it and he was dead. He was the last of our officers. Now we had none at all. Off to the right, next to a small house, we saw our platoon commander, with a group of men. We called over that Zitzewitz was dead and he just shook his head.[11]

"The cannonade continued with undiminished intensity, accompanied by the crack of small arms fire. Many, many of our men, dead and wounded, lay strewn around the open fields as far back as the hop poles. There was no way forward; there could be no way forward, the fire was too intense and the enemy infantry had such clear targets that they could have picked us all off one by one. They had us on a presentation platter. The men could not be kept in line. The platoon commander gave the order, 'Back to the start line!' Zig-zagging back and forth, running to avoid incoming shells, we made our way back individually. We could hear bullets striking the ground and the artillery fire harried us all the way. Once more we passed the hop field with its black corpses, now joined by many of our comrades ... "

What an unmitigated disaster. Survivors and lightly wounded men crawled in well into the night; a night whose stillness was broken by the piteous groans of the seriously wounded and the shouts of men trying to alert their comrades not to fire at them as they returned. As Pouplier remarked, 'We could not credit that we had been ordered to assault in broad daylight, without artillery preparation' – but they had been and all they could do was gather in the wounded and count the cost to their rapidly shrinking band of effectives.

About four to five kilometres to the west of 51st Reserve Division, the battered, severely reduced, regiments of 46th Reserve Division made yet another attempt to capture Bikschote. The situation was complicated. The front line wandered in all directions and both regiments of 89 Reserve Infantry Brigade, Reserve Infantry Regiments 211 and 212, were forced to sit impotently and wait whilst Reserve Infantry Regiments 209 and 210 of 90 Reserve Infantry Brigade tried to fight their way forward until they were level with them. This was a particular problem for Reserve Infantry Regiment 212, whose front line was several hundred metres in advance of the rest. In view of this, there was a certain amount of re-subordination of units of 89 Reserve Infantry Brigade to reinforce the weak formations of the other brigade and assist them to get forward, but these moves and other preparations were spotted by the French defenders, who were on high alert and who even launched minor thrusts of their own to disrupt the attack.

Despite the difficulties, 90 Reserve Infantry Brigade moved forward promptly after their bombardment lifted at 7.30 am – and equally promptly ran into trouble. The lift of the gun fire was the signal for a huge defensive fire plan to be fired by the Allied artillery. It hammered down on the forward German trenches and raked backwards and forwards across No Man's Land. Nevertheless, some courageous German infantrymen from Reserve Infantry Regiment 210 managed to get forward and even to secure a foothold on the far bank of one of the many beeks – the Markejevaert, a minor canalised stream – and to link up with Reserve Infantry Regiment 212, though their total strength amounted to less than one weak company.[12] That was the extent of the advance, heavy flanking fire was brought down by French machine guns, which prevented further movement and their reserves could be seen massing and threatening the right flank of Reserve Infantry Regiment 210. All troops less one platoon, which had been given a junction point role with Reserve Infantry Regiment 212, were withdrawn and the remainder of the regiment was deployed to face down the new threat. In the end this did not materialise, but it had been sufficient to call a halt to the attack.

Reserve Infantry Regiment 209 had much the same experience. Struck by extremely heavy artillery fire, which caused many casualties, the regimental history states that the advance continued until casualties were so heavy that nothing more could be done. '2nd Battalion lost all its runners except one to a single shell . . . the machine guns could only be moved forward with great difficulty, but the effort continued until, finally, the weapons were left lying, with all their crews gone. The enemy rifle fire was well aimed and tore great gaps in our ranks without our being able to reply in any way, because we never located the enemy . . . The attack came to an end. Those who were a little more to the rear crawled or ran back panic-stricken to our trenches . . . '[13]

Despite the unpromising situation, it was decided at about 10.00 am to start the attack of Reserve Infantry Regiments 211 and 212. The deciding factor was the arrival of the men of Reserve Infantry Regiment 210 across the Martjevaert and orders then arrived for the advance to begin. That of Reserve Infantry Regiment 212 was also doomed from the start. As soon as movement forward of the German trenches was detected, heavy concentrations of artillery fire were directed on it by the French artillery observers and, before long, the forward elements of this regiment were either digging in or being directed elsewhere to deal with other threats developing along the divisional front. In an attempt to encourage his men, the commander of Reserve Infantry Regiment 212, Major von Heyde, was right forward with the leading sections and fell victim to a shrapnel ball, which wounded him.[14] His evacuation was merely the heaviest blow amongst many casualties incurred for no useful purpose.

On a day when progress was extremely limited, the push by Reserve Infantry Regiment 211, supported by parts of Reserve Infantry Regiments 209 and 216, into Bikschote was one of the more successful aspects of the operation, but even this slight success was short lived; the village had to be evacuated once more the following night. It is not completely clear how the men of Reserve Infantry Regiment 211 managed to get forward through the heavy curtain of artillery fire when other struggled, but succeed they did. Setting out at 10.00 am, within an hour 1st and 2nd Battalions had pressed up to the outskirts of Bikschote, but were stalled there by the weight of enemy shell fire. Once it lifted, better progress was made and, by the early afternoon, 2nd Battalion had pushed right through to its southwest corner. Attempts to press on beyond were, however, completely thwarted by torrents of fire, in particular from the area of Hill 10, just south of Bikschote.

Whilst trying to maintain contact with 1st Battalion, the regimental adjutant, Leutnant Münzer, was mortally wounded and, with officer casualties rising almost by the minute, Hauptmann Brauchitsch, commanding officer 2nd Battalion, was forced to assume command of 1st Battalion as well as his own as he tried to drive the French defenders back off the dominating positions on Hill 10.[15] The task was not made easier due to the fact that ill directed German guns were pounding the area where his troops were trying to organise themselves for an attack. Despite all efforts, this proved to be impossible to carry out. As night fell, the total number of German troops still in and around Bikschote was down to about 500 and both their flanks were in the air, with wide gaps to the nearest friendly forces. Because of the constant fire the built up area was attracting, the regimental commander, Oberstleutnant Puttkammer, decided to evacuate it so, leaving strong patrols behind, Hauptmann Brauchitsch reluctantly withdrew his men about 150 metres to the north and had them dig in.

Nobody could deny the courage displayed by the men of 2nd Battalion in particular, but it was all in vain. Apart from Oberleutnant Müller, Hauptmann Brauchitsch was the only officer still on his feet and, in the words of the regimental history, 'His battalion had been totally decimated and so was disbanded'. His men were distributed to the other battalions and Brauchitsch assumed command of 3rd Battalion the following day when its commanding officer, Major Birkenstock, was medically evacuated. In addition to earlier losses, the battles around Bikschote cost the regiment twenty four officers and 674 men. As well as Leutnant Münzer, the regiment also lost Oberleutnant Harder and Offizierstellvertreters Kabisch, Baumunk, Huth, Wernicke, Knopf and Philipp killed in action.[16] It was a very high price to have paid for an operation designed to do little more than provide a diversion to cover attacks elsewhere and one which achieved nothing more than the gain of a few useless metres of blasted terrain.

Sandwiched between 45th and 51st Reserve Divisions, the regiments of 46th Reserve Division, together with Reserve Jäger Battalion 18, conducted an attack all along their sector. The previous day, like many other formations, they had been reorganised into two brigades. Reserve Infantry Regiments 214 and 216, together with Reserve Jäger Battalion 18 formed 92 Reserve Infantry Brigade, whilst 91 Reserve Infantry Brigade was created from Reserve Infantry Regiments 213 and 215.[17] It is not clear why this particular breakdown was chosen. It may have been connected with strengths at the time or, possibly, was due to the layout of the regiments on the ground and in contact with the enemy. For 30 October, orders were given to the regiments to attack with four of them in the front line, viz. from west to east, Reserve Infantry Regiment 216, Reserve Jäger Battalion 18, Reserve Infantry Regiments 213 and 215 (which adjoined Reserve Infantry Regiment 234). Reserve Infantry Regiment 214 filled in behind Reserve Infantry Regiments 213 and 215, with its units fulfilling a variety of roles throughout the day.

Information concerning Reserve Infantry Regiment 216 is scanty, because it never published a history. However, it is known from that of Reserve Jäger Battalion 18 that its direction of attack was southwards, passing Bikschote on its eastern side and, because Reserve Infantry Regiment 213 attacked Weidendrift directly, the Jägers were forced to fill in the gap more to the southwest than originally planned. When, finally, Reserve Infantry Regiment 213 after three attempts closed up to the Bikschote – Langemark road, Reserve Jäger Battalion 18 found itself locked in a close fight for the higher ground to the southwest of Weidendrift, where it eventually dug in.[18] Reserve Infantry Regiment 215, for its part, did not even receive the attack orders until 4.00 am 30 October, which provided little time for either planning or preparation.

Nevertheless, the regiment crossed the start line on time and to begin with made reasonably rapid progress, the French forces in outposts immediately north of the

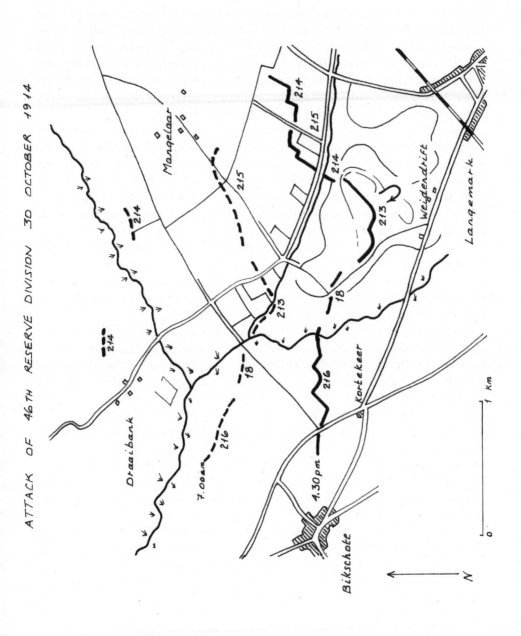

ATTACK OF 46TH RESERVE DIVISION 30 OCTOBER 1914

Broenbeek pulling back swiftly as the men of Reserve Infantry Regiment 215 bore down on them. Eventually bayonets were fixed about fifty metres short of the forward French positions, which were being manned by men of the 96th Regiment. At the cost of a number of casualties, prominent amongst which were Major Saksofski and Oberleutnant Hoffmann, a farm occupied by the French was stormed and captured, together with fifty prisoners, who emerged from the cellars.[19] However, already by mid morning the regiment was suffering from being exposed forward in a salient in the enemy lines, Reserve Infantry Regiment 234, as has already been noted, did not get forward to any meaningful extent and the companies of Reserve Infantry Regiment 213 were continually being repulsed as they attempted to advance.

To be fair to Reserve Infantry Regiment 213, the mission they had been given was extremely difficult. In essence their left flank subunits had to cross the Kortebeek, which at that point ran at an acute angle to the direction of the attack. The sub units on the right had their own problems to overcome, including the fact that they had to cross the Draaibank – Langemark road, which also ran at a sharp angle. As a result, the risk existed from the outset that the two halves of the regiment would tend to drift apart and cohesion would be lost, or at least be difficult to maintain. Just to add to the problem, the ground was difficult geographically. Both sides of the Kortebeek were very boggy and Weidendrift itself stood on high ground, which was liberally supplied with hedges and fences and which the French defenders had exploited to provide defence in depth, with several lines of trenches and interlocking arcs of fire from mutually supporting strong points.

It was already clear that the French resistance would be tough and hard to overcome, especially by troops who were near exhaustion after ten days of continuous operations. They lacked leaders (many of whom had been killed, wounded, or evacuated sick), their ranks had been thinned considerably and, like many other regiments, they had frequently gone hungry during the past few days. Nevertheless, it was their duty to do their utmost to overcome the difficulties and to capture Weidendrift. Promptly, at 7.05 am, the German artillery opened up but, typical of much of the poor performance of this arm within the new reserve corps, most shells fell short, crashing to the ground only a few metres forward of the start line in some cases. As if that were not bad enough, the opening of this attempt at a bombardment served as an alarm call to the French defenders. Within minutes the Allied artillery brought down defensive fire all along the German front line and on the approach routes to the rear.

Before the attack even jumped off there were casualties. Within 3rd Battalion Offizierstellvertreter Heß was killed,[20] there were ten casualties from the already weak 5th Company and Offizierstellvertreter Fröse, a platoon commander in 7th Company, was also killed. All this disruption and the heavy weight of French artillery fire meant that the start time was delayed considerably. Then, once the advance began against a fully alert enemy, problems arose immediately. A storm of small arms fire caused the attack to stall very quickly. The left flank was unable to cross the Draaibank – Langemark road and the centre and right of the attack, pressing on towards the heights at Weidendrift, were quickly pinned down and unable to move. In the centre, 7th

Company pushed forward reserves and some progress was made, but at high cost, including the deaths of Oberleutnant Grimsehl and Offizierstellvertreter Mackprang of 8th Company.[21]

The loss of Grimsehl, known throughout the regiment as 'Papa Grimsehl' on account of his advanced age (53 at the time of his death), was deeply felt by all ranks.

Vizefeldwebel Robert Thiemann 8th Company Reserve Infantry Regiment 213[22] 5.

> "Calmly, Oberleutnant Grimsehl advanced into battle with my platoon (3rd). In a copse to the east of the Draaibank – Langemark road at about midday I met up with him again, when he called me over and I took cover next to him. Our wood was under a dreadful weight of enemy fire, especially from the artillery which was showering us with shells. Many a brave comrade already lay there on the ground, dead or wounded. I had just left him for a few moments to go to the aid of a wounded man nearby when I was wounded myself, as was he. I crawled over to him and found that he had a wound to his left hand which I bandaged up. This would be about one minute after the shell landed. He had also been wounded in the head by a rifle bullet, which caused his death. Even as I treated him, I could see that death was approaching. Without giving any sign of pain, or even opening his eyes, our good and courageous leader left us. The day cost 8th Company considerable casualties, but those who survived felt as one with our honoured fallen . . . During the evening of 30 October, before I went back to the dressing station, I once more sought out the place where he had met his fate and found him in exactly the same position, leaning back against a tree as though he was having a gentle nap. A rare and beautiful death brought an end to a life of many blessings. Honour his memory!"

Meanwhile the battle continued. The regimental commander, Oberst Ottmer, who had only been in command for fourteen days, was hit and seriously wounded in the chest near to the mill southeast of Draaibank and was succeeded by the commanding officer 1st Battalion, Major von Loesen. Early in the afternoon another major effort was made. All the reserves available were thrown into the battle, but progress was painfully slow and it was not until about 4.00 pm that small parties of Reserve Infantry Regiments 213 and 209 closed right up on the French positions. Hauptmann Lange, commander of 3rd Company and temporarily standing in as commanding officer 1st Battalion, was wounded in the thigh as he led a charge on a heavily defended hedge row near Weidendrift. He was only saved from capture by the heroism of Gefreiter Karl of 1st Company, who rushed forward and carried him to safety under heavy small arms fire.

As night fell on the battlefield, the remnants of the regiment halted and dug in where they were. Nobody could accuse them of not having tried their hardest; they had advanced further than any other regiment that day, but their gains were still meagre. Weidendrift was still firmly in French hands and nowhere had they forced a crossing of the Bikschote – Langemark road. It was a miserable return for all the casualties they and the other regiments of the division had suffered and, thanks to the heroic defence of the French, Langemark lived to fight another day. What had this fresh round of sacrificial attacks achieved? Probably very little directly, but they did form part of a pattern which the Allies were forced to take into account. In its summary of the events of the day, the French Official History emphasised the influence of the operations by Army Group Fabeck, pointing out that the opening of a major new front south of Ypres changed the dynamics of the battle entirely. Whilst not ignoring events in the north, 'The French commander, abandoning the attempt to break through on the German right [flank], did his best to hold the attack by propping up and consolidating the threatened British front'.[23]

For the time being the German offensive on this sector of the front had run its course, with both sides exhausted.

Hauptmann von Hammerstein 5th Company Reserve Infantry Regiment 213[24] 6.

> "It was completely chaotic. I attempted to establish links left and right and found that I was furthest forward. To my right rear were Oberleutnant Pagenstecher and 6th Company. Off to the left, after a one kilometre gap, were elements of Reserve Infantry Regiments 214 and 215, all hopelessly mixed up. As an emergency measure I tried to cover the gap with small outposts, but, apart from that, I was extremely cautious. Had the French realised my true situation and had they attacked, I have no idea what might have happened. As far as possible, I arranged for the wounded to be brought into the shelter of the trenches; there was absolutely no contact with the rear by day. The battlefield all around us presented an appalling picture. Everywhere the moans and groans of the wounded could be heard; from everywhere came desperate cries for help and, in most cases, any thought of help was completely out of the question. That evening the Rationing Officer, Offizierstellvertreter Schröder, managed to get through the shelling, which was still quite heavy and brought us at least something to eat. We were in an unenviable position – right up against an enemy in overwhelming strength. However, after the experience of the past few days we could be reasonably sure that the old French territorials and colonial troops would not attack. We, too, were too weak to launch another assault. For the time being, it was just a matter of holding on as best we could".

North of Ypres, as November opened, the formations and units engaged against the Belgian and French forces were very worn down, severely reduced in numbers and exhausted from the pace of events and the inclement weather. Nevertheless, such was the pressure from the Army High Command that there could be no question of easing the demands on the troops all the time that the slightest chance remained of breaking through the Allied lines in the direction of Calais and St Omer. The risks were equally clear to the Allied commanders and every effort was made to hold firm along the line Bikschote – Langemark – Geluveld – Hollebeke. Already certain parts of the line were identified as being of particular importance: hence the tiny hamlet of Kortekeer Cabaret found itself transformed into a field fortification of considerable strength, which was defended obstinately by French troops under the overall command of General d'Urbal.

Realistically, nothing much more could be expected of the regiments clinging precariously to their trenches hard up against the French defenders, but something had to be done to try to reduce the Langemark position and, fortunately for Fourth Army, the inundations further north, with the consequent redeployment of substantial forces, seemed to offer a possible solution. As a result, the formations pulled back across the Ijzer at the end of October were not left in their initial positions very long. It was soon evident that there was no intention on the part of the Allies to attempt to launch attacks east of the flooded area, so 38 Ersatz Brigade 4th Ersatz Division and elements of 43rd Reserve Division were given a screening role, under command of XXII Reserve Corps, to cover the inundations and the remainder of III Reserve Corps, mainly 5th and 6th Reserve Divisions, were redeployed to the south, as were the regiments of 44th Reserve Division.

Having moved south, a determined attempt was made by all three divisions to link up with a view to thrusting more or less southeast, so as to render the task of holding Langemark impossible for the Allies. By 1 November, for example, formations of 5th Reserve Division were already assembled in rear of XXIII and XXVI Corps, ready to move forward as required. On 2 November the first battle casualty replacements were arriving, but there was little time to absorb them or to undertake additional training, because a series of counter-attacks launched by newly arriving reserves against divisions weakened seriously by the bloody battles for and around Langemark represented an unacceptable level of threat to the German lines, which had to be countered urgently. The experience of the first night in close contact with the front line was described in a letter home a few days later.

Ersatz-Reservist Häfner 7th Company Reserve Infantry Regiment 52 [25]

"I am writing this letter sitting in a village very close to the enemy troops accompanied by the thunderous noise of the guns. The racket is truly shocking. There are enemy aircraft circling above us with shells exploding over them. Our airmen, whom we can observe very clearly, are pursuing them and driving them off. I am sitting in the small garden of a poor house whose occupants have abandoned it. I do not know the name of the village and I can see no trace of it anywhere. There are forty men quartered in this house. 150 men have come to the regiment from the 8th Regiment [Reserve Infantry Regiment 8 – part of the same division], which has suffered some casualties recently. The entire regiment comprises men aged between twenty eight and thirty three years old. We are delighted because younger men tend to become rather overwrought, whilst the older ones are calmer.

"We are ready to move. Our equipment is placed ready to be put on.

Knapsacks are packed constantly and our belts can be fastened at a moment's notice. We are wearing our boots and our helmets. At any moment the bugle call to depart could sound. Then it will be a matter of an approach march of one hour and we shall be manning the trenches. I have not been in bed since Wednesday morning and do not expect to see one during the coming months. Yesterday, Sunday, all we had to eat and drink were two cups of coffee and dry bread then, at night, we were able to get under cover. Today I feel fully refreshed. The midday meal was really quite good: a rice soup with plenty of meat. In the evening we brewed some coffee and ate ham. However, I expect thinner pickings during the next few days. Crikey! How the guns roar! Even the air is trembling. Now I am going to smoke another cigar (a present) then, as far as I am concerned, we can get going. With God, for King and Country!"

Sure enough, when he wrote those words Häfner did not have long to wait. During the night 2/3 November, the regiments of 5th Reserve Division marched to the front to relieve the hard pressed forward troops and to attempt to resume the attacks. One of the great difficulties of operating in this very flat terrain, with little opportunity to find good positions from which to observe, was incomplete information about the enemy and the layout of their positions. Forward elements of Reserve Infantry Regiment 48 spent the entire day on 3 November trying to establish exactly what was to their front but, even after strenuous efforts, Hauptmann Moeller, commanding 9th Company, had to report that afternoon, 'There is nothing to be seen of the enemy, [but] if we as much as show the point of a helmet we bring down a torrent of fire, including machine gun fire, on ourselves.'[26] For once some notice was taken of this report, Reserve Infantry Regiment 8, its sister regiment noting later, 'An order by 9 Reserve Infantry Brigade for an attack to be launched at 4.15 pm was rescinded at the request of Reserve Infantry Regiment 48, who reported that the enemy showed no signs whatsoever of being shaken and that it had not been possible to obtain any details about the enemy positions.'[27]

The situation was little better a short distance away when, in a day of fighting, involving repeated charges, Reserve Infantry Regiment 52, 10 Reserve Infantry Brigade, gained a mere 150 metres of ground; their assault being brought to a halt right on the enemy positions, when a final attempt was made after dark to press it home. A member of the 1st Platoon of its 7th Company later reported: **7.**

"During the evening, orders came to attack the enemy position. The Frenchies were on high alert but, at long last, with the company commander, Leutnant Voß, Offizierstellvertreter Spannaus and Vizefeldwebel Schubert in the lead, we left our trenches and stormed forward. Inspired by the thought of being able to report a fresh success to everyone at home, we pressed on single-mindedly, each determined to be in the van. During our first bounds forward, we did not come under enemy fire and we believed that we had succeeded in surprising the French. Then, all of a sudden, absolutely murderous fire was opened. Despite this we continued until we were just short of the enemy position. Here all of us who were left had to halt and dig in. The second platoon then arrived to reinforce the position. The French reacted by bringing our sector under systematic fire. Fine drizzle started to come down, making our situation even more unpleasant. The following morning we were relieved. At roll call it was brought home to us that this attack had torn great gaps in our ranks. It was extremely painful for us to learn that our company commander, Leutnant Voß, Offizierstellvertreter Spannaus and many other comrades had died a hero's death for the Fatherland.[28] Leutnant Legeler was also seriously wounded. The company was more or less wiped out; this included many members of the latest draft, who also did not return."[29]

Unfortunately for the German army this attack, so courageously pressed home, but inadequately prepared and totally lacking in effective fire support, was entirely typical of much of the fighting in the later stages of the battle. Losses were being incurred for very little; truly the law of diminishing returns was beginning to apply and it was becoming clear that all the impetus was draining out of the offensive. Following this disastrous incident, one member of 3rd Platoon, 7th Company Reserve Infantry Regiment 52, wrote sadly to his family:

Ersatz-Reservist Häfner 7th Company Reserve Infantry Regiment 52 [30] **7.**

"The rifle fire was quite extraordinary. Countless high explosive and shrapnel shells were exploding, but we could not fire, because our comrades were located directly between us and the enemy. I cannot describe how it feels to have to lie there and not react when enemy bullets are whistling past. When the fire had eased slightly, we received the sad news that only a few men from the two platoons that went forward returned, the remainder were all dead. We had to hang on for another day and the fire which roared overhead was far worse than that which we had experienced during earlier days. One shell crashed down not two metres from me. If we as much as lifted our heads, bullets cracked by, just missing."

The situation was much the same for the formations of 6th Reserve Division. Its orders were, '12 Reserve Infantry Brigade is to relieve 51st Reserve Division and occupy its positions: right flank on the Staden – Langemark railway line where it crosses the Kortebeek; left flank approximately by the Haenixbeek (one kilometre southwest of Poelkapelle). The inter-regimental boundary is to be where the northern Poelkapelle – Langemark track bends to the southwest for the first time. Reserve Infantry Regiment 35, because its strength is weaker, is to occupy the right hand sector, whilst Reserve Infantry Regiment 26 moves into the left hand sector. The relief of 51st Reserve Division is to be complete by 7.00 am.'[31] The relief was actually over by 6.00 am, with 51st Reserve Division extremely happy to part company with the dismal, roughly dug and shallow trenches, which made up the position.

Where the ground was slightly low lying there was already water twenty centimetres deep in the trenches and it was rising due to the inclement weather. The clay here was so sticky that it held boots in a vice-like grip. Reserve Infantry Regiment 35 described it as 'an Eldorado for frogs' and one of the forward commanders, Hauptmann Bartsch, commanding officer 3rd Battalion, reported that the entire place resembled, 'pea soup on top of a base of *Syndetikon*'.[32] There was an almost complete lack of wood to provide support for rudimentary overhead cover against shrapnel attack. What little could be obtained from nearby buildings had also been pressed into service to provide shelter for dry tobacco leaves found in an abandoned farm building and earmarked by those who found them for German use. To the front were the remains of Langemark, sitting on slightly higher ground and therefore in a drier place. Elsewhere and as far as the eye could see, was a battlefield of dreadful aspect. Thousands of corpses, some roughly buried, some not buried at all, littered the ground, competing for space with large numbers of dud shells. The slightest movement brought an instant response from machine gun or artillery fire and, from this unpromising place, another attempt was to be launched to take Langemark.

Before this could be attempted, further reorganisation was necessary. XXII Reserve Corps, some of whose units had been operating west of the Ijzer were, like III Reserve Corps, withdrawn because of the inundation. Its 44th Reserve Division was then also diverted to the south to assist in the operations against Langemark, coming under command of General der Infanterie von Beseler for the purpose. All these moves and regroupings took some time to complete, so it was not possible to make a first full scale attempt until 3 November, when an attack all along the line from Diksmuide to the Ypres – Menen road was ordered and when it was hoped that the presence of III Reserve Corps units and formations would add additional impetus to the attack. The plan was for 5th and 44th Reserve Divisions to advance during the night 2/3 November until they drew level with 6th Reserve Division, at which point all three divisions were to strike forwards.

In the event the move forward during the night proved to be problematic. The formations of 44th Reserve Division became disorientated in the dark, arrived too late and with elements echeloned behind 5th Reserve Division. This delayed the relief of 46th Reserve Division and matters became even worse. XXIII Reserve Corps, which was meant to be involved, did not attack at all, whilst 45th Reserve Division became tangled up in a defensive battle of its own and was not ready to participate until the afternoon. Once it did get started, it tried to push on through Bikschote and on as far as the enemy positions. 5th Reserve Division managed to get forward a few hundred metres in the first rush but then, in accordance with its orders, went to ground to await the arrival of 44th Reserve Division on its left.

Towards evening the attack was then renewed and it was possible to close right up to the first of the enemy defences. Off to the left, XXVI Reserve Corps could not move, having been pinned down by heavy artillery fire and the situation was not much better for XXVII Reserve Corps down near Veldhoek. In general, the German losses were heavy this day and certainly not proportionate to any success gained. Lack of artillery support was blamed for the failure to produce even the glimmer of a breakthrough, but battle weariness and wariness was also playing an increased part in the failure of the combined effort of over four corps to make any useful progress.

Despite all these difficulties, completely mindless orders to renew the attack against Langemark and all points to the west on 4 November were passed down, but concentrated French artillery and small arms fire meant that all efforts were in vain and no progress was made. Nevertheless, these failures had a bad effect on the morale of those who witnessed them, as is clear from a subsequent report by 11th Company Reserve Infantry Regiment 52.[33] **7.**

> "Kassube's platoon was first onto the position. Gefreiter Fabian, an excellent man, was first through the hedge but was cut down within a few steps. The second man lost all the fingers of one hand and the third man was wounded as well. It was all a bit much to take for the young soldiers, with no experience of battle – as the latest draft had to be described. However, there was nothing else for it, we had to get forward and, fortunately, everything went somewhat better. At 4.30 am 5 November, orders arrived that there was to be an immediate attack. Our lines were still rather thin but the battalion was ready at 7.20 am to storm forward. The companies made their final preparations.
>
> Wrampe's platoon from 11th Company set off first and advanced towards a copse to our front which had been evacuated by the French. Bullets cracked over our heads constantly, so it seemed as though there were still enemy in position up the trees. Feldwebel Goltz and three sections were sent into the wood in order to clear the trees, whilst the remainder pressed on forwards. To our front was a paved road, behind that a ditch, followed by a rise in the ground. There was no sign of the enemy, but they were certainly shooting large amounts. Within the copse, which was about fifty meters wide by one hundred metres long, there were at least one hundred dead. The majority of them were French, but there were also some men of our 7th Company."

The second attack mentioned was part of a major effort all along the line on 5 November, when further determined attempts were made to storm both Langemark and Kortekeer Cabaret by 44th and 46th Reserve Divisions, together with 5th Reserve Division. The way forward having been sufficiently cleared by subunits of 3rd Battalion, 1st Battalion Reserve Infantry Regiment 52 also began to advance beyond the copse and towards the higher ground to the south of the Kortebeek. This part of the operation was equally difficult and demanding as the after-action report of 2nd Company makes clear.[34] **7.**

> "On the morning of 5 November as dawn was breaking, we received a whispered order, 'Make ready, we are going to attack!' Silently we crept along the communication trenches towards the front line; however, before we reached that point, led by Feldwebel Schröder, we launched up out of the trench and, with loud shouts of *Hurra!* we threw ourselves at the enemy. Countless bullets cracked past our ears, but nothing could put us off. Over there a comrade would be falling silently, mortally wounded; here another would be moaning with

pain, but nobody could or should have helped. 'Onwards, ever onwards' was the cry. 'Up and at the enemy!' We were threatened with death and destruction from a nearby copse, where a machine gun was firing away from one corner. Swiftly sizing up the situation and seizing the moment, our feldwebel raced towards this target. With great courage he stormed forwards through a hail of bullets, spotting that the crew was laying the machine gun on us. Quickly, before that could happen, Schröder was on them, swinging his sword through the air and bringing it down on the gunner. His skull smashed, the men collapsed and a second cut dealt with the other man. Shouting *Hurra!* our feld-webel seized the machine gun. It was the work of a few moments and he was oblivious to the bullets. That, however, was not sufficient and we pushed on into the wood, which was teeming with Frenchmen. With Feldwebel Schröder leading us on, we continued the advance where the blood-drenched sword saw further action. On we went through the undergrowth until the opposition was mown down or captured. On several occasions we saw our feldwebel surrounded by Frenchmen, but he thwarted their bayonet thrusts with deadly slashes of his sword. So it continued until the wood was cleared and the enemy had taken to their heels. We called a halt in the next trench, where the heroic act of our feldwebel was discussed by everyone."

Schröder's action was typical of many others during a day of intense but ultimately frustrating battle for the German troops, who found themselves confronted constantly by very strong resistance, as these additional eyewitnesses later related.

Leutnant Uth 2nd Company Reserve Jäger Battalion 3 [35] *8.*

"An attack on the enemy positions at Kortekeer Cabaret was ordered for 6.30 am. Under the overall command of Hauptmann Müller, 9th Company Reserve Infantry Regiment 48, I led my company forward in single file through the trenches of 3rd Battalion Reserve Infantry Regiment 48 onto a start line immediately to the right of 9th Company Reserve Infantry Regiment 48. We were in position by approximately 6.00 am. I had contact to my left, but not to my right, [because] 10th Company Reserve Infantry Regiment 48 was about one hundred metres distant. I therefore ordered 1st and 2nd Platoons (commanded by Leutnant von Luckowitz and Leutnant Wagner respectively) to form the first line, shaken out into very open order, whilst 3rd Platoon, under Leutnant Rasmus, was ordered to take up a deeply echeloned position in rear and to advance whilst providing flank protection.

"The two forward platoons were to advance with fixed bayonets as quietly as they could, making use of dead ground as far as possible and, without shooting or speaking, gain ground and break into the enemy positions silently. The 3rd Platoon was to make its way forward, making use of a track along the bottom of a trench-like depression between two fields of sugar beet. Leutnant Rasmus, a calm, collected, hunter and a first class shot, protected my right shoulder and ordered contact patrols to link up with the company hanging back to my right. I had sufficient time to work my way along my line of jägers and to talk encouragingly to them. All watches were carefully synchronised and, at exactly 6.30 am, I quietly gave the order, 'Forwards!' I myself advanced with the 3rd Platoon, which was to allow the leading platoons about an eighty metre start, then to follow up.

"Once the forward line began to move, all that could be heard was a slight mysterious rustling of beet leaves and so I was convinced that we should achieve surprise. I then set off with 3rd Platoon and we stalked our way forward. I suppose that we had closed up to a final assault position about one hundred metres [from the enemy] when, suddenly, rapid machine gun fire opened up – initially without causing casualties amongst 3rd Platoon. Together with company headquarters I attempted to get forward by running, walking and finally crawling, but I found myself pinned down by all-too-accurate fire. However, I eventually managed to crawl as far as the well, which was just immediately to the north of the road; whilst the enemy trench was located just to the south of it.

"I was now roughly in the centre of my forward two platoons and was in a position to shout and wave to them. They had indeed achieved surprise. In some places the enemy were surprised while brewing coffee and those who did not surrender were bayoneted. However the jägers were suddenly pinned down to the ground when they found themselves enfiladed by an enemy machine gun. This meant that within seconds few of them were still alive and even fewer unwounded. At 7.00 am the situation was roughly as follows: On either side of the mill the jägers were in control of the enemy position. The mill itself was still in the hands of the enemy, which housed machine guns all the way up to its upper story. Oberjäger Hoff was located just in front of the miller's house. Displaying exemplary courage he and his jägers made several attempts to storm the dwelling. Each time almost every man who followed him was shot down. Finally, miraculously still unwounded, he had to accept that he could do nothing against such odds . . .

"The behaviour of Kriegsfreiwilliger von Heynitz was outstanding. His bayonet bent, he was finally stood all alone on the edge of the trench, fighting for his life and firing standing in the open. When he fell wounded into the trench, Sanitätsoberjäger Bröcker threw him across his shoulders and, despite a hail of bullets, carried him to the aid post . . . His selfless act was of even greater merit, because he could only assume that he was laying his life on the line for a dying comrade. In fact in so acting he saved him . . . The devotion to duty of Jäger Menzel did not have such a happy outcome. Despite heavy enemy fire, he tried to lead two enemy prisoners to the rear but, struck by numerous bullets, the brave man fell, together with those he had captured.

"The situation became more critical. As a result of flanking fire from the west, we suffered heavy casualties, which we could not neutralise, even when we threw up hasty parapets. In addition there were a good many prisoners in our positions and there was a real danger that we should soon be exchanging roles. So, at about 8.00 am and especially in view of the fact that the infantry to our right had not got forward, I came to the bitter conclusion that we had to yield everything we had achieved or the company would be lost, right down to the last jäger. At 8.00 am I gave the order to crawl back to the start line, taking the prisoners with us. By 9.00 a small band of about twenty jägers had made it back.

"Meanwhile 3rd Platoon, to the west of the road, was acting independently. Leutnant Rasmus led his platoon brilliantly. It was entirely thanks to him that the courageous Grünröcke returned alive. Despite the fact that 3rd Platoon was absolutely isolated, despite the fact that there was a threat of enemy envelopment from the west and the south, Leutnant Rasmus provided excellent fire support to the two other platoons and protected their open flank. Later, when the prospect of encirclement seemed to be ever more certain, Rasmus personally fired with great accuracy at every worthwhile target. He was a brilliant shot and had nerves of steel. Not until after dark did this courageous little band return. The company had suffered the most appalling casualties; that evening it mustered only sixty one rifles.

"All the survivors of the assault on Kortekeer Cabaret were amazed that they had escaped that hell in one piece. The pain of the losses made them heavy hearted; but, above all, they were proud to have been there and to have done their duty."

Oberjäger Roche 3rd Platoon 2nd Company Reserve Jäger Battalion 3 [36] *8.*

"A drizzly, misty morning began to dawn. Silently, dressed in assault order, the company climbed out of its trenches. Anything which could have rattled was fastened securely. Final handshakes were exchanged: *Comrade, if I should fall . . .* Quietly we crept towards the French trenches. The occupants seemed to be asleep. Everything went well then, just as we reached the trenches, every-thing broke loose . . . tack! tack! The fire came from a house off to a flank and to the rear. Then the French in the trench to our front woke up and began to bring down lacerating fire. Oberjäger Rusch and Jäger Waldau came with me up the trench and we fired down into it. I can still see them falling dead into the trench. When the call, 'Jägers, pull back!' came later, we raced to the rear in bounds. I felt something hot on my hand and quickly threw myself down. A bullet had pierced my wrist and torn my hand open. I raced to the nearest trench like a man possessed and there I came across Leutnant Rasmus and six other men. We found ourselves in an old British trench, which contained numerous dead highlanders.

"Enemy artillery fire began to fall on our trenches. Leutnant Rasmus spoke firmly to us, 'Lads, we have got to hold out until evening. Keep tight in against the side of the trench!' I suppose we must have been there for some hours when we heard heart rending groans coming from our left. Leutnant Rasmus said, 'Perhaps we can help save a comrade. Who is coming with me?' I crawled forward on all fours with the Leutnant and we located three wounded jägers, amongst them Jäger Kriesbach, who, apparently, was seriously wounded. As we tried to bandage him the unfortunate man was hit by another shot. Leutnant Rasmus waved his handkerchief constantly but the French fired on rapidly. We laid Jäger Kriesbach to rest as best we could then crawled back to our unwounded comrades.

"As we pulled back we shouted the password constantly, because we had no wish to be shot by our own men and none of them knew that there were still unwounded men to their front. Once we got back to our positions Leutnant Uth embraced Leutnant Rasmus and shook us all by the hand."

In order to give the assault the maximum chance of success, a major effort had been made by all the supporting artillery to get well forward and so be able to suppress not only Allied defences but also gun positions over as wide an area as possible. Reserve Field Artillery Regiment 44 had a particular responsibility for the neutralisation of heavy guns and also the bridges at Het Sas and Steenstraat. When, by midday, the infantry had closed to within fifty metres of the Bikschote – Langemark road, with Reserve Infantry Regiment 48 making progress towards Kortekeer Cabaret, it was decided to move 1st and 6th Batteries forward across St Jans Beek, whilst 5th Battery closed up, so as to soften up targets around Kortekeer Cabaret itself. To facilitate this, the German infantry was withdrawn 150 metres, so as to be out of the danger zone, whilst one gun and two ammunition wagons of 7th Battery moved to where it could bring the group of houses under direct fire. This hazardous operation was subsequently described by an NCO of 7th Battery, who was later given a reserve commission.

Reserve Leutnant Nebel 7th Battery Reserve Field Artillery Regiment 44 [37] **8.**

"During the afternoon of 5th November, orders arrived to harness up and move, 'Four guns and four ammunition wagons to move into fire positions!' Because some days earlier I had been allocated the fourth wagon, I also took part. On the gun lines we were told what was to happen. The fourth gun was to be shifted to one side behind the trenches, so as to be able to bring down effective fire against the French machine gun positions. Ten men with picks and spades and an infantry protection party were detailed to accompany us and off we went for over an hour through the confusion of the battle. Hauptmann, now Freiherr, von Reitzenstein, was in command. The new position was behind a hedge, but was otherwise completely open, adjacent to an approach road and it had a reserve trench in front of it. The team of horses drove to the rear and then it was a matter of digging in. The work progressed rapidly. A defensive wall was thrown up and cover constructed. Twigs and branches were cut off to camouflage the position then, all of a sudden, we heard Ping! Ping!

Ping! – over and over again and at an increasingly rapid rate. We were under small arms fire. When this happens to twenty five men in the open, it is a matter of taking cover. Luckily, just in rear of the gun was a stack of straw, which were found frequently in this area. We rushed to get to the side of it away from the enemy and to seek its protection, which was absolutely essential. Two houses, located very close by, played a full part in proceedings as well. Bullets hitting them flew off as ricochets and stone chips disappeared at all angles. This cracking, whistling and whirring lasted a full hour, then we were able to get back to work."

With the outcome of the continuing desperate attempts to force a decision in the Ypres area still believed to be in the balance, orders were issued in early November, directing 9th Reserve Division of V Reserve Corps to proceed north immediately to Flanders, there to reinforce III Reserve Corps in its efforts to make progress across the Ijzer. By 8 November, the majority of units and formations were in position ready to go into action. It was said that all ranks hoped for a return to the victorious advances of the previous August but, even if true, it is quite evident that there were dissenting voices in the ranks.

Oberleutnant von Schauroth Adjutant Reserve Infantry Regiment 19 [38]

"Headquarters XXVI Reserve Corps (Commander, General der Infanterie Freiherr von Hügel) was located in Westrozebeke. The information that filtered out concerning the previous battles dampened spirits considerably. It appeared that the newly arrived regiments of 9th Reserve Division were to make the eighth attempt at an assault which had already failed seven times. When we then met up with the remnants of the young regiments we heard about the utter lack of success of their operations. Amongst the very few surviving officers there was an air of deepest depression. Our morale then sank to zero."

However the decision to proceed was taken at a much higher level and during the evening of 9 November 1914, Commander Fourth Army issued a special Order of the Day.

Duke Albrecht of Württemberg, Commander Fourth Army [39]

"The enemy, who are still defending their current positions obstinately, are to be thrown back on 10 November by means of a general attack, launched by Fourth and Sixth Armies, which will envelop them. Every man of Fourth Army is to be aware that the very highest standards are expected of him during this attack."

It is worth bearing in mind, as the events of the day are described, that this was the attack which led to Supreme Army Headquarters issuing a communiqué claiming a whole range of successes up and down the line and giving birth to the legend of Langemark through its reference to the singing of the National Anthem. An extract of this sophistry reads:

> "We made good progress yesterday along the Ijzer. Diksmuide was assaulted. More than 500 prisoners and nine machine guns fell into our hands. To the south our troops pressed on over the canal. To the west of Langemark [the men of] some of our young regiments charged forward towards the first line of French trenches, singing *Deutschland, Deutschland über alles*, and captured them. About 2,000 Frenchmen of the infantry of the line and six machine guns were captured. To the south of Ypres we drove the enemy out of St Elooi, a place that has been bitterly fought over for several days. About 1,000 prisoners and six machine guns came into our possession there."[40]

Concealing more than it reveals, this report skims glibly over the fact that this day of battle for Langemark and Bikschote simply amounted to the final sacrificial blood letting of the unfortunate formations involved. Despite all the courage displayed, nothing at all of lasting value was achieved. Here the original high hopes of a break through across the Ijzer north of Ypres finally sank into the mud and rain of the approaching Flanders winter.

Oberleutnant von Schauroth Adjutant Reserve Infantry Regiment 19 [41]

> "An increasing number of reports from the front line indicated that an assault in the prevailing conditions offered no prospect of success. All attempts to convince higher authority of the hopelessness of a frontal assault through the morass of the Flanders clay, in the face of complete lack of clarity regarding enemy, ground or even our own positions and to dissuade them from sticking to their plans failed totally. The order to attack early on 10 November was confirmed; it was fated to run its course."

So, flanked by 6th Reserve Division on its right and 51st Reserve Division on its left, the formations of 9th Reserve Division attempted to launch an attack in a south west-erly direction from a start line west of Poelkappelle. There was no fixed moment for the start of the attack. The infantry was to advance once the artillery firing on their front had lifted to targets to the rear. Reserve Infantry Regiment 6, advancing to the west of the Poelkapelle – Kerselaar road, unfortunately left no history, so its fate is unclear. For Reserve Infantry Regiment 19, advancing to its left in the first wave, it is evident that it was a day of frustration and tragedy. 1st and 2nd Battalions stormed forward as ordered, each with three companies leading. The bombardment completely failed to suppress the French defences so, the moment that the attack stepped off, it was met by a hail of fire from the artillery and every other weapon which could be brought to bear.

The 1st Battalion recorded that the shells buzzed amongst the attacking troops like flies and could have added that the men died like flies as well. Nevertheless, even with their ranks thinned and in the face of desperate defence, leading elements of both battalions closed with the French trenches and the survivors pushed on into the depths of the

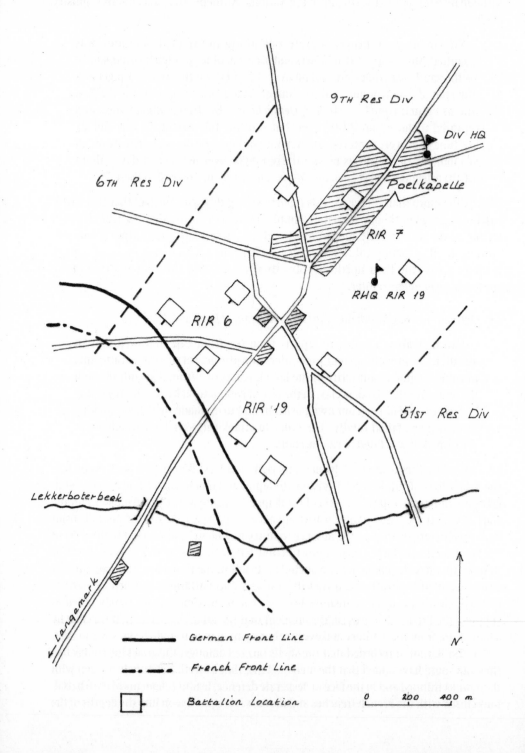

ATTACK OF 9TH RESERVE DIVISION 10 NOVEMBER 1914

9TH Res Div

DIV HQ

Poelkapelle

6TH Res Div

RIR 7

RHQ RIR 19

RIR 6

RIR 19

51ST Res Div

Lekkerboterbeek

Langemark

German Front Line

French Front Line

Battalion Location

N

0   200   400 m

positions. The cost was enormous. Major Horn, commanding officer of 1st Battalion, fell at the head of his men as the position was being penetrated; Hauptmann Sattig, commanding 1st Company, was killed and Oberleutnant Blasius of 2nd Company was seriously wounded. The only officer to survive the day unscathed was Landwehr Leutnant Dreyer of 2nd Company. The 3rd Company ran into uncut barbed wire and had no means to pass it. The entire sub unit was cut to pieces there. The company commander, Hauptmann von Mutius, was wounded and all his platoon commanders killed. An attempt by a platoon of 4th Company to assist 3rd Company failed when its platoon commander, Reserve Leutnant Otto, was killed.[42]

Landwehr Leutnant Dreyer 2nd Company Reserve Infantry Regiment 19 [43] *2.*

"By now it was 7.30 am and completely light. Suddenly the air was filled with a howling sound and the crash of an impact. A great cloud of dark smoke shot up over the poplar trees alongside the road by which we were lying. Shell splinters whistled past our ears and branches crashed down from the trees. Sergeant Heise was taking cover with a section on the far side of the road. Suddenly another shell crashed down. The shells of our own artillery landed in front, behind and beside us; some smashed down in the trenches, killing the men there.

"I caused the remainder of the company, approximately twenty five men, to take cover under the bridge, there to await the end of this lengthy shelling. I then despatched a gefreiter back along the line of the stream. He returned to report that the French trenches were all occupied. So, together with remnants of the company, I was sitting in a mousetrap. Something had to be done. Towards 11.00 am I had [the men] occupy the edge of the road and opened fire against the French, who were withdrawing from their rear trenches. Wherever red trousers appeared, they were blasted – and always with good effect. My men were displaying outstanding calm and cold blooded control as they fired and observed. We continued to fire until about 3.00 pm. Finally we could hold out no longer, because we were under heavy fire from the flanks and rear, so we took cover in a French trench which was about one hundred metres to the rear and which offered more protection. About thirty men came with me and the rest of 1st Company arrived after dark."

On the 2nd Battalion front, three companies – 5th, 6th and 7th, led the attack. On the right flank there was initially little resistance, it was relatively easy to enter the trenches and the assault stormed past the first two lines of trenches, before being halted by a wire obstacle in front of the third line, where many of them perished. In the centre and right, the attackers were subject to an appalling weight of fire and, for the 5th Company on the left flank, the situation was made worse by thigh deep water in the Lekkerboterbeek, 150 metres short of the position. Having negotiated that obstacle, at the cost of the death of their commander, Hauptmann Grüttner,[44] to cap it all they then came under heavy fire from German field guns as they closed on the enemy position. The final casualty count was again heavy. Of the nine officers of 6th and 7th Companies who stormed forward, seven, including Landwehr Hauptmann Homuth, commanding 6th Company, were killed. Fortunately for its members, 8th Company, in reserve, was never committed but, occupying forward trenches, they had to sit and watch as the dreadful scenes to their front were played out.

Offizierstellvertreter Baltz 8th Company Reserve Infantry Regiment 19[45] **2.**

"As the company moved up through the communication trenches we were not all in very high spirits. We had seen nothing of the promised powerful artillery bombardment. Holding our breath we lay in wait. Suddenly the first waves made ready to climb out of the trenches. From the sector to our right came the sound of rapid rifle and machine gun fire. Immediately the assault force set out in our sector as well, though it was also under heavy small arms fire that dominated it. Just as we were pushing forward to the place from which the assault had been mounted, there to stick it out and wait for the order to advance, shells coming from our rear impacted in endless succession immediately in front of our trenches. No Man's Land was strewn with dead and wounded. Individual wounded men crawled back to our trenches. There was nothing else to be seen of the once proud three companies. It was simply dreadful."

The attack of Reserve Infantry Regiment 6, conducted to the west of the Ypres – Poelkapelle road, also failed. The divisional commander launched his reserve formation, Reserve Infantry Regiment 7, forward in an attempt to inject fresh momentum into the attack, but this, too, soon encountered difficulties, even before the divisional front line had been reached. As it became light there could be no question of advancing across the open ground in the normal way. Nevertheless, the battalions of Reserve Infantry Regiment 7 made every effort to work their way forward, exploiting every piece of cover available in an attempt to reach the communication trenches leading forward, but without conspicuous success. Even where small parties managed to reach the forward trenches and attempted to launch onward out of them, they came under immediate fire from the French and no progress could be made. In addition, the available trenches soon became crammed with the walking wounded who were flooding to the rear, the dying and the dead and it was impossible to move in either direction.

Commanders still clung to the hope that the start of the attack of 51st Reserve Division, scheduled for 7.30 am, would lead to an improvement in the situation, but it proved to be in vain. The right flank units of this division made no progress at all, spending the entire day echeloned back in rear of Reserve Infantry Regiment 19 and totally pinned down. Of course it is important to place this failure in context. The newly raised regiments of 51st Reserve Division, which had been action before Langemark since 20 October without relief, had suffered dreadful casualties assaulting Langemark or holding the line ever since. Already by 1 November, Reserve Infantry Regiment 235, for example, had suffered seventy percent casualties, but was still in the line over a week later, admittedly having received a draft of reinforcements in the meantime.[46] As a result, when the orders were issued, it was hard for the brigades to respond. The best that could be achieved by 101 Reserve Infantry Brigade, for example, was to concentrate the survivors of Reserve Infantry Regiments 234 and 235, together with those of Reserve Jäger Battalion 23, under the Brigade Commander, Oberst von Busse, then prepare to send them into action.

In order to set the tone and, seemingly, in blissful ignorance of the parlous state of the forward troops, Headquarters 51st Reserve Division prefaced its orders as follows:

"Tomorrow morning a general assault is to be launched against the enemy opposite us, who are to be attacked and thrown back. The Army Commander expects the attack to be pressed home with the utmost determination. Every man is to be made aware that he is expected to give of his best and to close with the enemy come what may. The infantry attack is to begin tomorrow at 7.30 am. Oberst von Busse is to command the attack within divisional boundaries. All his currently available troops are subordinated to him for the attack, together with the battalion of Reserve Infantry Regiment 235 which I have been holding in reserve."[47]

101 Reserve Infantry Brigade then added its guidance and direction:

"1. The men are to be briefed about the high importance attached to the success of this attack. Every effort is to be made to make sure that they are fully keyed up to succeed.

2. In the right hand sector, the attack will be mounted by Reserve Jäger Battalion 23 and 2nd Battalion Infantry Regiment 235, led by Major von Mengersen. In support and arriving at his command post tomorrow morning by 6.00 am, will be 3rd Battalion Reserve Infantry Regiment 235. This battalion is to be deployed so as to be able to reinforce the right flank of Reserve Infantry Regiment 234 if necessary. The left sector will be the responsibility of Reserve Infantry Regiment 234 led by Major Krumbiegel-Möllmann.

3. During the advance, contact it to be maintained to the right, so that the attack is coordinated with Reserve Infantry Regiment 19.

4. As soon as possible after the start of the assault, our forward trenches are to be occupied by supporting troops in order to guard against counter-actions. Similarly, until the success of the attack is certain, machine guns are to remain in their [current] positions.

5. If the forward trench is captured, it is initially to be occupied and developed for defence. Only then is the advance to be continued in conjunction with neighbouring units. There will be pauses in the artillery fire. These are to be used for reconnaissance and to enable engineers to work. All successes are to be reported.

Signed von Busse."[48]

On the basis of this order, preparations began to be made. Makeshift bridges arrived, together with forty engineers from Reserve Pionier Company 51. They were distributed among the five assaulting companies across the front and given the task of dealing with any wire obstacles encountered the following morning. Patrols had established that the enemy had erected some strong wire obstacles to protect their trenches and that these had not yet been destroyed. There would also be a need to deal with low level entanglements wherever they were encountered. As intended, artillery preparation did begin in the early morning, but it was more or less ineffectual and served primarily to warn the enemy that something serious was afoot. In addition H Hour was set for 7.30 am, when it was already broad daylight, so the defenders, in this case men of the British 2nd Division, had no trouble identifying targets and engaging them with devastating effect as soon the attack was launched.[49]

No Man's Land was only about one hundred metres wide on this part of the front, but not one man of the brigade made it across the open ground. Every single attempt to move was simply shot to pieces and even the depth positions came under accurate and unpleasant artillery fire. During the morning 3rd Battalion Reserve Infantry Regiment 234 lost 150 men and more during a further abortive attempt that same afternoon. There were no further attempts to advance on this sector of the front and although the Corps Commander, having commended them for their earlier efforts, when he called on 'Brigade von Busse', on 11 November to take, 'every opportunity to damage the enemy to the front and to gain ground in coordination with 9th [Reserve] Division, there was no possibility whatsoever of the worn down troops responding and they were soon all relieved. Every formation has its limits and this one had been called on to attack too often and for too long.

The situation was the same on the 9th Reserve Division's right flank on 10 November, when almost all the troops of 6th Reserve Division never even managed to get clear of their own trenches. In a day of almost unrelieved failure, a few isolated parties did penetrate the French lines but, unsupported, their fate was sealed from the start, though generally they managed to resist until they were captured. Back in the starting positions and suffering throughout the day from the effects of heavy harassing shell fire, the sub units of 3rd Battalion Reserve Infantry Regiment 19 were hopelessly mixed with the 8th Company, still in support, and the few individuals who had survived the abortive assault.

Offizierstellvertreter Baltz 8th Company Reserve Infantry Regiment 19 [50]

"The long hours up until we were relieved were torture. Our morale was at rock bottom. The men were very nervous; the sentries were constantly opening fire, without being able to make out any sort of target, until they were finally calmed down. The condition of the forward trenches was the cause of great concern. In stretches they were completely indefensible. The firing steps had slid down into the mud in places, so it was impossible to see out, never mind to open fire effectively. Once it went dark there was a constant procession of wounded crawling back one by one. It was also possible, despite constant small arms fire, to bring in several of the wounded who were lying forward of our trenches, unable to move. In the end we were so exhausted that we were able to sleep standing up, with our heads leant against the damp wall of the trench. At long last relief arrived.

"During the march to the rear, we passed our gallant battalion Medical Officer, Oberarzt Dr. Wolff, who, assisted by Heumann, who later became a Feldunterarzt, was operating in the area of the support trenches. Within the confines of a hole in the ground, roughly covered with planks of wood, they worked tirelessly to treat the victims of the battle. All the wounded of the division owed their lives to the self-sacrificial efforts of our doctors."

During this catastrophic day for 9th Reserve Division, Reserve Infantry Regiment 19 suffered no fewer than twenty four officers and 213 other ranks killed, clear indication of how hard the junior officers attempted to inspire their men to get forward. Five officers and 293 other ranks were wounded, whilst no fewer than two officers and 590 other ranks were missing. Although a few of this last category were captured, the greatest number was also killed. It is small wonder that recriminations followed as men tried to come to terms with the extent of the sacrifice and sought explanations for why matters had turned out so badly. The after action report of 9th Reserve Division had this to say:

"In accordance with orders, extremely heavy artillery preparation was to have been expected between 5.15 am and 6.15 am. In fact it was noticeable that there was hardly any artillery fire to be heard; merely the odd shell now and then. All attempts to increase the rate of fire foundered, because none of the artillery commanders could be located sufficiently quickly in the close country. Concerns about lack of ammunition also appear to have been an additional cause for the slowness of the fire. Finally, it was also impossible, because of lack of time, to ensure that all the places from where well directed fire against the French trenches could be observed could be exploited. The most careful reconnaissance would have been essential in view of the fact that the French trenches were scattered extraordinarily widely amongst the countless hedgerows. As a result, the assault in fact went in without any artillery preparation . . . [In addition] there had been insufficient time to permit thorough reconnaissance of the ground over which the attack was to take place. There was a total lack of information concerning the location and strength of the obstacles. According to the troops who were relieved, the information was simply not available. In the event it transpired that there were well constructed obstacle belts everywhere, even though they were not continuous and, furthermore, each was covered to its immediate rear by trenches, camouflaged with brushwood and occupied by French troops. Even in daylight they were difficult to spot, because they were hidden away in hedges and folds in the ground." [51]

One anonymous soldier of Reserve Infantry Regiment 19, who took part in the disastrous attack, later summarised the day as follows:

> "Amongst the men, the order to attack did not raise the slightest bit of enthusiasm, in complete contrast to similar situations previously. There was general amazement that such an order could have been issued when there was absolutely no information about terrain or enemy. At daybreak I looked out from our trenches over the battlefield. My heart sank within me when I saw that the ground in front of the enemy positions was covered with field grey, whilst the whole area was strewn with our men, lying dead individually or in twos and threes. Confronted by this sight, which I shall never forget, the involuntary thought came into my head, 'Was this really necessary?' Here the commanders had launched something with no consideration for the consequences: they had simply sent entire regiments – the best men – to their deaths. Could they ever provide a justification for this entirely foreseeable bloodbath?" [52]

More in sadness than anger, the adjutant of Reserve Infantry Regiment 19 later wrote:

Oberleutnant von Shauroth Adjutant Reserve Infantry Regiment 19 [53]

> "Hundreds of our finest men gave their lives for something which was completely hopeless. It is indicative of the spirit of 1914, however, that the sacrificial courage displayed enabled the attack to be driven into the depths of the enemy position. That was the tragedy of Poelkapelle: each participant, imbued with a highly developed sense of duty, tried his sacrificial best, even though he was convinced of its hopelessness right from the start. The men of Poelkapelle did not go to their deaths through any sense of bravado; rather the deeds and performance of Reserve Infantry Regiment 19 bore the stamp of the old inherited Prussian sense of duty and faithfulness unto death."

On 9 November the most prominent member of 6th Reserve Division to have to report sick was Oberstleutnant von Ernst, the commander of Reserve Infantry Regiment 35; his place being taken by Major Fischel.[54] The commanding officer 2nd Battalion, Major zu Strohe, also fell ill and had to be evacuated and there was general concern, despite generous issues of rum and red wine, that the cold, wet weather was taking a severe toll on the state of health of the men of 6th Reserve Division. Already that day, Reserve Infantry Regiment 26 had been withdrawn from the line, to be replaced by Reserve Infantry Regiment 6 of 9th Reserve Division. Despite any concerns for the physical state of the troops, III Reserve Corps also issued orders for a resumption of the assault for 10 November. On this sector of the front, the plan was for 3rd Battalion Reserve Infantry Regiment 35 to be left in reserve, initially because it was positioned too far back and there was a chance that an attack by it might endanger Reserve Infantry Regiment 12 to its right. However, 2nd Battalion Reserve Infantry Regiment 35, with 1st Battalion echeloned in rear of it in depth, was intended to launch forward simultaneously with Reserve Infantry Regiment 6.

However, at 6.00 am, when the attack had been due to begin, the German front line was under such heavy fire that it was impossible to leave the trenches and advance. On the right, benefiting from the ability of Reserve Infantry Regiment 12 to take a few hundred metres of ground and an abandoned enemy trench, a little ground was gained. On the left, however, it was different story. At the appointed time, Reserve Infantry Regiment 6 made one attempt to get forward, but was swiftly driven back to its start line, having suffered numerous casualties. This put paid to any attempt by 2nd Battalion Reserve Infantry Regiment 35 to launch an assault. The general impression was that there was a risk that the enemy might launch counter-attacks, so reserves were called forward to man depth positions – even 1st Battalion Reserve Infantry Regiment 26, which had only just been relieved, was not exempt and the day ended here with a whimper.

By the end of 10 November no significant progress had been made anywhere along this front. At Langemark and Bikschote the German lines had been pushed forward to the edge of the villages during previous days, but that was all. Exhaustion, previous losses and shortages of artillery ammunition combined to make it impossible to drive in the enemy defences, which became ever more solid and difficult to take with each passing day. Since the redeployment south, Reserve Infantry Regiment 24 of 6th Reserve Division, already having suffered particularly heavy casualties, had spent several days in reserve and so had not been involved in the hard attritional fighting undertaken by Reserve Infantry Regiment 26 and 35 then, when the call for reinforcements came later in the battle, those elements of it which did become committed tended to be sent forward to come under the command of others.

This is what occurred to the 1st Battalion, a composite company formed by amalgamating 9th and 10th Companies and the Machine Gun Company, on 10 November, when they were sent to reinforce 9 Reserve Brigade of 5th Reserve Division and found themselves deployed in support of Reserve Infantry Regiment 48. Their assistance was urgently required, because the forward troops were becoming very worn down by the conditions, as indeed were those in support.

"Several days in the Second Line", recorded an anonymous member of Reserve Infantry Regiment 52, "were almost worse than time spent in the front line, which is only a few metres from the enemy. Not many shells land right in the trenches, but in front and behind them they tear out great holes. As well as the shells, shrapnel rounds explode in the air, showering their iron down at us. Then there is the constant rifle fire, so you could imagine that all of the pits of Hell had opened in order to shower us with sulphur. The companies have shrunk to ninety men from their original strengths of 250. Then comes the certainty that at any moment we may be called on to take part in yet another attack; that is to say we lunge forward few metres then, shouting *Hurra!*, we charge the enemy trenches with our bayonets fixed and eject the [occupants]. The casualties in such attacks are appalling. Ground has to be gained step by step. The enemy always have good targets, whilst the attackers can hardly ever open fire. Anybody who survives a storm attack can count himself lucky."[55]

Oberst von Kleist Commander Reserve Infantry Regiment 48[56]

"The terrain around Weidendrift was covered in a labyrinth of trenches. Opposite the right flank, at a distance of 120 metres, were the enemy positions, which they seemed to be reinforcing. On the left flank, opposite the 'farmhouse group', the distance was more like eighty metres. For over eight days my men had been hanging on in holes in the ground lined with a bit of straw and only a stretched groundsheet as shelter from the rain. They had to obtain their water by digging holes a little deeper in the bases of the trenches. Fetching rations from the field kitchens, which were located some two and a half kilometres away as the crow flew, was an awful experience. The ration carrying parties were forced to stick to certain paths, where the mud was still knee deep and where they were affected by both the 'evening blessing' and the constant harassing fire. The return journey lasted about four hours and reduced them to a terrible state when they eventually returned to the forward positions, worn out and carrying food which had gone cold."

Ingenious methods of avoiding this dangerous and tiring routine were introduced. One company even devised a three day routine which involved only one round trip to the field kitchens in that period, but which reduced the company having to exist on cold tinned rations and the occasional cup of coffee brewed forward. The very existence of such a system showed that mobility was fast disappearing from the battlefield, but there was still another major effort to be made by 5th Reserve Division, directed like its neighbouring formations to attempt to deflect Allied attention from the major thrust planned for 11 November. Launched primarily by Reserve Infantry Regiment 48 on 10 November, it made little progress at high cost. The Corps Commander, General von Beseler, had stated, 'The enemy are to be driven back against the canal by a thrust to the south by the reinforced III Reserve Corps. Without waiting for further orders, the attack is to begin promptly at 6.30 am. Weapons are to be unloaded.'[57]

Already by 4.00 am it was clear that the enemy had an idea about what was going to happen, because they opened up with such heavy defensive fire that Major Hauß doubted if it would be possible, after all the assaults of the previous days, to attack at all. In order to increase fire support, he ordered 3rd Battalion Reserve Infantry Regiment 48 and Reserve Jäger Battalion 3 to stay in their forward trenches and to bring down fire to help the neighbouring troops forward. For its part, 2nd Battalion was pinned down in its trenches. However, once the men of 44th Reserve Division began to advance to their right at 10.30, Major Hauß issued a revised attack order.

"3rd and 12th Companies, commanded by Reserve Leutnant Graeff, are to launch an attack astride the northern Bikschote – Langemark track against the northernmost extremity of the enemy position. Hauptmann Mathieu, to whom these companies are subordinated, is to follow up with his three companies and further press home the attack as necessary. As soon as the enemy salient is driven in and on my order, 3rd Battalion Reserve Infantry Regiment 48 and Reserve Jäger Battalion 3, under Hauptmann Rohrbeck, is to advance against the area Kortekeer [Cabaret] crossroads – windmill 250 metres to the west of the crossroads".[58]

It was intended that 2nd Battalion would conform to this movement once the attack gained some ground. Meanwhile artillery observers came forward and began to bring down fire against Kortekeer Cabaret. All this took time and, impatient to be off and not waiting for the executive order to move, Leutnant Graeff launched forward at 12.15 pm. He was killed almost instantly and the attack stalled. Two companies of Reserve Infantry Regiment 24 arrived to reinforce and finally, at about 3.00 pm, Hauptmann Mathieu managed to get his attack going forward, capturing Kortekeer from the north. At long last this strongpoint had fallen and Major Hauß ordered a combined force of his own 1st Battalion, Reserve Jäger Battalion 3 and the remaining elements of 1st Battalion Reserve Infantry Regiment 24 to begin a frontal assault. A short, but heavy, concentration of artillery fire was directed at the enemy beginning at 3.55 pm and the assault troops set off towards the clouds of smoke and dust.

Unfortunately, as was so often the case, not every enemy position had been destroyed or suppressed. A pair of machine guns opened up, threatening to stop everything, but an accurate fire mission by the experienced Bavarian Foot Artillery Battalion 2 silenced the guns and, protected by the fire of their own machine gun company, the assault force set off and the line of Bikschote – Langemark road was secured up to a point 200 metres east of Kortekeer Mill. The enemy also pulled back from a rudimentary defensive position just south of the road in one place and Reserve Infantry Regiment 48 was able to occupy that as well after dark. An advance of sorts had been achieved, but it was not much of a success and it did not lead to any subsequent gain. The Allied artillery continued to harass the forward troops and, despite orders to advance further the following day, it transpired that this attack was the last dying gasp of the German effort on this sector of the front.

On the extreme right [west] of the attack, advancing with its right hand sub unit brushing the east bank of the Ijzer, were the remnants of 44th Reserve Division. Severely worn down after three weeks of continuous action, they were nevertheless able to participate. Reserve Infantry Regiment 205 and Reserve Jäger Battalion 16 were deployed on the right flank, with Reserve Infantry Regiment 206 on the left. Bearing in mind that it was these particular regiments which were referred to specifically in the Supreme Army Headquarters communiqué of 11 November; and the fact that the history of Reserve Infantry Regiment 205, for example, did not appear until 1937 (by which time the Langemark myth had achieved an unassailable position in the German consciousness), it is no surprise to find that the accounts of the events of the day contain a higher than usual percentage of purple prose. According to Reserve Jäger Battalion 16,

"The forceful conduct of this attack will be the decisive factor of the day for the Army', stated the attack order of Excellenz [Generalleutnant] von Dieringhausen. 'Forwards at all costs!' – and the jägers did go forward. Once again they did their duty; once again they paid the price of heavy casualties. In the early dawn the artillery opened up, preparing the enemy positions for the assault. At 7.40 am, the first to rush forward out of the trenches was Feldwebelleutnant Nausester. *Horridoh!* he bawled at the top of his voice. He launched the entire divisional attack, because there was some delay to the right and left. His long sandy beard blew in the wind. His drawn sword was in his hand; the proud old sword, which had proved itself to be so impractical in this war. Most officers had abandoned them from the very first days of battle. He had been unwilling to do so.

"Leading his jägers from the front, he hurled himself at the enemy. He could only provide his leadership and example for a very short time. Just after he left the trench, he was hit in the chest by an enemy bullet. Silently he collapsed, still clutching his sword, his black and white ribbon in his buttonhole.[59] He had been one of the first of the battalion to be able to wear it. The jägers were leaderless! The last of the officers was down! There was not a moment's delay. The senior Vizefeldwebel, Siecke, sprang into the breach. More and more the battle split into the series of individual actions which had so often been the case during the previous days. The battalion bore off southwest, so as to drive back the enemy in the direction of Steenstraat . . . "[60]

In conformity with the orders of III Reserve Corps, 44th Reserve Division was meant to be seizing crossing points over the Ypres Canal and, to that end, it was the task of Reserve Infantry Regiment 205 and Reserve Jäger Battalion 16 to advance as far south as Steenstraat and Het Sas. This would have been challenging in any context. As it was, the experience of Reserve Infantry Regiment 205, unsurprising to note, mirrored that of the jägers. Every effort was made to prepare carefully for the assault. The engineers worked right through the night to push the jumping off trenches as far forward as possible, to set up mortars and assist in softening up the forward French positions. Ammunition resupply was complete, as was rationing of the forward troops so, as the attack began in the gloom of early dawn, everything was as well prepared as possible. Unfortunately, the defenders were equally well prepared and fully alert. A decision had been made not to open with artillery in this sector until 6.35, a full five minutes after H Hour. The thinking had been sound enough. This time surprise was intended to be a key element of the initial move forward, but it was a risky decision. Often success or failure was determined very early and, on this occasion, heavy suppressive fire would certainly have been the better choice.

Promptly at 6.30 am, bayonets fixed, the infantry of 1st Battalion launched forward out of their trenches – to be greeted by a storm of fire at close range. The last two officers of 1st Battalion Reserve Infantry Regiment 205, the commanding officer, Hauptmann Dabis, and the commander of 1st Company, Leutnant Herrmann, were killed almost immediately, together with a great many of their men.[61] It was total slaughter. The regimental commander, Oberst Freiherr von Schleinitz, who had placed himself on this flank of the attack, reported the melancholy news to brigade by telephone, 'Attack carried out. 1st Battalion destroyed, with the exception of the regimental commander, the adjutant and a few men.'[62] The brigade commander, Generalleutnant von Dieringshofen, sent forward about twenty men as reinforcements. Half an hour later, they joined the survivors of the attack, who had crawled back to their start line. By now it was starting to get light and the French could see the dire situation to their front where No Man's Land was littered with the dead and dying and an immediate counter-attack was launched.

This could have led to total disaster but, in fact, was a bad decision by the French commander. 2nd Battalion Reserve Infantry Regiment 205 had not advanced simultaneously with the 1st Battalion. Its position was slightly in advance of the other forward battalion, so its commanding officer, Hauptmann Klos, had planned to move forward when the companies of 1st Battalion drew level. Due to the intensity of the fire and its appalling consequences, his men had never left their trenches so, when the French troops went forward in large numbers, they poured heavy flanking fire into them, then charged forward, scattering the French and taking a large number of prisoners. The survivors of 1st Battalion joined in and swiftly the final remaining French machine guns were silenced, the French were bundled out of their trenches and they headed rapidly to the rear, with the men of Reserve Infantry Regiment 205 in hot pursuit.

Gefreiter Lewerenz 5th Company Reserve Infantry Regiment 205[63] **9.**

"We had gone quite a long distance when I, together with several comrades spotted a number of Frenchmen running into a house. We pursued them and fired into the house, then we dashed over and gathered by one of the walls. Shots were then fired from the house and one comrade was killed. There were twelve to fifteen of us. I leapt over to the door of the house and put several bullets through it. We then heard shouts coming from inside. We had a prisoner with us who could speak German, so we sent him inside with instructions to tell the occupants to surrender. The prisoner emerged from a window, saying that they did not want to. This was followed by firing from the window, the cellar and the ground floor. We could not think of anything other than to smoke them out. Some comrades stayed to keep watch, while others went to get some straw. This was set alight then thrown through the window. The Frenchmen then tried to make a bolt for it as a group, but our shots drove them back. Gradually the flame and smoke in the building became too much and the occupants came out one by one without their weapons. There were fifteen of them and we took them prisoner. Whilst some of us escorted them to the rear I, together with the remainder, pushed on until we reached our new position and began to dig in."

What the advancing German soldiers had butted up against was a depth French position on better ground which was strongly manned – or at least held in greater strength than the men of 44th Reserve Division could tackle. They had run out of manpower, as demonstrated when the brigade commander could only send forward twenty uncommitted reinforcements earlier in the attack. The necessity to escort quite substantial numbers of prisoners to the rear had also reduced the front line strength available and, although further reinforcements had been despatched forward from holding positions somewhere near to Draaibank three hours after the attack had begun, there was still no sign of them. One of the reasons for this was that the French defenders were by now fully aware of the situation which had developed on the east bank of the Ijzer and were pouring fire from every gun within range onto the German positions and the associated approach routes. There was nothing for it but to consolidate in a position short of Steenstraat, about 400 metres from the canal.

The position in which the attackers found themselves was extremely precarious and dangerous. The regimental commander, Oberst Freiherr von Schleinitz, was wounded in the neck. His adjutant, Leutnant Freiherr von Wachtmeister, escorted him back to a dressing station at St. Jan and then went to report the situation to the brigade commander. Not being aware that Hauptmann Klos was still on his feet, the brigade commander appointed Wachtmeister, who was believed to be the only surviving regimental officer, as temporary regimental commander. Rounding up all the previous prisoner escorts and any other man he could find, Wachtmeister headed back forward. His little band, buoyed up by the knowledge that they had captured fourteen French officers, 1,154 other ranks and five machine guns,[64] nevertheless were near exhaustion, after nine days and nights spent in their wet, muddy trenches, followed by this costly attack.

On the way forward, the regimental history claims that the following improbable incident occurred:

> "During the march forward through the thick, sticky mud, it was necessary to call a halt for a short breather in the ruins of Bikschote. One man discovered a piano in a half-collapsed building. Freiherr von Wachtmeister had it brought out. One man who could play it sat down and began to play a folk melody. Too uninspiring for men on the verge of exhaustion! Then came a dance tune, which brought life back to tired limbs! Military marches. Hey, that was the stuff to lift the spirits! Then, when the commander gave the signal to continue the march, came the only piece which could truly match the glory of this great day. Singing, *Deutschland, Deutschland über alles*, they set off for the front line trenches".[65]

What few reserves were available to 44th Reserve Division eventually made it forward, but there were too few of them to do other than fill some of the gaps in the much thinned ranks of Reserve Jäger Battalion 16 and Reserve Infantry Regiments 205 and 206. The last named had benefited from the lunge forward by 2nd Battalion Reserve Infantry Regiment 205 and had also managed to make some progress before becoming bogged down in costly close quarter fighting in the wooded area south of Bikschote. For its part, Reserve Infantry Regiment 208, already withdrawn into reserve on 7 November, having suffered unsustainable losses, reduced as it was from 3,000 to 270 all ranks, did provide a composite company under Leutnant Seevers, which joined in the general pursuit and the end of the day saw it eventually digging in some 500 metres north of Steenstraat. No reinforcements were available to follow up, so there the advance halted.[66]

It was no easy matter to attempt to construct a continuous defensive line. No element of 5th Reserve Division was much further forward than the Langemark – Kortekeer Cabaret road, the resulting salient formed by advance of the 44th Reserve Division was vulnerable to enemy counter-action and so the entire garrison spent the night stood to. There were indeed half-hearted French attempt to snuff out this protuberance in the German line the following day and the whole area was kept under incessant artillery fire. With its left flank securely anchored on the Ijzer, the left flank was bent back to conform and the severely depleted regiments spent another two days forward in truly grisly conditions. Both here and in the adjacent 5th Reserve Division sector, losses through enemy action and increasing rates of sickness continued to be serious, so the newly gained positions were only held as a result of the timely arrival of reinforcements scraped up from throughout the III Reserve Corps area.[67] The Machine Gun Company of Reserve Infantry Regiment 24 was one such sub unit pressed into service in this manner and their after action report shows just what an effort this intervention cost men themselves very close to the limit of endurance. **10.**

"At 10.00 am on 10 November, the company was ordered to move forward to 1st Battalion Reserve Infantry Regiment 48, together with 1st and 2nd Companies. Initially we moved into a trench about one hundred metres further right, where enemy artillery fire pinned us for a lengthy halt. Towards midday we moved off again. The march of about two kilometres took us through a tangle of trenches. For the most part these were full of fresh mud, so moving through them with heavy loads under intermittent shell, shrapnel and small arms fire was extraordinarily strenuous and difficult. In between we also had to dash across country in places. Despite everything the company suffered no losses and we arrived on the position of the 48th about 3.00 pm. This was about one kilometre northeast of Bikschote.

"It rained heavily during the night. The platoons were unable to get any food, because it was impossible to link up with the vehicles . . . The platoons had to attempt to obtain some sort of cover from enemy fire in a half-dug French trench, which offered a flank to the French, was full of mud and water and was equipped with no dugouts or other shelter. We fed ourselves from tinned rations which we took from the bodies of dead British and French soldiers who were lying around. We could not do any work on the trench by day, because the French maintained a rapid rate of fire on it. This was particularly marked at midday each day, when we were also shelled. The battle continued unabated through 13 November, when it rained all day and throughout 14 November as well.

"The trenches became ever muddier. It was impossible to arrange weather protection and bundles of straw were soaked through in a very short time. Rationing was extremely difficult to arrange. A combination of artillery fire and the bottomless mud meant that the field kitchens could get no more than half way to the positions from their locations in Houthulst Wood. As a result, it took the carrying parties one hour each way, so the food was cold when it arrived in the trenches. It was completely impossible to warm it up; there was not a single dry item of combustible material, so the health and strength of the men began seriously to be reduced. Morale was at a very low ebb, especially following the assaults, which had achieved nothing and of which there seemed to be no end in sight.

"At dawn each morning, the battle, which had faded somewhat during the night, increased once more in intensity. One day our artillery fired six heavy shells short, landing them in our trenches and forcing us back. Once the error was corrected we regained our old positions. About seventy five Frenchmen, followed a little while later by an officer, came along one of the communication trenches which led to the enemy position, surrendered to us and were moved back to the rear. The French artillery fired on this group, killing and wounding several Frenchmen. At long last, at midday on 16 November, orders arrived stating that III Reserve Corps was to be relieved complete by VIII Corps in an operation which was to be complete by 11.00 pm.

"It poured with rain all day! The platoon positions came under heavy artillery fire again and the relief was delayed, not being completed until 3.00 am. The march back through heavy enemy artillery fire, carrying the weapons and ammunition boxes to the wagons and the continuation of the march along bottomless tracks, where the vehicles sank up to their axles in the mud, was very difficult and strenuous. Progress was extremely slow. It was not until 2.00 pm that the company arrived at its billets and both men and horses were utterly exhausted."[68]

In its way, this report typifies the entire battle. It never really ended, not for another four years. It just ground to a halt, descending into dangerous stalemate, where death was random, daily life was eked out amidst a sea of filth and mud and the dreary routine was punctuated by periods when the fighting flared up once more. Brushing over the overwhelming defensive victory achieved by the Allies at Langemark, conveniently overlooking the fact that the original aim had been to capture that place, with barely a pause, *en route* to a huge outflanking manoeuvre west of the Ijzer, XXVI Reserve Corps summed the situation at the end of the battle in this way:

"If the battles of October and November had proved to be a superhuman test of the sacrificial courage, physical and mental strength of the young kriegsfrei-willigen, the battle now became one with the elements, which bore down equally on friend and foe and ruled out any major operations. The battle trenches and communications trenches filled with water and mud, the walls of the trenches slumped in and the hitherto harmless little streams swelled into wide rivers. However, the young kriegsfreiwilligen had by now turned into battle-hardened fighters. Undaunted, they began to develop their positions. With enormous effort, they carried the necessary material forward along muddy tracks and over narrow footbridges. They had endured the 'Days of Langemark' and now they patiently manned the 'Flanders Watch', protecting the Homeland through their silent heroism."[69]

Notes
1. Mayer History Reserve Infantry Regiment 236 pp 117–118.
2. Brendler *Kriegserlebnisse* pp 25–26.
3. Hennig History Reserve Infantry Regiment 235 p 28.
4. Knieling History Reserve Infantry Regiment 234 pp 81–82.
5. Tiessen History Reserve Infantry Regiment 213 p 90.
6. The rifle companies of Reserve Infantry Regiment 235, prior to temporary amalgamation, were down to sixty to seventy five men, for example. Its losses had been 1,900 from over 2,700, or something in excess of seventy percent in just over a week of battle. Hennig *op. cit.* p 29.
7. Mayer *op. cit.* p 120.
8. *ibid.* p 120.
9. Partial confirmation of this appears in Willers History Reserve Infantry Regiment 215 p 98. In describing the situation at 10.00 am 30 October, the history states that, 'There was no sign of any involvement by Reserve Infantry Regiment 234. 215 had no contact to the left or right. The situation of the 215th was dangerous. There was no sign of any activity by Reserve Infantry Regiment 214 to the right whilst, on the left, Reserve Infantry Regiment 234 was at least 600 metres to the rear.'
10. Knieling *op. cit.* pp 84–85.
11. Leutnant Hermann von Zitzewitz is buried in the *Kamaradengrab* of the German cemetery at Langemark.
12. Gieraths History Reserve Infantry Regiment 210 p 45.
13. Schulz History Reserve Infantry Regiment 209 p 32.
14. Makoben History Reserve Infantry Regiment 212 p 66.
15. Leutnant Horst Münzer is buried in the German cemetery at Langemark Block A Grave 3141.
16. Fuhrmann History Reserve Infantry Regiment 211 p 45. The only additional men of this group to have known graves are Oberleutnant Helmuth Harder and Offizierstellvertreter Walter Huth, who are buried in the German cemetery at Langemark in Block A, Graves 1441 and 3351 respectively.
17. Bastanier History Reserve Infantry Regiment 214 p 42.
18. Stoffleth History Reserve Jäger Battalion 18 p 42.
19. Willers *op. cit.* pp 95–96.
20. Offizierstellvertreter Adolf Heß is buried in the German cemetery at Menen in Block F Grave 2125.
21. Oberleutnant Ernst Grimsehl and Offizierstellvertreter Wilhelm Mackprang are both buried in the German cemetery at Langemark in the *Kamaradengrab* and Block A Grave 2838 respectively. Grimsehl, a well known physicist in Germany before the war, was the headmaster of a science based secondary school in Hamburg before volunteering for front line service,

despite being in his fifties. Leading his men with great courage in the earlier battles, he had already been one of the first of his regiment to be awarded the Iron Cross.

22. Tiessen *op. cit.* pp 105–106.
23. FOH p 352.
24. Tiessen *op. cit.* p 108.
25. Ulrich History Reserve Infantry Regiment 52 p 76.
26. Schakert History Reserve Infantry Regiment 48 p 58.
27. Rohrbeck History Reserve Infantry Regiment 8 p 65.
28. Leutnant Hans Voss and Offizierstellvertreter Hugo Spannaus are buried in the German cemetery at Langemark in Block A, Graves 1811 and 5256 respectively.
29. Ulrich *op. cit.* p 77.
30. *ibid.* p 76.
31. History Reserve Infantry Regiment 35 p 67.
32. *ibid.* p 68. *Syndetikon* was a fish-based universal glue made in Germany from 1889 by Otto Ring Ltd. By 1914 it was one of the best known household adhesives on the German market.
33. Ulrich *op. cit.* p 78.
34. *ibid.* pp 78–79.
35. Repetzky Reserve Jäger Battalion 3 pp 56–59.
36. *ibid.* pp 59–60.
37. Boesser History Reserve Field Artillery Regiment 44 pp 77–78.
38. Schwenke History Reserve Infantry Regiment 19 p 64.
39. Unruh *Langemark* p 151
40. *Frankfurter Zeitung* 313 11 November 1914, quoted in Unruh *op. cit.* p 9.
41. Schwenke *op. cit.* p 65.
42. Reserve Leutnant Alois Otto is buried in the *Kamaradengrab* of the German cemetery at Langemark but, for some reason, Major Karl Horn and Hauptmann Karl Sattig lie in the German cemetery at Menen in Block D Grave 3541 and Block A Grave 60 respectively.
43. Schwenke *op. cit.* p 71.
44. Hauptmann Erich Grüttner is buried in the *Kamaradengrab* of the German cemetery at Langemark.
45. Schwenke *op. cit.* p 69.
46. Hennig *op. cit.* p 29.
47. Knieling *op. cit.* p 94.
48. *ibid.* pp 91–92.
49. For some reason, possibly poor reporting by 2nd Division, the BOH (p 413) asserts that nothing apart from an attempt to dig some trenches occurred in this area at this time, yet Reserve Infantry Regiment 234 states firmly (History p 94) they were opposed by the British. The FOH (p384), however, talks of capturing, 'between Poelkapelle and Langemark', men identified as belonging to the 'German V Reserve Corps (9th Reserve Division) withdrawn from the Verdun region; the prisoners declared that they had been ordered 'to attack at all costs' and that, 'the order had been carried out at the price of heavy casualties'.
50. Schwenke *op. cit.* p 72.
51. *ibid.* p 75.
52. *ibid.* p 76.
53. *ibid.* p 76.
54. History Reserve Infantry Regiment 35 p 72.
55. Ulrich *op. cit.* pp 80–81.
56. Rohrbeck *op. cit.* pp 66–67.

57. *ibid.* p 62.
58. *ibid.* p 62.
59. This is a reference to the award of the Iron Cross Second Class. Feldwebelleutnant Nausester was carried back by his men and buried near the church in Bikschote that night. His remains were later reburied in the German cemetery at Langemark Block A Grave 1281.
60. Atzrott History Reserve Jäger Battalion 16 pp 37–38.
61. Hauptmann Ulrich Dabis is buried in the German cemetery in Langemark Block A Grave 1277.
62. Appel History Reserve Infantry Regiment 205 p 38.
63. *ibid.* pp 38–39.
64. *ibid.* pp 39–40
65. What are we to make of this unlikely yarn, so reminiscent of similar insertions in novels produced during the Soviet First Five Year Plan? The regimental accounts make it clear that the initial assault was met by a hail of fire the moment the men left the trenches. Even if they could have heard themselves speak, let alone sing, they had little time available to do so, before they were cut down. Yet the Supreme Army Headquarters communiqué had stated clearly that the 'young regiments' had gone forward singing *Deutschland, Deutschland über alles* so, by the time the Nazis were well entrenched in power, there had to be some written proof that the incident had happened; the 'Spirit of Langemark' was a central pillar in the continuing effort to spur on the new generation. There were hardly any survivors to provide personal recollections, so this strange paragraph was inserted into the history of Reserve Infantry Regiment 205, produced at a time when there were strict controls over what could be published in Germany. It does not require much imagination to visualise a requirement for a reference to the singing to appear. So we are invited to believe that on a battlefield, under heavy fire and when they were needed desperately at the front, a band of men stopped for some time to listen to a folksong, some dance music and military marches before joining in for a jolly sing song round a miraculously surviving piano in the mud of a blasted village. Hmm.
66. Haleck History Reserve Infantry Regiment 208 p 15. When Reserve Infantry Regiment 208 was eventually relieved during the evening of 12 November by elements of Landwehr Infantry Regiments 34 and 36, its total strength, including all the rear duties men, was down to two officers, fourteen offizierstellvertreters and 213 other ranks. Assuming that the regiment did not raise a band, it would have comprised 3,178 all ranks on deployment. To have suffered 2,949 casualties implies that the battalions were more or less wiped out at Langemark. As it is, measured against its starting strength, the overall casualty rate was 92.8% – a staggering thought.
67. By the time Reserve Infantry Regiment 205 was withdrawn on 13 November, its losses since 19 October had been more than 1,700 killed or wounded, with hundreds more evacuated sick. Back in billets in Houthulst, only two officers, one offizierstellvertreter, fifteen unteroffiziers and 202 other ranks were there to answer their name at roll call.
68. History Reserve Infantry Regiment 24 pp 26–27.
69. Reich *Langemark* p 16

CHAPTER 8

Stalemate on the Menen Road

As night fell on the wrecked village of Geluveld on 31 October, the regiments who had fought for it and finally wrested it from its British defenders began to count the cost of their success. In addition to its commander, Oberst List, Bavarian Reserve Infantry Regiment 16 also had to mourn the loss of hundreds of its men. Hauptmann von Lünebosch, commanding officer 3rd Battalion, had had to be evacuated with appalling wounds, including his face carried away by a shell splinter, and almost every single one of his platoon commanders was dead or wounded. It was the same story for Reserve Infantry Regiment 247. With casualties, living and dead, strewn all over the battlefield and piled up where the fight had been hottest, the survivors tried to rally around and at least get the wounded evacuated. However, three days of incessant battle had taken a terrible toll on the men. Suffering from an overwhelming physical and emotional reaction, the majority were numbed into listless apathy and it was extremely difficult for the few surviving officers and NCOs to motivate men whose sole desire was for food, drink and, above all, rest.

With a huge effort, the tangled sub units were reorganised, patrols and listening posts were sent forward to ensure against surprise and orders were issued for the following day, when it was certain that the advance would have to be resumed. At around midnight there was one significant boost to morale. The company feldwebels back with the rear echelons had used their initiative and mobilised the cooks and sundry other administrative personnel who, loaded up with large containers of coffee, bottles of wine and sacks of cured bacon and biscuits, had come right forward to bring some urgently need comfort to their comrades in the rifle companies. Even with all the losses, there was little enough to share round but, although there was a mere half mug of coffee per man and a small handful of food, this was one occasion when the thought counted and there was general gratitude for the determination shown by the carrying parties involved. Refreshed and grimly determined, a group under Vizefeldwebel Hörstmann, of Bavarian Reserve Infantry Regiment 16, spent the rest of the night gathering together corpses and burying them roughly in shell holes. There was little time for ceremony and they could only deal with a small part of the problem, but at least they had not left them to rot in the open.[1]

The senior man on the spot, Oberst von Hügel, commander of Reserve Infantry Regiment 248, issued a written order to Bavarian Reserve Infantry Regiment 16 during the early hours of 1 November:[2]

> "I am assuming command of all the detachments located to the right of the main road running through Geluveld. The attack will be continued today. Bavarian [Reserve Infantry] Regiment 16, with its left flank anchored on the

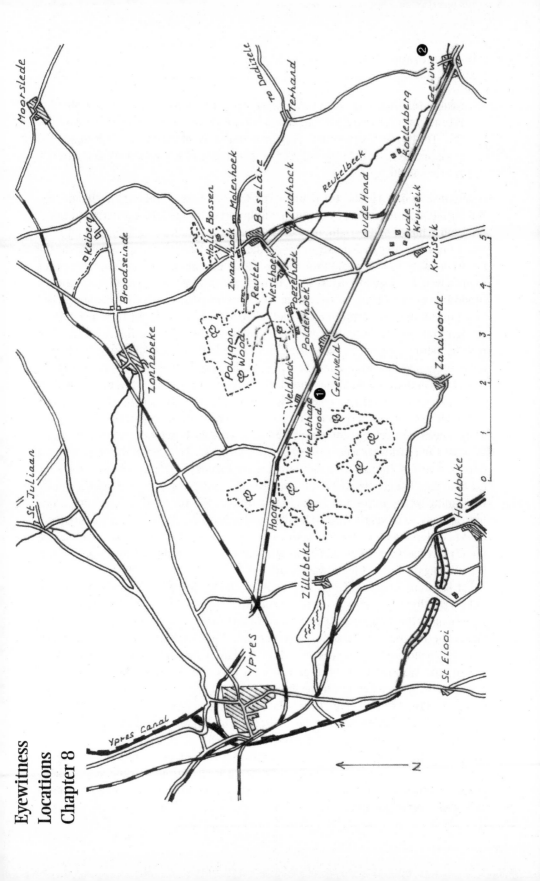

**Eyewitness
Locations
Chapter 8**

road and maintaining contact with Reserve Infantry Regiment 249 on its right, is to advance via Geluveld Chateau towards the Geluveld – Poezelhoek railway line. The intervening wooded areas are to be cleared of the enemy. Reports are to be sent to Geluveld Chateau. Today, after battle of several days, a decision is to be sought."

In response, as dawn broke, the remnants of Bavarian Reserve Infantry Regiment 16 – 3rd Battalion, commanded by Hauptmann Butterfaß on the left, 1st Battalion under Leutnant Schmidt on the right, near the grounds of the chateau, each formed into two firing lines and prepared to advance.[3] As the British had previously withdrawn, the Bavarians were soon moving through the parkland around the chateau, where they found a well developed trench system. Here they captured large quantities of *materiel*. In addition to entire crates of small arms ammunition, there were stocks of maps, brand new rangefinders, waterproof coats and telephone equipment, not to mention large stocks of rations. Box after box of corned beef was recovered, together with crates of biscuits, tobacco, cigarettes and spirits. This caused the morale of all concerned to rise, not only because they were able to benefit from the items found, but also because it indicated to them that the British had intended to make a firmer stand forward in Geluveld.

The park of the chateau was, naturally, in a dreadful state. The shelling had not spared one single tree. Everywhere there were bare trunks with the upper parts of the trees shot away. The magnificent greenhouses and formal gardens were totally destroyed, whilst the lawns and pathways were littered by the intermingled corpses of the defenders and dozens of men of 3rd Battalion Bavarian Reserve Infantry Regiment 16 killed there the previous day. The chateau itself was not too badly damaged at that time though, during the coming weeks, it, too, was reduced to a ruin; as was the nearby church and cemetery. Already, at this early stage, it had been so badly hit that the cemetery was one great mass of craters and wrecked graves. However, there was little time to take in the sights, the advance had to continue and, by around mid morning, leading elements were established along the line of the railway as ordered.

For Bavarian Reserve Infantry Regiment 16, the battle was over for the time being. They were directed to advance no further and to prepare to be withdrawn that evening. Buoyed up by the thought that Geluveld now lay to the rear and was securely in German hands, the 1st and 3rd Battalions, together with 2nd Battalion, which had been operating independently for the past few days, withdrew into rest at Wervik after dark, leaving the Württembergers responsible for this crucial sector. Reserve Infantry Regiment 245, deployed to the north, was involved in a further attack which, in the event, amounted to little more than a line straightening exercise, but the British were driven back from Polderhoek Chateau to the edges of Polygon Wood. The attack cost the regiment the lives of Hauptmann Käusler and Oberleutnant Arnold but there were relatively few other casualties.[4] After the events of 1 November, there was virtually no activity on this section of the front for the next week, apart from near-incessant digging as both sides attempted to improve their positions and provide themselves with as much overhead cover as possible.

The withdrawal into rest of Bavarian Reserve Infantry Regiment 16 meant that, from 2 November, Reserve Infantry Regiment 248 was located to the left of Reserve Infantry Regiment 245, with Reserve Infantry Regiment 242, supported by Reserve Jäger Battalion 26, to the left. The remains of Reserve Infantry Regiment 247 remained in reserve for the time being. Casualties amongst key personnel continued to rise and, on 2 November, Oberst von Hügel, who seemed to bear a charmed life, had to assume responsibility for forward command of the left forward troops of the division in addition to his own responsibilities. This was only possible because the casualties meant that the various formations were much reduced in size. On paper, Hügel commanded Reserve Infantry Regiment 248, Detachment Pudor (Reserve Infantry Regiment 242 and Reserve Jäger Battalion 26), Reserve Infantry Regiment 247, Landwehr Infantry Regiment 77/78 (the so-called Detachment Waxmann) and Reserve Field Artillery Regiment 54 but, in practice, Reserve Infantry Regiment 248 was down to ten companies, Reserve Infantry Regiment 242 five companies, Reserve Jäger Battalion 26 two companies, Landwehr 77/78 one company and Reserve Infantry Regiment 247 three companies – an organisation only achieved on 1 November when about 180 men, drawn mostly from 3rd Battalion, which had been operating independently, arrived, led by Offizierstellvertreter Baur, late on 1 November.[5]

Following the death of Oberst Feucht during the morning of 31 October, command of the artillery of 54th Reserve Division had changed hands rapidly. Oberst von Kreßman of XV Corps, who happened to have been with Feucht when he was hit, was appointed to the role, but he, too, was wounded a short time later. His (very temporary) replacement was an officer from the artillery staff of XV Corps, but then Oberst Bleidorn, commander of Field Artillery Regiment 84, was sent for. Nobody in these days before reliable means of communication had a clear idea of what assets were actually available, so it was then decided that Major Klotz, commanding officer 2nd Battalion Reserve Field Artillery Regiment 54, would assume the role. In becoming the fifth commander of Reserve Field Artillery Regiment 54 in twenty four hours, Klotz must have broken some sort of record, but it was decided between he and Oberst Bleidorn that the latter would stand in temporarily whilst Klotz spent the night 31 October/ 1 November touring round the various units and sub units, so that he knew for sure what he was about to command.

The situation resolved, he joined Oberst Freiherr von Hügel in the late morning of 1 November in a small network of British trenches near Geluveld Chateau. It is an extraordinary thought, but Reserve Field Artillery Regiment 54 owned no telephones at that stage of the war, so co-location with the infantry commander was essential in order to ensure that Klotz would have a means of communicating back to Headquarters 54th Reserve Division and across the inter-corps boundary to XV Corps. All other links, including those to the battalions and gun lines, was by runner or despatch rider.

Despite the staggering losses, the attack was continued on 2 November, but little of lasting significance was achieved, despite the fact that the operations caused considerable alarm to the British. There had been slight progress forward of Polderhoek Chateau whilst, on the left flank, there had been a link up by the so-called Group Mühry, with

Infantry Regiment 99 of 30th Infantry Division, operating on the right flank of XV Corps near Veldhoek. There is no doubt that Mühry's men benefited from the advance of the still relatively fresh XV Corps which, further south, closed right up to St Elooi that day, a mere three kilometres from Ypres. There was also a decisive intervention from Reserve Field Artillery Regiment 54, a formation which appears to have been of high quality and led with considerable aggression and determination. Feuerwerkleutnant Bley,[6] commander 7th Battery, went right forward, then crawled into a position in a farmhouse in front of the infantry and only 150 metres from the enemy. From this vantage point he was able to direct the fire of his battery to such effect that he caused the crews of a section of guns, those who were not killed or wounded by his fire, to abandon their positions, leaving behind the weapons and piles of ammunition. This, in turn, caused a local withdrawal, which the German infantry was able to exploit, but only temporarily. The gun positions were abandoned once more that night.

The British account[7] claims that even the limited German success was, in effect, lucky, the British guns having been directed to cease firing at midday (German time). As a result, Infantry Regiments 99 and 143 were able to push up the road boldly in groups of thirty to forty men, overpower what was left of the Coldstream Guards and then attack the King's Royal Rifle Corps and capture more than four hundred men. Towards the end of the afternoon, a threat began to build up from the northeast, so 2nd Battalion Infantry Regiment 99, which had been in reserve, was introduced north of the Menen – Ypres road, together with a platoon of the Machine Gun Company. Between 5.00pm and 7.00pm, when reinforcements from Infantry Regiment 143 arrived, a rather scratch force of 2nd and 3rd Battalions Infantry Regiment 99, together with elements of Reserve Infantry Regiment 248 and what remained of Landwehr Infantry Regiments 77 and 78, managed to beat off this counter-attack, though losses amongst the defenders had been quite severe.[8] A brief outline of this eventful day was later written by the brigade commander.

Generalleutnant von Altrock Commander 60 Infantry Brigade [9] **1.**

"During the afternoon of 2 November, Infantry Regiment 99 captured British trenches in front of Veldhoek, taking 400 prisoners, including ten officers of the 'Rifles, Buffs, Coldstreams and Guards Regiments' [*sic*]. A French attack threatened from the right, but General von Altrock directed artillery fire against it. Reinforcement was requested from Headquarters XV Corps. Infantry Regiment 143, Reserve Hussar Regiment 8 and two companies of engineers were despatched and were sent into action. Infantry Regiment 143 advanced south of the Geluveld – Veldhoek road and succeeded in capturing two British guns, together with their crews.[10] These were the only ones taken by XV Corps on the Ypres front."

Reserve Oberleutnant Lentz and the men of 3rd Company Infantry Regiment 143 were credited with this important seizure. The guns were taken back to Strasbourg, where they were displayed for some weeks on Kaiserplatz, then claimed by Infantry Regiment

143 and placed in their barracks. Both Lentz and Unteroffizier Rüther, who had been prominent during the capture of the guns, were awarded the Iron Cross First Class. Later on the afternoon of 2 November, 2nd and 3rd Battalions Infantry Regiment 143 were also launched in the attack, supported by the Machine Gun Company, but it was too late in the day to achieve much and the only result was to compound an already confused situation in the forward area.

Reserve Leutnant Hagedorn 9th Company Infantry Regiment 143 [11] **1.**

"The two battalions advanced across open country on a broad front, a row of trees denying the enemy observation. At one point the progress of the forward companies came to a halt, but those following up continued. The consequence was that these troops ended up alongside the companies which had halted and the entire landscape was full of masses of troops. Luckily, all this was hidden from the enemy, otherwise they would have been able to cause a major bloodbath with their artillery. Only one, apparently stray, shell landed amongst a section of 11th Company, killing Reserve Leutnant Hoffmann and several men.[12] Once orders arrived, the companies were able to disentangle themselves and occupy the designated positions."

The three weak companies of Reserve Infantry Regiment 247 did not take part in this action. One company, under Vizefeldwebel Barthlomä, was at readiness in rear of the Beselare – Geluveld railway, near to the chateau, Offizierstellvertreter Baur with the second company occupied the grounds of Geluveld chateau, whilst the third company, commanded by Offizierstellvertreter Mayer, who was promoted to Reserve Leutnant on 6 November, was given the grisly task of clearing the battlefield. This job was far from easy. A mass of weapons and equipment had to be salvaged and the many dead buried. There were also very large numbers of dead cattle to be disposed of. A high percentage of the Landwehr reinforcements in Mayer's company were farmers or agricultural workers, who were extremely upset at the sight of all these dead animals (which included fourteen who had burned to death in a single byre, still chained to their stalls) and they had to be excused this particular duty, which fell to the townsmen instead.

Towards evening first Bartholomä's, then Baur's, companies were launched forward on the right, pressing on up to to the Polderhoek – Veldhoek road and digging in under heavy fire. In order to ease the pressure on the infantry, Major Klotz of Reserve Field Artillery Regiment 54 ordered his 2nd Battalion forward in immediate support of the front line. Galloping forward in the order 6th, 5th and 4th Batteries, fire was opened up on the British positions at almost point blank range. The German infantry benefited considerably from this daring action, but it came at a high price that evening and in the days which followed. Hauptmann Probst, commanding 6th Battery, Offizier-stellvertreter Rilling of 4th Battery and Reserve Leutnant Körner of 5th Battery were killed, whilst Reserve Leutnant Kienzle, commanding 5th Battery, was wounded, together with Offizierstellverterter Lorenz and numerous other ranks.[13] A member of 6th Battery later provided a graphic account of this intervention.[14]

"As the leading battery, Battery Probst, was closing in on the crossing over the narrow gauge railway, the infantry bawled at them, 'Hey! Where are you going? We are manning the front line!' We certainly did not project the most intelligent of images, but we were at least right in front of the entrance to the grounds of the chateau. The gates were swiftly pulled open, then in we went, crossing over the most beautiful flowerbeds, past the chateau itself in the direction of Veldhoek and took up position at the end of the parkland. Fortunately the enemy had evacuated this area, otherwise they would have given us a most unpleasant reception. They were located a few hundred metres to our front which, at that time, was regarded as almost normal battle range.

"Towards evening we asked for infantry protection. For a long time this was in vain but, finally, about sixty dismounted cavalry had been assembled. They promised to protect us but, by morning, they had all disappeared. Crammed tightly together, 3rd Battery was right in the chateau grounds. 5th Battery was to the right, hard up against the chateau, then came 6th, with 4th Battery on the extreme left. The enemy had pulled back to a point about half way to Polygon Wood and our infantry, on seeing our arrival, decided to push forward as well until it was in close contact with the enemy out in front of us. Our battalion immediately opened fire on the enemy infantry which, during the course of the day, was forced back into Polygon Wood but then made a stand there.

"Apparently the enemy artillery had been changing positions simultaneously with us and so passed up the opportunity to exploit what was a critical moment for us. However, they now came into action and soon shrapnel balls were whistling past our ears. The fire was then supplemented by high explosive shells. These were the loathsome shells filled with lyddite, which crashed down on our positions, filling them with yellow smoke. It really was unpleasant and we soon began to realise that war really was a serious business. That evening, after it went dark, a stack of straw on the western edge of the chateau grounds caught fire and illuminated the 4th Battery positions against the night sky. Things then began to get dangerous.

"The enemy could see our every movement so, naturally, there were soon casualties as the enemy began to make use of this lucky situation. An enemy battery began to fire at 4th Battery at the rapid rate and with wonderful precision. Thank heavens, however, the bursting point was a few metres too high, so this 'blessing' did not achieve any notable success. On the other hand, the lack of experience of some of our men repeatedly offered the enemy opportunities to cause damage so, by the time that the rations were distributed at 10.00 pm, the house was already overflowing with wounded men. The 5th Battery in particular suffered heavy casualties. They had placed their guns under some high trees and believed that they were well hidden. Unfortunately, the enemy had still located them and there was one concentration of fire whose shells, bursting in amongst the trees, sent down great showers of splinters and caused much worse casualties than doubtless would have been the case if they had been directed at a position in the open. Many a comrade paid with his life because of this inexperience."

On 3 November there was, inevitably, a further effort along the Menen road, but the presence of French reinforcements to bolster the almost exhausted British troops in this area had an effect. At various places, they launched their own attacks and the result was a day of near stalemate, a 'day of marking time', as a French writer put it subsequently.[15] German accounts complain of the weight of artillery fire directed at them that day, both French and British artillery causing severe casualties and the explosive gases from the British lyddite-filled shells having an almost suffocating effect on those troops affected by them. There was also a great deal of damage done to depth targets and, for example, much of the materiel captured when Geluveld Chateau was taken was damaged or destroyed by repeated concentrations of fire. Then, in the ensuing confusion, all the war records of Reserve Infantry Regiment 248 to date went missing: orders, reports and war diaries.[16] Nothing was ever recovered.

In addition to general harassment and routine destruction, it was quite often the case that speculative shelling of rear areas had an effect. A supporting member of Reserve Field Artillery Regiment 54 later described one such incident.

Kanonier Hurtig Light Ammunition Column II Reserve Field Artillery Regiment 54 [17]

"At about 3.00 am, II Light Ammunition Column arrived at the location of the main column. There had been casualties amongst both men and horses. I was the first member of the main column to be detailed to transfer to the light ammunition column. We rode off at about 4.00 am to Terhand via Dadizele and there I received my baptism of fire and was lucky to escape with my life. We had just ridden by a tobacco shed where the heavy artillery was storing shells for their four 210 mm howitzers, which were located to the right of it. There was a dummy battery position to the left. Airmen had observed this shed and, suddenly, shells came roaring and howling through the air. This made us all duck. It was always like that the first time people heard shells explode nearby. Over time you got used to it.

"Suddenly there was direct hit on the shed, followed by a terrible explosion. Everything was cloaked in black smoke. How I parted company with my horse I do not know to this day. There were about 170 rounds in the shed. These shells, which weighed hundredweights and not all of which exploded, were scattered for hundreds of metres. The men who had been collecting ammunition were blown to pieces. Later their remains were gathered up in groundsheets and buried there. I stood by this grave for a long time afterwards and repeated the Lord's Prayer. The dummy battery position to the left was absolutely smashed. I shall never forget that day. That was where I really understood what war was about. All around houses were burning and shells were crashing down. In the middle of all that fire was the covered command post of Light Ammunition Column II and we reported in to its commander, Hauptmann Pfeiffer."

Once more Feuerwerkleutnant Bley of Reserve Field Artillery Regiment 54 had an outstanding day on 3 November. He organised and led the recovery of the French guns engaged on 2 November. He had hoped to turn these guns round against the Allies but the prize money proved to be too tempting and they were taken further to the rear by some infantrymen, so the opportunity was lost. Nevertheless, Bley continued to provide outstanding fire support and, at one point later in the day, he brought such devastating fire to bear on a British position near Veldhoek that a large group of soldiers surrendered, came marching towards him with their hands up and were escorted away by a few infantrymen. For his overall performance during these critical days, Bley was awarded the Iron Cross First Class, the first man from his regiment to be so honoured.[18]

On either side of the Menen road, the villages, hamlets and countryside had taken on a stricken appearance following the days of intense fighting and shelling. The houses, barns and farms were flattened, burnt out and in ruins, whilst next to countless fallen of both sides the entire area was littered with the stinking cadavers of dead horses, cattle and domestic animals. The roads and tracks were blocked with wrecked vehicles, which had been developed into improvised obstacles, but still the grim battle continued and casualties continued to mount. Infantry Regiment 143, 30th Infantry Division, like many other regiments, was forced to amalgamate the reduced ranks of pairs of its companies in order to produce one viable manoeuvre unit and, in the cold grey foggy dawn of 3 November, what was left of its 2nd and 3rd Battalions resumed the painful advance towards Veldhoek. In bitter fighting for every hedge, ditch and fold in the ground and at the cost of yet more serious casualties, following hard on the heels of the mortal wounding of Hauptmann Dierke whilst conducting a reconnaissance the previous night, a precarious foothold was obtained in the outskirts of Veldhoek.

Reserve Leutnant Hagedorn 9th Company Infantry Regiment 143 [19] 1.

"Hauptmann Dierke, officer commanding 10th Company, who had already been wounded at Schweighausen and who had only returned to the regiment on 16 October, was totally careless of his personal safety and made an outstanding impression. The regimental commander, Oberstleutnant Linker, called over to him (prior to his departure to reconnoitre), 'Be careful, you are my last hauptmann!' This was quite true. Of the twelve who had marched off to war, he was the last still serving with the troops. He did not shrink from the situation and, waving to his platoon commanders, he set off to spy out the situation and the ground to the front. Hardly ten minutes later he was being carried to the rear past Oberstleutnant Linker, terribly wounded by a shell splinter. When [Linker] grasped the sad truth he involuntarily dropped a water glass, which fell from his hand to shatter on the cobbled country road. A few hours later, Dierke died, never having regained consciousness. Reserve Leutnant Kutscher took over command of the company which, that very same day, lost an entire section to a direct hit. Those killed included Musketier Keilholz,[20] who had already been awarded the Iron Cross Second Class for his bravery in Lorraine and at Hurtebise."

Reserve Oberleutnant Lentz 3rd Company Infantry Regiment 143 [21] **1.**

"On 3 November at 5.00 am the commander of the Bavarian Cavalry Division requested orders and then his men were committed to the battle. There was heavy fire throughout the day, but at 6.30 pm Veldhoek was captured. Suddenly there were Frenchmen to our front once more (4th Zouaves), whom we had fought previously on numerous occasions in other places. To the left of us, in the sector of 85 Infantry Brigade [also part of 30th Infantry Division], there was extremely heavy fire. On 4th November we received orders from the commander of XV Corps: 'At all costs and disregarding losses due to fire from the flanks or rear, progress forwards is to be made.' During the morning Field Marshal [Freiherr] von der Goltz [at the time, Governor General of Belgium] visited us, as did liaison officers from XV Corps and 30th Infantry Division, who did not choose to do us the honour later. Due to strong obstacles, fortified houses and wiring in front of and within the wood to the west of Veldhoek, no progress worth the name was achieved.

North of the road, the worn down regiments of 54th Reserve Division, which were effectively fought out, found themselves less able with each passing day to contribute to maintaining the impetus of the offensive. It was not only the BEF which was feeling the pain of this protracted battle. However, the following day both they and the formations of 30th Infantry Division were ordered to continue to press on towards Ypres, so as to give the defence no time to recover. Reserve Infantry Regiment 248 of 54th Reserve Division was ordered to capture Pottyn Farm, whilst Infantry Regiment 143 was given the task of taking the forward edge of Herenthage Wood to the south of the main Menen – Ypres road. Both these tasks were easier said than done. Herenthage Wood was being stoutly defended by British dismounted cavalry which, taking advantage of the dense cover from view it offered and in conjunction with the Royal Artillery, was exerting firm control over the approaches. Despite the ringing call for 'energetic attack', 60 Infantry Brigade directed a more methodical approach, this to begin by sapping forward and preparing good jumping off positions. By dint of hard digging in difficult conditions, Infantry Regiment 143 gained about fifty metres that day, the work being matched by equally determined improvements to their defensive positions by the British cavalrymen.

Reserve Leutnant Hagedorn 9th Company Infantry Regiment 143 [22] **1.**

"The driving forward of saps went on throughout the night as well. The demands, both physical and mental, on the fighting troops were immense. However, the extraordinarily tense situation as both sides struggled to achieve a decision meant that the troops could be permitted no rest. By day the strain of battle told on their nerves, whilst by night these exhausted men had to keep on working on the trenches. Checking for progress one night, a platoon commander of 10th Company discovered that, instead of a complete section, only the section commander, Fahnenjunker Strauch, was working. Asked where his section was, [Strauch] replied that he had simply been unable to wake his exhausted men, so he had left them to sleep and instead dug single handed, without a pause, throughout the night, so as to carry out the section's allotted task. The sense of duty of this courageous fahnenjunker was fully recognised, but the demands of the situation required the full involvement of the entire section; the very last reserves of strength had to be called on."

The orders directing Reserve Infantry Regiment 248 to capture Pottyn Farm reached them during the morning of 4 November. There was a reasonably thorough artillery bombardment then, at 3.15 pm, its 1st Battalion stormed forward, took the farm and surrounding buildings and then dug in.[23] This was virtually the last successful offensive act of this tour of duty by 54th Reserve Division, though elements of Reserve Infantry Regiment 247 played a part in an attempt by 30th Infantry Division to press home their attacks in Herenthage Wood, by intervening to support the operations of Infantry Regiment 143. Meanwhile, the painfully slow work of sapping forward continued right through the next two days and nights and gradually the gap between the opposing lines was reduced – but at the cost of a steady trickle of casualties on both sides. During the remaining days before the arrival of the *ad hoc* Guards Infantry Division, this amounted to some hundreds of metres in total, but Reserve Infantry Regiment 247 later commented, 'that the casualties were disproportionate to what was achieved'.[24]

Selected men who were known to be good shots maintained surveillance over the British lines throughout the next few days. They sniped whenever a target appeared and enjoyed a certain amount of success. However, this was easily matched by the work of British marksmen. To the south of the Menen road, Offizierstellvertreter Schenk of the combined 7th/8th Company Infantry Regiment 143, for example, received an arm wound as he returned from a reconnaissance patrol, which was so painful that he had set off as fast as he could for the rear towards the dressing station, only to fall, mortally wounded, before he gone more than a few paces. That same night Reserve Leutnant Redecker was killed as his men continued to work on communication trenches to link up the scattered company positions.[25]

Feeding was once more causing great concern. The rationing situation with 54th Reserve Division had been chaotic for some considerable time and, within 30th Infantry Division, the company field kitchens had not been able to get forward for several days. By now the iron rations had all been eaten, including those of the living and the dead and, furthermore, whenever prisoners were captured, none was allowed to proceed to the rear until every scrap of food on his person had been seized. Nevertheless, the steady progress forward was with difficulty maintained as one isolated house or dominating point after another was incorporated into the positions, regardless of the cost.

Reserve Oberleutnant Lentz 3rd Company Infantry Regiment 143 [26] **1.**

> "Throughout 5th November there was heavy artillery fire. The edge of the wood to the west of Veldhoek and the intervening ground were brought under fire by the howitzers. There was meant to be a full scale assault after this. In the event there was an advance of only about three hundred metres to the right [north] of the Veldhoek – Ypres road and a mere 150 metres to the left of it. The commanders reported that the men were utterly exhausted; it was inadvisable to attack the edge of the wood, especially because we were under enfilade fire from the right and rear. Our evening patrols rounded up one hundred shirkers out of the farmsteads and cellars of Geluveld. On 6th November, Reserve Rittmeister Minderop, on the staff of 60 Infantry Brigade, discovered that the enemy trenches west of Veldhoek were protected by hedges reinforced with wire and barbed wire obstacles and that British troops were present. During the afternoon we witnessed the greatest exchange of artillery fire that we had ever experienced.

It was not just the front line that was receiving attention from the Allied artillery. Although ammunition shortages were becoming a source of increasing concern to the Allies, there were still sufficient stocks on hand to permit harassing fire to be brought down on likely targets well to the rear, as this diary entry makes clear:

Major Collet Commanding Officer 2nd Battalion Infantry Regiment 143 [27]

> "About 5.30 pm [on 6 November] I was sitting with my adjutant, Leutnant Klein, in a room at the rear of the house. Because shells began landing very close by, I said to my adjutant that we ought to move into the hall, where we would at least have two walls to protect us. We had only been outside it for a short while when a great big shell bored down into our room, wrecking every-thing. It exploded with an almighty crash, deafening and blinding us and we were covered in a hail of stones, pieces of wood and iron and dust, which almost suffocated us in this tiny, narrow hallway. Eventually I found a door and realised that I was uninjured. I could hear shouts, but could still see nobody. Then another shell exploded right in front of me and just outside the door, covering me with earth but without wounding me. Leutnant Klein and my battalion trumpeter, Unteroffizier Krumkühler, were wounded but, luckily, the wounds did not seem to be too serious. A little while later I re-entered the villa, but my former room looked absolutely dreadful; everything was smashed, so I transferred to the room on the other side. The battalion staff of 3rd Battalion had been operating out of the cellar of the same house for some days. Once we were over the initial shock, we took refuge there, whilst

Leutnant Klein's wounds were dressed and then yet another shell landed right
in front of the cellar opening in the courtyard, enveloping everything in smoke
and dust once more."

On 6 November 312 Landwehr soldiers arrived at the rear echelon of Infantry Regiment
143. Initially it was not intended to deploy them at once but then orders arrived for a
continuation of the attack on 7 November to conform with the thrust by 39th Infantry
Division to the south, so one hundred of the new arrivals were distributed to the
companies of 1st Battalion, which was to carry out the assault. It is not clear if the Allies
were expecting an attack that morning, but their artillery fire was noted as being particularly heavy. The German guns were only able to make a limited reply because shortages
of ammunition were already being felt keenly in Flanders. Nevertheless, at 5.00 am, 1st
and 2nd Companies, advancing together with 3rd Battalion Infantry Regiment 136, did
manage to storm and take a British trench, capturing thirteen prisoners. Elsewhere
there was little or no success; indeed, with the attack on the right being beaten back, the
regiment found itself in the uncomfortable position of having its 2nd Company a mere
ten metres from the enemy lines, but its 9th Company, which had also attempted to get
forward, stranded 200 metres to the rear.

Many of the troops were out on a limb, pinned down throughout the day and had to
await nightfall before they could move and close up to the British lines. Infantry
Regiment 143 found that they were still losing a lot of men to snipers, despite moving
along communications trenches wherever possible so, following a piece of advice from
Reserve Leutnant Bein, formerly with Infantry Regiment 171, the decision was taken
to unscrew the spikes from their helmets. This was done, the practice spread very
rapidly and soon the spikes of the *Pickelhauben* were things of the past, even though it
led to accusations that it made everyone look like firemen. During the next thirty six
hours the regiment was going to need all the help it could get as it bore the entire weight
of the attacks along the Menen road. 54th Reserve Division had given its all. It was
capable of no more offensive action, merely of holding on to what it had captured, with
particular emphasis on its right flank, until it was relieved; this despite the fact that
Reserve Infantry Regiment 248, for example, received reinforcements from Germany
on 8, 9 and 10 November, thus enabling it to revert to a twelve company organisation.[28]

Orders arrived during the evening of 7 November and by dawn on 8 November all the
companies of Infantry Regiment 143 were in position on their start lines, ready to
resume the assault on Herenthage Wood, which by now was developing a fearsome
reputation. At daybreak all the low lying ground was shrouded in mist whilst, roaring
overhead, the German bombardment crashed down. The medium artillery engaged
known strong points and isolated farm buildings, whilst the field artillery poured fire
down on the edge of the wood itself, where the enemy trenches were thought to be
located. Out on the right, where Becker's 7th/8th Company were operating two grenade
launchers, the French soldiers manning the trenches opposite placed their kepis on their
bayonets and waved them in an attempt to surrender, but nobody took any notice.

This was an all-out effort by the regiment and, in an attempt to encourage the troops, the commander had ordered the regimental band forward to play military marches once the attack began. Everywhere the participants were lying flat, their faces pressed close to the ground to avoid all the incoming fire. This applied to the band as well, as they took cover amongst the men in the second wave. Unfortunately for them, they too suffered some casualties from the fire, a number of instruments were damaged and, in the event, they did not actually play when, at 11.30 am, the mist having cleared, the signal was given and the companies stormed forward.

Unteroffizier Berndt Regimental Band Infantry Regiment 143 [29]

"The regimental band, led by Obermusikmeister Fischer, was attached to the reserve battalion in Amerika, where we were waiting for further orders. Towards evening [7 November] . . . the 'alarm' call was blown. Under enemy aerial observation, we marched forward to the positions. On the down slope of a hill to the left of the Ypres road the order came, 'Halt, lie down'. Simultaneously, enemy artillery fire began to come down. We marched up and down until, finally, somewhere to the right of the main road we arrived at a railway embankment, where we paused for a long time. In the early dawn of the following morning, down in our hastily dug trenches, we were suddenly subject to a hail of iron. This is where Sergeant Barth of the band was wounded and drained the Obermusikmeister's brandy flask and where we ended up staying for several days.

"The band was ordered to pull back about fifty to seventy metres to a position in rear of a building on the right hand [north] side of the road and from there play the troops forward into battle when the attack began. Orders: 'During the attack, play the *Yorck[scher]-Marsch*,[30] followed by *Deutschland, Deutschland über alles* when the objective is reached'. However, even before the assault, came a fresh order from one of the battalion commanders: 'The band is to advance immediately!'. We bumped into the regimental commander in a communication trench on our way forward. He sent us back firmly, saying, 'It is impossible to advance through this fire.' He was killed just after that.

"We gathered once more at the original spot. Quite why we did not play from that place, I do not know. Here we suffered another man wounded, Oboist Wilebinsky, and one killed, Oboist Waldmeyer.[31] At that, we handed our instruments in, just as at Craonne earlier and later at Verdun, on the Somme and at Cambrai, then we went onto stretcherbearer duty."

Despite earlier casualties and the tiredness felt by all ranks, the initial assault was conducted with great aggression and some localised success. There was hand to hand fighting in places, but a lodgement was gained on the edge of the wood. It was claimed that the French reservists, who had attempted to surrender earlier, did not put up much of a fight and were captured by follow-up waves, but the British troops who were encountered fought with desperate courage, firing their rifles from the standing position at very close range and inflicting numerous casualties on the attackers. It had been intended to pause and reorganise on the edge of the wood whilst a further bombardment paved the way for a further advance, but 7th Company Infantry Regiment 143, sensing an opportunity, stormed on into the wood towards Veldhoek Chateau at its northern tip.

This thrust was beaten back. Reserve Leutnant Bein, commanding one half of the company, was shot through the lung and collapsed, seriously wounded, whilst the company commander, Oberleutnant Becker, who gone into action accompanied by a large dog which had befriended him, was cut off and killed, together with his dog. A member of the 1st Battalion later described the build up to the second phase of the attack and its confused aftermath.

Reserve Oberleutnant Lentz 3rd Company Infantry Regiment 143 [32] **1.**

"On 7th November the artillery duel continued. The previous night Infantry Regiment 99 was pulled back to Timbriele in Corps reserve. Towards 5.00 pm there was an intense battle, telephone lines were shot through and it was difficult to make ourselves heard. Gunners racing to the rear shouted, 'Fire needs to be brought down further forward'. Infantry Regiment 143 made some progress to the left of the main road, but there was no success to the right of it. That night heavy howitzers in Veldhoek bombarded the enemy positions and there was a failed attempt by the reserve division on our right to get forward. At midday 8 November our howitzers fired once more but there was still no success right of the road. Attempts to persuade the reserve division to get forward or to go into reserve behind our right flank also foundered.

"Oberst[Leutnant] Linker, Infantry Regiment 143, was killed during an assault designed to encourage the reserve division to press forward.[33] Our slight success was bought dearly. Prisoners, both British and 4th Zouaves, were taken. They [were members of] Royal Fusilier, Lionhardt [*sic*.], Lancastire [*sic*], Duke of Wellington, Grenadier Guards, Scotts Guards [*sic*], Badford [*sic*], Norfolk and 4th Reserve Battalion 4th Zouaves. However, despite all efforts and all the casualties, the wooded edge west of Veldhoek could not be reached. On 9 November, at 10.00 am, General von Altrock was directed, together with the adjutants, to move to Kruiseke to 30th Infantry Division. 60 Infantry Brigade was to be relieved. Elements of the Guards moved into position for this purpose. A later attempt to storm the wood to the west of Veldhoek caused them painful casualties. The *Leib* Company of Footguard Regiment 1 was reduced to nine men and 3rd Battalion Regiment 'Franz' [Grenadier Guard Regiment 2] was completely wiped out in the woods."

In fact, it appears that Oberstleutnant Linker was killed when he went right forward to observe progress. Noting at about 1.30 pm that a counter-attack seemed to be developing around the western exit to Veldhoek and conscious that, if it succeeded, his assault risked being taken in the flank, he summoned his final immediate reserve, a platoon of previously uncommitted Landwehr reinforcements, gathered up numerous stragglers in his vicinity and, with himself leading, launched a wild charge at the would-be attackers. This had the desired effect, but Linker fell, shot through the head. His artillery liaison officer, Leutnant Kaphengst of Reserve Field Artillery Regiment 51, was also killed[34] and Leutnant Fricke, adjutant 3rd Battalion, went down, shot through both cheeks.

It also appears that Linker originally intended to launch a stronger attack, but was forced to move earlier than he intended because the situation was rapidly becoming critical. It is definitely the case that further to the rear Leutnant Schnarrenberger, originally commanding 11th Company, but now in charge of a newly arrived group of *Ersatz-Reservists* (for whom there had not even been time to record their personal details on the regimental roll), also received orders to move forward and reinforce the later stages of the attack. Moving up, his men came under heavy fire and he suffered considerable losses before he ever reached the cover of the wood. Unaware of the situation, only of the need for haste, he and his men plunged on, becoming split up and disorientated in the wood, before ending up in amongst a group of men from 2nd Battalion. In one of the day's minor tragedies, by the end of the day only thirty two of an estimated 200 reinforcements were still available for duty. To make matters worse, because the men lost were unknown to the regiment, it was completely impossible, then or after, to establish how many were killed or missing or who they were. This incident does not reflect well on Infantry Regiment 143, but it remains a striking demonstration of the utter desperation displayed by both sides during this life or death struggle for possession of the Menen road.

On the extreme right, hard up against the road itself, the advances of 30th Infantry Division and 54th Reserve Division were intended to be coordinated. As has already been noted, however, 54th Reserve Division was already effectively fought to a standstill as a result of its efforts to capture Gelvueld, so little could be expected in the way of support from that quarter and, in addition, the defences were known to be formidable close by the road itself. Despite their difficulties, however, Reserve Infantry Regiment 247, having been ordered to move in support of Infantry Regiment 143 at about 3.40 pm, was able to react. A short time later four rifle companies did push forward. They claimed subsequently that they had managed to obtain a foothold in Herenthage Wood, but that the Allied artillery fire was so heavy that they were soon forced back to their former positions to the west of Veldhoek.[35] Two companies – 9th Company Infantry Regiment 143, reinforced by 10th Company Infantry Regiment 99 under Reserve Leutnant Cadé, were given the task of attempting to push the attack forward in this sector.

Reserve Leutnant Hagedorn 9th Company Infantry Regiment 143 [36] **1.**

"On this particular day, 9th Company was under a very unfavourable star. According to the order for the attack, the assault was to begin as soon as the enemy position was shattered by the arrival of twelve heavy mortar bombs. However, by the time the seventh bomb had been launched, both heavy mortars were wrecked by a direct hit. Neither 9th Company, nor 10th

Company Infantry Regiment 99, further off to the right, were aware of what had happened and, as a result, both missed the moment the general assault began. Once the companies received explicit orders to advance at once against Herenthage Wood, [we realised] that, in the face of strongly occupied trenches and an alert enemy, the attack was impossible. Reserve Leutnants Hagedorn and Cadé, the company commanders, and all their platoon commanders were in agreement that such an attack was completely out of the question during the hours of daylight.

"This was especially the case because it could be established beyond doubt, indeed it could be seen with the naked eye, that every metre of the enemy trenches was lined with a rifle ready to be fired in defence. A report to this effect, complete with sketch map, was sent to Hauptmann Hoffmann, who was commanding the sector to the left of the road. As a result of this report, the attack was postponed until after dark. The two company commanders agreed that, in view of the distance to the enemy – about 150 meters, the assault would begin at a walk and that only when Reserve Leutnant Hagedorn shouted *Hurra!* would the charge begin.

"It duly went dark and the attack began to develop as planned. Then, far too early, somebody shouted *Hurra!* and the entire assault line joined in, even though they were still eighty to one hundred metres short of the enemy trenches. The assault was then met by a storm of British fire from sharp shooters and in the interlocking curtains of fire of two machine guns, which did enormous damage. Shouts of *Hurra!* were drowned out by the racket of the defensive fire and the groans of the wounded. Reserve Leutnants Goedicke and Schmidt were killed, Reserve Leutnant Dedreux was severely wounded in the spine and Reserve Leutnant Cadé of 10th Company Infantry Regiment 99 was captured. Reserve Leutnant Hagedorn got to within fifteen metres of the enemy trenches, then was pinned down for a full thirty minutes by a machine gun firing continuously [*sic*]. Only then was able to crawl away and return to his starting point.

"The attack was totally shattered. Of the 125 men of 9th Company, twenty six men were killed, three officers amongst them [because] Reserve Leutnant Dedreux died of his wounds.[37] About sixty men were wounded to some degree. Hardly one third of the company got back in one piece."

It was not only 9th Company which suffered grievously on 8 November. By the end of that day there was barely one single officer still on his feet. 1st Company was commanded by Vizefeldwebel Bormann, the Machine Gun Company by Offizierstellvertreter Aurisch. The casualty list was enormous and, which was worse, all those killed, wounded or missing were experienced men, impossible in the short term to replace. All that this sacrifice had achieved was the capture of the nearest edge of Herenthage Wood. This was a small return for the effort expended on a piece of ground, the possession of which was asserted only precariously. Finally, during the evening of 9 November, utterly exhausted and temporarily finished as a fighting force, Infantry Regiment 143 was relieved by Grenadier Guard Regiment 4. Just across the road Reserve Infantry Regiment 247 was also pulled out of the line; the regiment later describing their total surprise when, immaculately turned out and equipped, the battalions of Grenadier Guard Regiment 2 arrived silently at about midnight to relieve them. Having wished the Guards the best of luck, Reserve Infantry Regiment 247 marched back to rest, smiling to themselves at, 'the bold statements by the Guards that they would be in Ypres by the following day'.[38]

Every effort was of course made to maximise the fire support available to the advance down the main road to Ypres and Field Artillery Regiment 53, which had been operating south of the Ypres – Menen road, found itself switched sideways ready to move forward and thicken up the concentration of artillery deployed to fire in support of what was by now clearly the main German effort.

Kanonier Drescher 3rd Battery Field Artillery Regiment 53 [39] *2.*

"After three days spent at readiness, teams in harness, in the streaming rain along the road Wervik – Amerika, both officers and men were delighted when we moved into quarters in Geluwe, three kilometres northwest of Menen. We arried in Geluwe dripping wet. The village was overflowing. 2nd Battalion Field Artillery Regiment 53 had already spent three days under canvas and we were to share the same fate, but then our battery commander, Oberleutnant Hofrichter, discovered a station of the Menen – Ypres narrow gauge railway at the northwest exit of the place. The horses were stabled in the engine sheds, whilst the NCOs and men were accommodated in the carriages which were dotted about. Having, at long last, a roof over our heads raised everybody's spirits. Our carriage was soon made really comfortable through the use of plenty of straw.

"Jopp Krebs, the gunner on our observation wagon and battery barber, kept us entertained with tunes on the harmonica that he carried everywhere. It meant that from time to time there was a bit of home, a bit of peace. Often, if we were fed up or tired on the march, on the gun lines or in our billets, or if there was a stormy night and the mud was deep, or if some sort of dispute flared up, Jopp used to pull his harmonica out of his pocket. Then, when he played some sort of march or folk song we were soon in good spirits once more. A little bit of music worked like magic.

"Of course we were all well aware that this happy situation would not last very long. We dried our coats and our groundsheets in front of great wood fires and our uniforms on our bodies. Apart from that we just ate and caught some shut eye. In the evenings we headed for one or other of the numerous *estaminets* of the village, where we had a great time together with the men of Footguards Regiment 1, who were also billeted here. The grenadiers also spoke often respectfully of their high appreciation of their commander, Prinz Eitel

Friedrich of Prussia. It was here that we first heard sung that most beautiful of all the German front line soldiers' songs: *Argonnerwald, um Mitternacht* [In the Argonne Forest at Midnight]. This song, with its wonderful melody, which was completely new to us, made a deep impression. It really was the only soldiers' song which genuinely emerged from the front line troops themselves and always, whenever we heard this song, which grabbed at the emotions, we embraced its words and tune close to our hearts.[40]

"One evening – we had just received post, read our letters and tasted some of the things in the parcels from home – something suddenly came howling and roaring overhead and crashed into an open field a few hundred metres behind. Now then! What could that be? Had the Tommies not always left us in peace so far? Then a second 'coal box' came over. This was really heavy stuff! Sitting in our railway carriages, we flinched involuntarily as the 'heavies' roared over our heads. Already the impacts were getting closer, but we sat tight. By now we had become thick skinned and we did not believe that the Tommies had actually spotted us in our station. That really would have been sick-making.

"The third shell was on its way. From the alteration in its roaring sound, we felt that this time the trajectory was somewhat shorter, that the round was heading straight for us and was going to land right in amongst us. We were gripped by a sort of paralysis; it took two crashing impacts in our immediate vicinity to break the spell. Get out! We dived out of the carriage through doors and windows. Outside was a great chaos of wooden planking and bits of metal. Two unoccupied carriages right next to ours had been totally destroyed. The second long range shell went straight through the roof of the engine shed and exploded in one corner.

"Our officers, who were billeted right next to the station, came rushing up and we all ran into the engine shed to rescue the horses. Only a few of them were even slightly hurt because the shell had landed right in a corner where the supplies of hay and straw were being kept. Our battery commander shouted, 'Get out of the line of fire! Move to the right into open ground, together with the horses!' In amongst this we also heard the calm voice of our Offizierstellvertreter through the darkness, 'Supply column horses over here!' We succeeded, without incurring further casualties, in getting all the horses away from the station. Remarkable to relate, the British ceased firing as abruptly as they had begun. We did not quite trust the peace and quiet and stayed out in the open for a solid hour. We then harnessed up and went into open bivouac behind the village. We all realised that we were bidding a swift farewell to our warm, dry quarters and that we were forced once more to brave the rainy November weather. We were sad to be taking our leave from our comfortable 'sleeping car'. Of course the very next day other columns arrived at the station and, knowing nothing of the firing, were delighted, in the midst of the crammed Geluwe, to find themselves in such excellent quarters. They probably thought they were in clover."

The renewed operation along the Menen road was to be controlled by the newly formed Group Linsingen, based on Headquarters II Army Corps and comprising XV Army Corps, commanded by General der Infanterie von Deimling, and the so-called *Korps-Plettenberg*. Plettenberg's command was made up of Headquarters Guard Corps, with 4th Infantry Division and the *ad hoc* 'Guards Division Winckler', commanded by Generaleutnant von Winckler, normally head of 2nd Guards Infantry Division. In order to accommodate the new forces, the boundaries of Army Group Fabeck were adjusted, so as to concentrate on the sector to the west of the Comines – Ypres canal and to include Hollebeke, St Elooi, Wijtschate and Messines. Group Linsingen was deployed to the east of Army Group Fabeck and, forming the southern flank of a more general Fourth Army attack, was given an axis of advance to Ypres via Hooge Chateau.

The fact that the Guards were to take over the main thrust down the Menen road to Ypres was a calculated risk. On the one hand the Allies were known to have taken very high casualties and to be such under enormous pressure that one more concerted blow from the élite Guards regiments might just be sufficient to bring about a decision in favour of the German army. On the other, it was a 'one shot weapon'. If it did not succeed, there was nothing else available to take over the task and some of the finest remaining troops on the Western front would have been sacrificed for nothing. The stakes, therefore, could not have been higher as the regiments were withdrawn from Monchy, south of Arras and rushed north to Flanders. It is also worth pointing out that the Guards had been in action continuously since the beginning of the war, almost always on critical parts of the battlefront and their casualties had already been high. The regiments bearing down on Ypres were not comparable with those which had marched away the previous August. Oberstleutnant von Rieben of Grenadier Guard Regiment 2 commented, 'Our ranks were filled out with refugees from East Prussia, who knew nothing more of the regiment than our drill shed where they were quartered when their flight from their homeland was over. However, we had received more officers than the Augusta Regiment [Grenadier Guard Regiment 4]. As our commander, Oberst von Roeder, remarked as they marched slowly past one day, 'All tradition has been completely shot away!'[41]

Major Schering Commanding Officer 3rd Battalion Grenadier Guard Regiment 2 [42]

"We reached Menen on 9 November. Further along the main road we could see a high ranking officer wearing the uniform of the 1st Dragoon Guards, his staff around him. As we got closer we saw that it was Reichschancellor von Bethmann Hollweg. Oberst von Roeder rode up to him and saluted. Later he told us that the Chancellor had informed him that several corps were massed around Ypres, preparing to break through the following day. Somewhere or other, somebody would manage to achieve it. 'Herr Oberst', he said later, having ridden up to my commander, "That is the way I have always wanted it; to be there at a time and place where I can really give the lads *die letzte*

Ölung.'[43] . . . Just then a despatch rider arrived with the order, 'Battalion and company commanders forward to Brigade [Headquarters].

"In Geluwe, General von Gontard informed us that the Fusilier [3rd] Battalion was to relieve Infantry Regiment 143 that same evening in the front line . . . As I rode forward with the company commanders to Oude Kruiseke . . . it became clear to me that this was going to be tough. Everywhere there were rubble heaps and ruined buildings, abandoned trenches full of bodies and the intensity of the bitter fighting was underlined by the presence of huge shell holes everywhere, For some considerable distance the area was under fire from British long range guns, so it was only by following the less shelled areas that it was possible to close up on the front line by day. We also made the unpleasant discovery that, in contrast with the situation around Arras, the high water table here meant that the mud was almost unbelievable.

"The Sector Commander in Kruiseke was General von Altrock, though I hardly recognised him with a full beard. Whilst Oberst von Roeder was being briefed about the battle positions in general and given the details of his command post in a piece of dead ground just behind the front, I counted my company commanders and found – only three. The fourth had been unable to follow on the bicycle he had used for the purpose. This did not matter much, because we did not have to take over the positions until the evening. In thoughtful mood we rode back to the battalion, which had been fed and issued with rations at Koelenberg. The November night sky, upon which the shades of evening were falling, looked grey and foreboding. I took leave of my magnificent horse and, as it began to go dark, set off forwards once more.

"There were supposed to be unteroffiziers waiting in Kruiseke to guide us forward. We had a wait a long time before they appeared; some never came at all and those who did were insufficiently familiar with the routes over which they were meant to be leading us. I was not without concern about how the relief would go because the enemy trenches were in some places very close to ours. In addition the Menen – Ypres road that we had to use in places was covered for much of its length by machine guns and we could not use the ditches; they were full of corpses. A great weight was lifted off me when the order came through stating that the assault on the enemy positions was to be postponed from the 10th to the morning of 11 November.

"Despite the designation of several routes forward, most of the companies ended up on the main road, plodding forward through the pitch darkness in one long snake towards the enemy machine guns. Soon the regimental staff was turning off to the left, then we came across a small, ruined farmhouse: Veldhoek. This was my command post; this was where the final approach to the trenches led off and the long column disappeared slowly towards them. I suppose that we were about 400 metres from the enemy and I expected at any moment to hear the rattle of the machine guns. It was a comfort during these tense moments to come across numerous members of the 143rd who, reacting on their own initiative to the announcement of the relief, had quietly and cheerfully begun to make their way back along this route.

"Down in my cellar I could not settle. There was nothing I could do to help, so I stood outside by the sandbagged breastwork and simply waited, longing for the arrival of the report that the trenches had been fully occupied. Hours went by and still the Fusiliers were stalled in the communications trenches, unable to move forwards or backwards. No orders could be got forward and no reports came back. In the confusion of old trenches all orientation was lost. Pressing on round hundreds of nooks and crannies, men suddenly found that they were back at their start point. What on earth would happen if the sun rose on this chaos? At long last – it was well after 3.00 am – the muddle was sorted out. Movement into the trenches began and soon I began to get reports that the companies had manned the position, albeit in some cases in sectors completely different from those intended.

"Given that the enemy had noticed nothing of this 'Polonaise' and not taken the opportunity to inflict a thorough drubbing on us, it appeared that they had had enough for the time being so, as dawn broke, I found myself in a far more upbeat mood that had been the case before we had embarked on that merry dance the previous night."

One of Schering's company commanders later provided a first hand description of this extraordinarily difficult relief in the line.

Reserve Leutnant Baehreke 11th Company Grenadier Guard Regiment 2 [44] **1.**

"Carefully, flitting like shadows, the companies crept through the ruins of Veldhoek. Here and there dim light glimmered amongst the heaps of rubble; otherwise the place was utterly dead. On the far side of Veldhoek was a typical Flanders landscape: trees, hedges and buildings laid out in a confusing tangle. It was cold and rather misty but, nevertheless, reasonably light. The immediate front was restless. Now and then the British flayed the area with shrapnel, flares guttered through the night sky and the small arms fire was incessant. As a result we frequently had to halt and get down. It appeared that the guiding arrangements were either a flop or were not going to materialise. Lying down between some British corpses I noticed, somewhat bemused, that German infantrymen were making their way to the rear and greeting us ironically with comments such as, 'Enjoy yourselves'.

"For the most part we took cover behind the many detached houses and then, in rear of one of them, we linked up with our guide, an extraordinarily small soldier, but a man possessed of amazing self-confidence. The communication trench began by this house. Pleased to be entering proper cover, the company climbed down into the trench and began following the guide who, moving forward rapidly, gave the impression of wanting to get his task finished as soon as possible. The trench was very deep and festooned with heaps of corpses, over which we often had to climb. In some places the whole trench was covered with boards or doors, so it was like moving through a tunnel. But in these tunnels it was very hell. Countless wounded men had dragged themselves into them and, in fear that we might tread on them, called out to us piteously through the darkness.

"I struck a match and, by its light, saw the anguished bearded face of a Zouave, who reached out a hand toward us. Beside him lay one of the 143rd, unconscious and with his head bandaged. Then my match went out and we groped our way forward through the awful darkness. Suddenly my guide announced that we must have gone wrong and that he would have to find the correct route. I climbed out with him and quartered the surrounding houses and gardens without coming to any conclusion. Unfortunately, at that moment the British artillery opened up and, when it had lifted, I found that my little man had vanished. I rushed around desperately, but could locate neither my own men nor my guide. Typical of what could happen in positional warfare, I cannot say how long this incident lasted.

"Bathed in sweat I finally found my man again and was heartily glad to find that he was still there when he would obviously have preferred to be away from that place. Unfortunately the entire company had to get out of that trench, cross a piece of open ground, then climb down into another trench. Only one hundred metres from the enemy, this was a very risky manoeuvre and I was sweating blood with anxiety. However, it all worked perfectly. The trench was somewhat shallower, but it contained no corpses, so we could get forward more quickly, then we soon found that we reached a point where the trench ended. Once more the guide was uncertain and he paused to have a good look round. Suddenly he grabbed my shoulder and indicated a place where, between the trees, a black shape loomed. He explained that that was a hedge and that the fire trench ran along it; at least he was fairly certain that it did.

"There was no communication trench, so the men had to crawl forwards, very careful and quietly because the Tommies were very close, a fact confirmed by the crackle of their fire. It must have been about this moment when I received the fatal news that the larger part of the third platoon was missing... I decided to occupy the trench without them, climbed out of the communication trench and advanced carefully to the hedge. To my amazement I found that the trench was completely empty. I followed the trench in the direction of the main road, but found nobody, not even any wounded. My first reaction was to climb out of the trench and advance towards the enemy, assuming that this was not the correct trench but, at that moment, my men came rushing up, making an unusual amount of noise and under heavy fire from the British, the accuracy of whose shooting was confirmed by loud cries.

"With some effort I brought order to the confused mob, which I had to split into two separate trenches that were not connected, forcing us to crawl between them, because the British were by now fully alert. I immediately despatched patrols to round up the missing third platoon and to bring in the wounded. In the meantime I examined the 'position' more closely and discovered that it comprised a shallow trench, about eighty centimetres deep with an impenetrable hedge immediately in front of it, and we were supposed to be launching an attack from this hopeless position the following day! I sent men off to get hold of the engineers, telling them of the need to pierce gaps through the hedge . . .

"Shortly after midnight the third platoon turned up and to my extreme annoyance made a great racket and rushed into the small section of trench on my right flank. Of course the British opened fire at that and killed the platoon commander. My men were now crammed into this small section of trench and I ordered an 'evacuation'. At that, too many men left that trench and I had to strain everything to restore order. Worn out by my exertions and bathed in sweat once more, I had just laid down when rifle fire began on my left flank. There was a heart rending cry and a short time later a captured British officer was brought to me. He shook my hand warmly and declared, 'This is my first battle but no great success for me'. [*sic.*] A report then arrived announcing that the attack would not take place until 11th so, just before dawn, everything calmed down.

"It was still dark when I was woken. It was an unteroffizier from the right flank, who informed me that a man with a huge head had been seen and that this had unsettled his men. I sent him packing and threatened his section with dire consequences if they attempted to flee again at the sight of men with large heads. Just after that there was a crash and the unteroffizier turned up excitedly and explained that the man with the big head had been shot and that his head was in fact of normal size; it was his turban [*sic.*] that made it look large.[45] As soon as it became light I had a most unpleasant surprise. Out on my left flank a British machine gun was firing almost in defilade into my trench and had already accounted for ten of my men. This was a serious loss for my small group. Naturally everyone pushed up to the right and there was nothing that could be done about this monstrous opponent. About midday a British corporal was brought into the trench then, just as I was talking to him, the twigs of the hedge parted and a Zouave in a woollen hat peered through in to the trench, shouting in French, 'Don't shoot. I am the father of a large family with many children'. At almost the same instant, he grabbed the water bottle of one of my men and, to the laughter of the grenadiers, drained it."

On the south side of the Menen – Ypres road, Grenadier Guard Regiment 4, once more under the command of Oberstleutnant von Walther, who had just recovered from wounds sustained earlier, also encountered problems moving into position. In its case, however, this was more to do with the immense volume of traffic on the main road, rather than obstacles to moving into the forward trenches, though there were some difficulties comparable with those encountered by Grenadier Guard Regiment 2. Having arrived at Koelenberg during the afternoon of 9 November, its 2nd and Fusilier [3rd] Battalions were left in reserve in a large copse to the south of the village, whilst 1st Battalion moved up into the line. Weaving their way through felled trees, collapsed trenches and around wrecked buildings, Hauptmann von Franke's men occupied two lines of trenches. The first, less than one hundred metres from the enemy, was manned by 3rd and 4th Companies under Leutnants von Scheele and von Krosigk respectively, whilst 1st and 2nd Companies, commanded by Leutnant von Wedel and Leutnant Wolf von Unger, were in immediate reserve behind them.

So, after a long, frustrating and tiring night, the relief in the line was complete and the forward troops settled down to await the dawn on 10 November.

Major Schering Commanding Officer 3rd Battalion Grenadier Guard Regiment 2 [46]

"With the dawn came a resumption of British artillery fire. It came from the right, from north of the wood to our front. Some of the shells crashed down through the roof of the house, in the cellar of which I had established my command post. The flat countryside could be observed clearly from the roof of the house. 400 metres to the front was the edge of the wood which the 143rd had repeatedly captured and then lost once more and which housed the British positions.

"To the immediate left was the main road to Ypres. On the far side the Augusta Regiment [Grenadier Guard Regiment 4] had moved into position. Enemy machine guns were located where the road disappeared into the wood. This was the place where Baehrecke, in his insatiable desire to add fresh laurels to his already legendary victor's crown, had insisted that his company be placed. From there, to the right and bending back sharply to the rear, came Unruh's 10th Company, which linked with 4th Company of Footguard Regiment 1. 9th Company, commanded by Leutnant Kurt-Erich Freiherr von Boenigk, which could not find a place in the front line, was back in the second line, together with Eckermann's 12th Company, which had always been designated in reserve . . . [47]

"The short November day was spent by the troops getting organised within their trenches and ranging in on the enemy trenches. The adjutant of the battalion of field artillery which was firing on my sector was constantly on the telephone as, tirelessly, he corrected the fire of his guns and impressed on his battery commanders the seriousness of the situation. From time to time shrapnel burst overhead, the balls rattling down on the tiles of the house like handfuls of dried peas. When this happened we rapidly left the tripod binoculars which were stuck up through a hole in the roof and retreated to the lower floors. Enemy fire was concentrated more on the front line, particularly on the 10th Company sub-sector, where for long periods the yellow smoke from the lyddite-filled shells clung to the damp ground. Through the concert of detonations of all kinds could be heard occasionally the loud thump of a 305 mm howitzer, firing from a position somewhere back in depth.

During the day a series of orders for the attack on 11 November, issued by Guards Division Winckler, arrived at the various regimental headquarters, where they were studied and detailed orders for the forthcoming major operation were swiftly prepared and then passed down to the numerous attacking units and sub units.

"Divisional Order for 11 November

"1. Fourth Army has captured Diksmuide and crossed the canal south of Diksmuide in several places, taking 2,000 prisoners and six machine guns. In the area of Hollebeke numerous French soldiers have deserted to us. XIX Corps has beaten off the bitterly contested attacks of the British. A captured order is encouraging French soldiers to endure a few days longer in their trenches, by which time the attacking power of the Germans will have been reduced considerably. This order is an indication of how exhausted the enemy is already. This information is, as far as possible, to be transmitted to the front line trenches.

"2. Tomorrow at 10.00 am there is to be a general assault. Should there be any sign before that time that the enemy is withdrawing then attacks are to be launched without waiting for artillery preparation and are to be driven forward with the utmost energy. All neighbouring formations will be participating in the attack.

"3. Oberst Janke (Commander 7 Infantry Brigade) will assume command of the Army Group Reserve, comprising 3rd Battalion Footguard Regiment 1 and 3rd Battalion Grenadier Guard Regiment 4, at Keiberg

"4. From 8.00 am I shall be located at Oude Kruiseke [two kilometres southeast of Geluveld]."[48]

A short time later the Division issued a supplementary order:

"1. The infantry is to press on with the construction of their saps, in order to gain ground. It is of particular importance that 1 Guards Infantry Brigade gets far enough forward to permit artillery observation of the western edge of Polygon Wood and Verbeek Farm.

"2. The artillery is so to deploy its guns that it can open fire at 7.30 am. The artillery is then to fire from 7.30 am to 10.00 am precisely. From 7.30 am to 9.00 am this fire is to be moderately heavy, but between 9.00 am and 10.00 am significant quantities of ammunition are to be fired.

"3. At exactly 10.00 am, by synchronised watches, artillery fire is to cease. This sudden silence by our artillery is the signal for our entire forward line of infantry to launch the assault ... " [49]

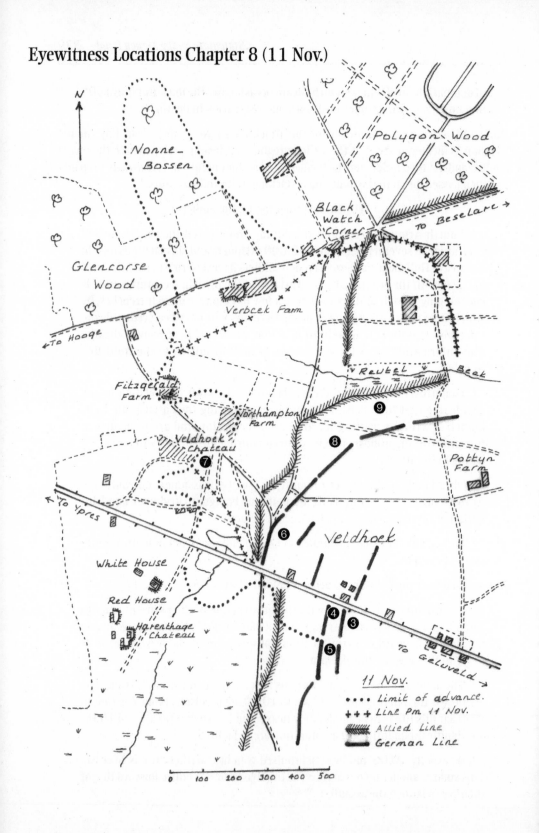

The map overlays which accompanied these orders showed that, in some ways, the attack as planned carried within it the seeds of its own failure. 1 Guards Infantry Brigade was to thrust northwest with, on its right flank, Footguard Regiment 3 passing the southwest corner of Polygon Wood; whilst the boundaries of Footguard Regiment 1 were defined as: right Pottyn farm, passing Verbeek Farm to hit the southwest edge of Nonnebossen; left passing the northern edge of Herenthage Wood. 4 Guards Infantry Brigade was directed to thrust rather more to the west. This would create a gap early on, which was meant to be filled by the divisional reserve – one battalion from Grenadier Guard Regiment 2. This somewhat makeshift solution could not disguise the fact that the attack frontage was too wide, there was insufficient strength in depth and that there was simply not enough artillery to support it properly. As though that were not sufficient impediment, not only did the guns have to provide fire along axes of attack which diverged, they also had to cope with not knowing the location of the British batteries, which they should have concentrated on neutralising as the attack went in.

There had also been insufficient time to permit proper reconnaissance to take place and, in consequence, there was little or no information about the precise locations of British infantry positions or, more important, where their machine guns had been placed. In general, it was known that the British were occupying trenches along the forward edges of Herenthage and Veldhoek Woods and that the front line then ran away from the northeast corner of Veldhoek Wood to the southwest corner of Polygon Wood, which later became known as Black Watch Corner. It was believed that the positions in the open were dug in depth, that there were a number of wired strong points to be dealt with and that there were probably reserve, depth positions in the woods. With the exception of the general line involved, much of the remaining assessment was inaccurate and exaggerated, not that that prevented the same assertions from being repeated when the histories came to be written later.

From their start line in and around Veldhoek, the Guards planned to launch their attack north of the Menen – Ypres road with all four regiments in line: Grenadier Guard Regiment 4, Grenadier Guard Regiment 2, Footguard Regiment 1 and Footguard Regiment 3. The prospect was unappealing. The flat terrain was criss-crossed with hedges, copses and farms, all of which reduced visibility and fields of fire dramatically. The ground, which had been fought over intensely previously, was littered with collapsed primitive trenches; and the dismal, windy weather, which varied between rain and sleet, was made worse by the large numbers of unburied, decomposing corpses everywhere which filled the air with a foul smell. There was no time to worry about any of that. From the moment the orders arrived, all ranks were kept extremely busy preparing for the following day. Oberstleutnant von Walther, Grenadier Guard Regiment 4, extracted his orders and passed them quickly down to battalion commanders. During the evening of 10 November, Hauptmann von Franke, commanding Officer 1st Battalion, whose companies were to be in the first wave, called together his company commanders to discuss the attack and to give out his own orders.

"The battalion will attack at 10.00 am tomorrow morning, the moment that our artillery ceases firing. 3rd and 4th Companies will form the first wave and are to prepare assault steps in the trenches. Each company is to be reinforced by twenty engineers, equipped with wire cutters and hand grenades. As soon as 3rd and 4th Companies have left their trenches, 1st and 2nd Companies, forming the second wave, are to occupy the positions and be prepared to follow up."[50]

A similar scene was taking place north of the road. Believing, or at least fervently hoping, that the potential gap the following day would be covered readily by the move forward of reserves, and confident that the availability of two battalions to cover 150 metres of attack frontage would provide the necessary weight to maintain the impetus of the forthcoming attack, the mood was confident as company commanders assembled for their orders groups.

Major Schering Commanding Officer 3rd Battalion Grenadier Guard Regiment 2 [51] **1.**

"Evening fell early and, as it did, orders arrived for the attack the following day. From 7.30 am the artillery was to begin bringing moderate fire down then from 9.00 am was to fire at intense rates on the enemy positions. This fire was to lift at 10.00 am and the assault was to be launched. The wood edge opposite was to be charged, with no consideration of the situation to the left or right, and unteroffiziers were to be placed in rear of the leading troops to goad forward anybody who was hanging back.

"The company commanders assembled in my cellar at 8.00 pm, so I could pass on the orders and Hauptmann Freiherr von Sell, commanding 1st Company, was also present. I stressed the need to charge forward regardless, leaving our reserves to fill any gaps or mop up overrun enemy. Our left hand boundary was on the main road, so it was going to be necessary for Unruh's [10th] company to change direction as it advanced. 10th and 11th Companies would advance in the first wave, with 9th and 12th following up. Battalion headquarters and the signals section was to move with 12th Company. I asked for reports to be made when preparations for the assault – cutting of steps in the trench walls and gaps in the hedges – were complete. We then shook hands. I only ever met up with two of these comrades again – five years later.

"The night hours passed but slowly. I was occupied in writing a letter with the aid of dismal lighting when Fähnrich von Weiher was brought to me on a stretcher. During the critical days at Monchy I had learned to appreciate the calm and focussed way he went about his duties. So it shocked me all the more to see him again in a state of collapse. He was only half conscious and delirious, struggling with all his strength, despite his serious injuries, with our Oberarzt, who was trying to give him an injection of morphine. He kept trying to go back into the trenches; our main concern was how to quieten him down and evacuate him to the rear. Eventually the Oberarzt, who was a good friend of his, succeed in injecting him and arranging for him to be moved back while he was half asleep.

"Just after that another guest was brought to me. He was a strange looking enemy, a black man, blacker than the November night and unusually large. He took care to emphasise to us that he was harmless and was moved back to the regimental command post. Hardly has this been dealt with than a British officer was brought in. He had blundered into the 11th Company trenches. A tall, upright man, he stood before me so determined to present a correct impression that he hit the cellar roof hard. Examination of his papers showed that this was a worthwhile capture. He was an artillery forward observation officer who was carrying exact sketches of the British gun lines on his person which, naturally, were passed on at once. We then all lay down for a short rest: my faithful adjutant, Obernitz, my batman, Bültemeyer, the big doctor and the telephonist."

In accordance with divisional direction, the positions continued to be pushed towards the enemy trenches, which were very close in this sector. This caused few problems and a further fifty metres was gained during the night then, exactly as planned, the artillery opened up early the following morning at 7.30 am, the explosions of the bursting shells flashing eerily through the early morning mist. During the final hour, large quantities of ammunition were fired by every gun and howitzer in range, right up to the huge 305 mm shells, known as *Zuckerhüten* [sugar loaves], which were directed against depth targets in Ypres itself. As the British responded to the German shelling, the yellowish smoke of their lyddite-filled rounds mingling with the fog, the attackers crouched in their trenches, smoking a last cigarette or pipe, rolling up their overcoats and fixing their bayonets. Some men could not resist putting their heads above the parapet to watch the spectacle and at least one, Leutnant von Spiegel of Footguard Regiment 1, paid with his life for his curiosity.[52]

Major Schering Commanding Officer 3rd Battalion Grenadier Guard Regiment 2 [53] **1.**

"The grey dawn saw us standing in a position from which we could observe the artillery bombardment, scheduled to begin about 7.00 am. Through the roof, which had more holes than a sieve, we could watch as the smoke clouds from the explosions thickened and crept closer until they enveloped the edge of the wood. The final corrections were applied once the curtain of fire was in the correct place and then the process of softening up the positions began; the crashes as the shells exploded on and beyond the British positions were very noticeable. Through the tripod binoculars we could clearly see British soldiers here and there leaving their positions and running to the rear.[54] We took that as a good omen, even though we knew that the hard work would begin once we were in the woods.

"Through the ear splitting racket of our gun fire we were completely oblivious to the occasional shot fired by the enemy. The hands of the clock ticked towards 10.00 am. From the front line came a report that everything was ready for the assault. It was five minutes to ten when the harsh clatter of our machine guns began to blend with the detonation of the shells. I threw off my cloak and drew my sword. To my faithful Bültemeyer – later killed as an unteroffizier in Gorlice – I gave my personal property and asked him to pass my greetings back to my home. After taking my leave briefly of my comrades from the artillery and von Sell, who was also ready to go, we moved outside.

"All around everything was quiet. This was doubly impressive after all the tumult of the past few hours. To our front nothing was to be seen across the flat ground. The 12th Company, to which we were going to attach ourselves, was already moving forward in the trenches, so my staff began to pick their way forward across a landscape which appeared to have been turned over by rabbits. We got split up, but found each other after fifty metres. Then at long last we were free of the confusion of trenches and raced across the shortest gap to get to the wood edge, which appeared to be in our hands."

Across on the far side of the Menen – Ypres road the situation was slightly different. Initially the bombardment proceeded precisely as it did in front of Grenadier Guard Regiment 2, but there was a problem with the way it lifted in this sector.

Leutnant Wolf von Unger 2nd Company Grenadier Guard Regiment 4 [55] **4.**

"In the morning at 7.00 am, the artillery began to fire slowly; gradually the noise grew until it resembled a howling hurricane. The shells came down very accurately. With enormous crashes the shells landed between the trees and the whole wood appeared to be on fire. Despite this the British risked returning fire now and then. We could clearly make out our fallen from earlier failed assaults. How would it turn out for us? 10.00 am ... 10.05 am ... 10.07 am ... the artillery did not cease firing as one. Now and then the odd stray shell came over."

Despite the proximity of the opposing trenches and the fact that the British counter-fire appeared to slacken somewhat as 10.00 am drew near, the failure to achieve an immediate transition from bombardment to infantry assault meant that any potential surprise was lost and in most places the attack was a catastrophe for the Grenadier Guards. However, that was still in the future when, with just a few minutes to go, the Guards' machine guns opened up rapid fire on the enemy lines and final handshakes were exchanged.

Leutnant von Scheele 3rd Company Grenadier Guard Regiment 4 [56] **5.**

"One daring lad leapt out of the trench. I blew my whistle and launched myself forward. In order not to be recognised as an officer, I was carrying a knapsack and a rifle. Right and left of me the men were going down in rows. How I myself got as far as the first line trench I do not know. It was like a miracle. I was one of the first there. The British were still firing at us, cutting us down, but some were surrendering. Only twenty five of my men succeeded in getting into the trenches. The remainder were all shot down, the two flanking platoon mowed down by machine gun fire. About twenty men, commanded by Feldwebel Fernau, charged forward on the far side of the road with the *Franz-Regiment* [Grenadier Guard Regiment 2]. I pointed my revolver at the chests of two British soldiers who were trying to escape, but I could not bring myself to shoot them; they were human beings after all. Together with my twenty five men I was completely cut off – off to the right towards the *Franzers* there was no link. Between them and us there was a hedge concealing Zouaves; to the left the British were occupying the same trench as we were. There was no communication to the rear. The battalion had absolutely no idea that we had captured the trench."

Off to the left, the attack of 4th Company achieved absolutely nothing. The company commander, Leutnant von Krosigk, shot through both eyes on leaving his trench, was put out of action right at the start, as was the remainder of his company, allegedly the victims of four machine guns protected by barbed wire and sited in rear of a hedge only forty metres distant. Unsuppressed, they dominated No Man's Land totally; the attack had no chance whatsoever of succeeding; and much the same happened when Hauptmann von Franke committed his two reserve companies. Hardly any progress was made and the entire attacking force soon found itself pinned down, unable to move and decimated, initially by 1st Battalion Lincolnshire Regiment but later by a British counter-attack and because reverses north of the road exposed its flank to British enfilade fire.

On the Grenadier Guard Regiment 2 front, profiting from the withdrawal of British troops from the wood edge, the Fusilier [3rd] Battalion made swift progress initially, plunging in to Veldhoek Wood as far as the chateau, located about five hundred metres inside the wood and defended by a company of Zouaves. The 10th Company was particularly fortunate in this respect, despite the fact that it had to deal with the problem of having to advance westwards from a start line pointing northwest. Leading his men out promptly at 10.00 am, a platoon commander, Leutnant von Trossel, simply shouted, 'Move now and go left!', and it worked.

Leutnant Unruh 10th Company Grenadier Guard Regiment 2 [57] 6.

"I watched and saw the company rise up as one behind me and launch forward. Then, a few minutes after ten, I was hit by shell splinters in the hand, right thigh and left boot, which drew blood and prevented me from moving. So I remained in the trench and saw, after about half an hour, first individuals, then a few more men come back, saying that they had been outflanked to the right by the British. I ordered all of them forward once more and the men all carried out this order without the slightest hesitation. I put their action down to being somewhat overwrought, because my information was that reserves were poised ready to intervene at the threatened point. It seemed that the battle was moving forward, because returning wounded men told me that the wood had already been crossed. Nothing whatever could be seen of the action due to the cover from sight the ground afforded, but it appeared that the trenches to the left [south] of road were still occupied by the enemy, because every attempt to evacuate the wounded was met by rapid fire."

9th Company Grenadier Guard Regiment 2, which had had difficulty in squeezing into the trenches allocated to it earlier, attempted as it advanced to ease over to the right and then swing left so as to get into its correct position. Such manoeuvres are desperately difficult on the battlefield and it enjoyed only partial success, finding itself heading not for the wood edge but the trenches to the north of it. This area had not been hit as hard as other sectors by the preliminary bombardment, so the trenches were more strongly manned and, to complicate matters further, elements of 9th and 10th Companies Grenadier Guard Regiment 2 became mixed up with 4th Company Footguard Regiment 1 and then came under fire from a combination of 2nd Battalion Duke of Wellington's Regiment and 1st Battalion Scots Guards.

Oberleutnant Freiherr von Boenigk 3rd Battalion Grenadier Guard Regiment 2 [58] 6.

"We soon reached two British trenches, located one behind the other. The right flank bumped into even more, because here the untouched British forces put up considerable resistance. In particularly a machine gun caused us many problems. The centre and left flank of the company had fewer difficulties. The British here were surprised and had too little time to mount a vigorous defence. They did not hold us up for long and I stormed forward with my company towards the section of the wood we had been ordered to take. In front of this wood was a thick hedge which cut off all observation of the wood. Because I did not want to plunge into the unknown, I lay down on the ground where the hedge was thinner and could be penetrated, to check what could be seen within the wood. I had hardly lain down than I felt a sharp pain in my face, as though somebody had stuck something sharp into it. At the same time a gout of blood came from my eye and nose and it was not until somewhat later that I realised I had lost an eye."

For Boenigk the battle was over for the time being, but other members of the battalion were in position to assume the command responsibilities as the attack developed through the wood towards the chateau.

Feldwebelleutnant Rosenberg 3rd Battalion Grenadier Guard Regiment 2 [59] 7.

"The defenders had not suffered any casualties and were not immediately overrun, because they defended themselves desperately. However we managed to take up positions to a flank and fired into the trench, each reinforcing the other's efforts, until we had shot down the last of the defenders, who fought with great bravery to the end. Reserve Vizefeldwebel Lentz performed in an outstanding manner until he fell through [the roof of] a dugout and was seriously injured. Once we had broken the main line of resistance, we turned our attention to the individual dugouts, from which the enemy was still firing at us, and mopped them up. We were only able to take a few men prisoner.

"There were five lines of trenches, one behind the other and all linked to the front line, then came a group of French [Zouaves – defending Veldhoek Chateau] and we shot them down as they tried to run off. Off to my left I witnessed the battle for an enemy machine gun. This turned into a real ding dong scrap, which was eventually decided in our favour. Once the forward enemy trenches were firmly in our hands, the advance through the thick undergrowth and the debris of fallen tree crowns went relatively swiftly, but the thickness of the vegetation made it difficult for us to observe the enemy withdrawal. Despite the fact that the majority of the junior commanders had fallen, the fusiliers pressed on determinedly with their daring advance, until they came to an impenetrable hedge and a swamp just before the chateau in the middle of the wood. Here a man brought an order to me from my commander, directing me to assume command of the company because he had been wounded."

This point represented the furthest advance of Grenadier Guard Regiment 2 and it had been bought at a very high price.

To the right the attack was an equally desperate business for Footguard Regiment 1, commanded by Prince Eitel Friedrich, the second son of the Kaiser. It was intrigued to find that it had faced '1st Guard Brigade, under [Brigadier] General FitzClarence, so élite troops from both armies were facing one another. In the sector from the road to Polygon Wood, battalions of the following famous British regiments were deployed: Royal Fusiliers, Duke of Wellington, Blackwatch Grenadiers, Skotchguards and Cameroon Highländers.' [*sic.*][60]

Prinz Eitel Friedrich's men had also profited by the delay in launching the attack by spending the day on 10 November preparing for the assault and improving their positions. One particular problem was the average height of the guards, which necessitated deepening their trenches quite considerably, a task made harder by the inclement weather and the propensity of these trenches in low lying places to fill with water. Mention has already been made of the death of Leutnant von Spiegel, but there was no time to mourn his passing, as the minutes leading up to 10.00 am were spent in final preparations and checks. As was the case further south, the initial rush of the leading companies, which launched forward, with Hauptmann von Hahnke and Leutnant von Trotha well to the fore, as the final shells of the bombardment were falling, enabled them to overrun the British front line in their sector.

However, as the attempt was made to press on, strong enfilade fire from both right and left hammered the advancing lines. The consequent splintering of the attack was also exacerbated by the early loss of Leutnant von Trotha, shot through the head. Those men of 4th Company, who continued under Feldwebel Mazur, found themselves veering off towards what was later described as 'the White Chateau' [Veldhoek Chateau] in Herenthage Wood, where Hauptmann von Hahnke, commander of the *Leib* Company, was seen to fall. Others who carried on in the correct direction, i.e. most of the *Leib* and 3rd Companies, then attempted to press on beyond the captured trenches and came under fire in their turn from the right. They then found themselves heading for the heavily defended Verbeek Farm, just to the south of Nonnebossen. Anxious to escape the concentration of British small arms and artillery, they rushed on into Nonnebossen itself, driving what few British defenders there were in that place backwards out of the wood, with the exception of one troublesome pocket of resistance in its southeast corner.

There had already been high casualties amongst the junior leadership, but the grenadiers of Footguard Regiments 1 and 3 carried on forward on their own initiative. On reaching the northern edge of the wood, they were dismayed to find that no German artillery fire was coming down to their front and that they were therefore vulnerable to British gun fire. Hauptmann von Weiher led the men of 2nd Company in the wake of the *Leib* Company as far as the Verbeek farm area where, in the course of bitter fighting, it became split up. Some men remained in the immediate vicinity of the farm, while others either followed the *Leib* Company into Nonnebossen or became entangled with the extreme left hand elements of Footguard Regiment 3.

2nd Battalion had an equally torrid time of it that day. The moment its assaulting troops stood up ready to move off, they came under a hail of shrapnel and small arms fire, which took a very heavy toll of their ranks. Within only a few metres of the start line, Hauptmann von Stutterheim, Leutnant von Ketler, Hauptmann von Helldorf, Hauptmann von Moltke and Reserve Oberleutnant von Dobbeler were lying dead on the battlefield. Lacking their officers and NCOs, the companies lost direction and began to drift to the right,[61] so that some of them, too, became involved later with Footguard Regiment 3. Pinned down out in front, Major von Goerne, commanding officer 1st Battalion, managed to get a message back to the regimental commander, 'I am out here with 4th Company and six machine guns. I am unclear as to the situation to my front because all contact has been lost with *Leib*, 2nd and 3rd Companies. Where is 2nd Battalion? Where is Footguard Regiment 3? Runners whom I have despatched to the three companies appear to have been killed. Leutnant von Busse has just been killed and Leutnant von Trotha slightly wounded in the head.'[62]

Prinz Eitel Friedrich was in the unenviable position of not being able to help Goerne. Despite numerous requests, his 3rd Battalion had still not been re-subordinated to him, whilst the divisional reserve from Grenadier Guard Regiment 2, which had been given the task of filling the inter-brigade gap, was so badly shot up on its march forward that only a few of its men reached the front line and those that did were too few in numbers to act independently. As a result, the troops pinned down forward were effectively beyond help and could only hold on and await nightfall, trusting that the cover of darkness would arrive before they were either wiped out or encircled and captured. As the day wore on there were attacks and counter-attacks at various points and, gradually, the attackers were forced back from the high point of their advances earlier in the day. The survivors were gathered together, so as to be able to fend off any British counter-actions.

It does appear[63] that Brigadier General FitzClarence had some such operation in mind once Nonnebossen was back in British hands after a vigorous action by 2nd Battalion Oxfordshire Light Infantry, but lack of reserves, coupled with the risk to the advancing troops from German flanking fire once they were clear of the cover of the woods, ruled it out and he had to content himself with reorganising his much depleted front line. Inspirational in his leadership to the last, Brigadier General FitzClarence was still trying to coordinate an attack by the Irish Guards and 2nd Battalion Grenadier Guards in the early hours of 12 November when he was cut down and killed by what was probably a stray rifle bullet. Commenting on his death, Prinz Eitel Friedrich later wrote, 'He was an opponent before whom we dip our swords in respectful salute'.[64] For the Germans, too, there was no possibility of continuing the attack as directed, so the only option, as 11 November drew to a close, was to dig in wherever the ground permitted it. One of the relatively few survivors later left a full description of the way events unrolled in his sub-sector.

Unteroffizier Quest 2nd Company Footguard Regiment 1 [65] *8.*

"At precisely 10.00 am a whistle blast signalled the start of the attack. As one man, we left our trenches at the double, charging forward hard up behind the *Leib* and the 4th Companies. The first assault wave protected us initially to some extent from the enemy fire. However, once we had covered one hundred metres and were hard up against the British trenches, we were greeted with lacerating machine gun fire. Many of our dear comrades sacrificed their lives for the Fatherland at this point. Because the *Leib* and 4th Companies had already captured the British front line trenches, we were able, together with the *Leib*, to clear the second trench. To begin with we were taken aback by the sight of the Scots in their extraordinary uniform of short pleated knee length skirts and thought that we must have women to our front. When it transpired that these were obstinate fighters and excellent shots, in order to protect ourselves, we had to capture the trenches out to the sides. This did not produce many prisoners.

"In the meantime our ranks were thinned very considerably. Those who remained stormed forward against the third line of trenches. To have attempted to have pressed on any further would have been in vain because, on a front of twenty to thirty metres, there were only two of us left. Over to my left was my pal, Unteroffizier Göbels. We had to strain every sinew to obtain cover from view because the enemy was manning a hedge only about thirty metres away. All we could do was to press ourselves flat on the ground and attempt to scrabble away with fingers and toes as best we could. We had reasonable quantities of ammunition with us, so we laid it out in front of us, so that we should be able to respond effectively in the event of a counter-attack.

"Any movement from us was enough to unleash a hail of fire from the British. By now it was 2.00 pm and Göbels called across to me, 'I am going to see what the Tommies are up to'. Raising himself upright, he was hit with an enemy bullet in the head. His loss was a heavy blow to me. Now I lay completely alone, with no contact either to the right or the left. Almost simultaneously my bayonet was shot off my rifle and the weapon itself was damaged. My mess tins had already suffered similarly and bore several holes. My comrade's rifle now had to render me further good service. This unforgettable Monday afternoon seemed to stretch out to eternity. A counter-attack could be expected at any moment and there were absolutely no reserves on hand. Eventually the ammunition had all been fired and slowly the longed-for evening began to fall. Once it was dark I was able to crawl away from my position in order to link up once more. In the late evening I arrived back in the second trench which we had attacked and there we established a weak defensive line."

Located between Footguard Regiment 1 and Reserve Infantry Regiment 248, on the extreme right flank of the attack by the Guards Division, Footguard Regiment 3 spent 10 November in rather exposed, poorly dug, trenches. As a result, it suffered a steady trickle of casualties throughout the day, including the commanding officer of 2nd Battalion, Hauptmann von Phiseldeck, wounded and the adjutant 1st Battalion, Leutnant Elstermann, killed. Because of the lie of the land and a lack of width within its boundaries, its commander, Oberstleutnant von Schultzendorff, decided to attack on a one battalion frontage in three waves, in the order 1st, 2nd and Fusilier [3rd] Battalions. In an attempt to obtain more information about the layout of the British positions which, in this sector, were held by 1st Battalion Cameron Highlanders, the 1st Battalion pushed forward several strong patrols during the night 10/11 November. Little was gained. The British may have not have had much in the way of defence stores, but they had managed to stretch trip wires and strands of barbed wire forward of their positions and equip them with stone filled tin cans and other devices to make a noise if they were snagged. As a result the night was punctuated by bursts of firing as patrols stumbled into these obstacles and, eventually, they were withdrawn, not much the wiser about what opposed them.

At 10.00 am 11 November the 1st Battalion rushed forward, with 2nd Company right forward under Oberleutnant von Marck and 3rd Company, commanded by Reserve Leutnant Henderkost, left forward. These two companies easily succeeded in overrunning the lightly manned forward trenches of the Camerons and 1st Company, under Hauptmann Freiherr von Marschall, following up the first wave very closely, also traversed the strip of No Man's Land with some ease. However, the defence soon recovered and fire from 1st Battalion King's Regiment, located on the edge of Polygon Wood, took a huge toll on Footguard Regiment 3 and the rest of the day's attacks on this part of the front were a fiasco, including that of 6th Company launched during the afternoon directly at the position of the Kings. Footguard Regiment 3 had been relying on the fire of Reserve Field Artillery Regiment 54 to suppress the defences in the wood, but this had not been very effective, despite the fact that 6th Battery Guards Field Artillery Regiment 1 had been subordinated to its artillery commander, Major Klotz, and performed well. Some slight progress was, nevertheless, made in the direction of Polygon Wood, but the stout resistance put up by two companies of the Black Watch in the southwest corner of that wood – at the cost of their virtual obliteration – deflected what was left of the German thrust in this area northwest into Nonnebossen, which was effectively undefended.[66] One of the company commanders of Footguard Regiment 3, who was awarded the Iron Cross First Class for his work that day, later left a detailed account of events on its front.

Reserve Leutnant Henderkott 3rd Company Footguard Regiment 3[67] **9.**

"During the day we had sufficient observation over the ground to our front to be able to take the correct decisions. Immediately to the front of the company was a damp meadow overlooked by the enemy. Beyond that, at a distance of about 150 metres, were individual houses, gardens and a stack of straw. The crossing of this meadow would certainly have cost heavy casualties so, during the night, I had a communication trench dug which was to spare us the necessity. The night 10/11 was very dark, the ground was mostly clay, so no noise was made and, by between 3.00 and 4.00 am, the trench was complete. During the 11th and 12th it was used by almost all advancing supports. At 8.30 am, during the artillery preparation, I stood together with Hauptmann von Hahnke of Footguard Regiment 1 at the corner of a wood and agreed the precise axis of advance. At 9.45 am, under cover of thick smoke from the heavy artillery barrage, I entered the communication trench with the 1st and 2nd Platoons of my company. At 10.00 am precisely, the 3rd Platoon went over the top, led from the front by the platoon and section commanders.

"For about fifty metres they were not under fire, but then they were hit by small arms fire, which caused many casualties. Firing from the garden hedges, camouflaged by web-like festoons of grey string and daubed with clay, barely visible, were hidden machine guns, which mowed down the attacking troops. Looking back at my company I saw that those on the left flank were still pushing forward, despite being under machine gun fire. I and the troops behind me closed in on the flank of the machine guns and were able to assault and capture two of them. The crews went on firing to the last minute and several courageous men fell victim to their lead when they were within a few metres of the death-dealing weapons. As we continued to storm forward, we caught fleeting glimpses of the small gardens, noting that they had all been turned into miniature fortresses by the digging of trenches and small fire positions. We were up against tough enemies, big strapping Scotsmen – Scots Guards [*sic*] who, despite the lateness of the season, were fighting in their characteristic uniforms with bare knees and thighs.[68] This caused my batman to shout, 'Leutnant! There are women there!' They fought on to the last, but soon were lying on the ground dead, or seriously wounded.

"However there was yet another position to the rear occupied by the enemy; a hail of deadly lead claimed more victims. It was now essential to pull together all the men who were taking cover behind garden hedges or folds in the ground and beginning to dig in and, instead, set about clearing the final section of trenches. The task was not as difficult as the first because my 3rd Platoon and 2nd Company had come up on our right and were beginning to roll up the trenches from right to left. We did the same thing from left to right and so dealt with the enemy infantry. To my left I saw other men disappear behind a hedge whilst to my front was a lengthy stretch of open meadowland leading forward into the wood. In attempting to avoid the open section and to gain to the wood to our half left, we came under artillery fire, which forced us to take cover in a patch of low scrub. I still had about fifteen men with me. To our right I saw many of the men of our 2nd Company who had been cut down. The enemy artillery fire began to have an ever greater effect on us and soon some of the men with me were blown apart by direct hits, as the scrub was too low and offered insufficient cover.

"When the heavy artillery fire began to ease somewhat, I attempted to find out what was to my left and right. In this, Cyclist Kalisch, who had acted as an absolutely fearless runner to me all day, distinguished himself by crawling to the left under enemy fire along what remained of a trench and establishing that there was nobody to our left but, off to the right, there were about thirty men, mostly from 2nd Company. I linked up with these men and saw that they were all united in their unshakeable determination to hold on to the position at all costs. In the meantime I failed, despite despatching runners, to make contact with those in rear, so I decided to go back myself, accompanied by two men and to seek reinforcements. We succeeded; I came across a platoon of 1st Company in the communication trench and had them guided forward by Kalisch under cover of the gathering darkness. Further on I found the commander of 10th Company and had him agree to send forward one of his platoons. With the aid of these supports the former British trench was held and consolidated."

Consolidated it may have been, but at appalling cost, to both sides. The khaki-clad, kilted defenders lay where they were, unburied until the snows of winter covered them, together with enormous numbers of the guards. Of Footguard Regiment 3, Major von Arentschild, Reserve Hauptmann Freiherr Marschall von Bieberstein, Oberleutnant

Marck, Feldwebelleutnant Strelow and Offizierstellvertreters Fahlenberg of 1st Company and Bauerschmidt of 11th Company were dead, together 112 other ranks. The 3rd Company alone had lost a full third of its strength killed and across the regiment the numbers wounded were enormous.[69]

Taking charge of the local situation, Major von Goerne of Footguard Regiment 1 drew together elements of his own 1st and 2nd Battalions, men from Grenadier Guard Regiment 2 and Footguard Regiment 3 and established a thin line of resistance, supplemented by six machine guns, roughly in the area of the former British Second Line. The right hand sector was commanded by Hauptmann von Weiher, the left by Feldwebel Mazur, the first man of the regiment to win the Iron Cross First Class. It was an extremely difficult night. On top of the traumatic day of battle, the weather was dreadful, with rain filling the shallow trenches and neighbouring shell holes more and more as time went by. The night air was filled with the moaning of those who had been severely wounded and, although stretcherbearers worked through the night to rescue them, many succumbed to exposure and a lonely death isolated between the positions.

There had been a few successful moments in an otherwise appalling day of reverses. Gefreiter Quade, a runner with the *Leib* Company Footguard Regiment 1, for example, won an Iron Cross First Class for coolly capturing an entire enemy platoon, which was attempting to evade the German attackers and regain its own lines. It was said subsequently that morale remained intact, but that is at least questionable, bearing in mind that Footguard Regiment 1 alone lost about 800 officers and men killed, wounded or missing. Of the seven officers killed, only Oberleutnants von Busse and Dobbeler have known graves and the proportion of other ranks subsequently identified was equally low on this confused battlefield. When Prinz Eitel Friedrich later summed up the fighting on 11 November 1914, he wrote, 'Ypres was the end of the peacetime regiment',[70] a statement which held good not only for his own regiment, but every other one of both sides which fought at Ypres in 1914.

There had been some harassing fire during the day but comparatively little aimed counter-battery fire by either side, both of whom lacked precise knowledge of the location of the opposing guns, so casualties within the batteries engaged had been relatively light. The adjutant of Guards Field Artillery Regiment 2, Leutnant Matthius, however, was killed whilst manning an observation post right forward with the infantry in an attempt to overcome this problem and his assistant, Unteroffizier Knust, was wounded at the same time.[71] Of all the supporting artillery, it is probable that 6th Battery Guards Field Artillery Regiment 1 had one of the most prominent roles that day. Subordinated to Reserve Field Artillery Regiment 54 and working his guns forward to where they could fire in the direct role against enemy trenches, its commander, Hauptmann von Buch, ensured that the one thousand rounds fired were generally well placed. His audacity came at a price, however. One British high explosive shell landed in amongst the cartridges and set off a large explosion. Another shell burst through the overhead cover of the crew of Number 1 gun, wounding Kanoniers Stieg, Degen and Holz and shaking up Kanonier Döhlung so badly that he had to be evacuated with shell shock.[72] Unpleasant though these incidents were for those directly involved, they paled into insignificance compared with the traumatic experience of the infantry, which had effectively been fought to a standstill.

That evening the scene was the same all along the sector the Guards had attacked from Polygon Wood to the Menen-Ypres road. The previous British front line was firmly in German hands, but behind that the enemy had either held their positions or won them back by means of a series of counter-attacks. As it went dark both sides were more or less exhausted and the British did not attempt to press any further forward. This meant that, for the time being at least, No Man's Land was fairly broad and it was possible for wounded men to crawl back or be recovered to their own lines as late as the following night. Gradually the full extent of the check became known up the chain of command and consequently a highly optimistic order was issued by Headquarters Guards Division Winckler at 5.15 pm 11 November in an attempt to achieve at least some progress south of the main road.

> "Regiment Augusta [Grenadier Guard Regiment 4], together with Infantry Regiment 49 and supported by Regiment Franz [Grenadier Guard Regiment 2], is to capture the trenches to their front. 1 Guards Infantry Brigade is to remain in its current positions and support the attack of 4 Guards Infantry Brigade." [73]

Needless to say, there was absolutely no hope of this attack succeeding where previous efforts by fully battle ready troops had failed and this order came to nothing. Nor did a second one, issued at 7.00 pm, directing Grenadier Guard Regiment 4 to launch a frontal attack at 9.00 pm with its 1st Battalion, supported by a flanking attack from north of the road by one half of 2nd Battalion. The regiment pointed out the sheer impossibility of the enterprise and the order was cancelled at 8.25 pm. The question might legitimately be put why it was ever issued in the first place. Here, between Veldhoek and Polygon Wood, the final attack of significance in the current campaign had failed. All the courage displayed by the German attackers had been for nothing. They had attacked with the utmost determination, but the British defenders pressed, severely pressed, had fought back hard and had just avoided being broken.

Some ground had been gained and numerous prisoners were captured during the hours that the battle had raged. But, unfortunately for the German army, the disadvantageous starting position had worked against any chance of the attack developing synergy. Cohesion was lost early on, when the links left and right could not be maintained. Intense fire and a fragmented battlefield meant that orders and reports failed to arrive and the day swiftly degenerated into a host of individual battles by companies, platoons and even smaller groups. The lack of coordination and battlefield isolation of the various fighting troops worked in favour of the defence, despite the fact that it had itself also been considerably disrupted. As a battle, it had been yet another example of what the Duke of Wellington once called 'a damn'd close run thing', especially in Nonnebossen, where parties from Footguard Regiments 1 and 3 had only been prevented from breaking through by the very last of the British defenders and point blank fire from the guns of XLI Brigade and 35th Heavy Battery Royal Artillery. The

Prussian Guards had done their best, but it had not been good enough. Ypres was still a tantalising four kilometres away.

Notes
1. Sollider *Vier Jahre Westfront* p 40.
2. *ibid.* p 41.
3. So heavy had been the losses that command of the regiment devolved on Hauptmann Rubenbauer, previously commanding officer 1st Battalion.
4. Krämer History Reserve Infantry Regiment 245 p 17. Käußler has no known grave, but Oberleutnant Gerhard Arnold is buried in the German cemetery at Menen Block N Grave 1871.
5. Herkenrath History Reserve Infantry Regiment 247 p 21.
6. It is extremely unusual to come across a Feuerwerkoffizier serving with a field unit. Bley was a specialist ammunition technical officer, whose duties would normally involve supervision or expert tasks in major ammunition depots or permanent fortresses.
7. BOH p 368.
8. Petri History Infantry Regiment 99 pp 28–29.
9. Bossert History Infantry Regiment 143 pp 159 – 160.
10. The section of guns was from 116th Battery Royal Artillery. The BOH (p368) dismisses this loss in a couple of words, but it was a rare event and probably the first time that the Royal Artillery had lost field guns since the battle of Le Cateau ten weeks earlier. Reserve Oberleutnant Lentz and the men of 3rd Company Infantry Regiment 143 were credited with this important seizure. The guns were taken back to Strasbourg where they were displayed for some weeks on Kaiserplatz, then claimed by Infantry Regiment 143 and placed in their barracks.
11. Bossert *op. cit.* pp 168–169
12. Reserve Leutnant Ernst Hoffmann is buried in the German cemetery at Menen Block G Grave 2293
13. Of these, two have known graves in the German cemetery at Menen. Hauptmann Theodor Probst is buried in Block D Grave 153, whilst Reserve Leutnant Ernst Körner, a native of Stuttgart, born on 13 Feb 1893, is buried in Block D Grave 2564.
14. Klotz History Reserve Field Artillery Regiment 54 p 21.
15. Quoted BOH p 376.
16. Reinhardt History Reserve Infantry Regiment 248 p 14.
17. Klotz *op. cit.* p 18.
18. *ibid.* p 23.
19. Bossert *op. cit.* pp 168–169.
20. Unlike Hauptmann Dierke, who has no known grave, Musketier Wilhelm Keilholz is buried in the German cemetery at Menen Block L Grave 443.
21. Bossert *op. cit.* pp 160–161.
22. *ibid.* pp 170–171.
23. Reinhardt *op. cit.* p 15.
24. Herkenrath *op. cit.* p 22.
25. Reserve Leutnant Friedrich Redecker is buried in the *Kamaradengrab* of the German cemetery at Langemark.
26. Bossert *op. cit.* pp 160–161.
27. *ibid.* p 172.
28. Reinhardt *op. cit.* p 15.

29. Bossert *op. cit.* p 180.
30. Composed by Ludwig van Beethoven in 1808 as March Number 1 in F major, this march was rededicated in 1813 to Johann David Ludwig Graf Yorck von Wartenburg who, in complete defiance of government policy and without authority, signed the Convention of Tauroggen in 1812 on behalf of Prussia, which permitted Russian forces to pass into East Prussia and tie down French forces there, an act which though almost treasonable at that time, marked the beginning of the War of Liberation of the German States against Napoleon. Ever since that time, it has been regarded as one of the most important marches in the German repertoire. To this day it is the first march played when German military bands beat retreat and it is the march of the ceremonial *Wachbataillon* in Berlin.
31. Both these men were temporary musicians, seconded from other parts of the regiment. The loss of two together like this would have had a bad effect on the sound quality of the band. Musketier Arthur Waldmeyer is buried in the German cemetery at Menen Block I Grave 995.
32. Bossert *op. cit.* pp 160–161.
33. Oberstleutnant Friedrich Linker is buried in the German cemetery at Menen Block G Grave 1725.
34. Leutnant Hans Kaphengst is buried in the German cemetery at Menen Block F Grave 1692. The *Volksbund* has wrongly recorded the date of his death as 9 November 1914.
35. Herkenrath *op. cit.* p 23.
36. Bossert *op. cit.* pp 178–179.
37. During the attack, Dedreux was wrongly reported to be wounded and lying in a British trench by Reserve Leutnant Notwodworski of 3rd Company Infantry Regiment 143. In fact he was evacuated with great difficulty and in considerable pain to a field hospital in Halluin where he succumbed to his injuries on 11 November.
38. Herkenrath *op. cit.* p 23.
39. Drescher History Field Artillery Regiment 53 pp 108–109.
40. It is highly improbable that Drescher heard this at the time and place he claims, though the song was extremely popular in the front line and widely sung. The song is generally credited to Hermann Albert von Gordon and dated 1915, but other authorities attribute it to Pionier Andreas Schott of 2nd Company Engineer Battalion 30, who was stationed in the Argonne Forest in November 1914 and heard a variant of the song sung by a Pionier Nissen, who in turn had obtained it from a German sailor while serving a sentence in a military prison! The sailor had learned it in the Far East and sang it as *Zu Kiautschou um Mitternacht*. Nissen was killed in action on 15 November and Schott is said to have written it in his memory. It then, allegedly, appeared in published form in a newspaper in the Rhineland in early 1915. The claims do not end there, however. Others link it to a member of Infantry Regiment 135 who served in the Forest in autumn 1914. The official version is all about the experiences of an engineer in front line service against the French and it has a good tune, also used for other songs. Unfortunately, the melody was hijacked later by the Nazis, given new words as *SA marschiert* and orchestrated to sound like the first cousin to the *Horst Wessel Lied*, so putting it later beyond the pale. This is unfortunate, because it would be hard to take exception to the original words of the song, though it is suspected that the final verse was also a Nazi addition of the late 1930s.
41. Rieben History Grenadier Guard Regiment 2 p 203.
42. *ibid.* pp 203–205.
43. This may seem a strange thing for Bethman-Hollweg to say. He was not a priest and it would not have been his business to administer the last rites. To the modern mind *die letzte Ölung,*

as practised by the Roman Catholic Church, is (wrongly) seen as a death rite. This is not the case; the idea has grown up because priests historically have often been summoned too late to minister what is meant to be a healing rite to a seriously sick patient. To make its purpose clear, the name of the rite has been changed in recent times to 'The Anointing of the Sick'. The use of holy oil for this purpose is founded in the scriptures and in antiquity was seen as definite means by which healing could be brought about. Interesting to note, at the specific insistence of the Elector of Saxony, who had been repeatedly petitioned on the subject, the anointing rite had been retained by the Lutheran Church at the time of the Reformation. Furthermore, in German *die letzte Ölung* has a second association. It harks back to combat in the arena where it was the practice for gladiators and wrestlers to oil themselves, not only to make it harder for an opponent to take a firm grip, but also to speed up healing in the case of wounds. The assumption must be that this secular meaning is what the Chancellor had in mind.

44. Rieben *op. cit.* pp 206–208.
45. The original eyewitness report refers to a 'turban', but of course there were no Indian troops as far north as this at that time. The subsequent mention of a Zouave suggests that the man was from the French colonial forces.
46. *ibid.* p 205–206.
47. The fact that the reinforcing Guards had such a superiority of numbers over the men of Infantry Regiment 143 whom they were relieving is clear proof of the extent to which that regiment had been worn down during the previous days. Almost without exception the survivors had been manning the front line only when the Guards arrived.
48. Rieben *op. cit.* p 208.
49. *ibid.* p 209.
50. Unger History Grenadier Guard Regiment 4 p 67.
51. Rieben *op. cit.* pp 210–211.
52. Leutnant Karl Freiherr Spiegel von und zu Peckenheim is buried in the *Kamaradengrab* of the German cemetery Langemark.
53. Rieben *op. cit.* pp 211–212.
54. What Schering observed were men of FitzClarence's Brigade from I Corps being sent further into the woods to shelter from the worst of the bombardment. BOH p 421.
55. Unger *op. cit.* p 68.
56. *ibid.* p 68.
57. Rieben *op. cit.* pp 212.
58. *ibid.* p 213.
59. *ibid.* pp 213–214.
60. Eitel Friedrich History Footguard Regiment 1 p 57.
61. Of these officers, only Oberleutnant Karl von Dobbeler has a known grave. He is buried in the German cemetery in Menen Block O Grave 1249.
62. *ibid.* p 59. Oberleutnant Hermann von Busse is buried in the German cemetery at Menen Block B Grave 414.
63. BOH p 443.
64. Eitel Friedrich *op. cit.* p 60.
65. *ibid.* pp 61–62.
66. Brice *The Battle Book of Ypres* pp 149 – 155.
67. Ditfurth History Footguard Regiment 3 pp 59–61.
68. Henderkott was mistaken. The Scots Guards were deployed nearby, but were opposite Footguard Regiment 1 and in any case the Scots Guards did not wear kilts. It is most probable

that the men were from 1st Battalion Cameron Highlanders, though it is also possible that Footguard Regiment 3 also encountered men of the Black Watch.

69. *ibid.* pp 58–59. Of those killed, only Offizierstellvertreter Albert Bauerschmidt has a known grave. He is buried in the German cemetery at Menen Block I Grave 911.

70. Eitel Friedrich *op. cit.* p 63.

71. Luyken History Guards Field Artillery Regiment 2 p 54.

72. Köhn History Guards Field Artillery Regiment 1 p 117.

73. Rieben *op. cit.* p 226.

Postscript

"It is impossible ever to describe the facts in their full reality. To do that it would be necessary to describe them as they unfold. That, naturally, is impossible and yet, the very next minute – and thank heavens – their memory is softened. So nobody else can ever really experience how desperate things can be before a mixture of a sense of duty, desire to get the job done and manly ambition overcomes sunken morale and spurs us on with renewed strength!" [1]

So wrote a young kriegsfreiwilliger of Reserve Infantry Regiment 201 in a letter home in the wake of the battles around Diksmuide – and a good thing too many would say, following such an experience. However, it is fortunate that so many were willing and able to commit their thoughts to paper and thus enable us to gain at least an impression of what occurred at Ypres one hundred years ago.

A great many battles of the First World War ended, or, rather ground to a halt, with both sides temporarily exhausted. Nowhere was this more so than around Ypres in late 1914. Officially, the battle went on for another ten days after the final major efforts at Diksmuide, Langemark and along the Menen road but, in reality, these final skirmishes were little more than that. The odd section of line was straightened here; the occasional point of local tactical importance was disputed there but, essentially, the lines had settled down in their final form before the fighting died away and the focus of the chain of command shifted onto the solution of pressing administrative issues before the onset of winter, capturing and disseminating the lessons learned and doing all in its power to boost sagging morale.

This last point was all too necessary, because anecdotal information concerning associated problems was already beginning to accumulate in higher headquarters, leading in one case to instructions from XXIV Reserve Corps to 6th Bavarian Reserve Division on 16 November to put its house in order and to do something about the excessive numbers of stragglers dodging front line duty.

"The daily infantry casualty returns, though only estimates, are in stark contrast to the nature of the battles which have occurred since 13 [November]. With the exception of the taking of the park at Wijtschate on the 13th and the capture of the buildings at the southern tip of the axe-shaped wood, the casualty figures for which have still not arrived here, operations have been confined to a slight pushing forward of our own lines without noticeable resistance from the enemy infantry. So, when for 14 November it is estimated that losses in killed and wounded for three regiments were forty percent, the report

FINAL SITUATION

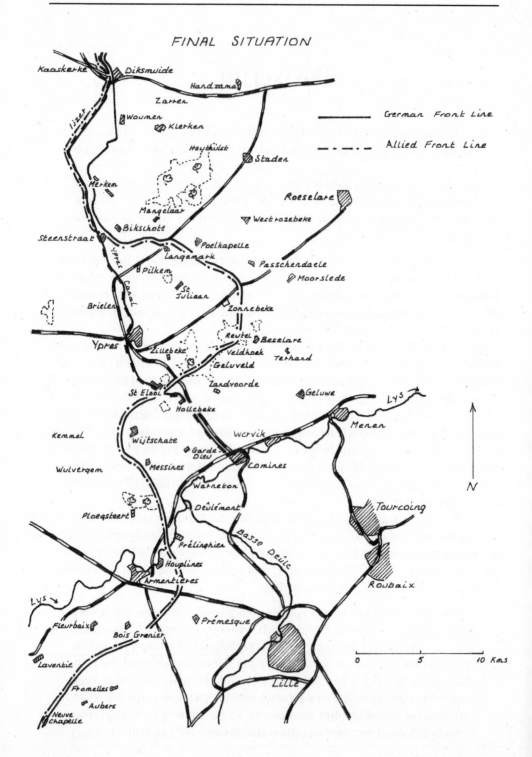

German Front Line
Allied Front Line

Kaaskerke
Diksmuide
Handzame
Zarren
Woumen
Klerken
Houthulst
Staden
IJzer
Merken
Roeselare
Mangelaar
Westrozebeke
Bikschote
Steenstraat
Poelkapelle
Ypres Canal
Langemark
Passchendaele
Pilkem
Moorslede
St Juliaan
Brielen
Zonnebeke
Ypres
Reutel Beselare
Zillebeke
Veldhoek
Terhand
Geluveld
Zandvoorde
St Elooi
Geluwe
LYS
Hollebeke
Menen
Kemmel
Wijtschate
Wervik
Garde Dieu
Wulvergem
Messines
Comines
Warneton
Deûlémont
Ploegsteert
Frélinghien
Basse Deûle
Tourcoing
Houplines
Armentières
Roubaix
LYS
Fleurbaix
Prémesque
Bois Grenier
Laventie
Fromelles
Lille
Aubers
Neuve Chapelle

N

0   5   10 Kms

is not self-evidently explicable. This is all the more striking because, according to reports from the field and base hospitals, together with those of the main dressing stations, the flow of wounded [from those regiments] has not been particularly high during the past few days and it significantly trails behind the regimental casualty figures.

"It must be assumed, therefore, that included amongst the estimated and reported losses, are large numbers of men who, for whatever reason, have absented themselves from the firing line without permission and evaded the controls. This is to be countered by every means possible. To that end, the following measures are to be introduced:

1. A constant watch is to be kept on the numbers of men employed with the quartermasters and field kitchens, or on stretcher bearer duty.

2. The movement of personnel to the divisional rear is to be supervised constantly by military police, cavalry patrols and officers of the divisional staff. Checks are to be made to ensure that all unwounded personnel are in possession of written permission given them by an officer, or a certificate signed by the medical officer.

3. The doctors manning the aid posts, dressing stations and walking wounded collecting points are to ensure, by the way they conduct their duties, that they strive always to act as a check on dilution of forward strength.

4. All casualty returns are to differentiate clearly the dead and wounded from the missing.

5. Infantry elements located clear of the battle area are to be subject to controls by means of daily roll calls."[2]

Naturally, the strain was not only being felt on one side. The head of the intelligence branch at Sixth Army produced the following intelligence report on 9 November.[3]

"In an order dated 3 November, the British commander in chief, Field Marshal Sir J French, praises with extravagant language the brilliant performance of his troops during recent days. He believes that no other army in the world would be tough enough to withstand the appalling weight of German artillery fire. He then calls on his troops for renewed effort, claiming that it is likely to be only a few days or, perhaps, a few hours before the enemy will be beaten off with terrible losses. The Field Marshal concludes by stating that he is fully confident that his appeal to the troops will not be in vain.

"Whether the British commander in chief really has such trust in his troops would appear to be doubtful, in view of two orders which have been captured. One Routine Order from the British headquarters reveals that there have been numerous cases of cowardice in the face of the enemy, which have been tried by court martial. One man has been condemned to death for cowardice and the sentence has been confirmed. For the same offence and from the same brigade, fifteen men have been sentenced to imprisonment for three months. A further man from the same brigade has been punished for dressing himself in civilian clothes and deserting, whilst another man from a different part of the army, has been shot for the same thing. According to an order from 10 British Brigade, there have been numerous cases of self-inflicted wounds amongst the men, who sought to be admitted to hospital, because they could no longer face up to the risk of battle."

By the end of October, prisoner interrogation was already beginning to yield results and anything negative concerning the Allies was also seized on eagerly. 'The French complained bitterly about their Allies, the British. The French were just cannon fodder, constantly despatched into the front line by the British. The reality was that the French were the last reserves available, after the British had long since been worn out by the dreadful battles, which had been going on for days . . . '⁴ Announcements, accompanied by instructions to distribute the information, 'right down to the front line trenches', also appeared regularly, particularly towards the end of the battle. One such, originating at Sixth Army during the evening of 10 November, reads in part:

> " . . . II Bavarian Army Corps has captured the heights at St Elooi and occupied St Elooi itself. The enemy have withdrawn to Voormezele. The Corps has taken 800 prisoners and captured six machine guns. There are reports from Hollebeke that large groups of Frenchmen have deserted to us. Further details are not yet available. There has been no other progress along the Army Group Fabeck front. XIX Corps has beaten off eight bitter assaults on the strong points they have established around Le Gheer. The attacks were repeated four times last night . . . Fourth Army has captured Diksmuide. It has pushed on across the Ypres Canal south of Diksmuide in several places [*sic.*] and has captured about 2,000 prisoners.⁵

There is a note of desperation in all these reports because, no matter what gloss was placed on the plans and dispositions ordered by Supreme Army Headquarters, or the way the battle unfolded, the failure of the German army in Flanders was so complete that it is small wonder that Falkenhayn was subject to a great deal of criticism subsequently for his handling of the campaign; in effect he committed the raw formations of Fourth Army to battle with nothing but their own high courage to sustain them. Even the later deployment of more experienced formations made no difference to the outcome. Such was the scale of problems they faced in the final battles, that they stood no greater chance of succeeding than had the reserve corps engaged earlier and the experience scarred them and those who commanded them deeply. During the summer of 1915 a soldier by the name of Renner, a member of Reserve Infantry Regiment 19, had occasion to visit Headquarters 9th Reserve Division, where he spoke to the commander, General von Guretzky-Cornitz.

Renner later reported that he was asked, 'Were you at Poelkapelle?' When he replied in the affirmative, the general continued, 'Are the men still of the general opinion that

I volunteered the division for Flanders and that, therefore, I bear the blame for the casualties of 10 November?' Renner looked him in the eye and, hard though it was, replied, *'Jawohl, Herr General!'* At that, the commander said, 'Try to persuade them it is not true. It was not for me to decide what to do with my division; I was subject to the orders of higher authority.'[6] This may seem to have been an extraordinary exchange, but it clearly made an impact on Renner, was generally believed within the regiment and, if true, simply goes to show how setbacks suffered in this campaign continued to haunt the army long after they were over. The whole concept was always a gamble and even accepted as such by Falkenhayn after the war. 'The prize to be won was worth the stake,' he wrote in his memoirs,[7] but, as the battle died away and winter descended on the cold, sodden Flanders battlefield, there were many who would have disagreed – and with more than a little justification.

During the twenty five years which followed these events, the sacrifice of the men of Fourth Army and Army Group Fabeck was subverted and distorted by the Nazis for their own ends, but their passing into history and the experience of another world war, meant that Nazi triumphalism was replaced by lasting and universal feelings of bereavement, nowhere better encapsulated than in the sculpture *Die Eltern* [The Parents] by Kathe Kollwitz, dedicated in 1932 and still on display in the German cemetery at Vladslo. Kollwitz was expelled from the Prussian Academy of Arts by the Nazis, she was banned from exhibiting and her work condemned as 'degenerate'. However, her great masterpiece, created with raw emotion and placed close to the grave of her young son Peter, who was killed in action near Diksmuide on 23 October 1914, while serving with Reserve Infantry Regiment 207, has comfortably outlasted them and will continue to be admired and respected by generations to come, as one of the finest and most moving expressions of grief and loss ever captured by an artist.

None of those involved was left unmarked by the experience of autumn 1914 in Flanders and some carried the memories of those bitter days with them for the rest of their life. One young Bavarian soldier who fought at Wijtschate, gave expression to his feelings and spoke for countless others in this short poem, written in the 1920s and found unpublished and deposited amongst the archived documents of his regiment.

Die toten Kameraden!

In manchen stillen Nächten,
Zieht's grau an mir vorbei,
Die toten Kamaraden,
In langer, langer reih,

Ziehn bleich an mir vorüber,
Und jeder sieht mich an,
Als wollt' er zu mir sagen,
Es ist für dich getan!

The Fallen Comrades!

In silent watches of the night,
A grey stream past me flows,
Of all my fallen comrades,
In never-ending rows.

They march past, pale and silent,
Staring at me, too
As though to me they're saying,
We did it all for you!

Für dich, der mit uns kämpfte,	*For you, who fought alongside,*
Dich, der wohl nie vergisst,	*For you, who won't forget*
Wie bitter uns Soldaten	*Our bitter lot as soldiers*
Der Tod geworden ist.	*And violent deaths we met.*
Sie ziehen still vorüber,	*They march past me in silence,*
Und jeder sieht mich an.	*Each with a staring eye*
Und endlos ist dies Schreiten	*A never-ending cortège*
Der Toten, Mann für Mann.	*Of fallen, passing by.*
Mit ihnen aber schreiten	*With them, too, come marching,*
Die Stunden ohne Zahl	*The hours – far from few,*
Voll Grauen, Bluten, Sterben	*Of cruelty, of blood and death,*
Und namenloser Qual	*And nameless tortures too.*
Das greift mir nach dem Herzen.	*That tugs at my own heartstrings,*
Das rüttelt Stoss um Stoss.	*Delivers blow on blow,*
Die toten Kamaraden	*The fate of fallen comrades,*
Sie lassen mich nicht los.	*Who never let me go.*
Sie ziehen still vorüber,	*They march past me in silence,*
Und jeder sieht mich an,	*With stares that linger on,*
Wie lang? – marschier'n wir wieder,	*How long? – Until we march again,*
Zusammen, Man für Mann.	*Together, all for one.*

Kriegsfreiwilliger E Kramer 8th Company Bavarian Reserve Infantry Regiment 20

Notes
1. Hayner History Reserve Infantry Regiment 201 p 49.
2. Kriegsarchiv München 6. Res. Div. Bd 87 *Generalkommando XXIV Reservekorps No. 1844IIa von 16.11.1914.*
3. Kriegsarchiv München Gen-Kdo (wk) II AK Bd. 6 *Armee-Oberkommando 6. Armee Nachr. Offz. Br. Nr. 153 von 9.11.1914.*
4. Kriegsarchiv München HS 1360 *Geschichte des RIR 20* p 24.
5. Kriegsarchiv München 5. Inf. Brig. Bd. 2 AOK 6. *Armee Armeebefehl für 11.11.1914.*
6. Schwenke History Reserve Infantry Regiment 19 p 78.
7. Falkenhayn: *General Headquarters* p 28.

Approximate German – British Comparison of Ranks

Generalfeldmarschall	Field Marshal
General der Infanterie	General of Infantry} General
General der Kavallerie	General of Cavalry} General
	N.B. The holder of any of these last two ranks was at least a corps commander and might have been an army commander.
Generalleutnant	Lieutenant General.
	N.B. The holder of this rank could be the commander of a formation ranging in size from a brigade to a corps. From 1732 onwards Prussian officers of the rank of Generalleutnant or higher, who had sufficient seniority, were referred to as *'Exzellenz'* [Excellency].
Generalmajor	Major General
Oberst	Colonel
Oberstleutnant	Lieutenant Colonel
Major	Major
Hauptmann	Captain
Rittmeister	Captain (mounted unit such as cavalry, horse artillery or transport) It was also retained by officers of this senority serving with the German Flying Corps
Oberleutnant	Lieutenant
Leutnant	Second Lieutenant
Feldwebelleutnant	Sergeant Major Lieutenant
Offizierstellvertreter	Officer Deputy
	N.B. This was an appointment, rather than a substantive rank.
Feldwebel	Sergeant Major
Wachtmeister	Sergeant Major (mounted unit)

Vizefeldwebel	Staff Sergeant
Vizewachtmeister	Staff Sergeant (mounted unit)
Sergeant	Sergeant
Unteroffizier	Corporal
Korporal	Corporal (Bavarian units)
Gefreiter	Lance Corporal
Musketier	}
Grenadier	}
Garde-Füsilier	} N.B. These ranks all equate to
Füsilier	} Private Soldier (infantry). The
Schütze	} differences in nomenclature
Infanterist	} are due to tradition, the type of
Jäger	} unit involved, or the class of
Wehrmann	} conscript to which the
Landsturmmann	} individual belonged.
Soldat	}
Ersatz-Reservist	}
Kriegsfreiwilliger	Wartime Volunteer. This equates to Private Soldier.
Kanonier	Gunner}
Pionier	Sapper} N.B. These ranks all
Fahrer	Driver} equate to Private
Hornist	Trumpeter} Soldier.
Tambour	Drummer}

Medical Personnel

Oberstabsarzt	Major (or higher)
Stabsarzt	Captain
Oberarzt	Lieutenant
Assistenzarzt	Second Lieutenant

N.B. These individuals were also referred to by their appointments; for example, *Bataillonsarzt* or *Regimentsarzt* [Battalion or Regimental Medical Officer]. Such usage, which varied in the different contingents which made up the German army, is no indicator of rank.

Sanitäter
Krankenträger

Medical Assistant} N.B. These two
Stretcherbearer } ranks both equate
                    to Private Soldier.
Frequently the prefix 'Sanitäts-' appears in front of a normal NCO rank, such as Gefreiter or Unteroffizier. This simply indicates that a man of that particular seniority was part of the medical services.

Bibliography

Unpublished Sources

Kriegsarchiv München

Gen-Kdo (w.k) II AK Bd. 6	*A.O.K. 6.Armee <u>Weisung an die Armee</u> von 30.10.1914.* *Fernsprechmeldung von Fabeck 30.10.14* *Fernsprechmeldung Wilhelm 5.11.14* *Armee-Oberkommando 6. Armee Nachr. Offz. Br. Nr. 153 9.11.1914*
3. Inf. Div. Bd 6	Generalkommando II. Bayer. A.K. <u>*Korpsbefehl*</u> *29.10.1914*
6. Res. Div. Bd. 5	XXVII. Reserve-Korps Generalkommando Nr. 451 Ia. 4.11.14 *An Kgl. Bayr. 6. Reserve-Division.*
6. Res. Div. Bd 87	Generalkommando II. Bayer. A.K. <u>*Korpsbefehl*</u> *2.11.1914* Generalkommando XXIV. Reservekorps No. 1844IIa *R. 6.bayr. Reserve-Division 16.11.1914.*
5. Inf. Brig. Bd. 2	Armeeoberkommando 6. Armee A.H.Qu. Lille, 10.11.1914 7 Uhr Abds. *Armeebefehl für 11.11.1914*
HS 1360	*Geschichte des RIR 20 & Beilage III*
HS 1928	*Auszug aus einem Briefe des Einj. Gefreiten Ludwig Klein 11./ Res. IR.16*
HS 1972	Generalkommando II. Bayer. A.K. An das Armee-Ober-Kommando 6. Nr 1560 von 3.11.1914 *Betreff: Besondere Taten [Zott]*

Published Works (German: author known)

Appel Dr Friedrich *Das Reserve-Infanterie-Regt. Nr. 205 im Weltkrieg* Berlin 1937

Atzrott Leutnant d.R. Hans *Das Reserve-Jäger-Bataillon Nr 16* Oldenburg 1923

Bastanier Lt. d.Res. a.D., Jakobi Oblt. a.D. v., Krüger Lt. d.Res. a.D. Dr., Mangel Lt. d.Res. & Tegtmeier Lt. d.Res. a.D. *Geschichte des Großherzoglich-Mecklenburgischen Reserve-Infanterie-Regiments Nr. 214* Dessau 1933

Beckh Oberst a.D. Dr. Emil *Das Reserve-Feldartillerie-Regiment Nr 6 im Weltkrieg 1914/1918* München 1940

Bergeder Hauptmann d.R. Dr. Fritz *Das Reserve-Infanterie-Regiment Nr. 202 auf den Schlachtfeldern des Weltkrieges 1914–1918* Berlin 1939

Beumelberg Werner *Ypern 1914* Oldenburg 1925

Boesser Oberstleutnant a.D. Karl *Geschichte des Reserve-Feldartillerie-Regiments Nr. 44* Berlin 1932

Bossert Hauptmann Hans *Das 4. Unter-Elsässisches Infanterie-Regiment Nr 143 im Frieden und im Weltkrieg Band I* Berlin 1935

Böttger Hauptmann Karl, Schönberg Oberst a.D. Kurt, Bock von Wülsingen Generalmajor a.D. Georg & Melzer Oblt. Walter *Das Kgl. Sächs. 7. Infanterie-Regiment 'König Georg' Nr. 106* Dresden 1927

Brandenstein Oberst v. *Das Infanterie-Regiment 'Alt-Württemberg' (3. Württ.) Nr. 121 im Weltkrieg 1914–1918* Stuttgart 1921

Brase Dr. Siegfried *Bei den 241ern. Kriegserlebnisse* Dresden 1915

Braun Generalmajor a.D. Julius Ritter von *Das K.B. Reserve-Infanterie-Regiment Nr. 21* München 1921

Brendler Wilhelm *Kriegserlebnisse 1914 bis 1918 im Reserve-Infanterie-Regiment 233 (Regimentsgeschichte)* Zeulenroda 1929

Dellmensingen Königl. Bayer. General der Artillerie z.D. Konrad Krafft von & Feeser Generalmajor a.D. Friedrichfranz *Das Bayernbuch vom Weltkriege 1914–1918 II. Band* Stuttgart 1930

Ditfurth Major v., Primus Lt. d.R., Krause Lt. d.R., Naumann Hauptmann d.R., Michaelis Lt. d.R. & Loebell Major v. *Das 3. Garde-Regiment zu Fuß im Weltkriege* Berlin 1926

Drescher Paul *Unser Kriegserlebnis! Das Königlich Preuß. Hinterpommersche Feldartillerie-Regiment Nr. 53 im Großen Kriege 1914–1918* Zeulenroda 1938

Dreysse Wilhelm *Langemark 1914: Der heldische Opfergang der Deutschen Jugend* Minden i.W. 1934

Eitel Friedrich Kgl. Pr. Generalmajor a.D Prinz von Preußen *Das Erste Garderegiment zu Fuß im Weltkrieg 1914 – 18* Berlin 1934

Etzel Generalmajor a.D. Hans *Das K.B. 9. Infanterie-Regiment 'Wrede'* München 1927

Foerster Oberstleutnant a.D Wolfgang & Greiner Hauptmann a.D. Helmuth *Wir Kämpfer im Weltkrieg* Berlin 1929

Frauenholz Dr. phil. Eugen *Das K.B. 2. Kürassier- und Schwere Reiter-Regiment (Ergänzungsband)* München 1922

Fuhrmann Major d.R. a.D. Hans, Pfoertner Leutnant d.R. a.D. Otto & Fries Leutnant d.R. a.D. Nikolaus *Königlich Preußisches Reserve-Infanterie-Rgt. Nr. 211 im Weltkriege 1914–1918* Berlin 1933

Gebsattel General der Kavallerie Ludwig Freiherr von *Das K.B. 1. Ulanen-Regiment 'Kaiser Wilhelm II. König von Preußen'* München 1924

Gemmingen-Guttenberg-Fürfeld Oberst Freiherr von *Das Grenadier-Regiment Königen Olga (1. Württ.) Nr. 119 im Weltkrieg 1914 – 1918* Stuttgart 1927

Gerok Hauptmann *Das 2. württ. Feldartillerie-Reg. Nr. 29 'Prinzregent Luitpold von Bayern' im Weltkrieg 1914–1918* Stuttgart 1921

Gieraths Dr. phil. Günther *Geschichte des Res.-Infanterie-Regiments Nr 210* Oldenburg 1928

Glogowski Oberlt. d.R. a.D. *Das Kgl. Sächs. 6. Infanterie-Regiment Nr. 105 'König Wilhelm II. von Württemberg'* Dresden 1929

Glück Generalmajor a.D. & Wald Generalmajor a.D. *Das 8. Württembergische Infanterie-Regiment Nr. 126 'Großherzog Friedrich von Baden' im Weltkrieg 1914–1918* Stuttgart 1929

Goertze Generalmajor a.D. von *Das Marine-Infanterie-Regiment 2 im Weltkrieg 1914/18* Oldenburg 1926

Gonnermann Karl Ritter von *Das K.B. 1. Schwere Reiter-Regiment 'Prinz Karl von Bayern' im Weltkriege 1914–1918* München 1936

Gottberg Kgl. Pr. Generalmajor a.D. Döring v. *Das Grenadier-Regiment König Friedrich Wilhelm IV. (1. Pommersches) Nr. 2 im Weltkriege* Berlin 1928

Großmann Generalleutnant a.D. August *Das K.B. Reserve-Infanterie-Regiment Nr. 17* München 1923

Haleck Oberleutnant Fritz *Das Reserve-Infanterie-Regiment Nr. 208* Oldenburg 1922

Hansch Oberleutnant Johannes & Weidling Leutnant Dr. Fritz *Das Colbergsche Grenadier-Regiment Graf Gneisenau (2. Pommersches) Nr. 9 im Weltkriege 1914–1918* Oldenburg 1929

Hayner Oberst a.D., Frantzius Major a.D. von & Zorn Otto *Geschichte des Reserve-Infanterie-Regiment Nr. 201* Berlin 1940

Hennig Leutnant d. Res. Otto *Das Reserve-Infanterie-Regiment Nr. 235 im Weltkriege* Oldenburg 1931

Herkenrath Oberleutnant d.Res. a.D. Dr. August *Das Württembergische Reserve-Infanterie-Regiment Nr. 247 im Weltkrieg 1914–1918* Stuttgart 1923

Hutschenreuter Rittmeister a.D. Richard *Das K.B. 1. Chevaulegers-Regiment im Weltkriege 1914–19* München 1922

Joermann-Düsseldorf Leutnant d.R. a.D. *Geschichte des 4. Lothringschen Infanterie-Regiments Nr. 136* Duisburg am Rhein

Kaiser Generalmajor a.D., Buchholtz Major & Renovanz Hauptmann a.D. *Das Infanterie-Regiment Nr. 171 im Weltkriege* Oldenburg 1927

Kastner Oberleutnant d.R. *Geschichte des Königlich Sächsischen Reserve-Infanterie-Regiments 242* Zittau 1924

Klotz Oberst a.D. *Das Württembergische Reserve-Feldartillerie-Regiment Nr. 54 im Weltkrieg 1914–1918* Stuttgart 1929

Knieling Lutz & Bölsche Arnold *Reserve Infantry Regiment 234* Zeulenroda 1931

Kohl Leutnant d.Res. a.D. Hermann *Mit Hurra in den Tod! Kriegserlebnisse eines Frontsoldaten 17. bayer. Infanterie-Regiment 'Orff'* Stuttgart 1932

Köhn Hermann *Erstes Garde Feldartillerie-Regiment und seine Reitende Abteilung* Berlin 1928

Kollmann Generalmajor a.D. Walter & Loch Hauptmann Herbert *Das Kgl. Bayer. 5. Feldartillerie-Regiment 'König Alfons XIII. Von Spanien' I & II Teile.* München 1926

Krämer Max *Geschichte des Reserve-Infanterie-Regiments 245 im Weltkriege* Leipzig

Lennartz Oberstleutnant d.Sch. a.D. J & Nagel Postrat a.D. *Geschichte des badischen (später rheinischen)Reserve-Infanterie-Regiments 240* Zeulenroda 1938

Loßberg General der Infanterie Fritz v. *Meine Tätigkeit im Weltkriege 1914–1918* Berlin 1939

Luyken Oberregierungsrat Walter *Das 2. Garde-Feldartillerie-Regiment im Weltkriege* Berlin 1929

Makoben Leutnant d.R. Ernst *Geschichte des Reserve-Infanterie-Regiments Nr. 212 im Weltkriege 1914–1918* Oldenburg 1933

Mayer Hauptmann d.L. Arthur & Görtz Kriegsfreiwilliger Joseph *Das Reserve-Infanterie-Regiment Nr. 236 im Weltkriege* Zeulenroda 1938

Moser Generalleutnant Otto v. *Die Württemberger im Weltkrieg* Stuttgart 1928

Niemann Oberstlt. a.D. Johannes *Das 9. Königlich-Sächsische Infanterie-Regiment Nr. 133 im Weltkrieg 1914–18* Hamburg 1969

Orgeldinger Leutnant der Reserve Louis *Das Württembergische Reserve-Infanterie-Regiment Nr. 246* Stuttgart 1931

Osman Leutn. d.L. Hans *Mit den Kriegsfreiwilligen über die Yser* Bielefeld 1915

Partzsch Oberst a.D. *Das Kgl. Sächs. 3. Feldartillerie-Regiment Nr. 32* Dresden 1939

Paulus Oberst a.D. Karl *Das K.B. Jäger Regiment Nr. 1* München 1925

Petri Oberstleutnant *2. Oberrheinisches Infanterie-Regiment 99* Oldenburg 1925

Pflugbeil Hanns *Das Kgl. Sächs. 15. Infanterie-Regiment Nr. 181* Dresden 1923

Plathe Hauptmann a.D. W. *Das Reserve-Infanterie-Regiment Nr. 26 im Weltkriege* Zeulenroda 1932

Reich Polizeioberst a.D. Gustav *Langemarck: Die Kämpfe des XXVI. Res.-Korps ('Grünes Korps') in Flandern 1914* Köln 1934

Reimer Major a.D. *I. (Kgl. Sächs.) Abteilung des Res. Felda. Rgt. Nr. 54 später III. Abteilung des Kgl. Sächs. Res. Felda. Rgt. Nr. 32* Dresden 1927

Reinhardt Generalleutnant a.D. Ernst *Das Württembergische Reserve-Inf.-Regiment Nr. 248 im Weltkrieg 1914–1918* Stuttgart 1924

Repetzky Leutnant der Reserve *Geschichte des Reservebataillons der Brandenberger Jäger* Berlin 1929

Rieben Oberstleutnant a.D. Oberarchivrat Dr. von *Kaiser Franz-Garde-Grenadier-Regiment Nr. 2* Oldenburg 1929

Riegel Hauptmann a.D. Johann *Das K.B. 17. Infanterie-Regiment 'Orff'* München 1927

RitterMajor a.D. Dr. Phil. Albrecht *Das K.B. 18. Infanterie-Regiment 'Prinz Ludwig Ferdinand'* München 1926

Rohrbeck Oberst a.D. Karl-August *Reserve-Infanterie-Regiment Nr. 8 im Weltkriege* Zeulenroda 1934

Rutz Hauptmann d.R. *Bayernkämpfe: Einmarsch in Frankreich; Mit der Kavallerie in Flandern; Grabenkrieg vor Arras* München 1917

Sanftleben Major a.D. Eduard *Das 1. Garde-Ulanen-Regiment im Weltkriege* Berlin 1929

Schakert Oberleutnant der Reserve a.D. Walter *Reserve-Infanterie-Regiment Nr. 48* Oldenburg 1925

Schatz Oberleutnant a.D. *Das Kgl. Sächs. 10. Infanterie-Regiment Nr. 134 Heft 3, I. Teil* Dresden 1922

Schatz Leutnant d.R. Josef *Geschichte des badischen (rheinischen) Reserve-Infanterie-Regiments 239* Stuttgart 1927

Schulz Oberleutnant d.R. a.D., Kißler Oberstleutnant a.D. & Schulze Leutnant d.R. a.D. *Geschichte des Reserve-Infanterie-Regiments Nr. 209 im Weltkriege 1914–1918* Oldenburg 1930

Schwedt Major d.R. *Das Reserve-Infanterie-Regiment Nr. 204* Zeulenroda 1929

Schwenke Oberstleutnant a.D. *Geschichte des Reserve-Infanterie-Regiment Nr. 19* Oldenburg 1926

Schwink K. bay. Hauptmann Otto *Die Schlacht an der Yser und bei Ypern im Herbst 1914* Oldenburg 1918

Solleder Dr. Fridolin *Vier Jahre Westfront: Geschichte des Regiments List R.I.R. 16* München 1932

Steuer Major a.D. Joseph *Das 1. Unter-Elsässische Infanterie-Regiment Nr. 132 im Weltkriege* Berlin 1931

Stoffleth Major a.D. *Geschichte des Reserve-Jäger-Bataillons Nr. 18* Berlin 1937

Stuhlmann Oberstleutnant a.D. Dr. Friedrich *Das Kgl. Sächs. 6. Feldartillerie-Regiment Nr. 68* Dresden 1927

Stühmke General *Das Infanterie-Regiment 'Kaiser Friedrich, König von Preußen' (7. Württ.) Nr. 125 im Weltkrieg 1914–1918* Stuttgart 1923

Thimmermann Hermann *Der Sturm auf Langemarck* München 1933

Tiessen Studienrat Max *Königlich Preußisches Reserve-Infanterie-Regiment 213: Geschichte eines Flandernregiments* Glückstadt 1937

Tschischwitz General der Infanterie von *General von der Marwitz: Weltkriegsbriefe* Berlin 1940

Ulrich Oberleutnant d.R. a.D. *Res.-Inf.-Regiment 52 im Weltkriege* Cottbus 1925

Unger Major a.D. Fritz v. *Das Königin Augusta Garde-Grenadier-Regiment Nr. 4 im Weltkriege 1914–1919* Berlin 1922

Unruh Karl *Langemarck: Legende und Wirklichkeit* Koblenz 1986

Vogt F *Das Res.-Feldart.-Rgt. Nr. 51 im Weltkriege* Kassel 1932

Wagner Oberstleutnant a.D. Rudolf *Das. 2. Ober-Elsässische Feldartillerie-Regiment Nr. 51 im Weltkriege 1914/1918* Berlin 1936

Weniger Generalmajor a.D. Heinrich, Zobel Oberst a.D. Artur & Fels Oberst a.D. Maximilian *Das K.B. 5. Infanterie-Regiment 'Großherzog Ernst Ludwig von Hessen'* München 1929.

Willers Lt. d.R. a.D. Studienrat Hans *Königlich Preußisches Res.-Inf.-Regiment Nr. 215 I. Teil* Oldenburg 1926

Winzer Lt. d.R. Richard *Das Kgl. Sächs. Res.-Infanterie-Regiment Nr. 243 im Weltkriege1914–1918* Dresden 1927

Wolff Hauptmann Ludwig *Das Kgl. Sächs. 5. Inf-Regiment 'Kronprinz' Nr. 104 (Erster Band)* Dresden 1925

Wurmb Major a.D. Herbert Ritter von *Das K.B. Reserve-Infanterie-Regiment Nr. 8* München 1929

Published Works (German: author unknown)

Der Weltkrieg 1914 bis 1918 Fünfter Band: Der Herbst-Feldzug 1914 Im Westen bis zum Stellungskrieg Im Osten bis zum Rückzug Berlin 1929

Freiburger Zeitung 15 January 1915.

Garde-Jäger-Bataillon Oldenburg 1934

Geschichte des Reserve-Infanterie-Regiments Nr. 24 1914 bis 1918: Von Antwerpen zur Düna und über Verdun bis zur Avre Berlin 1931

Geschichte des Reserve-Infanterie-Regiments Nr. 35 Berlin 1935

Langemarck: Ein Vermächtnis München 1932

Published Works (French)

Les Armées Françaises dans la Grande Guerre: Tome Premier, Quatrième Volume[FOH] Paris 1934

Published Works (English)

Beckett Ian F W *Ypres The First Battle 1914* Harlow 2004

Brice Beatrix *The Battle Book of Ypres* Stevenage 1987

Corbett Sir Julian S *Official History of the War: Naval Operations Volume I* London 1920

Edmonds Brigadier General Sir James E *Official History of the War [BOH]: Military Operations France and Belgium 1914: Antwerp, La Bassée, Armentières, Messines and Ypres October-November 1914* London 1925

Falkenhayn General Erich von *General Headquarters 1914 – 1916 and its Critical Decisions* London 1919

Farrer-Hockley A H *Ypres 1914: Death of an Army* London 1967

Poseck Lieutenant General M von *The German Cavalry 1914 in Belgium and France* Uckfield 2007

Pul Paul van *In Flanders Flooded Fields: Before Ypres there was Yser* Barnsley 2006

Index